SOLDIERS OF THE SEA

GREAT
WAR
STORIES

Two different flags were raised atop Mt. Suribachi during the invasion of Iwo Jima. This was the first. The historic event occurred at 10:31 in the morning of February 23, 1945, and was photographed under enemy fire by Staff Sergeant Louis R. Lowery, then a 25-year old combat cameraman for *Leatherneck,* the Marine Corps' official magazine.

SOLDIERS OF THE SEA
The United States Marine Corps, 1775-1962

by Robert Debs Heinl, Jr., Colonel, USMC

Foreword by B. H. Liddell Hart

Foreword to Second Edition
by General Alfred M. Gray, USMC Commandant

The Nautical & Aviation Publishing Company of America
Baltimore, Maryland

Reprinted in 1991 by The Nautical & Aviation Publishing Company of America, Inc., 101 W. Read Street, Suite 314, Baltimore, Maryland 21201. Originally published in 1962 by The United States Naval Institute. All rights reserved. No part of this publication may be reprinted, stored in a retrieval system, or transmitted in any form by any electronic or mechanical copying system without the written permission of the publisher.

Library of Congress Catalog Card Number: 90-49078
ISBN: 1-877853-01-1
Printed in The United States of America
Second Edition

Library of Congress Cataloging-in-Publication Data

Heinl, Robert Debs, 1916–1979
    Soldiers of the sea: the United States Marine Corps, 1775–1962
  by Robert Debs Heinl, Jr.; forward by B. H. Lidell Hart.—2nd ed.
      p. cm.—(Great war stories)
    Includes bibliographical references and index.
    ISBN 1-877853-01-1
    1. United States. Marine Corps—History. I. Title. II. Series.
  VE23.H4 1990   90-49078
    359.9'6' 0973—dc20   CIP

All photos are official U.S. Marine Corps unless otherwise noted.

Art at end of chapters courtesy of Lieutenant Colonel J. H. Magruder III.

Art on pages 215 and 313 courtesy of Mrs. John W. Thomason, Jr.

Cartography by Steve Oltmann

To

The Class of 1937

and to the Instructors

U.S. Marine Corps Basic School, Philadelphia

★

WE ENTERED AS MANY, WE DEPARTED ONE

We have compelled every land and every sea to open a path for our valor, and have everywhere planted eternal memorials of our friendship and of our enmity.
    —THE "FUNERAL ORATION" OF PERICLES,
      THUCYDIDES, *History of the Peloponnesian War*

THE MARINES' HYMN

From the Halls of Montezuma
To the shores of Tripoli,
We fight our country's battles
In the air, on land, and sea.
First to fight for right and freedom,
And to keep our honor clean,
We are proud to claim the title
Of United States Marine.

Our flag's unfurl'd to every breeze
From dawn to setting sun;
We have fought in every clime and place
Where we could take a gun.
In the snow of far-off northern lands
And in sunny tropic scenes,
You will find us always on the job—
The United States Marines.

Here's health to you and to our Corps
Which we are proud to serve;
In many a strife we've fought for life
And never lost our nerve.
If the Army and the Navy
Ever gaze on Heaven's scenes,
They will find the streets are guarded
By United States Marines.

FOREWORD TO SECOND EDITION

When *Soldiers of the Sea* first was published in 1962, the United States was in the midst of the Cold War. Our conventional defense efforts were focused on providing the ground based land and air forces needed to counter the threat posed by the Soviet Union on the continent of Europe. For the first time in our Nation's peacetime history, a large standing army was being maintained outside our borders for a prolonged period of time. The enormity of the ground threat in Europe also caused many of our defense planners to lose sight of the maritime character of our Nation and the role that naval forces had in the day to day protection of our interests and the achievement of our objective around the globe. As a result, some began to view maritime forces as not having the same usefulness as continental forces in the achievement of our national security objectives.

In 1962, not unlike today, although the Congress only ten years previously had recognized the requirement for the Marine Corps to peform the mission as our Nation's force-in-readiness, the aggregate utility and purpose of the Corps were not understood completely. Once again the role of the Marine Corps was being questioned. Some, to include Colonel Heinl, wondered if the United States Marine Corps could survive within a defense establishment that was focused on the continental defense of Europe. Accordingly, when Colonel Heinl wrote *Soldiers of the Sea*, it seems that he had several objectives in mind. First, he was writing the history of the United States Marine Corps. Second, he was explaining the role and mission that this elite amphibious expeditionary military force performed, and should continue to perform, for a Nation dependent on global stability, access to the world's markets and resources, and unimpeded use of the seas for its political, economic, and security well being. And, third, he was attempting to preserve the identity of his Corps of Marines. When one reads his work, it becomes apparent that Colonel Heinl was successful in achieving all of his objectives.

On the last pages of *Soldiers of the Sea*, Colonel Heinl questioned whether the role and identity of the Marine Corps as an expeditionary crisis response force could survive in a security environment that was dominated by an unprecedented strategic and conventional arms race. He believed the Corps could, provided it continued to focus on its legislated roles and missions as a force-in-readiness and avoid becoming a "second land army." In 1962, Colonel Heinl provided visionary instructions for the Corps to achieve this end. First, the Corps must be "ready to fight any time, anywhere, and to perform such other duties as the President may direct." Second, the Corps must be "a ready amphibious expeditionary force, whether for police action during peace or for the seizure and defense of advanced naval bases in war." And, third, the Corps must "preserve and enhance its professional quality and thereby retain its position in the defense establishment as a professional elite force, military but not militaristic, an example and soldierly standard of comparison for all comers."

Over the ensuing 28 years, the Corps has remained true to the purpose and identity which Colonel Heinl sought to preserve. The Marine Corps continues to provide our Nation with a maritime expeditionary force that is specifically organized, trained, and equipped for sustained operations in austere and hostile environments. A force which can be task organized to the mission, and a force which can deploy by multiple means. Most importantly, a force which possesses a unique and an unmatched forcible entry capability. As evidenced by over 40 crises since the original publication of *Soldiers of the Sea*, these Marine Corps forces have been ready when called. Missions performed have ranged from disaster relief and humanitarian assistance to sustained combat operations across the spectrum of conflict.

The history of innovation detailed within the book's chapters continues to flourish. Our focus remains on expeditionary warfare. We have avoided the temptation to become a specialized amphibious force. We have continued to develop new ways to capitalize on the aggregate capability within our integrated combined arms force structure. Driven by operational requirements, the Marine Corps has steadily improved its ability to influence world events and project power from the sea over extended distances.

The proliferation of sophisticated weapons around the globe has led to the development of an over-the-horizon assault capability. This operational maneuver concept has been the operational basis for our research and development programs. Although improvements continue, we now possess the capability to project power from over-the-horizon beyond the range of the threat to strike an opponent where he is most vulnerable at a time of our own choosing. Innovation also can be found within our training and education programs. Marines are taught to out-think their opponents and to seize and exploit the initiative in any type of engagement. We have preserved and ehanced those qualities of dedication to duty and military professionalism that since 1775 have established Marines as an elite military force.

Why is *Soldiers of the Sea* still worthy of reading today? It is relevant because the history of our Corps reflects the future of the Corps. Throughout our history, we have remained an expeditionary force with global missions. As the world security environment has changed, the mission of the Corps has remained constant. The history of our Nation and the history of our Corps have proven the vital need of a maritime nation for a maritime expeditionary force-in-readiness. The strength and value of the Corps to our Nation will continue to be its versatility and readiness; characteristics which have been hallmarks of the Corps for over 200 years.

As our Nation debates its requirement for military forces in light of the changes that have occurred within the world's security environment, we should focus on the lessons contained within the title Colonel Heinl chose for his book. Marines are truly "Soldiers of the Sea." Using the sea as an operating base, not just for transportation, Marines can project sustained combat power ashore or maintain sustained presence anywhere around the globe.

The standard of excellence which Marines have established in the performance of their crisis response mission is the result of an organizational structure and institutional ethos focused on maritime expeditionary operations. Accordingly, as we shape our future military force structure, we would do well to remember that our Nation has been successful when it has employed its military forces in a manner consistent with the roles and missions for which they were organized, trained and equipped, or as Colonel Heinl would have stated "in a manner consistent with their identity." Herein is found the true value of his work.

A. M. Gray
Commandant of the Marine Corps.

FOREWORD TO FIRST EDITION

THE UNITED States Marine Corps has made an outstanding contribution to the development of amphibious operations in this era. It has also been, and remains, an outstanding example of the value of an elite professional force, combining a qualitative superiority and state of readiness which can only be attained by a force of such kind. Moreover, it has gone further than any armed force in any country towards demonstrating the potentialities of a three-in-one force, combining sea, land, and air action. As these are three points that I have been urging for many years, it has been an exhilarating experience to see them so strikingly demonstrated as they have been by the United States Marine Corps.

This history of the Marine Corps, written by Colonel Robert Debs Heinl, Jr., ably fulfils its purpose. It covers the story of the Corps from its birth in 1775 up to the present time, in 1962. Unlike most histories of this kind, it is a pleasure to read. The author has the rare gift of marshalling an immense amount of detail and presenting it in a continuously interesting way, so that the reader gets not only the flavour of the episodes, but also a sense of their underlying significance. That is a remarkable achievement in dealing with the story of a Corps which embraces such a multiplicity of experience in such a variety of operations and situations over so long a period.

The title, *Soldiers of the Sea*, is apt—epitomising the adaptability, and thus the flexibility, that such an amphibious fighting service possesses. The history of warfare shows that the basic strategic asset of sea-based peoples is amphibious flexibility. In tackling land-based opponents, they can produce a distraction to the enemy's power of concentration that is advantageously disproportionate to the scale of force they employ and the resources they possess.

But for full advantage this flexibility needs to be coupled with rapidity in exploitation. For the distraction-effect is likely to diminish once a landing takes place, since such commitment to a particular sector naturally tends to narrow what had been a widespread threat.

The best prospect of such rapidity, especially in the crucial first stage, lies in employing an expert amphibious force—and the need for it is now greater than ever before. Although Britain has, by force of geographical circumstances been more amphibious in action than any other power, her performance has been much poorer than her experience. That deficiency is due to her failure to develop her marines into a special "lock-opening" force of adequate scale. The United States has been wiser in this important respect.

The value of such a force is proved by experience with elite troops. Their key importance as lock-openers has been repeatedly proved in the history of warfare, and more than ever in recent times. No fresh problem in war has been tackled effectively if treated in a "general purpose" way, and entrusted to a service or arm primarily concerned with other and more familiar problems.

These lessons were emphasized, and the conclusions reinforced, by the experiences of World War II—both positive and negative. The Pacific campaign very clearly demonstrated the strategic value of amphibious flexibility. But for the distracting and the by-passing power it conferred—the ability to vary the thrust-point while keeping the opponent on the stretch—the penetration of Japan's successive outlying defence lines would have been a far slower and more costly process.

There is a tendency to view the war in Europe as mainly a continental struggle, in which sea power played merely a secondary part as the means of conveying troops and supplies to nourish the fighting on land. But an analysis of the distribution of Germany's strength at successive stages of the war leads to very different conclusions and changes the picture. For it becomes evident that the amphibious flexibility provided by sea power, which the Western allies possessed, exerted a much greater influence than would appear on the surface.

It was sea power that made possible the surprise landings of the Western allies in Algeria and Morocco, in November 1942. It was sea power which subsequently trapped the German and Italian forces in Tunisia, ensuring that the whole of them were captured, in May 1943. That "bag" cleared the way for the Western allies' re-entry into Europe, by wiping out the bulk of the Axis forces that would otherwise have been available to resist and perhaps rebuff the Allied cross-sea jump into Sicily. The landing in Sicily, two months later, produced the downfall of Mussolini and the swiftly following capitulation of Italy.

Soon after the Allies landed in Italy in September 1943, however, the distraction-effect began to diminish. In the later phases of the campaign the Allies were employing a much larger force than the Germans used to oppose their advance.

This turn was due partly to the narrowness of the Italian peninsula. Offensive distraction is most effective when it carries a wide strategic threat, and where there is ample room for its development by attack to be expanded easily and quickly into a widening tactical threat. But the relatively poor distraction-effect of the Italian campaign, after the landing, was due also to the Allies' reduced amphibious power in that theatre of war. Italy would have been a more suitable site for attack if there had been plenty of assault shipping, and if it had been available for a long enough time. But when the decision was made to land there, the Allied planners were already committed to shift most of the assault shipping back to Britain in readiness for the landing in Normandy. The need for adequate amphibious means is another basic lesson of modern warfare.

This need is more than a matter of shipping. Skilled personnel are of no less importance, and they must be available in adequate numbers if landing operations are to be executed smoothly *and* exploited quickly. The necessary skill is the product of special training in amphibious techniques, and of constant practice in the combination of the different elements in such a force.

From a study of the African, Sicilian, and Italian landings it becomes evident that many hitches and delays stemmed from lack of knowledge and experience in dealing with amphibious problems, and from differences of view between the Army and the Navy commanders and staffs respectively. In seeking the explanation, and in comparing the execution with the better performances among Pacific landing operations, a clue can be found in a significant factor that was absent in the European theatre. For here there was no expert amphibious force such as the divisions of the Marine Corps provided in the Pacific. Such a spearhead could have made a striking difference and great improvement in the initial rapidity and general effectiveness of the landings in Europe.

A study of British landing operations—not only those in World War II, but throughout the past 300 years—tends to confirm that deduction. From Britain's amphibious superiority during those centuries arose the world-wide empire which this small island gained. Yet for all their success at sea, and in expanding overseas, the performance of the British in amphibious warfare did not reflect their amphibious experience. When they met any serious opposition their expeditionary forces more often failed than succeeded.

A study of the record shows that the most frequent cause of failure lay in a mutual misunderstanding of the other Service's problems. All too often, the attack miscarried or evaporated in a wrangle among the "co-operating" Services.

British amphibious operations furnished further disappointments in World War I. At that time, the leaders of the British Army had become so continentally-minded that their guiding idea was simply to provide a direct reinforcement to France by shipping the bulk of the Army across the Channel to fight alongside their ally. They frowned on arguments for continuing to follow the historic principles of British strategy, a strategic tradition which had now in soldiers' eyes become heresy. As a result, few amphibious operations were attempted, and they did not fulfil expectations.

The only important amphibious operation of the war took place in 1915, with the aim of opening the Dardanelles by capturing the Gallipoli peninsula, dominating the gateway to these straits, and thereby knocking out Turkey, which had become Germany's ally. Amphibious flexibility and its distraction-effect enabled the British to throw the enemy off balance both in the original April landing and again in the fresh August landing further up the peninsula. But on each occasion, a promising opportunity was forfeited on landing, and stalemate ensued, so the British government decided to withdraw the expeditionary force.

That was a dismal ending to a move which by its original threat had upset the whole war plan of the Germans for 1915. What the opening of the Dardanelles would have meant was summed up by General von Falkenhayn, then the directing head of the Germanic alliance, when he said that: "If the straits between the Mediterranean and the Black Sea were not permanently closed to Entente traffic, all hopes of a successful issue of the war [for Germany] would be seriously diminished. Russia would have been freed from her strategic isolation which . . . ensured that the forces of this Titan would eventually and automatically be crippled."

Tsarist Russia lacked the industrial resources to equip her manpower adequately, so that her prospects depended on the inflow of supplies from her Western allies. The consequences of their failure to open up the Dardanelles were far-reaching. The terrific losses suffered by Russia's ill-equipped armies led to the Revolution there, and the establishment of the Communist regime. Moreover, the Dardanelles failure turned the British against the idea of renewing amphibious strategy, and committed them more fully to a slow-grinding attrition campaign on the deeply entrenched Western

Front—a long-drawn effort which left both Britain and France exhausted.

During the 20 years' interval which followed, before World War II, the introduction of some measures of joint staff training raised hopes that amphibious operations would be better conducted if war came again. But in 1940, the seaborne moves to counter the German invasion of Norway were as badly bungled as almost any of those in the past. The next important amphibious thrust, that against Dieppe in 1942, was another depressing fiasco. The subsequent operations have already been discussed.

Historians may well be puzzled that Britain's performance in amphibious operations during these centuries should have been so poor in comparison with the achievements of her Navy on the high seas, and also of her Army ashore. A clue to the puzzle may be found in a missing factor. For although Britain formed a force of marines as far back as 1664, and although its value was soon proved, it has always been confined to a very limited scale and scope. It has never been developed, like the United States Marine Corps, into a strong amphibious fighting force embodying all the different arms and elements required for effective attacking power and capable of carrying out a large-scale landing operation. No other explanation becomes apparent in studying the record.

This conclusion leads to the question of why in Britain, the country most dependent on sea power, the marines have never been developed in adequate scale and scope. The basic hindrance has been that opposing vested interests, which are strong everywhere, are reinforced by the distrust of specialisation that is a British characteristic. The Services, and particularly the Army, have always been inclined to resist specialist claims and specialised forces. If compelled by necessity to accept these, the Army has sought to discard them as soon as possible—and usually too soon. It maintains its faith in the general-purpose concept—the idea and ideal that *every* man should be capable of fitting *any* job, and be a "jack of all trades."

Linked with such disregard of differing aptitudes has been an ingrained distrust of those who mastered any special technique, often prompted by an underlying fear that recognition of its importance would disqualify for promotion those who had not acquired it. This very common attitude is reinforced by the repugnance which armies have shown constantly towards new methods and new instruments. Even when something new could no longer be resisted, its further development has too often been handed over to a general handyman who would not be likely to make the most of its potentialities.

Yet from Gideon to Guderian, the value of elite forces has been repeatedly demonstrated in warfare. The 300 that formed "The *sword* of the Lord, and of Gideon" in defeating the host of Midian were picked, out of 10,000, by the way they gave evidence of exceptional dash. Alexander the Great's Royal Companion cavalry, Cromwell's Ironsides of the New Model, Napoleon's Imperial Guard, Ludendorff's storm troops in the German breakthrough attacks of 1918, and Guderian's Panzers in 1940, are among many successive links in the chain of evidence that shows the value of having elite forces for tasks of key importance. The British, however, have long shown an obstinate disfavour for the concept, except in its application to the social sphere. Although the Foot Guards have a very fine military record, they would hardly have survived but for their intimate association with the monarchy. In war, the British have paid heavily for their reluctance to recognise the need and value of special skills—and in no respect have they paid so heavily as in amphibious operations.

The Americans have adjusted their forces far better to changing conditions and new needs, especially in the amphibious sphere. The development of the Marine Corps, embodying all the various elements required for timely effect, has been a striking example.

In World War II it was sea power and its companion, the power to throw a force ashore wherever desired or needed, that was basically the decisive factor in liberating Europe from Hitler's tyranny, as well as in liberating the Far East from Japan. By itself the land power of Russia was not enough to overthrow Hitler.

After World War II, the older kinds of military power were overshadowed by the development of nuclear power. But this was too drastic and dangerous for use except as a last resort, even while it remained a monopoly. Moreover it was obviously unsuitable as a counter to insidious or limited forms of aggression. Thus sea power and its amphibious companion continued to be the operative means for curbing aggression against any of the free countries on the Eurasian land mass.

Since Russia has developed nuclear weapons in quantity to match America's, a nuclear stalemate has developed. In such a situation, local and limited aggression becomes more likely, and amphibious forces become more necessary, both as a deterrent and as a counter to aggression—a counter which can be used without being suicidal, and a deterrent which is therefore credible.

Although airborne forces may seem a better counter, as being quicker to arrive, their speed of strategic movement, and their effect on arrival, are subject to many limitations. Many of the spots where an emergency may arise are far distant and cannot be reached by air without flying over foreign territory or making a long circuit to avoid it. Most of the Asiatic and African countries are acutely sensitive to any infringement of their recently acquired independence, resentful of Western interference in those regions, and insistent on preserving neutrality—or apt to side with the opponents of the West. A circuitous air approach, even where possible, increases the need for intermediate bases where aircraft can be refueled and serviced, while their establishment and maintenance are subject to similar political difficulties.

As strategic movement by air is so liable to the political risks of being blocked or impeded by countries in its path, it is becoming strategically unreliable as a way of meeting the world-wide problems of the Atlantic Alliance—which more truly should be called the Oceanic Alliance. Moreover, on arrival, an airborne force needs airfields for its disembarkation and logistic support. Adequate fields for large aircraft and a large force do not exist in many areas, and even when they do, they may be in hostile hands. If they are well defended, an attempt to capture them by parachute drop can easily turn into disaster, while a ground approach may be checked through lack of tactical mobility and of weapon-power sufficient to overcome strong resistance, for an airborne force is narrowly limited in the vehicles, heavy weapons, and ammunition it can carry. If it is held up and has to wait for these requirements to arrive by sea, it loses its main advantage—rapidity of intervention. Another of its drawbacks is its vulnerability to interception while in transit.

To meet emergencies, two hands are better than one, and essential when one is unreliable. While it is *desirable* to have an airborne force, which enables quicker intervention where its use is possible, it is *essential* to have a marine force. An amphibious force of modern type, operating from the sea and equipped with helicopters, is free from dependence on airfields, beaches, ports, and land bases, with all their logistical and political complications. The use of an airborne force, or of any land-based force, is a more irrevocable step than the use of an amphibious force, since its commitment is more definite and its withdrawal more difficult. A self-contained and sea-based amphibious force, of which the United States Marine Corps is the prototype, is the best kind of fire-extinguisher because of its flexibility, reliability, logistic simplicity, and relative economy.

These conclusions lead on to a further reflection. It has come to be recognized that the old distinction between land and sea operations is no longer suitable. But the recent three-fold division into land, sea, and air operations fits no better and is already out ot date. Rather than dividing them into arbitrary and obsolete land, sea, and air components, problems need to be tackled in a more integrated way, blending the functions of the three Services. The United States Marine Corps is a three-in-one Service in embryo. It has gained so much experience in combining land, sea, and air action that it forms a nucleus and a pattern for further development. Logically it should be the basis for further progress in integration.

B. H. LIDDELL HART

PREFACE

THIS HISTORY is an attempt to convey what the Marine Corps is, and how it came to be that way; and to recount the achievements and doings of the Corps, and why. This is the history of the Marine Corps as an institution —a story not confined to "Expeditions, Engagements, and Distinguished Service," but also one of planning, policy, command, administration, traditions, and personalities. Because this is Marine Corps history, I have chiefly focused attention on the Corps and on its members; for so doing, I hope I shall not be taxed with narrowness, or for failure (even when sorely tempted) to enlarge upon surrounding events which merely set the stage. Activities of the other Services, for example, however interesting or inspiring, receive mention only as they impinge on those of the Marine Corps. But, of course, an exception must be noted on behalf of the Navy. Just as our story is their story, so theirs is ours. The Marine Corps is one of the Naval Services, and —though some naval historians forget it—the history of Marines is naval history.

"No historian, no matter how he tries," wrote John P. Marquand, "can be neutral." The same can be said of Marines. And when one is both Marine and historian, non-involvement becomes difficult indeed. I have, nevertheless, tried to see things clearly and see them whole. Mistakes, blemishes, and lapses—like Oliver Cromwell's mole—appear from time to time, even on the brighter pages.

The sources of this history consist of executive documents, Congressional proceedings, official reports and records, the memoirs, biographies, and private papers of officers and statesmen, contemporary journals and Service publications, and, of course, the works of other military and general historians. Original documents, where available, have in all cases been freely consulted; but, to the maximum extent, citations have been made to printed works, for they are more easily available to the reader. Quotations, except where obvious in origin or trivial in nature, have been documented either by footnote or in the text, as have other matters of fact likely to arouse question or curiosity. I have, however, made no attempt to document facts which, in Garrett Mattingly's phrase, "lie within history's public domain." In my selection of illustrations I have followed the principle of using contemporary material only and generally have avoided after-the-fact pictures done in later times. A bibliography containing the most important sources is appended. Finally, as the work moves forward into my own era as a Marine, I have not hesitated, where necessary, to rely on direct recollection, impressions, and conclusions, since, like Virgil, "These things I saw, and a part of them I was."

Among the many who have assisted, informed, advised and (on occasion) cautioned me, I must single out for special thanks Lieutenant Colonel J. H. Magruder III, Director of Marine Corps Museums, whose encouragement, unsparing criticism, and rich fund of historical resource have aided me at every turn. Colonel Magruder's expert hand will also be recognized in the art work of the dust jacket and chapter tailpieces. For equally unsparing critical reading and for long hours thereby diverted from his own studies, I am deeply grateful to my old friend and company commander, Brigadier General S. B. Griffith, as I am to General Thomas Holcomb for sessions of invaluable reminiscence and criticism.

The heavy chore of reviewing, correcting, and commenting on the initial draft of this history was cheerfully accepted and painstakingly executed by "a multitude of witnesses," including Generals A. A. Vandegrift, C. B. Cates, L. C. Shepherd, Jr., R. McC. Pate, H. M. Smith, H. Schmidt, O. P. Smith, G. C. Thomas, V. E. Megee, and R. E. Hogaboom; Lieutenant Generals J. T. Selden and W. M. Greene, Jr.; Major Generals E. A. Ostermann, R. C. Mangrum, and V. H. Krulak; Brigadier Generals S. R. Shaw and W. R. Wendt; Colonels DeW. Schatzel, R. C. McGlashan, J. C. Murray, Roger Willock, H. N. Shea, H. M. Hoyler, and A. M. Fraser; Lieutenant Colonel E. L. Smith; Major J. E. Greenwood; Messrs. Robert Sherrod and N. J. Wilson, and Professor W. H. Russell.

Others to whom thanks or special acknowledgment are due include Lieutenant General J. C. Smith; Rear Admirals H. W. Osterhaus, E. M. Eller, and S. E. Morison; the late Major General R. C. Berkeley and his son, Major General J. P. Berkeley; Colonels J. J. Farley, T. G. Roe, W. M. Miller, and J. R. Blandford; Lieutenant Colonel P. N. Pierce; Commander T. K. Treadwell; Major T. A. Tighe and his son, Lieutenant Colonel T. B. Tighe; Major D. E. Schwulst; Captains W. A. Merrill, R. H. Westmoreland, and R. B. Asprey; First Sergeant R. F. Lee; Dr. Louis Morton; Messrs. Jonathan Daniels, David Lawrence, D. M. O'Quinlivan, LeRoy Whitman, and T. R. Butler (for permission to use hitherto unpublished correspondence of General Butler); Mrs. John W. Thomason, Jr. (for permission to reprint passages and unpublished drawings from the works of her distinguished husband), and Mrs. Iva Holland. The Historical Branch, G-3 Division, Marine Corps Headquarters, has been unfailing in assistance, criticism, and support, while the Photographic Section has been equally prompt, painstaking, and helpful. All photographs are Marine Corps or Navy, many from the Marine Corps Museum, and the cartography is the work of Mr. W. J. Clipson. For hours of tedious work on the final draft and proofs, and for domestic forbearance throughout, I must thank my wife, Nancy, and my daughter, Pamela.

Finally, nothing I can say about this book expresses so completely my feeling toward it as the sentences penned 33 years ago by one of the Navy's ablest officers, Holloway H. Frost, in the Preface to a history of his own:

> There will doubtless be detected upon every page and along every line of this volume a love of my own Service which I have made no effort to suppress. I venture to hope that some of this sentiment may be communicated to the reader.

This having been said, and having testified to the aid and encouragement of so many, I must underscore that the conclusions, not to speak of the defects, of this history are wholly my own. In the time-honored wording of *Navy Regulations,* "the opinions or assertions . . . are the private ones of the writer and are not to be construed as official or reflecting the views of the Navy Department or the naval service at large." This book, therefore, is in no sense an official or even a "semi-official" work. It is the history of the Marine Corps as I have come to understand it.

R. D. HEINL, JR.
Colonel, U. S. Marine Corps

Port-au-Prince
Haiti
15 May 1962

CONTENTS

CONTENTS

MAPS

CHAPTER ENDPIECES

These drawings of Bits and Pieces of Marine Equipment were prepared by Lieutenant Colonel John H. Magruder, III, U. S. Marine Corps, who is Director of Marine Corps Museums, Quantico, Virginia.

ABBREVIATIONS

The following is the system of abbreviations used in this book. Officers' ranks and enlisted ratings are those contemporaneous with the event. Officers and men named will be presumed to be of the U. S. Marine Corps or Marine Corps Reserve unless otherwise indicated, or when possessing a distinctively naval rank. Other Service abbreviations are: USA, U. S. Army; USN, U. S. Navy; USCG, U. S. Coast Guard; USAF, U. S. Air Force; CSMC, Confederate States Marine Corps; CSN, Confederate States Navy; CSA, Confederate States Army; RN, Royal Navy; RM, Royal Marines; KMC, Korean Marine Corps; IJN, Imperial Japanese Navy; NKPA, North Korean People's Army; CCF, Chinese Communist Forces.

AA—Antiaircraft
AAF—Army Air Forces
ACAF—Amphibious Corps, Atlantic Fleet
ACPF—Amphibious Corps, Pacific Fleet
AEF—American Expeditionary Forces
AirFMFPac—Aircraft, Fleet Marine Force, Pacific
AirNorSols—Aircraft, Northern Solomons
AKA—Attack cargo ship
APA—Attack transport
APD—High-speed transport
BAR—Browning automatic rifle
BLT—Battalion landing team
CAM—Composite Americal-Marine Division
CG—Commanding general
CinC—Commander in Chief; CinCFE, Commander in Chief, Far East; CinC-Pac, Commander in Chief, Pacific.
CMC—Commandant of the Marine Corps
CNO—Chief of Naval Operations
CO—Commanding officer
Com—As prefix, means Commander; Com-NavFE, Commander, Naval Forces, Far

East; ComSoPac, Commander, South Pacific.
ComInCh—Commander in Chief, U. S. Fleet
CP—Command post
CSMO—"Close station—march order" (field artillery command)
CV—Aircraft carrier
CVE—Escort carrier
CUB—Naval advance base unit, medium size (World War II)
D- —As prefix, followed by numeral, assistant chief of staff at division level (1) for personnel, (2) for intelligence, (3) for operations and training, and (4) for logistics; alternatively, may refer to number of days before or after D-day, commencement of an operation.
DD—Destroyer
DI—Recruit drill-instructor
DSC—Distinguished Service Cross
DSO—Distinguished Service Order (British)
DUKW—Amphibian truck

FEAF—Far East Air Force

FLEX—Fleet landing exercise

FMF—Fleet Marine Force

FMFPac—Fleet Marine Force, Pacific

FO—Forward observer

G- —As prefix, followed by numeral, assistant chief of staff at division or higher level (post-1944) for staff sections as indicated under D- (*q.v.*)

GHQ—General headquarters

Gd'H—Gendarmerie (Garde) d'Haiti

GNN—Guardia Nacional, Nicaragua

HMS—His (Her) Majesty's Ship (British); HMAS, His (Her) Majesty's Ship (Australian); HIJMS, His Imperial Japanese Majesty's Ship.

HMX-1—Marine Helicopter Experimental Squadron 1

HMR—As prefix, followed by numeral, Marine helicopter transport squadron

IMAC—I Marine Amphibious Corps

III AC—III Amphibious Corps

JAG—Judge Advocate General

JASCO—Joint assault signal company

JCS—Joint Chiefs of Staff

JTF—As prefix, followed by numeral, Joint Task Force

LCI—Landing craft, infantry

LCM—Landing craft, mechanized

LCP—Landing craft, personnel

LCVP—Landing craft, vehicle and personnel

LCT—Landing craft, tank

LFASCU—Landing force air support control unit

LSD—Landing ship, dock

LST—Landing ship, tank

LVT—Amphibian tractor

MAG- —As prefix, followed by numeral, Marine Air Group

MAW- —Preceded or followed by numeral, Marine Air Wing; MAWPac, Marine Air Wings, Pacific Fleet

MB—Marine Barracks

MC—Member of Congress, or Medical Corps, U. S. Navy

MCI—Marine Corps Institute

MD—Marine detachment

MGC—Major General Commandant

MLR—Main line of resistance

MP—Military police

MSR—Main supply route

NAP—Naval aviation pilot (enlisted pilot)

NCO—Noncommissioned officer

NGF—Naval gunfire support

NTLF—Northern Troops and Landing Force

OCMH—Office of the Chief of Military History, U. S. Army

O.D.—Officer of the Day

OinC—Officer in charge

ONRL—Office of Naval Records and Library

OSS—Office of Strategic Services

P.I.—Parris Island, S.C.

RCT—Regimental combat team

ROK—Republic of Korea

SCAT—South Pacific Combat Air Transport Command

SNLF—Special Naval Landing Force (Japanese)

S.O.S.—Services of Supply, American Expeditionary Forces

SSN—Personnel specialty designator number

TAF—Tactical Air Force

UDT—Underwater demolition team

VAC—V Amphibious Corps

VMF—Marine fighting squadron

VMF(N)—Marine night-fighting squadron

VMO—Marine observation squadron

VMS—Marine scouting squadron

VMSB—Marine scout-bombing squadron

VMTB—Marine torpedo bombing squadron

VO—Observation squadron (Navy)

VS—Scouting squadron (Navy)

Aircraft Designations

Unless otherwise indicated, aircraft are U. S. Navy types. Numeral in parentheses indicates number of engines.

AD—Skyraider, Douglas (1)

B-17—Army Flying Fortress, Boeing (4)

B-29—Army/Air Force Superfortress, Boeing (4)

DH-4—"Flying Coffin," DeHavilland (1)

F2A—Buffalo, Brewster (1)

F4F—Wildcat, Grumman (1)

F9F—Panther jet, Grumman (1)

F2H2—Banshee jet, McDonnell (2)

F4U—Corsair, Vought (1) (monoplane, World War II, Korea)

GV-1—Hercules, Lockheed (4)

HRP-1—"Flying Banana," Piasecki helicopter (1, but 2 rotors)

HRS—Sikorsky helicopter (1)

J2F—Duck, Grumman (1)

JN—Jenny, Curtiss (1)

L-4—Army designation for the OY Sentinel, Stinson (1)

O2U—Corsair, Vought (1) (biplane, 1927-34)

OL-8—Loening amphibian (1)

OP-1—Pitcairn autogiro (1)

P-51—Army Mustang, North American (1)

P-400—Army Airacobra (export), Bell (1)

PBJ—Mitchell, North American (2) (Army B-25)

PBY—Catalina, Consolidated (2)

PBY5A—Catalina (amphibian), Consolidated (2)

PB4Y—Liberator, Consolidated (4) (Army B-24)

PV—Ventura, Lockheed Vega (2)

R4D—Skytrain, Douglas (2) (DC-3, Army C-47)

R5D—Skymaster, Douglas (4) (DC-4, Army C-54)

R4Q—Flying Boxcar, Fairchild (2)

SBD—Dauntless, Douglas (1)

SB2U—Vindicator, Vought (1)

TBF—Avenger, Grumman (1)

TBM—Avenger, General Motors (1)

1 THE OLD CORPS *1775-1815*

There shall be raised and organized a Corps of Marines . .
—ACT OF CONGRESS, 11 July 1798

M*ARINES* are as old as war at sea.

When Themistocles mobilized Athenian sea power against the invading Persians in 480 B.C., one of his first decrees was:[1]

. . . enlist Marines, twenty to a ship, from men between 20 and 30, and archers.

These men, called *Epibatae,* fought the Greek triremes at Salamis which turned back Xerxes and saved Athens. Later, Rome had her separate legions of *milites classiarii* ("soldiers of the fleet") who served aboard the quinqueremes of the line, one legion to each fleet.[2]

Modern Marines came into being during the 17th century. In 1622 Cardinal de Richelieu raised a *Compagnie de la Mer* composed of French sailors trained to fight on shore. But it was not until 42 years later on 28 October 1664, during the Dutch Wars between England and Holland, that the first true corps of Marines was formed. On that date King Charles II organized "The Duke of York and Albany's Maritime Regiment of Foot" by an Order in Council which decreed:[3]

That twelve hundred Land Souldjers be forthwith raysed, to be in readinesse, to be distributed into his Ma⁺ˢ Fleets prepared for Sea Service wᶜʰ twelve hundred men are to be putt into One Regiment. . . .

The new regiment differed from Richelieu's Frenchmen in that it was to be made up of soldiers who would be bred to the sea, and it was to come under command of the Admiralty. Within a year, Holland followed suit with the Royal Netherlands *Korps Mariniers,* and soon after, Richelieu's seaman-company won a new name: *1er Régiment de Marine.*

The first American Marines were four colonial battalions raised in 1740 to fight the Spaniards in the War of the Austrian Succession. Alexander Spotts-wood of Virginia was their first colonel, but he died a few weeks after assuming command. The regiment, 3,000 strong, then passed to Colonel William Gooch and became known as "Gooch's Marines." Under Admiral Edward Vernon ("Old Grog" to his sailors), Gooch led his regiment and was wounded at Cartagena in April 1741, following which, in July, the Marines landed unopposed at Guantanamo (then known as Walthenham) Bay, Cuba, to secure a base for the British fleet. Although the campaign achieved little, it gave America, if nothing else, the name "Mount Vernon," chosen for his Potomac home by one of Gooch's Marine officers, Captain Lawrence Washington, who had become a staunch admirer of his admiral.

By the end of the Seven Years' War, during which British Marines again served in North America, Marines had a well-established place in the naval scheme of things. Every fighting ship had a Marine detachment whose job it was to stiffen the sailors and, if necessary, enforce discipline among them. During sea fights, Marines headed boarding parties and fought from the tops and rigging as sharpshooters and grenadiers. And Marines were then, as now, the spearhead and backbone of the landing force.

THE CONTINENTAL MARINES

After the outbreak of the American Revolution, John Adams and his Marine (or Maritime) Committee of Congress tried from the outset to pattern our navy on the familiar and eminently successful British model. To do so, of course, required Marines. More specifically, an initial if unrealized project of the Continental Congress was a seaborne invasion of Nova Scotia, for which, as early as May 1775, the raising of Marines was proposed.[4]

Sitting in Tun Tavern, on King (or Water) Street in Philadelphia, after daily debate at the State House (now Independence Hall), the Marine Committee worked out the purchase of ships, wrote *Rules for the Regulation of the Navy of the United Colonies*, established a "Naval Pay List," and drafted a resolution which, enacted by Congress on 10 November 1775, created the Continental Marines:[5]

Resolved, That two Battalions of Marines be raised consisting of one Colonel two lieutenant Colonels, two Majors & Officers as usual in other regiments, that they consist of an equal number of privates with other battalions; that particular care be taken that no person be appointed to office or inlisted into said Battalions, but such as are good seamen, or so acquainted with maritime affairs as to be able to serve to advantage by sea, when required. That they be inlisted and commissioned for and during the present war between Great Britain and the colonies, unless dismissed by order of Congress. That they be distinguished by the names of the first & second battalions of American Marines, and that they be considered a part of the number, which the continental Army before Boston is ordered to consist of.

Anticipating Congress, George Washington had already fitted out a squadron of his own, including soldiers detailed as Marines. Likewise, eight colonies—Massachusetts, Rhode Island, Connecticut, Pennsylvania, Maryland, Virginia, North Carolina, and Georgia—had their own Marines as adjuncts to state navies. All these but Maryland's were in being before Congress formed the Continental Marines. Indeed, as early as July 1775, the Massachusetts sloop, *Interprise*, on Lake Champlain (then the frontier of western Massachusetts), had one Marine officer (Lieutenant James Watson) and 17 enlisted Marines on her rolls. How well these and other Massachusetts Marines served Benedict Arnold, who was in command on the lake, may be judged by his description of them as "the refuse of every regiment."[6]

Samuel Nicholas of Philadelphia, owner of a prosperous inn, Conestoga Wagon, was commissioned a captain on 28 November 1775 and charged with raising the Marines provided for by Congress. Nicholas remained senior officer in the Continental Marines throughout the Revolution and is properly considered the first Marine Commandant.

Recruiting, to the tune of "Drum, Fife, and Colours," promptly began at Philadelphia, the recruiting rendezvous being Tun Tavern. Because of his prowess as a recruiter, Robert Mullan, the innkeeper, was also commissioned a captain.

The pay of a private of Marines was six and two-thirds dollars a month. His daily ration, the prescribed Navy ration, was a pound of bread, a pound of beef or pork, a pound of potatoes or turnips or a half pint of peas, and a half pint of rum. Butter was served out once a week, pudding twice, and cheese thrice. Uniforms, when available, were green and white.

OPERATIONS DURING THE REVOLUTION

By early 1776, Captain Nicholas had the Continental Marines ready for their first expedition. Their objective was New Providence Island in the Bahamas, where the British were known to have large supplies of arms and gunpowder, both much in demand in Washington's army.

With Nicholas in command, 268 Marines sailed from the Delaware on 17

February 1776 aboard Continental warships under Commodore Esek Hopkins. On 3 March, Nicholas landed his battalion and marched on Fort Montague, one of two forts guarding old Nassau Town. After a feeble show of resistance (three rounds from one of the fort's guns), the garrison withdrew, whereupon the Marines secured the fort and bivouacked for the night. The remaining work, Fort Nassau, was still to be occupied. Captain Nicholas wrote of this action:[7]

> The next morning by daylight we marched forward to take possession of the Governor's house . . . and demanded the keys to the fort, which were given to me immediately, and then took possession of Fort Nassau. In it there were 40 cannon mounted and well loaded for our reception with round, langridge, and canister shot. All this was accomplished without firing a single shot from our side. We found in this fort a great quantity of shot and shells, with 15 brass mortars, but the grand article, powder, the Governor sent off the night before. . . .

All told, the Marines took 88 guns, 15 mortars, 16,535 shells and cannon balls, but only 24 barrels of powder. Even so, it was a welcome haul for the Continental Army.

Homeward bound, on 6 April, the Marines had their first taste of battle when Hopkins' squadron fell in with HMS *Glasgow*, 20 guns, off Block Island. In the confused and lubberly night action which followed, Captain Nicholas' ship, *Alfred*, lost her second lieutenant of Marines, John Fitzpatrick (probably the first U.S. Marine, and certainly our first Marine officer, ever killed in action), "a worthy officer, sincere friend and companion," wrote Nicholas, "that was beloved by all the ship's company." Six other Marines were killed and four wounded aboard ships of the squadron, while the *Glasgow* reported four killed and wounded, all by the Continental Marines' musketry.[8]

After the fleet's return to home waters, the Marines were landed and Nicholas (who had been promoted to major, at $32 a month, for his work in the Bahamas) was ordered to "discipline four companies of Marines" at Philadelphia. In December 1776, leaving one company behind, but reinforcing the other three from ships' detachments, Nicholas and his battalion were attached to Cadwalader's division of Pennsylvania militia in Washington's army. Although ice floes prevented Cadwalader from getting across the Delaware to join in the Christmas night attack on Trenton, he rejoined Washington next day, in time for the Marines to fight in the second battle of Trenton (Assunpink) where the Continentals slipped through Lord Cornwallis' fingers by the ruse of false campfires at night. Then, on 3 January of the new year, the Army fell on the British flank and rear at Princeton, scoring a victory in which the Marines were proud to share. After this came the winter camp of 1777 at Morristown, New Jersey (not to be confused with the more publicized succeeding winter at Valley Forge). Camp life at Morristown, where the Marines shared the icy fortunes of the Continental Army, was as arduous as any fighting.

In March 1777, the Marine battalion was detached from the Army and returned to Philadelphia to provide ships' detachments and perform various shore duties for the Continental Navy. Among the most conspicuous of these was participation in the defense of Fort Mifflin and the Delaware River operations of October and November 1777. Fort Mifflin, below Philadelphia on the Delaware, together with other works and naval river forces, prevented the British fleet, under Admiral Lord Richard Howe, from supporting and reinforcing the army of his brother, Major General Sir William Howe, in Philadelphia. From 22 October until 15 November, 12 British ships of the line, frigates, and sloops-of-war, co-ordinating with siege batteries and Hessian infantry ashore, battered Fort Mifflin, the adjacent Fort Mercer, and the river obstacles defended by the tiny American squadron. Continental Marines formed part of the 450-man garrison of Mifflin, and Continental and Pennsylvania Marines served aboard the American ships. After a prolonged and obstinate defense in which Fort Mifflin was literally leveled by sustained bombardment and some 250 of the defenders killed or wounded, the position was abandoned, and the remaining magazine blown up. The defense of Fort Mifflin was the last shore action, exclusive of amphibious raids and landings, on the part of the Continental Marines.

At sea, Marine detachments played their role in the naval actions of the war. Aboard the *Reprisal,* commanded by Captain Lambert Wickes, a detachment of two officers and 30 enlisted men shared in her daring raids on British shipping in European waters in 1777, and Captain Miles Pennington, Wickes's Marine officer, was lost when the ship finally went down. The junior Marine officer, Lieutenant John Elliott, who "had a Musquet ball lodged in his wrist" in one of the ship's actions, survived.

Under John Paul Jones, during the *Ranger's* cruise in April 1778, the Marines, commanded by Lieutenant Samuel Wallingford, took part in the two raids on British soil (at Whitehaven and St. Mary's Isle, where the Countess of Selkirk's silver was carried off)—among the few hostile landings in Great Britain since 1066. During the Selkirk affair, Lieutenant Wallingford apparently deported himself as a model Marine. Lady Selkirk, while describing landing force of 300 Marines (under Captain John Welsh) and 900 militia attempted to expel a British garrison from what is now Castine, Maine. The Marines executed two successful assault landings: the capture of Banks Island and four British guns on 26 July, and the storming of Bagaduce Heights on 28 July. The latter engagement demanded a 200-foot ascent up a steep cliff, with the troops clinging to trees and shrubs to keep from falling, while the British fired down at them. Despite 40 killed and 20 wounded, the Marines gained the heights and, reinforced by the militia, ultimately drove the defending Highlanders back into their fort with 70 casualties. Among the American dead, and remembered by his people as "a brave officer," was Captain Welsh. Despite the Marines' good work, the campaign degenerated into a fiasco. Commodore Dudley Saltonstall (who was afterward cashiered) failed to support the landing force, and, on 13 August, a British squadron arrived and made short work of the American ships, leaving the Marines and militia on the beach. Their southward retirement on foot provided an end to what one participant described as "a most disheartening affair."

After the Peace of Paris, which concluded the Revolution, both the Continental Navy and the Marines (which had attained a peak strength of 124 officers and about 3,000 men) waned rapidly and finally disappeared. The last warship was sold in 1785. Samuel Nicholas returned to business, his last recorded service on active duty being as a member of a court-martial. Although records show that Marines enlisted for and served in the few American armed vessels of the period (revenue cutters after 1791), there was no Corps organization, and little survived of the Continental Marines but a few gallant memories.

THE FOUNDING OF THE CORPS

In May 1798, Alexander Hamilton wrote to Secretary of War James McHenry:[10]

I presume you will have heard before this reaches you that a French privateer has made captures at the mouth of our harbor. This is too much humiliation after all that has passed—Our merchants are very indignant—Our government very prostrate in the view of every man of energy.

After some years of such pressure to protect American commerce against depredations by France, as well as by the Barbary pirates in the Mediterranean, Congress in 1794 passed a Naval Act which provided for six frigates (among them, the *Constellation, United States,* and *Constitution*) and for "the vile blackguard look" of one of the American naval officers, remarked the good behavior of "a civil young man in a green uniform, an anchor on his buttons, which were white [who] seemed naturally well bred. . . ."⁹ Alas, within 24 hours Wallingford was dead, killed in the action between the *Ranger* and HMS *Drake* on 24 April, the one American officer lost in this well-fought fight.

Aboard the *Bonhomme Richard,* Jones's Marine detachment was a foreign legion—three Irish officers and 137 French Marines whom John Adams described in his diary of 13 May 1779:

> After Dinner walked out, with Captains Jones & Landais to see Jones's Marines—dressed in the English uniforms, red & white; a Number of very active & clever Sergiants & Corporals are employed to teach them the exercise, and Manevous & Marches, &c.

The red coats were not British, however; they were the French *Corps Royaux d'Infanterie et d'Artillerie de Marine,* whom King Louis XVI assigned to Jones. French though they were, the *Bonhomme Richard's* Marines played a leading part in Jones's victory over HMS *Serapis* in the battle off Flamborough Head on 23 September 1779; 67 were killed or wounded, and their marksmanship at close quarters virtually cleared the British deck of its gun crews. There is no truth, however, in the story that the grenades which touched off the British ready-service powder at the height of battle were hurled by a Marine; this was the feat of a seaman.

At any rate, both before and after his great victory at Flamborough Head, John Paul Jones relied strongly on Marines, whether French or American. According to his biographer, Admiral Samuel E. Morison, Jones was partial to Marines because they understood military discipline, while the average officer of the Continental Navy was an ex-merchant mariner who didn't. At one point, Jones even tried to persuade Congress to recruit a Marine regiment with headquarters at Boston as a pool from which ships' guards could be drawn, but, despite its merit, the proposal was never acted on.

The last overseas expedition of the Continental Marines was another descent on New Providence in early 1778, when, with 28 men, Captain John Trevett (whose commission even antedated that of Nicholas) again captured Forts Nassau and Montague, again carried off ordnance and munitions for Washington, released 30 American prisoners, and took four ships into the bargain.

The Continental Marines had one more amphibious operation before the end of the war: the abortive Penobscot Bay attack in July 1779. There, a "officers, seamen, and Marines" to man them. Four years later, in one of his last acts before Congress removed naval affairs from the War Department, Secretary McHenry urged the creation of a "regiment of infantry . . . enlisted to act in the double capacity of Marines."[11] Before this recommendation could be acted on, Congress, on 27 April 1798, established the Navy Department. Within a month, the House Naval Committee was at work on a bill to raise "a battalion, to be called the Marine Corps."[12]

Committee chairman Samuel Sewall from Massachusetts took the lead: economy and discipline argued for a single Corps rather than an amalgamation of separate "minute detachments"; under a Corps headquarters Marines could be better trained and controlled when ashore between cruises; the "Major Commandant" could co-ordinate recruiting, superintend all Marines, and deal with complaints. Moreover, contended Sewall, the new Corps must be separate—"in addition to the present Military Establishment," read the Naval Committee's resolution of 22 May. Taking the House bill in hand, the Senate amended out all references to a battalion organization and increased the enlisted strength initially authorized. The House concurred, and on 11 July 1798, Congress sent to President John Adams "An Act for Establishing and Organizing a Marine Corps." Samuel Sewall might well be called its father.[13]

The Corps of 1798 was to consist of 33 officers and 848 "noncommissioned officers, musicians, and privates."[14] Its missions—"of amphibious nature," noted the Secretary of the Navy—were: sea duty; "duty in the forts and garrisons of the United States"; and perhaps most important for the long run, "any other duty on shore, as the President, at his discretion shall direct." Marines were to be immune from arrest for debt and were to be governed by the Articles of War or by *Navy Regulations* according to whether they were ashore or afloat (a bothersome duality inherited from the British Marines). Within 24 hours after signing the bill into law, President Adams appointed William Ward Burrows as Major Commandant of the Corps.

Major Burrows, a firm and polished Charlestonian who had done well in the Revolution, was a good example of the right man in the right place. He commenced recruiting energetically and handpicked a group of outstanding officers. Within six months (despite the fact that Marine privates got 40 per cent—$4 per month—less pay than seamen), he had the new Corps up to authorized strength; by the end of the year, he had gained an increase of eight officers and 196 men, and soon after, a promotion to lieutenant colonel— a proper recognition of the energy and common sense with which he had impressed both the President and the first Secretary of the Navy, Benjamin Stoddert. Where the efficiency of the Corps demanded, he cut red tape and set his own precedents. Dissatisfied with "The Vagabond, Matthew Spillard," as he described an Army quartermaster initially assigned to the Corps, he established his own supply system, and in fact served almost a year as Paymaster of the Corps (drawing the added pay and allowances of the empty billet) until a suitable officer, Lieutenant James Thompson, was appointed.[15]

Before Christmas 1798, Major Burrows took another step with long future consequences when he organized the U. S. Marine Band by the simple expedient of assessing every officer $10 (a second lieutenant drew $25 a month), although the matter of manning the band with suitable musicians was something else again, as we shall see. In any case, the officers paid up in good heart, one writing to Headquarters:[16]

If my brother officers in general have subscribed ten dollars as a fund for music, I'd thank Major Burrows to place ten to my Acct. and throw in my mite.

The Commandant's forthright attitude stands out in a letter he wrote in 1800 to Second Lieutenant Henry Caldwell, who, he heard, had been insulted by an officer of the Navy:[17]

Sir, When I answer'd your Letter I did not Know what Injuries you had received on board the *Trumbull*. . . . Yesterday the Secretary told me, that he understood one of the Lieutenants of the Navy had struck you. I lament that the Capt of y^r Ship cannot Keep Order on board of her. . . . As to yourself I can only say, that a Blow ought never to be forgiven, and without you wipe away this Insult offer'd to the Marine Corps, you cannot expect to join our Officers.

I have permitted you to leave the Ship, after settling the pay of the Marines &^{c} that you may be on an equal Footing with the Captain, or any one who dare insult you, or the Corps. I have wrote to Capt Carmick, who is at Boston to call on you & be your Friend. He is a Man of Spirit, and will take care of you, but don't let me see you 'till you have wip'd away this Disgrace. It is my Duty to support my Officers and I will do it with my Life, but they must deserve it.—On board the *Ganges*, about 12 Mo^s ago, Lt Gale, was struck by an Officer of the Navy, the Capt took no notice of the Business and Gale got no satisfaction on the Cruise: the moment he arrived he call'd the Lieu^t out, and shot him; afterwards Politeness was restor'd. . . .

Y^r obed^t Ser^t

W W B
Lt C.C
M.C

Under the iron guidance of Captain Carmick, whom we shall meet again, Mr. Caldwell "call'd out" his man (Lieutenant Charles Jewett) and "Politeness was restor'd." Happily no blood was shed; the Navy officer apologized.

Unfortunately, not all Marines won their causes even when Captain Carmick was at hand, as witness the fate of Captain James McKnight, Stephen Decatur's brother-in-law and the *Constellation's* Marine officer. McKnight became embroiled in a dispute with one of his shipmates on 14 October 1802 at Leghorn. As Carmick wrote next day to Colonel Burrows:[18]

He [McKnight] then left me and went on board his own Ship where they unfortunately renewed the Quarrel and aggravated each other to the highest pitch when they consented to fight at the distance of Six Paces with a Brace of Pistols and advance and should both fail then to take Cutlasses. Capt. McKnight received the Ball directly through the Center of his Heart; he had but time to say he was shot and expired. . . . We had him conveyed to the American Hotel but the laws of the place obliged us to convey him to a Vault near the Burial Ground that the Coroner might sit over him, and where I was witness to a scene I shall ever remember, that of being obliged to see a Brother Officer's heart cut out, that I might certify that the Ball had passed through the center of it. . . .

Aside from his almost parental supervision of his officers, the most lasting and tangible mark left by Burrows while establishing the Corps was his move of Marine Corps Headquarters from Philadelphia to Washington, the new capital, in July 1800, two months after his promotion to lieutenant colonel.[19] Coming to Washington by ship and by road, the Marines first bivouacked on Prospect Hill, Georgetown; then they crossed Rock Creek and set up a more permanent camp on the commanding hill between what is now 23d and 25th Streets, N.W., and Constitution Avenue and E Street, presently the site of the Navy's Bureau of Medicine and Surgery. On 31 March 1801, accompanied on horseback by his friend, President Jefferson, Colonel Burrows selected a seat for Headquarters and a depot for the Corps "near the Navy Yard and within easy marching distance of the Capitol."[20] In June 1801, contract was let for a Marine Barracks in the block bounded by 8th and 9th, and G and I (Eye) Streets, S.E.[21] Thus did "Eighth and Eye," at a cost of four cents a square foot, become the oldest post in the Corps, and the Commandant's House, on its G Street face, the oldest public building in Washington (except the White House) still in use in 1962. Of this destiny Burrows was indifferent at the time; reporting to Secretary Stoddert, he wrote:[22]

. . . but I care not for myself where my house is, so I can get my men comfortably provided for.

Early in 1804, ill health and financial difficulties forced Burrows to resign; within less than a year he was dead. His six-year commandancy had done much to fix the place of the Marine Corps in the scheme of things in spite of some senior naval officers with other ideas, as well as a few economy-minded congressmen who wished to whittle down the Corps.[23] But most important of all, Colonel Burrows brought to his office a style and tone which could serve as models for every future Commandant.

"TO ARMS, ESPECIALLY BY SEA"

Somewhat ahead of Congress, President Adams had realized that America could not call herself a nation until she could protect her commerce against French privateers bent on strangling our trade with Britain. On 22 May 1798, in response to a patriotic address by the students of Harvard, he replied, "To arms, then, my young friends—to arms, especially by sea." More practically, as Congress neared adjournment, Secretary of the Navy Stoddert wrote Captain John Barry, USN:[24]

Congress will break up on Monday, without a declaration of war against France. We shall not on that acct. be the less at war, against their armed vessels.

A series of victories followed for the spirited little United States Navy. The USS *Constellation* (with 41 Marines commanded by Lieutenant Bartholomew Clinch) shot to pieces two French frigates, *Insurgente* and *Vengeance*. The *Constitution,* whose Marine officer was that "Man of Spirit," Captain Carmick, took three prizes and cut out a captured British ship, *Sandwich,* held by the French in Puerto Plata, on the north coast of Santo Domingo. This affair, one of the most deft cutting-out expeditions of the early Navy, likewise involved the first landing on a foreign shore by Marines of the new Corps. The *Sandwich* lay in the harbor of Puerto Plata (where Marines would again land 116 years later) under the guns of a Spanish fort and in water too shallow for the *Constitution*. To get the prize, Lieutenant Isaac Hull, USN, the *Constitution's* first lieutenant, embarked 80 Marines and bluejackets aboard a commandeered American coaster which could enter the harbor without suspicion. Captain Carmick and his junior officer, First Lieutenant William Amory, had the Marines well hidden below, and, as Carmick related, "It put me in mind of the wooden horse at Troy."[25]

Entering Puerto Plata in broad daylight on 12 May 1800, Hull put his schooner alongside the *Sandwich,* and, in Carmick's words, "The men went on board like devils." Then the Marines landed (some in water up to their necks) and stormed up to the fort where, again in Carmick's account, "It was not half an hour after the ship was taken that I had possession of the fort and all the cannon spiked." As soon as the prize could be gotten ready for sea, Hull re-embarked the Marines and took her out. Unfortunately, the raid, though widely acclaimed, turned out to be a breach of Spain's nominal neutrality and the *Sandwich* had to be returned.

Following her earlier drubbing by the *Constitution,* the French frigate *Vengeance* limped into Dutch Curacao, where the local authorities refused to assist in repairs or succor. The French thereupon sent an expedition against Curacao from nearby Guadeloupe; this force beset the small Dutch garrison, who appealed for help to United States naval forces operating in the vicinity of St. Christopher. The USS *Merrimack* and *Patapsco* responded, the latter boldly entering the harbor on 23 September 1800 to shell the French ashore and attack their ships. Under command of Lieutenant James Middleton, the *Patapsco's* Marine officer, the combined Marine detachments from the two ships, 70 men in all, landed and went to the aid of the Dutch. During the night the French broke off action, re-embarked aboard their remaining ships, and made off, the American force staying to protect American interests ashore. This landing was the second and final shore action in our naval war with France.[26]

An aside, which again foreshadowed the future, was America's support of Toussaint l'Ouverture, the former Haitian slave who was fighting to control his own country and expel its French masters. In early 1800 United States ships and Marines helped Toussaint capture Jacmel, on the south coast of Haiti, and defeated his principal rival, a mulatto general named Rigaud, in several sharp actions off Léogane, the two Goâves, and St. Marc.

When peace was concluded with France in February 1801, the U. S. Navy had taken 85 French sail and established itself as a force to be reckoned with. As would so often happen again, the Navy was quickly reduced, and, on 21 May 1802, President Jefferson ordered widespread discharges of Marines which reduced the Corps to 26 officers and 453 enlisted men.[27]

TO THE SHORES OF TRIPOLI

Within three months after peace with France, trouble flared in the Mediterranean. The Barbary pirates, who for years had exacted tribute from the United States and from European powers, had become intolerable. Yusuf Caramanli, Bey of Tripoli, was the principal offender. When his demand for larger bribes was refused, he chopped down the flagpole before the American consulate on 14 May 1801 and began war on our commerce.

Four United States men-of-war—the *President, Philadelphia, Essex,* and *Enterprise*—including in their companies two-thirds of the small Marine Corps, were organized as a Mediterranean Squadron with orders to bring Yusuf to heel.

Amid many minor landings, desperate sea fights, and cutting-out expeditions (such as the brilliant recapture and destruction of the USS *Philadelphia* by Stephen Decatur), the overland campaign against Derna, spearheaded by a squad of Marines under First Lieutenant Presley Neville O'Bannon, was one of the outstanding events of the war.

The object of the march on Derna, Yusuf's capital, was to support Hamet (or Ahmet) Bey, rightful claimant to Yusuf Caramanli's throne, who was exiled in Egypt. This scheme was the brain child of an American diplomatic agent, William Eaton. After persuading the Navy to assign to him Lieutenant O'Bannon, a midshipman, and seven Marines, Eaton recruited a motley force of 67 "Christian" adventurers (mainly Greek mercenaries), about a hundred Arabs, and some two hundred native camel drivers and bearers.[28] In a seven-week desert march which has few parallels in the history of the Corps, Eaton, O'Bannon, Hamet, their assorted companions, and 107 camels covered the 600 miles from Alexandria. Despite religious altercations, Arab thievery and mutiny, and thirst, the column deployed before the walls of Derna on 25 April 1805. Next morning, in answer to Eaton's demand for surrender, Yusuf snapped, "My head or yours."[29]

The terms were completely acceptable to Eaton and O'Bannon.

On the 27th, following a cannonade by the USS *Argus, Hornet,* and *Nautilus,* which had arrived offshore, Eaton posted his Arabs, under Hamet, on the shoreward side of Derna, while the "Christians," under O'Bannon, some 50 altogether, formed for an assault. In Eaton's words:[30]

A little before 2 PM the fire became General in all quarters where Tripolitans and Americans were opposed to each other. . . . Mr. O'Bannon, accompanied by Mr. Mann of Annapolis, urged forward with his Marines, Greeks, and such of the Cannoniers as were not necessary to the management of the field piece, passed through a shower of Musketry from the walls of houses, took possession of the Battery, planted the American Flag upon its ramparts, and turned its guns upon the Enemy, who being now driven from their Out Posts fired only from their houses, from which they were soon dislodged by the whole fire of the Vessels, which was suspended during the charge being directed into them. The Bashaw Hamet soon got possession of the Bey's Pallace; his Cavalry flanked the flying enemy, and a little after four o'clock we had compleat possession of the Town.

Two of the seven Marines were killed, and one was wounded, while O'Bannon had the honor of being the first American officer to raise the Stars and Stripes over a captured fortress in the Old World. The Mameluke sword, subsequently carried by Marine officers, takes its pattern from an Arab sword which Hamet Bey presented to O'Bannon after the battle. Unfortunately, the sword was almost the whole extent of O'Bannon's reward; when he returned home, his native state, Virginia, gave him another sword, but the government did nothing. After two years, when no brevet or other promotion had materialized, O'Bannon left the Corps and ended his days in Kentucky.

A comical side show of the Tripolitan War (which ended on American terms on 3 June 1805) was the affair of the Sicilian musicians.

One of Lieutenant Colonel Burrows' last orders in 1803, before being succeeded as Commandant by Franklin Wharton, a Philadelphian, had directed Captain John Hall, Marine officer of the *Constitution*, "to enlist 14 good Musicians for the Marine Corps"[31] in Italy. These instructions Hall carried out in Catania, Sicily, by landing a sergeant's guard and, so legend says, impressing a band of 18 strolling musicians, families and all. Meanwhile, however, Commandants had changed, and Hall's mission had apparently been overlooked or forgotten in Washington. When Hall, well pleased, reported his coup to the new Commandant, Wharton gnashed his teeth and dispatched a reply evidencing official displeasure seldom equaled:[32]

I have received your letter . . . that part of it which relates to a band of music, I cannot comprehend. You observe the Commandant had ordered a band procured. . . . He could not order it for the Corps. You then remark that you have engaged it. . . . This must be equally incorrect. I have never given any orders for the collection of a band in the Mediterranean, and it will not be mentioned as belonging to the Corps. The expenses already arising, I am well assured, will not be paid. The Secretary of the Navy can never assent to two bands for one Corps.

But Hall and his Sicilians were already on the way and reached Washington in late 1805. History fails to record exactly how Hall got out of this scrape, but he somehow managed to attain the rank of major in 1814. As for the Sicilian bandsmen, they formed an "Italian Group" of the Marine Band until disbanded a year later; several, however, were promptly re-enlisted, and one, a 12-year-old clarinetist, Venerando Pulizzi, served for the next 47 years in the successive capacities of music boy, bandsman, drum major, line sergeant, and, from 1832 to 1852, as sergeant major at Marine Corps Headquarters.

WAR WITH BRITAIN

Although the United States had won political independence in 1783, the great belligerents of the Napoleonic Wars continued to treat American maritime commerce as if it were that of a colony. Spain, France, and Britain all gave the United States ample cause for war by their abuse of belligerent rights, but of these the actions and attitude of Great Britain were the most arrogant and highhanded. In the words of President Madison:[33]

British cruisers have been in the practice of violating the rights and peace of our coasts. They hover over and harass our entering and departing commerce. To the most insulting pretensions, they have added the most lawless proceedings in our very harbors, and have wantonly spilt American blood within the sanctuary of our territorial jurisdiction. . . .

By 1809, apprehensive of forthcoming war, Congress authorized, but failed to appropriate for, enlargement of the Marine Corps to 1,869. Even though Wharton only received funds for two-thirds of the authorized increase, every extra man was a godsend, for the Corps, as would often happen again, was overworked and overcommitted.

While most Marines had been at sea, mainly with the Mediterranean Squadron, Captain Carmick had been sent to New Orleans in 1804 with a hundred Marines to set the seal of possession on the Louisiana Purchase. In East Florida, which Congress feared England would lift from Spain's failing grip, another detachment, commanded by Captain John Williams, campaigned amid palmetto swamp and rattlesnakes against Indians, pirates, and Spanish soldiers. On 11 September 1812, at the head of a 20-man convoy escort near St. Augustine, Williams was ambushed by a large body of Indians. In the words graven on his tombstone, his men fought "as long as they had a cartridge left"; then, carrying their captain, pierced by eight wounds, the Marines retired. Eighteen days later, Captain Williams died. On the monument raised for him by the officers of the Corps and now over his remains in Arlington is the inscription:

EMINENTLY CHARACTERIZED by cool Intrepidity, Captain Williams evinced, during this short but severe contest, those Military requisites, which qualify the Officer for command:—and if his sphere of action was too limited to attract the admiration of the world, it was sufficiently expanded to crown him with the gratitude of his country; and to afford his brethren in arms an example as highly useful as it has sealed with honor the life of a Patriot Soldier.

When war finally broke out with England, on 18 June 1812, about half the understrength Marine Corps was on sea duty. The balance was distributed meagerly among the Marine Barracks at Boston, New York, Philadelphia, Washington, and Charleston; in the field in East Florida and at New Orleans; and aboard one warship (USS *Oneida*) on Lake Ontario.

During the first two years of war, the principal achievements of the Marine Corps—and of the American cause as a whole—were at sea and on the Great Lakes. Shipboard Marines distinguished themselves aboard such gallant ships as the USS *Enterprise* (commanded by a son of former Commandant Burrows), *Wasp, United States,* and *Constitution.* When ordered to duty in 1812 as commanding officer of the *Constitution's* Marines, First Lieutenant W. S. Bush wrote a friend:[34]

I am ordered to the *Constitution.* . . . Should an opportunity be afforded for boarding the enemy, I will be the first man upon his deck.

On 19 August 1812, in the first decisive naval action of the war, Bush's ship, commanded by Captain Isaac Hull, USN, engaged the British frigate *Guerrière.* As the two ships ground together at close quarters, Lieutenant Bush swung onto the hammock nettings, called out to his captain, "Shall I board her?" and fell dead, shot by a Royal Marine. But Bush's marksmen in the tops—six men loading and the best shot firing—swept the British decks; shot to pieces by American gunnery and musketry, the *Guerrière* struck, the first British man-of-war to surrender to Americans since the days of John Paul Jones. When news of the manner of Bush's death reached Washington, Colonel Wharton published the following:

Orders!—In testimony of respect to the memory of the late Lieut. William S. Bush, who gallantly fell in the action with the *Guerrière* on the 19th Ulto., it is ordered that crape be worn by the Officers of the Corps on the left arm and hilt of the Sword for one month. . . .

F. Wharton
Lt. Col., Comt. M. Corps

Hd.Q's of the M. Corps
Washington Sept. 6th, 1812

The small force of Marines on Lake Ontario was obviously insufficient, and Marine Corps Headquarters attempted to remedy this by closing down the barracks at Charleston, South Carolina, and marching the barracks detachment to Sackets Harbor on Lake Ontario, 800 miles northward. Captain R. D. Wainwright, the commanding officer, was told to build up his force by recruiting as he advanced, and by drafts on Marine Barracks en route. A similar march, from Washington, D.C., via Pittsburgh, to Lake Erie (400 miles) was the fortune of First Lieutenant John Brooks, Jr., handsome son of the Governor of Massachusetts and Marine officer aboard the *Wasp* during her smashing victory over HMS *Frolic* in 1812. Despite similar injunctions to do his recruiting from the roadside, Brooks reached Lake Erie with only his 12 original men, who were nevertheless a valuable reinforcement to the few trained Marines and backwoods recruits already there. Unfortunately, Lieutenant Brooks's long march was to a rendezvous with death; he was killed in action by a British round shot during the battle of Lake Erie, on 10 September 1813, aboard Commodore Perry's flagship, the USS *Lawrence*. Little is known to this day about the part taken by the few Marines on Lake Erie, who were supplemented, on board two ships, by Army detachments. Seventeen, however, were killed or wounded in action, among them five officers and NCOs; three soldiers, acting as Marines, were also wounded. Lieutenant Brooks and his 34-man detachment must have done well, for Congress honored him with a posthumous silver medal.

On Lake Ontario, where a force of three officers and 121 enlisted Marines was present, no decisive naval action was fought, but the Marines took part in the defense of the naval base at Sackets Harbor against the British attack on 29 May 1813. In addition, a detachment of Marines under Captain Samuel E. Watson was attached to Colonel Winfield Scott's fine brigade of Army regulars in their campaign along the Niagara.[35] On Lake Champlain there were no Marines whatever to man Thomas Macdonough's small squadron, so, as on Lake Erie, officers and men were borrowed, from the 6th, 15th, and 33d Infantry, and these served as Marines in the battle of Lake Champlain, seven being killed and ten wounded. Apparently the British suffered from the same deficiencies: in addition to the one Royal Marine officer listed among Macdonough's prisoners were members of the 39th Foot, an Army regiment. It was not until almost the end of the war that the Marine Corps won an increase sufficient to meet the pressing demands of the hour.[36]

THE INCREDIBLE CAPTAIN GAMBLE

The outstanding record among seagoing Marines during the War of 1812, if not for all time, was that of 23-year-old Lieutenant John Marshall Gamble, three of whose brothers were naval officers. Gamble was commanding officer of Marines aboard Captain David Porter's *Essex*, the frigate which virtually destroyed Britain's whaling fleet in the Pacific. He was also the only officer of the Marine Corps ever to command a ship of the United States Navy.

The *Essex's* history-making cruise began on 28 October 1812 when she set sail from the Delaware Capes. From that time until the next April, Gamble discharged his routine duties as ship's Marine officer. Then the pattern changed. Lieutenant Gamble, with a prize crew of 14 Marines and seamen, was given command of a ship taken in the Galapagos Islands and commissioned by Porter as the USS *Greenwich* (". . . I had much confidence in the discretion of this gentleman," said Porter).

In July 1813 the *Greenwich*, cruising in company with the *Essex*, spied a strange sail (one of three); Gamble gave chase and soon found himself in action against *Seringapatam*, a British raider which had been giving American whalers a dose of the *Essex's* medicine. The battle was anxiously watched aboard the *Essex*, as one of Gamble's messmates wrote him soon afterward:[37]

Capt Porter chewed as much tobacco and kept his poor spy-glass as constantly employed as ever I knew him to. At one time, when the *Seringapatam* tacked, Capt Porter became more anxious than ever; fearful you would tack at the same time and receive a raking shot, he exclaimed, "Now, Mr. Gamble, if you'll only stand on five minutes and then tack, I'll make you a Prince." You stood on a while, when he again exclaimed: "Now is your time;" just then we observed your ship in stays, which gave you the raking shot that did the enemy so much injury. So now, my dear fellow, you stand a chance of being princed, knighted, or something else. The Captain was much pleased, put the spy-glass under his arm, walked aft, and appeared to think all safe.

In October 1813 Captain Porter took his force, including several prizes thinly manned by American prize crews and sullen British prisoners, into Nukuhiva in the Marquesas Islands. There, with three prizes left behind, and but 22 American officers and men, and some of the British prisoners, Gamble was to defend Fort Madison, an advance base built by Porter, while the *Essex* and her consort, *Essex Junior* (another prize), proceeded to the coast of Chile.

Gamble's assignment proved to be beyond the capabilities of his force. Gamble later reported:[38]

The frigate had not got clear of the Marquesas before we discovered in the natives a hostile disposition towards us, who in a few days became so insolent, that I found it absolutely necessary, not only for the security of the ships and property on shore, but for our personal safety, to land my men and regain by force of arms the many articles they had in the most daring manner stolen from the encampment; and what was still of greater importance, to prevent, if possible, their putting threats into execution, which might have been attended with the most serious consequences on our part.

On Christmas Eve 1813, less than two weeks after Captain Porter's departure, Gamble learned that several thousand native Typees were massing to attack Fort Madison. Grasping the nettle, Gamble promptly landed 35 men, including British prisoners; then, under covering fire from his ships' guns, he attacked the Typees' stronghold and imposed an uneasy peace.

Beaten though they were for the moment, the Marquesans recognized Gamble's weakness in numbers, which was compounded by four desertions for the sake of native sweethearts. And meanwhile, on 28 March 1814 off Valparaiso, the *Essex* had come to grief under the long guns of HMS *Cherub* and *Phoebe*. Such a possibility had been reflected in Gamble's orders, which allowed him to abandon Fort Madison should the *Essex* not return by May 1814. While making preparations to depart, on 7 May 1814, Gamble was set upon by mutinous prisoners from his first prize, *Seringapatam,* and was wounded and taken to sea, where he was set adrift in an open boat with two midshipmen, after being given one pair of oars, some powder, and three old muskets. Despite his wound, Gamble managed to bring the boat back to Nukuhiva and there boarded the *Greenwich,* where his few remaining loyal seamen and Marines were quartered. Then, shifting all hands to the most seaworthy prize, *Sir Andrew Hammond,* he repelled a native attack which cost further casualties, and got the ship under way with no charts and a seven-man crew too feeble to sail.

Now a captain (though he didn't know it until a year later), Gamble decided to run before the trade winds in the hope of reaching the Sandwich Islands. He succeeded, but only to fall in with HMS *Cherub,* Porter's nemesis at Valparaiso. Gamble and his surviving men (three seamen and three Marines) were taken by the British to Rio de Janeiro and there, when news of peace arrived, they were released penniless and five thousand miles from home. It was August 1815 before Captain Gamble, still limping from his wound, found a ship to take him back to New York with his remaining men. For his gallantry, leadership, and seamanship, he was soon brevetted major and died a lieutenant colonel in 1836. As David Porter wrote the Secretary of the Navy:[39]

No Marine officer in the service ever had such strong claims as Captain Gamble, and none have been placed in such conspicuous and critical situations, and none could have extricated themselves from them more to their honor.

DEFENDING WASHINGTON AND BALTIMORE

Napoleon's defeat and abdication in 1814 was a serious blow to the American cause, for it made thousands of seasoned redcoats and many more warships available for service across the Atlantic. The objective of British strategy toward America in 1814 seems to have been attainment of a strong position from which to bargain at the peace negotiations already under way at Ghent. The main effort was planned along the Richelieu-Lake Champlain waterway, to divide the country and give Britain a claim to New England. Raids against Washington, Baltimore, and New Orleans were also included in the plan. Although, as we have seen, Marines took no part in Macdonough's victory on Lake Champlain, they saw their share of action in the Chesapeake and on the Gulf Coast.

As early as June 1813, Rear Admiral Sir George Cockburn, RN—that harsh and overbearing officer who later had his official portrait painted with its background the United States Capitol in flames—had entered the Chesapeake. Amid uninterrupted success in raiding and pillage, his one setback

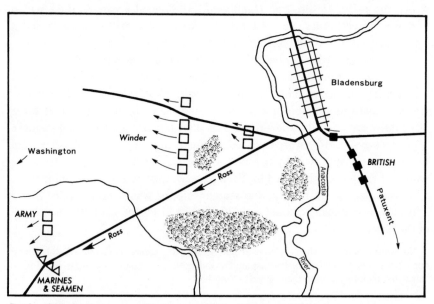

Battle of Bladensburg, near Washington, D.C., 24 August 1814

was the defeat of a British landing attack against Craney Island, guarding the mouth of the Elizabeth River and hence the Norfolk Navy Yard. There, on 22 June, a mixed force of soldiers, seamen, and Marines from the USS *Constellation* and the navy yard, stood off two successive landing attempts by British infantry and Marines, inflicting 81 casualties mainly by intense and accurate fire from naval guns manned by the American seamen and Marines.

On 19 August 1814 Major General Robert Ross landed 4,000 men—The King's Own Royal Lancasters, Shropshire Light Infantry, Royal Scots Fusiliers, East Essex Regiment, and a detachment of 50 Marines armed with Congreve rockets—at Benedict, Maryland, about 20 miles north of the future site of the Patuxent River Naval Air Station. There Ross joined forces with two battalions of Cockburn's Marines and set out for Washington.

American plans to defend Washington were, to say the least, disorganized and conflicting. Brigadier General Henry Winder, USA, had a force, mainly militia, which on paper numbered 10,000; actually, he could muster little more than half that number. No defenses had been erected. Among the few experienced fighting men available were Commodore Joshua Barney's "flotilla men"—seamen who had been waging estuarial war against Cockburn's gunboats—and a battalion of 114 Marines organized by Lieutenant Colonel Wharton from the ranks of the Marine Barracks, Washington. The battalion commander was Captain Samuel Miller, friend and contemporary of Captain Gamble, and Adjutant of the Corps. Miller's battalion was no stranger to Barney since the Marines had been under the Commodore's command during recent operations in Southern Maryland. While Winder attempted ineffectually to shape up his army, Secretary of the Navy William Jones had a look at the seamen and Marines. He noted:[40]

. . . whose appearance and preparations for battle promised all that could be expected from cool intrepidity and a high state of discipline.

Five days after landing, impeded only by the Maryland sun which prostrated 12 men, Ross quickstepped his force toward Bladensburg, a village just outside Washington. Confronting Ross and his Peninsular veterans were General Winder's nondescript troops, numbering about 6,000. On first sight, recounted a supercilious British officer, "They might have passed off very well for a crowd of spectators come out to view the approach of the army."[41]

On the refused right wing of this assembly were formed Barney's seamen with five guns and Miller's Marines, on the right of the line. Shortly after their arrival on the field, the British had begun to cross the Anacostia River, which separated the two armies.

At the first whoosh of Congreve rockets fired by the British to cover their crossing, Winder's militia threw away their muskets and fled. The Marines and seamen stood fast. The old commodore busied himself with his guns, while Captain Miller deployed the Marines and some of the sailors as infantry.

With the Shropshires in the van, Ross pushed on unconcernedly until his advance guard reached the rising ground on which Barney and Miller had sited their guns and formed the Marines. The commodore himself checked the laying of each piece. As the British charged, Barney reported afterward:[42]

I reserved our fire. In a few minutes the British advanced, when I ordered an 18-pounder to be fired, which completely cleared the road.

The commodore was guilty of no overclaim. The British afterward credited the seamen-gunners' initial blast of grape and canister with blowing an entire company off the road. As the bluejackets stood to their guns in man-of-war style, a hail of musketry swept down on the advancing foe from the Marines. Twice more the British courageously re-formed and charged; twice again they were thrown back. The last repulse was actually followed by a counterattack by the Marines and by cutlass-swinging sailors shouting, "Board 'em! Board 'em!"

But by now both the commodore and Captain Miller had been wounded. And General Ross, having seven times Barney's force, worked flanking columns expertly around the thin line of Marines and seamen. With more than a fifth of the Marines killed or wounded, and with a bullet through his own thigh, Commodore Barney gave orders to retire. Although the redcoats had been stopped for two hours and had suffered 249 casualties, they could not be kept from their goal. Almost every public building in Washington was put to the torch, including the White House and the Capitol. The Commandant's House was one structure that escaped, however; legend has it that General Ross spared the house out of a soldier's respect for its status as married quarters.

Ignominious as the defeat at Bladensburg was, it could not overshadow the contribution made by the Navy and Marines. "Great praise is due to Barney's men," wrote a contemporary observer, "[they] fought with desperation, as did the Marine Corps." Still another reported:[43]

The people of the flotilla, under the orders of Capt Barney, and the Marines, were justly applauded for their excellent conduct on this occasion. No troops could have stood better; and the fire of both artillery and musketry has been described as to the last degree severe. Capt Barney himself, and Captain Miller of the Marines in particular, gained much additional reputation.

"They have given us our only real fighting," was General Ross's terse report.[44]

Unfortunately, the professional reputation of Lieutenant Colonel Commandant Wharton did not share the advancement gained at Bladensburg by the rest of the Corps. As he himself recorded:[45]

Whilst the enemy was in the city, I was with the Paymaster at Fredricktown. . . . The events of the past few days seem as a bad dream.

True it was. As General Ross marched on Washington, Wharton commandeered a wagon and, with the Paymaster and all cash on hand, headed for Frederick, Maryland, where he remained until the British had departed.

After their stand at Bladensburg, instead of falling back on the doomed capital, the Washington Marines retired north to Baltimore, where American forces, including other Marines from the Philadelphia Navy Yard and from the newly launched USS *Guerrière*, were concentrating to defend the port. Here, from 11 to 13 September 1814, the British attacked Fort McHenry by land and by sea. An early casualty to a random shot was none other than General Ross, the victor of Bladensburg. The British assaults were all thrown back. Among the defenders, both at Sparrows Point and at Fort McHenry, were the Marines under Lieutenant J. L. Kuhn, who, by the "red glare" of the Congreve rockets, saw to it that "our Flag was still there."

BATTLE AMONG THE BAYOUS

Ever since 1804, with a brief respite in healthier latitudes, Captain Daniel Carmick, at New Orleans, had been fighting Indians, Spaniards, and, in particular, the Creole pirates along the Gulf Coast. Carmick's command, Marine Barracks, Navy Yard, New Orleans, originally numbered 122; in 1809 he was promoted to major and his force increased to 300, an indication of the importance attached to the Gulf Coast by the Navy.

Although the British Navy was active in Gulf waters, the main concern of the U. S. Navy and Marines at New Orleans throughout the War of 1812 was the suppression of Jean and Pierre Lafitte, the smugglers and slavers of Barataria Bay. On 16 September 1814 a naval force under Master Commandant Daniel Patterson, USN, engaged the pirate squadron and landed

Carmick's Marines (reinforced by 70 soldiers from the 44th Infantry) at Barataria. After working through the settlement at bayonet point, the landing force put Barataria to the torch and returned to New Orleans.

But a more dangerous enemy was approaching. Vice Admiral Sir Alexander Cochrane, RN, the British commander in chief on the American Station, was charged with the capture of New Orleans, and under him the Duke of Wellington's brother-in-law, Sir Edward Pakenham, commanded 9,000 Peninsular veterans, including some who had fought at Bladensburg. The British approached New Orleans via Lake Borgne on the same day arrangements were concluded to sign the peace treaty at Ghent, 5,000 miles away.

After dark on 23 December 1814, with Carmick's Marines and Army regulars on his right, Andrew Jackson, commanding the defenders, probed sharply at the British. Five days later, Pakenham's first attack spent itself against an American line with Marines in the center. There, while leading a counterattack, Carmick received the wound of which eventually he died.

Pakenham tried again, on 8 January of the new year. Posted east of the river under Jackson, most of the Marines were with Major Plauché's Creoles, while some served as artillery on the left of the mixed army which included everything from United States regulars to the "hellish banditti" of Jean Lafitte, who generously made common cause with the troops who had burned his base.

Despite brave assaults by English redcoats, Marines, and Highlanders, Jackson's line held. Before noon it was over. As Pakenham fell, hit thrice and mortally wounded, the attack ebbed: 2,036 British soldiers lay dead or wounded, and more than 500 were prisoners. The British lost three major generals, eight colonels, and 78 other officers. New Orleans was saved.

Amid the general glory, Congress resolved its thanks "for the valor and good conduct of Major Daniel Carmick, of the officers, noncommissioned officers, and Marines under his command."[46] But the thanks were to no avail; Carmick, who might have survived to become a great Commandant, died in November 1815 as a result of his wound.

THE CORPS SCENE

During early years no one was quite sure whether the Marine Corps appertained more to the Navy or to the Army. This was the result of language in the 1798 law which placed Marines under *Navy Regulations* when afloat and under the Articles of War ashore. Neither the Secretary of the

Navy nor the Secretary of War fully controlled or administered the Corps. Ashore, Marines drew fuel, straw, and forage in accordance with Army regulations; afloat, they subsisted on a Navy ration. In 1812 the Army abolished flogging, but Marines afloat could be flogged until 1850 when the Navy reluctantly followed suit. The oath of enlistment taken by Marines was the same as that for the Army. And both Army and Marines used the same drill manual, von Steuben's *Regulations for the Order & Discipline of the Troops of the United States.* One Secretary of the Navy, writing to the Secretary of War, alluded to "your own regiment of Marines,"[47] and Secretary Stoddert tried to persuade the War Department to assist the Navy in the upkeep of the Corps.

Despite these confusions, Marine discipline in the early days was stern and unrelenting. In 1776 a court-martial headed by Captain Mullan awarded Private Henry Hasson ". . . fifty Lafhes for Defertion & Twenty one Lafhes for Quiting his Guard without leave of his Officers, on his bare back well laid on at the head of his Company." Thirty-two years later, a deserter received "50 lashes, by the Taps, hard labor, Ball & Chain." In the same year a more aggravated case of desertion got the sentence, ". . . 4 times run the Gantlope & drummed out." And to Private Michael Duggatt, convicted on the specification—

Drunk & riotous, and after being confined, using seditious language in Damning the Marine Corps, and all the officers belonging to it & saying he hoped to have the pleasure of seeing their Souls roasting in Hell—

fifty lashes and a month's hard labor.

But the worst was reserved for a wartime deserter. On Friday, 13 January 1815, the Marine Band, playing the "Dead March" from *Saul,* escorted him from the barracks at 8th and Eye Streets to Hospital Square (near Gallinger Hospital in later Washington), where he was stood up beside an open grave and shot in hollow square.[48]

In addition to being a stiff disciplinarian, Colonel Wharton established the first formal training for Marine officers and men, as witness this order of 6 September 1808:[49]

Headquarters of the Marine Corps at Washington considered as the school where young officers and recruits are to be instructed in the various duties which they may be called upon to perform, it is expected that in future the Commanding or Senior officer in Barracks will order such Parades as he may think necessary to insure the same, exclusive of those already ordered; and that he will require the attendance of such officers on them as he may think proper.

Even in those early days the Navy hospital corpsman was part of Marine Corps life. Known as "Loblolly Boys," corpsmen were detailed to assist the surgeons and surgeon's mates, ashore or afloat. Daily sick call aboard ship was signaled by a loblolly boy whose duty was to go fore and aft on berth and gun decks ringing a bell to give notice to "those slightly indisposed and with ulcers" to attend the surgeon at the mainmast.[50] Before battle afloat, the corpsmen were to provide the cockpit (ship's sick bay) with water, with containers for amputated limbs, and with braziers to heat irons for searing amputations and for melting tar to stop hemorrhage. In addition, corpsmen on deck were responsible for buckets of sand to absorb blood underfoot. When Marines went ashore to fight, the corpsmen went too. To pay for the costs of medical care, commencing in November 1799, all members of the Navy and Marine Corps had their pay assessed 20 cents a month, a practice which continued for the next 148 years, until after the Second World War.

The routine duties of Marines afloat, which comprised most of the life of the Corps in this era, appear in the guard orders for the detachment aboard the USS *Constitution* under Captain John Hall (he of the Sicilian bandsmen) in 1804.[51]

One [sentry] at the Cabbin door, who is not to permit any person to pass into the cabbin excepting a quarter-deck Officer, and such persons as are immediately attached thereto. One Centinel on each Gangway to give notice to the commanding Officer of the deck of the approach of any Boat or Vessel, and not suffer any boat to leave the Ship, without the knowledge of said Officer. They are to pay proper respect to the Officers entering or leaving the Ship. One Centinel at the Spirit Room to protect it at all times, that no theft or depredations are there committed. A Centinel on the Fore Castle in the night time, from 8 o'clock P.M. to 6 A.M. with the same orders that are given those on the Gangways. A Centinel at the Galley to keep Order at all times, and more especially at the time of cooking and serving out Dinner, and not suffer any fires being made after the Officers Dinners are served, but by permission of the Officer of the deck, and both by night and day, to take care that not any person leaves the Ship from the Gun Deck without permission.

The ranks and monthly pay of the Marine Corps of 1798 were as follows:[52]

Major	$50 and 4 rations
Captain	$40 and 3 rations
First lieutenant	$30 and 3 rations
Second lieutenant	$25 and 2 rations
Sergeant major; quartermaster sergeant	$10
Drum major; fife major	$9
Sergeant	$9
Corporal	$8
Fifers and drummers	$7
Private	$6

The supply system of the Corps under its first Quartermaster, Second Lieutenant Thomas Wharton,[53] was simple. Rations—originally at 21½ cents a day, later 28 cents—were provided by cash payments to individual commanding officers both in the Continental Marines and after creation of the Corps. Uniforms and equipment were contracted for by Marine Corps Headquarters and issued as required. One early clothing requisition read as follows:

April 11th 1778

On Board the Boston

Wanted, for the use and service of the Marines belonging to this ship:

40 green coats faced with white
40 white waistcoats, and
40 white breeches.

The buttons of the whole to be a plain white. Coats to be open-sleeved, and a belt for every waistcoat.

In behalf of the Captain of Marines,
William Jenison,
Lieutenant of Marines.

Although Lieutenant Jenison's requisition failed to include such other items, the Continental Marines wore short black gaiters (spatterdashes), round hats (for officers, tricornes), and leather stocks. The leather stock, or neckpiece—one of which Major Carmick wore for nine years "and then only laid it aside because it was out of fashion"—provides the origin of the nickname "Leatherneck."

Every known type of firearm must have been used by Marines during the Revolution. We find records of flintlock muskets (mainly British Tower muskets and French "Charlevilles"), pistols, blunderbusses, and hand grenades. In addition, Continental Marines also carried boarding pikes, cutlasses, even spears, and, at least once, tomahawks.

When the Marine Corps was reconstituted in 1798, its first uniforms and equipment were mainly those of the Army: Charlevilles left over from the Revolution, and surplus clothing remaining after disbandment of General "Mad Anthony" Wayne's Legion in 1796. These hand-me-downs were blue, faced and trimmed with scarlet, with scarlet vest, and tight blue trousers ("overalls") bearing thin scarlet stripes—and, of course, leather stocks.[54]

On 25 March 1804 the new Commandant, Franklin Wharton, with approval from the Secretary of the Navy, issued the first uniform regulations designed specifically for the Marine Corps.[55] These regulations prescribed pomponed shakos for enlisted men, and white trousers, blue double-breasted coats with gold lace and gilt buttons, and plumed chapeaux for the officers. Black boots replaced the officers' spatterdashes of what, no doubt, was even then being spoken of as "The Old Corps."

That Lieutenant Colonel Wharton warmly espoused "spit and polish" is evident from this order which accompanied the uniform regulations:[56]

Ordered that each NCO charged with a Squad be held responsible for their Dress and good appearance & that the men may appear on the Parade clean and properly dressed & in good uniform, a Non Com^d Officer is appointed to each Room who half an hour before the Parade is to turn the men out of their rooms, their hair dressed and powdered, their clothing & accoutrements clean, their arms in good order. The Sergeant Major is then to inspect; he is not to suffer a. man to go on Parade who is not fit for the inspection of the Adjutant & it is expected he will report those NCOs who are negligent in this duty, or he will be held responsible by the Adjutant who is himself answerable to the Commandant for the order & good appearance of the Parade, on which no man is to be marched without a Queue, & the most minute part of his uniform is agreeable to the General Order.

The "Queue," or pigtail, which Colonel Wharton mentioned was powdered with flour, one pound per man per month being the allowance. The stuff was apparently no treat for the users, as an 1805 requisition refers to the issue of "one barrel of *sour* flour for powdering."

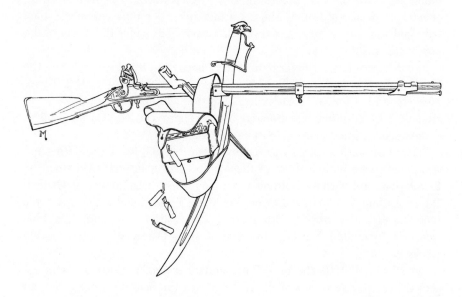

2 THE AGE OF
ARCHIBALD HENDERSON *1816-1859*

Take care to be right, and then they are powerless.
—BREVET BRIGADIER GENERAL ARCHIBALD HENDERSON

FRANKLIN WHARTON never lived down his absence when the British were devastating Washington. The third Commandant's flight to Frederick, while more resolute Marines fought at Bladensburg, was a blot which Wharton could not erase. From 1814 until his death on 1 September 1818, efforts were made to force his resignation. After a petition for his deposal failed, Captain Archibald Henderson, who had commanded the *Constitution's* Marines with distinction throughout the war, preferred charges against the Commandant—neglect of duty (five specifications) and conduct unbecoming an officer and a gentleman. ("In that, notwithstanding it was communicated to him that his military character had been assailed in its tenderest point, in consequence of the course he pursued at the time of the capture of the city of Washington by the enemy, he did decline and has ever since declined . . . to take any steps to put a stop to reports so highly injurious to his own character.")[1]

On 22 September 1817, Wharton was finally acquitted after a trial held at Davis's Hotel in Washington, which disclosed deep bitterness between himself and several of the principal officers of the Corps. Thus, Wharton's declining years in office were darkened and unhappy. In addition to personal troubles, he had also to contend with difficulties caused by the Peace Establishment Act of 1817 which cut the Corps back to a strength of 915 and forced the separation of many experienced officers. As a side effect, this act left its mark on the Marine Corps in lasting fashion by giving the Commandant a permanent staff consisting of the Adjutant and Inspector, the Quartermaster, and the Paymaster—a Marine Corps Headquarters organization destined to remain in effect for the next century and a quarter.

From Wharton's death until the spring of 1818, the Commandant's office lay vacant. Henderson, brevet major and second senior officer in the Corps, exercised command while the appointment of the next Commandant was debated. By right of seniority the place belonged to Major Anthony Gale, an officer of 1798, whose Irish hothead had won him no friends in the Navy after the duel in which he killed a naval officer who had insulted him aboard ship. Moreover, even though cleared by a court of inquiry, he had been in hot water over alleged mishandling of funds while in command of Marine Barracks, Philadelphia. With misgiving, on 3 March 1818 after six months' delay, Secretary of the Navy Smith Thompson approved Gale's appointment as Commandant.

The new Commandant's administration was stormy and unhappy. From the outset, Gale was at odds with Secretary Thompson, who meddled in Gale's command of the Corps and countermanded many of his orders. In August 1820, Gale appealed for a showdown to determine where his authority began and the Secretary's ended. This action having been taken, he hopelessly undermined his case by embarking on a prolonged jag which came to an end three weeks later with his arrest; charge: ". . . being intoxicated in common dram shops and other places of low repute."[2] On 17 October a court-martial, obviously not receptive to his plea of temporary insanity, found him guilty as charged. With the approval of President Monroe, Gale was then cashiered. As a sort of consolation prize for what may well have been a legal railroading, he was awarded a pension by Congress in 1835, which he lived to enjoy until 1843.

ARCHIBALD HENDERSON ASSUMES COMMAND

Whether so recognized at the time or not, the most important event for the Marine Corps following the War of 1812 took place when, after approving Gale's sentence, President Monroe appointed Brevet Major Archibald Henderson as fifth Commandant of the Marine Corps.

Age 38 (the youngest man ever to become Commandant), red-headed and forceful, Henderson was destined to dominate the Marine Corps through 39 years and ten presidential administrations. Born near Colchester, Virginia, almost within eyeshot of the future site of Quantico, Henderson created as his memorial the high military character which he imprinted upon the Corps. "Take care to be right," he once wrote, "and then they are powerless."[3] At the Commandant's pay and emoluments of $2,636.16 a year, Archibald Henderson was a bargain.

The new Commandant's clear head and firm hand were especially needed by the none-too-well established Corps. In addition to the legacy of ill-feeling and confusion left behind by Gale's differences with Secretary Thompson, the administration of the Corps was fraught with headaches stemming from the Marines' hazy status under the Act of 1798. Ashore, Marines still came under the Articles of War and, when not afloat, got Army pay. Among various suggestions for righting the muddles which continually arose, one brain storm that greeted Henderson was to abolish the offices of Commandant and Quartermaster and substitute civil servants instead.[4] Colonel Henderson scotched this proposition in short order, but his first days in office were not easy, as this excerpt from one of his early letters to Secretary Thompson bears witness:[5]

Our isolated Corps, with the Army on one side and the Navy on the other (neither friendly) has been struggling ever since its establishment for its very existence. We have deserved hostility from neither, more especially the Navy.

ADVENTURES ABROAD

Fortunately for Archibald Henderson the expanding interests of the United States provided enough employment for his $6-a-month privates to forestall all attempts to hamstring the Corps.

The years from 1817 to 1832 found Marines chasing pirates here and there, and showing the flag everywhere from the Falkland Islands to Sumatra.

In July 1817, nearly a century before Marines were destined to occupy Haiti, the guard from the USS *Congress* (1 officer, 47 enlisted men—little different from a cruiser's guard in 1962) landed at Port-au-Prince. There, the American consul had been sent packing by the touchy government of Alexandre Pétion. Under the ship's guns and the muskets of the Marines, diplomacy resumed its ordered course, and relations were re-established. Later that same year, again in 1818, and finally in 1821 during disorders following the death of King Henry Christophe in the north, Marine guards had to be landed briefly at Cap-Haitien, as well.

As Spain's empire disintegrated, Puerto Rico and northern Cuba became pirate hunting grounds, and American commerce in the Caribbean was as sore beset as that of the Mediterranean in the days of the Barbary pirates.

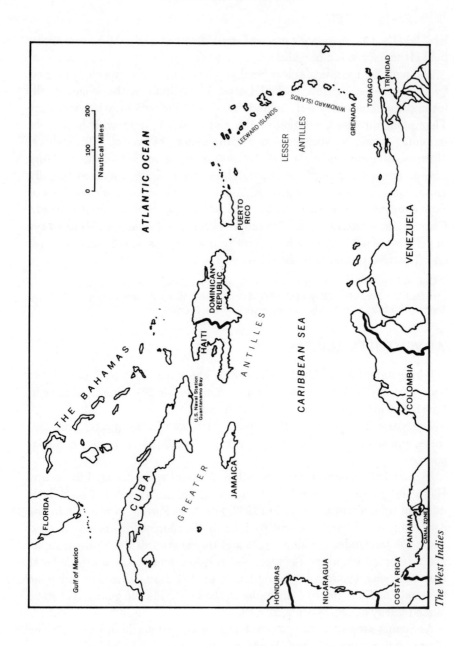

The West Indies

Operating from Pensacola and, for a time, fever-ridden Key West, the Navy's West India Squadron, including a landing force of almost 300 Marines, spent 1821 and part of 1822 in pacifying the north coast of Cuba. In the two succeeding years, Commodore David Porter waged equally relentless war against the pirates of Puerto Rico, who were hand-in-glove with the Spanish authorities. Unfortunately for Porter, his aggressiveness was his undoing. To redress the arrest and maltreatment of a naval officer by the authorities at Fajardo, a pirate stronghold under Spanish protection, Porter landed 200 Marines and seamen on 27 October, spiked the guns of the fort, and exacted an apology. Under diplomatic pressure, however, Porter was disavowed, tried, and reprimanded. No man to endure such treatment, the dashing commodore resigned from the Navy and offered his sword to the service of Mexico. Nonetheless, he was the founder of a long line of distinguished naval and Marine officers, including one who was destined to win the Medal of Honor and serve as Adjutant and Inspector of the Corps.

In spite of his rebuff, David Porter and his Marines had made their mark, and, with co-operation from the Royal Marines of a British squadron in the West Indies, they removed piracy from the list of paying occupations in that region.

Far to the south, the infant Argentine republic, always intransigent where the Falkland Islands were concerned, had been making difficulties for American whaling ships in the South Atlantic. In 1831, it was necessary to send the USS *Lexington*, a sloop-of-war, to the Falklands and land her Marines in order to secure the release of three American whalers held, in the words of Andrew Jackson's message to Congress of 6 December 1831, "by a band, acting, as they pretend, under the authority of the Government of Buenos Ayres." After the first of the new year, the *Lexington* evacuated some 38 Americans, whose persons and goods were safely seen on board under protection of the ship's guard.

Another such action in protection of American trade occurred in the same year more than ten thousand miles away, when the American merchantman, *Friendship*, was set upon by Malay pirates while loading pepper at Kuala Batu ("Quallah Battoo" in the reports of the day) in western Sumatra. This savage attack, in which the mate and two seamen were murdered, climaxed other depredations and demanded reprisal. The frigate, *Potomac*, under Commodore John Downes, was sent from Brooklyn Navy Yard to the southwest Pacific with a landing force of 250 Marines and seamen. Downes, who had served as Porter's first lieutenant aboard the *Essex*, was also the founder of an illustrious naval line, five successive generations of whom were destined to wear the uniform.

The pirates' lair was defended by four forts and numerous log palisades mounting cannon and manned by some four thousand Malay pirates. In the dawn of 7 February 1832, the *Potomac,* disguised in slipshod merchant dress, hove to off Kuala Batu, called away all boats, and landed the landing force. The Marines, who landed first, were led by First Lieutenant Alvin Edson; Edson's second-in-command was Second Lieutenant George H. Terrett, destined to distinguish himself at the San Cosme Gate of Mexico City.

Covered by Marines armed with the new Hall breech-loading rifles adopted in 1828, the landing force achieved surprise and marched on the forts. One of these was carried by a division of seamen under Lieutenant Irvine Shubrick, USN; the next one by Edson's Marines. Meanwhile, the remaining two divisions of seamen pressed into the town. After two hours' hot fighting across wet ditches, sharpened palisades, and earthworks, Edson carried his final position and hurried to support the bluejackets who were attacking the town. Amid the smoke and flames of burning huts, Marines and sailormen formed to assault the last fort. Edson having been wounded, Terrett assumed command. With a dash and a cheer, the Americans swarmed forward, and Kuala Batu was won. More than 150 pirates lay dead, including their rajah, Po Mahomet, who was killed among his men.[6]

EMERGENCIES AT HOME

While the bulk of the Corps was upholding American interests beyond the seas, Marines at home also had plenty to do.

In 1824, Marines from the Charlestown Navy Yard went to the aid of Boston when fire swept the town. In 1833, when the U. S. Treasury in Washington was set afire by arsonists, men from the barracks at Eighth and Eye Streets helped to quell the flames and guard the funds. During New York's great fire of December 1835, Marines and seamen from the Brooklyn Navy Yard fought fire, protected property against looters, and blew firebreaks which ultimately were credited with saving Manhattan. No doubt some of Lieutenant Colonel Gamble's Marines (for he commanded the barracks in Brooklyn at that time) who distinguished themselves in the New York fire had learned how to eat smoke when Marine and bluejacket fire and rescue parties landed to give aid during earlier conflagrations at St. Thomas in the Virgin Islands and at Smyrna in 1825.

But the outstanding Marine performance at home was unquestionably that by Major R. D. Wainwright and 30 men from Marine Barracks, Boston, in putting down the 1824 mutiny among inmates of the Massachusetts state prison in Charlestown.

Herded together into one end of "the long, dark, and damp" prison mess-hall, 283 "imprisoned wretches" held a guard as hostage in order to save three of their number from a flogging.

An appeal for help reached Major Wainwright, the Marine Barracks commander. Already breveted for bravery, Wainwright himself led 30 Marines inside the walls. Rejecting advice by prison guards that he blaze away into the messhall from outside, the major marched his detachment into one end of the room—31 against 283. Here Wainwright formed his troops in two ranks; he had them load with ball ammunition before the eyes of the armed convicts; then, he ordered the prisoners to disperse. The mutineers, said a contemporary account, responded with "a growl of determination,"[7] whereupon Wainwright gave the word for his men to level their muskets at the prisoners. The major then took out his watch and announced, "You must leave this hall. I give you three minutes to decide. If at the end of that time a man remains, he will be shot dead. I speak no more."

As *McGuffey's Eclectic Reader* (which made the story a schoolboy classic for the rest of the century) continued:

For two minutes not a person or a muscle was moved. . . . At the expiration of two minutes, two or three of those in the rear, and nearest the furthest entrance, went slowly out; a few more followed the example . . . and before the last half minute was gone, every man was struck by the panic, and crowded for the exit, and the hall was cleared as if by magic.

ANDREW JACKSON VS. THE MARINES

On 8 December 1829 President Andrew Jackson struck consternation throughout the Marine Corps by a recommendation in his message to Congress:

I would also recommend that the Marine Corps be merged in the artillery or infantry, as the best mode of curing the many defects in its organization. But little exceeding in number any of the regiments of infantry, that corps has, besides its Lieutenant-Colonel Commandant, five brevet lieutenant-colonels, who receive the full pay and emoluments of their brevet rank, without rendering proportionate service. Details for Marine service could well be made from the artillery or infantry, there being no peculiar training required for it.

The factors which had precipitated this recommendation into the President's message were: the continuing bother of having to administer the Corps more or less simultaneously (as the 1798 law required) under both Army and Navy regulations; discovery of extensive irregularities in the Pay and Quartermaster's Departments; and a vendetta against the Commandant and Marine Corps Headquarters by the Board of Navy Commissioners, a remote ancestor of the CNO organization of today.

As we have seen, serious confusions existed as to the legal and administrative status of the Corps. Some authorities held Marines to be part of the Army (ashore they were in many respects so—the courts-martial on both Wharton and Gale, for example, had been presided over and predominantly composed of Army officers). Other authorities thought Marines part of the Navy, and still a third opinion considered the Corps autonomous.

Partly as a result of the ambiguities of Marine Corps status, the pay and supply arrangements of the Corps had become badly muddled, a situation which came to the notice of Amos Kendall, Fourth Auditor of the Treasury, who fulfilled watchdog functions toward the Navy not unlike those of the Bureau of the Budget and General Accounting Office in after years. In concert with another Jackson appointee, Secretary of the Navy John Branch, Kendall held up Marine Corps accounts and made the Marine Corps the target of a series of indictments in both 1829 and 1830.[8]

In the minds of the Navy Commissioners—a group of senior captains performing the functions of a Board of Admiralty over the Navy—there existed the idea, first voiced as early as 1801 by Thomas Truxtun, that, if Marines were needed at all, they should be fragmented into local detachments wholly under the commanders of naval ships and shore stations. This notion brought the Navy Commissioners, headed by Captain John Rodgers, into collision with Archibald Henderson, whose office, headquarters, and Corps establishment were, from 1825 on, subject to repeated attacks by Rodgers and his colleagues. So bitter became the controversy that, in November 1829, the Navy Commissioners stripped the sloop-of-war *Erie* of her Marine guard and sent her to sea on a cruise to prove that Marines were unnecessary. Her captain, Master Commandant David Conner, brought in the desired finding:[9]

Should the Marine Corps be separated from the Navy, you will, in a very short time, hear every officer in command expressing his astonishment why such an absurdity had been so long tolerated. I often hear my officers remark, how much better we get along without Marines. . . .

It was against this background that Andrew Jackson called for abolition of the Marine Corps, and hearings on the proposal were held in both houses of Congress in 1830. Before the Senate Naval Affairs Committee, Secretary Branch supported the President's recommendation by presenting a somewhat selective list of anti-Marine views obtained from senior naval officers, but offset at the end by forcible pro-Marine expressions from such respected officers as Bainbridge, Jacob Jones, Charles Stewart, and Thomas ap Catesby Jones.[10] With Archibald Henderson active in the background, the Committee refused to act against the Corps. In the House, Jackson's recommendation went to the Military Affairs Committee which "did not think it proper to interfere with the status of the Marine Corps,"[11] and passed the buck to the Naval Affairs Committee, where the President's proposal died. Those who sought to abolish the Corps, or at least its separate organization and headquarters, however, did not give up. In his annual report for 1831, the Secretary of the Navy recommended "discontinuance of the Marine Corps or its transfer entirely" either to the Army or the Navy:[12]

In its present fluctuating condition, without any imputation on the character of the officers of the corps, frequent difficulties in relation to pay, allowances, trials, and orders, are necessarily happening; and part of which proceeded to such an extent as to require a special resolution of Congress in 1830, and a particular provision in the appropriation bill of 1831. But by placing this establishment, as in former years has been proposed, wholly under navy discipline and laws, most of these difficulties might, in my opinion, be obviated; all the present benefits of it to the service retained; its increase in numbers rendered unnecessary; its old associations preserved; and much greater economy, harmony, and energy infused into its operations, without derogating at all from the respectability and usefulness of the corps.

Although nothing further was done to resolve the status of the Marine Corps during the next two years, Congress, on 30 June 1834, finally passed "An Act for the Better Organization of the Marine Corps,"[13] which accepted the common-sense concept that, ashore or afloat, the Corps should be part of the Naval Establishment, but rejected the Navy Commissioners' attempt to merge it with the Navy proper and abolish the office of Commandant. Strongly supported by Henderson, and even by a petition from all Marine officers on duty at Headquarters, this law, in addition to establishing the relationship between the Navy and Marine Corps which exists to this day, increased the Corps to an unprecedented peace strength of 63 officers and 1,224 enlisted men; it forever prohibited Marine officers, like Gamble, from commanding any navy yard or vessel; and it promoted Archibald Henderson—still a relative newcomer as Commandant, with only 14 years in office

—to the rank of colonel. With inward feelings which will never be known, President Jackson signed the bill and made it law. More important than individual feelings of the time, however, was the essential soundness of what Congress had finally arrived at. As Henderson had written an earlier Secretary of the Navy in 1823:[14]

> The Marine Corps is, and must continue to be, an appendage of the Navy, participating in its prosperity or sharing in its adversity—in war braving with it the same dangers, and in peace asking of it nothing but sheer justice. In the latter we have harmoniously and sedulously performed our duties; in the former we have fought side by side with our brethren of the Navy, and if a Hull survived to reap the benefits and honors of the victory over the *Guerrière,* a Bush sealed it with his life's blood.

Thus ended the first outright attempt to abolish the Marine Corps. Congress supported and protected Henderson's "isolated Corps," and was destined to do so many times again.

Archibald Henderson's relations with other Presidents were not as difficult as those with Andrew Jackson. In 1845, Navy Secretary J. Y. Mason got the idea that Henderson's brevet as a brigadier general (acquired in the Seminole War, as will be seen) was illegal and tried to check his pay account $12,698.33 for previous "overpayments." The Commandant went directly to President Tyler, a fellow Virginian, who convened a special board headed by General Winfield Scott, USA, then senior officer in the U. S. Armed Forces, to look into the matter. Scott's board unanimously found for Henderson, President Tyler approved their decision, and Archibald Henderson kept his $12,698.33. So that the point would not be overlooked by any future Secretary of the Navy, General Henderson had the proceedings of the board printed and publicly distributed at his own expense. Unfortunately, economy-minded congressmen had the last word. A year later, the Naval Appropriation Act contained the proviso:

> No payment shall hereafter be made to the colonel, or any other officer of the Marine Corps, by virtue of a commission of brigadier general by brevet.

The resulting pay cut was one of Archibald Henderson's few recorded defeats.

"GONE TO FIGHT THE INDIANS"

A happy legend recounts that, after proffering the Army two battalions to fight the rampaging Creek Indians in 1836, Colonel Henderson tacked a notice on the front door of Marine Corps Headquarters, took firm grip on his gold-headed walking stick (fashioned from timber of HMS *Cyane*, taken in 1812 by Henderson's ship, *Constitution*), and sallied south. Henderson's notice, says the legend, read as follows:

> Gone to fight the Indians. Will be back when the war is over.
>
> A. Henderson,
> Col. Comdt.

Be the facts of this episode what they may, Colonel Henderson did leave behind him a well-authenticated letter of instruction to Lieutenant Colonel Wainwright, to whom he entrusted the responsibility of administering the Marine Corps while the Commandant took the field:[15]

> During my absence on the campaign against the Creek Indians, I leave you in command at Head Quarters. I leave you a most valuable soldier in the Sergeant Major. He is anxious to go, but as a matter of duty I have ordered him to remain, as I cannot take any other than able-bodied men on such arduous service. Sergeant Triguet is left to assist you in attending to the duties at Head Quarters. He is a respectable old man, and has no other failing than that which but too often attends an old soldier.
>
> Three Sergeants (for duty), one Corporal and 12 privates are left to furnish a guard for the Navy Yard, to consist of one Sergeant, one Corporal, and six privates. One of the Musics left behind will have to act as lance Corporal as a relief for the guard at the Navy Yard. The Sergeant Major will sleep in Barracks. . . .
>
> Since writing the above I have decided to leave the Band, and you will be pleased to divide it into guards to keep up one sentinel at Head Quarters. The Drum and Fife Majors will take alternate days with them, so that one of those non-commissioned officers will be at all times with them.
>
> My clerk, Mr. Fulmer, can take charge of the School in barracks until the regular teacher returns and can at the same time, attend to the business of this office.

The Creek Indians (in Georgia and Alabama) and the Seminoles (in the Florida Everglades) were on the warpath, attempting to resist deportation from their home lands to reservations beyond the Mississippi. The small regular Army, augmented by the usual levies of militia, was seriously over-committed, and Colonel Henderson's offer of Marines for the campaign was quickly accepted. On 23 May 1836, acting under a clause in the new Marine Corps law, President Jackson ordered all available Marines detached to service with the Army. The Commandant promptly put himself at the head of the "available" list, reported to the Secretary of War for duty, reduced all Navy Yards to sergeant's guards, and within ten days had a two-battalion regiment, including more than half the Marine Corps, on the way south. Of Henderson's regiment, which numbered 38 officers and 424 enlisted men, the *Washington National Intelligencer* reported on 2 June 1836:

> The detachment of Marines under the command of Colonel Henderson, which so

promptly and handsomely volunteered to go against the Creek Indians, will, we understand, leave here this morning in the *Columbia* for Norfolk, where they will take passage for Charleston, South Carolina, on their route to the scene of savage warfare. This is another striking evidence of the great value of this arm of the national defence; it has shown itself as prompt to defend its country on the land as on the water, the element in which it was designed, originally, exclusively, to act. Upon several occasions during the late war with England, detachments from this brave and highly disciplined Corps covered themselves with unfading laurels by their conduct while serving on land; and in every instance of conflict on the water its bravery and efficiency were attested by the official reports of the actions in which it bore a part. In the present emergency it did not wait even an intimation that its services would be acceptable, but promptly came forth, through its commanding officer, in the first hour of danger. . . .

Henderson's movement proceeded by ship, by steam cars (the first movement by rail in the history of the Corps), then 14 days on foot, and ended with the regiment in Indian country south of Columbus, Georgia, on the Chattahoochee River. One of the battalion commanders was Brevet Lieutenant Colonel Samuel Miller who had done so well at Bladensburg 22 years earlier. A company commander was Captain John Harris.

By the end of summer, the Army and Marines had pacified the Creeks. In the Everglades, however, a more difficult campaign lay ahead as Army, Navy, and Marines bent united efforts from 1837 to 1841 to resettle the less-than-co-operative Seminoles in what is now Oklahoma.

While the Army and Marines had been finishing off the Creek campaign in Alabama, virtually the only forces available to cope with the Seminoles in Florida had been landing parties from the Navy's West India Squadron. In January 1836, under First Lieutenant N. S. Waldron, 57 Marines and a few seamen from the USS *Constellation* and the USS *St. Louis* had been sent ashore to defend Fort Brooke (now Tampa) against Indian attacks. They held the fort until the Marine regiment was redeployed to Florida in September. The first offensive action by Henderson's Marines took place at Wahoo Swamp, site of the 1835 massacre of an Army column under Major Dade. Here, on 21 November, Marines and Creek Indian scouts, brought south from Alabama and officered by Marines, fell upon the Seminoles and inflicted a defeat in which First Lieutenant Andrew Ross, who died of wounds a fortnight later, distinguished himself and was mentioned in dispatches.

When the Army commander, Major General T. H. Jesup, had his forces concentrated for the Florida campaign, Colonel Henderson was given command of one of the two brigades into which the army was divided, a mixed force of regular Army infantry and artillery, Georgia volunteers, Creek scouts, and the Marine regiment. On 27 January 1837, on the Hatchee-Lustee

River, northeast of Tampa, Henderson won one of the few successful engagements of the campaign and was brevetted brigadier general as a result—the first general officer in the history of the Corps. On 22 May, when a truce with the Seminoles appeared to be concluded, all but two companies of the six-company regiment returned north with Henderson and his staff, which had included the Adjutant and Inspector, the Quartermaster, and the Paymaster. Lieutenant Colonel Miller remained in the field with the two companies and a small headquarters, 189 in all, until July 1837, when he was succeeded by Captain William Dulany. Sixty-one Marines lost their lives in the campaign. When the battalion finally returned to Washington in mid-1838, Henderson published the following order:

Accept the congratulations of your Colonel, on your return from a tour of duty equally honourable to yourselves, and to the Corps to which you belong. Capt. Dulany is relieved from the Command of the Battalion. To him, and to its other officers the thanks of their Chief are most cordially conveyed. He sincerely wishes they may find an ample reward for all their toils and privations in a return to their homes, and in the assurance that they have elevated their Ancient Corps in the estimation of the Country.

Head Q^trs of the M. Corps }
Wash^n 24th July 1838   }

Arch. Henderson
Col. Comdt.

While the Marine battalion had been operating ashore, based at Fort Brooke, ships' detachments and seamen from the West India Squadron had conducted numerous river and coastal patrols in Florida waters. In 1838, when hostilities were resumed, the Navy organized the so-called "Mosquito Fleet," made up of patrol craft, revenue cutters, barges, and even canoes. One hundred and thirty Marines, commanded until 1840 by First Lieutenant G. H. Terrett, and from 1840 to 1842 by First Lieutenant T. T. Sloan, formed about one-fifth of the flotilla's strength. For four years, under conditions of appalling hardship and disease, the Mosquito Fleet ranged the Florida coasts and probed the Everglades, but despite much hard fighting and patrolling and many contacts, the Seminoles had the best of it, and in 1842 the war subsided (peace was never formally concluded) on Seminole terms.

PACIFIC INTERLUDES

While much of the Corps was fighting Indians, 31 Marines, commanded by Quartermaster Sergeant Marion A. Stearns, were in the far Pacific with the Wilkes Exploring Expedition, which explored in the Pacific Ocean from June 1838 until June 1842. Under Lieutenant-Commanding Charles Wilkes,

USN, the expedition visited and charted anew the Fiji Islands, Samoa, parts of the Philippines, the Hawaiian Islands, the Pacific Northwest, and Antarctica.

At Fiji the five-ship squadron received an unfriendly reception. In July 1840 a surveying launch was fiercely attacked by Fijians in Sualib Bay. Although their powder had been drenched by a squall, the party managed to get away safely. On their return, Wilkes called away Marines and proceeded to burn the offending village, consisting of about 60 huts.

Later in the month, the same natives set upon a working party which was provisioning from the beach at Malolo. Two officers were killed (including Wilkes's nephew, a midshipman), and one seaman was wounded. This time Wilkes landed everyone but the duty sections aboard ship and formed two columns, one headed by himself and the other by Lieutenant-Commanding Cadwalader Ringgold. The two columns converged on the town of Sualib. Rather than fight his way across the town's coconut-log palisades and wet ditch, Wilkes engaged the natives in a fire-fight beyond the range of their spears and bows, and set fire to the town by rockets. Then, the whole force marched across Malolo, burning native gardens as they advanced, and ended by burning the other principal town, Arro, whereupon the entire populace sued for peace.

At Upolu, Samoa, Marines and seamen from the USS *Peacock* landed on 25 February 1841, after an American merchant seaman had been murdered. The ship bombarded Upolu Town, and the landing force without resistance burned that town and Fusi and Salesesi as well. Less than two months later, on 9 April, at Drummond Island in the Kingmill Group, the *Peacock's* landing force had a similar but more serious experience. In a vain attempt to recover a seaman who had been spirited away and probably murdered by hostile natives, an 80-man party, including all the squadron's Marines, fought more than 600 spear-throwing islanders at Utirod, which, with its neighboring village, Aita, was burned in reprisal.

Far to the northwest, Marines of the newly established East India Squadron engaged in the Corps' first brush with the Chinese. On 16 June 1844, an American trader on Whampoa Island, off Canton, became embroiled in a Chinese riot, and next day a mob laid siege to the American compound. On 19 June the USS *St. Louis* arrived and landed her Marines, augmented by a party of bluejackets. These forces pushed their way to the compound, dispersed the Chinese, and remained on guard ashore until the American consul at Macao had settled the dispute.

TO THE HALLS OF THE MONTEZUMAS

War with Mexico was the inevitable result of America's westward and southwestern expansion against the frontiers of the southern republic. The Texas War of Independence in 1836 was, in fact, a dress rehearsal for the war of 1846.

In the Mexican War there were several geographically distinct campaigns. Scott's march on Mexico City attracted most attention and ended the war, but the campaigns against California and the west coast of Mexico gave the United States its last major domestic territorial acquisition—California and the Southwest. In addition, the Navy waged a campaign against the Mexican Gulf Coast. Marines took part in all these campaigns.

As far as the Corps was concerned, the stage was set by the secret mission of First Lieutenant A. H. Gillespie, the red-headed diplomatic agent of President James K. Polk. Polk wanted New Mexico and California. In late 1845, Gillespie—originally an enlisted Marine and described as "an elegant, precise man with a stiff pointed beard, and a temper of the same description"[16]—received secret orders from the President to make his way overland from Washington, via Mexico itself, reporting on the west coast of Mexico to Commodore John D. Sloat, commanding the Pacific Squadron. Then, he was to deliver memorized instructions to two of the President's trusted agents in the far west, Consul Thomas Larkin at Monterey and Captain John C. Fremont, USA, who headed a "scientific expedition" then exploring California and Oregon, both watchfully coveted by Great Britain.

For the moment it is enough to follow Gillespie—disguised as a whiskey salesman—through Veracruz to Mexico City, unscathed through a revolution, to Mazatlan on the Pacific, and on board one of Sloat's ships, the USS *Cyane*, commanded by S. F. Du Pont. There, Gillespie gave the commodore President Polk's instructions should war break out; in the meanwhile, Sloat was to counter British intrigues on the Pacific Coast. Gillespie then set out to find Fremont, who was mapping the California border of the disputed Oregon Territory. On 9 May 1846, deep in Indian country beside Klamath Lake, Gillespie found his man and delivered Polk's message in the nick of time; war was brewing along the Rio Grande.

On 18 May 1846, after Zachary Taylor's Texas battles at Resaca de la Palma and Palo Alto, the invasion of Mexico commenced. The first American forces to set foot on the soil of Mexico proper were Marine skirmishers in a naval force commanded by Captain J. H. Aulick, USN. The place was

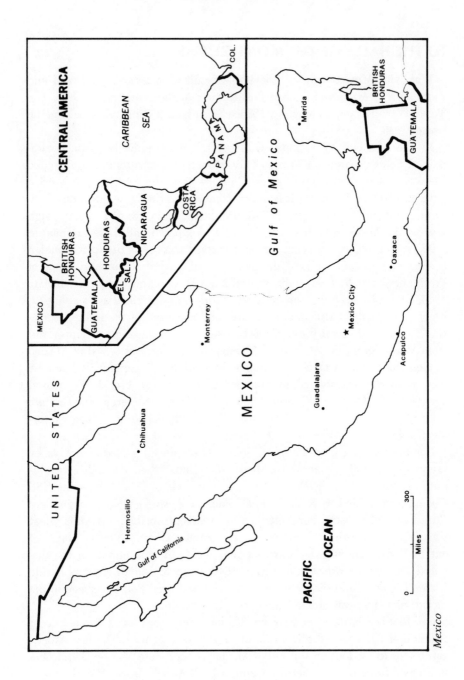

Mexico

Burrita, some 15 miles up from the mouth of the Rio Grande. This little incursion (which preceded "Old Rough and Ready" Taylor's crossing by about two hours) was soon overshadowed by more ambitious Gulf Coast operations in which Marines played their usual role as landing forces.

The immediate naval problem in the Gulf of Mexico was to establish an effective blockade and to provide secure seaborne communications for General Taylor as he marched south from the Rio Grande. Both requirements called for advance bases along the coast. Under Captain Alvin Edson, senior Marine officer in Commodore David Conner's Gulf Squadron, a 200-man battalion of Marines was formed by combining all ships' detachments in the squadron. Edson, veteran of Kuala Batu, employed his battalion with considerable effect. Augmented by sailors and supported by Conner's guns, the landing force raided Frontera and San Juan Bautista (October 1846), secured Tampico (14 November 1846), and made two unsuccessful efforts to capture Alvarado. These operations against Mexico's secondary ports were interrupted temporarily by the main landing at Veracruz, but were resumed with skill and vigor by Commodore Matthew C. Perry, younger brother of Oliver Hazard Perry, who relieved Conner as commander of the Gulf Squadron in March 1847. Perry organized a landing force brigade, 1,489 strong, the core of which was Edson's battalion and a battery of field artillery. With this force at his disposal, Perry, in concert with Army troops, finally secured Alvarado (1 April 1847), and on 18 April, in a briskly opposed landing attack, captured Tuxpan.

Following the Tuxpan operations, Commodore Perry determined to close the one important port which remained open (Frontera) and to occupy San Juan Bautista, almost a hundred miles up the Tabasco River from Frontera, a Yucatan town through which the Mexicans were receiving supplies from Central America. As a preliminary, he landed Marines from the USS *Mississippi* at Frontera on 15 May 1847. Then, in June, he concentrated his squadron at that port, and landed his naval brigade for the river campaign against San Juan Bautista (referred to as "Tabasco" in some accounts). Leaving his deep-draft ships outside the bar, the commodore formed a column of steamers, gunboats, and barges for the landing force, which included ten pieces of artillery and even a submarine explosive device aboard the USS *Spitfire* for underwater demolition of obstacles. On 14 June the force advanced more than 40 miles upstream without opposition, but on the following day enemy defenders were encountered in strength. Commencing with sniping from the wooded banks, Mexican fire grew heavier as the ships came to obstructions in the channel. Under cover of ships' gunfire the obstructions were cleared, but it was apparent that enemy batteries defended the river, and that these must be taken out by land attack. At a river bend called "Seven Palm Trees," with "three hearty cheers," the landing force pulled ashore to the left bank, and, within a few minutes, had formed for the advance after snaking their artillery up and over a 25-foot bluff. All day, capturing four successive batteries (Colmina, Acachapan, Independencia, and Iturbide), the Marines and seamen advanced under support of the gunboats working upstream beside them. In the late afternoon, having captured 12 guns, almost 600 muskets and many stores, and having ejected 400 Mexican defenders from San Juan Bautista itself, the force ran up the colors over the plaza and settled into garrison routine. Leaving three gunboats at the town to support a shore detachment of 115 Marines and 60 seamen-artillerists, Perry descended the river. Until the end of June, occasional skirmishing went on with Mexican troops in the vicinity, but, after the region had been pacified for three weeks, and because the yellow fever season was setting in, the landing force was withdrawn. On 22 July, colors were hauled down by a guard of honor, and, to the tune of "Hail, Columbia," the Marines and seamen marched aboard ship and descended the river. The capture and neutralization of San Juan Bautista—the town played no further role in the war—was the last important amphibious operation of the Gulf Squadron, since it closed the final port of entry remaining to the Mexicans. The campaign was conducted smoothly and expertly, and reflected a high degree of amphibious technique and mutual co-ordination between the fleet and its landing force.

As General Taylor advanced southward from Texas, it became clear that the terrain precluded penetration of Mexico much below Monterrey, and that subjugation of the country would require a thrust onto the central plateau. In early 1847 an expedition was therefore organized to capture Mexico City itself, and General Winfield Scott, the Douglas MacArthur of his day, was given command. As a preliminary, an advance base had to be established at Veracruz.

On 9 March 1847, supported by the Gulf Squadron, Scott's expeditionary force landed three miles southeast of Veracruz and invested that city. Edson's fleet Marine battalion, now at a strength of 180 men, was attached to the 3d Artillery, Worth's Division, which landed first. The Marines served siege guns throughout the 20-day bombardment and received Winfield Scott's thanks as "this handsome detachment of Marines."[17]

At home, while "Old Fuss and Feathers" (as the Army nicknamed Scott) was girding for the march on Mexico City, Archibald Henderson had repeated his feat of Creek and Seminole days. By stripping every navy yard to a sergeant's guard and by dipping into a 1,000-man increase voted the Marine Corps by Congress on 3 March 1847, Henderson again set out to form a Marine regiment, a project he had cleared with President Polk himself.

Regimental headquarters and the first battalion, 328 strong, sailed from Fort Hamilton, New York, a few days after being organized—a breathless schedule and one which would typify many another Marine expedition in the years to come. To form the second battalion, Henderson, with the approval of the Secretary of the Navy, planned to draw on the Gulf Squadron Marines under Captain Edson; Brevet Lieutenant Colonel Samuel E. Watson, who had commanded the Marines with Winfield Scott's regular brigade in 1813, was to command the regiment. Unfortunately, this ambitious plan did not suit Commodore Perry at all because he needed the Marines to garrison Alvarado and other Gulf Coast ports seized by the Navy. Accordingly, after consulting with Scott, Perry decided to disregard the Secretary of the Navy's orders and keep his Marines for further service in the Gulf Coast naval brigade. He did, however, give Colonel Watson one officer and 28 enlisted men, reporting as follows to the Secretary:[18]

> I have had an interview with Brigadier General Pierce, whose brigade the Marines ordered to be detached from the squadron are to join. General Pierce has fully agreed with me that the small force of Marines in the squadron, about 190 effective men, will be of little advantage to him, and that the consequences of withdrawing them . . . will produce a most pernicious effect with the enemy. . . . I shall await with much interest your communications, and hope that you will not only soon be able to replace the Marines withdrawn from the squadron, but add to their number.

The Marine regiment, which had arrived at Veracruz on 1 July, forthwith became the Marine battalion.

Attached to the division of Franklin Pierce (later to become President of the United States), the 357 Marines set out on 16 July on a three-week march to Puebla, Scott's forward base. Although the column was attacked six times by guerrillas, it arrived on 6 August in good order. Lieutenant Colonel Watson's battalion was thereupon incorporated into the 4th Division, commanded by Brigadier General John A. Quitman, and Watson himself was given command of the Army brigade to which the Marines were attached. Major Levi Twiggs, an 1812 veteran hardened in the Florida wars, inherited the battalion. Forty-eight hours later Scott marched his 10,738 men on Mexico City and against the 32,000-man Mexican army.

A month of hard fighting and marching brought Scott to the approaches of Mexico City. In the initial battles of Cherubusco, Contreras, and Molino del Rey, the Marines were saddled with the chore of protecting Scott's siege and supply trains—an unhappy job for Marines even though Scott attempted to soften their disappointment by asserting,[19] ". . . it might well become, emphatically, the post of honor."

While Scott hammered at Molino del Rey on 8 September, reconnaissance showed that the key to Mexico City was Chapultepec Castle, riding the precipitous crest of a long ridge which commanded the swamp causeways leading to the city's Belen and San Cosme Gates. In Chapultepec Castle was the Military Academy of Mexico; among the castle's 800 defenders were more than a hundred young cadets, ever afterward known in the history of Mexico as *Los Niños Héroes*. General Scott's plan was to make him main effort against Chapultepec's west face with one division (Pillow's) and to attack the southern face with another (Quitman's). The leading troops in each division were to be made up of picked "storming parties," specially selected and equipped. In Quitman's division, Major Twiggs was chosen to lead the storming parties for the attack from the south, while Captain John G. Reynolds, a Marine company commander and one of the ablest officers in the Corps, was selected to head the first wave—the "pioneer storming party" made up of 40 Army and Marine volunteers picked from the entire division.[20] General Quitman designated the remainder of the Marine battalion, under Colonel Watson—the only regulars in his division—to support the storming parties and lead the division in the attack. In preparation for the assault, planned for 13 September, Scott's siege batteries commenced pounding Chapultepec on the 12th. The same day, screened by a force of Marines headed by Major Twiggs, Quitman reconnoitered the ground over which the storming parties would advance; seven Marines were wounded in the process.[21]

At daylight on the 13th the artillery doubled its fire on Chapultepec. At 0800, after a two-hour cannonade, the guns fell silent for five minutes, then resumed fire. This was the signal for the assault.

Under a hail of musketry, grape, and canister from the fortress, Major Twiggs—armed with his favorite double-barreled fowling piece—moved out. Close behind followed Reynolds' pioneers carrying pickaxes, crowbars, and scaling ladders much like those Marines would use a century later on the slopes of Iwo Jima's Suribachi Yama and at Korea's Inchon sea wall. With the Marine battalion in support of the pioneers, Quitman's division followed.

Five Mexican guns on the Veronica Causeway east of Chapultepec, behind a deep ditch, forced the assault to take cover in the lee of some ruined houses and in another ditch near the base of the southeast face of the hill, where an aide reached Colonel Watson with orders from General Quitman to hold the Marine battalion at that point. After ten minutes waiting, while the Marines returned the enemy fire with their muskets, Twiggs exclaimed, "By God, I'm tired," and stepped into the open to give the command to ad-

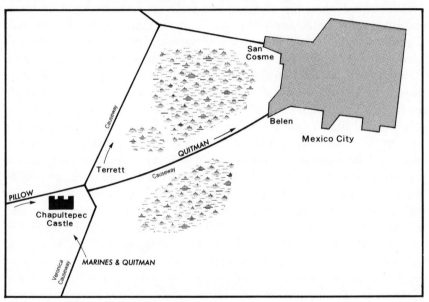

Assault on Chapultepec, Mexico, 13 September 1847

vance. An instant later he fell—"the brave and lamented Twiggs," Quitman reported[22]—killed instantly by a volley from the ramparts above. Reynolds urged Watson to forget his orders and attack, but the elderly battalion commander stood fast until the general charge was sounded. In a few moments, the storming parties of both Quitman and Pillow were over the castle walls, bayoneting the enemy as they swept in. Five hundred and fifty prisoners (including a general and ten colonels) were the reward, plus seven guns, a thousand muskets, and several stand of colors. Twenty-four Marines, including four officers, were killed or wounded in the assault on Chapultepec;[23]

among the wounded was Second Lieutenant C. A. Henderson, the Commandant's son. Indicative of the Marine battalion's performance was the fact that 13 of the 23 Marine officers present at Chapultepec received brevets for bravery.

Meanwhile, Captain George H. Terrett, whose Company C formed the right flank of the support, outflanked and carried the Mexican guns on the Veronica Causeway; then, instead of wheeling left toward the castle, pursued the fleeing enemy to his front, along the San Cosme road toward the city. Thus separated from the Chapultepec action, with 67 officers and men, Terrett annexed two light artillery sections of Magruder's Battery, which supported his push along the causeway and broke up a counterattack by Mexican lancers. Soon after, near a cemetery where the causeway turned east, Terrett encountered and routed a disorganized force of over a thousand Mexicans. Short of the San Cosme Gate, the Marines fell in with Lieutenant U. S. Grant, USA, and 26 men of the 4th Infantry. The combined force gained the gateway and set foot inside Mexico City, the first American troops to do so. When General Worth, into whose zone of action Terrett's attack had drifted, came up, he attached the Marine company to the 11th Infantry, with whom they remained until able to rejoin their own battalion.

On the other causeway, leading to the Belen Gate, General Quitman pushed his division, with the Marines still in the van, up to the city walls before night intervened. During darkness the Mexican forces evacuated the city. Early in the morning, Quitman led his men into the Grand Plaza and formed them in the shadow of the Cathedral. The Marine battalion (which had sustained 39 killed or wounded in the fighting on the 13th) was given the task of clearing the Palacio Nacional of thieves and vagabonds who were already plundering its halls. Atop this building, the Palace of the Montezumas, Second Lieutenant A. S. Nicholson, later to become Adjutant and Inspector of the Corps, cut down the Mexican colors and ran up the Stars and Stripes,[24] while the troops in the Plaza presented arms. And as Winfield Scott strode into the Palacio Nacional, the surrounding streets were guarded by United States Marines.

Until 1848 the Marine Corps standard bore only the traditional motto, *To the Shores of Tripoli*. On the return of the Marine battalion to Washington, the people of the city presented General Henderson with a blue and gold standard, blazoned with a new motto:[25]

From Tripoli to the Halls of the Montezumas

WINNING THE PACIFIC COAST

While the Marines with Winfield Scott and with the Gulf Squadron were molding traditions for the Corps, other Marines on the Pacific Coast were also making history.

Commodore Sloat's instructions required that he operate "with his finger on his number" until dead certain that war existed with Mexico. There was no room for repetition of the 1842 fiasco in which Commodore ap Catesby Jones, Sloat's impetuous predecessor, had landed Marines and seized the Presidio of Monterey only to discover that the news of war was false.

Sloat's caution, however, did not restrain Lieutenant Gillespie, President Polk's agent, who had remained with Fremont after delivering the President's instructions. As second-in-command and adjutant, with Captain Fremont, he joined the band of 224 California-American mounted riflemen under the "Bear Flag." This "California Battalion," as it was styled, had already seized Sonoma and the fort (on the site of today's Fort Winfield Scott) which commanded the Golden Gate.[26]

By 2 July, even Commodore Sloat (who had orders for home) was satisfied that shooting war was on. On the 9th, Marines and seamen landed without opposition at Yerba Buena and raised the colors over what was to become San Francisco. Monterey had been captured two days earlier by the USS *Savannah's* landing force including 85 Marines under Captain Ward Marston. Sloat's relief, Commodore Robert F. Stockton, immediately sent the California Battalion south to take San Diego, which was accomplished with support from the USS *Cyane* on 29 July, Gillespie being left in command. Eight days later, Stockton landed 350 Marines and seamen at San Pedro preparatory to marching on Ciudad de los Angeles; Stockton's Marines were under Lieutenant Jacob Zeilin, future Commandant of the Corps.

Within a week, Commodore Stockton, all energy and courage, had reached Los Angeles, joined a detachment under Fremont which had arrived from San Diego, and on 13 August scared Mexican General Jose Castro and his army out of town.

With Los Angeles, San Pedro, and San Diego in hand, Stockton sailed north again, as did Fremont, leaving Gillespie, now a captain, as Military Commandant of the Department of Southern California, with a garrison of California Volunteers at Los Angeles—". . . perfect drunkards whilst in this

Ciudad of wine and Aguardiente but serviceable Riflemen in the field."[27] Another Marine, Second Lieutenant W. A. T. Maddox (from the *Cyane*) was made commandant of the Middle Department with headquarters at Monterey.

So far, so good: but the Southern Californians, of Spanish extraction, soon realized the numerical weakness of Gillespie's force. On 23 September, Los Angeles revolted against the Americans who (including seven men hastily released from the brig) numbered but 59, with no artillery. Spying four spiked and rusty gun barrels in the yard of the *commandancia*, Gillespie set his gunner's mate to work, while melting down lead pipes for grapeshot. Within 48 hours, two guns were mounted and in action against the 600 attackers. Nevertheless, the odds were too great and, on 30 September, having capitulated honorably, Gillespie marched out of Los Angeles with his troops, guns, and full honors of war. The force boarded the USS *Vandalia* at San Pedro on 4 October.

When the USS *Savannah* arrived, on 7 October, a 310-man Navy and Marine landing force was put ashore with Gillespie's detachment in an attempt to retake Los Angeles. Under the fumbling command of Captain William Mervine, USN, the column suffered what Stockton curtly called, "A defeat, and a very bad defeat," which was followed by another reverse on the 27th.

Meanwhile, San Diego, held by a small seaman-garrison, was besieged. With the double intent of relieving San Diego and of establishing a base for operations against Los Angeles, Stockton sent Gillespie south and landed Marines from the *Savannah* and *Congress,* who fought a pitched battle on 18 November that raised the siege.

On 5 December, after a five-month march overland from Fort Leavenworth, Brigadier General Stephen W. Kearny, USA, with 100 dragoons and Kit Carson, the frontier scout, made contact with Gillespie and 39 mounted volunteers and seamen and a fieldpiece, in the Santa Maria Valley. Despite the worn-out condition of his troops, Kearny attacked the nearby Californian forces under Andres Pico at San Pasqual (not far from today's Camp Pendleton). This was a mistake. Pico's lancers cut the Americans to pieces, inflicting 38 casualties (including Gillespie) and were only driven from the field by fire from the Navy fieldpiece. But better days were ahead. At the San Gabriel River, south of Los Angeles, on 8 January, anniversary of the Battle of New Orleans, under Stockton's command, Kearny's dragoons, Gillespie's volunteers, and the Pacific Squadron's landing force, led by Zeilin, defeated the enemy main body, some 600 strong including cavalry and several guns. Gillespie was again wounded. Two days later, Los Angeles fell and resistance ceased. Gillespie then proudly raised over the city the same colors he had lowered in September. Both Zeilin and Gillespie were breveted major for their services.

The conquest of California illustrates how a numerically inferior but mobile force, prepositioned afloat for prompt action and possessing control of the sea and the means to land at will, was able to dominate and eventually subjugate an immense land mass.

With California uneasily at peace by early 1847, the Pacific Squadron proceeded to blockade and capture Mexico's west coast ports. Mazatlan, Guaymas, Muleje, San Blas, and finally San Jose, were the scenes of landing operations. The assault on Mazatlan was the most important, both in scale and in results. On 10 November 1847, 72d Birthday of the Marine Corps, 730 Marines and seamen-gunners landed in Mazatlan Harbor under the guns of the frigates *Congress* and *Independence,* and of the corvette *Cyane.* The Mexicans, more than a thousand strong, took to their heels and allowed Captain Zeilin, with the Marine detachments of the frigates, to establish himself as military governor in the abandoned presidio. Mazatlan was garrisoned by Marines until 17 June 1848.

At San Jose, while an eight-year-old boy who would one day command the Marine Corps waited at home in Maine, his father, Lieutenant Charles Heywood, USN, conducted a memorable defense. Landed on 9 November 1847 with four midshipmen, 20 Marines, and a 12-pounder, Heywood was given the job of holding San Jose mission, located at the southern extremity of Lower California. No sooner had Commodore W. B. Shubrick (who had relieved Stockton) weighed anchor and set sail than 150 Mexicans, equipped with artillery, laid siege to the mission. Attacking night and day for three days, they were only frightened off by the arrival of an American whaler which they took for a warship. Shortly afterward, the USS *Portsmouth* stood in with reinforcements which brought Heywood's command to 27 Marines, 10 seamen, and 20 California volunteers. They arrived in the nick of time, for, on 22 January, after the *Portsmouth* had sailed, San Jose was invested by 400 Mexicans, including cavalry and artillery. Drawing the siege lines closer, the Mexicans had the mission surrounded by the beginning of February and captured eight defenders, who were swooped up by a cavalry dash. On 6 February, Heywood led a sortie which dislodged the Mexicans from one of their most threatening positions, but he lacked the strength to hold it. Next day he made another sortie and again had to fall back. Meanwhile, the Mexicans continued to close in: on 10

February they gained a church tower from which they could snipe into Heywood's lines; on the 12th they captured his well. Heywood's men attempted to dig a well of their own, but struck no water. Then, on 15 February, just as the situation seemed desperate, the USS *Cyane* arrived. Led in person by her captain, Commander Du Pont, the ship's landing force came to the rescue, attacking the Mexicans from the rear, while Heywood and his men sallied from the mission. This action ended any further serious attempts to dislodge Heywood, although his detachment was harried by guerrillas until 20 April, when an Army garrison force relieved him.

The defense of San Jose was the last fighting ashore by sailors and Marines on the west coast of Mexico. Of the Marines' contribution to this remote campaign, Commodore Shubrick wrote in his final report:[28]

The Marines have behaved with the fidelity and constancy which characterizes that valuable Corps, and I embrace this opportunity respectfully to recommend that ships coming to this station be allowed as large a complement of these valuable men as possible.

"... THE MOST WIDELY EXTENDED DUTIES"

In spite of postwar cutbacks in the Corps to its earlier enlisted strength of 1,224, the decade which followed peace with Mexico was hardly one of peace for Marines. American foreign trade increased threefold between 1846 and 1860, and about two-thirds of this increase traveled in American bottoms. As a result, there was work throughout the world for both the Navy and the Marine Corps—first in the Far East and then in South and Central America.

Commodore Matthew Calbraith Perry had already showed his energy and imagination (and also his reliance on Marines) during the Gulf Coast operations in the Mexican War. Perry was therefore a logical choice to command our expedition to open relations with Japan, and, as might be expected, he called on the Marines to play a star role. In early 1853 Commodore Perry's seven ships sailed for Yedo (Tokyo), calling en route at two spots which would be well known to Marines of later days—Naha in Okinawa and Port Lloyd in the Bonins. Perry's squadron included almost one-sixth of the Marine Corps: a battalion of six officers and 200 Marines commanded by Major Jacob Zeilin, squadron Marine officer.

Although no fighting was called for in Perry's two ceremonial visits, both Zeilin and the commodore were prepared for anything that might happen.

Ships approached at general quarters, and the Marines were ready to land either fighting or parading. As it turned out, parading was the order of the day, a role which Zeilin's battalion, uniformed in white trousers, blue blouses, cross-belts, and tall shakoes, handsomely filled. Two bands (whose musicians wore loaded pistols) provided music. In the best traditions of the Corps, the Marines landed first and lined Perry's route to the ceremonial pavilion. One unforeseen episode provided a human bond between Americans and Japanese; Private Robert Williams of the USS *Mississippi* died and the Japanese permitted his burial ashore with full honors,[29] the first Christian burial on Japanese soil since 1550. It would be nine decades before ships' Marine detachments would emulate Zeilin's Marines by another "first" in Tokyo Bay: the landing at Yokosuka on 30 August 1945.

Hardly as peaceful as the landings of Commodore Perry was that at Shanghai on 4 April 1854, during the Taiping Rebellion that rocked China. When Chinese on both sides threatened to overrun the already important foreign concessions, the USS *Plymouth* landed her sergeant's guard of Marines, who were joined by Royal Marines and seamen from a British man-of-war. The two detachments formed a single force and swept the contending Chinese out of Shanghai. American casualties were one seaman killed, and two Marines and a seaman wounded. A year later, the USS *Powhatan* had to repeat the performance at Shanghai, landing her guard, under First Lieutenant J. H. Jones, on 19 May 1855, for a two-day stay. The *Powhatan's* landing force also took part, on 4 August 1855, in a combined British-American foray against a pirate base on Ty-Ho Bay, near Hong Kong. Seventeen pirate junks were made prize in an all-day fight, with two Marines and three seamen killed, and six more of the latter wounded.

As a climax in China waters, in the fall of 1856, the incident of the "Barrier Forts" brought Marines into their hottest fighting since 1847. In a trial of strength with the foreigners bent on "opening" China, the garrison of the Barrier Forts below Canton opened fire without warning on U. S. merchantmen and Navy ships' boats in the stream. These forts, designed by European engineers and mounting heavy guns, were sited to interdict the river approaches to Canton, where a small Marine detachment was already ashore guarding the American consulate; this detachment and the consulate depended on supplies delivered by pulling boat from men-of-war downstream.

On the afternoon of 16 November, Commodore James Armstrong, aboard the steam frigate *San Jacinto*, stood up the Pearl River toward the forts and Canton, accompanied by the sloops-of-war *Portsmouth* and *Levant*, to bombard the offending fort. The Chinese gunners showed fight (as well they might with ten-inch guns behind seven-foot granite-faced earthworks), and ships and forts dueled until nightfall.

On 20 November, Commodore A. H. Foote, the *Portsmouth's* stanch commander (who had succeeded Armstrong, laid low by illness), received Armstrong's final orders[30]—land and take whatever action might be required, "even though you may be led to the capture of the forts." This was enough for Foote. With a landing force of 287 seamen and Marines and four howitz-

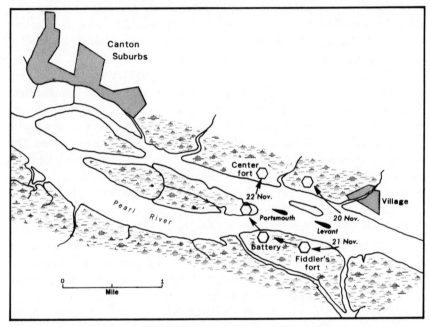

Battle of the Barrier Forts, Canton, China, 16-22 November 1856

ers, Foote stormed ashore. His senior Marine officer, Captain J. D. Simms, had won his brevet for gallantry at Chapultepec, and here was work of the same kind. After an hour's bombardment by the two sloops-of-war, the landing force outflanked the fort, rushed it from the rear, and routed the defenders, ". . . the Marines being in advance opened fire upon the fugitives with deadly effect, killing some forty or fifty."[31]

Two thousand Chinese then counterattacked from an adjacent village, "but," said the commodore, "they were both times repulsed by the Marines." Meanwhile, several of the 53 captured guns were put into action against the opposite fort, which was shelling both the captured work and the *Ports-*

mouth. Next, a 4,000-man column attacked from Canton. The Chinese charged three times and only fell back after being cut to pieces by Simms's fire.

At 0300 next morning, "Fiddler's Fort" (the troops' name for a work on the south shore) opened fire. Foote boated most of his landing force, bombarded the fort until daylight, and again assaulted. This time the attack led across swamp and paddy as the Chinese replied with everything from 68-pound shot to "rockets and stink pots."[32] The first man over the walls was Corporal William McDougal, USS *Levant,* who planted the colors on the rampart. While some of the fort's 41 guns were turned on the two adjoining works, Simms ordered the remaining guns spiked and their carriages burned.

That afternoon, supported by fire from Fiddler's Fort, Captain Simms captured a six-gun battery, and the landing force then stormed a third fort located on an island in mid-stream. Again leading the Marines over the parapet, Corporal McDougal implanted the colors atop the fort. Thirty-eight guns were taken, all of which were spiked and destroyed. Next morning the last remaining work—"Center Fort"—was the objective. Despite its 28 guns, fire from the ships and from Fiddler's Fort neutralized the defenders, and, as the storming parties clambered into Center Fort, the Chinese fled, leaving 250 dead. American killed and wounded were 42. Commodore Foote ordered demolition of the forts, which were blown up with their own powder, and the remaining Chinese guns were spiked and rolled into the Pearl River. In all, 176 Chinese guns had been taken and destroyed, and the most modern and well-built forts in China reduced to rubble. In reviewing these achievements, Foote was not unmindful of the work done by the Marines:[33]

It may be seen in this report how efficient our Marines are in service of this kind; and the inference is inevitable that an increase of that Corps, and of the number of officers and men attached to our ships, would tend to insure success in like expeditions. In all the advances, the men were ready, in perfect order and discipline, to respond to the call of their officers.

A hemisphere away, in Nicaragua, Panama, Paraguay, and Uruguay, Marines were hardly less active. With the discovery of gold in California in 1849, the Isthmus of Panama became the highroad to the Pacific coast. In 1855 a rickety American railroad was completed across the Isthmus, and Panama soon attracted hordes of sharpers, three-card artists, and fugitive desperadoes. Disorder inevitably followed. Transit of American passengers and cargo, guaranteed to United States citizens under the Treaty of New Granada, was interrupted. In September 1856, following a summer of unrest, Captain Addison Garland (who had been the first Marine officer to land on Mexican soil in 1846) went ashore at Panama City at the head of a 160-man landing force from the USS *Independence* and *St. Mary's*. Within a few days, Garland had restored peace, and travel across the Isthmus was resumed. Peace was not permanent, however; in September 1860, *St. Mary's* again had to land her Marines (who were followed soon after by a British detachment from HMS *Clio*) to neutralize Panama City during an outbreak of civil war.

From 1852 to 1854, Marines landed three times in Nicaragua, the most consequential operation being that at Greytown by the USS *Cyane* in July 1854, for the purpose of exacting an apology and indemnities for the illegal arrest and overnight detention there of the American Minister to Nicaragua. When the local authorities refused to take notice of the American demands, the *Cyane's* captain, Commander G. N. Hollins, landed his Marines, under Orderly Sergeant J. E. Thompson, on 12 July, and disarmed the town. The Nicaraguans still refused the required amends; Commander Hollins thereupon bombarded Greytown and burned it, a course of action which the State Department sustained.

In Uruguay and Paraguay the story was the same: unsettled times, immature governments. During November 1855, Brevet First Lieutenant Nicholson (he who had run up the colors over Mexico City) landed from the USS *Germantown* to protect the American consulate at Montevideo during a revolution. On the 27th, by interposing his detachment between two factions, he prevented the massacre of a group of prisoners who were in the act of surrender. Three years later, on 2 January 1858, Brevet Major J. G. Reynolds, likewise a veteran of Chapultepec, led American Marines in a joint landing with the British to safeguard the respective national interests during still another revolution at Montevideo. In Paraguay, in the same year, a show of force by ships of the Brazil Squadron, which steamed up the Paraná River to Asunción, carrying 300 Marines, was sufficient to bring about more mannerly dealings between local authorities and American representatives.

Across the South Atlantic, in Africa, February 1860 saw the last landing by U. S. Marines (in Kissembo, now in Angola) to guard American property and suppress slaving, an effort in which the Navy's African Squadron had engaged since 1843. Commodore Perry, one of the squadron's earlier commanders, indeed owed his life to a Marine sergeant who shot down Ben Crack-O, king of the Berribees, when the latter suddenly grappled with the commodore during a parley ashore in Liberia in 1843.

During these active years the Navy grew steadily, and even the Marine Corps, always financially straitened and held far below its authorized strength of 2,420 officers and men, received welcome increments in 1856 and the two years that followed. With these reinforcements, the Corps could muster 53 officers and 2,010 enlisted men. The modest increases in the Marine Corps, authorized by President Buchanan, were in response to persuasion by Archibald Henderson who, from 1852 on, had mounted a campaign to get the men he so badly needed. One of Henderson's techniques, which would often be repeated, was to amass testimonials from senior officers of the Navy, for use as ammunition in connection with personnel legislation and negotiations. The leading argument used by General Henderson was one calculated to appeal to the weathered naval officers of the day: enlargement of the Marine Corps was a necessity, as Henderson urged, "since the abolishment of flogging in the Navy." Favorable replies came in quickly from such eminent officers as Charles Stewart, M. C. Perry, Hiram Paulding, Josiah Tattnall, Charles Wilkes, and many others. Typical was the dictum of Commodore Joshua Sands:[34]

I should not deem a man-of-war complete without a body of Marines, imbued with that *esprit* which has so long characterized the Old Corps.

In his Annual Report for 1859 (the year in which Henderson died in office), Secretary of the Navy Isaac Toucey extolled Henderson's Corps in terms calculated to have gladdened the old Commandant:

The Marine Corps is an indispensable branch of the Naval Service. . . . It is a gallant little band upon which rests the most widely extended duties at home and in every sea and clime, without sufficient numbers to perform them.

"MEN, YOU HAD BETTER THINK TWICE . . ."

The 1st of June 1857 was election day in the District of Columbia, which in those days still enjoyed the franchise (only recently restored) and self-government (yet to be regained). That morning a gang of Baltimore toughs, who styled themselves "Plug-Uglies," arrived by train, intent on taking control of Washington's polls. As the *Washington Star* reported:[35]

Such an exhibition of murderous instruments as the party carried was sufficient to cause the peaceably disposed to keep as far as possible from them. One man was armed with a huge blacksmith sledge, another with a horse-pistol, a third carried an assortment of revolvers, bowie-knives, billies, and an iron bar, while a fourth carried, besides a sack filled with stones, brickbats, etc., a large maul of sufficient strength to fell an ox. The parties, armed with revolvers, billies, and slung-shots, brandished them about in a menacing manner, to the terror of all.

After putting Washington's police to flight, the Plug-Uglies produced a shotted brass cannon. With good reason for alarm, Mayor Magruder of Washington appealed for help. The Marines were called out. A two-company battalion responded from Eighth and Eye. Major H. B. Tyler, the Adjutant and Inspector, was in command, and Captain Zeilin had one of the companies. Brevet Captain W. A. T. Maddox who, as a second lieutenant, had almost singlehandedly kept the lid on northern California in 1846 and 1847, commanded the other. At the Northern Liberties Market (near 5th and K Streets today), the principal polling place, Plug-Uglies and Marines faced each other.

Across the interval dominated by the thugs' brass cannon strode an old gentleman in civilian clothes, carrying a gold-headed cane. None of the Plug-Uglies knew that that cane was made from a timber of His Britannic Majesty's late ship *Cyane,* nor could they know that the bearer of that cane had served as captain of Marines aboard "Old Ironsides" when she captured *Cyane* in 1815. But they stood aside, loaded pistols, billies, slung-shots, and all, as the brave old man faced the cannon's muzzle and said, "Men, you had better think twice before you fire this piece at the Marines."[36]

The speaker was Brevet Brigadier General Archibald Henderson, fifth Commandant of the Marine Corps, age 74. While the Plug-Uglies milled in indecision, a squad of Marines led by Lieutenant Henderson, the Commandant's son, rushed the cannon and dragged it clear. As the *Star* continued:[37]

A man ran up to the general, within two feet of his person, and was about to discharge his pistol, when a private with a musket struck his arm, causing the weapon to fall; at the same time, the general seized the villain and marched him off to the mayor, into whose hands he placed him. The pistol-shots now rattled around like hailstones, and the officers had great difficulty in restraining their men from returning the fire. General Henderson and all the officers were constantly admonishing the men not to fire until the order was given, but a shot coming from the crowd struck a private in the cheek, making a dreadful wound, and, several more being hit by stones, the soldiers could stand it no longer; they poured in an answering fire. . . . The battalion made a movement as if to pour in another fire, which the rioters seeing, took to their heels and fled. The force was finally drawn off to the City Hall; and then proceeded to the railroad depot, to intercept, if possible, any more of the murderous gang arriving from Baltimore.

THE CORPS SCENE

In a Corps run by Archibald Henderson emphasis could be expected on professional capability and discipline. To secure the first, Henderson resumed Wharton's policy of having new officers ordered to Eighth and Eye for basic training before being sent to duty elsewhere. Another type of training which Henderson instituted is described in his 1857 annual report to the Secretary of the Navy:

First Lieutenant Green, with your approval, passed a large portion of the summer at West Point engaged in securing a knowledge of artillery for the purpose of introducing it into the Marine Corps. A battery of light and heavy guns, directed by the Department to be turned over to the Marine Corps, will in a few days be at Headquarters, and instruction in artillery will immediately thereafter commence.[38]

West Point figured in other ways in Henderson's plans for improving the Corps: whenever, as frequently happened, the Army could not find room for all its Military Academy graduates, Henderson recruited them as Marine officers and thus instituted a practice, later interrupted, which finally became recognized in law a century after his death.[39]

With equal concern for the quality of the enlisted Marine, General Henderson systematized recruiting and issued the first published instructions for recruiters, the 1847 *Regulations for the Recruiting Service of the United States Marine Corps*,[40] which opened with the words, "No man is wanted who does not come voluntarily to the standard of his country"—a Marine Corps policy which has held good ever since even though draftees have been imposed on the Corps three times in the 20th century. After the recruit had passed inspection, been sworn in, and a two-dollar bounty paid to his bringer, the manual went on:[41]

The Recruiting Officer will have his hair cut close to his head and cause him to be well washed from head to foot.

The "shipping-over music" of Henderson's day was largely that of fifes and drums, as described by a veteran recruiter, Sergeant Major Edward Dunn, who ultimately survived to become, in 1915, the oldest living Marine:[42]

Yes sir, I was on recruiting duty in New York in 1852. I was off the old *Pennsyl-*

vania, ship of the line. There was the captain, the recruiting officer, the sergeant, my drummer and me. Along in the morning about ten o'clock, after the crowds would get out on the street, the drummer and I would put on our red full dress tunics, with swallow tails, form a procession and down the street we'd go. The captain bought some bright colored ribbons for the drummer and me, which we tied in bows on our arms and to the buttons on the sides of our shakoes, and when the wind blew we certainly made a fine sight as we marched down Broadway to the Battery, then up the Bowery and back to the rendezvous on Chambers Street, ribbons flying and playing quick-steps all the way. Then the captain would get up on a dry-goods box in front of the recruiting office and make a speech to the crowd, telling them what a fine place the Marine Corps was for a man and what a chance he'd have to visit foreign ports. That's the way we got recruits in those days.

After 1843 (when the Bureau of Medicine and Surgery was a year old), the person who gave the recruit his physical examination was no longer a loblolly boy but a "surgeon's steward" of the Navy, at the pay of $18 a month and one ration. While privates still drew $6 a month, the sergeant major (there was still only one) had gained a 70 per cent monthly raise by the end of Henderson's commandancy, from $10 to $17. In addition, each enlisted man received a yearly clothing allowance of $30, with which, during each enlistment, he was expected to maintain the following bag of clothing as prescribed in *Uniform Regulations, 1859:*

1 uniform cap	1 blanket
2 uniform coats	8 pairs of socks
2 sets of epaulettes, bullion	8 pairs of drawers
7 pairs linen trousers	4 fatigue caps
8 pairs woolen trousers	4 fatigue coats
12 shirts	8 blue flannel shirts
2 stocks, leather	1 greatcoat
6 pairs of shoes	

Discipline in the Marine Corps of the early 19th century continued to be simple and severe.

Troublesome drunks were straightened out, as one Commandant later noted, ". . . by making them drink one and two quarts of salt water, which has a greater effect on them than the Catt."[43]

Sleeping on watch called down such penalties as ". . . to walk post with iron collar and balls for two months."

Disregarding the orders of a sentry: ". . . 12 lashes with the cat" (cat-o'-nine-tails).

A deserter's punishment was ". . . to wear an iron collar round his neck for four months and with a 6 lb ball and forfeit all the pay—then to be drummed out of the garrison."[44]

The Marine's daily ration of a gill of grog (rum and water) played its part in discipline as well: minor offenders could expect to have their grog stopped from a few days to a month. A quart of salt water was a poor exchange for a noggin of rum and water.

As excerpted and somewhat modified from Metcalf's *History of the U. S. Marine Corps,* Archibald Henderson's Corps was distributed as follows in November 1855, on the Corps' 80th anniversary:

Station							Grades and Distribution				
	Brig Gen	LtCol	Maj	Capt	1stLt	2dLt	Sgt and above	Cpl	Music	Pvt	Aggre-gate
MarCorps Headquarters (MB, Washington, D.C.)	1		3	2	3	4	11	4	36	72	136
MB, Washington Navy Yard				1			2	2	2	22	29
MB, Brooklyn Navy Yard		1	1		4	2	7	7	7	75	104
MB, Boston Navy Yard		1	1				4	2	2	69	79
MB, Norfolk Navy Yard			1	1			4	3		33	42
MB, Philadelphia Navy Yard			1		3		6	2	3	50	65
MB, Portsmouth Navy Yard, N.H.			1				5	3	2	32	43
MB, Pensacola Navy Yard			1				5	2		47	55
Pacific Squadron			1			2	8	14	10	120	155
Home Squadron			1	1	2	6	10	15	79	114
Mediterranean Squadron			1	1	2	7	11	6	104	132
Brazil Squadron					1	2	4	7	4	63	81
Africa Squadron			1			1	4	7	6	58	77
East India Squadron					3	1	9	11	9	116	149
Aboard Receiving Ships					2		6	8	2	90	106
On the Great Lakes						1		1	2	11	15
Practice Ship, Annapolis								1	2	6	9
Totals	1	2	7	10	18	17	88	95	108	1047	1391

With few exceptions, the weapons, equipment, and drill of the Corps were those of the Army. But in 1828, the worn-out smooth-bore muskets which the Corps had been carrying since before the War of 1812 were replaced by Hall rifles, the first breech-loading weapon to be adopted by the United States Armed Forces, with parts machined for interchangeability and a rate of fire almost three times that of the Charleville musket.[45] The hand guns carried by Marines were those of the Army or the Navy, of which the best known was the renowned Navy Colt revolver. In 1826 the Mameluke sword (which had been unofficially carried since about 1805) was adopted for all officers. And the drill and tactics taught to Marines were those prescribed by Winfield Scott's *Infantry Tactics.*

One notable achievement of Major D. J. Sutherland, General Henderson's last Quartermaster, was the establishment in 1857 of the first Marine Corps Depot of Supplies. This depot, manned by a captain, one sergeant clerk, and five privates, was located at Philadelphia (the ancestor of today's depot at 1100 South Broad Street) in a four-story house at 226 South 4th Street. The equipment of the individual Marine, which Major Sutherland husbanded so jealously in his storerooms, included the following items of what a later Corps would describe as "782 equipment":[46]

Muskets, complete	Drums
Belts, bayonet	Fifes
Scabbards, bayonet	Knapsacks
Cartridge boxes	Haversacks
Belts, cartridge box	Canteens
Swords, NCO	Slings, musket
Swords, musician	Slings, drum
Belts, sword	

After Wharton, the third Commandant, issued his initial *Uniform Regulations,* few changes in Marine uniforms took place until 1822, when, for the first time, undress uniforms were approved for officers. The 1822 uniform orders also brought the first chevrons into the Corps. Not only did NCOs wear them, but so did lieutenants and captains; the wearing of chevrons by officers was, however, discontinued in 1830.

In 1834, by order of President Jackson, Colonel Henderson issued the first printed *Uniform Regulations.* The blue, white, and scarlet uniforms of the War of 1812 were shelved for green coatees with buff facings. Light grey trousers were to be worn with the green coat, officers and NCOs being distinguished by buff trouser stripes. This uniform lasted only a few years, however, because on 1 July 1839, Henderson promulgated a further change, which, while retaining much of the substance of the 1834 regulations, restored the color scheme of Wharton. These regulations of 1839 remained unchanged for two decades.

The blue coatee with red piping (with standing collar and leather stock) was made standard. Enlisted men wore white cross-belts. Trousers were either "white linen or cotton" (summer) or "sky-blue cloth from the 15th October to the 30th April." Dark blue trouser stripes edged with scarlet were worn by officers and NCOs. In 1851 officers adopted dark blue trousers to match their coats, and at this time the present scarlet stripe was restored. Then as now, the Marine Band wore scarlet coats, as did all field musics.

Headgear ranged from the blue cloth fatigue cap with black leather visor to the black shako with scarlet pompon, and the field officer's cocked hat with scarlet plumes.

The buttons retained by Colonel Henderson were even then old in the Corps, dating back before the War of 1812 and were the same pattern as the enlisted man's dress buttons worn into modern times until carelessly modified by the Uniform Board in 1956: "Gilt, convex, with eagle, anchor and stars, raised border." Officers continued to wear scarlet sashes when carrying side arms. Staff officers and aides had their "loafer's loops"—". . . gold aiguillettes, worn on the right shoulder under the epaulette."

Allowing for changes in cut and in some of the accessories—such as the cross-belt, sash, plumed hat, and shako—Henderson's dress uniforms of 1839 are the dress uniforms of 1962.

During early years Marine uniforms included various distinguishing devices or badges, mainly based on the American eagle or the foul anchor. In 1840, two Marine devices were accepted. Both were circled by a laurel wreath undoubtedly borrowed from the badge of the Royal Marines. One had a foul anchor inscribed inside the laurels, while the other bore the letters "USM." In 1859, a standard center was adopted—a U. S. shield surmounted by a hunting horn within which was inscribed an "M." From this time on, the bugle and "M" were worn as a Marine emblem on the undress uniform. This pattern of bugle was also the traditional badge for light infantry, in which category Marines were generally considered.

During the era of Henderson, the Corps had two mottoes, neither official. One was *By Sea and by Land*—obviously a translation of the Royal Marines' *Per Mare per Terram*. The second—which seems to have replaced the earliest known U. S. Marine motto, *Fortitudine*—had more authentic roots in U. S. Marine tradition. Until 1848, it was simply *To the Shores of Tripoli;* after the return of the Marines from Mexico City, as we have seen, it became *From Tripoli to the Halls of the Montezumas.*

Just exactly when "The Marines' Hymn" was adopted remains one of the mysteries of the Corps, but its melody dates from 19 November 1859, the date of the first performance of Jacques Offenbach's opera, *Geneviève de Brabant.* The famous "Marine theme" (of which Winston Churchill wrote,[47] "[it] bit so deeply into my memory [in Iceland, 1941] that I could not get it out of my head") comes from a duet, "Gendarmes of the Queen," sung by two comedians, Sergeant Grabuge (baritone) and Fusilier Pitou (tenor). Who wrote the words, and when they were adopted by Marines, remains undiscovered; the earliest appearance of the words so far found in print is on an 1898 recruiting poster.[48]

On 6 January 1859 an era ended for the Marine Corps. Archibald Hender-

Samuel Nicholas, 1st Commandant of the Marine Corps, 1775–1781.

William W. Burrows, 2nd
Commandant of the
Marine Corps, 1798–1804.

Franklin Wharton,
3rd Commandant of
the Marine Corps,
1804–1818

Archibald Henderson, 5th Commandant of the Marine Corps, 1820–1859.

John Harris, 6th Commandant of the Marine Corps, 1859–1864.

Jacob Zeilin, 7th Commandant of the Marine Corps, 1864–1876.

son died. The old Commandant had held office so long (39 years) that he is said to have willed the Commandant's House to his son. After a funeral at Eighth and Eye, attended by President Buchanan and the Cabinet, he was buried beside many other early dignitaries of the Republic in Washington's Congressional Cemetery.

The debt which the Marine Corps owes its fifth Commandant is incalcu-lable. General Henderson had taken over in a time of confusion and brought the Corps through many crises. Under his leadership, the Corps' status was clarified, its strength doubled, and its efficiency multiplied many times. To Archibald Henderson can be traced the Marine Corps traditions of readi-ness, of "make-do" and "can-do," and of soldierly professionalism. No Com-mandant served longer than Henderson, and none has left a better legacy.

Lieutenant Colonel John Harris, who as a new second lieutenant in 1814 had fought at Bladensburg and won his brevet majority at Hatchee-Lustee beside Henderson, was the next senior officer in the Corps. Since the office went by seniority in those days, Harris, with 45 years' service behind him (including 20 on sea duty), was duly appointed Colonel-Commandant. John Harris's record had been outstanding: War of 1812, company commander in Florida, battalion commander on the east coast of Mexico, and two brevets for bravery. In addition, he should be remembered as the seagoing Marine who casually introduced the Lima bean to the United States.[49] But Harris was already 66 years old when he finally became Commandant, and he was no Archibald Henderson.

3 OUR FLAG'S UNFURLED
TO EVERY BREEZE *1859-1897*

We have fought in every clime and place where we could take a gun . . .
—THE MARINES' HYMN

S*HORTLY AFTER* lunch on Monday, 17 October 1859, the new Colonel-Commandant, John Harris, sent for the Officer of the Day. First Lieutenant Israel Green, veteran of the Mexican War and future Adjutant and
Inspector of the Confederate Marine Corps, buckled on his sword, adjusted
his sash, and strode across the parade ground from the O.D.'s room in old
North Wing to the Commandant's office directly opposite.

With Colonel Harris was Major W. W. Russell, Paymaster of the Corps
and veteran of fighting in California and Mexico. On the Commandant's
desk was an order from Secretary of the Navy Toucey:[1]

Send all the available Marines at Head Quarters, under charge of suitable officers,
by this evening's train of cars to Harpers Ferry to protect the public property at that
place, which is endangered by a riotous outbreak.

John Brown, the Kansas abolitionist, had seized the United States Arsenal
at Harpers Ferry, West Virginia; Green was to report on arrival to the senior
Army officer present, or, in his absence, to act for himself.

Within an hour Lieutenant Green had 86 Marines, together with two 12-
pound Dahlgren howitzers and shrapnel, at the Baltimore and Ohio Railroad
station southwest of Capitol Hill. Here, accompanied at Secretary Toucey's
request by Major Russell (who, as a staff officer, could not command), Green
received further instructions from the Secretary himself and from Secretary
of War John B. Floyd. Brown might have as many as 500 Kansas desperadoes
and armed Negroes. He was barricaded at the Arsenal and held 40 hostages,
notably including Colonel Lewis Washington, George Washington's great-
grandnephew. Colonel Robert E. Lee of the Army was being ordered to the

scene to command all forces; 150 soldiers from Fort Monroe would follow as soon as the Army could get them there. Until then it would be up to the Marines. At 1530, with Green's howitzers on a flat car, the train pulled out. Like all Marines, as Green later related:[2]

. . . the men were exhilarated by the excitement of the occasion, which came after a long, dull season of confinement in the barracks, and enjoyed the trip exceedingly.

At 2200, as the detachment debarked a mile short of Harpers Ferry, Colonel Lee arrived by special train, accompanied by a bearded aide, Lieutenant J. E. B. Stuart of the cavalry. By 2300 the Marines were across the railroad bridge in Harpers Ferry, and the Arsenal was surrounded. Brown, his men (nowhere near 500), and the hostages were holed up in the Arsenal firehouse, a strong brick building 35 feet across, with massive wooden doors. The town was swarming with panicky militia from as far away as Frederick and Baltimore. Many were drunk; all were disorganized.

By daybreak Green had organized and briefed a 24-man storming party. Lieutenant Stuart would advance under a flag of truce and present the Colonel's surrender demand to John Brown (who was posing under the alias of "Smith"). If the demand were rejected, the Marines would move in.

After offering the cautious militia one last opportunity to regain face by driving Brown from the firehouse, Lee ordered Green and Stuart to proceed as planned. Still wearing civilian clothes, Colonel Lee then took post on a slight mound about 40 feet to one side.

Stuart stepped forward to the heavily barred doors and read the ultimatum:[3]

Colonel Lee, U. S. Army, commanding the troops sent by the President of the United States to suppress the insurrection at this place, demands the surrender of the persons in the Armory building. If they will peaceably surrender themselves and restore the pillaged property, they shall be kept in safety to await the orders of the President. Colonel Lee represents to them in all frankness that it is impossible for them to escape, that the Armory is surrounded on all sides by troops, and that if he is compelled to take them by force he cannot answer for their safety.

John Brown temporized (". . . with admirable tact," related Stuart[4]). Stuart stepped clear and waved his cap to Green.

In Green's words, "the men took hold bravely and made a tremendous assault upon the door" with sledge hammers and a heavy ladder. Lieutenant Green, with sword drawn, was first inside; Major Russell (". . . feeling great pride in his Corps, and his southern blood being up a little, too," said Stuart) followed instantly, armed only with a rattan cane. "Hello, Green," said Colonel Washington, who was an acquaintance, clasping the lieutenant's left hand and pointing out Brown, who was on one knee, reloading his carbine. Green struck him to the floor with a slash across the neck. The Marines behind Green, "rushing in," he said, "like tigers," bayoneted two of Brown's followers who showed fight, and John Brown's insurrection was over. One Marine, who had entered the firehouse on the heels of Green and Russell, was killed in the brief melee; another was wounded. Lieutenant Stuart was impressed by the attack "made so gallantly by Green & Russell well backed by their men."[5] Colonel Lee, Green afterward remarked, "treated the affair as one of no great consequence, which would be speedily settled by the Marines."[6] It was.

CIVIL WAR

Despite the Marines' readiness and prompt action at Harpers Ferry, the Corps played only a small part during the war years which followed. Like the regular Army, the Marine Corps was never expanded or mobilized commensurate with its professional talent or past performance. Like the other regular Services also, the Corps suffered its share of resignations and desertions by officers and men who felt they owed their first allegiance to their states. This loss was serious in the company grades: three captains and 13 lieutenants resigned or were dismissed after tendering resignations to go south. Only two field officers seceded, Major H. B. Tyler, the Adjutant and Inspector (who was accompanied by his son, Second Lieutenant H. B. Tyler, Jr.), and Major G. H. Terrett.

The drain on quality was more marked than the statistics by themselves indicate. The field officers of the Corps—who had inched upward by virtue of seniority and enduring health—were old and in some cases enfeebled. Among the officers who headed south were some of the best: Terrett (Kuala Batu and Mexico City); Tansill (California); Simms (Chapultepec and the Barrier Forts); and Green (Harpers Ferry). To make up these losses and meet expanded wartime requirements, Congress increased the strength of the Marine Corps to 93 officers and 3,074 enlisted men. The President boosted this increase by a thousand more under his discretionary power to enlist additional Marines instead of landsmen for the Navy. Neither augmentation was in any way adequate to meet the demands made on the Corps throughout the Civil War.

Nevertheless, since the Marines were among the few regular troops available when war broke out, it was in keeping with the traditions of the Corps that they would play a part in initial operations. Early in January 1861, reinforcements were sent to the garrison beleaguered at Fort Sumter in Charleston Harbor. This expedition, aboard the steamer, *Star of the West,* was partly composed of Marines. Not having adequate support from fighting ships, on 9 January 1861 the transport was compelled to turn back by the Confederate defenses in the outer harbor. Within a few days, 40 Marines from Washington were ordered to man Fort Washington, a picturesque 1812 relic across from Mount Vernon, which commanded the upper Potomac approaches to the capital. On the same day that the *Star of the West* turned back, 30 Marines occupied Fort McHenry at Baltimore, which Marines had helped to defend in 1814.

In April it became necessary to reinforce Fort Pickens, the last of Pensacola's defenses remaining in Union hands. To accomplish this, 110 Marines, commanded by First Lieutenant John C. Cash, landed, together with Army troops, on 12 April. Cash, a veteran of California and the west coast of Mexico, ultimately became Paymaster of the Corps and, despite a fusilade of puns, held the job 15 years, the best named paymaster in the history of American arms. A week after the reinforcement of Pickens, on 20 April, 100 Marines, under Lieutenant A. S. Nicholson, were sent to Norfolk Navy Yard, not to defend it but to destroy several ships and large stocks of arms and supplies there. This dramatic but heartbreaking task, involving the burning of seven ships and the destruction of several thousand carbines and revolvers and tons of explosives, took all night, while hostile citizens milled outside the navy yard walls. To provide light the Marines had to burn down their own barracks.

Once real hostilities were joined, the First Battle of Bull Run (21 July 1861) provided another opportunity for Marines from Washington to smell powder. A 353-man battalion was shaken together, mainly from recruits and new lieutenants in training at Eighth and Eye. Commanded by Major J. G. Reynolds, it included only 17 officers and NCOs with previous service. Among these, however, were the new Adjutant and Inspector, Major A. S. Nicholson (who had skipped the rank of captain on appointment as A & I); Major Jacob Zeilin, commanding a company; and a platoon leader to be noted, Second Lieutenant Robert W. Huntington.

After sustaining 44 casualties (including Major Zeilin) and three assaults on Henry House Hill, on that afternoon when the Federals broke, the Marines, too, gave way. This was reported with sorrow by Colonel Harris to

Secretary of the Navy Gideon Welles as "the first instance in [Marine Corps] history where any portion of its members turned their backs to the enemy."[7] In the gentler phrase of Major General Ben H. Fuller, 15th Commandant, the best that can be said of the Marine battalion at Bull Run was, "Surely they were among the last to run."

"BY SEA AND BY LAND"

During the remainder of the war, Marines served at sea in the amphibious stranglehold which U. S. sea power applied to the rimland of the Confederacy and ashore both in the Mississippi Valley and the defenses of Washington.

Along the Confederate seaboard, from North Carolina to Louisiana, Marines from aboard ship (or sometimes in provisional battalions) took part in the amphibious attacks, raids, and landings which enabled the Union Navy to tighten its grip on the South's coasts. This campaign was largely the fruit of a "confidential board of strategy" convened in June 1861 under Captain S. F. Du Pont and supported by Gustavus V. Fox, Lincoln's able Assistant Secretary of the Navy.

The first operation undertaken was to capture two forts (Clark and Hatteras) which guarded Hatteras Inlet, North Carolina. The object was to check Confederate privateering out of Pamlico Sound and close the sound to blockade-running. Although two Army regiments were embarked for the purpose, Hatteras weather prevented execution of the landing as planned. Instead, on 28 August 1861, a 250-man assault force of Marines and Army regulars landed from surfboats to storm Fort Clark, with the USS *Minnesota's* Marine detachment in the van. With bombardment support from the *Minnesota,* her sister steam frigate *Wabash,* and sloop-of-war *Cumberland,* the Marines and soldiers planted their colors on the ramparts of Fort Clark by two that afternoon. Before noon next day, Fort Hatteras, on the opposite side of the inlet, surrendered after its magazine had been exploded by a shell from one of the bombarding ships, and Major General B. F. Butler, the Army commander, went ashore by steam tug to assume command.

The next Union objective was to establish a base at Port Royal, South Carolina, future location of the Marine recruit depot at Parris Island. Port Royal Sound was a blockade-runners' stronghold; more important, in Union hands it would afford a fine advance base for the forces blockading Charleston and Savannah. The entrance to the sound was defended by two large works: Fort Walker on Hilton Head (a site well known to Marine defense battalions of World War II), and Fort Beauregard, opposite on Bay Point. Du Pont, now promoted to flag rank, headed an armada of 50 ships and 13,000 soldiers. At Du Pont's request, the force included a battalion of Marines, commanded by Major J. G. Reynolds and embarked in a specially assigned transport, SS *Governor*.

What might possibly have developed from grouping a fleet Marine battalion with a naval amphibious force (for such Du Pont's squadron really was) can only be conjectured, for on 1 November 1861 a Hatteras gale raked the fleet. Among the casualties was the Marines' transport. Aboard the sinking side-wheeler manned by a merchant crew, Reynolds' men manned pumps and fought for two days to save the ship. Finally, as the transport settled lower and lower, with flooded firerooms and no steam, orders were passed to abandon ship. In a feat of seamanship seldom equaled, the frigate USS *Sabine*, commanded by Captain Cadwalader Ringgold, USN, anchored, then got a line from her stern to the *Governor's* bow, and commenced whipping Reynolds' Marines across. After some 30 had been gotten over, the plunging of the two ships parted the tackle. Despite the fierce gale, Captain Ringgold then managed to maneuver the *Sabine* alongside the sinking *Governor* in close enough proximity for 40 Marines to make the jump. Following the inevitable glancing collision of the two ships, Ringgold had to stand clear and put out boats, which proceeded to pluck the remaining Marines from the sea as they went overboard from the transport. Miraculously, only seven of Reynolds' 300 men were lost; and all weapons, together with about half the organizational equipment, were saved. Major Reynolds, with the one naval officer on board, was the last to leave the ship. As Du Pont reported to the Secretary of the Navy:[8]

> The established reputation and high standing of Major Reynolds might almost dispense with any observation of my own upon the bravery and high sense of honor which he displayed.

Nevertheless, Reynolds' battalion was out of the fight at Port Royal. As it turned out, however, Du Pont's "beautifully accurate fire at short range" (a Confederate tribute) shot Forts Walker and Beauregard to pieces. On 7 November, after four hours' resistance, the Confederate gunners abandoned the works, and the Marines of the USS *Wabash* landed on Hilton Head amid a souvenir hunter's bonanza of abandoned equipment and even officers' swords.

After the capture of Port Royal, Du Pont spent early 1862 in extending his blockade southward. On 4 March 1862, Reynolds' battalion occupied Fernandina, Florida, without opposition. Two weeks later, St. Augustine likewise fell without a fight to the Marines of the USS *Wabash* and *Mohican*. The city fathers of St. Augustine expected the worst when the Federals descended and were so agreeably taken aback by the behavior of the Marines that they passed a resolution of thanks expressing the town's:

. . . heartfelt gratification and satisfaction at the polite and urbane course of Major [Isaac T.] Doughty and the officers of the U. S. Marines . . . and of the good conduct and discipline of the troops.[9]

Meanwhile, without Archibald Henderson's firm grasp to hold them together, the officers of the Corps were divided by rivalry between the Staff, well entrenched at Headquarters, and the Line. As Secretary Welles regretfully summed it up, "Almost all the elder officers [of the Marine Corps] are at loggerheads and ought to be retired."[10] Major Russell, the Paymaster, with the connivance of Colonel Harris, tried in 1862 to edge himself into position to succeed to the commandancy and was only headed off by a blast (in the form of an open letter to the Commandant) from Reynolds, now a lieutenant colonel and champion of the Line. Harris promptly brought Reynolds before a court-martial in May 1862 with charges of (1) drunkenness at Fernandina and (2) treating with contempt his superior officer in the execution of his office. Regarding the first charge, which may have been well founded, one of Reynolds' lieutenants, R. W. Huntington, later said,[11] "Colonel Reynolds always has everything about him in order, and, drunk or sober, duty must be carried on right." In any case the court, mostly anti-Harris and pro-Reynolds, acquitted the latter, whereupon he in turn preferred charges against the Commandant. This was the last straw for Gideon Welles, who foresaw "a series of courts-martial for a year to come,"[12] and closed the affair by sending "a letter of reproof" to both Harris and Reynolds. Lieutenant Huntington's comment was characteristic:

I know [Reynolds] is not perfect, but since I left his command, I have arrived at the opinion that I shall not again serve under any officer in the Navy or Marine Corps where discipline is better observed.

While Colonel Reynolds was being court-martialed in Washington, a more illustrious event for the Marine Corps took place in the James River below Richmond. On 11 May 1862, the USS *Galena*, bombarding Confederate works on Drewry's Bluff, was badly hit and sustained an ammunition explosion. Corporal John Mackie put out fires on the gun deck, dragged casualties clear, and got three guns back into action. For this he became the first Marine to win the Medal of Honor, from the hands of Abraham Lincoln himself.

Soon after, on 24 June 1862, Lieutenant H. B. Lowry led a 60-man detachment on a raid up the Santee River from Georgetown, South Carolina. Their mission, that of destroying a railroad bridge, was never achieved because of insufficient water to allow supporting gunboats within range. But the expedition fought a running battle with Confederate cavalry most of the way and destroyed a plantation being used by the secessionists as a base.

While Du Pont was thus bringing the coasts of the Carolinas, Georgia, and Florida under Union control, Flag-Officer David G. Farragut was preparing to force the mouth of the Mississippi and seize New Orleans. On the night of 24 April, Farragut's 17 ships fought their way past Forts Jackson and St. Philip. The next day, having destroyed a Confederate river flotilla and received word of the surrender of the forts, Farragut lay off New Orleans. The city, never a peaceable place, was volatile with anger and fear.

First ashore were the Marines from the USS *Pensacola*, a screw-sloop. Armed with two boat-howitzers, they were met on the levee by a mob brandishing clubs, pistols, and knives. Second Lieutenant J. C. Harris set up his howitzers to cover the mob, formed his men as though on parade, and marched them to the nearby U. S. Mint, where the Stars and Bars were hauled down and the Stars and Stripes broken out. Soon afterward the remainder of the squadron's Marines, formed into a 300-man battalion, landed under command of Farragut's squadron Marine officer, Captain J. L. Broome, then and later an officer of ability. Broome followed the same tactics as Harris. As though unaware of the mob, Broome led his battalion through the narrow streets, first to the customhouse, then to the city hall. At each place, for the first time since 1861, he raised the colors and left a guard. For three days Broome's battalion held New Orleans until General Benjamin Butler's soldiers arrived and the Army took over. This, as it turned out, was fortunate for the reputation of the Corps, which thereby escaped being associated in Southern eyes with Butler's occupation of New Orleans.

Earlier in 1862, in January, Marines had first come to the upper Mississippi, as a detachment for the USS *St. Louis*, flagship of the gunboats based, appropriately, at St. Louis. In the following November a detachment of four officers and 88 enlisted men was transferred from Washington to the newly established naval station at Cairo, Illinois, renowned along the length of the "Father of Waters" for its honky-tonks, saloons, and gambling halls. There are no complaints on record about the liberty in Cairo, but all good things must end, and in May 1864 the detachment, doubled in size, moved eight miles up the Ohio to Mound City, Illinois, which had gradually usurped Cairo's functions as a naval base. Marines from Cairo, as well as occasional drafts of soldiers, served aboard the Navy's gunboats which worked so hard for Grant and Sherman along the Mississippi and the Tennessee.

Another important service rendered by the Navy and Marine Corps to Grant was to convince him that Vicksburg, which obstructed the "Father of Waters," could only be reduced by attack from the south, instead of the fruitless operations against Chickasaw Bluff, Haines Bluff, and in the Yazoo Swamp, which had consumed the winter of 1863. Farragut—deeply anxious to open the Mississippi and simultaneously cut off the Confederacy from the west—felt, on advice from Captain Broome, his squadron Marine officer, that the only way to take Vicksburg was from down-river. Farragut sent Broome for a confidential meeting with Grant on 23 March at Milliken's Bend. Broome presented Farragut's strong views on closing off the Red River traffic across the Mississippi and on the urgency of opening the latter. The best terrain for attacking Vicksburg, he pointed out, was from the south, an area of which Grant frankly said he had little knowledge. To Grant's demur against placing Vicksburg between his army and their base at Corinth, Broome said all hands should march with a week's rations and live off the country like the rebels. Besides, once Grant was below Vicksburg, the Navy would support him. Within a month of his conference with Broome, Grant (who until then had been planning further operations up-river) was moving against Vicksburg from the south. In addition to its intrinsic interest, this episode is a classic example of the correct use by a naval commander of his staff Marine officer to influence military operations so as to support naval objectives.

The feats of real Marines in the west have not gone unsung, but the "Marines" on the Mississippi who basked in the publicity of the time were really Army troops—the Mississippi River Marine Brigade (". . . a set of courageous and picked men," commented Gideon Welles[13]) commanded by Lieutenant Colonel Alfred D. Ellet, USA.

Ellet's "Marines" were raised in the west in November 1862 (even preempting the birth month of their prototype) after the Navy Department had been forced by lack of manpower to turn down Admiral David Porter's request for an authentic Marine brigade. The local substitute, a real "task force," included infantry, light artillery, and four squadrons of cavalry. Seven New Orleans packets were pressed into service to lift the brigade, which was attached to Porter's Mississippi Squadron.

Meanwhile, a song writer's attention had lighted upon those four squadrons of Marine cavalry, and the result, in 1863, was a smash hit, "Ellet's Horse Marines." Sung by gaslight, one stanza seemed irresistible:

> I am Captain Jinks of the Horse Marines.
> I give my horse good corn and beans,
> Of course it is quite beyond my means,
> Though I am a Captain in the Army.

Although Ellet's brigade disbanded in 1864 after excellent service before Vicksburg, nobody could ever forget the Horse Marines, and the theme was still going strong 70 years later when the Marine mounted detachment at Peking included a pony named Captain Jinks.

One reason for the Ellet brigade's demise was an inter-Service difference which began in 1862. At that time, Congress ordered that all war vessels on the Mississippi and their crews should come under the Navy. With the backing of Secretary of War Stanton and of Army Chief of Staff Halleck, Ellet declined to transfer his ships and command to the Navy Department "or to recognize the Admiral in command of the Mississippi Squadron."[14] As Secretary Welles summed up:[15]

That Ellet should wish a distinct command is not surprising. It is characteristic. He is full of zeal to overflowing, but yet is not a naval man, but is very naturally delighted with an independent naval command. It is, however, a pitiful business on the part of Stanton and Halleck, who should take an administrative view and who should be aware that there cannot be two distinct commands on the river.

The last Civil War river foray in which genuine Marines took a hand was the expedition in November 1864 up Broad River from Port Royal, South Carolina. Like the Santee raid in 1862, this thrust had as its purpose the destruction of railroad bridges. Marines formed one battalion of a very mixed force made up of sailors acting as artillery and infantry, some Ohio and New York volunteers, and a regiment of freed Negroes. The Marine battalion, 182 strong, had less officer overhead than any Marine battalion before or since: its one commissioned officer was First Lieutenant G. G. Stoddard, who, unlike the salty 15- and 20-year lieutenants of the days just past, actually had only two years' service.

Despite his short time in the Corps, Stoddard behaved in the best style, no doubt with the assistance of many a seasoned NCO. On 29 November the Marine battalion screened the debarkation of the force, and next day fought in the front lines at the Battle of Boyd's Neck. On 6 December, the Marines took their part in the Battle of Tullifinney's Creek, for which Stoddard won a brevet as captain. This expedition cost the Marines 22 casualties; unfortunately, the Confederates had the railroad bridges well protected, and trains continued to run until the railroad ultimately fell into the hands of General William Tecumseh Sherman.

TWO REPULSES: SUMTER AND FISHER

During 1863 both Abraham Lincoln and Gideon Welles greatly desired the capture of Charleston, "hotbed of secession." As Charleston and its seaward approaches were defended by some nine major forts, this was a desire not readily to be consummated. From April until September 1863, nine monitors, the backbone of the Navy's new ironclad fleet, and more than 3,000 soldiers, invested Charleston Harbor, with shore siege operations against Fort Wagner, on Morris Island, which commanded the south side of the main channel. To reinforce the Army, a 300-man Marine battalion was added. This battalion included two future Commandants: Zeilin was in command, and one company was led by Captain C. G. McCawley. For once in his career, Zeilin did not last long. In August he took sick, had to be invalided north, and was succeeded by Captain E. McD. Reynolds, who in turn was relieved by his father, Lieutenant Colonel J. G. Reynolds.

On 7 September, after Fort Wagner finally yielded, the time was deemed ripe to storm Fort Sumter. Five 100-man "divisions" (four of sailors, one of Marines) were to make a night landing on 8 September. The Marine division, 106 officers and men, was commanded by Captain McCawley, but was apparently not a very distinguished body of Marines, since Zeilin, when originally asked to earmark men for the assault force, told Admiral Dahlgren he was assigning "150 men, such as they are."[16]

As is often the case when untrained and ill-prepared forces attempt a night landing, the assault on Fort Sumter failed miserably. The nocturnal shore-to-shore movement collapsed in confusion, the Confederate defenders proved unco-operatively alert, and the defending fire was deadly. Only 150 Marines and sailors ever landed on Sumter itself, and of these, 44 Marines were killed, wounded, or captured. First Lieutenant C. H. Bradford, one of the officers mortally wounded, fell into the hands of prewar friends in Charleston, but the most devoted nursing proved useless. Bradford's body, first buried in a family lot in Charleston's Magnolia Cemetery, was subsequently dug up and reburied by the authorities in the potter's field. When Charleston finally did fall, in February 1865, Flag-Officer J. A. Dahlgren, in his own words,[17] "took the necessary measures to reverse the savage and disgraceful act of the rebel community." Poor Bradford was again disinterred and conveyed with an escort of Marines, soldiers, and sailors, to St. Paul's Church, for an elaborate funeral, after which final reburial with full honors took place in Magnolia Cemetery.

By the end of 1864 the only remaining focus of large-scale blockade-running on the Confederate east coast was Wilmington, North Carolina, a few miles south of the present site of Camp Lejeune. To render the Union blockade fully effective, it was essential to close Wilmington. To close Wilmington, however, it was in turn necessary to capture one of the best constructed works on the seaboard, Fort Fisher, which commanded the entrance to the Cape Fear River. Fort Fisher—defended by 44 large-caliber guns and more than a thousand Confederates—stood on the tongue of land between the Cape Fear River and the Atlantic. The east face, 1,200 yards long, fronted the ocean; the north face covered the one narrow land approach. Forward of the north face was a log palisade and thick abatis fronted in turn by a field of buried "torpedoes," as mines were then styled.

In mid-December 1864, Rear Admiral David D. Porter concentrated 56 ships off Cape Fear, bearing a landing force of 6,500 soldiers commanded by Major General B. F. Butler, the Massachusetts politician. On 24 December, at Butler's suggestion, a powder-ship containing 150 tons of explosives was run close in and set off; the defenders, unscathed, thought a steamboat boiler had exploded. On Christmas Day, while the 100-pound Parrotts and 9-inch guns of Porter's fleet slugged at Fort Fisher, Butler landed 3,000 soldiers north of the fort and slowly advanced southward until his leading units were within a few hundred yards of the silent works. One daring officer mounted the parapet and walked back bearing a Confederate flag which had been shot down; a Confederate orderly carrying a message was captured inside the fort; and a Union soldier even returned with a Confederate officer's charger in tow.

But soldier-politico Ben Butler had little inclination to fight on Christmas Day and announced that the ships' gunfire had done insufficient damage. Troops were to be re-embarked and the assault canceled. Porter, a fighting admiral who had been used to U. S. Grant and W. T. Sherman as his military opposite numbers on the Mississippi, was disgusted. With well-turned irony he wrote Butler:[18]

> I wish some more of your gallant fellows had followed the officer who took the flag from the parapet, and the brave fellow who brought the horse out from the fort. I think they would have found it an easier conquest than is supposed. . . .

This performance was anything but a welcome Christmas present for General Grant, who was grappling with Lee in Virginia, and a relief for Ben Butler was not slow in coming. Major General A. H. Terry, USA, with reinforcements bringing the army to 8,500, would lead a new assault. Admiral Porter proposed two days' bombardment from seaward, followed by a diversionary attack by Marines and seamen against the east (Atlantic)

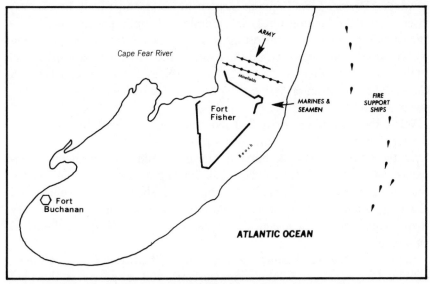

Capture of Fort Fisher, Wilmington, North Carolina, 13-15 January 1865

face of Fort Fisher, while Terry landed north of the fort and attacked southward as Butler should have done. Meanwhile, however, Fort Fisher's defenders had been more than doubled, and Confederate General Braxton Bragg had arrived to command the defenses of Wilmington.

On 13 January the softening-up process began anew. While Porter's guns thundered from 800 yards offshore, Terry landed his troops above the fort. Next day the bombardment continued, and preparations were made for the final assault to be launched at 1500 on the 15th. During the forenoon of that day, the diversionary force, comprising 1,600 sailors and 400 Marines, began forming for the attack. The Marines, armed with rifled muskets and distributed throughout the various ships' boats, were to land among the sailors, get themselves together and organize in companies, advance close to the fort, dig rifle pits, and then support the bluejackets in a final assault— all within close range of enemy weapons. While this was going on, the seamen, armed only with cutlasses and revolvers, were to "board" Fort Fisher as if it were a frigate in the War of 1812. Porter's order for the attack described the seamen's role as follows:[19]

> The sailors will be armed with cutlasses, well sharpened, and with revolvers. . . . When the signal is made to assault, board the fort on the run in a seamanlike way.

Admiral Porter's Fleet Captain, Lieutenant Commander K. R. Breese, was to command the landing force, an example, unhappily not the last, of the long-standing practice of entrusting to naval officers the command of important shore operations beyond the scope of their training and experience. In the words of Lieutenant George Dewey, USN, executive officer of the USS *Colorado,* one of Admiral Porter's ships, the whole plan was "sheer, murderous madness."[20]

While the landing parties milled about on the beach with their cutlasses, the Confederates, thinking this was the main assault, massed grimly behind their breastworks. Before the Marines could even form into companies, let alone reach their assigned supporting positions, the bluejackets, courageous but unco-ordinated, "rose up and dashed forward, yelling and cheering so loudly that no order could either be heard or passed."[21] Every steam whistle in the fleet emitted a whoop, and, on this signal, the naval gunfire lifted.

Relief from the naval gunfire was exactly what Braxton Bragg had been waiting for: a hail of Confederate musketry and grape swept the bare beaches, and the sailors went down in swathes. Forty yards short of the parapet, the seamen had taken more than flesh and blood could stand, and "the whole line commenced doubling up and flying, everybody for themselves."

Meanwhile, a succession of contradictory orders from Breese reached Captain L. L. Dawson, commanding the Marines, who was still trying to form the assemblage of ships' detachments into companies while simultaneously trying to carry out the Marines' part in the assault as prearranged. "Bring up the Marines at once . . ."; then, ". . . take the Marines down the beach"; then, "join the frontal assault."[22] Utter confusion. As the surviving sailors gave way, some of the Marines were swept back with them. More than 309 dead and wounded seamen and Marines littered the beach.

Fortunately for the Union, General Terry's soldiers had meanwhile launched their attack in fine style, and, profiting from the hot fight along the fort's seaward face, were soon over the breastworks, promptly supported, as the naval attack ebbed, by the ironclad *New Ironsides*. At 2200 Fort Fisher surrendered; 2,083 prisoners were taken.

With his attack routed and 309 casualties left behind, Lieutenant Commander Breese had considerable explaining to do; so, for that matter, did Admiral Porter. The resulting excuses, even from Porter, before and later a warm friend of the Corps, attempted to sluice the blame onto the Marines (who had sustained 59 casualties). "I can but attribute the failure of the assault to the absence of the Marines from their position," reported Breese.[23] "Had the covering party of Marines performed their duty, every one of the enemy would have been killed," was Porter's shrug of blame for the fiasco.[24] The phrase would be heard again as late as 1895, when certain naval officers questioned the continuing usefulness of the Marine Corps. What was unrecognized was that no amount of bravery can compensate for lack of training, practice, and correct organization on the part of all forces in an amphibious assault, especially, as in this case, when the plan was basically unsound. In any event, the failure at Fort Fisher had the effect of setting back the cause of amphibious progress at least a generation in the U. S. Navy, just as the later reverse at Gallipoli had a similar effect throughout most of the world.

GREY-BACKED MARINES

The CSMC—Confederate States Marine Corps—was established by act of the Confederate Congress on 16 March 1861. The original authorized strength was 22 officers and 660 enlisted men, organized into a headquarters and six companies. The headquarters was a miniature of the small U. S. Marine Corps Headquarters of 1861; the Commandant was a major. On 20 May 1861, however, the Commandant's rank was raised to colonel, and one lieutenant colonel was provided. At the same time the corps' strength was raised to 46 officers and 944 enlisted Marines to be organized in ten companies. Although the backbone of the Confederate corps was composed of former U. S. Marine officers, the Colonel-Commandant, Lloyd J. Beall, a Marylander, was a former U. S. Army paymaster with no experience whatsoever as a Marine. That the authentic Marine spirit animated the corps, however, can be recognized in the decision of Captain J. R. F. Tatt-nall (late USMC), who resigned a colonel's commission in the Confederate Army for a captaincy of Marines, saying he would rather command a company of Marines than a brigade of volunteers.

Duties, ranks, pay, and traditions in the CSMC were virtually those of the U. S. Marine Corps. Ashore they provided guard detachments for the Confederate naval stations at Mobile, Savannah, Charleston (where the CSMC had a tiny recruit depot), Charlotte, Richmond, and Wilmington. In addition, they manned naval shore batteries at Pensacola (opposite Fort Pickens, which was partly manned by U. S. Marines), Hilton Head, Fort Fisher, and Drewry's Bluff (at all of which they fought against U. S. Marines). The first naval engagement in which Confederate Marines took part was the battle between the ironclads *Monitor* and *Virginia* (ex-USS *Merrimack*), on 9 March 1862, when the *Virginia's* captain of Marines won a commendation; on the same occasion, Captain Charles Heywood won a brevet for personal gallantry and that of the U. S. Marines aboard the USS *Cumberland,* which was one of two wooden ships hammered to pieces by the former *Merrimack.* Thereafter, seagoing detachments of Confederate Marines served at one time or another in 33 warships.

On 7 December 1862 the raider *Alabama* attempted to obtain recruits for the Confederate Marines by stopping the unarmed Pacific Mail steamer *Ariel,* off Cuba en route to Panama with a draft of U. S. Marines headed for the newly established Mare Island Navy Yard on the West Coast. After the *Ariel* hove to under fire from the *Alabama,* the first demand by the Confederate boarding party was for volunteers to join the CSMC (which was represented aboard the *Alabama* by one officer, Lieutenant Beckett J. Howell, ex-USMC, and no detachment). When nobody stepped forward, a Southern prize crew took over the ship. But, on orders from Captain Raphael Semmes, CSN, commanding the *Alabama,* the U. S. Marines were kept on normal guard routine, mainly, it appears, to prevent the Confederate sailors from getting at the transport's supply of spirits. This anomalous relationship ended with ransom of the transport for $261,000 and parole of the U. S. Marines so that Mare Island could have its guard. The Confederate Marines got no recruits, and the sailors got no grog.

Throughout the war the CSMC operated on a perpetual manpower deficit because (shades of the 1820s) the Confederate Attorney General couldn't decide whether recruiting legislation applicable to the Confederate Army likewise encompassed the Marines. Up to 1864 the monthly pay of Marine

enlisted men was $3 less than for equivalent Army ranks, another draw-
back. The last known strength return of the Confederate Marines is dated
30 October 1864, when the actual strength (less 32 recruits in boot camp)
was 539 officers and men.

The Confederate Marine Corps is known to have lasted until the fall of
Richmond in 1865, and, in one of his last reports, the Secretary of the Confederate Navy voiced a tribute which echoed those received over the years
by their enemy brothers-in-arms, the U. S. Marines:[25]

Upon all occasions when the Marines have been called upon for active service they
have displayed the promptness and efficiency of well disciplined soldiers.

ZEILIN TAKES OVER

On 12 May 1864, John Harris, worn to pieces by a half century of service,
died and was laid to rest in Georgetown's Oak Hill Cemetery. This event
(and the problem it posed) was noted in Secretary Welles's diary as follows:[26]

Attended the funeral of Colonel Harris. His death gives embarrassment as to a successor. The higher class of Marine officers are not the men who can elevate or give efficiency to the Corps. To supersede them will cause much dissatisfaction. Every man who
is over-slaughed [*sic*] and all his friends will be offended with me for what will be deemed
an insult. But there is a duty to perform.

On 9 June, after the office had been vacant almost a month, and after
discussing the matter with President Lincoln, Welles noted gloomily:[27]

Concluded to retire the Marine officers who are past the legal age, and to bring in
Zeilin as Commandant of the Corps. There seems no alternative.

Next day, 10 June, the President retired every Marine officer senior to
Zeilin and appointed him seventh Commandant of the Marine Corps. Zeilin
thus became the first Commandant since Burrows to take office by selection
rather than seniority.

There have been few occasions when the Marine Corps so badly needed
ability at the helm, but, just as Welles had predicted, there were misgivings, not only among disappointed seniors but even some juniors. Lieutenant Huntington, blunt as ever, commented:[28]

A martinet like Colonel Reynolds, I think, would make a better Commandant than
so easy a man as Zeilin, though I have more respect for Zeilin.

The reputation of the Corps, by and large, was at low ebb; it had not been enlarged materially, even at the height of the biggest war ever fought in the Americas. More serious was the fact that, during the Civil War, Marines, as a corps, had not been called on to perform important amphibious or expeditionary duties, nor had they taken any prominent part in the consequential fighting of the war, as underscored by the fact that only 148 Marines were killed in action (plus 312 deaths from other causes) from 1861 to 1865. What Marine fighting there was had taken place aboard ship or ashore in auxiliary operations. Moreover, from the family point of view, the Marine Corps had been shaken not only by defections to the Confederacy and by increasing desertions, but by serious feuding between Staff and Line, which came to a head in the Reynolds court-martial already mentioned.

As early as 1863, all this had given rise to complaints against the Marine Corps and had prompted Colonel Harris to write letters, such as that which follows, to the most influential officers of the Navy:[29]

Sir:

In consequence of an effort which I understand is about to be repeated at an early day during the ensuing session of Congress, viz., to transfer the Marine Corps to the Army as an additional regiment, I am desirous of obtaining the opinion and wishes of some officers of high standing in the Navy. Will you be so good as to give me your opinion as to the necessity for and the efficiency of Marines on shore and afloat in connection with the Navy? Whether they have not generally been effective wherever employed; and if, in your opinion, they are not a necessary part of the crew of a vessel of war; also if an increase of numbers is not required by the exigencies of the service. . . .

Replies were prompt and favorable. Farragut was heard from ("I have always deemed the Marine guard one of the great essentials of a man-of-war . . ."); so was Du Pont ("It gives me pleasure to speak of the efficient character of the Marine Corps, its patriotism and devotion to duty . . ."); and Wilkes ("Instead of dispensing with the Marines, there should be, in my opinion, an increase . . ."); and Balch (". . . the integrity and faithfulness of the Marines . . ."). The encomia which the Commandant thus accumulated is typified by this letter from Admiral Porter, fortunately then on the Mississippi, some months before Fort Fisher:[30]

My Dear Sir:

Your communication of December 10 has been received, and in answer I beg leave to say that I would consider it a great calamity if the Marine Corps should be abolished and turned over to the Army.

In its organization it should be naval altogether. A ship without Marines is no ship of war at all.

The past efficiency of our Marine Corps fills one of the brightest pages in the history of our country, and the man who proposes such a measure cannot know the Service, or is demented.

When they take away the Marines from the Navy they had better lay up all large vessels. I wish anyone could see the difference between the Marines out here and the people they call soldiers; they would not talk of abolishing the Corps.

I can only say, God forbid that it should come to pass. . . .

Sure enough, in 1864 (after Colonel Harris's death), a Congressional resolution was introduced to transfer the Corps to the Army. When the proposal became known, the new Commandant followed his predecessor's lead and called on the Navy for help. The admirals' response was unanimous, as Harris's correspondence had foreshadowed, and, with the naval hierarchy firmly on the side of the Marine Corps, Congress tabled the resolution.

But on 18 June 1866, trouble again reared its head: Colonel Zeilin, now firmly in the saddle, was notified that the House of Representatives had just approved an ominous resolution:[31]

Resolved, That the Committee on Naval Affairs be directed to consider the expediency of abolishing the Marine Corps, and transferring it to the Army, and making provision for supplying such military force as may at any time be needed in the Navy, by detail from the Army.

Zeilin's reaction (and again, that of the Navy) was instantaneous. The committee received pro-Marine testimony or testimonials by Farragut, Porter, Rowan, Stribling, Stringham, Paulding, Du Pont, Sands, Rodgers, Foote, Davis, Wilkes, Worden, and Dahlgren.

The House Naval Affairs Committee, then and later a friend and protector of the Marine Corps, was not deaf to these petitions. The resolution was reported out adversely on 21 February 1867 in the following sentences:[32]

From the beginning, this Corps seems to have satisfactorily fulfilled the purposes of its organization, and no good reason appears either for abolishing it or transferring it to the Army; on the contrary, the Committee recommends that its organization as a separate Corps be preserved and strengthened . . . [and] that its commanding officer shall hold the rank of a brigadier general.

Perhaps if the measure had been introduced still another time, Zeilin would have ended up a major general.

"IN EVERY CLIME AND PLACE" 1867–1896

Although the latter part of the 19th century has sometimes been described as a period when the Marine Corps was marking time, this generalization hardly holds up under examination.

Marines conducted minor landings in Formosa (1867), Japan (1867 and 1868), Uruguay (1868), west coast of Mexico (1870), Colombia (1873), Hawaiian Islands (1874), Egypt (1882), Korea (1888), Haiti (1888), Samoa (1888), Hawaiian Islands again (1889), Argentina (1890), Chile (1891), Navassa Island (1891), Nicaragua (1894), Korea (1894), North China (1894-95), Isthmus of Panama (1895), and Nicaragua (1896). In Korea (1871) and on the Isthmus of Panama (1885), there were, by the standards of the day, major landings. Farther north, in 1891, Marines pursued Bering Sea seal poachers. And if all the foregoing operations were not enough to provide ample activity for the Marine Corps, events at home, as we shall see, were not exactly quiet.

In 1871, Korea, "The Hermit Kingdom," still merited its name. Foreigners were strictly excluded, and one shipwrecked American crew had been set upon and killed. To avoid any further such occurrences, the American Minister to China was thereupon instructed to visit Korea and negotiate a treaty of amity and commerce. For this purpose, in May 1871, the minister, Mr. Frederick Low, embarked aboard the USS *Colorado*, Asiatic Fleet flagship, which, with four other men-of-war, was to try to convey him to Seoul.

On 30 May 1871, Rear Admiral John Rodgers brought this squadron to anchor north of Inchon in what, 79 years later, would be a Seventh Fleet fire-support area for a landing. On 1 June, as a Navy surveying party worked its way up the channel (known in those days as the Salee River) between Kanghwa-Do and Kumpo Peninsula, it was fired on without warning by one of five forts with which the Koreans covered the approach to the Han River, and thus to Seoul. Later examination of the guns by scholars would indicate that the Americans had been attacked by the oldest active coast-defense weapons in the world, two of which dated from 1313 A.D., and the remainder of which bore Korean dates equivalent to 1607, 1665, and 1680.

An apology was demanded. Within ten days, none being forthcoming, the fleet was ordered to exact one. Preparations were made to land a brigade of bluejackets and Marines (the latter a two-company battalion commanded by Captain McLane Tilton, Asiatic Fleet Marine Officer). Tilton, who had served on the board which in 1869 had adopted the Remington "rolling-block" rifle as standard for the Navy, had apprehensions about going after the Koreans with the muzzle-loading muskets then in the hands of his men. Before sailing, he had written Headquarters Marine Corps:[33]

One man with a breech loader is equal to 12 to 15 armed as we are and in the event of any landing, or even chasing Coreans armed with an excellent repeater, what ever could Americans do with a blasted old *Muzzle Fuzzel?*

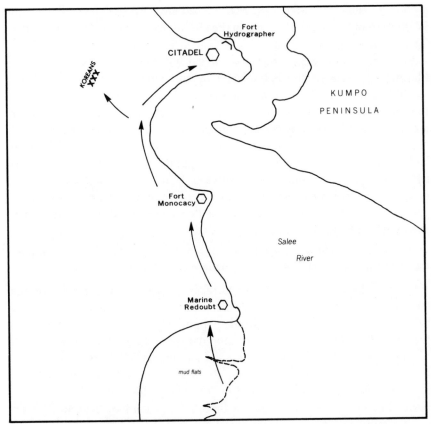

Battle of the Salee River Forts, Korea, 10-11 June 1871

On 10 June, muzzle fuzzels and all, the brigade landed on Kanghwa-Do, downstream from the nearest of the offending forts. The Marines (4 officers and 105 men) landed first. This debarkation might have been disastrous as the entire first wave sank up to its knees in the Korean mud, which future Marines would know only too well. For 200 yards the assault literally bogged down and might well have been stopped then and there but for support from the 9-inch guns of the USS *Monocacy* and the 24-pounders of the *Palos*. After a hasty volley the Koreans decamped, and the Marines finally thrashed free of the muck. Tilton then led his men forward into the fort, spiked its guns, and, on order, advanced up-river toward the next fort to establish an outpost, while the main body of bluejackets occupied what had

promptly been christened "The Marine Redoubt." As darkness fell, the first
Western troops to spend the night in the Hermit Kingdom made their bivouac
for an early jump-off next day.

Fortunately, the second fort was carried with equal ease, and here the
Marines "dismantled the battlements by throwing over the 50 or 60 in-
significant breech-loading brass cannon, all being loaded, and tore down
the ramparts."[34] While this demolition was in progress, Tilton's young field
music amused himself by rolling cannon over a cliff into the river.

Then followed the main assault, directed against "The Citadel," which
had originally opened fire on the surveying parties. This work was occupied
by O Chae-yon, governor of Kanghwa-Do. While a Navy detachment covered his left flank and rear against bodies of white-robed Koreans who began to appear on the ridges, Captain Tilton commenced his advance over
terrain which he later depicted as follows:[35]

The topography of the country being indescribable, resembling a sort of chopped
sea, of immense hills and deep ravines lying in every conceivable position.

Short of the fort a large force of Koreans opened fire from a ridge on the
left, which paralleled the advance; these "blazed away at us with their gin-
gals or matchlocks, their black heads popping up and down the while from
the grass."[36] A Navy howitzer put a stop to this, and the Marines pressed on.

The Korean citadel stood atop a 150-foot conical hill. There was no way
to get to the top except straight up. The Koreans opened with what Tilton
described as "a tremendous hail of bullets" which hit nobody, whereas the
return fire by the Marines' muzzle fuzzels toppled more than 40 Koreans
on the ramparts. As the Marines and bluejackets scrambled upward, the
Koreans began rolling down stones and giving vent to "melancholy songs."
Despite stones and songs, the assault parties finally reached the top. First
man over the parapet was Lieutenant Hugh W. McKee, USN, whom a
Korean killed with a spear. Inside, the Koreans fought with desperation
matched only by their disorganization and terrible marksmanship. Only
20 prisoners were taken, and 243 Korean dead were counted. Fifty Korean
standards and 481 cannon (ranging from 32- to 2-pounders) were likewise
captured. The chief Korean flag, a yellow banner 12 feet square, was hauled
down under fire by two Marines, Corporal Charles Brown and Private Hugh
Purvis, both of whom subsequently received Medals of Honor. The captured fort was named for Lieutenant McKee, whose father before him, a
colonel in the Army, had also been killed in action, at Buena Vista in 1847.

Remarkably, in view of the heavy Korean fire and stout resistance at the citadel, only 11 American casualties were sustained, two of these being Marines. Since six Marines were recommended for and ultimately received Medals of Honor for this action, the Korean expedition of 1871 goes down as the only campaign in the annals of the Corps in which there were three times as many Medals of Honor as there were casualties. In any case, despite their small numbers and slight casualties, Tilton's Marines received the lion's share of credit, which was generously accorded in the report of Commander L. A. Kimberly, the landing force commander:[37]

To Captain Tilton and his Marines belongs the honor of first landing and last leaving the shore, in leading the advance on the march, in entering the forts, and in acting as skirmishers. Chosen as the advanced guard, on account of their steadiness and discipline, and looked to with confidence in case of difficulty, their whole behavior on the march and in the assault proved that it was not misplaced.

"YOUR SMART, FAITHFUL FORCE"

In the summer of 1882 the USS *Lancaster*, flagship of the small (three-ship) European Squadron, cruised the eastern Mediterranean. Her detachment commander and squadron Marine officer was Captain H. C. Cochrane, who had already become a footnote in American history, when, as a new second lieutenant, he accompanied President Lincoln on his trip to dedicate the Gettysburg cemetery in 1863. The shipboard routine of Cochrane's Marines began at dawn, when hammocks were lashed up and stowed and all hands went to cleaning stations. After breakfast of coffee and sour bread at 0800, the detachment commenced squaring itself away for morning quarters and drill at 0930. Following inspection by Captain Cochrane or by Second Lieutenant L. W. T. Waller, the red-headed junior Marine, there would be an hour of drill, manual of arms, facings, and on the great guns. Then, dinner at 1130: salt beef or pork, peas or beans, perhaps some dried fruit, and tea or coffee. Until a few years earlier, a gill of spirits would have added zest to this fare, but in 1862 grog was stopped and a nickel a day was added to the ration allowance. After dinner, ship's work would go on until 1700, following which the boatswain's mates piped "Down Hammocks," and the day was done.

In late June 1882 a welcome break came in this routine. Alexandria, Egypt, was in the hands of an antiforeign movement headed by Arabi Pasha, the Nasser of his day. Along with the British Mediterranean Fleet, which was concentrating at Alexandria, the American squadron headed for the scene of trouble. On 11 July the British were forced to bombard the city. Conditions ashore could hardly have been worse. *Fellah* mobs were looting and murdering. The bombardment had set part of the city afire. Foreigners, including some Americans, were in peril.

On 14 July the three American ships landed 73 Marines and 60 blue-jackets, commanded by Captain Cochrane, who was later vividly character-ized in a vignette by one of his juniors, Frederic M. Wise:[38]

. . . distinctly a gentleman and always extremely courteous in his social contacts, but "ornery" and meaner than hell on duty. . . . A man of no sympathy and no affection, but efficient to an unusual degree. A magnificent barracks and mess officer. Cordially hated by officers and men alike.

For the situation in Alexandria, Henry Clay Cochrane was just the man. Marching his force directly to the Grand Square of Mehemet Ali, center of the town, he clamped a guard over the American Consulate and set about restoring order. When Arabi Pasha, who had momentarily retired, headed for Alexandria again, French and Italian landing forces prudently re-em-barked. Not so Cochrane, who announced that the Americans would "stick by the British and take their chances."[39] This decision was not as rash as might appear, because the British had by then landed some 4,000 troops, including 450 Royal Marines. Nevertheless, both the spirit and quality of Cochrane's landing force were much appreciated by the British press and by their commander ashore, Lord Charles Beresford, who wrote:[40]

To your smart, faithful force, great credit is due. . . . I have represented these facts to my government.

"... THE SITUATION IS WELL IN HAND"

At noon on 2 April 1885, the Commandant of the Marine Corps received orders from Secretary of the Navy W. C. Whitney to organize and dispatch a battalion of Marines to Aspinwall (now Colon), the Atlantic port on the Isthmus of Panama. Revolution had flared there against the Colombian government, and transit across the isthmus, vital to American security and guaranteed by treaty, had been stopped.

Within 24 hours a 232-man battalion, which had been collected from the barracks at Portsmouth, New Hampshire; Brooklyn, Philadelphia, and Washington, sailed from New York for Aspinwall. In command was Brevet Lieutenant Colonel Charles Heywood. Known as "the boy colonel" because he had broken all records by rising from second lieutenant in 1858 to brevet lieutenant colonel in 1864, Heywood held two brevets (*Merrimack* vs. USS *Cumberland* and Mobile Bay).

On 6 April, drafts on Marine Barracks from Pensacola to Boston had filled a second 265-man battalion, commanded by Captain J. H. Higbee, which sailed next day, accompanied by a bluejacket battalion and Commander Bowman H. McCalla, who was ordered by the Navy Department to command all forces ashore on the isthmus. Captain Huntington, later to win fame at Guantanamo Bay, had one company of this battalion; First Lieutenant George F. Elliott, a future Commandant, was with him.

Heywood lost no time on arrival. At daybreak, 12 April, his battalion landed. By nightfall they had crossed the 47-mile isthmus, were encamped outside Panama City, and had Marine guards on each train operated by the Panama Railroad. If not yet exactly on time, the trains were at least running again.

Three days later, when Commander McCalla reached Aspinwall, it was only necessary to extend the control which "the boy colonel" had already established. A renowned old-Navy sundowner and seemingly a resolute teetotaler, McCalla made his presence felt by the following order:[41]

Prohibit the use of wines, spirituous and malt liquors. Dispense with all unnecessary ceremonies and parades. Instruct your men in the early morning and late in the afternoon, avoiding the sun in the middle of the day.

Possibly McCalla's bone-dry order was a reaction to the snakes which all hands were (really) seeing on all sides. To prove they existed, Lieutenant Elliott passed the time on outpost at San Pablo by accumulating a fearsome collection of reptiles in a row of rum-filled fruit jars. "Fish stories are nothing to snake stories," said he.[42]

Augmented by ships' detachments from both the Atlantic and Pacific Squadrons and by another draft from Pensacola, a third Marine battalion, under Captain J. M. T. Young, was formed as the situation grew more tense. All three battalions were then grouped into a brigade under Heywood—the first U. S. Marine brigade ever organized.

On 20 April the revolution reached a crisis in Panama City, where the rebels had announced their intention to fight from house to house and, if need be, burn the town. Commander McCalla thereupon concentrated the brigade in Panama City and ordered the Marines to destroy all street barricades and neutralize the city, a process which included setting up a Gatling gun in the front entrance of the cathedral. On 30 April, enough Colombian troops arrived in Panama to control the situation, and, by 25 May, the U. S. expeditionary force was re-embarking at Aspinwall for New York and home stations. "We were all glad to clear out," grumped Elliott.

When informed, at the height of this excitement, that a U. S. Marine brigade was ashore, the captain of a British man-of-war lying off Panama City said, "Tranquility is then assured."[43] A better known observer coined a more well-known phrase: correspondent Richard Harding Davis simply reported, "The Marines have landed and have the situation well in hand."[44]

AFFAIRS AT HOME

In the years following the Civil War by no means all of the activity of the Marine Corps occurred abroad. Jacob Zeilin inherited numerous military chores at home. These ranged from guarding Abraham Lincoln's assassins to assisting the civil authorities during strikes and epidemics and whiskey raids.

After Lincoln's assassination, Washington was hysterical with panic and shock. Casting about for the most escape-proof means of detaining the Lincoln conspirators, Secretary Welles and Secretary of War Stanton determined to confine them on board the monitor *Montauk* at the Navy Yard, under a Marine guard, one of whose officers, First Lieutenant R. S. Collum, was a future historian of the Corps.

One by one, as captured, the conspirators were brought in closed carriages to the Navy Yard main gate and there transferred to Marine custody. Booth's body followed and, under the bayonets of Marines, was autopsied on board the monitor. The security arrangements for all this were among the most rigorous in the history of the Corps. In addition to holding the hooded prisoners in solitary confinement, the Marine guard could allow no visitors on board the ship without a pass signed jointly by Secretaries Welles and Stanton.

A somewhat similar case (which turned out less disastrously for the prisoner) was the detention of Captain Raphael Semmes, CSN, who had been a distinguished officer in the U. S. Navy, but had "gone South" and commanded the raider *Alabama*. Semmes, a hot-tempered, loud-voiced Alabaman, was ordered arrested by Secretary Welles, who sent First Lieutenant L. P. French and two sergeants from Marine Barracks, Eighth and Eye, to do the job. Their quest took them to Louisville, Vicksburg, New Orleans, and finally Mobile. Here, Semmes, found on his plantation, was routed out of bed, protesting every inch of the way. When, forgetting his altered circumstances, Semmes reprimanded French for "outrages" on an officer of his rank, French replied that Semmes no longer had any rank, and his treatment would be "measured only by his good behavior."[45] Momentarily cowed, Semmes was conveyed to Washington, where, for three months, before being restored to his parole by President Johnson, he was held for trial. During this period he was lodged in an attic room of old Center House, at Eighth and Eye, under custody of French, as well as of Lieutenants H. C. Cochrane and George C. Reid. Reid afterward recalled that Semmes made so much noise that he could be heard all over the barracks.

On more than half a dozen occasions between 1867 and 1871, Marines from Philadelphia and Brooklyn were called out to perform the unlikely role of prohibition agents and protect federal revenue officers trying to extinguish bootleg stills in those cities.

The year 1871 was the banner one for raids in Brooklyn's "Irishtown," which was aglow and fuming with the bouquet of illicit mash. After the New York police, and even the 8th Infantry from Governor's Island, had failed to quiet the Irish, Major General Israel Vogdes, the local Army commander recommended that Marines be called in from the Navy Yard. General Vogdes was no stranger to the Corps, having, as a junior officer, commanded an Army detachment which accompanied Lieutenant Cash's Marines in the relief of Fort Pickens. In January, July, September, and October, up Myrtle Avenue, York Street, and Dixon's Alley, Lieutenant Colonel J. L. Broome personally led Brooklyn's Marines against Brooklyn's Irish, under a hail of everything from pistol balls to brickbats, while federal "revenooers" smashed still after still. In the fragrant, ruinous aftermath, Broome received grateful compliments from the police, the Army, and the Collector of Internal Revenue—and, no doubt, the wry respect of the Irish.

Six years later the Marines again appeared in the role of guardians of law and order. On the blistering afternoon of 21 July 1877, Colonel Heywood was ordered to form a battalion from Washington's Marines (6 officers, 127 enlisted men) and proceed by train to Baltimore. The occasion for Heywood's orders was the railroad strike of 1877, one of the most violent labor disputes in American history. Strikers and their angry sympathizers were rioting, burning rolling stock, and stoning local authorities throughout nine states. Federal troops had been called in to restore order.

After a perilous ride to Baltimore (it was an hour before Heywood could find a railroader bold enough to take the throttle of a troop train), the battalion detrained and advanced on Camden Station. Night had fallen, fire bells were ringing, and the railroad yards were ablaze with burning tank cars. Baltimore police had already bagged some 300 rioters, and many more were at hand. All through the night Heywood's little battalion defended two stations (Mount Clare and Camden) against arson and pillage. Next morning, during a lull, they marched with drums beating and bayonets fixed, to breakfast at the elegant Eutaw House.

In the middle of the following night Heywood was awakened by a telegram from the Secretary of the Navy: move the battalion to Philadelphia, now the storm center. At noon, having been slowed by ripped-up trackage, the Marines deployed against un-Quakerlike mobs in the City of Brotherly Love. It was Baltimore all over again, and here, as in Baltimore, politeness was restored by nightfall. As an added complication the battalion was then inspected by Major General W. S. Hancock, the Army officer in command of the federal forces; the Marines (who hadn't had their uniforms off for three days) were chagrined at being caught in such sorry condition, but Hancock, a fighting soldier of the Civil War, had nothing but praise. A tangible bonus was the gift by Philadelphians of a pipe and tobacco for each enlisted Marine—and, for the officers, "some liquid nourishment. . . ."[46]

Thus requited, Heywood's battalion settled down for a week in Philadelphia, following which they were shifted to Reading. Here, the mere presence of Marines was enough; there was no fight. Heywood proceeded to make camp in regulation style, with a daily routine including a parade each evening at Retreat. The good people of Reading were amazed. When, on 13 August, the battalion was ordered home to Washington, it departed amid plaudits from Reading and from General Hancock, whose General Order 46 read in part:[47]

> The major-general commanding desires to express his high appreciation of the excellent conduct and soldierly qualities of the Marines. . . . Citizens and soldiers are united in admiration of the soldierly bearing, excellent discipline, and devotion to duty displayed by them at Baltimore, Philadelphia, and Reading. . . .

Meanwhile, a second battalion had been formed from 11 ships' detachments and from Marine Barracks, Norfolk and Washington. This battalion, under Brevet Lieutenant Colonel James Forney, restored order along the Baltimore and Ohio Railroad between Washington and Martinsburg, West Virginia. In addition, separate companies of Marines were requested by the Army to protect the arsenals at Watervliet, New York, and Frankford, Pennsylvania. This was the Marine Corps' last strike duty, except for brief service at Sacramento, California, by a battalion from Mare Island commanded by Major P. C. Pope, during the summer of 1894 incident to strikes on the Central Pacific Railroad.

In 1891 a 40-man detachment commanded by Captain H. C. Cochrane sailed the Bering Sea in a 6,600-mile cruise slightly reminiscent of Gamble's voyages in the War of 1812. Indiscriminate killing of Alaskan seals by British and American poachers threatened extinction of the species, and, by agreement between the two countries, U. S. and British naval forces undertook to suppress the practice. The SS *Al-Ki*, a merchantman, was chartered as depot and prison ship for the combined effort, and Captain Cochrane and his men were ordered aboard her. Only four poachers were actually made prize, as word of the drive had been intentionally well publicized, but two of these, with Marine prize crews, were towed over the 1,200-mile run to Sitka for delivery to the U. S. Marshal. Aboard the *Al-Ki*, toward the end of the cruise, the merchant crew, egged on by union agitators, virtually mutinied, and the master turned to the Marines for help. Cochrane, veteran seagoing Marine that he was, ended the affair with one sentence when he told the captain, "You can set every one of them on the beach, firemen and all, and we'll take the ship to San Francisco."[48]

To maintain the military tone of his detachment, as Cochrane reported to Colonel Heywood:

. . . drills and instruction were unremitting, and every officer and man is trained in boating, in the Army signal code, in skirmishing, the bayonet exercise, and target practice, in addition to his routine duties. The men were organized into boat crews from the first day, and did all of the boarding and pulling required. An excellent rifle range up to 300 yards and four signal stations were established on Amnak Island.

In September 1892 the dread rumor of cholera among immigrant ships caused more than 900 immigrants to be quarantined in a special camp at Sandy Hook, New Jersey. The Marine Corps was directed to enforce the quarantine, and a battalion of ten officers and 201 enlisted men, commanded by Major R. W. Huntington, got the unenviable job. For a month, Huntington maintained the *cordon sanitaire* and characteristically got in some field training, too, ". . . although [he reported] the ground is poorly adapted for drill and the woods are full of poison oak."[49]

PROGRESS UNDER THREE ABLE COMMANDANTS

If strength and appropriations were the only measure, the 34 years from the end of the Civil War until the outbreak of war with Spain would have been, for the Marine Corps, years in the doldrums. In 1867 the strength of the Corps was 93 officers and 3,652 enlisted men; by 1880 this had been cut to 78 officers and 2,000 enlisted men; and it was not until 1896 that the Corps recovered itself somewhat by a belated increase to 2,600 enlisted men.

Moreover, in 1874 Congress again had to decide whether the Marine Corps should continue to exist, and whether the shipboard duties of the Corps should be taken over by sailors or assigned to the Army. The proposals were, as a contemporary pamphlet noted,[50] "defeated by the efforts of better informed legislators," but the escape was a narrow one. The Marine Corps' thin budget of $1,105,961 was slashed to an even scantier $877,616, its officer strength was reduced to 78, the Commandant's rank was reduced from brigadier general to that of colonel (to take effect upon Zeilin's retirement), and even the existence of the Marine Band was only saved by a floor fight in the House of Representatives. Had not the most respected seniors in the Navy intervened, led by Farragut and Porter, the Marine Corps might well have been abolished.

As if organizational cuts had not bit deep enough, within three years Secretary of the Navy R. W. Thompson (a Hoosier politician who was dumfounded, on boarding his first ironclad, to discover that it was hollow) had to announce to the officers of the Navy and Marines in 1877:[51]

. . . that the amount of money found by him in the Treasury of the United States . . . is insufficient to pay the officers for the months of April, May, and June.

But in spite of these hard times, and in spite of the concurrent decay of the Navy, all but unnoticed changes and improvements were under way. These stirrings came about under the leadership of three able Commandants: Jacob Zeilin, Charles Grymes McCawley, and Charles Heywood.

Zeilin served as Commandant until 1 November 1876. He had attained the office through selection, rather than seniority, and he again broke ground, this time by voluntarily retiring after 45 years' service. Although characterized as "easy" by Huntington, the driving perfectionist, Zeilin was efficient and judicious. He it was who introduced annual inspections for all Marine posts, and he it was who in 1867 further standardized Army drill and tactics (*Upton's Tactics*) for the Marine Corps.

When McCawley (son of a Marine officer of the 1820s) came to Marine Corps Headquarters in 1871, he was the senior officer in the Corps after

Zeilin and the latter's heir apparent. With typical foresight, as his own retirement drew near, Zeilin had ordered his successor to Washington, where he could become familiar at firsthand with the problems of keeping the Marine Corps afloat in the 1870s. Despite the initial rebuff of seeing his new job downgraded in rank, the eighth Commandant took over with vigor. Among McCawley's contributions were:

The commissioning of Naval Academy graduates in the Marine Corps. This was a great advance, culminating four years' prodding of Congress and the Navy Department to improve the haphazard methods by which the Corps obtained its officers. Beginning with the Annapolis class of 1881 and continuing until 1897, the entire intake of Marine officers (50 in all) came from the Naval Academy—a notable line which included, among many fine Marines, five Commandants (Barnett, Lejeune, Neville, Fuller, and Russell) and 13 other generals.

The first standard tables of organization for the Marine Corps.

The first factory manufacture of uniforms, using mass production methods at the Philadelphia depot of supplies.

A shake-up in Marine Corps Headquarters: Once and for all, the Staff, headed by the Adjutant and Inspector, was in 1886 precluded from independent authority or succession to command; all officers were required to study and recite tactics; all officers had to apply for their leave to the Commandant himself.

For noncommissioned officers and privates, equally interesting news: establishment of a retired list for enlisted Marines; promotion examinations for sergeants and corporals (including "reading, writing, and the simple rules of arithmetic"); a warrant for each NCO; a single roster for NCO promotions throughout the Corps; and better maintenance and furniture for barracks (but meanwhile, for want of appropriations, even Eighth and Eye had so far crumbled that a board of survey reported the barracks "no longer habitable without extensive repairs": it was inhabited, nevertheless, and unrepaired, until 1901).

For the Marine Band, more in the doldrums than any other part of the Corps: the appointment of John Philip Sousa, at $94 a month, as Leader. Colonel McCawley had sighed, "The Band gives me more trouble than all the rest of the Corps put together,"[52] then in October 1880 dismissed Sousa's predecessor, Louis Schneider, after a board of investigation reported him "unfit for the Service." Poor Schneider's press had included such unkind cuts as, "Put a musician in the place of Schneider." The Marine Corps did.

And, finally, for what teetotaling Marines there may have been: permission for the Marines Temperance Union to use the Marine Band Hall for meetings. Not content with this gesture, McCawley cast a pall over the Corps by banning the sale of beer in Marine canteens.

Charles Heywood, "boy colonel" of years past, assumed McCawley's mantle on 30 January 1891. Within three months, Colonel Heywood launched his first major reform. On 1 May 1891, under Captain D. P. Mannix (a Civil War veteran rounding out 29 years' service), the School of Application, forerunner of Basic School, was established at Washington. Mannix (who had been torpedo instructor to the Chinese Navy for four years) prescribed a curriculum which included: infantry tactics, small arms, gunnery and torpedoes, high explosives, electricity, steam launches, administration, field service and modern tactics, and field entrenchments. As Captain Mannix reported at the end of his first year:[53]

Here student officers and men are comparatively free from the care of guard duty, except so much as may be necessary for instruction, and in consequence display more interest in their drills and studies and have more time to devote to them. The naval experimental ground for ordnance at Indian Head is of easy access, as is the naval magazine with its excellent range for target practice, and a few miles back of the Potomac's eastern branch the country is well adapted for field training. The navy yard and gun foundry are conveniently at hand, combining a water front admirably suited for instruction in boat pulling and sailing, with the advantages offered by the gun shops of acquiring a practical knowledge of the manufacture of guns, carriages, etc., not to be obtained elsewhere. The school has also the services of the Corps band, which it could enjoy at no other station. . . .

One other advantage not obtainable at other stations was Sergeant Major Thomas F. Hayes. Hayes, sergeant major of the Marine Corps, had served in the British Army and was a veteran of much combat service, including the expedition to relieve Khartoum. During his time at Eighth and Eye, Sergeant Major Hayes, following the British custom, was given charge of the initial parade-ground training of new lieutenants and served as drillmaster for such illustrious Marines as Smedley Butler, Thomas Holcomb, and many others. Probably because his successors had not been brought up with this usage, the practice died with him.

Not content with founding the School of Application, the "boy colonel," now a commanding gentleman with white hair, aquiline nose, and sweeping moustache, finally succeeded in 1891 in a project dear to McCawley before him—mandatory promotion examinations for officers. Hand in hand with all this went still more improvements: fitness reports (1891); detail in

1894 of a Marine instructor for the Naval War College; creation in 1898 of the rank of gunnery sergeant (". . . will without doubt produce a class of noncommissioned officers most valuable to the Service"); continual emphasis on more and better training—marksmanship especially (Sergeant Major Hayes was also a shooter)—an emphasis which would pay off brilliantly when the country went to war with Spain. Finally, in 1897, Heywood set up the modern post exchange system.

In addition to the administrative reforms, just summarized, of Zeilin, McCawley, and Heywood, the birth of the "New Navy," beginning in 1883, combined with the writings of Mahan, focused attention on the role of sea power. With this came interest in landing operations; and just as the "New Navy" progressed from sail to steam, the philosophy behind employment of U. S. Marines began to depart from 18th and 19th century concepts toward the fleet-centered United States amphibious doctrine of the century ahead.

"THE MARINE HAS NO PLACE . . ."

As McCawley turned over to Heywood in 1891, the Marine Corps never seemed more secure. Only a year before, the Admiral of the Navy, David D. Porter (whose son had become a Marine officer after the Civil War), had written: [54]

> I have had Marines under my observation since the year 1824, when I first joined an American man-of-war, a period of 66 years, and all during that time I have never known a case where the Marines could not be depended on for any service. Without that well-drilled police force on shipboard, an American man-of-war could not be depended upon to maintain discipline and perform the arduous duties assigned her. There is not an intelligent officer in the Navy who can speak anything but praise of the Marine Corps. . . .

Yet, it was in the same year that Admiral Porter lauded the Corps that a cabal of younger naval officers, led by Lieutenant William F. Fullam, USN, launched a campaign to force Marines off ships of the Navy and, ultimately, into the Army. Fullam's opening gun was a paper presented in 1890 to the United States Naval Institute, at Annapolis, advocating the removal of Marines from sea duty, a proposal which, to be fully understood, must be examined in the light of conditions in the "New Navy" of the 1890s. [55]

The transition from sail to steam had been a hard one for the Line of the Navy. As Admiral Porter had remarked a few years earlier, "Our seamen were transformed into coal heavers, our officers had little to do but walk the deck." [56] The new Navy had created a host of technicians in engineering and ordnance, and reduced the all-purpose line officer and the bluejacket to mere housekeepers on deck. In searching for expanded missions, some Navy line officers became interested in landing force tactics and organization, and raised the question whether such matters should not become the exclusive province of the line of the Navy. The leader among these officers, Lieutenant Fullam, was ambitious, energetic, articulate, and egocentric. He had stood first in his class at Annapolis and had later been in charge of the midshipmen's infantry drill while an instructor at the Academy. This, he evidently considered, made him a military expert. His thesis was that the Marine Corps was a superfluity: naval officers and bluejackets could and should take over the guard and landing force duties of Marines. Although Fullam seems to have been unaware of the fact, he was advancing the same general proposition, supported by many of the same arguments, as we have seen put forward in 1801 by the Marine Corps' earliest Navy foe, Thomas Truxtun.

Fullam's initial test case (there were destined to be several during the next 15 years) was a proposal in early 1894 that the Marine detachment on board the USS *Raleigh* be sharply cut in strength. This the Navy Department disapproved.

What next followed was later described by General Elliott, tenth Commandant, in the following words:[57]

> The movers of [Fullam's] proposition being thus frustrated by the Department, petitions were circulated for signature among the crews of the vessels of the Navy, addressed to the Congress of the United States, asking for withdrawal of Marines on board ship. The attention of the Department being called to said petitions, the Secretary deemed it his duty to issue a Special Order reprobating this procedure on the part of the enlisted men, which was nurtured by the few officers previously referred to.

Fullam, then serving in the cruiser *Chicago*, was admittedly the moving spirit behind the petitions, but an agitation of this kind obviously could not have gone on without countenance by the more senior officers in the background.

In August 1894 the sailors' round robins went to the Senate and were read into the record by Vice President Adlai Stevenson. Within three weeks, on 24 August, Senator Manderson of Nebraska, together with Senator John Sherman (William Tecumseh Sherman's brother), introduced Senate Bill 2324. Under the Manderson-Sherman bill, five regiments of Army artillery would be consolidated with the Marine Corps; the resultant amalgam would become a Corps of Marine Artillery and be transferred into the Army. This concept was in line with contemporary German and English employment of Marines as coast-defense and fortress-artillery troops.

On the same day that Secretary of the Navy Hilary A. Herbert loosed his special order at Fullam and the petitioners, the Senate Naval Affairs Committee pigeonholed the petitions. Soon afterward, the Military Affairs Committee dropped the Manderson-Sherman bill, and the Marine Corps was allowed to remain undisturbed. One influential voice in the decision was that of Captain Henry C. Taylor, USN, President of the Naval War College, who, in the words of Professor William H. Russell, the naval historian, "put a finger on the fallacy of the entire Fullam proposal." If the Marines were abolished, wrote Taylor:[58]

. . . I do not doubt that those seamen, and the officers [who] command them, would evolve . . . into a new corps, identical with the present Marines.

At this juncture Captain Robley D. Evans, USN, appeared on stage. Captain Evans had won his nickname, "Fighting Bob," in 1865 at Fort Fisher. Severely wounded, he clapped a Colt's patent revolver to the head of a surgeon who had disclosed his intention to amputate Evans's leg. After recovering, Evans, understandably soured on amphibious operations, joined others in blaming the Marines for the dismal failure of the ships' landing forces at Fisher.

In 1895, 31 years after Fort Fisher, "Fighting Bob"—still fighting and evidently undaunted by the Secretary of the Navy's already expressed views on the Marine Corps—asked that the Navy Department omit Marines from the complement of the new battleship *Indiana*, which he had been ordered to command.

On 1 November 1895 Secretary Herbert faced up to Evans. First, to make matters clear, the request was disapproved. Second, the Secretary prescribed that the *Indiana's* Marine detachment would consist of "one captain, one subaltern, and 60 noncommissioned officers, privates, and musics." These Marines were to be part of the working force of the ship; would man certain guns under their own officers; and would assist in such all hands evolutions as provisioning, coaling, and ammunitioning.[59] To the present day, this letter sets the pattern for the duties of Marines aboard ship.

By way of follow-up, Colonel Heywood promptly detailed First Lieutenant Lincoln Karmany, one of the most forthright and capable younger officers in the Corps, as Evans's Marine officer. Unfortunately, the relationship kept its initial chill, possibly because of Karmany's habit of referring to Captain Evans as "Frightened Bob."[60]

But the Navy opponents of the Marine Corps were still bound to have their way. In 1896 the honorable-mention paper in the U. S. Naval Institute's Annual Prize Essay Contest was another attack on Marines by Fullam. This time, harking back to recommendations of years past that Marines be regimented ashore and given a permanent training base, Fullam urged their withdrawal from sea duty in the hope that time would take care of the rest. The paper (which contained such statements as "the Marine officer has no *raison d'être* . . . ") was followed by a printed "Discussion," as was usual in the Naval Institute *Proceedings*.[61] This discussion not only disclosed strong anti-Marine bias in some Navy circles, but identified as avowed foes of the Corps a number of naval officers destined for renown. Among their views were the following:

Captain Robley D. Evans: That I am opposed to Marines on board ship is pretty well known. . . . The more Marines we have, the lower the intelligence of the crew.

Lieutenant H. S. Knapp: As regards the Marines, every day's experience strengthens my conviction that they detract from rather than add to the discipline of ship life, and that they are room-takers and idlers.

Lieutenant Bradley A. Fiske: I am strongly in favor of withdrawal of Marines from our modern ships. My reasons are exactly those stated by Lieutenant Fullam.

Lieutenant Harry P. Huse: The Marine has no place. . . .

Lieutenant A. P. Niblack: It would seem the part of real wisdom to draw on the artillery of the Army for Marine duty on board ship.

Lieutenant C. E. Colahan: They have no place aboard ship.

Commander J. N. Hemphill: Regarding the Marines, I think they should be turned over bodily to the Army.

It is of interest that every naval officer who thus recorded himself against the Marine Corps graduated from Annapolis before 1881, the first class from which Marine officers were commissioned. Of greater significance is that those who voiced such obviously emotional views were virtually all future admirals who would, for years to come, constitute an obstacle to the Marine Corps and, upon occasion, a threat to its very existence.

But the debate was not all one-sided. With Colonel-Commandant Heywood cheering from the sidelines, the Corps was vigorously defended by such naval officers of high standing as Luce, Wainwright, and Ellicott, and by two uncowed junior Marines, Lieutenants Lauchheimer and Doyen, both destined to be general officers.

Rear Admiral Stephen B. Luce, founder of the Naval War College and elder statesman of the Navy, stood his ground (and that of the Marines) without equivocation. In February 1894 he had written to Heywood:[62]

The Corps has always been so distinguished in its discipline and efficiency that I should regard the withdrawal of the guards from our ships and Navy Yards as a positive misfortune for the Navy. The proposition to supply these places with bluejackets is not worthy of serious consideration. When a system has worked well for over a hundred years it seems unwise, to say the least, to change it save through pressure of some marked and obvious necessity for improvement, and it does not appear that any such necessity exists in regard to the Marine Corps.

In 1896, the admiral again defended the Marines, closing his statement with the words:[63]

Sorry would I be, speaking as an American citizen not unacquainted with naval affairs, to see the backward movement of withdrawing the Marine guards from our ships. Had I ten thousand votes they should all be cast in favor of preserving their present status and increasing their numbers.

Admiral Luce's final phrase touched a point on which Colonel Heywood had been devoting much effort—the urgent need for more Marines. Serious undermanning had been a Marine Corps problem ever since the 1850s and, with the advent of the new Navy and its new ships and stations, was aggravated with the passage of each year. In 1894, more than 12 per cent of the enlisted strength of the Corps was lost through desertions, mostly, according to Major Nicholson, the Adjutant and Inspector, as a result of overwork and day-on day-off guard duty. Two years later, owing to Colonel Heywood's prodding (example: a table showing that 1,000 Marines cost the government $69,584 a year less than 1,000 bluejackets performing identical duties), Congress authorized an increase of 600 enlisted Marines.[64] Typical of the history of the Corps, this Congressional increase of about 30 per cent in Marine strength came when opponents of the Corps were most vocal and active.

The extent of the feeling behind this activity became evident in early 1897, when President McKinley, on assuming office, innocently chose as his naval aide a Marine officer—the dashing, socially peerless son of a former Commandant, Captain C. L. McCawley. In a vain attempt to salve quickly evident hurt feelings, the President asked for a naval officer to assist McCawley; no officer would volunteer, and two lieutenants actually declined the detail. Finally, an ensign was assigned to the White House, but the harm was done.

Not surprisingly, 1897 saw another assault on the Marine Corps, this time through the oblique medium of the personnel board which had been convened under the chairmanship of Assistant Secretary of the Navy Theodore Roosevelt to bring the Corps of Steam Engineers into the Line of the Navy. One member of the board, a Fullam man, proposed that the Marine Corps, too, should be amalgamated with the Navy. Another followed with a resolution which would have put the board on record against having Marine detachments aboard seagoing ships. Both ideas found favor with Roosevelt, but Colonel Heywood's arguments defeated or at least deferred these proposals.

In 1899, after the Spanish-American War, the Naval Personnel Bill incorporated the steam engineers into the Line, and, in Professor Russell's word again:[65]

. . . the Navy line officer got back what was rightfully his: full responsibility for the entire ship, hull, motive power, and guns.

This reform immediately eased Navy pressure against the Marine Corps, and, as we shall see, the same law gave the Corps its largest personnel increase since establishment. For a decade the future of the Corps was assured.

THE CORPS SCENE

A Marine veteran of the Civil War wrote:[66]

There were many kinds of uniforms to be seen in Washington during those war days, but they were shabby in comparison to those worn by the Marines. While out on liberty in the city, we were frequently taken for brigadier generals by the volunteer soldiers, and they would sometimes present arms to us. We returned the salute, of course, as we considered they were saluting the uniform and not the man.

If Civil War Marines made up somewhat in uniform what they undeniably lacked in numbers, credit must go to the *Uniform Regulations* of 1859. Under these regulations, while the service uniform was virtually that of infantry of the regular Army—blue blouse, with light blue trousers, and fatigue caps—the dress uniform was an eye catcher. Even privates wore gold epaulettes, white cross-belts, and high-crowned round hats complete with scarlet pompon and dress cap emblems the size of salad plates.

Officers were distinguished by even larger epaulettes, by boat cloaks like those worn a century later, and, for field officers in full dress, a feathered fore-and-aft hat with cockade. The quatrefoil, or "knot" atop officers' caps, was also adopted by the 1859 regulations, which, in this as in other details, tended to follow French military fashions.

During following years the most noteworthy addition to the officers' wardrobe was the introduction, in 1869, of evening dress. This handsome uniform with dark blue shell jacket, gold standing collar and shoulder-knots, was unique in the American armed forces and remained unchanged for 80 years, when some of its ornamentation had to be sacrificed on the altar of unification.

One of Jacob Zeilin's last acts as Commandant, in 1875, was to approve new uniform regulations. The 1875 changes continued to follow French styles which, whatever the fortunes of French arms at the time, remained in vogue. One British feature which crept in, however, was the unvisored "pillbox" forage cap, suggestive to later generations of the best in hotel service. An unmourned casualty was the leather stock, which was abolished after exactly a century about the necks of Marines.

By the time Charles Heywood became Commandant, spiked helmets (blue or white) were the dress headgear, and an all-white tropical uniform with standing collar had been adopted for all hands. A field uniform of coarse grey material, styled "cheesecloth," to be worn with blue flannel shirts of Army pattern, was also prescribed.

After the Civil War, Marine insignia assumed many features familiar today. The most important innovation, as of 19 November 1868, was the present Marine Corps emblem. This design was the handiwork of a board convened by Jacob Zeilin, consisting of Major G. R. Graham, and Captains R. W. Huntington and C. F. Williams. In arriving at their decision, the board borrowed the globe from the Royal Marines, but chose the western hemisphere instead of the eastern as worn by the British. The eagle and foul anchor were added to leave no doubt that the Corps was both American and maritime. Only a few years later, about 1883, *Semper Fidelis* became the motto of the Corps and was duly commemorated by Marine Band Leader Sousa in the march of that name, which he composed in 1888 as the Corps march.

Officer rank insignia identical with those of the Army had been worn from the 1840s on, but first appear in the 1859 regulations. The 1875 regulations added sleeve braid (gold lace or black mohair) which indicated rank and carried over into modern times as the sleeve insignia on evening dress. The last Marine uniform to carry such insignia (until 1952) was that of the Leader of the Marine Band.

The equipment with which Marines entered the Civil War was largely that used by the Army. This included the officers' sword, for in 1859 the Corps temporarily abandoned the Mameluke sword and substituted the Army infantry saber, a heavier weapon. The saber had a black leather scabbard with brass fittings and basket hilt, and was thought somewhat better in combat; the leather scabbard was also less likely to be dented in the cramped quarters aboard ship than the metal scabbard of the Mameluke. In 1875 (with some reservations, but under pressure from the officers of the Corps) Zeilin restored the traditional pattern, while keeping the Army saber as the Marine NCO sword. The officer and NCO swords of the Marine Corps today are therefore, respectively, the oldest and second oldest arms carried by United States forces, the one dating from 1826, the other from 1859.

Among several shoulder weapons used by Marines during the Civil War, the .58 caliber muzzle-loading musket was the most common; the officers usually carried Navy Colt revolvers. In 1870 General Zeilin approved adoption of the much improved breech-loading .50 caliber rifled musket, which was standard until 1884, when, with the Army, the Marines adopted an improved model of the Army's Springfield .45-70 breech-loader. In 1896 Marines received a radically new weapon, the Lee Navy rifle, a high-velocity, clip-fed, bolt-action .236 caliber arm using smokeless powder (the first such in the U. S. Armed Forces), and it was with the Lee that the Corps went to war in 1898.

Enlistments were for five years, and the Marine recruit had to be between 18 and 35 years old (though 14-year-olds were enlisted as field musics, or "music boys," as they were usually called). To qualify, the applicant had to be able to read and write, be unmarried, and be "well made, sound as to senses and limbs." There were four recruiting rendezvous in 1880: Philadelphia, New York, Boston, and Mare Island. From these the new Marine went to boot training at Eighth and Eye, and then ordinarily was transferred to a Marine barracks for polishing before being drafted to a ship's detachment. From 1885 on, his training was regulated by the *Marines' Manual*, the Corps' first handbook on general military subjects. On hygiene, this work advised:

Where conveniences are to be had, the men should bathe once or twice a week; the feet should be washed at least twice a week.

For rifle marksmanship, the following sure-fire procedure was prescribed:

Take the best position for holding the rifle. Aim it correctly, hold it steadily, and pull the trigger without deranging the aim.

On shore duty, Marines were trained at the school of the soldier, company, and battalion; in skirmishing; at target practice; at bayonet exercises; and in ceremonies. The seagoing Marine continued in these subjects as conditions permitted, but also had to practice "the great gun, or artillery drill"; and to become proficient in swimming, boats, signals, and broadsword.

To make certain that all the foregoing training was carried out, the Commandant himself annually inspected each post, except Mare Island. There were 12 barracks in 1891: Portsmouth, New Hampshire; Boston, Newport, Brooklyn, Philadelphia, Washington, Annapolis, Norfolk, Port Royal, Pensacola, Mare Island, and Sitka, Alaska. Between visits by the Commandant, the Adjutant and Inspector descended once a quarter. The cost to the government of supporting the Marine Corps shore establishment in 1891 was $27,500, which Congress parceled out as follows:[67]

For freight, ferriage, tolls, cartage, funeral expenses of Marines, stationery, telegraphing, rent of telephones, purchase and repair of typewriters, apprehension of deserters, per diem of enlisted men employed on constant labor for a period of not less than ten days, repair of gas and water fixtures, office and barracks furniture, mess utensils for enlisted men, such as bowls, plates, spoons, knives, forks, packing boxes, wrapping paper, oil cloth, crash, rope, twine, camphor and carbolized paper, carpenters' tools, tools for police purposes, iron safes, purchase and repair of public wagons, purchase and repair of harness, purchase of public horses, services of veterinary surgeons and medicines for public horses, purchase and repair of hose, repair of fire extinguishers, purchase of fire hand grenades, purchase and repair of carts and wheelbarrows, purchase and repair of cooking stoves, ranges, stoves, and furnaces where there are no grates, purchase of ice, towels, and soap for offices, postage stamps for foreign postage, purchase of newspapers and periodicals, improving parade grounds, repair of pumps and wharves, laying drain and water pipes, introducing gas, and for gas and oil for marine barracks . . . also straw for bedding. . . .

"Severe punishments are seldom inflicted," wrote Captain Cochrane. "Drunkenness and desertion are decreasing every year." In an era (the 1880s) when a typical court-martial sentence (for desertion) included, as an accessory to a year's confinement, the wearing of a 12-pound ball on a four-foot chain, Cochrane may have thought himself and fellow commanding officers an easygoing lot. But here is a description of Cochrane's methods while commanding a Marine barracks, as seen through the eyes of a junior officer:[68]

He was a tartar for discipline. A Marine who had been drinking but wasn't exactly drunk came into the Yard. The Colonel smelled his breath and ordered him on bread and water for five days for smuggling liquor into the Marine Barracks—inside himself!

He could not abide waste of any kind. He never permitted it in his command. He used to cut the backs very carefully from used envelopes for his memorandum pads. Once the Marine baker turned out a batch of poor bread. The Colonel promptly made him pay for a sack of flour. He was a product of the Civil War. To him, orders were to be obeyed, work was to be done. No excuses. No explanations. No quarter to be given or expected.

If the officers were stern and set in their ways, there was good reason. Promotion was glacially slow. In 1894, officers who had been first commissioned during the Civil War were mainly captains, having served an average of 18 years as lieutenants. They could expect to make major after about 21 more years in the grade of captain. If they lasted much longer, they would rise to lieutenant colonel for a few brief years. As Captain George C. Reid (age 53, thirty years' service) testified in 1894:[69]

> When an officer is young he does not so much feel the effects of onerous duty; but when he passes the age of 45 and still has the duty of officer of the day to perform one day on and two days off, he feels it very much. . . . He will not have that cheerfulness, that interest, that energy and industry that every officer should have.

Yet, Colonel Heywood managed to improve the lot of both officers and men.

From 1885 on, all Marines could look forward to retirement under the Military Retirement Act, a benefit not extended to the Navy until 1899 and, meanwhile, something of an irritant between Marines and sailors. One benefit which both shared from 1896 on, however, was the award of Good Conduct Medals. Authorized on 20 July 1896 by Secretary of the Navy Herbert, the Marine Corps Good Conduct Medal was designed by General Heywood himself, as anyone familiar with his character would immediately recognize from the medal's legend—*Fidelity, Zeal, and Obedience.*

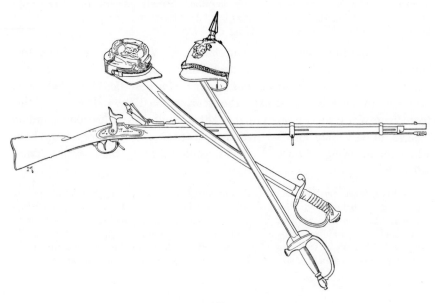

4 EXPEDITIONARY YEARS 1898-1916

No finer military organization than the Marine Corps exists in the world.
—GEORGE DEWEY, ADMIRAL OF THE NAVY

AT ELEVEN o'clock on the morning of 25 January 1898, the battleship *Maine* stood into Havana Harbor with Marines paraded on the quarter-deck and crew at quarters. She steamed past Morro Castle and up the channel, dropping anchor in the landlocked port. Although the visit had been advertised as one of courtesy, the battleship's captain, Charles D. Sigsbee, directed his Marine officer, First Lieutenant A. W. Catlin, to establish additional sentry posts for the security of the ship while at Havana.

Whether at this juncture the United States and Spain would go to war over Cuba was anybody's guess. And the real reason for the *Maine's* presence in Havana was to protect American lives and property and the consulate general, in case they did.

On the calm night of 15 February, 20 minutes after "Taps," as Marines settled down in their hammocks and Lieutenant Catlin prepared to write a letter home, the forward portion of the ship was riven by a tremendous explosion from below. While the stricken battleship settled rapidly by the head, carrying down 266 of her crew (including 28 Marines), the Captain's orderly, Private William Anthony, struggled aft between decks to the Captain's country. There, at attention while smoke rolled about him and the *Maine* shuddered in her death agony, Private Anthony reported to Captain Sigsbee, then calmly assisted him to the quarter-deck. When Sigsbee reported this to the Navy Department, Anthony was acclaimed a hero (and promptly rated sergeant by Colonel Heywood).

On 21 April 1898, despite President McKinley's efforts to restrain public opinion, war was declared on Spain. A fortnight later, on 4 May, Congress increased the Corps to the unprecedented size of 119 officers and 4,713 enlisted men. Forty of the new officers were to be temporary second lieutenants from civil life, and three—the first such in the history of the Marine Corps—were to be meritorious noncommissioned officers. With this increase came good news for Colonel Heywood: the Commandant was once again to be a brigadier general. Recruiting as fast as he could, Heywood set out to provide 40 ships' detachments, to man 15 shore stations, and, as we shall see, to field an expeditionary battalion which would make history for the Corps. Meanwhile the inflamed country, which had talked so much war during preceding months, suddenly found itself having to fight a war—a task for which not all of the Services were prepared.

"IF THERE HAD BEEN 5,000 MARINES UNDER MY COMMAND . . ."

Commodore George Dewey, commanding the Asiatic Squadron, was, however, conspicuously ready. Dewey, favorite and confidant of Assistant Secretary of the Navy Theodore Roosevelt, had on 25 February received orders by cable:[1]

Dewey, Hong Kong.

Secret and confidential. Order the Squadron, except *Monocacy*, to Hong Kong. Keep full of coal. In the event of declaration war Spain, your duty will be to see that the Spanish squadron does not leave the Asiatic coast and then offensive operations in Philippine Islands. Keep *Olympia* until further orders. Roosevelt.

Spirited stuff, and Dewey was the man for the job. On the morning of 1 May 1898, just nine days after the outbreak of war, Dewey took his seven ships into Manila Bay, and, even with time out for breakfast, managed to wipe out Spanish Admiral Montojo's squadron in one of the most rapid and conclusive surface actions of the age. Forty-eight hours later, Commodore Dewey landed Marines from the USS *Baltimore*, under First Lieutenant Dion Williams, to secure the Cavite Navy Yard. Williams' Marines were the first U. S. troops to land on Spanish territory, and he hoisted the first American flag to be raised on enemy soil in the war. After establishing outposts covering approaches from Manila, the Marines (subsequently commanded by Captain W. P. Biddle, Fleet Marine Officer) settled down in the former Spanish marine barracks. As Lieutenant Williams later recounted:[2]

In the barracks storerooms were supplies of clothing and rations which reminded us of our own barracks at home, one feature which greatly interested our men being several barrels of red wine as this formed an important part of the Spanish ration. Cavite was evidently an old-time "navy yard town" as shown by the number of liquor shops and other places of amusenent for sailors, and some of our Marines said "it was just like Vallejo," the *Baltimore* having gone in commission at Mare Island.

The different ships' guards rotated duty ashore at Cavite during the long wait (until July), when Army forces reached the Philippines. Pondering the nine-week delay, Dewey harrumphed:[3]

If there had been 5,000 Marines under my command at Manila Bay, the city would have surrendered to me on May 1 1898, and could have been properly garrisoned. The Filipinos would have received us with open arms, and there would have been no insurrection.

GUANTANAMO BAY

Another apostle of readiness, a hemisphere away from Commodore Dewey, was Lieutenant Colonel R. W. Huntington. On 17 April, four days before war was declared, Colonel Heywood, on orders of Secretary of the Navy John D. Long, had selected Huntington to command a Marine battalion to be organized for expeditionary service in Cuba. Huntington's selection was appropriate: as a second lieutenant, he had been a platoon leader in Reynolds' battalion, formed for service with the Atlantic Fleet in the Civil War.

As drafts from East Coast Marine barracks began arriving in New York, "composed [by Heywood's orders] of young, strong, and healthy men," Huntington formed them into six companies, five of infantry and one of artillery, the latter equipped with four 3-inch landing guns from the Brooklyn Navy Yard. While Huntington shaped his battalion, a former merchantman, rechristened the USS *Panther,* was being fitted out to serve as a transport for the Marines. To make sure that the creaky old *Panther* would be best equipped for her new job, Colonel-Commandant Heywood himself had come up from Washington to work with the navy yard and supervise Huntington's preparations. Under Heywood's sharp eye, the battalion:[4]

. . . was supplied with all the equipment and necessities for field service under conditions prevailing in Cuba, including mosquito netting, woolen and linen clothing, heavy and light weight underwear, three months' supply of provisions, wheelbarrows, pushcarts, pick-axes, shovels, barbed-wire cutters, wall and shelter tents, and a full supply of medical stores.

The day after war was declared, the *Panther* was ready. The Marine battalion, led by the navy yard band, paraded through the streets of Brooklyn, and embarked "amid a scene of marked enthusiasm on the part of a great

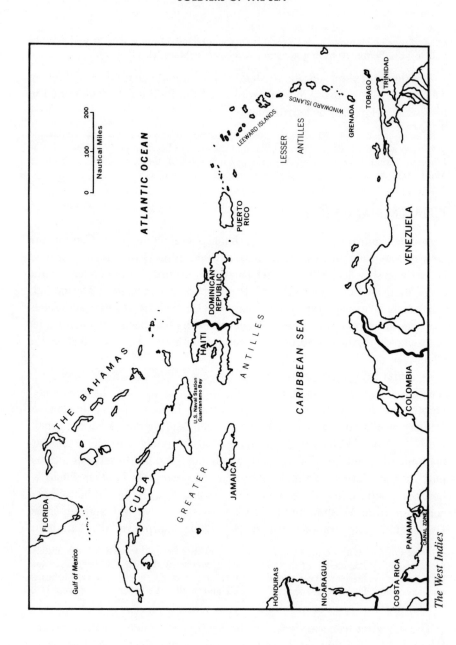

The West Indies

114

crowd of people." That afternoon, to the tune of cheers and whistles from passing ships, the battalion, composed of 24 officers and 623 men, sailed for Key West. Although Heywood and the navy yard had done a fine job in fitting out both the troops and their transport, one problem not solved, nor to be finally solved for some years, was the relationship between the transport's captain and the Marine battalion commander. Commander G. C. Reiter, who, like Huntington, had been in the service since 1861, thought the Marines and their gear were just as much a part of his ship as her main battery, a view which Colonel Huntington did not exactly share.

At Key West, on Commander Reiter's whim (". . . to put the Marines on their mettle") the battalion was dumped ashore at night and went into camp in a pestiferous swamp, a move which caused many junior officers to wring their hands for fear of being marooned on a Florida key while the war passed them by. Far from wringing his hands, however, Huntington immediately began tactical exercises and musketry while awaiting orders.

On 28 May, Commodore W. S. Schley's Flying Squadron had the Spanish Fleet cornered in Santiago de Cuba and the blockade had begun. To support the blockade, a nearby advance base was needed. "Can you not," cabled Navy Secretary Long, "take possession of Guantanamo, occupy as a coaling station?"[5] Rear Admiral W. T. Sampson, the Atlantic Fleet commander, cabled Washington, then Key West: send Colonel Huntington's Marines.

On 7 June, while the *Panther,* reloaded with Marines, was standing out of Key West, the small cruiser *Marblehead* and the converted merchant ship *Yankee* reconnoitered and shelled the defenses of Guantanamo Bay. These defenses consisted of one gunboat, *Sandoval;* a few mines in the upper harbor; and about 7,000 Spanish troops, commanded by General Felix Pareja, mainly concentrated inland about Guantanamo City.

Three days later, under the guns of the battleship *Oregon,* fresh from her dash around Cape Horn, the Marines began landing near Fisherman's Point, inside Guantanamo Bay. By afternoon, Huntington's companies, reinforced by Marines from the *Oregon* and *Marblehead,* were ashore and digging in under cover of intermittent shelling from the ships. These Marines were the spearhead of the American landing forces in Cuba.

While Huntington soon had his men ashore, landing his supplies was another matter. Although the ships' bands were willing to play while Marine working parties sweated, the crew of the *Panther* was conspicuously playing the role of spectators, not participants. Furthermore, because he didn't like the way his ship rode, Commander Reiter decided to keep the Marines' small arms ammunition on board as ballast.

When all this came to the attention of the senior officer present, Commander Bowman McCalla, the *Marblehead's* captain and veteran of the Panama expedition, there was an explosion that echoed through the bay. McCalla addressed the transport's captain:[6]

Sir, Break out immediately and land with the crew of the *Panther,* 50,000 rounds of 6-mm. ammunition. In future, do not require Colonel Huntington to break out or land his stores with members of his command. Use your own officers and men for this purpose, and supply the Commanding Officer of Marines promptly with anything he may desire.

Soon afterward, Huntington named the Marines' bivouac Camp McCalla.

During the next four days and nights the Spaniards sniped and harassed the battalion from the brush and scrub, killing, among others, the battalion surgeon and sergeant major. As a quick and sure cure, Huntington determined to destroy the Spanish water point at Cuzco Valley, two miles from the Marine camp. Under his most junior captain, George F. Elliott (age 52, 28 years' service), Colonel Huntington sent two rifle companies and 75 Cuban guerrillas to do the job. With fire support from the dispatch boat *Dolphin,* Elliott handily defeated more than 500 Spaniards and wrecked the well. At a total cost of 6 killed and 16 wounded in all operations, the Marines had bagged 18 prisoners and inflicted anything from 60 to 140 casualties, depending on which reports are to be believed. Noteworthy in the Cuzco action was First Lieutenant W. C. Neville, whose thunderous voice and dauntless courage were already making a reputation which would eventually gain him the commandancy.

But the unchallenged hero of the fight was Sergeant John H. Quick, who stood calmly amid United States and Spanish fire, to wig-wag the *Dolphin* to concentrate wholly on the Spanish positions rather than on ground already captured by the Marines. Quick's heroism was recorded by the novelist, Stephen Crane, who was, for the moment, a war correspondent:[7]

I watched his face, and it was as grave and serene as a man writing in his own library... I saw Quick betray only one sign of emotion. As he swung his clumsy flag to and fro, an end of it once caught on a cactus pillar. He looked annoyed.

For this, Sergeant Quick was awarded the Medal of Honor, while the hill overlooking the Marines' camp was later named for Stephen Crane.

The operations of Huntington's battalion highlight important developments of the new Marine Corps of 1898. Like Reynolds' battalion in 1861, the battalion was part of the Atlantic Fleet: an embryonic Fleet Marine Force—if anybody in those days had thought of the term. Its organization was not that of the casual ship's landing party of the 19th century, but that of a self-contained unit built around the combined arms. Its mobile base of operations was an 1898 attack transport, for the *Panther*, specifically fitted for expeditionary operations, was referred to repeatedly at the time as "the Marine transport." The mission of Huntington's battalion was to land on hostile shores to seize an advance base for the Fleet. The force moved quickly to the objective as part of the Fleet, and drew on the firepower and logistics of the Fleet to nail down its beachhead.

In other words, by action and not by theory, Colonel Huntington's fleet landing force had set a pattern for employment of U. S. Marines which would still stand more than half a century and three wars later.

Nor was the lesson lost on the public. The picture of the Spanish War was, in general, one of military unreadiness and inefficiency. The Army lost four men from disease for every one killed in combat, and 50 per cent of the soldiers who set foot on Cuba became casualties from yellow fever, malaria, or enteric disease. By contrast, the Marines moved fast and efficiently, did their job (suffering only two per cent casualties from disease, no deaths from sickness, and not a case of yellow jack) and, following several months of garrison duty and minor skirmishing at Guantanamo, returned home fighting fit. As a reward, when the Marine battalion came home for disbandment in September 1898, President McKinley had them march through Washington for a nationally applauded Presidential review to the strains of "The Marines' Hymn" and "A Hot Time in the Old Town Tonight."

More tangible evidence of national recognition was passage by Congress, on 3 March 1899, of the Naval Personnel Bill, which Theodore Roosevelt and the Fullam clique had originally hoped would finish the Marine Corps. Instead, Congress provided for a permanent Marine Corps of 201 officers and 6,062 enlisted men—more than a 100 per cent increase over 1896.

AFLOAT AND ASHORE

Although Huntington and Guantanamo stole the show, other Marines did their bit ashore and afloat while the short war lasted. Guam—reviled for the next 40 years as the hellhole of the Corps—was secured on 21 June 1898 by Marines from the USS *Charleston* under First Lieutenant John Twiggs ("Handsome Jack") Myers, soon to be one of the heroes in the defense of

Peking. The Guam landing, which was unopposed by the island's garrison of 56 Spanish Marines, had its funny side: the Spaniards, somewhat out of touch with world events, took the preliminary shelling from the *Charleston* to be a gun salute. Subsequently, occupation duty on Guam under an eccentric naval governor (Commander Seaton Schroeder, nicknamed "Satan" by his men) proved no treat: after solacing themselves with a stolen barrel of medical whiskey, some of the Marine garrison were reviled by the governor in a report to the Navy Department for their "detestable spirit of lawlessness."[8]

Five weeks after the occupation of Guam, on 28 July 1898, First Lieutenant H. C. Haines (having attained his rank in 15 years' service) landed the Marines of the battleship *Massachusetts* at Ponce, Puerto Rico, "with orders to deliver the town . . . to the first officer of the Army who came ashore."[9] This was duly done some three hours afterward when Lieutenant Haines turned over Ponce to Major General Nelson A. Miles, USA, commanding the Army's expeditionary force to Puerto Rico. Among others present that day was Captain John A. Lejeune, senior Marine officer in the USS *Cincinnati*, who got ashore to watch the landings and later followed the advancing American columns in a *carromato* commandeered for the occasion.

Serving in the 40 ships' detachments manned by the Marine Corps during the war were five future Commandants: Biddle, Barnett, Lejeune, Fuller, and Russell. Both at Manila Bay and at Santiago, and in lesser individual actions, the Marines won nothing but praise. Aboard the USS *Indiana*, at Santiago, Captain L. W. T. Waller's men got off 500 rounds of 6-pounder shell at Cervera's fleeing squadron during 61 minutes' action, and the other detachments were not far behind. Aboard the *Texas*, when the chase was at its height, Marines volunteered as coal-passers to spell the exhausted "black gang," while the *Brooklyn's* "music boys, Drummer Weisenberg and Fifer Stewart . . . behaved manfully."

SAMOA

Samoa, which ten years before had seen the loss of the USS *Vandalia* and the USS *Trenton* in a hurricane, was the scene of trouble in 1899. Under a joint British-American protectorate, the natives were divided by a contest over the chieftaincy of the island. This brought two British ships and the USS *Philadelphia*, a protected cruiser, to the scene. On 1 April a landing force of British and American Marines and seamen took the field against one of the factions. The immediate results were disastrous. After burning a hostile village near Apia, the column was heavily ambushed; Lieutenant P. V. H. Lansdale, USN, was mortally wounded beside the party's Colt machine gun, which had to be abandoned, and Ensign John Monaghan was killed while protecting Lansdale. First Lieutenant C. M. Perkins, with 20 Marines, rallied the force, put the surgeon in command of the bluejackets and conducted a hard-pressed retirement to the beach in which the U. S. Marines acted as rear guard and covered the withdrawal of both British and American parties. The hero of the day was Private H. L. Hulbert, who remained with Lansdale and Monaghan until both were dead and then made his way back under heavy fire to the main body. "His behavior throughout," reported Perkins, "was worthy of all praise and honor."[10]

This defeat brought heavy reprisals in the form of destruction of villages and punitive bombardments which imposed peace within a few weeks, following which, ultimately, Samoa was partitioned between Great Britain, the United States, and Germany. Still later, in 1904, when a naval station was established at Tutuila, there came into being a unique, Marine-trained native security force, the Fita-Fita Guard, commanded and trained by a succession of Marine NCOs. Thus the Naval Station, Tutuila, remained for many years the only outlying naval base which never had a Marine barracks.

INSURRECTION IN THE PHILIPPINES

Hardly had the smoke of Commodore Dewey's guns drifted to leeward before it became apparent that we would have to fight to hold the Philippines. Long oppressed by Spain, the Filipinos sought immediate independence. Three years would be required, in the hard-bitten phrase of the day, to "civilize 'em with a Krag" and convince such native leaders as Emilio Aguinaldo that the United States, like its Marines, had arrived to stay.

Trouble initially centered near Cavite, which had been converted into a United States naval station. Early in 1899, Dewey asked for a battalion of Marines to protect the base. Under Colonel P. C. Pope, who had been Huntington's executive officer at Guantanamo, 15 officers and 260 men were sent in April (the first overseas expedition in which officers were directed to leave their swords behind and arm themselves only with pistols). By September a second battalion, commanded by Major G. F. Elliott, was required and furnished. In December, still another, led by Major Waller, was dispatched to Cavite, and, by the end of 1900, six Marine battalions had been sent to the

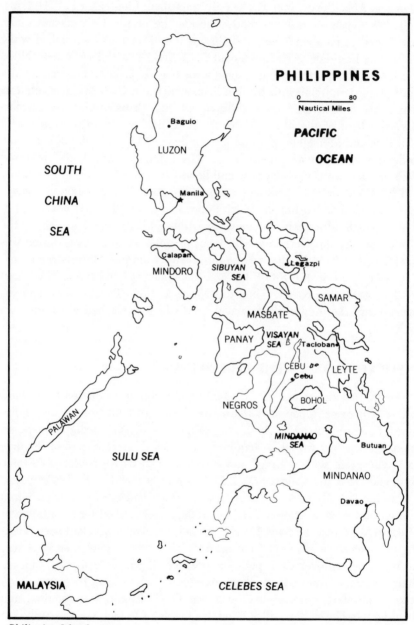

Philippine Islands

Philippines, where an improvised brigade was then converted into a real one: two rifle regiments and two artillery companies—58 officers and 1,547 enlisted men in all. Designated the 1st Marine Brigade (ancestor of an honorable line of brigades with that number), this one was rich in talent. Its battalion and company commanders included Major Elliott, Major W. P. Biddle, and Captain B. H. Fuller, not to speak of such renowned characters of the Corps as Waller. ("A most excellent officer," later reminisced one of his lieutenants,[11] "the only small man I ever knew who talked a lot about himself but who could always deliver the goods. The Marine Corps was his god. He never let you forget it.") In addition, the brigade's junior officers numbered among them Lieutenants Smedley D. Butler, David D. Porter, "Hiking Hiram" Bearss, George C. Thorpe, Louis McC. Little, and Robert H. Dunlap, to name only a few.

Marine operations in the Philippine Insurrection fell into two phases—that on Luzon, in 1899; and that on Samar, two years later. In between, the Marine brigade had part of its troops fighting Boxers in China, and the rest conducting pacification operations about Cavite and Subic Bay.

MARINES ON LUZON

The first recorded action by Marines in the Philippine Insurrection took place at Olongapo, on Subic Bay, on 23 September 1899. Seventy seagoing Marines led by Captain John T. Myers landed under gunfire support from three ships (*Concord, Baltimore,* and *Charleston*) and blew up a former Spanish coast-defense gun now most annoyingly active in the hands of "the little brown brothers."

Ten days later, under Captain H. C. Haines, 109 Marines and 24 bluejackets joined with the Army in a sweep through swamp and jungle toward Imus, south of Cavite. This action was a preliminary to more serious operations ahead.

Meanwhile the bulk of the brigade at Cavite chafed and champed. In the words of one lieutenant, Smedley D. Butler, who then and later was always ready for combat:[12]

We Marines harbored a special grudge against the 10th Pennsylvania [a silk-stocking militia regiment] who were encamped just outside the town of Cavite, between us and Filipinos. If there was a skirmish they hogged the show, and we were kept in the Navy Yard.

But an end comes to all troubles, and, in September 1899, the envied 10th

Pennsylvania struck their tents, leaving the war to the Marines.

Novaleta, between Cavite and Manila, had long been a running abscess of insurrecto activity. Set amid tidal lagoons, the principal approach to Novaleta was a long, narrow causeway. As the Spanish Army had heretofore learned to its cost, Novaleta was not easy to capture. In October the job was handed to Lieutenant Colonel G. F. Elliott, who, by virtue of the recent expansion of the Corps, had risen in about a year to this rank from the captaincy in which we saw him at Guantanamo Bay. While an Army column hooked south from Manila, Elliott's battalion, 376 strong, would beat its way into Novaleta and drive the insurrectos into the soldiers' arms. The USS *Petrel*, a gunboat, would support the attack with her 6-inchers, fire being coordinated by signal from a steam cutter lying close offshore, a very early example of naval gunfire liaison.

On 8 October 1899, Elliott's Marines hiked out of Cavite in two columns, led by Captains Ben H. Fuller and H. C. Haines ("rugged, gentle, and strikingly handsome," recalled Lieutenant Butler, who commanded one of the companies). As the Marines struggled through marsh, mangrove, and paddies, often up to their armpits in water, the Filipinos opened a withering fire. In a swirl of fighting, while the *Petrel's* shells clumped into the stronghold, the Marines carried the enemy defenses just as the Army column bored in from the flank. By noon Novaleta had fallen, and with it the heart of the south Luzon guerrilla effort. The Marines sustained 11 killed or wounded, some of the latter being barely rescued when the aid station was bushwacked from the rear at the height of the assault. "A great deal of personal bravery among officers and men was shown," reported Elliott, "even up to reckless bravado, of which I highly disapprove." The extent of the colonel's disapproval was made manifest in his report to the Commander in Chief, Asiatic Station, in which, after generously commending First Lieutenants Thorpe, Gilson, and Porter for bravery in action, he added:[13]

I respectfully request that the Admiral will admonish these young officers for bravado which might have caused a failure in carrying the fort provided these officers had been killed or wounded.

After Novaleta there remained only patrolling and pacification. For the Marine brigade this meant building up a force across Manila Bay and beyond Bataan, in Olongapo. Here, beginning in December 1899, three companies under Captain H. L. Draper chased *ladrones*, held elections, collected taxes, and gradually pacified the region. To finish the campaign, a naval expedition was sent to secure Vigan, on the northwest end of Luzon.

Headed by a company of Marines under Captain Dion Williams and the *Oregon's* detachment, commanded by First Lieutenant R. C. Berkeley, the column occupied Vigan without difficulty, as the insurgents had decamped, taking with them their lone American prisoner, a Navy lieutenant commander. His captivity cannot have been arduous, however, since Lieutenant Berkeley, detailed to close down the *cantinas* of the occupied town, picked up his chits all over Vigan, asking American liberating forces to settle his bar bills as he had run out of funds.

"STAND, GENTLEMEN, HE SERVED ON SAMAR"

The Samar campaign of 1901 included some of the most resolute and exhausting marching and fighting in the history of the Corps. Although the central role went to that "most excellent officer," Major Littleton Waller Tazewell Waller, he had a worthy supporting cast which included Gunnery Sergeant John H. Quick, hero of Guantanamo Bay, and Captains Bearss, Dunlap, and David D. Porter (". . . dashing, headstrong, full of the very Devil, and made for a leader of men," exclaimed a contemporary).[14]

In the fall of 1901 the Moros of Samar were aflame with insurrection. Parts of the 9th and 17th Infantry had proved unable to hold them down. In fact, Company C, 9th Infantry, had been caught eating breakfast at Balangiga on 28 September, and all but 26 fleeing survivors were wiped out.

In response to the Army's call for help, Major Waller's battalion, 315 officers and men, made up of companies from the 1st and 2d Regiments, was packed aboard the armored cruiser *New York* (destined, years later, as USS *Rochester*, to haul Marines to and from "banana wars" in the Caribbean), and sailed south for the scene of trouble. Waller proceeded separately with Rear Admiral Frederick Rogers, in a converted yacht, where they were joined off Samar by Brigadier General Jacob M. ("Hell Roaring Jake") Smith, USA, commanding the Army forces on Samar. The harassed island commander's orders to Major Waller were short and sharp: "I want no prisoners. I wish you to burn and kill; the more you burn and kill, the better it will please me."[15]

On 24 October, Waller landed his headquarters and two companies at Basey, just across from muddy Tacloban (on Leyte) where, 43 years later, Marine Air Group 12 would likewise support the Army. The remaining two companies, 159 men with a 3-inch landing gun and a Colt machine gun, under Captain Porter, landed at Balangiga, site of the massacre, on the opposite (south) coast of Samar. Operating in two concerted columns, the Marines were to take over and pacify southern Samar, which was entrusted to Waller's command.

During the first two weeks in November (in Waller's words) "we drove those devils from point to point," almost continually in contact along the trails, everywhere recovering Army weapons and gear and, heart-breakingly, ". . . little tokens of the 9th Infantry—photographs, cards, everything that a soldier cares for."[16]

Between 7 and 10 November, 126th Birthday of the Corps, Waller's and Porter's patrols burned 255 houses, killed 39 insurrectos, captured 18 more, destroyed a ton of hemp and a half ton of rice, and captured 50 native boats.

Under pressure from the Marines (who were frequently supported by the 4-inch guns of USS *Vicksburg*), the Moro leader, Vicente Lukban, pulled his men—who at one time numbered 3,000—back into a deep-jungle Moro stronghold in the bluffs of the Sojoton (Basey) River. Here in caves and terraces overlooking each other across the 200-foot river gorge, the natives. using captive labor, had spent years fashioning a defensive labyrinth. Hidden trails, camouflaged pits and traps, bamboo cannon, poisoned stakes, vine nets slung full of boulders—"everything that savage, treacherous minds could conceive"—encircled the tortuous approaches of the fortress. Although its existence was well known to the Spaniards, the place had never been reached by white men. Until the Sojoton fastness was penetrated and reduced, there would be no peace on Samar, and Major Waller knew it.

On 15 November 1901, Waller's battalion set out in three columns (Waller, Porter, and Bearss, who had been detached from Waller's main force). Next night all three parties bivouacked within striking distance of the objective. Before daylight Marines closed in from the river bed below and from the cliffs above. One NCO, Acting Corporal Harry Glenn, narrowly prevented the alarm from being given by snuffing out the burning fuze on a hastily lighted bamboo cannon with his bare hands.

As his machine gun clattered in support, Porter's people swept the left bank, then, in a headlong rush, crossed the river and scaled the cliffs on the opposite side—and that was that. The surviving Moros (who had gotten off only two volleys) melted into the *bosque* and resumed farming. Captains Porter and Bearss received Medals of Honor.

Now that peace of a sort reigned on Samar, General Smith ordered Waller to reconnoiter a telegraph route 52 miles across the unmapped island from Lanang to Basey on the west coast. The Marine party, besides Waller, included five officers (Captains Porter and Bearss, First Lieutenants Williams and Halford, and Second Lieutenant Lyles, USA) and 50 enlisted men with Quick as gunnery sergeant.

Setting out from Lanang three days after Christmas 1901, the expedition was dogged by disaster. Boats foundered in swollen rivers; provisions, even matches, were lost; bearers mutinied; and Marines dropped dead of fever and exhaustion, while one man went mad. To save the strongest, Waller divided the force and pushed ahead to Basey for help, leaving Porter to make the best of it with the weak. Not until 15 January 1902 were all survivors out of the bush. Ten Marines had perished.

Imperiled by repeated treachery of the Filipino guides and bearers, who were plotting to massacre the whole party, Waller convened a drumhead court at Basey on 20 January 1902. In his own words, "When I learned of the plots and heard everything, I sent them out and had them shot."[17]

All told, Waller conducted 11 summary executions in the town plaza of Basey, not only for the guides' gross betrayal of his Marines, but in reprisal for the slaughter of the 9th Infantry at Balangiga, where Moro bolo-men had ripped open the quivering entrails of butchered Army officers and poured in jam looted from the messhall.

Waller subsequently stated:[18]

Leaving Samar without the faintest suspicion of anything wrong, we reached Cavite. We looked forward to the meeting of our old friends—we expected a warm welcome home. This welcome we received from the flagship *New York*—the ship's sides were lined, and cheer after cheer went up for us. . . . I went to my Commander-in-Chief [Major General Adna R. Chaffee, USA] and was met with the charge of murder.

Literally he was. For his reprisals against "these devils," Waller, together with Lieutenant J. A. Day, was arraigned at Manila on 17 March by the U. S. Army (being, it was claimed, under Army legal jurisdiction for operations on Samar), and, on orders of General Chaffee, was tried by court-martial for murder.

To its abiding credit the Army's court under Brigadier General W. H. Bisbee, USA, a stalwart old Indian-fighter, acquitted Waller despite pressure from Chaffee, who in turn was under pressure from Washington. When Chaffee disapproved the acquittal, however, the Army Judge Advocate General threw the whole proceeding out as illegal, since Waller and his battalion had never been detached for service with the Army by order of the President. Even so, the episode unjustly shadowed the career of a fighting officer and was later given as an excuse for Waller's failure to become Commandant. As for the merits of the charge, Waller's own statement in the teeth of his accusers speaks for itself:[19]

As the representative officer responsible for the safety and welfare of my men, after investigation and from the information I had, I ordered the 11 men shot. I thought I was right then, I believe now I was right. Whatever may happen to me, I have the sure knowledge that my people know, and I believe the world knows, that I am not a murderer.

Even Chaffee, in a message to the War Department, reporting Major Waller's acquittal, commented:[20]

. . . impossible convey in words correct idea difficulties met with by officers in prosecution this war, nor can President fully comprehend that very much necessary success would have failed of accomplishment had not serious measures been used. . . . Some officers have doubtless failed in exercise due discretion, blood grown hot in their dealings with deceit and lying, hence severity some few occasions. . . . Waller acquitted by court.

In recognition of the ghastly ordeal of the Samar battalion, with its crown of persecution which followed so close on the victory of the Sojoton, it later became a custom in the messes of the brigade to drink a toast—standing— whenever one of the surviving officers of the Samar battalion was present: "*Stand, gentlemen, he served on Samar.*"

PHILIPPINE EPILOGUE

After the Samar campaign the Marine brigade was concentrated at Olongapo, with the exception of outlying detachments in southern Cavite and, curiously, several squad-sized outposts guarding lighthouses throughout the archipelago.

By 1905, when the Army finished its last serious fighting in Mindanao, the Philippines were pacified. The Marine brigade was thereupon set to work at base development in and about Subic Bay which, as Dewey had discerned in 1898, was the key to Manila Bay itself.

When Japan and the United States nearly went to war in 1907, the crisis speeded fortification of Subic Bay. On 1 July 1907, Washington cabled priority orders for the Marines to emplace 35 naval guns of 6-inch, 4.7-inch, and 3-inch caliber, stored at Cavite, for the defense of Subic Bay. Most of the guns were to be dug in on Grande Island.

At the height of the typhoon season the brigade sweated and slid, night and day, through jungle muck, setting in the pedestal-mount guns on massive timber advance-base platforms sunk below ground. During less than two months 30 inches of rain fell. As the climax, the first gun to be installed —a 4.7-incher taken from the rearmed *Albany*—blew up on the first round, killing one Marine and wounding several others. The rest of the guns, however, worked all right.

This employment of Marines for base-defense reflected the European practice by which, even today, foreign marines act as coast artillery troops. A feature of the 1894-96 attack on the Corps had been the proposition that it be transferred to the Army as a "Corps of Marine Artillery," and in those days even the Navy thought of Marines only as base-defense troops for the Fleet.

In any case, such was the final role of the Marine brigade at Olongapo, until, in 1914, when trouble hovered over the Caribbean, the brigade disbanded and its remaining duties were taken over by Marine Barracks, Olongapo.

"HELL IN CHINA"

As 1900 dawned, China was swept by a movement against the reigning dynasty on the part of groups—traditionally known as "Yao rebels"—who believed that they had been made invulnerable by sorcery and incantation. Although this uprising was initially against the regime, it was deflected by the Manchu leaders toward foreigners, and North China was soon convulsed by a surge of antiforeignism. Screaming mobs, determined to kill every Westerner, were egged on by a Yao society whose title, "The Fist of Righteous Amity," was translated by Americans and English into "Boxers."

On 28 May 1900, Boxers burned several railroad stations on the Belgian-built line between Peking and Paotingfu. Next day they hit Fengtai, principal junction below Peking, and destroyed the Imperial Railway shops there. In belated alarm the foreign legations in Peking telegraphed for help (the American Minister had already done so on 18 May), and the Asiatic squadrons of the great powers raised steam and set course for North China.

The first United States ship to reach Taku Bar, the Yellow Sea roadstead 40 miles down-river from Tientsin, was the USS *Newark*, a protected cruiser, which knifed through the Gulf of Chihli at her full 19 knots, and anchored on 27 May. The *Newark* carried a double-strength complement of Marines. On 24 May, while foreign ships lying at Nagasaki were helping the British celebrate Queen Victoria's 81st birthday, a signal had flashed to the USS *Oregon* to transfer 25 Marines and one officer to the *Newark* for service ashore in China. First Lieutenant R. C. Berkeley, who had redeemed the captive lieutenant commander's chits in Vigan, was alerted for the expedition when

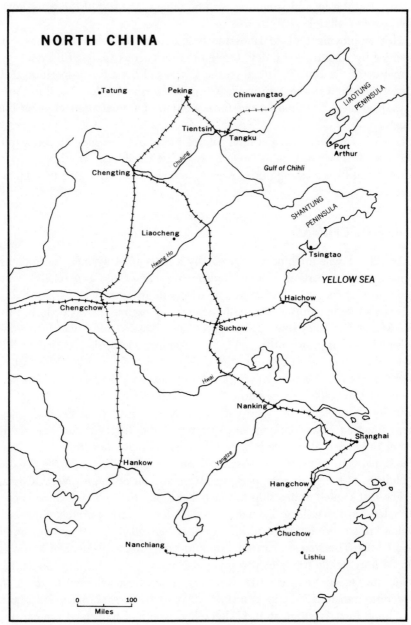

NORTH CHINA

North China

a second signal arrived, detailing the detachment commander, Captain John T. Myers, by name. Since "Handsome Jack" was in the midst of a guest night aboard HMS *Endymion,* Lieutenant Berkeley "had to send over to the British ship and break Captain Myers out of the party," as he later reminisced. Now, at Taku, Myers, senior to the *Newark's* captain of Marines, Newt H. Hall, was readying the combined detachments for landing.

From the *Newark's* quarter-deck the shore was barely in sight. Except for a French cruiser and gunboat, and three Chinese men-of-war, the dreary anchorage was empty. "A more desolate anchorage than off Taku," wrote one of the cruiser's junior officers, "cannot be imagined. The wide expanse of greenish-yellow water is depressing."[21]

At 0400, 29 May, Captain McCalla of the *Newark*—last seen at Guantanamo Bay—sent off 48 Marines under Myers and Hall, a 3-inch landing gun with bluejacket crew, a Colt machine gun, and Assistant Surgeon T. M. Lippett, USN, the *Newark's* junior medico. Following three hours later, as soon as the sailormen could wrestle themselves into white leggings and heavy marching order, were four naval officers, 60 seamen, and another machine gun.

Having joined forces at Tangku, inside the river bar, under personal command of Captain McCalla, the American column, traveling in junks towed by a commandeered steam tug, finally reached Tientsin at 2300 that night where the foreign colony had been waiting for them with a brass band. Among the welcomers was a 25-year-old American mining engineer, Mr. Herbert Hoover, who later recalled:[22]

I do not remember a more satisfying musical performance than the bugles of the American Marines [*sic*] entering the settlement playing "There'll Be a Hot Time in the Old Town Tonight."

The first foreign troops to arrive, they were billeted in Temperance Hall, ordinarily dedicated to an arid cause the futility of which has never been more often underscored than on the China station.

At Tientsin it was obvious that troops must push on to Peking despite stalling by the Chinese railroad authorities. Meanwhile, British, Austrian, German, French, Italian, Japanese, and Russian landing forces followed the Americans into Tientsin.

On 31 May, after considerable presssure (including a British threat to hang the Tientsin stationmaster), a train for Peking was arranged. On this entrained Captains Myers and Hall, Surgeon Lippett, the 48 Marines, five bluejackets, and the better of the two Colt guns with 8,000 rounds, plus 372 rounds per man. In addition to the U. S. Marines, this train and one other which followed carried 79 red-coated British Marines, 75 French sailors, 72 Russian sailors, 51 German Marines, 30 Austrian Marines, 39 Italian sailors, and 24 Japanese Special Naval Landing Force. Aside from individual weapons and the U. S. Marines' machine gun, the mixed trainload included an Italian one-pounder, an Austrian Mannlicher machine gun, and "an old-fashioned, clumsy" Nordenfelt machine gun belonging to the British. In some confusion, the Russians stowed a thousand rounds of ammunition for their field gun aboard the train, then forgot the gun.

All told, the troops bound for Peking numbered 22 officers and 423 enlisted men—for comparison, a force about the size of that on Wake in 1941.[23] They had no over-all commander. As they debarked that evening at Peking's "fire-cart stopping place," they were met not only by relieved representatives of the legations, but also by thousands of silent Chinese. "The dense mass which thronged either side of the roadway," reported Captain Myers from Peking, "seemed more ominous than a demonstration of hostility would have been."[24]

THE SEYMOUR EXPEDITION

By 10 June 1900 it was clear that the legations in Peking would need much more help. Boxers had severed the railroad to Tientsin; the last train had inched through on 5 June. Peking was cut off.

Meanwhile, Captain McCalla's bluejacket contingent at Tientsin had been reinforced by 50 more sailors and a couple of squads of Marines under a first sergeant. The whole eight-nation force in Tientsin now numbered 2,500. Senior officer present, and thus *de facto* commander in chief, was Vice Admiral Sir Edward Seymour, RN.

On 9 June, after a long-winded council of war, old Bowman McCalla faced the assembled senior officers and consuls at Tientsin and announced, "I don't care what the rest of you do. I have 112 men here, and I'm going tomorrow morning to the rescue of my own flesh and blood in Peking. I'll be damned if I sit here 90 miles away and just wait."[25]

That did it. Next day, leaving behind a detachment to protect Tientsin, Admiral Seymour, with McCalla second-in-command, set out for Peking, trying to repair the railroad as the column plodded forward, British and Americans in the van. The most essential man in the force soon proved to be a U. S. Navy coal-passer who had once been a section hand. He was the only man out of 2,129 who could set out a fishplate and spike down a rail.

Within a week the column—five trains in all—had made 65 miles and was at Langfang, only 25 miles from the besieged capital, but was in serious trouble. Harried by Boxers and by Imperial soldiers who had now joined in, the would-be rescuers had the choice of retreat or annihilation. At Anping, which was to be a place of ill omen for Marines 46 years later, the column turned back, abandoning its trains at a wrecked bridge.

From 18 to 22 June, Seymour and McCalla (the latter aboard a white mule) slogged back toward Tientsin while the red-scarved Boxers slashed at them from behind village walls and burial mounds. Finally, with more than 200 wounded, the force could neither retreat nor advance. In a last effort, the Royal Marines, supported by the Germans and Americans, carried the strongly fortified Hsi-ku Arsenal six miles north of Tientsin. Here, safe for the moment, they holed up with ample food, modern weapons, and sorely needed medical supplies, all inadvertently provided by the Chinese government. Of McCalla's 112, thirty-two were killed or wounded, including McCalla himself, thrice wounded. By percentage the small American contingent sustained almost twice as many casualties as any other in the force.

"BRAVE HEARTS AND BRIGHT WEAPONS"

First Lieutenant Smedley D. Butler, age just 20, wrote to his mother:[26]

Well, here we are about 200 miles from our destination and steaming 15 knots or about 17 miles an hour. We expect to arrive about noon tomorrow, but I doubt if we land until the next day. We were ordered away from Cavite in such a hurry that I did not have time to drop thee even a line so I asked Dunlap to send thee a note telling of our departure. To lead thee up to the situation as it now stands, I shall begin at the beginning. There has been a revolution in China, as nearly as we can make out, and all the European Powers have landed their Marines and bluejackets, and we are to represent the great American Republic. . . . It is needless to say that I am the happiest man alive and that for the last few days my feet have not touched the ground at all. . . .

Lieutenant Butler, far from his Quaker home in Pennsylvania, was in the Yellow Sea, aboard the USS *Solace*, with 106 Marines ("a very fine body of men") including two extra "that had sneaked aboard in the dark." These men, with eight officers, were the first American reinforcements which could be sent from the Philippines; they had been gloomily mounting out for Guam, under command of Major Waller, when the emergency diverted them to China.

As Lieutenant Butler recounted:[27]

Major Waller came ashore at 4.45 p.m. and told me that Company A was the one chosen for the expedition and that I was to go in command of it. He told me that I was to get the company ready by 8.45 that same night. For a while I seemed dazed and then it dawned on me and we all began preparations. Peter Wynn and myself first went out to the quarters and set all the men wild by the news and in my short but eventful life I have never seen such a howling mob. We then went back and packed ourselves and at 8.15 p.m. I started for the quarters to bring the company down to the boat. That was pretty quick work when you consider that I took out half an hour for dinner.

Following embarkation the ship sailed for Taku on 14 June. Hours later, the U. S. Minister in Peking got word through to Washington that the foreigners in Peking:[28]

... have been completely besieged within our compounds with the entire city in the possession of a rioting, murdering mob, with no visible effort being made by the Government in any way to restrain it. . . . In no intelligent sense can there be said to be in existence any Chinese government whatsoever.

Five days later, at 0330, Waller's Marines debarked, reinforced by 30 more Marines from the USS *Nashville*, armed with a 3-inch landing gun and a Colt machine gun. With the rough-and-ready help of machinist's mates and water tenders from the Civil War gunboat *Monocacy*, Waller coaxed a Chinese train back to life, loaded it with spare ties, rails, and Marines, and chugged from Tangku toward Tientsin. Repairing track as they advanced, the Marines joined forces with a battalion of 440 Russian infantry halted 12 miles short of Tientsin.

At 0200 on 20 June, within earshot of Chinese guns now shelling Tientsin, the Marines and the white-bloused, booted Russians resumed the advance. By seven they were in the outskirts of Tientsin, under heavy fire and counterattack by more than 1,500 Boxers and Imperial troops. This was more than the Russians—or, for that matter, the Marines—could stand, and with Major Waller covering the retirement, the forces disengaged.

The withdrawal was signalized by the rescue of a wounded Marine, inadvertently left behind, by a rear guard consisting of Lieutenants Butler and A. E. Harding and four enlisted Marines. Under continual Chinese pursuit and fire, by cavalry and artillery, the six Marines carried the wounded man seven miles without a stretcher. All four enlisted rescuers (two of whom were themselves wounded) got Medals of Honor. Since officers were not eligible to receive the Medal of Honor in those days, Butler and Harding were both brevetted captain for gallantry.

By nightfall, having hiked 30 miles, fought all day on nothing but hard-tack, and sustained 13 killed or wounded, Waller's battalion was back where it started, on the railroad 12 miles from Tientsin. Here, within two days there accumulated some 2,000 British, Russians, Germans, Italians, and Japanese. Waller now made common cause with the 600-man British naval contingent headed by Commander Christopher Cradock, RN, who was destined, as a rear admiral, to go down bravely in 1914 with his squadron at Coronel. On the 23d, at 0330, the column moved out, and in Butler's words:[29]

... after a terrible march in the face of a sand storm, and very severe fighting, we entered [Tientsin] about 1:30 p.m. ... I forgot to say that while crossing a bridge the Chinese exploded a mine under us, but outside of being plastered with mud and stones, none of us were hurt. Am well except toothache and sore feet.

The Marines led the way up Tientsin's Victoria Road with colors flying, while grateful Europeans, saved for the second time, plied the troops with beer.

After the rescue of Tientsin's foreign concessions, two jobs demanded immediate action: (1) relief of Admiral Seymour's column still besieged in Hsi-ku Arsenal (known to later China Marines as the French Arsenal); and (2) reduction of the fast-strengthening Boxer stronghold within Tientsin's walled Chinese City. Here Western-trained Chinese had mounted modern cannon on the walls and maintained a steady fire on the foreign concessions a mile or so distant.

On 25 June, after moving out before dawn, the relieving force reached Hsi-ku Arsenal, raised the siege, ". . . said goodbye to the Boxers by setting fire to the Arsenal" (related Butler), and "marched back to Tientsin loaded down with souvenirs." In addition, however, they brought in some 300 of Seymour's sick and wounded, including McCalla, who for once was glad to turn over command to Major Waller, who thereby became the American commander in chief ashore in North China.

But more Marines were on the way. Under mustachioed old Colonel Robert L. Meade, veteran of the abortive assault on Fort Sumter and of the Panama expedition in 1885, the remainder of the 1st Regiment at Cavite had embarked in the cruiser *Brooklyn,* and were at Taku Bar on 10 July. Meade brought one more infantry battalion, regimental headquarters, and an artillery company (three 3-inch landing guns and three Colts)—318 Marines in all.

Meanwhile, Waller's Marines in Tientsin had been in another fight. As a preliminary to a showdown with the Boxers in the Chinese City, the Tientsin East Arsenal (not to be confused with Hsi-ku Arsenal), held by some 7,000 Boxers, had to be captured. Cradock and the Russians determined to do the job and asked for Waller's help. This was given with alacrity, and, on 27 June, Russian soldiers, British sailors, and British and U. S. Marines (the latter led by First Lieutenant Harding) charged the parapets, and the East Arsenal was captured.

Taking a needed breather while the thoroughly alarmed powers built up their forces for the campaign ahead, Waller reported on operations to date:[30]

Our men have marched 97 miles in five days, fighting all the way. They have lived on one meal a day for six days, but they have been cheerful and willing always. They have gained the highest praise from all present, and have earned my love and confidence. They are like Falstaff's army in appearance, but with brave hearts and bright weapons. . . .

On the outside of this report, Waller scribbled to the captain of the *Monocacy*:

Captain Wise—Please open and read and add Russian casualties, 2 killed, 9 wounded. I need whiskey.

L.W.T.W.

Forwarding Waller's report, Rear Admiral Kempff, who commanded the China Squadron, added a resounding plaudit:[31]

I would suggest a suitable medal for Major Waller and five percent additional pay for life in various grades he may reach. . . . It is with our Marines under Major Waller as with the force under Captain McCalla—foreign officers have only the highest praise for their fighting qualities.

". . . AND SAINT DAVID"

The world's excitement over the plight of Peking and Tientsin was intense, and, while the Marines and sailors on the spot were doing their best, reinforcements streamed towards Taku.

The first substantial American force to augment the Marines was the 9th Infantry, which reached China on 6 July. The 9th was immediately sent up to Tientsin via the railroad which was now being operated by the bluejackets of the *Monocacy*.

Four days later, Colonel Meade's contingent of the 1st Marines followed. This gave the United States a brigade at Tientsin—1st Marines (including Waller's battalion), 9th Infantry (1st and 2d Battalions only), all commanded by Colonel Meade, senior U. S. officer present. This American force (about

1,000 officers and men) was brigaded with the 2,200-man British column made up of Ghurkas, Sikhs, Bengal Lancers, 2d Battalion, Royal Welch Fusiliers, and Royal Navy and Marines. All told, the foreign powers now mustered 5,650 troops before Tientsin, of whom more than half were British and American, the remainder being French, German, Japanese, and Russian.

In a council of war the respective commanders agreed that the next step was to clean out Tientsin's native city, with its 50,000 Boxers, and that this would be done on 13 July.

The native city was ringed by two walls—a 30-foot outer wall, relic of the Taiping Rebellion, and, about a mile inside, the stone city wall proper, 24 feet thick and likewise 30 feet high. On the latter the Chinese mounted the cannon with which they continued to shell the foreign concessions. Allied counterbattery fire came mainly from five British 12-pounder naval guns brought ashore, from HMS *Terrible*. These had, earlier in 1900, been hammered together on boiler-plate carriages and hauled across South Africa for the defense of Ladysmith.

At 0300, 13 July, under command of British Brigadier General A. R. F. Dorward, DSO, the American, British, and Japanese forces attacked the south face of the native city. The Marines had the left flank; on their right were the Royal Welch Fusiliers; still further right were the 9th Infantry (in support of the British naval brigade). Mr. Hoover, so he later related, accompanied the Marines "as a sort of guide in their part of the attack on the Chinese City."[32] The heat was suffocating (temperatures of 140 degrees Fahrenheit were recorded within the next fortnight), and the terrain between the two walls consisted of rice paddies, huge salt mounds, Chinese graves, and muck from sewage canals. Second Lieutenant Frederic M. Wise (son of the old *Monocacy's* captain) later wrote:[33]

> The sky was turning slightly grey. Chinese snipers across the river began to fire as fast as they could pull the trigger. Now they were shooting into our backs. We marched on, pouring out onto that plain. Snipers on our side of the river, behind those salt mounds, took up the chorus. Artillery began to blaze from the walls. . . .

Lieutenant Butler related:[34]

> We charged over the mud wall at seven in the morning and began our advance. The whole country was flooded. The Chinese had diverted the water from the canals into the open space between the two walls. We struggled through this filthy swamp, with bullets splashing and whining around us. The low mud walls of the rice paddies provided some slight protection. We crouched behind them, firing furiously, slipping, sliding, and stumbling from one to another.

George Barnett, 12th Commandant of the Marine Corps, 1914–1920.

John A. Lejune, 13th
Commandant of
the Marine Corps,
1920–1929.

Thomas A. Holcomb,
17th Commandant of
the Marine Corps,
1936–1943.

Alexander A. Vandergrift,
18th Commandant of
the Marine Corps,
1944–1947.

Clifton B. Cates,
19th Commandant of the
Marine Corps, 1948–1951.

Lemuel C. Shepherd, 20th Commandant of the Marine Corps, 1952–1955.

Butler's company, as well as some of the Welch Fusiliers, made it to the stone wall. There they were stopped and Butler was wounded in the thigh—"as pretty a hole as you ever saw." Sustained by brandy from a British offi-cer's canteen, and aided by First Lieutenant Henry Leonard (who lost an arm shortly after), he made it back to the field hospital.

While the rifle companies of the 1st Regiment and the Royal Welch Fusiliers were thrashing through mud and debris, the artillery company, under Captain B. H. Fuller, went into position behind the mud wall. Here the 3-inch landing guns opened fire on the stone wall and the Chinese City itself. This fire soon drew attention from the Chinese 4.7-inch Krupp guns, whose counterbattery proved so effective that the Marine battery had to shift position. After firing all ammunition—in a tradition that would dis-tinguish Marine artillery on many another battlefield—the battery reformed as infantry to shore up the right flank of the 9th Infantry, who were in trouble. For the rest of the day Captain Fuller screened the 9th and that evening covered their withdrawal, an action which the 9th's report gen-erously mentioned as follows:[35]

Our final withdrawal was handsomely covered by the British naval troops and United States Marines sent to our aid by General Dorward. These gallant men also aided us in the removal of our wounded.

By eight that night, after a day of inconclusive action under intense though inaccurate fire, all hands pulled back behind the outer wall, and the operation was no further ahead than at dawn. Of 451 Marines engaged, 21 had become casualties, including four officers (Captain A. R. Davis, killed; Captain W. B. Lemly and Lieutenants Leonard and Butler, wounded). The 9th Infantry, which never got beyond the mud wall, suffered more heavily (18 killed, 77 wounded). Worse still, their gallant commander, Colonel E. H. Liscum, USA, was killed with the regimental colors in his hands. His last words were, "Keep up the fire!"

Before dawn next day, the Japanese broke the stalemate. In a skilful night attack, they blew in the gate of the Chinese City and swarmed through. By daybreak the whole allied force was inside, sweeping the Boxers before them. The native city was afire, and looting was rampant.

"Soldiers of all nations joined the orgy," wrote Lieutenant Wise. "Men of the allies staggered through the streets, arms and backs piled high with silks and furs and brocades, with gold and silver and jewels."[36] As the ashes cooled, Marines guarded the yamen of the salt commissioner, where $800,000 in melted silver bullion clotted the wreckage. In reporting this trove to Washington, Admiral Remey, the Asiatic Station commander stated (a little gratuitously), "My obtainable information clears Marines of any imputation burning houses or looting Tientsin."[37]

A by-product of the fighting on the 13th was the friendship which forthwith sprang up between the 1st Marines and the Royal Welch Fusiliers (a regiment which had fought at Bunker Hill and Yorktown). Ever since the Boxer Uprising, it has been the annual custom of the two corps that, on St. David's Day (1 March), the national holiday of Wales, the Commandant of the Marine Corps and the Colonel of the Royal Welch exchange the traditional watchword of Wales—". . . and Saint David!"

THE DEFENSE OF THE LEGATIONS

While turmoil reigned from Taku to Tientsin, Peking, in the eye of the storm, remained ominously calm. On 20 June, however, the Chinese government, in answer to the Allied bombardment and landings at Taku, dropped its pretended neutrality and demanded that the foreign legations pack up and leave Peking within 24 hours. On his way to the foreign office to protest this impossible demand, the German Minister, Baron von Ketteller, was shot down by an Imperial Chinese soldier.

Precisely 24 hours after delivery of the ultimatum, Chinese troops opened fire on the Austrian and French lines. The French replied with a volley. The siege of the legations had begun.

All foreigners, including some 300 women and children, were concentrated in the British, Russian, American, German, Japanese, and French Legation compounds. The area, comprising the Legation Quarter, was bounded on the south and dominated by the immense Tartar Wall, 60 feet high and 40 feet wide. The American Legation lay in the shadow of the wall, as did the German compound just east. Thus the key to the American sector was the Tartar Wall which, for the next eight weeks, was in the hands of the U. S. Marines. "Captain Myers's post on the wall," the British Minister would soon write, "is the peg which holds the whole thing together."[38]

The immediate efforts of the besieged foreigners were to erect barricades and to get in provisions. The latter, fortunately, posed no problems in most respects. More than 150 ponies, assembled for a race-meeting, guaranteed fresh meat; the Peking Hotel's ample cellars included more than a thousand cases of Dry Monopole champagne and vast stores of anchovy paste. Such bonanzas, however, fell somewhat short of making up for the Russians' forgetfulness in leaving their field gun on the station platform at Tientsin.

The first sortie was on 23 June, to clear out the burning Hanlin Yuan (". . . at once the Oxford and Cambridge, the Heidelberg and Sorbonne of the 18 provinces of China rolled into one," observed a civilian diarist), which the Boxers had ruthlessly set afire in an attempt to burn out the neighboring British Legation. As this noble academy perished, taking with it half the recorded culture of China, British and U. S. Marines assaulted through the flames to drive off Boxers who were interrupting bucket brigades trying to dowse the fire with chamber pots full of water.

Next evening the Boxers again probed with fire. Outbuildings south of

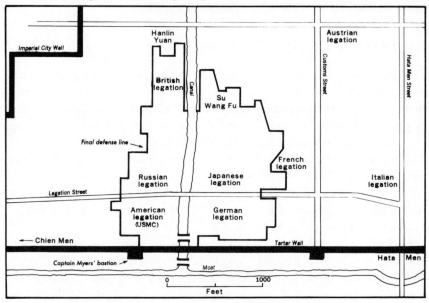

Defense of the Legations, Peking, 21 June to 14 August 1900

the British Legation were touched off, and brands were rolled to one gate of the British compound. In the counterattack which had to follow, Captain Halliday, the Royal Marines' commanding officer, was desperately wounded, shot through shoulder and lung, but still Marine enough to drop three Chinese with his revolver while covering his people's withdrawal, and then to stagger under his own power to the hospital—a feat which won him the Victoria Cross.

Taking advantage of the excitement in the British sector, Captain Myers, who had gotten up a barricade facing west toward the Chien Men (*Men* means "gate" in Mandarin), led a party of Marines forward along the wall. Before long he hit resistance in force. One foreign observer estimated that 2,000 Chinese were massed behind six successive barricades with "several big guns." This showed the power confronting the American position—"29 men against the Chinese Army," Myers subsequently reported[39] in a scrawled chit to Sir Claude MacDonald, the British Minister, who had been elected commander in chief. Needless to say, Myers took no ground that night; but, more important, he lost none.

The Marines' position across "the Wall"—as everyone called it—opened on its immediate south (left) front into a huge bastion, 40 yards across, overgrown with grass and brush from years of neglect. A ramp, inside the American lines, led up to Myers's barricade. Down the wall, to the west, with a corresponding ramp, a Chinese barricade confronted the Marines. Five hundred yards in Myers's rear, facing toward Hata Men, another gate, to the east, the German Marines had a barricade manned by about 15 men. On both Hata Men and Chien Men towers, the Chinese had observation posts, and cannon which shelled the American and German positions. Altogether, a tight spot, but, as Myers reported to American Minister E. H. Conger, "We will hold out until I give out."[40]

On 27 June, in broad daylight, Boxers attacked the American rampart. The Colt gun clattered away, the Lee rifles cracked, and the Chinese fell back, leaving more than half their number to augment the accumulated "human and equine carrion" about the lines. "So long as the Americans can hold the Wall," noted one diarist, "I think our Legations will be in no very serious danger."

The next night, although Myers's barricade was again probed, it was the Germans' turn to receive the Chinese main effort. At dawn on 1 July the Germans discovered that the Chinese had placed three guns in embrasures immediately facing them. Shortly after, under heavy shellfire, the German detachment, which had only a corporal in command, took flight. What was worse, they signaled to the Marines in their rear, facing the other way, that they had been overrun. By prearrangement the Americans withdrew, abandoning the Wall for a lower barricade covering the ramp.

Captain Myers was not the man to submit, however, and, after obtaining reinforcements from the British Marines, counterattacked. The rush succeeded, and, with three casualties, the American position was retaken. The Germans, however, were less successful and had to be content with an intermediate holding position instead of the one they had yielded. Meanwhile the Marines built a barricade of their own across the Wall to their rear.

By now, Myers was completely worn out. He had taken to himself the responsibility of the Wall, leaving to Newt Hall the less arduous posts guarding the American compound below. For more than five days he had gone without sleep. After reoccupying the Wall on 1 July, he was ordered by Sir Claude MacDonald to turn over his post to Hall and go below for sleep. This he did, and Captain Hall thereupon assumed command of the upper barricade, with a curious written order from Minister Conger. In writing, the American Minister threatened to prefer charges against Hall ". . . if you leave until you are absolutely *driven out*."[41] A strange order, and one which would become part of an equally strange dossier against Hall.

Just 24 hours later, at dusk on 2 July, Myers returned to his barricades and resumed command. In his absence the Chinese had been permitted to score an ominous gain—by advancing their wall 40 yards across the open front of the no-man's bastion which flanked both Chinese and American barricades, they were now within a few feet of the left (south) end of the U. S. position, and had just erected a 15-foot tower overlooking it.

Here was a turning point. If foreign troops expected to stay on the Tartar Wall, the Chinese would have to be ejected. At 0130, in a heavy rainstorm, Captain Myers collected 30 of his own people, 26 British Marines, and 15 Russian sailors. At the simple command, "Go!" the attack jumped off, Myers leading the Anglo-American main effort against the bastion and tower, the Russians making a secondary attack on the right.

Luck was with Myers. The Chinese had failed to man their tower, and by following the Boxer barricade across the bastion, Myers was able to lead his party into the rear of the enemy position, where the Chinamen were still blazing into the darkness to their front. Though Myers was wounded by a Chinese spear, the attack succeeded completely. Within a half hour the Boxer barricade, reversed, was the new front line. Thirty-six Chinese lay dead, and two flags were taken. Total Allied casualties: two U. S. Marines killed (". . . two of the best men in the Guard," noted Myers), one wounded (Myers); one Royal Marine and one Russian, wounded.

Small as this night attack may seem, it proved to be a turning point.

"The bravest and most successful event of the whole siege was an attack led by Captain Myers," reported Minister Conger.[42]

"This has been the only effectual offensive measure accomplished during the siege," wrote one diarist. ". . . It eventually proved to be one of the most important factors in the successful conduct of the siege and turned our precarious foothold on the Wall into a sound defensible position," noted another. "The pivot of our destiny," said still a third.

"Perhaps the most critical situation during the siege," stated Halliday (who survived his wound to become a lieutenant general and Adjutant-General, Royal Marines). Other Royal Marines thought so, too, and the bronze bas-relief commemorating the British Marines' role at Peking depicts this combined assault with the figure of Myers conspicuous to the front—a very pretty tribute.

His victory very nearly finished Captain Myers, however, for his wound became badly infected and worse still (as with Surgeon Lippett, also wounded in the leg, on 29 June), he came down with typhoid. This left the U. S. Marines under command of Captain Hall.

THE CASE OF CAPTAIN HALL

Here we are confronted by an unresolved mystery. Was Captain Newt H. Hall guilty of cowardice at Peking, or, as some delicately put it, "overcaution"?

Civilians in Peking pointed out after the siege that Hall had served below while Myers wore himself out on the Wall; that the Chinese had been permitted to advance their barricade across the bastion in a single day while Hall spelled Myers; that Minister Conger had admonished Hall against leaving the Wall until (these were the very words) ". . . absolutely *driven out*." Typical of the talk against Hall within the besieged legations (where Myers was liked and admired, and Hall was not) was the diary entry by Dr. G. E. Morrison, the *London Times* correspondent, who took a leading part in the defense:[43]

10 July—Today on the Wall there were 13 men under Captain Hall. He is never put on the Wall, his men having no confidence in his judgment. He has no control over his men. . . .

Still other charges circulated that he had hesitated to lead his men forward over the barricade on the final day when relief was in sight.

Ugly talk it was. And when the relief did take place, this talk came quickly to the ear of General Chaffee, commanding all United States forces in China. Chaffee immediately detailed his inspector-general, Captain (later Major General) William Crozier, a hero of the relieving assault, to look into this. Crozier's investigation, completed within 12 days after the relief of Peking, accumulated a smog of nasty statements—virtually all by civilians—but recommended against further action. Myers, incidentally, was still too ill to testify, and his subsequent report makes little mention of Captain Hall. Chaffee approved Crozier's view, but sent the whole bundle of trouble back to General Heywood.

Charles Heywood, winner of two brevets for "distinguished gallantry in the presence of the enemy," was one of the bravest men ever to wear the globe and anchor. His comment was that Hall (his own nephew by marriage) should have been court-martialed on the spot if only for his own protection.

Hall, meanwhile, was seeking such redress. First he asked for a court-martial. General Chaffee refused. Then Hall asked Admiral Remey, Commander in Chief, Asiatic Station, to convene a court of inquiry on his conduct. This time the answer was yes.

To complicate matters, Captain McCalla, Hall's commanding officer aboard the *Newark*, neither fool nor faint heart, recommended Hall for a brevet and to be advanced ten numbers in grade for his conduct at Peking. But at almost the same time, the *Century Magazine* published a damning, widely read attack on Hall by W. N. Pethick, an American civilian who had been at Peking.

On 1 March 1901 the Hall court of inquiry convened at Cavite. After a searching investigation, which disclosed "great caution" on his part, the court cleared the unhappy captain but in terms of which no officer could be very proud—"for the reasons that he has already suffered sufficiently for the world-wide publication and criticism of his conduct in Peking."[44]

Then, as if to compound the enigma, the Secretary of the Navy approved brevets to major for both Myers and Hall (but advanced Myers four numbers in grade for "eminent and conspicuous conduct," giving no such accolade to Hall).

Finally, in a public letter on 28 August 1901, Minister Conger denied that he had ever preferred charges against Hall (which was true), said he had personally defended Hall's conduct to Chaffee and Crozier, and referred with emotion to ". . . great injustice."[45]

There the matter lies. Hall, officially cleared and stoutly defended by many friends in the Marine Corps, got his brevet, stayed on, and ultimately retired a colonel.

LAST DAYS OF THE SIEGE

After the Myers attack the defense settled into a snipers' war between the barricades. As the Chinese made more and better use of their artillery, the need for a counterbattery weapon became acute. On 7 July, an ancient cannon was found in the ruins of an ironmonger's shop. Navy Gunner's Mate Mitchell, with true bluejacket ingenuity, concluded that this muzzle-loading relic might be adapted to shoot the Russian sailors' gunless ammunition. In two days of tinkering, Mitchell mounted his find on a pair of ricksha wheels and gingerly test-fired it (whereupon the first round dismounted barrel from carriage).

Besides the Russian shells, which worked quite well, Mitchell tested it with a bag of nails: the lethal charge exceeded all hopes. The gun was at first christened "The International," but finally the appreciative troops just called it "Betsy" or "The Old Crock." "Betsy" shared honors with the Marines' machine gun, of which one Englishman noted, ". . . it has killed more men than all the rest put together."

On 15 July activity flared briefly on the Wall, where Captain Hall was building a new barricade to cover the rear (Hata Men) face of his position. Here, under heavy fire, Private Daniel Daly won his first Medal of Honor for coolly holding an advance position alone while Captain Hall went back for reinforcements.

After 16 July a kind of truce, punctuated by pot shots, prevailed until Peking was relieved on 14 August. By this time, 17 of the original 56 Marine and Navy defenders had been killed or wounded. Of the officers, Captain Hall alone was unwounded.

THE RELIEF OF PEKING

After five weeks on the way from the States, Major General Chaffee finally arrived at Tientsin on 30 July and assumed command of all United States forces. Accompanying General Chaffee were substantial reinforcements: one more battalion of Marines (from San Francisco, under Major W. P. Biddle); two battalions of the 14th Infantry; the 6th Cavalry; and Riley's Battery, 5th Artillery. By order of President Roosevelt, all Marines in China thereupon came under the Army, and, Colonel Meade having been invalided to Mare Island, Major Biddle—nicknamed "Sitting Bull" by his juniors because of his "love of a comfortable chair"—succeeded to command of the 1st Marines.

To protect Tientsin, still far from peaceful, Chaffee peeled off a detachment of six Marine officers, two Navy surgeons, and 177 enlisted men. This left the 1st Marines still with two battalions, total strength 482 (out of 2,500 U. S. troops in the Peking relief column). Counting its commanding officer, the regiment included three future Commandants: Major Biddle, Captain W. C. Neville, and Captain B. H. Fuller. The regimental surgeon, a veteran of the fighting on Samoa in 1899, had the highly suggestive name of Lung.

On 3 August the 18,600-man international column set out for Peking. Although there were two Boxer stands (one at Pei-Tsang, the other at Yang-Tsun), the main enemy was the heat. As Lieutenant Butler related:[46]

> There was no shade, not a drop of rain, nor a breath of air. The cavalry and the artillery kicked up clouds of dust which beat back in our faces. The blistering heat burned our lungs. Nearly 50 percent of our men fell behind during the day, overcome by the sun. In the cool of the night they would catch up with us and start on again next morning. Our throats were parched, our tongues thick. We were cautioned not to drink the water, but no orders could keep us from anything that was liquid.

Ten days later the column reached the eastern outskirts of Peking. When the legation guards heard machine guns (which the Chinese didn't have), they knew Western troops were at hand. Throughout the 14th, the successive walls of Peking fell before American, British, and Japanese assaults. The 14th Infantry led the attack, and theirs were the first colors in the relieving force to be unfurled on the walls of Peking. As Chaffee had assigned the 2d Battalion, 1st Marines, the inglorious role of guarding the American pack train, only the 1st Battalion was in the forefront of the battle, where it covered Riley's Battery in breaching the Chien Men.

For political reasons, General Chaffee was compelled to check the American assault short of the Forbidden City, which had never been entered by foreigners. Since organized resistance was over anyway, it remained only for the relief force to go into billets. The 1st Regiment was assigned the southwest quarter of the Tartar City, with Major Waller as Provost Marshal. Regimental headquarters occupied the Palace of the Eighth Prince, an accession which one officer described as follows:[47]

> It was the usual Chinese succession of quadrangular courtyards with buildings on all four sides. The men were alloted sleeping quarters in some of the buildings. Officers took others. Yet another was converted into a galley where the men's food was cooked, and they ate. The courtyard, paved with flagstone, was drill ground and recreation hall. . . .

By noon we were all established, sentries posted, Officer of the Day appointed, the Marine Corps routine in full swing.

To underscore, for Chinese benefit, the moral of the campaign, it was decided that, on 28 August, a representative column of foreign troops should march across the Forbidden City to erase its legendary inviolability by foreigners. The Marine Corps contingent was one company from each battalion, 1st Marines; the company commanders, respectively, were Captain Neville and Lieutenant Butler, who wrote home:[48]

This is the first time within the memory of man when such a march occurred and it certainly was a wonderful sight to see Russian, Japanese, English, American, French, German, Italian, and Austrian troops marching in the order named in one column. We went through all the holy temples and palaces where foreigners have never set foot before.

As the last troops cleared the north gate, a 21-gun salute proclaimed the fall of the Forbidden City.

After a month of oddly mixed looting and policing, affairs in North China were quiet enough to allow the Marines to return to the Philippines, where General MacArthur (the elder) badly needed troops. On 3 October the 1st Regiment marched south from Peking and on 10 October sailed for Cavite in the *Brooklyn* and two transports, the *Zafiro* and *Indiana*.

Considering the heavy Chinese fire, all casualties, including those of the Marines, had been light. Probably the most noteworthy was that sustained by Lieutenant Butler (his second in the campaign): a bullet hit him in the chest and clipped off part (South America) of the Marine Corps emblem tattooed over his heart.

As the Marines marched out of Peking, General Chaffee shipped the Marine defenders' homemade cannon to the museum at West Point, and, on orders from Secretary of War Elihu Root, established a company of the 9th Infantry as the U. S. Legation Guard—an act which evoked a protest to the Secretary of the Navy from General Heywood:[49]

It has always been the custom to furnish guards for the legations in a foreign country from Marines, and this custom has not been departed from until the present guard at the legation in China was established, which was furnished by the Army. Army troops are never supposed to be sent to a foreign country except in time of war, and, for this reason, legation guards and other guards required in foreign countries have always been furnished by the Marine Corps. It is respectfully submitted that it is eminently proper that the guard to be kept at the legation in Pekin should be furnished by the Marine Corps.

Regardless of Heywood's reclama, Marines had to wait until 12 September 1905, five years almost to the day after the relief of Peking, before (at the specific request of American Minister W. W. Rockhill) a Marine detachment resumed the guard, thus restoring the safety of the American Legation to the Corps which had preserved it in time of trouble.

A NEW COMMANDANT

On 3 October 1903, Charles Heywood retired as Major General Commandant—the first major general in the history of the Corps, so promoted by special legislation in July 1902. At the same time, Congress increased the strength of the Corps by 750 enlisted men, bringing its total strength to 201 officers and 6,812 enlisted. These figures were further increased the following year. Taking a last look at the Corps in his final report, General Heywood gave himself a fully justified pat on the back:[50]

> Considering the fact that at the time I assumed command of the Marine Corps on 30 January 1891, it consisted of but 75 officers and 2,100 enlisted men, stationed at 11 posts in the United States and on board ships in commission, and that the Corps now [1903] consists of 278 officers and 7,532 enlisted men, stationed at 29 posts in the United States and in our colonial possessions, and on board ships in commission, I think I may be pardoned for stating that the Corps is at the present time in much better condition than when I was appointed Commandant.

One step backward (of which Heywood complained to the last and which was unquestionably due to the Fullam clique's influence) was that, beginning with the Class of 1896, the Naval Academy ceased to meet its quotas for Marine officers, and, from 1898 until 1914—in flat disobedience of an 1899 Act of Congress which required the annual commissioning of at least one midshipman in the Marines—not a single Annapolis graduate entered the Corps. Still another discordant note (recalling the dark days of 1874) was the legislative proviso that, on Heywood's retirement, his successor would wear not two stars, but one. Physically speaking, General Heywood was the first Commandant to have his headquarters in an office building. In 1901, Congress at last approved a long overdue reconstruction of Eighth and Eye. While the new construction was in progress, on 10 June 1901, Marine Corps Headquarters moved to the Bond Building, 14th and New York Avenue. Within a year it was clear that all the new buildings at Eighth and Eye would be needed for barracks, and Headquarters moved, on 28 March 1903, to the Mills Building, 17th and Pennsylvania Avenue, just across the street from the State, War, and Navy Building.

George F. Elliott, an Alabaman, only five years earlier a captain at Guantanamo, was the new Commandant. Elliott—a West Pointer and one of the last of his breed to become a Marine officer for almost a century—probably holds an all-time record in rising from company commander to Commandant in five years, but this becomes more explicable in light of his previous 22 years as a lieutenant. To his juniors "he was one of the kindest men in the world" (Smedley Butler), even though "the old boy had the worst temper I've ever known" (Thomas Holcomb). During his tenure the new Brigadier General Commandant was destined not only to lead and launch Marine expeditions throughout the world, but also to defend his Corps against enemies at home.

"I TOOK THE CANAL ZONE . . ."

Within three years after the 1st Regiment had added Chinese laurels to the Corps, trouble was afoot in Panama, where revolution against the government of Colombia was irritating a sensitive area in the foreign policy of the United States. Ever since 1846 the United States had guaranteed (and been guaranteed, in turn) the right of free transit of the isthmus, and, from 1901 on, had been negotiating with Colombia to construct a canal. These negotiations fell through in 1903, causing wide discontent among the inhabitants of the isthmus and extreme frustration to President Theodore Roosevelt, who already had Congressional authority to start digging whenever terms could be arrived at. On 3 November 1903, to no-one's great surprise, revolution broke out in Panama City, object—the independence of Panama from Colombia.

The USS *Nashville,* a gunboat, rushed at her full 14 knots to Colon (formerly Aspinwall), on the Atlantic side, put ashore a token landing force within hours after the outbreak, with orders to "prevent landing of any armed forces with hostile intent" (in other words, Colombians). Coincident with the *Nashville's* arrival was that of 474 Colombian soldiers sent to cross the isthmus and subdue the rebels on the Pacific side. By judicious bluff, assisted by the American superintendent of the Panama Railroad (who demanded an individual ticket for each Colombian soldier), the *Nashville's* people held off the Colombians until 5 November when the USS *Dixie,* transport, arrived with Major Lejeune's floating battalion of Marines. Lejeune immediately landed two companies "in one of the hardest downpours I ever experienced," he related, and the Colombians realized that they were balked. Fortunately, a merchantman lying in Colon consented to receive the

Colombian force, which embarked under the guns of the *Nashville* and the rifles of Lejeune's battalion.

After a month on board ship, the battalion was ordered ashore to garrison the isthmus and went into camp at Emperador, near Colon, on 12 December 1903. As American relations with Colombia were, to say the least, delicate (the United States having recognized Panamanian independence four days after the revolt), three more battalions, totaling 946 Marines, were sent to Panama, under personal command of the new Brigadier General Commandant. These reinforcements arrived aboard the *Dixie* on 3 January 1904, and were grouped with Lejeune's battalion to form a provisional brigade under General Elliott, who was revisiting the isthmus for the first time since 1885. This was the first instance since Archibald Henderson's day that a Commandant of the Marine Corps had taken personal command in the field and the last until the time of this writing. As Lejeune reminisced some years later:[51]

General Elliott was a very strenuous commander and kept his brigade actively engaged in drilling, hiking, rifle-shooting and map making.

General Elliott retained command in Panama until 16 February 1904, when it became clear that no matter how little the Colombians liked the situation, they had neither the stomach nor the means for a contest with the U. S. Marines and Navy. The brigade thereupon disbanded, General Elliott returned to Washington, and Lejeune's battalion remained. Diplomacy gradually assuaged the abraded feelings of Colombia and tempered the high spirits of newborn Panama, and the duties of the Marine garrison increasingly became those of routine security for the Canal Zone, a duty which the Army assumed in October 1911 (although a Marine battalion stayed there until 1914). For a final word on the Canal Zone, there is no better authority than Theodore Roosevelt who summed up the episode as follows: "I took the Canal Zone and let Congress debate, and while the debate goes on, the Canal does also."[52]

"... HE LENDS A HAND AT EVERY JOB"

From the pest-hole of Cavite
To the Ditch at Panama,
You will find them very needy
Of Marines—that's what we are;
We're the watchdogs of a pile of coal
Or we dig a magazine.
Though he lends a hand at every job,
Who would not be a Marine?

So wrote Colonel H. C. Davis in an added stanza of "The Marines' Hymn" which, although sung for some years afterward, was dropped when General Lejeune copyrighted the original three stanzas in 1929. Whatever their poetic merit, Colonel Davis's lines give a bird's-eye glimpse of Marine Corps duty in the early 20th century. In addition to the major "jobs" undertaken by the Corps, there were many minor ones, too.

Among these an outstanding one was the 1903 journey to Addis Ababa, capital of Ethiopia, by a detachment under Captain G. C. Thorpe. Captain Thorpe's detachment was the escort for an American diplomatic mission bent on negotiating a treaty with Emperor Menelik II. The march, which extended more than 300 miles inland from a jungle railhead, was—not unlike O'Bannon's—made with a train of 46 camels and 45 mules, through desolate mountains populated by savage tribesmen. At one point the *haban*, or native camel master, wished to take a route different from that chosen by Captain Thorpe, and a serious dispute ensued. At the climax, Thorpe ordered his men to seize the *haban* and bind him hand and foot. Then, turning to the interpreter, he said:[53]

Tell that man he is going with us over the route we have selected, and going feet foremost at the end of that rope, the other end being made fast to a mule.

For his arrival in Addis Ababa, Thorpe shifted his 19 men into special full dress (which until 1912 was a blue blouse with scarlet collar and a cap with scarlet band) and made a grand entry in the style of *Aida*, surrounded by Abyssinian warriors mounted on zebra-mules and draped in leopard skins. For ten days the Marines were billeted in a palace and, on 24 December, were inspected by the Emperor himself. On departure, Menelik decorated all enlisted men with the Menelik Medal and awarded the Star of Ethiopia to Captain Thorpe. The detachment returned to the coast on camel-back (bearing two live lions as gifts from Menelik to President Roosevelt) and embarked aboard the USS *Machias* at Djibouti on 15 January 1904, the first American troops ever to set foot in Ethiopia.

In 1903 and 1904, Marines landed in Honduras, Syria, and twice in Santo Domingo, to protect American nationals during civil disturbances. In May 1904, when the North African bandit, Raisouli, kidnapped an American citizen, Ion Perdicaris, and held him for ransom, the USS *Brooklyn's* Marines were landed at Tangier as part of the pattern of pressure to secure Perdicaris' release. This was the episode in which Theodore Roosevelt cabled, "Perdicaris alive or Raisouli dead"—and then landed Marines. Fortunately, Perdicaris was surrendered alive without the need for operations in the field.

In 1905, on the other side of the globe, Marines from Cavite were sent north to Seoul, capital of Korea, to establish a legation guard during the Russo-Japanese War. This detachment stayed on until the Japanese took over Korea at the end of the war.

In April 1906, when earthquake and fire ravaged San Francisco, the first U. S. troops on the scene were Marines from Yerba Buena (later renamed Treasure) Island, followed in short order by a Marine battalion, under Lieutenant Colonel Karmany, and ships' landing forces from Mare Island. These units fought fire, saved lives, salvaged property, and halted looting in much of the city. One establishment they failed to save, however, was the Marine Corps Depot of Supplies, opened in December 1903, and then located on Mission Street.

Finally, the Marine Corps exhibition detachment at the Pan-American Exposition in Buffalo provided the honor guard and funeral escort for President McKinley's body after his assassination there in September 1901. The custom of having Marine guards at such expositions had grown up before the Spanish war. Marine detachments guarded the American pavilions at the Paris expositions of 1878 and 1889, and were conspicuous at the Chicago World's Fair in 1893. Following the war, in addition to Buffalo, Marines served at Charleston (1902), St. Louis (1904), and the Jamestown Exposition on the site of what later became the Naval Operating Base, Norfolk. These units made model camps, performed exhibition drills, provided security for valuable displays, and rendered help in emergency. At Chicago, the Marine guard, commanded for a time by First Lieutenant George Barnett, served as "ship's detachment" for a mock-up battleship, "USS Illinois," which was the Navy's exhibit.

MARINE CORPS SHOOTING

It is hard to imagine a Marine Corps in which systematic marksmanship training was not a commonplace, but such was the Corps in the 1890s. To General Heywood it was a reproach that in 1899, only 98 officers and men were qualified as sharpshooter or marksman (the two qualifications then in use). Although he had planned to field a Marine Corps team in the Hilton Trophy Match in 1898, war intervened. In 1899, however, the Commandant appointed Major C. H. Lauchheimer as Inspector of Target Practice, a step with far-reaching effects, for Lauchheimer's energy and imagination were to be reflected in the Marine Corps marksmanship program for years to come.

Under Lauchheimer's impetus, and with coaching from Sergeant Major

Hayes, the Corps finally got a team into the Hilton Trophy Match at Sea Girt, New Jersey, in 1901, finishing sixth. The Marine shooters didn't even understand the use of the rifle sling at this time until civilian competitors explained it to them. Even so, one Marine, Second Lieutenant Thomas Holcomb, won a gold medal for the highest individual score, an omen of better days ahead.

In 1903, when Elliott succeeded Heywood, marksmanship found an even more enthusiastic supporter, and the hot-tempered new Commandant is usually thought of as the man who put Marine shooting on the map. One of Elliott's first steps, at Lauchheimer's urging, was to obtain a skilled shooter as full-time team coach. The choice was a 56-year-old, bearded Maryland dentist, Samuel T. ("Doc") Scott. Scott was enlisted in 1903 as a private, then promoted to gunnery sergeant, and served by arrangement as team coach until after the 1905 National Rifle Matches, in which the Marines finished fourth, after which he received, with many thanks, a special order discharge.

In 1906 Marines began receiving the M1903 Springfield rifles, and, in the same year, Congress established marksmanship qualification pay for the Army and Marine Corps—$1 a month extra for marksman, $2 for sharpshooter, and $3 for expert rifleman. With the advent of this "beer money," the troops discovered a much heightened interest in good shooting, and, within three years, more than a third of all officers and men were qualified as marksman or higher. Better still, in 1910 the Marine team, led by Captain W. C. Harllee, placed second in the National Matches, and a Marine, Corporal G. W. Farnum, for the first time won the President's Trophy Match. To top this next year, Captain D. C. McDougal led the Marine team to first place, while a young corporal, Calvin A. Lloyd, again captured the President's Trophy for the Marine Corps. Marine Corps shooting had arrived.[54]

PACIFYING CUBA

As if the Philippines, China, and Panama were not enough, Marines soon found themselves on expeditionary service in Cuba, over which the United States had established a protectorate. Under the terms of the so-called "Platt Amendment," the United States was responsible for maintaining stable government in Cuba.

In August 1906 rigged elections touched off a revolt. Reluctantly, President Theodore Roosevelt decided to intervene. Ready to go was Major

A. W. Catlin's floating battalion of Marines which had been aboard the USS *Dixie* since June and which reached Havana on 12 September. Havana Harbor held no novelty for Catlin—he had been blown into it from the *Maine* in 1898.

Four days after Catlin's arrival a provisional battalion was organized at Marine Barracks, Norfolk, and was en route to Havana. Within another 48 hours, still a third battalion was formed at Philadelphia and was on its way south aboard a cruiser. On arrival at Havana these battalions were grouped with Catlin's to form the 1st Regiment, under Lieutenant Colonel George Barnett. Like Catlin, Barnett was no stranger to Cuba, having served in Cuban waters throughout the war with Spain.

Beginning with a series of minor landings by ships' detachments on and after 13 September, full-blown intervention became a fact on 29 September. Meanwhile, two more battalions had been ordered down from East Coast Marine barracks, and two had been shaken together from the Atlantic Fleet. One of these went to Barnett's 1st Regiment, and the remaining three formed the 2d Regiment under Lieutenant Colonel F. J. Moses, who had commanded a battalion in the Peking relief column and was described years later as "the smartest man in the Marine Corps."[55] To command all, General Elliott, this time unable to take the field himself, sent his best colonel, "Tony" Waller, who reached Havana on 1 October with orders to form all Marines in Cuba into a brigade. This he did, and set up headquarters at Camp Columbia, outside Havana. At top strength the brigade (which never was assembled in one place) totaled 97 officers and 2,795 enlisted men.

The next four weeks were active ones. Marines fanned out to 24 key localities, guarding railroads, ports, and plantations. The 1st Regiment even had an armored train, probably the first piece of mobile armor ever used by the Marine Corps. Meanwhile, on 10 October, with the major jobs of pacification and disarming the insurgents well on to completion, U. S. Army units began to arrive under the title of Army of the Cuban Pacification. Apparently overlooking the effect and presence of some 3,000 Marines already on the scene, the Army Chief of Staff stated in his annual report for 1906 that the force "landed without opposition" (which was certainly true). As so often happened, the Army brought rank with it, and the Marines passed on 1 November to Army command.

Routine garrison duty was now the order of the day. With more than 5,000 American soldiers in Cuba, General Elliott pled for release of the

Marines but was only partially successful. The War Department retained the 1st Regiment but permitted disbandment of the brigade.

Although Cuba was pacified and tranquil when the Army of the Pacification went home in 1909, it was only three years before "The Pearl of the Antilles" reverted to internal disorder. In 1912 explosive revolts by Cuban blacks (only wholly freed from slavery since 1886) shook the country. On 22 May the 1st Provisional Regiment was organized at League Island Navy Yard, Philadelphia, and, by nightfall of 23 May, was standing down the Delaware aboard the USS *Prairie*.

Reinforced by a second regiment, which caught up with the 1st at Guantanamo on 5 June, a provisional brigade was again formed, this time under Colonel Lincoln Karmany, still forthright and blunt as when he was "Frightened Bob's" Marine officer. ("There may be a few good men who don't drink," he growled, "but they've got to prove it.")[56] Alarms and excursions were the order of the day all over Oriente, Cuba's eastern province, then and later the breeding place of revolution. Twenty-six towns, all near Santiago and Guantanamo, had to be occupied, and all trains east of Camaguey carried Marine guards until order was restored in July. As soon as the Cuban authorities were able to relieve them, Marine garrisons were progressively pulled back to Guantanamo Bay, where Karmany maintained headquarters. Within a month, transports began the homeward voyage of Karmany's efficient force. Although this brigade boasted no such exotic weaponry as its own armored train, it did include artillery and other brigade special troops. As a ludicrous aftermath the *Ferrocarril Nacional de Cuba* hopefully sent the Navy Department a bill for tickets for each and every Marine train guard during the revolt.

"NO VESTIGE OF THEIR ORGANIZATION SHOULD BE ALLOWED TO REMAIN..."

For seven years, the group headed by Lieutenant Fullam of the Navy had been relatively inactive in its maneuvers against the Marine Corps. It will be remembered that the stated object of Fullam's campaign was to end Marine detachments aboard ships of the Navy. Fullam's real object unquestionably was abolition of the Corps, or, virtually synonymous, its transfer to the Army.

On 10 November 1906 (131st Birthday of the Marine Corps) Rear Admiral G. A. Converse, the flinty-eyed Vermont-born Chief of the Bureau of

Navigation, advised the House Naval Affairs Committee that Marines should be taken off sea duty and grouped ashore for expeditionary duty and to safeguard Navy property. Less than four months later, Fullam, now Commander Fullam, was back in the ring, breaking his (official) silence of recent years by a letter to Secretary of the Navy Victor H. Metcalf himself, reiterating his own and Admiral Converse's proposals. As endorsed by General Elliott, the Marine Corps' views indicate a sense of weariness after more than a decade of such nagging:[57]

> The continued desultory agitation of this subject simply tends to injure the efficiency of both the Navy and Marine Corps, and causes dissension amongst its various officers, which cannot but be injurious to the service as a whole.

If General Elliott really believed that Fullam's idea was unworthy of concern, he was whistling in the dark, for he had already received intimations both from Secretary Metcalf and from T.R.'s attorney general that trouble was brewing for the Marines. Another storm signal was an open proposal in 1908 by Major General Leonard Wood, soon to be Chief of Staff of the Army, that the Marines should be absorbed into the Coast Artillery.

Even more significant than the uniformed opponents of the Corps, however, were two gentlemen in civilian clothes—Theodore Roosevelt and his Secretary of War and successor, William Howard Taft.

In October 1908 the Fullam clique, realizing that President Roosevelt's span was nearly run, determined on a final campaign which, they hoped, would end their long vendetta against the Marines. Rear Admiral J. B. Pillsbury, Admiral Converse's successor, fired the opening gun—a letter to the Secretary of the Navy:[58]

> *Sir:* The time has arrived when all Marine detachments should be removed from United States naval vessels, substituting bluejackets instead. . . .

Exactly one week after Pillsbury laid down his pen, on 23 October 1908, President Roosevelt directed the Secretary of the Navy to begin withdrawal of Marines from all ships of the Navy. In reply to an agonized reclama from General Elliott, the new Secretary of the Navy (Truman H. Newberry) merely quoted the President: "I know all about it—take them off!"[59] On 12 November, unmoved by a final personal plea from the Commandant, President Roosevelt signed Executive Order 969, a document long to be remembered by Marines:

EXECUTIVE ORDER DEFINING THE DUTIES OF THE UNITED STATES MARINE CORPS

In accordance with the power vested in me by section 1619, Revised Statutes of the

United States, the following duties are assigned to the United States Marine Corps:

(1) To garrison the different navy yards and naval stations, both within and beyond the continental limits of the United States.

(2) To furnish the first line of the mobile defense of naval bases and naval stations beyond the continental limits of the United States.

(3) To man such naval defenses, and to aid in manning, if necessary, such other defenses, as may be erected for the defense of naval bases and naval stations beyond the continental limits of the United States.

(4) To garrison the Isthmian Canal Zone, Panama.

(5) To furnish such garrisons and expeditionary forces for duties beyond the seas as may be necessary in time of peace.

Theodore Roosevelt

THE WHITE HOUSE, November 12, 1908,
(No. 969)

Just seven days after signing this document, Roosevelt confided to his military aide, Captain Archibald Butt, USA:[60]

[The Marines'] downfall is largely due to themselves. They have augmented to themselves such importance, and their influence . . . has given them such an abnormal position for the size of their corps that they have simply invited their own destruction. I do not hesitate to say they should be absorbed into the Army, *and no vestige of their organization should be allowed to remain.* They cannot get along with the Navy, and as a separate command with the Army, the conditions would be intolerable.

This private outburst against the Corps was in some contrast to T.R.'s silk-glove approach for public consumption a week later. In an open letter to his friend, Leonard Wood, the President blandly described the Marines as:[61]

. . . an excellent corps. It would be of great benefit to both services that the incorporation [into the Army] take place.

Thus, by the end of 1908 it was apparent that, in the curlicued rhetoric of General Elliott, ". . . elimination and absorption were casting, unknown to us, their shadows at our heels."[62]

With three months to act before the 1909 Naval Appropriations Bill, a group of officers generaled by "Tony" Waller and including Lauchheimer, Major Neville, and Colonel Frank L. Denny, the Quartermaster, banded together to save the Corps. Not the least important of those in the background was Captain Smedley Butler, whose father, Representative Thomas Butler, was Chairman of the House Naval Affairs Committee.

Against the drumroll of the Secretary of the Navy's order to withdraw Marines immediately from 13 major combatant ships, Congressman Butler's committee on 7 January 1909 summoned before it Secretary Newberry;

Admiral Pillsbury, the offending Chief of the Bureau of Navigation; Commander Fullam, Peck's bad boy of the whole affair; and General Elliott.

During the next week the fur flew. After carefully reviewing the functions of the Corps and hearing more than 20 witnesses, Congress stopped Theodore Roosevelt in his tracks and jolted the Navy to its keels on 3 March 1909 by an appropriations rider which began with the words:[63]

Provided, that no part of the appropriations herein made for the Marine Corps shall be expended for the purposes for which said appropriations are made unless officers and men shall serve as heretofore on board all battleships and armored cruisers and also on such other vessels of the Navy as the President may direct. . . .

Despite T.R.'s wrath, his own Attorney-General pronounced the rider legal, and the Marine Corps was still among those present in 1909. This would have been a good time for the Navy and the administration to listen to Admiral Luce, whose comment after the struggle was, as usual, sound:[64]

The Marines have won out. It is now the duty of all friends of the Navy to accept the situation cheerfully and in good faith and do everything possible to allay the ill feeling caused by the attempt to obliterate a fine Corps.

Alas, President Roosevelt's successor, William Howard Taft, felt differently. The new President was no more friendly than his predecessor. Taft had been Governor-General in Manila during Waller's court-martial, and his dislike of the Marines dated from that time.

On 24 July 1909, after a round of golf at the Chevy Chase Club, Mr. Taft sent for Captain Butt, who was Taft's aide as he had been Roosevelt's.

"Archie," said Mr. Taft, "seeing Colonel Denny and Colonel McCawley at the Club reminds me that I am getting tired of having the orders of the Navy Department curtailed by Marine officers, and the next time I hear of any such influence being used to check the Government in its plans for this Corps, one gentleman will find himself in the Philippines and the other at Guantanamo. If you are interested in these gentlemen, you might give them a hint to this effect."[65]

The meaning of Taft's ominous phrase—to check the Government in its plans for this Corps—was only too clear, as Butt recorded that very afternoon in a letter to his sister:

I knew of course what he meant. He referred to the influence which the Marine Corps has built up in Washington by admitting sons of every Congressman who happens to have a boy who has failed at everything else. The Corps is very unpopular with the Navy, and, at the request of this department, President Roosevelt ordered the Marines off the ships. Such was the influence of the Corps that Congress set aside the order and directed that they be used first aboard the naval vessels. They are now attempting to secure additional advantages, and this is what the President intended to hit. . . . The President said that sooner or later the Marines would have to leave the ships; that as a distinct body the Corps had become almost useless, and as far as the Navy was concerned it was an actual detriment.

Butt's sneer at Congressmen's sons was obviously aimed at Smedley Butler, who was to be one of the few men in American history to win two Medals of Honor. In retrospect it would seem that Captain Butt—a Quartermaster Corps captain who spent more than a third of his Army career as a White House functionary—had picked a somewhat inappropriate target in Butler, who had already been wounded twice, and had, before his twenty-first birthday, been brevetted captain and advanced on the Navy List for conspicuous gallantry in action.

"WE FORMED THE MARINE CORPS ASSOCIATION"

As the Taft administration ran its course, Marines realized in grim clarity that the ordinarily jovial, 250-pound President was pursuing his "plans for this Corps" with relentless tenacity. Moreover, naval officers who had launched their assault on the Marines as two-stripers in the 1890s now boasted many stripes or even stars.

Meanwhile, however, the Marine Corps had its daily business to conduct. This business, in 1911 as previously and subsequently, was as a national force in readiness. Early that year, revolution headed by Colonel Francisco Madera had shaken the long-standing regime of Mexico's venerable dictator, Porfirio Diaz. As American lives and interests were endangered, an expeditionary force—the 1st Provisional Marine Brigade—was organized forthwith for service in Mexico should the situation require. Of this force, John A. Lejeune, then in command of Marine Barracks, Brooklyn, recalled:[66]

It consisted of a brigade, made up in the usual way by assembling detachments from all eastern posts at the embarkation point [Philadelphia Navy Yard]. My first information of the proposed movement was a long distance call from Washington about 10 o'clock one evening. Colonel McCawley, who was on the other end of the line, gave me advance information to the effect that a detachment, consisting of certain officers, whom he named, and 200 men of the various grades, would be transferred to the brigade at Philadelphia the next day, to arrive at its destination not later than noon. . . . It was an all night party. At 8 o'clock the next morning all the details had been completed and the detachment marched to the tug which transported it to Jersey City, where it entrained. . . . The destination was Guantanamo Bay [where] it would remain in camp for two or three months.

Thus came into being the 1st Provisional Marine Brigade. Its commander was Colonel Waller; the 1st Regiment was commanded by that "remarkable man," F. J. Moses, while Colonel Barnett had the 2d Regiment. After arrival at Guantanamo Bay, whose familiar Deer Point camp served as a perennial staging point for West Indian expeditions, the brigade was reinforced by the 3d Regiment, composed of 16 Marine detachments from the Atlantic Fleet, under the Fleet Marine Officer, Lieutenant Colonel B. H. Fuller. Despite the casual way it had been organized, this brigade was the largest force of U. S. Marines that had ever served together. It included 93 officers, more than 25 per cent of the commissioned strength of the Corps.

Among those officers it was common knowledge that the Marine Corps, out of favor in Washington, might soon meet its end if President Taft persisted in his "plans for this Corps." And on 26 April 1911, Colonel Moses called a meeting attended by every officer in the brigade, ". . . to discuss defenses against being abolished by the Navy," as one later wrote.[67] Another participant stated, "An association was formed with the general mission of preserving our existence and status."[68] This was the origin of the Marine Corps Association.

The revolution against Porfirio Diaz failed, and the Waller brigade was disbanded. In 1912, William Howard Taft was defeated by Woodrow Wilson. The efforts of the Corps' most persistent opponent continued, however. In 1913, Fullam, now a captain, obtained a private audience with Navy Secretary Daniels' Aide for Operations (predecessor of CNO), Rear Admiral Bradley A. Fiske. Here, with himself in mind, Fullam recommended that the newly formed Marine Advance Base Force be placed under an officer of the Navy. "The Marine Corps," said Fullam, "would never successfully accomplish the very difficult task assigned to it, of its own volition, but would have to be driven to do it."[69]

Fullam's demand was soundly rebuffed by another naval officer of quite different kidney, Rear Admiral Charles J. Badger, Commander in Chief of the Atlantic Fleet (who had been one of the few Navy witnesses to take the Marines' side during the 1909 controversy). Badger dismissed Fullam's proposal as "an uncalled-for humiliation of the Marines' officers and men," and said, as Fleet commander, that he would not stand for it. Exit Captain Fullam.

And on 25 April 1913 the infant Marine Corps Association—which in a perverse sense was Fullam's offspring—got its written charter and a standing executive committee consisting of Lieutenant Colonel Lejeune, and Captains H. C. Snyder and D. B. Wills:[70]

For the purpose of recording and publishing the history of the Marine Corps, publishing a periodical journal for the dissemination of information concerning the aims, purposes and deeds of the Corps, and the interchange of ideas for the betterment and improvement of its officers and men.

In reviewing the circumstances that brought the Marine Corps Association into being, it is amusing to see the repeated attribution of the Marine Corps' preservation to "influence," political legerdemain, and like arts. Apparently it never penetrated home even to Theodore Roosevelt or Taft (let alone Captains Fullam or Butt) that the already enviable combat record of the Marine Corps, its notable economy, and its reputation as ready, hard-hitting expeditionary troops, might conceivably exert "influence" (of a different sort) on the attitude of Congress and the public toward their Corps of Marines.

THE ADVANCE BASE FORCE

On the afternoon of July 8 1901, the Marines (including the specially instructed Newport detachment) were landed from the battleships *Kearsarge, Alabama,* and *Massachusetts,* and occupied a position near Greatpoint, Nantucket, Massachusetts. . . . At this camp, lines of defense were immediately established; guns from the fleet were mounted on shore and fired; trenches were dug, a magazine built, etc.

These sentences from General Heywood's 1901 Annual Report chronicle the germination of seedlings from which modern American amphibious doctrine and amphibious victories would ultimately spring. "The specially instructed Newport detachment" was headed by Major H. C. Haines and included four other officers, 20 NCOs, and 20 privates, all of whom—at the behest of Heywood—had spent two months at Newport studying the mysteries of advance base operations.

Ever since Huntington's success in securing a Fleet base at Guantanamo, Marines, and some naval officers, had realized that projection of the Fleet's power ashore to seize and defend advance bases was a natural role for Marines. After the 1901 exercises at Newport and Nantucket, the next year saw winter maneuvers at Culebra, an island off Puerto Rico's eastern tip, where Marines again landed, as a regiment commanded by Colonel P. C. Pope. Many years later, commenting on the hundreds of landing exercises in Culebra's history, General H. M. Smith mused:[71]

If the battle of Waterloo was won on the playing fields of Eton, the Japanese bases in the Pacific were captured on the beaches of the Caribbean.

In this first exercise at Culebra, two battalions of Marines, reinforced by an artillery company, landed 4-inch and 5-inch guns, set them in on advance-base platforms, and fired them. In competition with sailor parties the Marines raced to get the first gun in and the first round off. Unfortunately (according to Smedley Butler, then a captain) the first (and winning) Marine salvo bracketed the Fleet flagship, a breach of etiquette which earned the troops a blast for their gunnery rather than a commendation for their sweat and energy.

Succeeding years saw increased use of floating battalions and regiments aboard transports. Though their remote ancestor was Reynolds' unfortunate unit that almost went down with the *Governor* in 1861, the floating battalions really took hold with Huntington's battalion in 1898. When in home waters, they usually based at League Island, Brooklyn, or Pensacola, but they spent a good deal of time at Guantanamo and around the Caribbean with the Fleet. They never were abolished as such, but the development of the Advance Base Force and events in the Caribbean and Europe overtook them, and after 1914 they vanished for many years.

In February 1903, after the Culebra maneuvers, Major Haines's battalion embarked aboard the USS *Panther* (which had served as Huntington's "APA" in 1898). The situation aboard the *Panther* was not ideal, far from it in fact, not only because of the captain's personality (a different officer from 1898, but no improvement), but, fundamentally, because the Marine battalion commander's authority was limited to drills and instruction, and he was considered merely an advisor to the ship's captain, even when his battalion was ashore. In mid-1903, Haines was relieved by Lejeune, and, to everybody's relief, the battalion was detached to the USS *Dixie*, a larger ship and a happier one. Here, Lejeune worked out a sensible relation with the ship which set a pattern followed to this day between embarked landing forces and the naval authorities: the battalion commander to be wholly responsible for the military command, discipline, efficiency, and readiness of the Marines, and all dealings with and from the ship to be conducted through the battalion headquarters.

In 1908, a by-product of the Fullam clique's drive to scuttle the Marine Corps was discussion of organization of the Corps "into regiments, battalions, and companies . . . embarked, or ready to embark, in a suitable vessel . . . attached to the fleets," as a leading naval officer put it. As such possibilities began to be realized, General Elliott, in his annual report for 1908, proposed "transports for the sole and exclusive use of the Marine Corps." Then, in 1910, a further logical step—establishment of a Marine Corps Advance Base School, at New London, Connecticut. The missions of this school were: (1) to train Marine officers and men in the handling, installation, and use of advance base materiel; (2) to investigate what types of guns, gun platforms, mines, torpedo defenses, and other equipment might be best suited for advance base work; and (3) to study such military and naval subjects as pertained to the selection, occupation, attack, and defense of advance bases, or to expeditionary service in general.

Founding the Advance Base School, Elliott's last major act as Commandant, was a significant step. Although the school was a logical development of the times, it was nevertheless the first institution of its kind ever established, and therefore a milestone in U. S. naval history. From 1910 on, the Marine Corps had a professional school to focus thinking on amphibious warfare, and, possibly even more important, to perfect the already well developed expeditionary capabilities of the Corps.

After a year at New London, the Advance Base School moved to League Island Navy Yard, which was already the springboard of Marine expeditions. Within two years after its founding, the School had trained 1,700 officers and men, no small fraction of the Corps' 1912 strength of 351 officers and 9,921 enlisted men.

The Navy's plans for the 1914 maneuvers of the Atlantic Fleet called for seizure and development of Culebra by a Marine Advance Base Force (organized 23 December 1913) under Colonel Barnett. The composition of this force, as Lejeune (who commanded the 2d Regiment) described it, was as follows:[72]

. . . a small brigade composed of two regiments, the 1st, or Fixed Defense Regiment, consisting of one battery of Navy landing guns, one signal company, one engineer company, one harbor defense mine company, and two batteries of Navy 5-inch guns (four guns each); and the 2d, or Mobile Regiment, consisting of one battery of Navy landing guns, one machine-gun company, and four rifle companies.

Lejeune, however, omitted an important fledgling: Marine Corps aviation.

From the needling of an air-minded enthusiast, Second Lieutenant A. A. Cunningham, the first Marine to qualify as a naval aviator, there had come to birth the Aviation Detachment, Advance Base Force, commissioned 27 December 1913. This detachment of two officers and seven enlisted

Marines, equipped with two Navy flying boats, was for the time being commanded by First Lieutenant B. L. Smith because Cunningham's new bride had forbidden him to fly and he had perforce (temporarily) turned in his wings.

Airplanes and all, the 1914 maneuvers were a success for the Advance Base Force and a total rebuttal to Fullam, as the report by Captain W. S. Sims, USN, chief umpire, underscored:[73]

[I] was greatly impressed with many evidences of the very high degree of efficiency on the part of the men and officers comprising the [Advance Base] Detachment. They appeared to be in splendid physical condition. Their morale was very high. They entered into their work not only with interest but with admirable enthusiasm. . . . Attention is invited to the very complete outfit of the Advance Base Detachment and to the great variety of military work required of officers and men. Rifle pits and bomb proof shelters have been dug, 3″ and 5″ guns have been landed in transports, dragged up steep declivities and installed ready for firing. Methods for both direct and indirect fire have been perfected for both fixed and field artillery. Mine fields have been laid, and an aviation camp has been established. The problems of supply to the numerous outlying camps have been well worked out in a waterless country almost devoid of supplies. A very complete system of communications, including almost 24 miles of telephone system, a radio plant, night and day heliograph system, and flag semaphore system have been established. All parts of this work seem to have been done in an extraordinarily efficient manner. . . . Such results could have been accomplished only by a harmonious combination of thorough planning and admirable administration, actuated by the driving force of an enthusiastic devotion to duty extending throughout the entire command.

Colonel Barnett's reward for this fine performance came with unusual timeliness. On the evening the maneuvers ended, word came through by radio that he had been selected as Commandant. In a later phase of the celebration which followed, one of his staff approached him from the rear and gave him an affectionate kick, explaining immediately afterward that he wanted to be able to boast that he was one officer who had kicked a Commandant in the stern sheets.

VERACRUZ

The 1914 maneuvers soon paid off. Trouble had been making up in Mexico ever since the death of Porfirio Diaz, whose most recent successor, Huerta, our government had refused to recognize. The result was an increasing strain in relations which, on 9 April 1914, came to a head in the so-called "Tampico Incident" when the paymaster and a boat's crew from the USS *Dolphin* were clapped without cause into the jail at Tampico, on the Gulf of Mexico. Although the prisoners were soon released with apologies, the Mexicans refused to render the salute to the American colors which Rear Admiral Henry T. Mayo, senior officer present, demanded as an amend.

As tension heightened, the Advance Base Force, now commanded by Lejeune (one of seven newly promoted colonels), was held in readiness for trouble. The 2d Regiment, under Lieutenant Colonel Neville, was ashore at Pensacola Navy Yard, ready to embark in the USS *Prairie* alongside. The 1st Regiment (Lieutenant Colonel C. G. Long) and brigade headquarters were embarked in the USS *Hancock* at the Naval Station, Algiers, Louisiana. In addition, Major Butler's Panama battalion had been aboard the cruiser *Chester* (most appropriately bearing the name of Butler's home town) ever since the new year.

On 20 April it was learned that, in violation of a United States embargo, a German merchantman, SS *Ypiranga,* was about to land a shipload of arms for the Huerta government at Veracruz. Next day, on President Wilson's orders, naval forces were ordered to land and seize the customhouse at Veracruz.

The first unit ashore was Neville's 2d Regiment, which had been standing by offshore. In support of Neville, together with bluejacket landing parties, was a provisional 3d Regiment made up of ships' detachments from the Fleet, commanded by Lieutenant Colonel A. W. Catlin. On the night of the 21st, Butler's battalion went ashore to join the 2d Regiment while the remainder of the Marine brigade steamed south to Veracruz and landed the next morning. Ultimately, more than three thousand bluejackets, wearing whites dyed with ships' coffee, were added to the landing force.

On the 22d, fairly stiff resistance developed. This took the form of house-to-house fighting for the Marines, and, briefly but dramatically, volley firing from the Mexican Naval Academy on the seaman regiment which was debouching onto a large plaza. This was abruptly halted by quick and intense fire from the 5-inch guns of the *San Francisco, Chester,* and *Prairie,* which blew much of the second story off the offending building.

The three Marine regiments under Lejeune, together with the seaman brigade, totaled 6,429 officers and men, of whom 2,469 were Marines. The whole landing force came under Rear Admiral Frank Friday Fletcher, while the Fleet commander in chief, Admiral Charles J. Badger, lay offshore.

By 24 April, Veracruz was pacified. In addition, a Marine battalion held an outpost at El Tejar, source of the city's water supply. Four days later, with peace restored, Army troops arrived, under Brigadier General Frederick Funston, USA, and took over the town from the Navy. As the Fleet weighed anchor, however, the Marine brigade, now 3,141 strong, remained behind under Army command and stayed quietly at Veracruz until 23 November 1914, most of the time commanded by Colonel Waller, who had arrived on 1 May.

This expedition provided useful field training for the Marine regiments and exercised all hands in working with larger formations than the Corps had ever assembled in one place before. A side development was formation of the first Marine field artillery battalion: three 3-inch artillery companies of the Advance Base Force were, on Lejeune's order, grouped as a battalion, drawn by Mexican mules. Major R. H. Dunlap was the battalion commander and thus, as far as Marines are concerned, may be called the father of his arm. Another first was tactical motor transport. Three Benz trucks were found in the Veracruz customhouse and, with "U. S. Marine Corps" hastily painted on them, were pressed into service.

The efficient services of the Advance Base Force were not overlooked by the public, as this editorial from *Collier's* shows:[74]

We have heard a great deal about the man behind the gun in turret or fighting top, and much also about the brave lads who shovel the coal, or stand in the front of the regiment's firing line, but recent events at Vera Cruz have shown that the amphibious branch of the service is no less to be counted on in time of trouble. "The Marines were there," as the slang saying is. Their maneuvers throughout were precise, skilful, and effective. . . . As Kipling has said in his ballad of "Soldier and Sailor Too"—"There isn't a job on the top of the earth the beggar don't know nor do." Kipling was right about it. We are proud of the Marines and don't mind saying so.

Harper's made a related point more succinctly:[75]

There wasn't any fuss about *their* mobilizing. There never is. Just an order issued and . . . one regiment after another are on their way to Cuba, or Mexico, or the world's end. Where they are going isn't the Marine's concern. Their business is to be always ready to go.

NEW COMMANDANTS: BIDDLE AND BARNETT

On 30 November 1910, George F. Elliott stepped down as Commandant, the first permanent major general commandant; in 1908, Congress had finally accorded the rank of major general to the commandancy. General Elliott had busied himself with many matters aside from the central problem which dogged his closing years, that of keeping the Marine Corps in existence. From 1906 on, he continually sought schooling for the Corps. In 1907, having been balked in a project to set up the School of Application and "a preliminary school for recruits" at New London, Elliott then persuaded the Navy to let him move the School of Application to Port Royal, South Carolina. To provide for the higher education of officers, General Elliott made arrangements to send Marines to both the Naval War College and the Army's Command and General Staff College, and, in addition, sent Marine language students to China. One administrative innovation on General Elliott's part was fingerprinting all enlisted men, a device which uncovered more than a hundred former deserters, fraudulent enlistees, and dishonorably discharged Marines who had pathetically stolen back to the colors. Another innovation: purchase in July 1909 of a 4-cylinder Studebaker "30," at a cost of $3,635, for Marine Corps Headquarters—the first motor vehicle ever owned by the Corps.

It had been generally supposed that Elliott's successor would be Colonel Waller, and Theodore Roosevelt had so intimated. In addition to being the outstanding troop leader of the period, Waller had the support of Representative Butler, Chairman of the Naval Affairs Committee, whose son had served admiringly under Waller in China. As General Elliott's tour neared its end, however, an even more powerful Pennsylvania Republican, Senator Boies Penrose, intervened. Going to the White House, Penrose asserted that his political future in Pennsylvania was linked to the Biddle family of Philadelphia, and got from Taft (who as ex-Governor General of the Philippines remembered Waller's court-martial) the appointment of Colonel W. P. Biddle. This was a blow from which Waller never fully recovered.

General Biddle, the 11th Commandant, a Marine since 1875, was an amply proportioned officer whose tenure, beginning 3 February 1911,[76] was mainly of routine character. But Biddle, too, had his special aims and interests, among which training ranked first. On assuming command of the Corps, Biddle made three months' recruit training mandatory and set up four recruit depots (Philadelphia, Port Royal, Mare Island, and Puget Sound). Port Royal had the largest capacity and would have become the sole East Coast depot but for the Navy's sudden choice of that lonely spot as a disciplinary barracks—a development which in late 1911 precipitated both recruit depot and School of Application into tents on the parade ground at Norfolk Navy Yard.

Another of General Biddle's changes was to divide every Marine barracks into a barracks detachment containing men ineligible for expeditionary duty, and one or more numbered companies, each composed of two officers and 100 men, liable for immediate expeditionary service. Biddle also came out in 1912 (without results) for concentrating the shore-side Marine Corps in ". . . one large post on each coast, eventually to be capable of housing a brigade of two regiments at war strength."[77]

As the last non-Annapolis graduate to be Commandant for a quarter of a century, General Biddle labored under the carry-over of Navy and administration hostility to the Marine Corps from the Roosevelt and Taft administrations. His tour of duty was therefore not personally easy, and, on 24 February 1914, he retired on his own application, clearing the way for appointment of Colonel George Barnett as 12th Commandant.

When General Barnett took office, Marine Corps Headquarters, traditionally small and informal, had begun to find itself faced with more complex administrative problems as the Corps built up to its strength of more than 10,000, authorized by Congress in August 1912. To give more depth to the headquarters, one of Barnett's first moves was creation of the billet of Assistant to the Commandant. Its first incumbent was Colonel Eli K. Cole, who was superseded (by arrangement) by Lejeune as soon as the brigade returned from Veracruz. But Marine Corps Headquarters still had no staff other than the Commandant's aides, the Adjutant and Inspector (Colonel George C. Reid), the Quartermaster (McCawley), the Paymaster (Colonel George Richards), and perhaps 20 enlisted clerks (who had to take a reduction to private on being ordered to Headquarters). Amid this tiny nucleus—located since 18 April 1914 in the Walker-Johnson Building, 1734 New York Avenue —Barnett and Lejeune formed a staff (Barnett's aides) whose names would be prominent in Marine Corps history: Captains Earl H. Ellis, Thomas Holcomb, and Ralph S. Keyser. These three bright captains, to whom the Corps would owe much for its development, became the new Commandant's executive staff.

Austere George Barnett was the first Annapolis graduate to become Commandant of the Marine Corps. In this capacity, he was destined to bring the Navy and Marine Corps to far closer mutual understanding. One of his first important steps in this direction was to re-establish the annual increment of Naval Academy graduates into the Corps; as a result of the new Commandant's negotiations, ten graduates of the class of 1915 entered the Marine Corps, and each year afterward (except 1918) a reasonable number followed. Barnett was also a stout advocate of the advance base role for the Corps, having been promoted to the commandancy directly from the Advance Base Force. Finally—and this was no doubt a reflection of his standing as a member of a vintage Naval Academy class (1881)—General

Barnett was promptly made a member of the Navy's General Board, the high policy body which had heretofore been the preserve of line officers of the Navy.

NICARAGUA

Nicaragua had long been a trouble spot in Central America. On seven occasions before 1910, Marines had been compelled to go ashore there, mainly to protect U. S. citizens and diplomats from violence during civil wars or revolutions. During the early 20th century the dictator, Zelaya, not only oppressed and misgoverned his own people, but fomented uprisings and invasions in El Salvador, Guatemala, and Honduras. Most of these forays were in open and contemptuous violation of treaties urged on Nicaragua by the United States and other Latin-American nations. To aggravate the situation, Nicaragua was deeply indebted to both American and European financial concerns who were pressing their governments for action. From a strategic viewpoint, the Nicaraguan isthmus, perennial rival of Panama's, was a tender spot to the United States. The dangerous instability in Central America was one of the main reasons that a mobile Marine battalion had been stationed in Panama.

In 1909 revolt flared against Zelaya—a long overdue explosion insofar as the views and interests of the United States were concerned. As a show of support, in December 1909, the State Department called for Major Butler's Panama battalion, then for a 750-man provisional regiment from Philadelphia, under Colonel J. E. Mahoney. For three months these forces lay off "the hottest place this side of hell," as Butler described Corinto, Nicaragua's west coast seaport—and then went home. Momentarily, events had quieted.

Hardly had the Panama battalion returned to camp at Bas Obispo, Canal Zone, when away they were called again, this time to Bluefields, on Nicaragua's east coast. Here, in May 1910, Zelaya's forces were gaining against rebel defenders of the city, and, in the process, endangering U. S. citizens and property. After the 12.5-knot gunboat *Paducah* had failed to inspire sufficient awe, Butler was ordered to land and neutralize the town, which he duly did on 30 May, remaining ashore until September. Both factions took to the swampy interior, leaving behind an assortment of "high-ranking bums"—some 50 New Orleans filibusterers who had been recruited to bolster the rebel army and were now bearing the style and title of colonel or gen-

Nicaragua.

eral. The Bluefields hotel where they congregated was nicknamed "the War College" by the Panama Marines, who one morning herded the whole crew aboard a tramp steamer and sent them packing—a distinct contribution to the peace and dignity of Nicaragua.

More serious trouble came to a head in 1912. All Nicaragua was in civil war, and the American Legation at Managua was well-nigh besieged. A seaman guard was sent up from Corinto, while the Panama battalion, 13 officers and 341 enlisted men, was again sent for. On 15 August 1912, Major Butler's people reached Managua only to find that the rebels, this time against a United States-supported government, had just stolen a whole railroad train (apparently the last on hand) in which the Navy legation guard had been embarked, forcing the footsore sailors, led by a crestfallen commander, to walk 12 miles back to town. After recapturing the train, the Marines set about neutralizing and repairing the railroad lifeline between Managua, on Lake Managua, and Corinto.

The railroad was the axis of revolution, with loyal and rebel areas checkerboarded along its length, each determined to block the other. Since American policy favored the Diaz regime in office, efforts were directed against the rebels headed by Generals Mena and Zeledon, whose headquarters were in Leon and Masaya.

On 4 September, Colonel J. H. ("Uncle Joe") Pendleton arrived at Corinto in the USS *Buffalo* with the 780-man 1st Provisional Regiment from Philadelphia. Meanwhile, the Pacific Fleet had reinforced Butler with two battalions made up of ships' landing forces, Marine and sailor, from the USS *California* and *Colorado,* both armored cruisers. Pendleton, senior officer ashore, assumed command of all.

To clear the coastal route to Managua, Pendleton stationed a battalion at Leon, then set out for Granada, at the end of the line on Lake Nicaragua. Between Managua and Granada lay Masaya, rebel stronghold where the railroad threaded a canyon-like defile between two fortified hills, Barranca and Coyotepe. Major Butler headed a column made up of his battalion and that of Major W. N. ("Wild Bill") McKelvy and one artillery battery from the 1st Regiment; Butler's mission was to relieve Granada, invested by the rebels.

After alternating negotiations and skirmishes with rebel forces, the Marines reached Granada on 22 September 1912 and disarmed the rebels headed by General Mena. The other leader, Zeledon, still held his two hilltops outside Masaya, however. "Those little hills," later commented Smedley Butler,[78] "were a tough nut to crack." They commanded the valley and effectively guarded the approach to Masaya. To complicate matters, Zeledon's men—more than a thousand—had wrecked a train so as to block the railroad within the fields of fire of the two hills.

On 2 October, Butler's battalion, with the artillery, deployed west of Coyotepe. All day on 3 October the artillery shelled the hill, but Zeledon hung on. After Pendleton came up with McKelvy's battalion and a seaman battalion from the *California,* the force moved to jump-off positions for a pre-dawn attack on 4 October. At 0330 the Marines and bluejackets moved out and were ready for the final assault at 0515.

On orders from "Uncle Joe" Pendleton the Americans swarmed forward and the artillery banged away. Despite "devilish hot blazing" by Zeledon, and barbed wire near the crest, McKelvy's battalion made it to the top in less than 40 minutes, with the others close behind. The rebels streamed clear while Marines and seaman gunners turned Coyotepe's cannon onto adjoining Barranca and shot the few remaining insurgents out of their positions there. Zeledon himself was killed by his own men. The battle was over in time for breakfast. Eighteen Marines had become casualties, and at least 60 Nicaraguans were killed.

The victory at Coyotepe broke the rebellion in Nicaragua, even though considerable mopping up remained. At Leon, for example, the town had to be taken in hand by a force of Marines and seamen under Lieutenant Colonel C. G. ("Squeegee") Long, who sustained six casualties before the rebels were dispersed. After that, the 1st Regiment was withdrawn, except for Colonel Long and a battalion which stayed in uneasy Leon until January 1913. At Managua a legation guard settled down for what was destined to be a 12-year tour. The situation was well in hand.

INTERVENTION IN HAITI

By late 1914 the Negro republic of Haiti was on the brink of collapse. Since 1886, only 28 years before, the country had run through ten presidents: four murdered, and the remainder driven from office by revolution. Haiti's finances, underwritten for years by foreign banks (mainly in France, Germany, and the United States) had finally petered out when the government was unable to collect or keep enough revenue to meet its interest payments or payrolls. In December 1914 the Marine detachment of the USS *Machias,* a coal-burning gunboat of the nineties, landed on State Department orders in Port-au-Prince and transferred the last $500,000 of Haiti's gold reserve to the vaults of the National City Bank in New York.

In March 1915, Haiti was wracked by a revolution which brought about the brief but bloody presidency of Vilbrun Guillaume Sam. Later in the year as summer descended, bringing rains and mosquitoes, still another revolution, led by Dr. Rosalvo Bobo, brewed up north. As Smedley Butler wrote:[79]

> Revolutions followed a definite procedure in Haiti. They always started in the north near the Dominican border so that the rebels could skip over to the sister Republic when the odds were against them. The first battle was invariably fought at Kilometer Post 17 on the railroad to Grande Rivière. Don't ask me why. That's the way it used to happen in Haiti.

In addition to Haiti's money problems, the State Department had good reason to fear a breach of the Monroe Doctrine if the United States did not assert control. Germany—which for many years had been attempting to gain control of Haiti's customs and negotiate "commercial" coaling-station and base rights at Mole St. Nicholas—landed Marines at Port-au-Prince in the Zamor revolution of February 1914 (as did France, Great Britain, and the United States). And on 19 June 1915, when Bobo launched his revolt against President Sam, a landing force from the French cruiser *Descartes* virtually took over Cap-Haitien. It was this last event which forced the United States to put ashore the spearhead of what was to become a 20-year protectorate. As soon as Rear Admiral William Caperton could get to Cap-Haitien in the armored cruiser *Washington,* he landed one officer, 11 Marines, and a field radio set, such as had advised Barnett of his promotion on Culebra and which had seen good service at Veracruz.

On 27 July, at four in the morning, the president's palace in Port-au-Prince was fired on by a group of attackers. Hearing the firing, the military governor of the city, General Oscar Etienne, personally undertook the murder of 167 political hostages (mainly from the mulatto "elite" families of Port-au-Prince), who had been collected on President Sam's order in the National Penitentiary.[80] By nightfall the grim old *Pénitencier* had become an abattoir in which the executioners resorted to the machete and *coco-macaque* after running out of ammunition. Among those slaughtered was Oreste Zamor, a former president whom Sam had detained. Blood flowed under the prison gateway into the dusty street outside. With enemies clamoring outside the city and the townspeople in fury, President Sam sought asylum in the French Legation while General Etienne hid in that of Santo Domingo. Quickly discovered, Etienne was killed, mutilated, and left lying in a gutter. In the French Legation, President Sam, "in a perfect

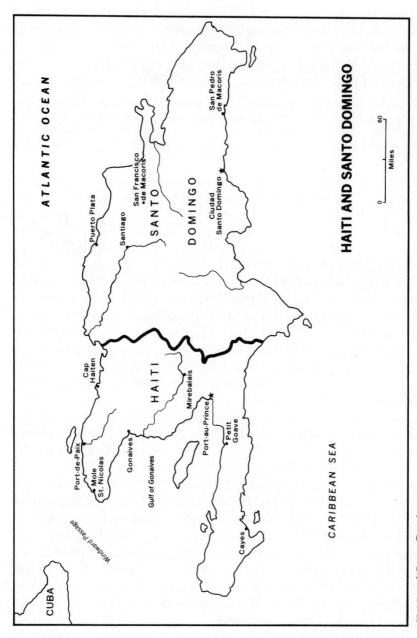

ATLANTIC OCEAN

Puerto Plata

Santiago

San Francisco
de Macoris

SANTO

DOMINGO

San Pedro
de Macoris

Ciudad
Santo Domingo

Cap
Haiten

HAITI

Mirebalais

Port-de-Paix

Mole
St. Nicolas

Gonaives

Gulf of Gonaives

Port-au-Prince

Petit
Goave

Windward Passage

CUBA

CARIBBEAN SEA

Cayes

HAITI AND SANTO DOMINGO

0   60

Miles

Haiti and Santo Domingo

frenzy of fear, creeping about the house like a hunted animal," was hunted down, dragged out of a locked bathroom, and thrown over a wall to the mob. In the words of the American chargé d'affaires:[81]

> I could see that something or somebody was on the ground in the center of the crowd, just before the gates, and when a man disentangled himself from the crowd and rushed howling by me, with a severed hand from which the blood was dripping, the thumb of which he had stuck in his mouth, I knew that the threatened assassination of the President had been accomplished. Behind him came other men with the feet, the other hand, the head, and other parts of the body displayed on poles, each one followed by a mob of screaming men and women.

With two foreign legations violated by the mob and with two presidents murdered within 36 hours, government in Haiti had ceased to exist.

Next day, while mourning crowds were leaving the interment ceremonies for Sam's victims, the USS *Washington* reached Port-au-Prince. After consulting with the American, British, and French Ministers, Admiral Caperton landed Marines under Captain George O. Van Orden, and a bluejacket landing force, at Bizoton, west of the city. The admiral then radioed Guantanamo for help, which arrived within 24 hours, in the form of the 24th Company aboard the collier USS *Jason*. Five days later, the battleship *Connecticut*, which had completed a record run south with regimental headquarters and five companies of the 2d Regiment under Colonel E. K. Cole, steamed in and Colonel Cole took command ashore. On 15 August, Colonel Waller arrived aboard the armored cruiser *Tennessee* with 1st Brigade headquarters and eight more companies of the 1st Regiment. On State Department orders, Waller assumed command in Haiti, his brigade being meanwhile reinforced by the field artillery battalion (Lejeune's recent offspring), from Annapolis.

Waller had two immediate tasks. His first was to take over the ten customhouses of Haiti, thus assuring fiscal control. Following that, the brigade had to pacify the country and re-establish enough order to permit a Haitian government to be reconstituted.

Securing the customhouses was quickly and smoothly accomplished. Within a month Marines had garrisoned Port-au-Prince, Port-de-Paix, Cap-Haitien, Gonaives, St. Marc, Petit-Goâve, Miragoâne, Jérémie, Cayes, and Jacmel. With 88 officers and 1,941 enlisted Marines ashore in Haiti, the 1st Marine Brigade bit into the job of restoring peace.

On 12 August, a new president, Sudre Dartiguenave, was elected with the understanding that he would negotiate a treaty regularizing existing relations with the United States. This was done in due course, providing for an American Financial Advisor, Receiver of Customs, Director of Public Works and Sanitation, and a United States-officered native gendarmerie.

The source of many of Haiti's headaches was a species of political bandits, known as *cacos*, who were most active in the mountains of the north. Their title came from a bird of prey with a red plume, which lives off weaker birds. Since the human cacos lived off the weak, the name came naturally; every caco wore red somewhere on his ragged clothes as a badge of identification and warning. As Colonel Waller commented:[82]

. . . the cacos have been the controlling element in all revolutions; they were purchased by first one candidate and then another. Finishing a contract with one man, they, having put him in power, would immediately sell their services to the next aspirant and unseat the first.

Thus the north of Haiti was a kind of black Sicily, and the cacos its Mafia. In the present instance, a defeated presidential candidate, Dr. Bobo, had obtained caco support and was resolved to bring down the Dartiguenave government if he could. This put Bobo and his cacos squarely in opposition to the American authorities.

The first step in controlling the cacos was elementary—run them out of Port-au-Prince, where hundreds had, in true bird-of-prey fashion, concentrated during the breakdown of government. On 6 August 1915, three days after landing, the 2d Marines had swept every known caco across the city limits, disarming many, locking up a few, and exchanging scattered shots in the process.

Gonaives, principal seaport north of Port-au-Prince, was the first trouble spot. To test the mettle of their new opponents, cacos began a blockade of Gonaives in September. Under "General" Rameau, they first cut off food, then the town water supply, and finally laid complete siege, 400 strong. The 7th Company, at Gonaives, was greatly outnumbered, and the USS *Castine*, another old-time gunboat, chugged in to help. At the same time Colonel Waller ordered Major Smedley Butler to take command. Butler immediately commenced a two-pronged campaign of patrolling and negotiating. The high point was a completely unforeseen fracas with Rameau's men, who were trying to burn a narrow-gauge railroad bridge outside town. It was early evening, and the Marines in their quarters were mainly sweltering in their "skivvies." When "Call to Arms" sounded, they poured out as they were, with rifles, cartridge belts, field hats, shoes, underwear, and nothing else. Led by Butler (and a young lieutenant, A. A. Vandegrift), the Marines chased the cacos far and wide. Next day, this time with their trousers on, Butler's people caught up with Rameau at Poteaux, 11 miles north of Gonaives. Rameau—"a sour looking, vicious little devil"[83]—was yanked off his horse by Major Butler and sent south for a sojourn at the *Pénitencier National*, now under new management.

Meanwhile hotter trouble was erupting around Cap-Haitien in the north. Here again the cacos tried a blockade, this time against the 1st Battalion, 1st Marines, under Colonel Cole, whom Colonel Waller had sent to take charge of the uneasy north.

On 20 September a Marine patrol was ambushed south of Cap-Haitien when it pushed through the caco lines. Two more patrols came to the rescue and were in turn attacked. Cole called in the landing force of the USS *Connecticut*, lying offshore, and headed for the scene with the rest of his battalion while the *Connecticut's* people held the town. Cole's reinforcements turned the tide, and the cacos melted away leaving 40 dead behind. Total Marine casualties were 10 wounded.

The following week, Colonel Cole marched his battalion down the railroad on Quartier Morin, southeast of Cap-Haitien. Here, in the form of a large caco headquarters, was the immediate source of trouble. On 27 September, Cole took Quartier Morin, left a detachment to hold it, and sent patrols still deeper into bandit country.

Colonel Waller now gave the north of Haiti his personal attention. To control the key spot, Ouanaminthe, on the Dominican border, he left the 11th Company, having paid off the ragged Haitian garrison (most of whom, at the pay table, claimed rank as *Général de Brigade*—the highest paying grade—and were so paid). This sealed off the border. Waller concentrated two companies at Grande Rivière du Nord and Fort Liberté, making, with Ouanaminthe, a triangle of key towns garrisoned between Cap-Haitien and Santo Domingo. Then, after extracting promises of more peaceful behavior from some caco leaders and buying in more than a thousand rifles (at $10 per weapon), Waller returned to the capital, leaving Colonel Cole in command at Grande Rivière du Nord.

The next move was to send out Major Butler on a six-day mounted patrol, with Captain W. P. ("Deacon") Upshur, two lieutenants, a Navy surgeon, and 40 enlisted Marines. The gunnery sergeant was Daniel Daly, last heard of on the Tartar Wall in Peking. The patrol had one machine gun. Its objective was to locate and capture Fort Capois, reputedly the main caco stronghold.

On the afternoon of 24 October, led by a Haitian guide, Butler came in sight of Fort Capois:[84]

. . . a mountain peak about a mile away, towering 1,000 feet above us. The cone shaped peak was circled with rough stone walls and trenches. Every detail was outlined distinctly in the afternoon sunlight. Through my field glasses I saw men crawling over the ramparts.

This was a lot more than 40 men could handle, and Butler, who (correctly) suspected double-dealing by his guide, commenced what he hoped would be an unopposed withdrawal to Grande Rivière. After dark, while the patrol was negotiating a rushing mountain river, a blast of rifle fire ripped out from the bush. Some 400 cacos from Fort Capois and nearby Fort Dipitié, another lesser stronghold, had closed in. All night the column was surrounded and under steady fire. Moreover, the pack horse carrying the machine gun had been killed by the first volley while fording the stream. Once the patrol was in a tenable position, Gunnery Sergeant Daly made his way back alone in the dark, through the caco lines, located the dead animal, removed the machine gun and ammunition, and struggled back with them to the beleaguered Marines. For this feat Daly received his second Medal of Honor.

When day broke, instead of letting the cacos close the trap, Butler attacked with his entire force—in three directions. The astonished cacos broke and ran. Captain Upshur and First Lieutenant E. A. Ostermann (despite a painful wound) chased them to Fort Dipitié, stormed it without stopping for breath, and burned and demolished the fort. Eighteen caco dead and wounded were counted, and Upshur and Ostermann (both destined to be general officers) were awarded Medals of Honor.

After this night of thrills, Major Butler led his patrol back to Grande Rivière du Nord where a column, under Captain Chandler Campbell, was at once organized to take Fort Capois. With five companies of Marines and two companies of seamen from the *Connecticut*, Captain Campbell surrounded the fort, only to find that the cacos, after initial resistance, had cleared out in the nick of time. On November 7th and 8th, two more forts, Selon and Berthol, were captured by a column under Major Butler. These victories, with another fight outside Grande Rivière, for the time being brought peace to the Plaine du Nord. As Waller reported:[85]

The mobile columns have averaged 15 miles a day for nine days, are as hard as nails and fit for anything.

CLIMAX ON MONTAGNE NOIRE

As the pressure built up, the cacos pulled back deeper and deeper into the mountains. Their final stronghold was Fort Rivière. As Smedley Butler related:[86]

It was an old bastion fort with thick walls of brick and stone, built in the latter part of the 18th century during the French occupation . . . on the peak of Montagne Noire, 4,000 feet above the sea, midway between Grande Rivière, Dondon, San Rafael and Bahon. On three sides the masonry of the wall joined the rock of the mountain, thus forming a steep precipice into the valley. On the fourth side, a gentle slope led to the sally port.

Fort Rivière had been located by a reconnaissance sent out by Colonel Cole, who entrusted the job to Major Butler. For the assault, Butler was given the 5th, 13th, and 23d Companies, the Marines from the *Connecticut*, and one seaman company from the same ship—". . . a splendid crowd," said Butler.

During the night of 17 November 1915 the force converged on Fort Rivière over three trails and began the all-night climb up Montagne Noire. At daybreak the Marines were in jump-off positions around the fort, which was 200 feet square with 30-foot walls. On a whistle signal from Butler the assault commenced.

While one company maintained a steady fire on the south face, another company worked its way across the bare, fire-swept west slope leading to the sally port. The storming party consisted of 24 enlisted Marines with two Benet automatic rifles, led by Major Butler, First Lieutenant John Marston, and Second Lieutenant George Stowell.

To their consternation, on reaching the shelter, such as it was, of the dead space under the walls, the Marines discovered that the sally port had been bricked up. The caco entrance was via a slippery masonry drain four feet high, three feet wide, and more than 15 feet long. Just inside was a caco sentry taking pot shots at all and sundry.

For an interminable moment, all hands waited poised. Then Sergeant Ross L. Iams spat out, "Oh hell, I'm going through," and rushed the tunnel entrance. Immediately behind him were Private Samuel Gross and Major Butler. As the caco sentry fired wild shots down the masonry tunnel, the three scrambled up, miraculously unhit. In a few seconds they were at the inner end. Sergeant Iams caught the caco sentry reloading, and shot him down. Gross and Butler were on his heels as some 70 bandits rushed wildly toward them. Covered by the three Marines fighting hand to hand at the tunnel mouth, the 13th Company swarmed up the passage and into Fort Rivière.

In the Donnybrook that followed, the Haitians threw away rifles and fought with machetes, sticks, and stones, only to be shot and bayoneted by the Marines. "General" Josephette, their leader, who had once been a cabinet officer, was killed in his habitual garb—black frock coat, plug hat, and brass watch chain. Within 15 minutes of Iams's rush, 50 cacos lay dead in Fort Rivière, and the caco movement in the north was dead with them. A ton of dynamite blew the fort sky-high.

For this assault, Iams and Gross received well-deserved Medals of Honor, and Major Butler was awarded his second Medal of Honor (his first had been won at Veracruz). More than a year later, the fame of Butler's assault was still sufficient to prompt Assistant Secretary of the Navy Franklin Roosevelt to ask to have Fort Rivière included in his itinerary during an inspection of Haiti planned for early 1917. Accompanied by General Barnett and Captain R. S. Keyser, Roosevelt got as far as Port-au-Prince, only to have the rest of the trip canceled because of increasing tension with Germany. Even so, the future President retained lifelong interests in Haiti and in the Marine Corps —both to be manifest as the years went by.

GENDARMERIE D'HAITI

Under Article X of the treaty which was finally ratified in December 1915 between the revived Haitian government and the United States, it was agreed that the United States would organize a Haitian constabulary officered by Americans. This force would replace Haiti's Army, later described by General Russell, the American High Commissioner, in the following terms:[87]

The Haitian Army before 1915 consisted of 38 line and 4 artillery regiments of a total paper strength of over 9,000, a *gendarmerie* of over 1,800, plus 4 regiments of the President's guard, and the whole was officered by 308 generals and 50 colonels, not to mention the honorary generals created by the President, *pro tem*, among his friends. The pay of the private was 20 cents a month, plus 80 cents for rations, none of which was ever received, with the exception of a few troops selected for honor duty. The soldiers' pay, plus appropriations for medical service and uniforms, went into the pockets of the generals. . . . The former method of recruiting without legal basis was performed to line the pockets of the generals who sent their soldiers out to impress all young men, whether of military age or not, to join their army. Those who would pay a bribe of around $2 were released from serving, and members of the *élite* families were allowed to engage in the fire brigade or the parade companies. The others were forced into service. With these conditions obtaining, it is small wonder that revolutions were never suppressed by the standing army, that many of the recruits for these insurrections came from the army itself, and that oppressive lawlessness was the rule.

To replace the predecessor organization, just described, formation of the Haitian Gendarmerie commenced in September 1915, with a strength of 336, mostly privates. On 1 February 1916, the Gendarmerie assumed police responsibilities for the entire country. As a cadre of leaders, French-speaking Marine and naval officers with the brigade were transferred to the senior posts as Gendarmerie officers, while Marine NCOs and Navy corpsmen became junior officers. The first commandant of the Gendarmerie was Major Butler, who for his new job was commissioned a major general in the Haitian service.

The 336 gendarmes had to take over the internal security of a country covering 10,714 square miles with a population of 2,500,000. Pay, promptly and fully paid, even though modest, and decent rations were the principal means of making the service attractive to Haitian recruits. These were novelties in Haiti where corrupt politicians and senior officers routinely diverted all pay and left soldiery and police to fill their pockets and stomachs at the expense of fellow citizens. The gendarmes drilled in English by commands out of the *Infantry Drill Regulations,* a system which prevailed until the end of the occupation, almost two decades later. They were equipped with surplus Marine uniforms and gear, and armed with Krag carbines (ultimately with early-model Springfields). As training progressed rapidly, the size of the Gendarmerie increased to 2,533 Haitian troops and 115 Marine and naval officers. From June 1916 on, by act of Congress, these American personnel were seconded to the service of Haiti and drew, in addition to United States pay, the prescribed Haitian pay of their grades, a feature which made Gendarmerie service highly attractive. Under such leadership, the Gendarmerie became, in amazingly faithful detail, a Haitian replica of the occupying Marines, not merely in uniforms and equipment but, more important, in discipline, courage, and fidelity. That this was so resulted mainly from Marine Corps willingness to invest good United States officers and NCOs in the Gendarmerie. As Butler later related:[88]

It's not easy to build up an efficient organization out of a population speaking a language you don't know with customs you don't understand. But Colonel Waller, with his usual generosity, contributed the pick of the Marines. I have never found their equal anywhere in the United States service. . . . The native gendarmes were good soldiers too. Their most difficult job was to learn to keep shoes on their enormous feet. Out on the trail they often slung their shoes over the muzzles of their rifles. But they wore their footgear with pride when they had an audience, and walked with a swagger, those black soldiers. With shoes and buttons shining and hats cocked over one eye, they strutted along the street and basked in the admiring glances of strapping Negro women. . . . A few months after the new treaty between Haiti and the United States in 1916, the Gendarmerie was sufficiently drilled and disciplined to take over the whole policing of the republic.

What results were soon being achieved by the American occupation, of which the Gendarmerie was the spearhead, can be measured in a 1916 appraisal by the Episcopal Bishop of Haiti, the Rt. Rev. Charles B. Colmore:[89]

The reconstruction work of the United States Marines in Haiti provides one of the most thrilling and gratifying chapters in contemporaneous American history. . . . The Marines have literally taught the Haitians how to live decently. Before their coming, sanitation, save in the crudest and most unsatisfactory forms, was unknown; fevers and epidemics were as plentiful as revolutions, a press gang was in vogue and the country was the victim of continuous uprisings engineered by political scoundrels, each of whom ravaged the customs money drawer as each in turn came into short-lived power. The entry of the United States Marines ended this sorry story.

TROUBLE IN SANTO DOMINGO

In eastern Hispaniola, events were coming to a boil. Santo Domingo, Haiti's Spanish-speaking neighbor, was under a United States-sponsored financial receivership which dated back to 1904 when Theodore Roosevelt had intervened to avert action by Santo Domingo's European creditors, principally France, Belgium, Germany, Italy, and Spain. The succeeding 12 years, although intermittently peaceful, saw increasing political dissension and some discontent over the stupidity and ineptitude of a politically appointed United States ambassador, as well as the acts of the American financial advisor, who stubbornly insisted on using the national revenue for national improvements and to liquidate Dominican indebtedness.

In April 1916, civil war again broke out in the capital, and the government, though not defunct like that in Haiti, was powerless. Reluctantly, Secretary of State William Jennings Bryan, pacifist though he was, advised President Wilson that the United States should intervene.

Although the Advance Base Force was fully committed in Haiti, there was no alternative but to detach units for Santo Domingo next door. On 5 May 1916, the 6th and 9th Companies (the latter a field artillery battery) were transferred aboard the USS *Prairie* from Port-au-Prince to Ciudad Santo Domingo, under command of Captain F. M. ("Dopey") Wise. Quickly sizing up a bad situation in the city proper, Wise landed his Marines and some bluejackets at Fort San Geronimo outside town and established a base for further operations under the 4-inch guns of the gunboat *Castine*. Meanwhile, seven more companies were shaken together from Port-au-Prince, Cap-Haitien, and the Marine Barracks at Fisherman's Point, Guantanamo Bay. These landed on 12 May from the USS *Culgoa*, but still weren't enough. As rebel forces held the city and the American landing force sheltered President Jiminez in their camp, three ships' detachments and more seamen were landed. Admiral Caperton, fresh from the pacification of Haiti, arrived and assumed over-all command. Accompanying Caperton from Haiti, was Major Newt Hall, last seen during the defense of the legations in Peking. With Wise as his executive officer, Hall made ready to assault Ciudad Santo Domingo with 375 Marines and 225 bluejackets at dawn on 15 May. Wise recalled:[90]

> It was Vera Cruz all over again, minus the first day of fighting. House by house, block by block, we combed Santo Domingo City clear to the beach. Not a shot was fired at us. Not one of our men fired a shot. We never found a weapon in all those houses. Arias [the rebel leader] and his army had departed the night before.

The dearth of weapons in what had been a menacingly armed town was not due to any overestimate of the situation by Hall and Wise. In fact, before the occupation of Santo Domingo was 18 months old, Marines had captured 53,000 stand of arms and 14,000 knives and machetes, and armed banditry was still going strong. The rebel Arias had decamped with at least a thousand armed men for the hill town of Santiago and there proclaimed his government.

To get at Arias and sustain the existing lawful government, it was necessary to extend United States control to the north coast of the island (which is divided by a central east-west mountain range). On 26 May, Wise landed with the Marine detachment from the USS *Louisiana* (embarked in the old *Panther*) and took over Monte Cristi on the north coast near the Haitian frontier. While guarding the town waterworks, the Marines were fired on by about 150 rebels. Wise had one machine gun, but held his fire as the bandits closed in.

> In a ragged, irregular group holding their rifles high and free arm, and shooting as they came, they ran down the hill toward the road. . . . When they reached the road, we opened up with the machine-gun. . . . I could see sheer amazement on their faces. The gun was functioning properly. All up and down the line I could see them dropping. Then they turned and ran. . . . I went over to the road to see what damage we had done. I found 39 casualties. . . . The food blockade ceased. Life in Monte Cristi went back to normal.[91]

Due east of Monte Cristi lies Puerto Plata, where Carmick had landed in 1800. Communications running inland from the two coastal towns converge in the mountains at Santiago, headquarters of Arias. On 1 June, under Major C. B. Hatch, Marines from the *Rhode Island* and the *New Jersey* (sent down aboard the cruiser *Salem*), accompanied by a seaman landing force, hit the beach at Puerto Plata under sharp rifle fire from hostile Dominicans. Before the steam launches and cutters could touch down, Captain J. H. Hirshinger was mortally wounded. But the Marines and bluejackets pushed ahead, and the fire of the USS *Sacramento*, a new gunboat, soon knocked the starch out of the defenders. The rebels then abandoned their fortifications and fell back southward into the high mountains toward Santiago.

Thus ended the first phase of a hot campaign. Santo Domingo City was occupied, and, in the north, Marines held the two ports necessary for operations against Arias in his mountain capital.

"UNCLE JOE" PENDLETON TAKES SANTIAGO

The thoroughly inflamed state of affairs demanded reinforcements. The only Marines left were "Uncle Joe" Pendleton's 4th Regiment, now designated as "The West Coast Expeditionary Force." Early in 1916, Marine Barracks, San Diego, had been made the permanent station of this force, but events in Santo Domingo were to prevent the 4th Marines from seeing San Diego for some time.

On 4 June the Major General Commandant ordered Pendleton to proceed by rail with the 4th Regiment to New Orleans. Two days later the regiment was rolling eastward on the Sante Fe. On 9 June the Marines were swinging their seabags and expeditionary gear into the compartments of the USS *Hancock* at New Orleans, whence the 4th Marines—reinforced by the 8th Company—steamed for Santo Domingo.

On 18 June, Colonel Pendleton relieved Colonel T. P. Kane (who had been senior Marine officer ashore), and organized the heterogeneous collection of Marines in Santo Domingo into the 2d Brigade, 47 officers and 1,738 enlisted men. Although not a balanced outfit like the 1st Brigade in Haiti, Pendleton's homemade brigade included a mounted reconnaissance detachment, a field artillery battalion, and motor transport. Among this last were all 12 Model "T" Fords in stock at the Ford agency in Monte Cristi, purchased outright by the brigade paymaster, and a dazzling windfall for the dealer.

The advance on Santiago presented "Uncle Joe" with a problem strikingly like that which he had solved so efficiently in Nicaragua in 1912—operations deep inland through mountainous enemy country with a determined foe entrenched in his path.

Leaving five officers and 230 men (25th Company and two ships' detachments) to safeguard his base at Monte Cristi, Pendleton hit the road, "little more than a muddy trail through a jungle of cactus and thorny brush," with the remainder of the 4th Marines, 33 officers and 800 men, organized into two rifle battalions, an artillery battalion, and a combat train. The latter was under command of Captain Wise, who recalled:[92]

> Our main reliance was the San Dominican cart, a two-wheel springless affair with one mule between the shafts, and two other mules, one on each side. . . . Then, through the aid of a civilian we got a Holt tractor, five Studebaker wagon trailers, two White motor trucks, two Quads, and 12 Ford touring cars. It was one of the strangest transport systems in the history of the Corps.

On 26 June, the first day out of Monte Cristi, the 4th Marines covered 25 kilometers without opposition. Two miles east of their bivouac lay the frowning ridge, Las Trencheras. Here in 1864 Dominican rebels had whipped a Spanish army. Now they were lying in wait for the Marines.

In characteristic style, as he had done at Coyotepe Hill, "Uncle Joe" carefully planned his fire support. While the artillery were to neutralize the Dominican trenches on the ridge, the one machine gun company was sited to enfilade. By daylight 27 June, the 4th Regiment was deployed in line and ready to attack. With Major R. H. Dunlap (Pendleton's executive officer) personally co-ordinating the attack, both battalions worked forward as the 3-inch landing guns pounded away. The final assault on the first line of trenches was handsomely pushed home with fixed bayonets. As the Dominicans bolted, Marine riflemen picked them off, then pursued and shot them out of their second line. Las Trencheras belonged to the U. S. Marines.

Pendleton continued his advance but broke no speed records, not only because the Dominicans—like the Haitians—had failed to build or maintain decent roads for many years, but also because they had burned all bridges on the Marines' route. On 28 June the rebels tried an unsuccessful night attack (believing that Pendleton's machine guns—dubbed "sprinklers" by the Dominicans—didn't work at night). During the next two days the Dominicans again fruitlessly attempted to halt the column by continual sniping and two daytime skirmishes which served only to demonstrate ill will.

The final and decisive fight occurred on 3 July at Guayacanas, a well-organized, strong ridge lying across the road like Las Trencheras. Here, under short-range enemy fire, Marine machine gun crews were shot down one after another as they supported the attack. Corporal Joseph A. Glowin, after being hit twice, fell beside his gun, being relieved with a second gun and crew by First Sergeant (later Colonel) Roswell Winans, who singlehandedly raked the enemy lines, cleared a stoppage under a hail of musketry, and finally achieved fire superiority. When the Marines carried the final trenches, a recently emptied rum barrel explained the recklessness of the defense. Both Winans and Glowin were awarded Medals of Honor.

Meanwhile, Major "Hiking Hiram" Bearss, with the 4th and 9th Companies and the *New Jersey* detachment, was advancing inland from Puerto Plata up the railroad which led to Santiago. No Dominican trainmen could be found, so two members of the USS *Sacramento's* black gang were brevetted engineer and fireman. The train consisted of all four of the road's boxcars, the engine, and, pushed ahead as the spearhead, a sandbagged flat car with a landing gun on the business end.

The "railroad battalion" highballed south on 26 June and had somewhat the same experiences as Pendleton, continual sniping and occasional exchanges of volleys. On 29 June, when the rebels massed on La Cumbre mountain through which the railroad tunneled, Bearss mounted a handcar (to guard against mines) and led his train through the tunnel in a subterranean envelopment. Although the handcar detonated no mines, the Dominicans foiled this maneuver by a quick getaway. As one fellow Marine reported, "It was the most fun Hiram had enjoyed in a long time."

On 4 July, at Navarrete, Pendleton (who had severed communications with his base at Monte Cristi) encountered the railroad and found Bearss waiting for him with his train. Bearss's battalion, augmented by the 24th Company, up from Puerto Plata, then reinforced the 4th Marines for the final advance on Santiago, which Pendleton occupied without further opposition on 6 July 1916. At a total cost of 23 officers and men killed and wounded, the Marines had broken the back of the rebellion.

POLICING THE DOMINICAN REPUBLIC

After the fall of Santiago, ten principal Dominican towns were garrisoned, and the 2d Brigade settled down for what was destined to be an eight-year stay. The Department of State had concluded that an American military government was the only solution to Santo Domingo's chronic inability to govern itself. Captain H. S. Knapp, USN, arrived from home with instructions to that effect, and on 29 November 1916 became the first Military Governor of Santo Domingo.

On the same day, at the inland town of San Francisco de Macoris, First Lieutenant E. C. Williams, commanding a small detachment, found himself confronting a large, hostile garrison occupying the local *fortaleza* with no intention whatever of surrendering to the new government. Leading 12 men in a sudden dash, Williams charged the fort. Although eight of the party were wounded, Williams gained the door just as the Dominicans tried to bar it. Forcing his way inside with his remaining Marines, Williams subdued the 40-man garrison and took possession—a feat which won him the Medal of Honor.

Following the proclamation of military government, Colonel Pendleton remained as commander of the 2d Marine Brigade, with additional duties as Minister of War and Navy, Interior, and Police. The portfolios of Foreign Relations, Justice, and Public Instruction were assigned to Colonel R. H. Lane. Since anti-American sentiment remained general during most of 1916 and 1917, few responsible Dominicans would assist the military government, and Marine and naval officers thus had to assume political duties far afield from any taught at Annapolis or the School of Application.

On 7 April 1917, Admiral Knapp, the Military Governor, formally dissolved the remaining shreds of the Dominican armed forces and ordered the Marines to form a national police force for Santo Domingo, the Guardia Nacional Dominicana. Like the Haitian Gendarmerie, the Guardia Nacional was commanded by Marine officers and NCOs. Its first commandant was Lieutenant Colonel George C. Thorpe. The new Guardia had an authorized strength of 1,234, replacing an army which had previously included 461 generals and 479 colonels. Its officer corps now comprised about 40 U. S. Marine and Navy personnel seconded by permission of Congress, like those in Haiti, to the Dominican government's service. Naturally, in organization, training, uniforms, administration, and discipline, the Guardia Nacional took the Marine Corps as its model, and this impress lasted for many years. Both in courage in combat and in faithfulness to its leaders, whether U. S. or native, the Guardia Nacional Dominicana lived up to its parent Corps. One unforeseen offspring of the Guardia, marked for his efficiency as a junior officer, was Leonidas Rafael Trujillo, destined to rule the country with a ruthlessly efficient hand in years ahead.

THE CORPS SCENE

With the end of 1916, the Marine Corps had reached a momentary pause after an era of great growth, not only professional but physical. In August of that year, with prompting from Colonel Lejeune and Assistant Secretary Roosevelt (who was charged with Marine Corps affairs), Congress increased the strength of the Corps to 596 officers and 14,981 enlisted Marines. Moreover, Congress wrote into law a standby provision to permit the President to augment the Corps to 17,400 enlisted men, when "it becomes necessary to place the country in a complete state of preparedness."

The growth and high standing of the Marine Corps had not gone unnoticed. Under General Barnett's skilled and perceptive administration, the Navy had relegated to the past some of its earlier attitudes towards the Corps, and the Navy-Marine team was once again firm. On the other hand, 1916 saw a foreboding gesture on the part of the Army. This took the form of a War Department General Staff proposal to the Joint Army and Navy Board (premise: "officers of the Marine Corps are *ipso facto* less fitted for high command than are officers of the Army") that, in case of operations involving mixed forces of Army and Marines (or Navy, if present), command should always be vested in the senior Army officer. This suggestion was referred to Colonel Lejeune, who torpedoed it in a trenchant rejoinder:[93]

It is, I believe, an incontestable fact that officers of the Marine Corps, grade for grade, are as well qualified for command on shore as are officers of the Army. . . . Under the acid test of actual experience in the field, Marine officers, as a class, are in no respect inferior to officers of the Army. . . . There is nowhere on record any comment of an unfavorable nature by officers of the Army concerning organizations of Marines which have served with the Army, but there are on file many communications from officers of the Army expressing commendation of the services of Marines. . . .

For the time being the proposal and its invalid premise were shelved, but both were destined to be repeated in the decades ahead.

The enlarged Marine Corps continued to pursue General Biddle's preoccupation with recruit training. After once losing hold of the old Naval Station at Port Royal, the Marine Corps, on 28 October 1915, regained the post, which then became the Parris Island recruit depot, with a 14-week standard course. Recruit quarantine posed no problems in those days since the only means of access to the island was by Navy tug or motor-sailer. To obtain the right kind of recruits in sufficient numbers, new methods appeared. In 1907, for example, the first local recruiting publicity bureau was established in Chicago; its equipment: one rotary mimeograph, one type-writer. Four years later, General Biddle set up the Marine Corps Recruiting Publicity Bureau in New York. The bureau's original mastermind was Gunnery Sergeant Thomas G. Sterrett, one of the pioneer public relations men of his day. Sterrett was succeeded by Master Technical Sergeant Percy Webb, a devoted and ingenious practitioner who summed up his creed in the simple sentence:[94]

I had the utmost faith in the Service I was writing about, and there was no need to gild the lily.

The same law that increased the Corps' strength in 1916 created new ranks. Among the officers, the grade of brigadier general was re-established, and the warrant ranks of Marine gunner and quartermaster clerk were created. Enlisted ranks and monthly pay, effective from 1908 on, were as follows:

Sergeant major, drum major, first sergeant, quartermaster sergeant, gunnery sergeant	$45
Sergeant	$30
Corporal	$21
Drummer, trumpeter, private	$15

On 17 June 1898, after establishing the Navy Hospital Corps, Congress created the warrant rank of pharmacist and the enlisted grades of hospital steward (chief petty officer), hospital apprentice 1st class (equivalent to 3d class petty officer), and hospital apprentice. In August 1916 these ratings gave way to a modern structure of hospital apprentice ranks equivalent to seaman ratings, and of pharmacist's mates in all the normal petty-officer ratings.

As might be supposed, with T.R. as President, physical fitness was a live subject. On 4 January 1909, General Order No. 6, issued at the President's personal direction, required that, once a year and whenever examined for promotion, each officer walk 50 miles in three days, or cover 90 miles on horseback, or 100 miles by bicycle in the same time. When Captain Henry Leonard, one-armed but vigorous, walked the whole stretch in one day, he was reprimanded and made to do it over, according to the book, in three days. Like a good officer he complied with his orders, walking 49 miles the first day and a half mile on each of the succeeding two.

Still another Roosevelt (Assistant Secretary Franklin D.) took an equally active but not so strenuous interest in Marine Corps matters. A typical excursion, recorded in a letter to his wife in 1915, was to the rifle range at Winthrop, Maryland (the first range ever built for the Marine Corps):[95]

Yesterday we had a most successful trip on the *Sylph* to Indian Head or rather Camp Winthrop, the rifle range just below there. General Barnett, Capt. McLean, Capt. Harlee and John McIlhenny went with me and we spent an hour going over the range and watching the rifle and machine gun drill. Then we drove over the reservation and had supper with Capt. & Mrs. Price.

Aside from such trips as this, Secretary Roosevelt kept in close touch with the Marine point of view through a weekly golfing round at the Chevy Chase Club in a foursome which included his good friend Colonel Mc-Cawley, Quartermaster of the Corps.

The natural development of 18 years' campaigning which began in 1898 was a new family of Marine Corps uniforms designed for field service, a family which, although now retired from combat duty, is mainly still used for routine service ashore.

In mounting out Huntington's battalion for Guantanamo, General Heywood quickly concluded that undress blues or whites with white helmets were not exactly suited for tropical campaigning. In a logistic blitz, the Philadelphia Depot of Supplies therefore turned out "campaign suits of brown linen" in a matter of weeks, while the Quartermaster turned to the Army for "campaign hats." Of the summer underwear obtained at the same time, Colonel Huntington later commented, "The so-called light weight underclothes would be much better if they were lighter in weight."[96] In any case, both field hat and khaki had now joined the Marine Corps.

The post-Spanish war uniform consisted of cotton khaki trousers; first blue, then mustard-colored flannel shirt; field hat (with fore-and-aft dent and emblem worn on the left side of the crown until 1901); and no field scarf. An English observer of the Boxer relief expedition opined:[97]

It is doubtful whether there was a more sensibly clothed or better armed body of troops in China than the Americans. The Marines wore soft brown felt hats, blue flannel shirts, warm and comfortable, and khaki trousers with dust-colored leggings.

In 1903, a standing-collar khaki blouse, cut like the blue and white blouses, was adopted, primarily for wear aboard ship. So were a khaki cap cover and a flannel field scarf of the same material as the shirt. In 1912 the so-called "Montana" four-dent peak supplanted the fore-and-aft shape of earlier field hats.

In 1912 it was also realized that a winter field uniform was needed to match the khaki summer outfit. Drawing on the Corps' traditional status as light infantry (which had been symbolized years before by the hunting-horn insignia), it was decided to adopt forest, or rifle green, with bronze hardware, as the winter field uniform of the Marine Corps. The combination of forest green and low-visibility bronze could be traced back to the first rifle or jäger regiments of the 18th century, when light infantry were principally recruited from huntsmen, foresters, and gamekeepers, who wore green livery. The first "greens" to be generally worn were issued to Marines in 1914. Again, the cut of the uniform was the same as that of undress blues. Soon after the war with Spain, the frogged and braided blue fatigue blouse for officers gave way to the present type. The accompanying headgear was a conductor-type item with an abbreviated visor. Except for the cut of the cap and a few other minor differences, Marine Corps blues had become what they are today. One change in the enlisted blues waited until 1915, how-ever. This came about when Colonel McCawley, the Quartermaster, was riding to the office in his carriage and noticed two enlisted men on the street wearing blues. "That uniform needs something to smarten it up," he mused to his niece, who was with him. "Why not white belts, Uncle Charlie?" she suggested. "That's a good idea," he replied, and the dress white belt, which late in the 19th century had been reserved exclusively as a duty belt, was thereupon restored to enlisted men's blue as an item for liberty wear.[98]

The rifle which Marines carried in the Spanish war, Boxer Uprising, and part of the Philippine Insurrection, was the Lee 6 mm., described earlier. In adopting this high-velocity rifle using smokeless powder, the Marines were a jump ahead of their Army comrades in Cuba who (except for some Regular units) were mainly armed with single-shot, black-powder .45s. De-spite the Lee's advanced design, it lacked shocking power, and, in 1900, the Marine Corps began conversion to the Army's .30 caliber Krag-Jorgensen, which Marines carried for the next six years. Then, in 1906, the Corps got its first Springfield 30-'03s. The era of the '03 had begun.

From the 1850s, when the first Navy Colts were issued to Marine officers, the Marines' hand gun had mainly been the Colt revolver in various stages of development. The last such revolver, a USMC Colt .45, was superseded in 1911 by the Colt .45 automatic pistol, which had been adopted by the Army as a result of numerous instances in the Philippines when the Army .38 had failed to stop fanatic *juramentado* natives. Failure to drop anyone it hit would never be charged to the Colt .45.

In the late 1890s the most modern crew-served weapon in the hands of Marines was the Colt-Browning machine gun, nicknamed, because of its action, "the potato-digger." This was mounted on wheels like a field gun. The first Marine artillery, the 3-inch landing gun, came in the Spanish war. Its technique of employment was, to say the least, primitive. Much more advanced and original was the Marines' adaptation of naval guns to serve as coast artillery—an art which, little changed, was still in use during World War II.

Although, as we have seen, the first Marine Corps automobile was purchased in 1909, the Advance Base Force employed oxen on Culebra in 1914 to haul guns into position. Between 1909 and World War I, however, the Marine Corps acquired 72 assorted motor vehicles, including two King armored cars, the first motor vehicles ever to be adopted for tactical use by any United States service. In addition to automobiles, the Advance Base Force had many other modern refinements, previously noted, and, for its day, was highly sophisticated in equipment and organization.

By its high degree of readiness and expeditionary knack, and by its status as one of the Naval Services, the Marine Corps had come by 1916 to be a natural arm of American foreign policy—the national force in readiness. In addition, seeds had been sown for amphibious developments still to come.

For the immediate future, however, the best fruits of the years from 1898 to 1916 were the series of far-flung, fighting expeditions in which the rank and file of the Corps had become hard, proficient, and versatile, and in which the leadership had fallen into such hands as those of Barnett, Lejeune, Pendleton, Butler, and Neville.

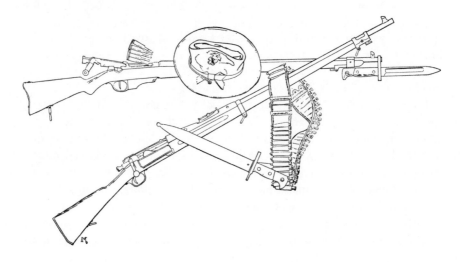

5 OVER THERE *1917-1920*

They never failed me. I look back on my service with the Marine Brigade with more pride and satisfaction than on any other equal period in my long Army career.
—MAJOR GENERAL JAMES G. HARBORD, USA

*T*HE MARINE CORPS being always ready for expeditionary duty," recounted General Barnett, "no extraordinary steps were taken to prepare it for the World War until it seemed probable in December 1916 that the United States would be involved."[1]

Although this statement was true enough, events had been at work to bring the Marine Corps to notable readiness for a role undreamed of by most members of the Corps.

The 1916 Naval Personnel Bill, as we have seen, had enlarged the Marine Corps by nearly 50 per cent, and the resultant recruiting campaign had progressed well. By the same law the grade of brigadier general had been re-created for Marines, and seven notable promotions were made—Lejeune, Waller, Pendleton, and Cole, in the Line; and the three heads of the Staff departments, Lauchheimer, McCawley, and George Richards, the Paymaster. Finally, President Wilson had authority to enlarge the Corps by 2,400 whenever the need arose.

Under the eye of his successor, General Biddle's scheme of recruit depots was now functioning efficiently at Parris Island and Mare Island, and the new base at San Diego was taking shape. A small Marine Corps Reserve had been founded in 1916. By thrift and wise management, General McCawley, perennial Quartermaster of the Marine Corps (1913-1929) and pillar of social Washington, had laid by equipment and supplies to outfit 8,500 additional Marines for field duty.

Thus, it came about that, in early 1917, the U. S. Marine Corps was larger, better trained and organized, more combat experienced, and better led, than at any time in its previous 142 years' service.

MOBILIZING THE MARINE CORPS

On 26 March 1917, with the sands of peace running out, President Wilson enlarged the Corps to 693 officers and 17,400 enlisted men. Eleven days later, the United States was at war with the Central Powers.

As far as the Navy was concerned, the Marine Corps existed for its usual purposes: the Advance Base Force, and ships' guards and security forces for the Fleet and Shore Establishment. To meet these demands, a wartime Marine Corps of 31,197—larger than the regular Army at the beginning of the Spanish war—was voted by Congress on 22 May 1917. In the previous month, on 16 April, the Marine Corps Reserve (three officers and 33 enlisted men) had been mobilized.

Marine Corps recruiting, spurred on by the electric effect of the slogan, "First to Fight," went into high gear. Major A. S. McLemore, in charge of recruiting, who had selected the phrase, was almost overpowered by his own success. By capitalizing on the general desire to get overseas, the Corps found itself swamped by a rush of recruits whose quality was unequaled in the history of the Corps. Parris Island and Mare Island were engulfed, and temporary training stations had to be set up at Philadelphia and Norfolk Navy Yards. Parris Island (which was destined to train 46,000 recruits before the end of the war) handled the lion's share. So many high-spirited young men volunteered that, by 4 June 1917, General Barnett closed down on officer appointments from civilian life and, for the rest of the war, filled the officer corps from the rich talent in the ranks.

To provide operational training and permit organization of tactical units, the Marine Corps badly needed an East Coast base of its own. The Navy had upset long-standing mobilization arrangements by pre-empting barracks and facilities previously allocated for Marine units at Algiers, Louisiana; at Annapolis; and at Winthrop, Maryland. A new site at Quantico, Virginia, seemed, however, to provide all that was needed: training areas, deep-water approaches for transports, and a main railroad line. On 14 May 1917, 6,000 acres were leased and Marine Barracks, Quantico, with four officers and 91 men, commanded by Major Chandler Campbell, was in business. Some of Quantico's original frame buildings had to be lightered across the Potomac from the abandoned rifle range at Stump Neck. Several of these ancient structures were still in use forty years later, having survived World Wars I and II, and the Korean War.

The first regiment to be raised for war service was the 5th Marines. This was mainly organized at League Island Navy Yard with a substantial cadre of experienced Marines in each company. All other units, except the 7th Marines, another Philadelphia regiment, were shaken together and trained at Quantico. Quantico, therefore, was the birthplace of the 6th, 8th, and 9th Marines (all infantry regiments); of the 10th Marines (artillery), the 11th (first artillery, then infantry), the 12th (artillery); the 13th (infantry); and of numerous machine gun battalions and replacement drafts. Of the regiments, the 7th, 8th, and 9th were allocated to the Advance Base Force, while the rest were intended for the American Expeditionary Forces (AEF) in France. As will be seen, not all of them got there.

The new 3,600-man Marine infantry regiments were bigger and different from anything of the kind in the past. In addition to three battalions, each about 1,100 strong, there was a regimental machine gun company armed with Hotchkiss guns, and headquarters and supply companies. Transportation included one automobile (for the colonel), three motorcycles, 59 chargers for officers, and an array of wagons, water carts, and rolling kitchens, drawn by 332 obstinate mules.

As an appropriate preparation for France, mud was the order of the day on the new post of Quantico, which grew by leaps and bounds. The second issue of *The Quantico Leatherneck* (later to become famous as the *Leatherneck*) reported:[2]

> Approximately $250,000 is being spent at Quantico by the government in constructing some of the finest concrete roads in Virginia. In all, eight miles of roadway are being paved. Perhaps the greatest achievement is the building of a concrete road, three and a half miles long, from the head of Potomac Avenue at the river to the Washington-Richmond highway. Other work includes paving of the company streets in the infantry and artillery camps and a concrete road all the way to the range. . . . The road connecting with the Washington-Richmond highway begins at the post garage and extends a short distance northward and thence due westward. It is a much favored road for hikes. . . . Quantico soon will no more be known as "Slippery Mud, Va."

"FIRST TO FIGHT"

In the minds of Generals Barnett and Lejeune, the Marine Corps possessed far greater war capabilities than as a mere satellite to the Navy. General Barnett thus set to work to convince both Secretary of the Navy Josephus Daniels and President Wilson that Marines must not only join the AEF in France, but that they must accompany the first convoy. "We had used the slogan 'First to Fight' on our posters," recalled Barnett, "and I did not want that slogan made ridiculous."[3]

Despite the desperate shortage of trained Army regulars, the Commandant's initial proposals got a cold shoulder from the War Department. Before Marines could be accepted for service in France, Major General John J. Pershing, commanding the American Expeditionary Forces, would have to approve, said Secretary of War Newton D. Baker. General Hugh Scott, the Army Chief of Staff, was more explicit: the Army had enough soldiers of its own.

Then followed eight days during which General Pershing, supposedly consulted, was reportedly preparing a cabled reply. Barnett again queried the Secretary of War, this time to be met with demurrers that the Marine Corps used different rifles and ammunition from the Army, different tactics, different drill regulations, and the like—all, needless to say, with no foundation in fact. Having firmly set the record straight, the Commandant was then assured by Secretary Baker that General Pershing had really wanted the Marines all along and that a Marine regiment could now go to France. "Personally, I do not think the original telegram to Pershing was ever sent," sniffed Barnett. "I think they intended to forget it."[4]

That such indeed was the disposition of the War Department toward having any Marines in France at all was later confirmed by Secretary Daniels, who wrote:[5]

When war was declared, I tendered, ready and equipped, two regiments of Marines to be incorporated in the Army. Some Army officers were not keen to accept them.

At any rate, on 29 May 1917, the President took a hand in the matter, and issued the following order to Secretary Daniels:[6]

My dear Mr. Secretary:

In pursuance of the authority vested in me by law, it is hereby directed that you issue the necessary orders detaching for service with the Army a force of Marines to be known as the Fifth Regiment of Marines.

This force will serve with the first expedition which has been directed to proceed to France in the near future, and will consist of such officers and men as may be required for such an organization by the instructions issued by the War Department.

You will direct the Major General Commandant of the Marine Corps to report to the Secretary of War for this duty.

By early June the 5th Marines, under Colonel C. A. Doyen, were ready to embark for France with the first convoy, as directed by President Wilson. Just before the day scheduled for embarkation, however, when no orders had yet been received from the Army regarding the 5th Regiment, Barnett opened a note from Secretary Baker which began:[7]

I am very sorry to have to tell you that it will be utterly impossible for the War Department to furnish transportation for a Marine regiment with the first outfit sailing. . . .

To a lesser man than Barnett, this dampening message would have spelled the end, as obviously seemed intended, of the Marines' hopes of getting to France "with the first expedition." But the Commandant, who had foreseen just this eventuality, merely replied to the Secretary of War:[8]

Please give yourself no further trouble in this matter, as transportation for the Marines has been arranged.

And so it had, quite independently, with the help of Barnett's friend, Admiral W. S. Benson, Chief of Naval Operations, who had held out the Navy transports *Henderson, Hancock,* and *DeKalb* for the Marines.

Thus it happened that the 5th Marines sailed for France on 14 June 1917, joined up with the first convoy at sea, and were ashore at St. Nazaire on 27 June, ready and anxious to get on with the war.

Once "Over There," the Marines were supposed to go into intensive training for trench warfare alongside the Army troops of the 1st Infantry Division. Alas, General Pershing had other ideas. The Marine regiment was parceled out through the length and breadth of France (with even one company in England) as line-of-communication troops, mainly military police, to support the Army division, always the apple of Pershing's sharp eye. The excuse given for dismembering the 5th Marines was that somebody "had to be scattered" in order to keep the 1st Division intact; that the Marines should be the ones chosen to be scattered, wrote General Pershing, "was the natural thing to do."[9]

In a wry, perhaps unintended sense, Pershing's decision was a compliment to the Marine Corps; at least this was the opinion of one war correspondent, Frederick Palmer:[10]

. . . the regiment of Marines which had come with the first convoy in June was withdrawn from the 1st Division. Although this was most depressing to every officer and man, in that it meant that they would not be among the first in the trenches, the service to which they were assigned was in one sense a compliment to qualities which are as inseparable from them as their gallantry. The Marines have traditions, associated with ships' orderliness, which are kept up by competent veteran noncommissioned officers, that make them models in soldierly deportment. . . . From all directions our widespread organization was calling for details of this dependable character, and the Marines were chosen to meet the demands. Marines acted as couriers across the channel; they guarded our construction projects and our property; kept order on piers and in laborers' quarters; acted as police in Paris and at the ports, carrying out Provost

Marshal's instructions with polite firmness in keeping with the impeccable neatness of their uniforms.

As long as only one Marine regiment was in France, it seemed likely to remain an orphan, as the Marines' treatment from the moment of arrival clearly demonstrated. With the backing of Secretary Daniels, General Barnett persuaded Secretary Baker, and finally President Wilson, that another Marine regiment and a machine gun battalion should be sent to France so that a full Marine brigade could be integrated into the combatant structure of the AEF. The 6th Marines, Colonel A. W. Catlin, and 6th Machine Gun Battalion were therefore organized and shipped out for France in late 1917. Early in 1918 the Marine brigade (assigned the designation of "4th Infantry Brigade" by AEF headquarters[11] but immediately self-styled as "4th Marine Brigade") was commissioned under Doyen, now a brigadier general. The brigade then commenced intensive training, with instructors from the renowned French *chasseurs Alpins,* as part of the newly formed 2d Infantry Division (which also included the 9th Infantry, veterans of Peking) destined to become the top fighting division of the AEF.

The Marine brigade, with its 280 officers and 9,164 enlisted men, the largest formation of Marines ever fielded up to this time, was about three times the size of the entire Corps in the war with Spain. Two companies of the new brigade were larger than Archibald Henderson's regiment of 1836. As it completed preparations for battle, the 4th Marine Brigade bore on its shoulders the honor of the Marine Corps.

INTO THE FRONT LINES

By the spring of 1918, the time had come for the Marine brigade to complete its training by a tour of trench warfare in the front lines. As was customary for new units, a relatively stable sector with well developed defenses was chosen—Toulon Sector, on the heights of the Meuse southeast of Verdun, where, commencing on St. Patrick's Day, the 5th and then the 6th Marines relieved French battalions in the line. The brigade's first casualty, sustained from long-range enemy shelling as the Marines detrained at the railhead behind the lines, was the 5th Regiment's bass drum, though the drummer went unscathed.

The initial arrangement, to sandwich Marine battalions in between experienced French battalions, lasted four days until unexpectedly terminated by the great Amiens offensive which the Germans unleashed on 21 March

1918, attempting to drive a wedge between the British and French armies. As Marshal Foch committed his reserves and pulled units out of quiet sectors to plug the ominous gap, the 5th Marines were shifted eastward to join with one remaining French regiment in taking over a sector vacated by a French division. The 6th Regiment stayed where it was, but expanded its frontage to cover trench lines similarly cleared by the French. Before the end of the month, by an exchange with intervening French units, the 6th, too, displaced eastward and went into line beside the other Marine regiment, giving the Marine brigade, which was virtually as large as one of the smaller French divisions, a sector of its own, supported by its own (Army) artillery, the 12th Field Artillery.

In the trenches the Marines quickly settled into a life of raids, night patrols, box barrages, carrying parties through the mud, cooties, gas alarms, and rats. One company of the 5th Marines, whose mascot was an ant-bear who had somehow come along from Haiti, found their friend a champion ratter, but there was no defense against the cooties, and, as the 74th Company bitterly discovered, little against gas: a surprise noctural bombardment by gas shells caught the company asleep in billets, and one shell, bursting inside a building occupied by a platoon, killed 39 men.

During the week of 9 May, having lost 128 killed and 744 wounded during 53 days in the trenches, and having played an honorable though minor part in the Aisne Defensive, the Marine brigade was relieved and rejoined its parent division for final training at Chaumont-en-Vexin, between Paris and Beauvais.

BELLEAU WOOD: "U.S. MARINE CORPS ENTIRELY"

In May, after coming out of the lines, two events of signal importance befell the Marine brigade.

The first event was the relief of General Doyen, on account of illness (he was dead within five months to the day), by an Army brigade commander, a veteran cavalryman and until then Pershing's chief of staff. Brigadier General James G. Harbord, USA, even though not a Marine, could hardly have been a better choice. Between Harbord and the brigade it was love at first sight. Pershing had laid the groundwork. In giving Harbord his send-off, the commander warned, "Young man, I'm giving you the best brigade in France —if anything goes wrong, I'll know whom to blame."[12] This encomium was considerably more than General Pershing, whose postwar memoirs were

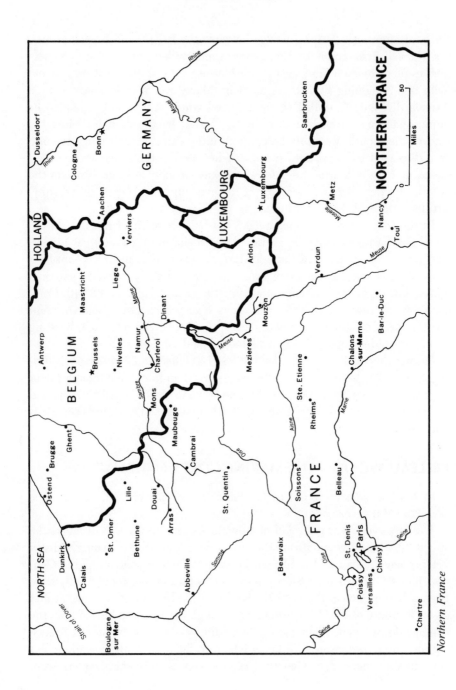

Northern France

conspicuously sparing in praise of Marines, ever got around to expressing on record, although in private he was frank to praise "the high state of discipline and excellent soldierly appearance" of the Marines.[13]

Harbord's reaction when sent to command a brigade of Marines set the tone of the Marines' relation with their favorite Army general. As Harbord later reminisced:[14]

As we neared Somme-Dieu, which was 2d Division Headquarters, I confess to having had a few misgivings. I was a National Army brigadier. By long custom, temporary rank in the Regular service had become known as "Mex rank," reference being had to the Mexican silver dollar in comparison with the U. S. dollar redeemable in gold. National Army rank was not yet taken as seriously as it became later. It was still a little bit "Mex" in Regular eyes. The two regimental commanders in the Brigade were both Regular colonels in the Marine Corps; I was a new Regular lieutenant colonel of Cavalry. They were both winners of the Medal of Honor, proud of their Corps and of its splendid traditions dating from the earliest years of the Republic. How warmly they would welcome an untried National Army brigadier as a superior officer might well give me some solicitude. They were losing a Regular brigadier of their own Corps to whom they were devoted. . . . They never failed me. I look back on my service with the Marine Brigade with more pride and satisfaction than on any other equal period in my long Army career.

The second event of importance which befell the Marine brigade was one which the German army withheld until Harbord was well in the saddle. On 27 May 1918, General Ludendorff launched his Chemin des Dames offensive against the Aisne heights, sliced the northern front in two, and all but reached Paris. Ludendorff certainly never intended it, but this great attack was in some sense responsible for today's Marine Corps.

Four days after the German stroke, as the French government prepared to flee Paris, the 2d Division was on the road from its training areas, slogging eastward toward the Marne. General Harbord later wrote:[15]

Everything that a terrified peasantry would be likely to think of bringing from among their humble treasures was to be seen on that congested highway. Men, women, children, hurrying to the rear; tired and worn, with stark terror on their faces. Many were walking, an occasional woman wheeled a perambulator with the baby in it. Sick people were lying exhausted beside the road. Some were driving carts piled high with their worldly goods. . . . Little flocks of sheep, a led cow, crates of chickens on carts. We passed many French officers and soldiers, but all coming from the front . . . the motley array which characterizes the rear of a beaten army.

To another observer on the Paris-Metz road that day, however, there was a different but equally striking sight—U. S. Marines marching toward the sound of the guns. A U. S. Army officer recalled:[16]

They looked fine, coming in there, tall fellows, healthy and fit—they looked hard and competent. We watched you going in, through those tired little Frenchmen, and we all felt better. We knew something was going to happen.

On the night of 5 June, the Marine brigade found itself astride the Paris-Metz highway only a few kilometers northeast of the spot where Marshal

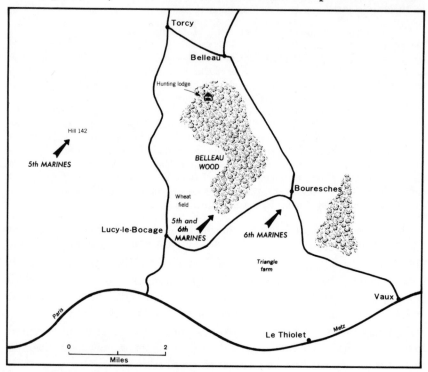

Battle of Belleau Wood, 6-26 June 1918

Gallieni, with his Paris taxicabs, had turned back von Kluck in 1914. Fragments of the French army trickled in retreat through the Marine assembly areas, often advising *les américains* to join them.

"Retreat, hell," was the reply, "we just got here."[17]

To the left of the highway, in the zone of action of the 5th Marines, lay a rolling wheatfield backed by an ominous square mile of rocks, woods, and huntsmen's trails—the Bois de Belleau. Belleau Wood was a carefully organized center of resistance held by the 461st Imperial German Infantry, more than 1,200 strong—the largest single body of combat-seasoned regular troops which Marines had confronted since Bladensburg. To Marines who would later know what it was to storm a small island held by comparably trained and resolute defenders, Belleau Wood and neighboring Bouresches could be likened to a well-fortified atoll, but one which must be captured by flesh and blood without benefit of ships' gunfire or close air support.

During the preceding two days the Marines and regular soldiers of the 2d Division had dug in across the Paris-Metz highway. Even as the French shredded back, the first Germans had hit the American line. There had been local infiltrations, each blunted in turn by rifle fire and by pelting bursts from the massed machine guns of Major E. B. Cole's 6th Machine Gun Battalion. Now, on 6 June 1918, the 4th Marine Brigade was tensed for counterattack.

The honor of the first assault fell to the 1st Battalion, 5th Marines, commanded by Major Julius S. Turrill. At daybreak the battalion surged forward through the wheatfields toward a hill a half mile north. When high noon's sun beat down, Hill 142 was in the hands of surviving Marines of the 49th and 67th Companies. The 1st Battalion, 5th Marines, in its first attack, had taken 410 casualties since dawn.

The second phase of the day's attack took the 3d Battalion, 5th Marines (Major B. S. Berry), and 2d and 3d Battalions, 6th Marines (Majors Thomas Holcomb and B. W. Sibley, respectively) into Belleau Wood itself. For a toehold in the edge of the wood and for the neighboring village of Bouresches, the Marine Corps paid 1,087 casualties in a late afternoon attack. Bouresches would not have stayed in Marine hands but for the heroism of two lieutenants, J. F. Robertson and C. B. Cates, who held it despite determined counterattacks, and of Sergeant Major John H. Quick. Quick, already a Medal of Honor man, now gained the Army's Distinguished Service Cross for driving a Model "T" Ford truck loaded with small-arms ammunition and grenades through intense German fire, in order to resupply fragments of Holcomb's battalion which clung to the ruins. Naturally he then joined the fight. Another Medal of Honor man who once again distinguished himself at Belleau Wood was Gunnery Sergeant Daniel Daly. In the later account of war correspondent Floyd Gibbons, who was wounded in action with Daly's platoon:[18]

> The oats and wheat in the open field were waving and snapping off—not from the wind but from rifle and machine-gun fire of German veterans in their well-concealed positions. . . . The sergeant [Daly] . . . swung his bayoneted rifle over his head with a forward sweep. He yelled at his men: "Come on, you sons-of-bitches. Do you want to live forever?"

Among other casualties of the fierce attack was Colonel Catlin of the 6th Marines, shot through the right lung as his regiment swept forward. Major B. S. Berry, commanding the 3d Battalion, 5th Marines, also fell wounded.

It would be 20 November 1943, on the beaches of Betio, before Marines again sustained such heavy casualties in a single day's assault.

On 8, 9, and 11 June, battalions of the 5th and 6th Marines—notably Lieutenant Colonel F. M. Wise's 2d Battalion, 5th Marines—hammered their way up the long axis of Belleau Wood. By nightfall on 12 June, Wise had broken through the third and final German defense line, and, except for some ground about a battered prewar hunting lodge in the northernmost edge of the wood, the Marines held the Bois de Belleau.

At daybreak on 13 June the German IV Corps struck back behind a storm of artillery and mustard gas. As the German attack rolled in, hitting first Bouresches and then the line of Marines on the rising ground in the edge of Belleau, the Germans encountered a new experience: aimed fire from Marine '03 rifles which began dropping men at 400 yards. But the Germans, good soldiers, too, kept coming.

Bouresches, briefly, was given up for lost by higher echelons, though not by the 1st Battalion, 6th Marines (Major John A.—"Johnny the Hard"— Hughes). Despite 450 gas casualties, Hughes held fast, so that General Harbord, true Marine despite his crossed sabers, could report to the division: "There is nothing but U. S. Marines in the town of Bouresches."[19]

After this, the mop-up of Belleau Wood proceeded slowly, stubbornly, and surely. From 15 to 22 June, to rest the tired and depleted Marines, the 7th Infantry, a new regiment from army reserve, took over from the 4th Brigade. Colonel "Buck" Neville, of the 5th Marines, was kept in command of the wood, however.

When the Marines returned to the fray, they found the front lines unchanged. On the night of 23 June, the 3d Battalion, 5th Marines, made another try at ejecting the enemy (now the 87th Infantry Division), but the results were discouraging. Next day, all day, the 2d Division artillery plastered the Germans. This did the job, and a final attack by the 3d Battalion, 5th Marines, now commanded by Major Maurice Shearer, carried the far tip of the wood. In much the same vein as Harbord's earlier report, Shearer announced, on 26 June, "Woods now U. S. Marine Corps entirely."[20]

Other than the fact that the battle of Belleau Wood, in Clemenceau's phrase, "saved Paris," there are several reasons why this bloody, hard-fought action constituted a turning point in the history of the Corps.

With the exception of the War of 1812, the Marine Corps had spent most of its previous 142 years in small actions or expeditions against native or informally trained enemies. At Belleau Wood, large formations of Marines encountered a professional, veteran antagonist, equipped and supported with everything in the book. This antagonist had been specifically directed, in corps operation orders, to inflict severe, exemplary loss on the Americans in their first big battle. By courage, discipline, *esprit,* and typical small-unit initiative, the Marine brigade had come out on top, and, in the process, many thousand Marine officers and men learned a lot in a hurry about a new kind of war. This was important, because it would shape the thinking, the spirit, and the quality of the Marine Corps during the years leading up to World War II.

One abiding by-product of the Belleau Wood action was a new term in the soldier's argot: as the Marines scratched out shallow rifle pits wherever the front lines lay, somebody called them "foxholes." The name caught on, a correspondent heard and reported it, and the era of the foxhole had arrived.

Another abiding by-product of Belleau Wood was one wholly unforeseen by any Marine in France. That was the explosion of publicity over the Marine brigade's achievements, which resulted in part from a florid dispatch by Floyd Gibbons. To add impact to the story, Gibbons had been wounded not once but three times, losing his left eye in the wheat on 6 June. "I am up front and entering Belleau Wood with the U. S. Marines," his story opened. That was enough for news-hungry folks at home, and, in a very different sense, quite enough for many in the other Services, who afterward went through life convinced that the Marines were a corps of publicity hounds. As General Harbord put it:[21]

The Marines have been taunted with having thought they had won the war, and there have been some unkind and unjust comments from Army officers of high enough rank to be above such pettiness. . . . The wounds inflicted by publicity received by someone else do not rate a wound stripe, but they are a long time healing.

Sad to relate, even this acid exorcism by so respected an officer as Harbord failed to lay the ghost, and it still rises to confront Marines unborn when Belleau Wood was taken.

Among those who did accord the Marine brigade unstinting praise for the superb fighting in Belleau Wood were two of its superiors: Assistant Secretary of the Navy Franklin Roosevelt and French General Joseph Degoutte, under whose Sixth Army the 2d Division had gone into battle.

In the War of 1812, U.S. Marines performed valiant service with Winder at Bladensburg and with Jackson at New Orleans. This painting by J. J. Capoline depicts the great victory of Lake Erie, where Marines served Commodore Perry when he offered the courtesy of an honorable surrender to the British Admiral Robert H. Barclay.

Marines battle Seminole Indians in the Florida War, 1835–42.

General Quitman entering Mexico City with a battalion of Marines during the Mexican War, 1847.

On the steps of the commandant's quarters, left to right: private (dress), first lieutenant (fatigue), the commandant (dress), fife-major (dress), major of staff (dress). This painting by D. L. Dickson is dated 1846–48.

U.S. Marines storming the engine house fort in John Brown's Raid, 16-18 October 1859. From *Thunder at Harper's Ferry*, by Allan Keller, Prentice Hall, Inc., 1958.

Federal Marines who fought in the Civil War. The figure at left is an officer, others are enlisted men.

On the deck of a gunboat on the Mississippi, 1864, a Marine as a member of the gun crew. The photo is by Mathew Brady.

Roosevelt inspected the brigade in August 1918 at Nancy, after having visited Belleau Wood. On the spot, the future President directed that Marine Corps uniform regulations be changed to authorize Marine enlisted men to wear the Corps emblem on their collars (only officers had done so before) "in recognition of the splendid work of the Marine Brigade," as he recorded in his journal.[22] He then cabled Secretary Daniels:[23]

Have returned to Paris from a visit to the Marine Brigade. American and French commanders are equally enthusiastic over their magnificent showing. Have also visited Belleau Wood, a most difficult position which Marines held against picked German troops, and finally cleared.

As for General Degoutte, a hard-fighting officer whose Croix de Guerre bore seven palms, the orders of his Sixth Army published the following citation on 30 June 1918:[24]

In view of the brilliant conduct of the 4th Marine Brigade of the 2d U. S. Division, which, in a spirited fight captured Bouresches and the important strong point, Belleau Wood, fiercely defended by the enemy in force, the Commanding General, VI Army, decrees that henceforth in all official papers, Belleau Wood shall bear the name, "Bois de la Brigade de Marine."

That this generous gesture seemingly caused some heartburn on the part of American higher headquarters is evidenced by the following entry from Secretary Roosevelt's journal:[25]

General Degoute [sic] commanding the whole army in this sector, arrived a few minutes after we did. . . . He was especially nice about our Marines and told me that he had been the one who had issued the order changing the name of Bois de Belleau to Bois de la Brigade de Marine. (I have later learned that there was a mean piece of hokus pokus by some narrow-minded army officer in this connection. Degoute, as he told me with his own lips, announced the change in a general order to his entire army, in which among other things he gave especial praise to the Marine Brigade. . . . Somewhere down the line, whether it was in the Corps Headquarters, or in the Division Headquarters, or perhaps even back at American General Headquarters, a public announcement was made that the French had changed the name of the wood to Bois des Americains. I put this on record because some other jealous individuals may seek further to prevent the Marine Brigade from getting this official recognition. . . .)

From the other side of the lines, German intelligence had its own verdict on the recent fighting:[26]

The 2d American Division must be considered a very good one, and may perhaps even be reckoned as storm troops. The different attacks on Belleau Wood were carried out with bravery and dash. The moral effect of our gunfire cannot seriously impede the advance of the American riflemen.

SOISSONS

As the 4th Marine Brigade (less 4,677 killed and wounded) filed rearward to rest areas along the Marne after Belleau Wood, great changes were in the making. On 14 July, Harbord, having been given a well-deserved second star, assumed command of the 2d Division. Neville, senior Marine regimental commander, was promoted to brigadier general and became brigade commander. Two days later the 2d Division went into action for the second time in less than a month.

On 15 July 1918 the German Army commenced its last offensive of the war—a thrust by 13 divisions, under General von Hutier, to capture Rheims and then Paris. To reduce the deep salient which resulted, Marshal Foch (at Pershing's urging) determined to counterattack near Soissons, in the Aisne-Marne region. The 1st and 2d Infantry Divisions were attached to the French XX Corps, composed of Moroccans, Senegalese, and the Foreign Legion—the elite shock troops of the French Army.

Starting on 16 July, the XX Corps began concentrating for its attack. The 2d Division was to jump off from the forest preserve of Retz (Villers-Coterets), with the 5th Marines in assault and the 6th Regiment in XX Corps reserve. As the 28,000-man American division tramped forward into the Forêt de Retz on the black night of 17 July, it rained. All night it rained. Beset by every conceivable tribulation, the Marine brigade staggered forward. Mud deepened, transport collapsed, stomachs were empty, rifle companies had to double time to reach the line of departure for a dawn H-hour.

Guns and caissons slewed sideways across the files, or irate machine-gun mules plunged across the tangle, the column slowed and jammed and halted on heavy feet; then went on again to plunge blindly against the next obstacle. Men fell into the deep ditch and broke arms and legs. Just to keep moving was a harder test than battle ever imposed. . . .

So wrote First Lieutenant Thomason, 49th Company, 5th Marines.[27] And another burdened Marine recounted more matter-of-factly:[28]

Cold, hungry, and wet, on we marched, hour after hour, each man bearing a pack weighing about 45 pounds, consisting of two blankets, a supply of underclothes, a pair of trousers, emergency rations of hardtack and "monkey meat" (canned corn beef), besides a heavy belt with 100 rounds of ammunition, a canteen, wire cutters, gas mask, helmet, rifle and bayonet. Yes, and each man had around his neck, next to his body, two identification tags one of which would mark his grave and the other his body. . . .

At 0435 on 18 July the massed artillery of the XX Corps opened fire, and the 5th Marines jumped off behind the barrage with the 1st Battalion on the left and the 2d Battalion on the right. Within a few hours the Marines had paced, passed, and outdistanced even the swirling Moroccans. By noon, the 5th Marines were at Beaurepaire Farm, two miles forward; by nightfall, they had gained three miles more, having driven a shaken enemy before them. Among the heroes of the day was a Serbian-born gunnery sergeant, Louis Cukela. By a series of headlong assaults on three machine gun positions in the Forêt de Retz, the last of which he silenced with captured German grenades, Gunnery Sergeant Cukela (66th Company, 5th Marines) thereby won both an Army and a Navy Medal of Honor. Later commissioned, Cukela delighted succeeding decades of Marines by his unique brand of English—"Next time I send a goddam fool, I go myself," was his blurted reprimand for a job badly done.

Next morning the 6th Marines, commanded by Colonel Harry Lee, pushed through another mile and a half against rapidly solidifying resistance backed by sheets of well-adjusted artillery fire. Without realizing it, the 6th Regiment had run head-on into a German corps counterattack.

The situation reported by field message from First Lieutenant C. B. Cates was typical:[29]

I am in an old abandoned French trench bordering on road leading out from your CP and 350 yards from an old mill. I have only two men left out of my company and 20 out of other companies. We need support but it is almost suicide to try to get it here as we are swept by machine gun fire and a constant artillery barrage is upon us. I have no one on my left and only a few on my right. I will hold.

When the regiment's casualties hit 50 per cent and Major Sibley's 3d Battalion (originally in reserve) had melted into Hughes's and Holcomb's 1st and 2d Battalions, the Marines finally dug in within rifle shot of the Soissons-Chateau Thierry road, main artery of General von Hutier's salient. "That was a bad day," said General Holcomb.[30] After nightfall a fresh division took over, and the 2d Division headed out of the lines. The Marine brigade had vacancies for 1,972 more replacements.

Of the battle as a whole—a battle in which the Marines had rendered stellar services—Marshal von Hindenburg was to write: "From the purely military view, it was of the greatest and most fateful importance that we had lost the initiative to the enemy...."[31]

Based on interrogation of the few Marine prisoners gained by this stage of the war, German intelligence had arrived at certain conclusions:[32]

The Marines are considered a sort of elite Corps, designed to go into action outside the United States. The high percentage of Marksmen, Sharpshooters, and Expert Riflemen, as perceived among our prisoners, allows a conclusion to be drawn as to the quality of the training in rifle marksmanship that the Marines receive. The prisoners are mostly members of the better class, and they consider their membership in the Marine Corps to be something of an honor. They proudly resent any attempts to place their regiments on a par with other infantry regiments. . . .

FRUSTRATIONS OF 1918

Little more than a week after the brigade had taken off their packs and stacked arms in rest camps northeast of Paris, General Harbord was again promoted. This time, Harbord was to trouble-shoot immense difficulties in the AEF's Services of Supply. Harbord's ill luck in losing a fine combat command, however, spelled good fortune for the Marine brigade and, personally, for Brigadier General Lejeune.

General Lejeune, last encountered as assistant to Commandant Barnett, had made his way to France, where, like many other Marine officers who got overseas, he was treated as a casual replacement and was ordered to a National Guard brigade. After this somewhat cavalier reception, considering his recent place in the high councils of the Marine Corps, Lejeune at length gained command of the Marine brigade. That command was short-lived—three days, to be exact. On 29 July 1918, when Harbord was detached, Lejeune (a graduate of the Army War College and well known by senior Army officers) was elevated to command the 2d Division—the first and only Marine officer ever to command a U. S. Army division in combat.

When Lejeune reached France in June 1918, he brought for General Pershing proposals from General Barnett that the Marine Corps be allowed to provide one or more divisions for the AEF. He also brought Barnett's earnest recommendation that Lejeune be given a Marine command. Pershing dismissed both recommendations, the former (after a final plea from Lejeune) in a message to the Secretary of War:[33]

Referring to my conversation with Secretary of War on this subject, I am still of the opinion that the formation of such a unit [a Marine Division] is not desirable from the military standpoint. While the Marines are splendid troops, their use as a separate division is inadvisable.

Pershing was willing to accept another Marine brigade in France, but not for combat: there were rear-area jobs he could think of, such as provost guards, service troops, base detachments and such. And when the 5th Marine

Brigade (11th and 13th Marines, 5th Machine Gun Battalion) reached France in September 1918, it was spread out from Tours to Brest. The brigade commander, Brigadier General E. K. Cole, was detached and put in command of an Army depot division. His successor, Brigadier General Smedley Butler, one of the most distinguished fighting soldiers in American history, was, in his own sulphurous phrases, ordered:[34]

. . . to sit in the rear and run this filthy mudhole [Camp Pontanezen, outside Brest]. Although 97 per cent of my men were expert riflemen or sharpshooters, troops that hardly knew which end of the gun to shoot were sent to the trenches. My crack regiment [the 13th Marines] was broken up to do manual labor and guard duty.

In confirmation of Butler's plaint, General Barnett pointed out that:[35]

A Marine could not hope to go abroad and go into the firing line unless he was qualified "Marksman" or better. Later on I crossed on a transport with 11,000 Army troops, and I do not think I am exaggerating in saying that almost all of these so-called soldiers had never fired an Army rifle.

In such a context, the keen edge of training given to the 5th Marine Brigade deserved better use than digging drainage ditches and toting duckboards at Camp Pontanezen. On the other hand, Marine Corps Headquarters deserves criticism—especially in light of General Barnett's previous experience with AEF Headquarters and the War Department in connection with the 5th and 6th Marines—for not taking positive steps at the Washington level to insure that the 5th Brigade, if sent to France, would be given an appropriate combat assignment within the divisional structure of the AEF.

Frustrating as was the case of the 5th Brigade, the history of the 10th Marines was worse. As has been seen, General Barnett, veteran of the Advance Base Force, was keen to field a Marine force of combined arms, preferably a Marine division. Essential to such a project would be Marine field artillery with both light and medium batteries to match the AEF divisional artillery organization.

In January 1918, the War Department asked the Navy to organize naval artillery units armed with 14-inch railway guns and 7-inch field mounts. The Secretary of the Navy directed Rear Admiral C. P. Plunkett to command the five 14-inch railway guns, which would be manned by bluejackets. There would be twenty 7-inch guns, he continued, to be manned by a Marine artillery regiment under Colonel R. H. Dunlap, who had commanded the artillery at Veracruz. On 14 January 1918, Dunlap's force was designated the 10th Marines and commenced training as the Navy speeded mounting and test firing of the 7-inchers (taken from predreadnought battleships of the old "Crab Fleet") at Indian Head Proving Ground.

Meanwhile, the 10th Marines retained the 3-inch field guns of the Advance Base Force, and, in April, General Barnett, overlooking no opportunity, offered the regiment for service in France, where, at least, it could support the Marine brigade. The War Department's chilly reply was, "no [Marine] artillery regiment could be accepted," although General Pershing would take Marine artillery officers as individual replacements in the AEF.[36]

As summer wore on, the Navy commenced mounting out the superb 14-inch railroad guns for France. On 23 August 1918, when Barnett reported that the 10th Marines were ready for duty as a 7-inch regiment, the Army Chief of Staff, now General Peyton C. March, replied that no more artillery was needed by the AEF, but that the Army would like nevertheless to take over the 10th Marines' newly acquired guns and just happened to have a regiment of soldiers trained to man Navy 7-inch guns. General Barnett's reaction is clear enough from this statement:[37]

When the Secretary of the Navy informed me of this, I very strongly protested. I told him that we had a splendid regiment, well drilled, and used to the naval guns, and that to allow the guns to go without the men would be most discouraging to the Marines, and furthermore, if the guns were needed by the Army, that I saw no reason, except prejudice, why the Marines were not wanted; this particularly as General Pershing's original request had specified that the guns should be manned by naval personnel.

Although Barnett kept the 10th Marines in commission and made strenuous efforts to rearm the regiment with the French 75s which were standard in the AEF, the regiment never got out of Quantico. "This instance and numerous others," wrote Colonel Dunlap to General Barnett,[38] "can be used to arrive at the conclusion that it was the intention of the Army not to utilize Marines if it could possibly be avoided."

To get around the obvious impasse which had developed, and to enable more of the Marine Corps to get into the war, Allied planners in London even proposed that additional U. S. Marine units be committed to operations in Italy outside Pershing's command. To implement this concept, Admiral William S. Sims, the U. S. Naval Commander in Europe, cabled in May 1918 for immediate establishment of a divisional-scale Marine expeditionary force, with a strength of 20,000, for service on Italy's Adriatic front, but the project failed to materialize.

In reviewing Marine Corps attempts to go to war in France, it is difficult to escape the conclusion that, from the outset of the war, there existed a deliberate Army policy to minimize, if not prevent, Marine participation in the AEF. This policy was realized through denying Marine units opportunity to serve in the front lines; through discouraging formation of Marine units equipped with the combined arms; through dispersion of well-trained Marines into noncombatant chores throughout the communications zone, while Army units with inferior training went to the front; and through outright refusal to accept Marine units for service in France.

The one senior Marine officer who went overseas with Pershing's original headquarters group in 1917 and, as it proved, the only Marine to serve on the staff of General Headquarters, AEF, had this to say: [39]

I was attached to General Headquarters, A.E.F., on several occasions, where I had opportunities for discussing the question of the utilization of the services of Marines in the Army, and I was forced to the conclusion that the Army believed (those who controlled the policy in this matter) that it was an Army war—that Marines had no business in it—that they were not desired for such service.

That behind this attitude and these actions of the Army toward the Marine Corps lay such an official policy was tacitly confirmed after the war on no less authority than that of Frederick Palmer, official biographer of Secretary of War Newton D. Baker, and confidant and biographer of Pershing, who wrote:[40]

Our Army staff, with all appreciation of the Marines' superb spirit, considered that Marine training for landing parties, policing occupied ports, and operating as forces of pacification in backward countries, had not fitted their officers in the same way as those of the Army for army operations.

In other words (just as the General Staff had suggested to the Joint Board in 1916), Marines might be good enough for minor operations, but, as for real war, leave it to the Army. This was a refrain which Marines would hear again in years to come.

ST. MIHIEL

Two such fights as Belleau Wood and Soissons called for a breather. The 2d Division got it by a ten-day assignment in August 1918 to a quiet sector with headquarters at Marbache, on the Moselle. Aside from one German probe—the customary treatment for each new division coming into the sector—the visit was a rest cure. The enemy raid on 8 August collided with the 2d Battalion, 5th Marines, still commanded by the irrepressible Lieutenant Colonel "Fritz" Wise. That was the end of the Germans. In a sense it was also the end for Wise: a few days later, he was promoted to colonel, and, as the Marine brigade was overstrength in colonels, Wise was detached to command an Army infantry regiment in another division, a task for which he was ultimately given the Distinguished Service Medal.

In the next month, September, there was to be another big offensive—the first all-American show, in which two United States corps were to eliminate the St. Mihiel salient along the Meuse River. For a change, the Marine brigade was to comprise the divisional reserve, or "support," as it was then styled. After its summer battles the brigade was still 2,500 men understrength, with every Marine replacement draft already aboard.

Thus General Lejeune's first problem was to get the brigade up to fighting strength without having to accept Army replacements—a situation which Lejeune rightly estimated would be "disastrous to the *esprit de corps* of the 4th Brigade."[41] Now was the time to have a friend in court, in this case General Harbord, latterly engaged in putting the Service of Supply, or "S.O.S.," on a paying basis. Since the preponderance of Marines who got to France had ended up in the S.O.S., Harbord was in a position to help. On Lejeune's grapevine appeal, Harbord looked the other way during a mass delivery of Marine castaways from the S.O.S.

Lejeune recalled:[42]

Very soon thereafter they began to arrive in small details or detachments. . . guards from base ports and supply depots; the company from GHQ at Chaumont; a detachment from England; men detained at hospitals for use as orderlies, chauffeurs, etc.; individuals assigned to duties of all descriptions; men who had got lost—every variety of Marine came home!

With the replacement problem solved, at least for the next battle, the brigade trained, rehearsed, and rolled packs. On the dark and rainy night of 11 September, the Marines, now led by General Neville, filed into their supporting positions for the attack. Aside from his notable standing as a combat soldier, the new brigade commander enjoyed, at least by repute, one special advantage from the communications point of view: Marines swore he could be heard—without a telephone—between his front line command post and GHQ at Chaumont.

At 0100, 12 September, the American artillery, including Admiral Plunkett's 14-inchers, crashed down with the opening volleys of a four-hour preparation. Sharp at 0500 the artillery lifted, and the 2d Division jumped off behind a rolling barrage. The Marine brigade followed on the heels of the Army assault units, who did themselves proud. By nightfall the soldiers had taken 3,300 stunned German prisoners and 120 guns.

After the Army brigade's splendid leap forward, the Marines passed through late next day, and chewed into the job of reducing the thickening enemy outpost positions which screened the dread Hindenburg Line. A member of the 6th Marines recounted:[43]

These were strong fortifications built of concrete with walls about two feet thick ranging in size from about five feet to 20 feet square. They were about five feet underground with about two feet extending above the surface, were well camouflaged and the larger ones were designed for four or more compartments. We also came upon many large dugouts, some of them 50 feet underground, into which we entered with great caution.

Nevertheless, Colonel Logan Feland's 5th Marines, on the right, had fairly easy going and reached their objectives on 14 September, digging in handily to stand off the expected German counterattack, which was turned back, also as expected.

Colonel Harry Lee, who had inherited the 6th Regiment after Catlin had fallen, had somewhat more of a fight. In the Bois de la Montagne, which everyone said was unoccupied, the 2d Battalion, 6th Marines, found tenants whom it required a stiff fight to evict. Not content with being shown the door, the Germans counterattacked four times, using artillery and gas. Four times they were turned back, and, by nightfall of 15 September, when the 2d Division was relieved, the 2d Battalion, 6th Marines, was still there.

Compared to Belleau Wood and Soissons, St. Mihiel was an easy fight for the Marine brigade. Nevertheless, there were now 132 more dead Marines and 574 wounded, mostly from the 6th Regiment, which would never quite share the over-all assessment of St. Mihiel as a relatively minor action for the Marines.

"THE GREATEST SINGLE ACHIEVEMENT": BLANC MONT

When General Lejeune brought his division out of the lines from St. Mihiel, important news was waiting. The 2d Division would be temporarily detached from American command to the French Fourth Army, under General Henri Gouraud. Gouraud, veteran of Gallipoli (where one of his arms still remained), was a bearded old-timer of the *Infanterie Coloniale*. In his opening greeting to Lejeune, Gouraud styled himself a fellow Marine, since the *Infanterie Coloniale* (whose badge was the anchor) had inherited the traditions of France's vanished *Infanterie de Marine*. After a long and friendly conversation, Gouraud told Lejeune, that the American division was to be in reserve for the moment, but that it could count on its share of hard fighting that lay ahead.

The Meuse-Argonne offensive had begun on 26 September, with the

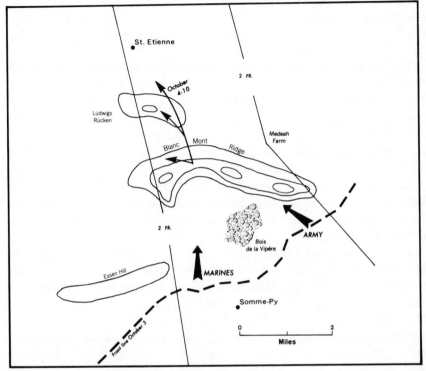

Battle of Blanc Mont Ridge, 2-9 October 1918

American First Army attacking beside Gouraud's troops. By the end of September the French had ground to a stop in the Champagne area near Somme-Py, against the outworks of the Hindenburg Line. The key terrain feature, German property since 1914, was Blanc Mont Ridge, a precipitous massif from which the Kaiser himself had watched the jump-off of Ludendorff's July offensive. The ground before Blanc Mont was a festering charnel house churned by four years' shelling and putrid with the flotsam of lost divisions: "a place," commented one Marine, "just built for calamities."[44]

Even at this moment, service politics were not dead. As their spent battalions hung onto hard-won enemy trenches, French staff officers grasped at General Lejeune's division, twice the strength of the frayed French divisions. Why not dismember it and use the big American brigades as replacements, whispered the French.

Lejeune was appalled. Quickly he appealed to Gouraud: Keep the 2d Division in one piece, and I can take Blanc Mont. Done, replied Gouraud. On 29 September orders were issued, and the 2d Division headed for the front. D-day: 3 October 1918.

The Marine brigade was to attack on the left and seize Blanc Mont Ridge itself. The 3d Infantry Brigade would angle in from the right. Between the brigade attacks, a well-entrenched German strongpoint would be by-passed and eventually pinched out, a demanding tactic "that was repeatedly utilized by the Germans during their major combats," observed one of the defending German battalion commanders, "and was much liked by the higher officers and much disliked by the troops."[45] While the Marine brigade advanced, the French would renew their attack along the brigade's left against a battered German position, the Essen Trench. An intermediate objective for the Marines bore the sinister appellation, Bois de la Vipère ("Viper Woods").

This time there was no prolonged artillery preparation; four years of such bone crushers had signally failed to do the job, as the chaos about Somme-Py testified. Instead, the 6th Marines struck out at 0550 after a five-minute thunderclap from 200 guns. Attached to the 6th Regiment, as well as to the 5th, which followed in support, were French tanks.

Within less than three hours, assault companies of the 1st and 2d Battalions, 6th Marines, were firing Very signals: "Objective taken." One company of the 5th Regiment (17th Company, Captain Leroy P. Hunt) had fought a war of its own across the brigade's left to capture the machine gun studded Essen position (stoutly defended by the Cologne Landsturm Battalion), which the French were still unable to take. Little good the 17th Company's fight did, though; before the battle was over, a German counter-attack got it back from the French, and the 5th Regiment had its work to do over again.

As the 6th Marines advanced, two men of the 78th Company spurred the attack. Private John J. Kelly, spotting a German machine gun whose fire was raking the Marines, dashed ahead through an American artillery barrage, killed two gunners, and brought eight prisoners back through the barrage. Corporal J. H. Pruitt successively knocked out two machine gun nests and finally captured 40 prisoners, being killed shortly after. Both men were awarded Medals of Honor.

The headlong advance of the 6th Marines carried the colors to the top of Blanc Mont, but not over its western slopes into the zone of the French, who were unable to keep pace with the Marines. This left the Marine brigade some two miles deep into German territory still being contested by the enemy 200th Infantry Division, with an open flank all the way back to Essen Trench. To plug this alarming gap and contain the stubborn German machine gunners in the French zone, the 5th Marines filled in, facing almost at right angle to the axis of advance.

"The advance realized by the American 2d Division during the course of the day was remarkable," reported the French Army operations summary of the Champagne battle, and so it was.

"Oh, Lordy! They've got us bracketed!" A drawing by Captain John W. Thomason, Jr., USMC.

October 4th was the 5th Marines' day. At dawn, in column of battalions, the 5th Regiment passed through the 6th Marines and drove forward toward St. Etienne, three miles ahead. The 6th Marines meanwhile took over the left flank gap and went to work against the 80 German machine guns still holding down the French from the west slopes of Blanc Mont.

By noon on 4 October, Major H. L. Larsen's 3d Battalion, 5th Marines, was within a thousand yards of St. Etienne. Here the Germans decided to counterattack, probing as usual into the deep, tender left flank of the Marine brigade.

The rear battalion of the 5th Marines was the 1st, commanded by Major George Hamilton. As the German flank attack revealed itself, Hamilton swung his battalion half left and counterattacked—a thousand Marines against the crack German 149th Infantry. Eight hundred yards up a hill which the Germans called Ludwigs Rücken, the four Marine companies advanced in line, with no artillery support. Halfway up, German shells crashed down:[46]

All along the extended line the saffron shrapnel flowered, flinging death and mutilation down. Singing balls and jagged bits of steel spattered on the hard ground like sheets of hail; the line writhed and staggered, steadied and went on, closing toward the center as the shells bit into it. High explosive shells came with the shrapnel, and where they fell geysers of torn earth and black smoke roared up to mingle with the devilish yellow in the air. A foul murky cloud of dust and smoke formed and went with the thinning companies, a cloud lit with red flashes and full of howling death.

What was left of the 1st Battalion, 5th Marines, little more than a hundred Marines, surged into the German counterattackers, and pushed them back onto St. Etienne.

For the next three days the attenuated brigade plugged toward the town. Since the 5th Regiment was spent, the 6th Marines, though in hardly better case, carried the assault. Finally the French XI Corps, long behind on the left, was drawn forward as the Germans (mainly an isolated battalion of the 149th Infantry) pulled back or died. On 8 October, the 75th and 76th Companies, 6th Marines, entered St. Etienne. In face of another violent counterattack, the two companies (one commanded by a sergeant, the senior Marine on his feet) hung on until reinforcements arrived. On 10 October 1918, the 2d Division was relieved by Army troops, and, for Marines, the Champagne battle was over.

Over, perhaps, but not forgotten.

The assault and consolidation of Blanc Mont cost 2,538 Marines killed and wounded. Rifle battalions that entered the fight more than a thousand strong marched out with 300 or less. In one company of the 5th Marines, as the battle waned, 230 rations came forward for the company's last reported ration strength. Twenty-two officers and men were left to eat them. The Marines used the extra cans of corned willy for revetments.

What significance the Blanc Mont assault held was reflected in a third citation of the Marine brigade in orders of the French Army. This was the highest collective citation of the French Army, and three such entitled a unit to carry the streamer of the Croix de Guerre on its colors, while individual members won the *fourragère* (known irreverently by Marines of later generations as "the pogey rope"). Thus did the 5th and 6th Marines and 6th Machine Gun Battalion earn their *fourragères*. Of the exploit by which they had earned this honor, a Marshal of France commented, "The taking of Blanc Mont Ridge is the greatest single achievement of the 1918 campaign."[47]

FINAL BATTLE

By October 1918 the reputations of the Marine brigade and its parent division were secure. The penalty of such reputation became apparent on 19 October when, without warning, the Marine brigade was detached, on French orders, and sent posthaste toward Leffincourt, with instructions to relieve a French division. The time and space factors were impossible; more than 60 kilometers had to be covered over congested, sodden roads in less than two days. The brigade made it all the same. Fortunately, the attempted dismemberment of the American division came to the notice of higher headquarters and was countermanded just as the Marines were making ready to enter combat again.

On 24 October, General Lejeune was summoned to First (American) Army headquarters for still another mission. Here he was told that the Meuse-Argonne offensive, launched in September by U. S. forces (minus the 2d Division), was stalled. To shatter "Brünhilde," a stronghold in the Hindenburg Line, and "Freya Stellung," an adjacent field fortification, the 2d Division was to be the point of a huge assault wedge comprising the United States V Corps. The attack was to jump off, west of the Meuse River, on All Saints Day.

At 0520 on D-day, 300 guns sounded reveille for Germans entrenched about the ruined village of Landres-et-St.-Georges and on the rearward heights of Barricourt. Ten minutes later, the 4th Brigade jumped off behind a creeping barrage, their objective to capture Barricourt and force the Germans behind the Meuse. The assault battalions of the brigade were 1st Battalion, 5th Marines, on the right, and 1st Battalion, 6th Marines, on the left. Succeeding battalions of each regiment, in column, would pass through the assault battalions on intermediate objectives.

Crushed by the massive artillery preparation and already smelling defeat, the Germans gave way before the Marines. At 0800 "Buck" Neville's troops had taken their initial objectives and were being leapfrogged by fresh battalions to maintain the momentum of the attack. By noon the process was again repeated, and still another relay of battalions was surging forward onto Barricourt Heights. Mid-afternoon saw the Marine brigade digging in on the crucial high ground. Once again, flanking divisions were left well behind, and the Marines had anxious moments until the adjacent 89th and 80th Infantry Divisions finally caught up. That night, the 3d Infantry Brigade relieved the Marines and continued the advance. Seventeen hundred German prisoners, including intact artillery formations, constituted the day's bag.

The 1 November attack by the Marine brigade set one of the speed and distance records of World War I. The impact of the assault may be measured in the admiring language of Major General C. P. Summerall, USA, the V Corps commander, who commended Lejeune for his: [48]

. . . brilliant advance of more than nine kilometers, destroying the last stronghold in the Hindenburg Line, capturing the Freya Stellung, one of the most remarkable achievements made by any troops in this war. . . . These results must be attributed to the great dash and speed of the troops, and to the irresistible force with which they struck and overcame the enemy.

The succeeding week was distinguished by a series of rapid advances by the 2d Division. On 9 November the division reached the Meuse River and was grouping for an assault crossing. Once again the Marine brigade was to lead the attack. The 6th Marines, reinforced by the 3d Battalion, 5th Marines, would seize one bridgehead near Mouzon. The remaining two battalions of the 5th Regiment were to cross at Villemontry.

On the dark night of 10 November 1918, 143d Birthday of the Marine Corps, the 5th Regiment's assault battalions, grouped under Major Hamilton, made a desperate attack across fire-swept footbridges built by the 2d Engineers under vicious shelling. By 2230 both battalions were across and consolidating. At Mouzon, meanwhile, enemy fire had prevented the construction of bridges, so the 6th Marines simply hugged their foxholes and hoped for a letup in the German shellfire.

Next morning, while high staffs on both sides prepared to ring down the curtain, the 5th Marines struck out undaunted, against slackening enemy resistance. "A few minutes before eleven o'clock," recalled General Lejeune, "there were tremendous bursts of fire from the two antagonists and then— suddenly—there was complete silence."[49]

The war was over.

"THE WHOLE NATION HAS REASON TO BE PROUD . . ."

The Marine Corps which emerged from World War I was different from anything ever known to Marines before. At the end of 1918 it had attained the unheard-of top strength of 79,524 (including 269 women reservists, or "Marinettes")—25 times the strength of the Corps only two decades before. Approximately 32,000 officers and men served in France. Since initial entry into combat in March 1918, Marine units had sustained more battle casualties in eight months' fighting than the entire Corps in its preceding 142 years. The total was 11,366 officers and men, of whom 2,459 were killed or missing in action. Only 25 Marines became prisoners of war.[50] "Surrendering," reflected Colonel Catlin, "wasn't popular at the time, and the only way to capture a Marine was to knock him senseless first."[51]

Twelve Army or Navy Medals of Honor were won by Marines, while six more (half of the 12 Medals of Honor awarded to members of the Navy during the war) went to Navy doctors and corpsmen with the Marine brigade. Seven hundred and forty-four Navy Crosses and Distinguished Service Crosses were awarded to other members of the brigade, together with 1,720 other American and foreign decorations. The colors of the brigade itself, of the 5th and 6th Marines, and of the 6th Machine Gun Battalion, came home bearing the streamer of the Croix de Guerre, which would forever symbolize the award of the *fourragère* to those units.

On 12 August 1919, after completing an uneventful tour of occupation duty along the Rhine, the 4th Marine Brigade reached Washington, D.C., en route to Quantico, where it was to be demobilized. Here, on arrival, all hands were warmly welcomed back into the Naval Establishment by Acting Secretary of the Navy Franklin Roosevelt (". . . a great friend of the Marines, and a virile, straight-shooting man as well," remarked Lejeune[52]). Then, as the August sun beat down, the brigade, with General Neville at its head, marched past the White House under the eyes of President and Mrs. Woodrow Wilson. When the Marine brigade, together for the last time after five major engagements, finally passed by and the strains of "Semper Fidelis" fell silent, the war President penned a brief note to General Barnett:[53]

. . . You may be sure it was a genuine pleasure to Mrs. Wilson and me to review the splendid body of Marines who have just been mustered out of service. We are intensely proud of their entire record, and are glad to have had the whole world see how irresistible they are in their might when a cause which America holds dear is at stake. The whole nation has reason to be proud of them.

"I'M HERE TO TAKE CARE OF YOU . . ."

If, as Woodrow Wilson wrote, the whole nation had reason to be proud of its Marines, there was an unsung group within the brigade of whom the whole Corps had reason to be proud, the Navy doctors and hospital corpsmen. In the words of one of their own, who soldiered from Belleau Wood to the Rhine:[54]

[medical personnel] splint broken bones; ligate bleeding arteries; support eviscerated entrails; perform merciful amputations with scissors or bayonets; neutralize agonizing burns; satisfy a searing thirst; stimulate and cheer a crushed body; rouse men from the brink of fatal shock; transfuse ensanguinated tissues; protect injuries against destructive infections; take a farewell word or note from those about to die. . . .

Although the Navy medical department had been with the Marines ever since the days of the loblolly boys, the problems of field medicine, even in Peking, the Philippines, or Nicaragua, were simple, and because of their simplicity, hardly recognized. Just as the World War opened new professional dimensions to the Marine Corps, so it brought recognition to field medical service as a distinct and major function of Navy medicine. In sheer volume and variety of casualties, let alone the conditions under which they were sustained and treated, the war added unprecedented experiences to the annals of the Medical Department.

In all, 331 Navy doctors, dentists, and corpsmen, the greater part of whom were trained at Quantico, served in combat with the 4th Marine Brigade, while many others were attached to the 5th Brigade and other Marine units which did not get an opportunity to fight. Among the former, 18 were killed and 165 wounded. Lieutenant Commander Joel T. Boone, regimental surgeon, 6th Marines, wounded at Belleau Wood, won the Army DSC, and, in his next action, Soissons, the Medal of Honor. With these and with a wide range of other well-deserved decorations, American and French, won by him, Commander Boone remained, until World War II, the most decorated officer in the United States Navy. Dr. Boone's fighting spirit was matched by that of an unnamed corpsman attached to a 5th Marines platoon at Belleau Wood which was confronted by a strongly defended German machine gun nest.

Several unsuccessful attempts to take it had been made with heavy losses. The handful of men left had drawn back prior to making another charge. The company hospital corpsman . . . yelled out in the thick of the hand-to-hand fighting, "Get that gun, you —— —— ——! I'm here to take care of you." The gun was captured shortly afterward.[55]

Once the fighting was over and the Marine brigade reached the Rhine, medical problems continued. Methyl alcohol appeared in cognac bottles. As in all military occupations of conquered territory, the disciplinary problem of "'fraternization with the enemy" presented itself in practical ways, so much so that the 2d Division surgeon, in reply to a request for a ruling, felt impelled to write:[56]

Office, Division Surgeon, 2d Division   14 January 1919
To: Surgeon, 6th Regiment, U.S.M.C.
   1. Returned. *Copulation is not fraternization,* and men will not be tried therefor.

Such aftermath of war aside, the 4th Brigade gave the nation ample reason to be proud of the Marines.

"BEYOND THE SEAS"

While the 4th Marine Brigade in France was adding immortal laurels to the colors of the Corps, many other Marines were performing less spectacular duties in other places at home and "beyond the seas."

Just because the United States was at war with Germany was no reason for Haitian cacos or the rebels in Santo Domingo and Cuba to ease their efforts. Quite the contrary.

Thus, the thinned-down 1st Brigade in Haiti—in reality, little more than the 2d Marines—had its hands full, as did the 2d Brigade in Santo Domingo, where the 3d and 4th Marines were stationed. In Cuba, the 3d Brigade, in the field since December 1917, was made up of the 7th and 9th Regiments. And in the newly purchased Virgin Islands, three rifle companies, reinforced in 1918 by a base-defense battalion from the 11th Marines, guarded St. Croix and St. Thomas against incursion or exploitation by German submarines.

Moreover, while the armies fought it out in France, the Navy, conditioned by Mahan, kept an anxious eye lest the tough German High Seas Fleet, held at bay by the British Grand Fleet, crash out of the North Sea into the Atlantic. The Navy's first step to avert any such possibility was to reinforce the Grand Fleet by five American battleships, grouped as the Sixth Battle Squadron. In all, some 19 officers and several hundred enlisted Marines served with the Sixth Battle Squadron while attached to the Grand Fleet between 7 December 1917 and 1 December 1919. There were sweeps of the fleet across the North Sea, escort missions for the minecraft which were laying the North Sea Mine Barrage between Scotland and Norway, and occasional brushes with U-boats (one of these was sunk when her hull was sliced open by one of the USS *New York's* propellers). There were no actions in which the American sailors and Marines aboard the battleships could show their mettle.

A breakout of the High Seas Fleet, though it would have brought the Grand Fleet into action immediately, might be a ruse under cover of which cruisers or armed merchant raiders could escape into the Atlantic and imperil American shipping along our coast from New England, through the Caribbean, and down to the Panama Canal.

Therefore, the Chief of Naval Operations' first requirements of the Marine Corps in 1917 was for a strengthened, reconstituted Advance Base Force capable of holding key points in the Caribbean against the German Navy, whether surface or submarine. With Haiti and Santo Domingo aflame in 1916, the force had been cut back to a skeletonized 1st Regiment left in Philadelphia to keep charge of the base-defense guns and gear at League Island Navy Yard, while the 2d Marines, an infantry regiment, soldiered in the West Indies.

To command the revived Advance Base Force, General Barnett looked to Brigadier General "Tony" Waller, just back from Port-au-Prince and sporting well-earned stars as a result of the 1916 Naval Personnel Bill. Although Waller, now 61, was too old for France, he was just the man to whip the Advance Base Force (or any other Marine force) back into shape.

The 1st Marines and Force Headquarters in Philadelphia were virtually the same in organization as the brigade which Barnett had put through its paces in the Culebra maneuvers of 1914, although motor transport had supplanted the oxen, horses, and mules of West Indian days. Now, in addition, there was an armored car company and a "Marine Aeronautic Company." Also, at Quantico there was a heavy artillery battalion made up of four companies of the 1st Marines, whose 5-inch naval guns had been repossessed by the Navy for arming merchantmen; 16 British 8-inch howitzers, highly unsuitable for base defense, had been scrounged from the Army instead.

The rifle units of the Advance Base Force consisted of two regiments, the 9th Marines (doing double duty as part of the 3d Brigade in eastern Cuba), and the 8th Marines, at Camp Crockett, Texas. This station was not as unlikely a place in which to find a Marine regiment as might seem. The Mexican oil fields were the Navy's primary source of fuel, and intelligence had been obtained, as early as 1915, that the Germans might take advantage of Mexico's chronic political upsets and anti-Gringo mood to disrupt this source. As a result, the 8th Regiment, ultimately reinforced by the 9th as Cuba settled down, remained poised to take over the oil fields and keep peace in Mexico.

As it turned out, the only true Marine Corps advance base operation in World War I was in the Azores, where, in 1917, the Navy had antisubmarine forces. To protect the base at Ponta Delgada, São Miguel Island, the Advance Base Force was ordered to send a 7-inch seacoast battery and an aviation unit, the 1st Marine Aeronautic Company, equipped with 18 assorted seaplanes from the Corps' 340 aircraft. The commanding officer of the aviation company, Captain Francis T. Evans, commanded the group, 11 officers and 188 men in all.

On 22 January 1918, the Marines landed at Ponta Delgada, installed their two 7-inch guns and scratched out a seaplane base from which flight operations commenced in a month. Unfortunately, no German submarines showed up within the 70-mile coverage of the Marine planes, and the only thrills were those normal to aviation in 1918. Lieutenant W. P. T. Hill, for example, received (and doubtless earned) a commendation for frequent flights in foul weather "without radio, pigeons, or Very pistols."[57]

Nevertheless, the little side show in the Azores furnished a crude prototype of the air-ground island-defense operations by which Marines helped to hold the Pacific in 1942—and the 7-inch guns which guarded Ponta Delgada were of the same type that Marines manned on Midway and Samoa 25 years later. The 1st Aeronautic Company, in the characteristic tradition of the Corps, was, incidentally, the first completely trained and equipped American aviation unit to go overseas.

MARINE AIR OPERATIONS IN FRANCE

Marine Corps aviation entered World War I with seven pilots—Major A. A. Cunningham, Captains B. L. Smith, W. M. McIlvain, F. T. Evans, and R. S. Geiger, First Lieutenant D. L. S. Brewster, and Marine Gunner W. E. McCaughtry—and 43 enlisted men. These pioneers were the cadre of the Aeronautic Company in the Advance Base Force.

After detachment of the aviation unit for duty in the Azores, the remainder of Marine aviation was designated as the 1st Aviation Squadron (24 officers, 237 enlisted). In 1918, training just about kept pace with receipt of flyable machines at the squadron's base, the Marine Flying Field outside Miami, Florida. One veteran reported: [58]

. . . living in tents, housing the machines in canvas hangars, which are about to fall down, using a landing field which is made of sand so soft that no grass can be made to grow in it and which is so near sea level that there is a possibility at any moment of having the whole field flooded.

On 15 April 1918 the squadron became the 1st Marine Aviation Force and split into four squadrons and a headquarters; at the same time, to the joy of chafing young aeronauts, it was alerted for movement to France.

The 1st Marine Aviation Force was earmarked to fly DH-4 pursuit bombers ("Flying Coffins" to the pilots of 1918) as the Day Wing of the Navy-Marine Corps Northern Bombing Group, based near Calais. The original mission of the group was to fly antisubmarine patrols over the North Sea and English Channel. Marine DH-4s would screen British and U. S. Navy bombers from German interceptors.

On 30 July 1918 the transport *DeKalb* debarked Major Cunningham and the 1st Aviation Force at Brest. The initial strength of the outfit was 100 officers and 657 enlisted Marines, but eventually rose to 1,095 officers and men. For the next ten weeks, Cunningham and his squadrons sweated to complete final training and assemble a complement of safely operable airplanes. Meanwhile, the submarine threat waned, and the force's mission was changed to support British and French ground units in Belgium and northern France.

Several officers of the Marine Aviation Force flew individually with the Royal Air Force, but the first all-Marine combat mission was a daylight raid on 14 October 1918 against Thielt by eight DH-4s led by Captain Douglas B. Roben, already wounded and distinguished in the Santo Domingo campaign. Everyone got back safely after dropping 2,218 pounds of bombs.

For the remaining weeks of the war, Marine air struck at the retreating German ground force, flew photo-reconnaissance missions, dueled with enemy fighters, and even provisioned a trapped French infantry regiment—a series of support missions not much different from those which Marine aviators would continue to fly in succeeding years. Lieutenant Ralph Talbot, a dashing youngster fresh from Yale, and his gunner, Corporal R. G. Robinson, shot down three German fighters out of 12 which jumped their lone airplane. Both received Medals of Honor, Talbot posthumously, while Robinson, despite three wounds, survived and eventually was commissioned a second lieutenant.

When the score was in, the 1st Marine Aviation Force was credited with inflicting 330 German casualties, shooting down 12 enemy planes, and dropping 52,000 pounds of bombs during 57 raids.

MARINES AT VLADIVOSTOK

In mid-1918, Vladivostok, although far away from the revolution in European Russia, became increasingly involved in violence and turmoil as freed Czechoslovakian prisoners of war fought to support an anti-Communist regime in the Far East. On 29 June 1918, the Asiatic Fleet flagship, USS *Brooklyn,* landed her Marine guard to protect the American consulate in Vladivostok. On 6 July, the Fleet commander in chief joined with the British and French, who had also landed troops, in assuming responsibility for maintaining "defense against dangers both external and internal."[59] The Marines, commanded by Captain A. F. Howard, meantime had also taken over security of the Russian navy yard, which adjoined the consulate. Six weeks later, on 16 August, a U. S. infantry brigade arrived from the Philippines, mainly as a counterbalance to a Japanese landing force which had occupied Vladivostok a few days before. On 28 August, once the Army units were established ashore, the *Brooklyn's* Marines were withdrawn, but a Marine guard was maintained until November 1922 at a U. S. Navy radio station on Russian Island in Vladivostok Bay.

THE RELIEF OF GENERAL BARNETT

In February 1918, General Barnett's tour as Commandant was running out. With the war at crescendo there was no question but that Barnett must be reappointed. As Major General Commandant he had made a distinguished record, and he enjoyed the esteem of President Wilson. Accordingly, on 12 February 1918, Navy Secretary Daniels announced, in a statement brimming with praise, that General Barnett had been reappointed for a second term:[60]

During the incumbency of General Barnett as head of the Marine Corps, that organization has attained its highest efficiency and this is due in a large measure to his personal efforts and to his ability as an organizer and administrator. . . . The reappointment of General Barnett is a merited reward for a record of extraordinary efficiency, and I am sure will be a source of gratification to the officers and men of the Marine Corps.

What Mr. Daniels did not announce was that, on the day he handed General Barnett his new four-year commission as Major General Commandant, he had also attempted to persuade the general to give him a signed, undated request for retirement, to be held on file awaiting the pleasure of the Secretary. Barnett, no easy mark for such a proposal, flushed and asked to see President Wilson. Mr. Daniels coughed, swallowed hard, and said never mind. For the time being the matter rested.

In June 1918, Congress had before it a Naval Personnel Bill which included one provision of extreme interest to the Marine Corps. If enacted, this legislation would increase the Commandant's rank to lieutenant general and would confer a second star on the Adjutant and Inspector, the Quartermaster, and the Paymaster.

As the time drew near for debate on this measure, the Secretary of the Navy was strangely silent. True, the Marines in France were winning laurels right and left, but—would "military necessity" be served by such promotions? Mr. Daniels just didn't know.

If Secretary Daniels seemed undecided, there was one Marine whose mind was made up, and that was Colonel Smedley D. Butler, who was desperately trying to lever himself up from Haiti to get into "the big parade." Butler noted that the promotions under the pending bill would go to the three principal staff officers of Marine Corps Headquarters, and to a Major General Commandant who, whatever his administrative merits, held no Medal of Honor and had few powder stains on his uniforms. Butler, as we have seen, was the cherished son of Representative Thomas Butler, Chairman of the House Naval Affairs Committee.

On 18 June the personnel bill came up for final action in the House of Representatives. Assured that the measure would pass, General and Mrs. Barnett and General Lauchheimer were in the gallery to hear the debate.

To their amazement, the all-powerful Representative Butler rose, majestic in a Quaker's wrath, to denounce the Marine promotions. General Barnett, claimed Butler and his fuglemen, was "a rocking-chair warrior," and "a swivel-chair hero." As for the Secretary of the Navy, Mr. Butler could state that he "refused to endorse" the promotions. Worse still, Barnett, it was charged, had gone over Daniels' honest head, had exerted "social and political pull"—a dig at Mrs. Barnett, doyenne of capital society—to get himself and his henchmen extra stars while braver and better Marines were in France. Et cetera. On a standing vote the Marine promotions failed, 73—49.[61]

General Barnett, a man of utter rectitude, to whom duty had been a lodestar for 40 years, was affronted. Lauchheimer was furious. Secretary Daniels said nothing and pursued the bland tenor of his daily relations with the Commandant.

Two years later to the day—18 June 1920—Secretary Daniels sent a sealed envelope to General Barnett, who was now (he thought) at midpoint of his second term as Major General Commandant. Mr. Daniels' letter was unlike any communication ever transmitted from the Secretary of the Navy to the Commandant of the Marine Corps: General Barnett was to be relieved as Commandant "one day next week most suitable" to him; meanwhile, before the end of working hours—within three hours, that is—would General Barnett please inform the Secretary of the Navy whether he intended to retire immediately or (as the law allowed) remain on the active list, taking a reduction to brigadier general?

General Barnett took a long breath, said he intended to stay on, didn't care whether he was reduced or not, and asked only two favors—could he be assigned to Quantico and could he catch up on his accrued leave (four months) as he had had none since early 1918? In reply, Mr. Daniels sent him to San Francisco (where Headquarters, Department of the Pacific, had been hastily set up as a kind of Elba for the deposed Commandant) and gave him half the leave he asked for.

Next day, General Barnett went to the Secretary's office, and, in Barnett's words:[62]

Mr. Daniels . . . appeared very much surprised that I was anything but pleased—that I had not expected it. . . . I remarked that even a servant was entitled to 30 days' notice and that he only gave me three hours. I told him that I had been treated unjustly after long years of faithful service. He then remarked, "Then that very materially lessens the sorrow of our parting." I said, "Good day, Sir," and left his office.

General Barnett's relief by a Democratic administration kicked up an immediate storm in a Republican Congress, but not enough to do Barnett any good. Mr. Daniels later asserted that the whole thing had been done by direction of President Wilson, a somewhat difficult assertion to confirm since Mr. Wilson had not yet recovered from the paralytic stroke which in late 1919 had cut him off from the nation and from almost all government business. And Woodrow Wilson had been General Barnett's friend.

The fact that the new Commandant, Lejeune, was enormously popular and respected undoubtedly helped to make Daniels' action stick. Nor should Smedley Butler's implacable hostility toward Barnett (and thus the demonstrated hostility of Congressman Butler) be discounted.

Exactly why Secretary Daniels chose to turn on General Barnett nevertheless remains something of an enigma. The most likely surmise is that Daniels had long entertained the advancement—certainly well deserved—of Lejeune, and that Barnett's refusal to facilitate his own deposal by tendering the blank resignation hardened the Secretary's heart. This, at any rate, was Barnett's opinion. "The only reason I can give for it," he wrote,[63] "is that the Secretary of the Navy wanted to appoint Lejeune."

At any rate, on 30 June 1920, Major General George Barnett was relieved as 12th Commandant of the Marine Corps and was succeeded by Major General John A. Lejeune.

THE CORPS SCENE

Aside from the obvious impact of World War I on the nation as a whole, in which the Marine Corps shared, the dominant factor in the Marine Corps scene was simply the fivefold expansion of the Corps throughout 1917, and its equally abrupt postwar contraction in 1919 to 17,400, as the 4th and 5th Brigades were demobilized at Quantico and Norfolk. Considering that the Haitian cacos and Santo Domingan bandits had by no means demobilized correspondingly, 17,400 Marines were simply not enough. In 1920, Congress authorized a Marine Corps of 1,093 officers and 27,400 enlisted men—and then in the next breath appropriated funds for 20,000. The situation in mid-1920 was summarized by General Lejeune in his characteristic way:[64]

When I assumed the duties of Commandant, demobilization had been completed and the entire Corps was suffering from the consequent let-down which invariably follows the return of a military organization to peacetime conditions. Nearly all of the splendid men who had enlisted for the period of the emergency had resumed their civil occupations; many wartime officers had separated themselves from the service; wholesale demotions in rank had taken place; recruiting was slow; there was much unrest among the officers owing to their uncertain status; and the lavish expenditures incident to war were to a great extent still prevalent.

As indicated by Lejeune, much uneasiness came from the problems of the officers. During the war most commissions had been awarded from the ranks (a policy dear, incidentally, to Secretary Daniels, who at one time had gone so far as to try to disqualify officers' sons for Annapolis appointments). In the 1919 cutback of the Corps from 75,000 to 17,400, the great question was, which wartime officers would retain their commissions and how would their permanent seniority stack up?

To make these all-important selections, General Barnett convened a board headed by Colonel J. H. Russell. Russell's opening charge to his fellow members, as reported by a survivor of those days, was to this effect—the officers you select for permanent retention in the Corps are those who will break bread with you and marry your daughters; choose accordingly.

Whatever may have been the effect of Russell's injunction, the findings of his board created bitter controversy, for the list which Russell sent in failed to include most of the hard-fighting former NCOs who, whatever their table manners might be, had unquestionably distinguished themselves in France. To exacerbate the matter, Russell himself had not been able to get to France. For the battle-knit alumni of the units which had served in France, the Russell report seemed a kick in the teeth. Hardly were the papers on the Secretary of the Navy's desk before they were held in abeyance. And General Lejeune's first action on becoming Commandant was to convene another board, this one headed by General Neville (who had conspicuously been in France). In January 1921 the Neville Board brought in a very different though equally controversial report which, promptly approved, retained as officers many colorful former enlisted men—most of whom ultimately had to be retired when promotion by selection finally probed its way into the Corps a decade later. In the nature of things, as the fate of the Russell Board had demonstrated, no proceeding of this character could satisfy everyone, and the Neville Board did not. For better or worse, however, it set a pattern of personal as well as professional relationships and rivalries that prevailed well into the future.

Physically speaking, although the Marine Corps had, by 1920, almost reverted to its prewar strength, it now found itself with three major bases of its own—quite a novelty to an organization whose posts (except for Eighth and Eye) had, for 140 years, been entirely ancillary to navy yards. Quantico, San Diego, and Parris Island—each a Marine Corps post in its own right—were symbols that the Corps was coming of age.

Few changes had taken place in the uniform. To be sure, the Army had ordered the Marines in France into olive drab—a much disliked imposition variously justified on grounds ranging from simplification of supply to the need to prevent the enemy (or perhaps our own war correspondents) from being able to identify individual American units. Once back in the Naval Establishment, however, Marines happily donned greens again. One war casualty was the old special full dress, a handsome blue frock-coated uniform with double rows of buttons (although this lingered for White House aides until the 1930s). The Sam Browne belt, originally worn only by officers assigned to the AEF, became, in 1921, the standard officers' belt. Otherwise—fortunately, most felt—the existing spectrum of Marine uniforms remained undisturbed.

Even in 1917, the pace of war, for officers, at any rate, remained ordered and somewhat sedate, as witness the following list of items (other than uniforms) which every Marine officer going to France was advised to take:[65]

1 bedding roll, pillow, and mattress	1 small rubber boots, pair
1 clothing roll	1 hip rubber boots, pair
2 blankets	3 shoes, with extra laces, pairs
1 overcoat	1 high lace leather boots, pair
1 coat sweater	1 puttees spiral, pair

1 puttees, leather, pair	6 socks, light, pairs
1 cap	4 suits, underwear, heavy, woolen
1 field hat	6 suits, underwear, light, woolen
1 canvas leggings, pair	6 suits, underwear, light, summer
12 handkerchieves, olive drab	2 garters
2 wrist watches	2 belly bands
1 note-book	1 Romeo slippers
2 pajamas, woolen	4 towels, face
1 polished mirror	2 towels, bath
1 knife	2 soap, face
1 compass	2 soap, shaving
1 whistle	2 toothbrushes
1 field glass	2 tooth-paste, tubes
1 leather gloves, buckskin, pair	1 raincoat
1 canvas bucket	1 bathrobe
1 rubber sponge	1 manicure set
1 Thermos bottle, unbreakable	1 set of brushes
1 nest, aluminum cups	1 jar, tobacco, with pipes and water-tight
1 poncho	matchbox
1 housewife	1 amber glasses
3 pillow cases	1 can-opener and corkscrew
4 sheets	1 Elliott ear protector, pair
6 socks, heavy, pairs	1 flashlight with extra batteries

In addition, every officer was advised to bring along *Field Service Regulations* and "whatever books he thinks he might need." Perhaps this last phrase was an omen of things to come, for the enlarged, professionally developing Marine Corps which emerged from the war needed many more books, more students, and more studies. Meanwhile, ahead somewhat dimly, lay peace, always a rather uncertain quantity for Marines, many of whom no doubt recalled the old gunnery sergeant's classic distinction between times of peace and war: "In peace, th' stuff flies around, and war looms ahead. In war, th' stuff flies around—and peace looms ahead."

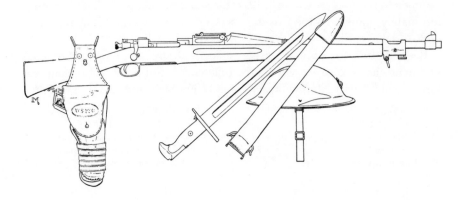

6 BETWEEN THE WARS *1919-1941*

The future success of the Marine Corps depends on two factors: first, an efficient performance of all the duties to which its officers and men may be assigned; second, promptly bringing this efficiency to the attention of the proper officials of the Government, and the American people.
—MAJOR GENERAL JOHN A. LEJEUNE

A*LTHOUGH* the Marines were home from France in 1919, the Corps still had its hands full of unfinished business in the West Indies, and, in different ways, at home, too.

Abroad, Marine brigades were engaged in varying degrees of activity in Haiti (major trouble since June 1918), Santo Domingo (steady rise in banditry beginning in early 1919), and Cuba (situation fairly stable). All these brigades had to be supported, if not reinforced, while at home the Marine Corps went through the contractions and convulsions which even the best conceived demobilization cannot prevent.

Aside from the physical trials of adjustment to peace, the stateside Marine Corps was patently in a time of change. After its great expansion and its heroic role in the AEF in France, the Corps could never be quite the same again. Although many officers and men looked forward (backward in reality) to a return to the old patterns of service, it was clear to thoughtful officers that the Marine Corps could not stand still; it must now go forward.

Regardless of the standing of the Marine Corps in the hearts of the American people, the Corps faced three serious internal problems at the conclusion of World War I.

The officers needed professional education for duties much broader, more technical, and more complex than those required only a decade before, and this requirement was compounded in many cases by the permanent retention as officers of former NCOs who had been hastily commissioned during the war.

A new type of enlisted man, younger, often more intelligent, and not as amenable to the traditional disciplines of the Corps as prewar Marines, had to be absorbed and properly motivated.

Most important of all, it was up to the Marine Corps to find its place and formulate a distinct role for itself as a service, a role which would enable the Corps to continue to make a recognizable contribution in its own right to the military needs of the United States.

How the Marine Corps dealt, in its own way, with all three problems while meeting the day-to-day demands and crises of its expeditions beyond the seas, we shall now see.

"SUGAR INTERVENTION": CUBA, 1917–22

After the 1912 revolt in Oriente province, Cuba enjoyed five uneasy years of superficial peace, peace which was really little more than ferment. Early in 1917, Oriente again erupted. Guantanamo City and Santiago, both familiar to U. S. Marines, were the eastern centers of revolt, while dissidence in western Oriente centered in the sugar-producing districts about Guacanayabo Bay. Aside from America's responsibilities for Cuban stability under the Platt Amendment, which permitted American intervention for the protection of Cuban independence, what lent special seriousness to the situation was the dependence of the United States and the other Allies on Cuban sugar, then as now a strategic material. To maintain the supply of sugar, it was vital that Cuba be preserved from anarchy.

On George Washington's birthday 1917, the U. S. consul in Santiago called for intervention. Three days later, U. S. Marines were ashore in two localities. At Guacanayabo Bay, Marines from the battleships *Michigan, Connecticut,* and *South Carolina* were formed into a provisional battalion commanded by Captain C. H. Lyman and landed to protect United States-owned sugar mills and plantations. Meanwhile, the Commandant of the Naval Station, Guantanamo Bay, sent the 24th Company from Fisherman's Point reinforced by Marines from the armored cruiser *Montana,* 220 in all, under Captain Harry Schmidt, to occupy Guantanamo City. Other Atlantic Fleet ships converged on Cuba, and the 1st Brigade, enjoying relative quiet at Port-au-Prince, contributed a six-company battalion which arrived in Cuba on 4 March. Within four days the Marine Corps had two companies (43d and 51st) in control of Santiago, assisted by Marine detachments from the cruiser *Olympia,* minelayer *San Francisco,* and gunboat *Machias.*

The mission of the Marines who fanned out into eastern Cuba and onto the north coast was simple and passive: protect United States-owned mills and leave the Cuban Army free to chase rebels. This was no problem. So successful were the arrangements that by May things seemed quiet enough to permit withdrawal, a course of action particularly timely since the formation of the 5th Marines at Quantico and Philadelphia required every regular who could be spared from the West Indies. And, on 25 May 1917, the 24th Company returned to Fisherman's Point, while the remaining companies were pulled back hastily to the States for further transfer to France. The first phase of the Sugar Intervention was over.

Whether or not the need for Marines in France swayed the decision to withdraw the companies from Cuba, it was soon apparent that withdrawal had been premature. Intelligence reported that German agents were backing rebel sabotage of key sugar-producing installations in Cuba. The U. S. government's first reaction was to organize an Army force, shaped around a regiment of cavalry, for antiguerrilla operations. Unfortunately, although staff officers drew up plans, the Army found itself unable to provide the troops. The Marines were then called in on short notice. On 17 August 1917, the 7th Regiment, commanded by Lieutenant Colonel M. J. Shaw, a veteran of Huntington's Guantanamo battalion, returned to the scene of its commander's early battle and then deployed through Oriente. Two companies and regimental headquarters encamped on San Juan Hill.

On Christmas Eve of the same year, the 9th Marines followed, bringing with them a brigade headquarters (3d Marine Brigade, Colonel J. E. ("Flip") Mahoney, who had been one of the leading spirits in the 1909 defense of the Corps). This regiment and brigade headquarters remained in reserve, at Deer Point, Guantanamo Bay, to back up the 7th Regiment. As one of the Advance Base Force regiments, however, the 9th was shifted to Galveston, Texas, on 31 July 1918, when the Navy decided to concentrate a ready reserve near the Mexican oil fields. Meanwhile, both the 7th and 9th Marines took advantage of the opportunity to train hard. Like their immediate predecessors, they confined their duties to protecting United States-owned property and showing the flag, while the Cuban Army took the field against the rebels. Again the arrangement worked to perfection, and the Marines for once had little if any shooting. Briefly (November 1918-May 1919) the 1st Marines were also stationed at Guantanamo Bay, together with the 2d Machine Gun Battalion. During this time the 1st was brigaded with the 7th Regiment to form the 6th Marine Brigade (Colonel T. C. Treadwell).

By August 1919, the need for Cuban stabilization had tapered off. World War I had ended. Accordingly, all Marines were withdrawn from Cuba, except a small battalion which held Camaguey, a key transportation center, until early 1922. Thus ended the Sugar Intervention. No fighting, much training.

THE CACO REBELLION

If service in Cuba was relatively peaceful, the same could hardly be said of Haitian duty during the same period. After two years of quiet, which resulted from Waller's wise administration coupled with Smedley Butler's decisive campaign in the north, the cacos were again up in arms. The immediate cause of discontent was enforcement by the American authorities of the *corvée*. The corvée, which Haiti had inherited from France, was the legal obligation of every citizen to perform unpaid labor to maintain the public roads. As Haiti had practically no roads before the Marines arrived, the requirement was traditionally honored in the breach. When the occupation forces began development of a long-overdue network of modern roads, the corvée suddenly assumed a different and far more onerous aspect to the average Haitian.

It was against this background of resentment towards what amounted to legalized, if temporary, peonage, that the figure of Charlemagne Massena Péralte entered the scene. Charlemagne, a man of spirit and intelligence, was a citizen of Hinche, focus of caco activity in central Haiti, and also an adherent of the Zamor family, who were powerful in the north of Haiti and had opposed the regime of President Dartiguenave, the American-supported chief magistrate. In January 1918, Charlemagne had been convicted of complicity in a caco raid on the Gendermerie headquarters at Hinche and sentenced to five years' hard labor. Cap-Haitien was his place of confinement, and the proud Charlemagne, who had received education in France, was assigned to street-sweeping under Gendarmerie escort. This was too much. On 3 September 1918, he induced his gendarme "chaser" to join him in flight to the mountains, where he immediately rallied local cacos to his banner with an appeal to drive "the invaders" into the sea and free Haiti. Ironically, the corvée was abolished throughout Haiti within less than a month after Charlemagne's flight.

Charlemagne's initial moves were directed against the numerous small outlying posts usually manned by detachments of the Gendarmerie, from three to six men. As the gendarmes were the visible symbols of the regime, these attacks served the double purpose of gaining comparatively modern weapons and of discrediting the occupation.

On the night of 17 October 1918, a hundred cacos, some armed only with machetes and sharpened wooden pikes, stole down toward Hinche. At ten o'clock they attacked. Fortunately, the two Gendarmerie officers at Hinche had been alerted. After a half hour of spirited fighting, the bandits fled, leaving 35 dead behind; two gendarmes were killed. The unquestioned hero of the fight was Lieutenant (First Sergeant, USMC) Patrick Francis Kelly, one of the most popular NCOs in the Corps. (The non-Marine Corps ranks are the Gendarmerie ranks in which Marines served.) "Even in a service where courage was taken for granted, his iron nerve and ice-cold daring marked him among his fellows,"[1] wrote an officer who served with him in Haiti. For his fine showing in this, the opening battle of the caco revolt, he was promoted to captain and awarded the Haitian Medaille Militaire.

Charlemagne's next strike was more successful. Sixty cacos hit Maissade, the next garrison northwest of Hinche, before dawn on 10 November 1918, routed the ten-man Gendarmerie detachment (no Marines were present), burned the barracks, and sacked the town.

For the next four months the pot boiled ever higher. More than 20 contacts with major caco forces were made by the hard-pressed Gendarmerie. Among these were toe-to-toe battles at or near Mirebalais, Cerca-la-Source, Mirebalais again, Las Cahobas, and St. Michel. In some instances, odds were 20 or 30 to 1; as at Ranquitte, where a Marine sergeant and two gendarmes, aided by a few townsmen, held their post against 70 cacos. On 21 March 1919, at Dufailly, a hundred cacos ambushed a patrol of five gendarmes commanded by Lieutenant (Sergeant, USMC) N. B. Moskoff. Moskoff fell at the first volley, mortally wounded, but his five men stood fast, lashed Moskoff to a *bourrique,* and began a two-hour fighting retirement on Mirebalais. When Moskoff's second-in-command was decapitated by a machete stroke, the remaining four nevertheless protected Moskoff and finally reached town. Unhappily, Lieutenant Moskoff was too badly hit and died soon after, but this showed how well the gendarmes would fight.

By this time, it was estimated, Charlemagne had some 5,000 active adherents. He himself was controlling operations in northern Haiti. Benoit Batraville, a caco chief almost as formidable as Charlemagne, kept things hot in the central part of the country, where once, as chief of police in Mirebalais, he had sullenly acquiesced in the occupation.

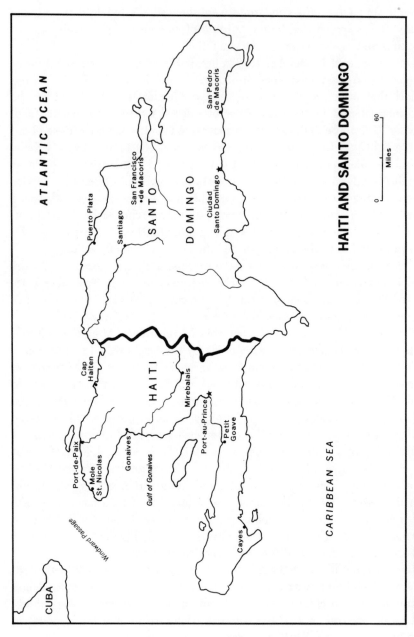

Haiti and Santo Domingo

On 16 March 1919, the commandant of the Gendarmerie, Lieutenant Colonel A. S. Williams, admitted what should have been realized much earlier, that he had a full-scale rebellion on his hands and that the Gendarmerie was most inadequate to the situation. Williams therefore requested that the 1st Marine Brigade be committed to the campaign.

Two factors compounded a situation already serious. Despite their loyalty, the Gendarmerie units outside Port-au-Prince, the showplace, were in poor shape, with ragged uniforms, ill-kept weapons, and low marksmanship ability. Moreover, the Marine brigade had been greatly weakened by transfers resulting from the demobilization process. On 31 December 1918, the brigade amounted to little more than a headquarters plus the 2d Regiment—64 officers and 884 enlisted Marines—not much to handle a national emergency.

Nevertheless, the brigade responded with all it had. Six companies of the 2d Marines were deployed to the hot spots—two to Hinche, two to Las Cahobas, one to Mirebalais, and one to St. Michel. The company which usually held Ouanaminthe was pulled south to Thomonde. Twenty-five per cent of the brigade was required to be on the trail patrolling at all times. Colonel Frederic M. Wise, an officer of extreme energy and combat experience, was ordered from the States in mid-1919 to assume command of the Gendarmerie. Less than a fortnight after Williams' admission of the extent of the trouble, four companies were transferred to the 2d Regiment from the 7th in Cuba. A more portentous reinforcement, even if not universally recognized as such, was Squadron E, Marine aviation, which, with seven HS-2 seaplanes, six Jenny landplanes, 11 officers, and 138 enlisted men, debarked at Port-au-Prince on 31 March. Squadron E, commanded for the moment by Captain Harvey B. Mims, USMC, would shortly come under the hand of Captain Roy S. Geiger, USMC, an aviator with a future.

During the months that followed, April through September 1919, Marines and gendarmes fought 131 actions ranging from skirmishes to pitched battles. Charlemagne's camp was overrun; three weeks later, Benoit Batraville's horse was captured—but Charlemagne and Benoit rode higher than ever.

On 6 October 1919, Charlemagne had a column of cacos in camp 15 miles north of Port-au-Prince. Here, with his force poised, using the superscription, "Chief of the Revolutionary Forces Against the Americans on Haitian Soil," he addressed an ultimatum to the British Legation, demanding the offices of the diplomatic corps to effect the surrender to him of the government of Haiti. Having received no reply by nightfall, Charlemagne launched 300 cacos at the capital city; they arrived at 0400 next morning, and were joined by sympathizers in the town.

The Marines and gendarmes were ready. Within minutes after the cacos began spilling into Port-au-Prince they came under sharp counterattacks. Soon the raid was converted into a pell-mell retreat. Next day, in their turn, the Gendarmerie found and attacked the caco camp, killing 30 bandits and capturing numerous weapons, including Charlemagne's prized field gun. Charlemagne himself, however, was nowhere to be found and was in fact well to the rear during the melee about Port-au-Prince.

CHARLEMAGNE'S DOWNFALL

As a long-term proposition, the suppression of the caco rebellion was getting nowhere and promised to continue to do so until Charlemagne Péralte could be laid by the heels.

None knew this better than Captain (Sergeant, USMC) H. H. Hanneken, in command of the district of Grande Rivière du Nord, a seedbed of cacos. Colonel Wise was also well aware of this. Within days after he assumed command of the Gendarmerie (19 July 1919), Wise sent word to Colonel (Major, USMC) James J. Meade, commanding operations in the north, "Get Charlemagne." To get Charlemagne thereupon became the highly secret mission of Captain Hanneken.

It was a pretty big order. It meant running down one Haitian out of several millions of Haitians in a country as big as the state of New York. And that one Haitian was surrounded by his friends, operating in a country almost entirely sympathetic to him, was protected by a fanatical body guard, never slept two nights in the same place, and must be run down in a tangled maze of mountains and valleys and jungles, of which there were no accurate maps.[2]

In August 1919, Captain Hanneken completed his plan, which he then communicated in its entirety only to Colonel Meade. Soon after, Jean-Baptiste Conzé, a leading citizen of Grande Rivière du Nord, left town in the night after letting it be known that he had had enough of the *blancs* and would thenceforth be found with the cacos. Accompanying Conzé were Cherubin Blot, another civilian, and a Gendarmerie deserter, Private Jean Edmond François. Conzé's destination and intended base of operations was Fort Capois, that same bandit stronghold which Smedley Butler had cleaned out in 1915. Since Conzé was well heeled with rum, rations, and money, cacos rallied quickly to his standard, and he soon became a leader of standing.

What nobody knew, except Colonel Meade and Captain Hanneken, was that Conzé and his two confederates were hand-in-glove with the authorities and were being supported with Hanneken's personal funds. Each week, or more often, Private François—sometimes even Conzé himself—would steal down into Grande Rivière du Nord for a secret meeting with Hanneken.

Charlemagne, like many Haitians, was suspicious by nature, a trait to which he owed much of his success and his continued survival. He was therefore slow to accept Conzé at face value. However, after the spectacular failure of a Gendarmerie attack on Fort Capois, led by Captain Hanneken, Charlemagne sent Conzé warm congratulations and a "commission" as *Général de Division* in his service. Publicly crestfallen and in notably poor standing with other Marines, Hanneken nursed a heavily bandaged arm stained with issue red ink from the Gendarmerie detachment's field desk. This, he reported, was a wound inflicted by Conzé's men.

Conzé now urged Charlemagne to join him in capturing Grande Rivière du Nord itself. To take a principal town would be a great thing for Charlemagne's cause, and he assented. On 26 October, Charlemagne arrived at Fort Capois, accompanied by his brother, St. Rémy Péralte, by the notorious "Papillon" (so called because he always carved the outline of a butterfly in the hide of each victim), and by a thousand cacos. The plan was to attack the town on Friday night, 31 October. Charlemagne would stand by just out of town to await the result.

On Thursday night, 30 October, while Grande Rivière slept, Colonel Meade brought in strong reinforcements of Marines and gendarmes, who were closely concealed during the day. Meanwhile, Hanneken briefed and disguised 16 picked gendarmes and his own second-in-command, First Lieutenant (Corporal, USMC) William R. Button. Disguised as cacos (Hanneken and Button being stained with burned cork) and armed with individual weapons and an automatic rifle carried by Button, the party laid an ambush at Mazare, where it was expected that Charlemagne would pass before the attack. After some 700 cacos had filed by unwittingly, but still no Charlemagne, Private François, the "deserter," made his way to the ambush with bad news—Charlemagne had decided not to come down but would wait and see what happened from a hideout back in the hills near Fort Capois.

There was only one thing Hanneken could do if he was to get Charlemagne. Setting out through the twilight, he led his patrol along the trail marked by Private François, who was to say that he was carrying messages from Conzé to Charlemagne. There were six caco outposts which the group had to pass, but Hanneken had the secret password of the day—"Général

Jean"—from Conzé. At the last outpost, manned by Charlemagne's personal guard, Button was almost unmasked by a bandit who noticed his BAR, but his luck held.

In the light of a small fire, Private François silently pointed out Charlemagne, dressed in a silk shirt. Hanneken drew his pistol, approached within 15 feet of the bandit, and put two .45 caliber slugs through his chest. Button emptied his automatic rifle into the swarming bodyguard, dropping nine of them before one of the caco women put out the fire. In the darkness, Hanneken grappled onto Charlemagne's body and stayed beside it during the intermittent counterattacks and shooting which went on until daybreak.

By morning light, the gendarmes ransacked the bivouac and found Charlemagne's headquarters files, which betrayed many secret supporters, some highly placed. Charlemagne's body, trussed over a captured mule, was brought down to Grande Rivière du Nord (where Colonel Mead had stood off the caco assault with no difficulty), then taken to Cap-Haitien.

At Cap-Haitien the bishop, who had known Charlemagne, publicly identified the body and gave it a Christian burial with the movingly Christian statement, "Moi, je suis le père des Haitiens, mais je suis aussi le père des cacos."[3]

To convince other cacos that Charlemagne was indeed dead, his body was photographed, laid out on a door, which gave rise to the canard that the *blancs* had crucified him against a door. Subsequently, to foil voodoo necromancy over the remains, his body was buried in concrete, but after the end of the occupation he was reburied with a state funeral, which was depicted in a painting by Obin, one of Haiti's leading artists.

AFTERMATH

As soon as Charlemagne's death was reported, a cordon of trail-blocks and ambushes was thrown across northern Haiti, from the Dominican border to the sea, to prevent any of the late leader's men from making their way south to rally on Benoit Batraville. More than 300 cacos were captured in the week after Charlemagne's demise. On 2 November, Captain Hanneken completed the clean up by leading an assault which carried Fort Capois and wiped out the cacos who had boasted of his repulse. This evened all scores.

Both Hanneken and Button were awarded thoroughly deserved Medals of Honor. Conzé, once again the respectable man of affairs at home, received the $2,000 reward posted on Charlemagne's head, while Jean Edmond

François—now Sergeant François—and Cherubin Blot also got substantial rewards. Moreover, by a government not yet ridden with doubting comptrollers and accounting office agents, Hanneken was promptly and fully reimbursed for his own highly irregular but vitally necessary out-of-pocket expenditures with which the coup had been financed.

SHAKEUP IN HAITI

Although the elimination of Charlemagne brought peace to northern Haiti, affairs in the central part of the country were far from quiet. Benoit Batraville was the cause.

Moreover, it was clear that, despite the windfall of Hanneken's enormous success, the existing organization, strength, and efficiency of both the Brigade and the Gendarmerie had not been adequate to deal with the caco uprising. This had already been recognized, at least in part, and was now being dealt with.

In mid-summer 1919, the Brigade commander, General Catlin, ailing ever since his wound at Belleau Wood, retired, and Lieutenant Colonel Louis McC. Little succeeded him for the time being. At about the same time Colonel Wise took over the Gendarmerie. Soon after, the State Department, which had been anxiously following the caco flare-up, asked Secretary Daniels to assign Colonel John H. Russell as the new Brigade commander, citing his past record as a successful military administrator in Haiti. This was promptly done, and Colonel Russell assumed command on 2 October 1919. Lieutenant Colonel Little, an able soldier with an excellent knowledge of French, was given charge of operations in the northern area.

Russell promptly shook up the Brigade staff to make it more effective in over-all co-ordination of antibandit operations. Among the first steps was creation of a far better intelligence organization. For operations, the whole caco country was divided into squares or areas of responsibility, with troops assigned to each, and measures were instituted to continue without letup the harrying of any caco group once located. General G. C. Thomas, who was a company officer during the caco rebellion, recalled:[4]

McCarty Little really drove us. We would come in from a 15-day patrol at daybreak, and he would have us exchange our enlisted and be off by dark.

The 8th Regiment, which had just disbanded after an uneventful tour at Galveston during the war, was reconstituted on 17 December 1919 and ordered to Haiti. On 5 January of the new year, Lieutenant Colonel Little was given the regiment. This added another rifle regiment to the Brigade, whose strength at year's end was 83 officers and 1,263 enlisted men. The Gendarmerie, too, was strong; it numbered 2,700. Furthermore, the last enlisted men of the World War had been demobilized, and the units in Haiti now had full complements of peacetime regulars.

In March 1919, an aviation squadron had joined the brigade. In August, with the assistance of one of the aviators, First Lieutenant L. H. M. Sanderson, Captain E. A. Ostermann, in command at Mirebalais, persuaded Colonel Little to assign him two airplanes, a Jenny and a DeHavilland, for which Ostermann and Sanderson laid out a grass landing field. On Ostermann's orders, although the planes had machine guns, caco bands were not fired on when seen from the air, and the bandits became quite used to Marine air patrols. Soon afterward, Ostermann, veteran and Medal of Honor winner of the 1916 campaign, learned that Benoit Batraville planned an all-night *bamboche,* a Haitian drinking party, on a mountaintop outside Mirebalais. During the night he posted Marines and gendarmes on all trails leading down from the mountain. As Ostermann later wrote:[5]

> I took up a position where with my field glasses I could observe without being seen. . . . At dawn our two airplanes came over and circled the clearing where the party was still going strong. They then made an approach low over a wooded area and opened up with the machine guns. The Cacos were taken completely by surprise and stampeded in all directions down the mountain trails where they were met by more machine-gun and rifle fire from my patrols. . . . We killed or wounded more than two hundred by actual count.

"We had no more trouble from Benoit Batraville in my area," concluded Ostermann, unaware until long afterward that he had brought about the first recorded instance of co-ordinated air-ground combat action in the annals of the Marine Corps. Another air-ground first for Haiti was experiments in glide bombing, also by the Mirebalais detachment. After the cacos became habituated to aerial strafing, Ostermann and Sanderson decided to bomb but found that no bomb racks were available. While waiting for one to arrive from the States, Sanderson rigged a mailbag between the Jenny's wheels and tried releasing a 25-pound bomb from inside by yanking the pucker-string. His target was an old caco hilltop fort. When the proper rack and release finally arrived, this was substituted and worked much better.[6]

Most of these fruitful changes, from reorganization to air-ground teamwork, were effected under the aegis of Russell, Wise, and Little during the closing months of 1919. Their object was to prepare all forces, both Marine and Gendarmerie, for an all-out campaign in January 1920.

THE END OF THE REVOLT

Since Benoit Batraville, who had not been killed on the mountaintop, was known to have some 2,500 active adherents, central Haiti was declared an emergency area, and a maximum effort by all forces, including aviation and Navy coastal craft, was launched by Russell to stamp out cacoism.

Batraville's reaction to Russell's offensive was prompt and characteristic of the caco leader, who was later characterized as "a much more aggressive man than Charlemagne but lacking in intelligence and leadership."[7]

At 0340 on the morning of 15 January 1920, Benoit marshaled more than 300 cacos north of Port-au-Prince, some disguised in stolen Gendarmerie uniforms. Then, in the words of Colonel Russell's son-in-law:[8]

The cacos, advancing into town in column and with flags and conch-horns blowing, divided . . . one column going along the water front and reaching town by way of the slaughter house, the other two columns turning farther inland and advancing around Bellair [sic] Hill, by the radio station. When the troops had nearly reached town our Marines opened fire with Brownings and machine guns, but the natives broke ranks and fired from around corners, and rushing into houses, fired upon the Marines from windows . . . enroute they had fired some of the native cailles [shanties], in the poor section of the town and the light from this lit up the entire surrounding country.

The speed and sharpness with which both Marines and Gendarmerie reacted came as a shock to the cacos and proved the soundness of Russell's new organization. Aggressive patrols and riot squads combed Port-au-Prince. One of these—ten men, a gunnery sergeant, and two BARS, under First Lieutenant G. C. Thomas—collided head-on with Benoit's waterfront column, which was making for the National Bank:[9]

Near the Iron Market we saw a large number of Cacos coming down this street. We detrucked and opened fire. I had one man killed and six wounded in five minutes, but we mowed the Cacos down.

Other Marine columns ranged out into the Cul-de-Sac, the great plain north of the city, which the retreating cacos had to traverse in order to reach the shelter of the mountains. One caco column was hemmed into a valley near the radio station, and, vainly resisting, was wiped out almost to a man. By break of day, 66 cacos had been killed and many more had been cut off, captured, and wounded, including the leader of the assault, Solomon Janvier, a native of Port-au-Prince who was found hiding in his own house. Well might the surviving bandits refer to this action as *la débâcle,* which became its name in caco parlance.

Following *la débâcle* it became clear to most that Benoit's days were numbered. Various chiefs began to surrender and were, in turn, required by Colonel Russell to take the field with Marine patrols in order to prove their sincerity and manifest their change of heart to the people of the countryside. Even Papillon came in and was taken on a tour through central Haiti by Captain Kelly. One officer who was particularly successful in capturing caco chiefs alive and converting them into *bons habitants* was Lieutenant (1st Sergeant, USMC) J. M. ("Spic") Darmond. Darmond, who was credited with bringing in some 20 caco "generals," observed:[10]

> A reformed bandit does us more good than a dead one. Dead men tell no tales, but live ones, treated right, tell tales, and they tell the tales we want them to tell. They told that the white man wasn't such a bad lot and that the Haitian people could have confidence in them, but they must behave themselves.

Faced with trouble on all sides, Benoit nevertheless fought on. He also consulted a renowned *bocor,* or sorcerer, Ti Bouton of Arcahaie, from whom he received counsels about how he might invoke supernatural aid in what was plainly becoming an uneven fight.

At daybreak on 4 April 1920, a small patrol consisting of Second Lieutenant (Sergeant, USMC) Lawrence Muth and three enlisted Marines breasted the slopes of Morne Michel, near Las Cahobas. Sighting a few cacos ahead, they opened fire. A few seconds later the entire hillside blazed with a hail of bullets from a powerful ambush. Lieutenant Muth was hit in the stomach and head by the first volley. As he went down he gasped orders to retire to his second-in-command, a private who was also wounded. Using their automatic rifle, the two unwounded Marines shot their way out, helping the wounded second-in-command and leaving Muth for dead. Led in person by Benoit Batraville, the cacos closed in and dragged Muth into the bush.

As soon as the three survivors reached Las Cahobas four hours later, 21 patrols were sent out from there and from Mirebalais. That afternoon a patrol, led by Colonel Little himself, hit a large body of cacos, and, after killing 25, recovered all that was left of Lieutenant Muth. According to a prisoner, Muth had partly revived after being hauled away. He was thereupon beheaded by machete to the accompaniment of Voodoo rituals laid down by Ti Bouton. Benoit himself then cut out, roasted, and ate the lieutenant's heart and liver, said to be the seats of courage and military sagacity. Bits of Muth's brain were smeared on each caco's rifle to make the weapon shoot straight and true. By this necromancy, Batraville expected to restore his fortunes and drive the *blancs* into the sea.

Magic or no magic, Benoit had only 45 days left to live. On an informer's tip, two patrols headed by Captain J. L. ("Si") Perkins and Second Lieutenant E. G. Kirkpatrick closed in on Benoit at daybreak 19 May in a wooded bivouac outside Las Cahobas. When the bandit leader opened fire, he was cut down by a blast from the automatic rifle of Sergeant W. F. Passmore. As he struggled to rise he received the *coup de grâce* from Sergeant A. A. Taubert. Thus ended the career of Benoit Batraville, and with it the last hopes of the caco revolt. The 1st Marine Brigade had sustained 23 casualties, and the Gendarmerie 75 (including five Marines).[11] The best count of caco casualties indicated that 2,006 were killed.

GENERAL RUSSELL'S PROCONSULSHIP

Much of the ultimate success of the 1st Brigade in quelling the second caco uprising may be attributed to Colonel Russell's skill and Little's drive. Russell was one of the intellectuals of the Corps (as early as 1916 he had called for "a conference of field officers" to determine a fixed set of missions for the Corps). It was therefore logical that, in seeking a more efficient way to administer the *de facto* protectorate over Haiti, the government should turn to Russell, who had served there, with one brief interruption, since 1917. In February 1922 the treaty services in Haiti were reorganized, and, following promotion to brigadier general, Russell became United States High Commissioner (with rank of ambassador), a post which he combined with command of the Marine brigade.

After the end of the caco revolt and the abolition of the corvée, which had started it, Haiti began a period of peace and great progress. Generally speaking, the country was prosperous as never before, healthy, and honestly governed. Literacy rose from two per cent in 1915 to over ten per cent. The Gendarmerie reached an efficiency which was destined to endure for some years after the Marines finally left. This efficiency was underscored in 1924 when, to the world's surprise, Haiti fielded a national rifle team (coached and sparked by Colonel D. C. McDougal) which won second place, only behind the United States, in the Olympics of that year, defeating 17 other countries including Great Britain, France, and the other great powers.

Nevertheless, General Russell had two serious headaches. One was a series of "scandals" and resultant investigations, mainly of political origin, which were provoked in 1920 by an unfortunate phrase in a private letter by General Barnett[12] which unintentionally suggested that "indiscriminate killings" of Haitians had taken place on the part of Marines. Needless to say, this charge was never established to be true. Russell's second headache has been well described by Dana G. Munro, career diplomat and historian who served as American Minister to Haiti after General Russell's departure:[13]

The American occupation was nonetheless disliked by the majority of the Haitian *élite*. Though this group had returned to power with the intervention, after the long period of subjugation to black military leaders and Caco chieftains, they felt that they had derived little benefit from the change. In the past, the government's revenue had nearly all found its way, through one channel or another, into the pockets of the ruling class. Now it was being spent by foreigners on projects that benefited the masses of the people.

This discontent found voice in late 1929 when it appeared that President Louis Borno, who had co-operated fully and openly with the United States, was planning to succeed himself for another term in office. The resultant disorders were quelled within a month, almost wholly by Gendarmerie forces while the Marine brigade remained mostly in the background. The lone clash involving Marines took place on 6 December 1929, at Marche-à-Terre, outside Les Cayes, where a drunken mob of some 1,500 peasants, incited by local politicians, charged and stoned a small Marine detachment which was finally forced to open fire, killing and wounding 34. A year later, with the country quiet, General Russell was allowed to come home as a first step in restoration of full sovereignty to Haiti. A most fitting send-off for General Russell was voiced in the report by President Hoover's Forbes Commission, which had investigated and recommended U. S. policies regarding the Haitian protectorate:[14]

The Commission desires to record its high praise of General Russell's wholehearted and single-minded devotion to the interests of Haiti as he conceived them, his unremitting labor, and his patient and painstaking efforts to bring order out of chaos and to reconstruct a governmental machine which had been largely destroyed by years of abuse, incapacity, and anarchy.

By the turn of the 1930s an era of American political intervention was coming to an end. This was reflected in Haiti (as it would be in Nicaragua) by realization that military occupation of small Caribbean countries had served its greatest use and must now be replaced by a policy of nonintervention. On 21 August 1934, after being relieved by the Garde d'Haiti, as the Gendarmerie had been redesignated, the 1st Marine Brigade hauled down its colors over Casernes Dessalines in Port-au-Prince and filed aboard transports for the voyage home.

SANTO DOMINGO, 1917–18

After Pendleton's campaign in 1916, and the capture of the principal rebel leaders in early 1917, a sullen peace prevailed in Santo Domingo. For the moment, although the country was far from friendly to the American military government, political strife had subsided. This had no effect on banditry as such, which was one of the main occupations of much of the male populace. To worsen the situation, Santo Domingo, like the Old West, had a long-standing tradition of gun-toting, feuding, and assassination.

That this was so was proven in January 1917 when two Marine officers, sitting aboard a patrol craft alongside in San Pedro de Macoris, were set upon by a band of gunmen who murdered one and wounded the other. During the rest of the year there were 14 major contacts with bandit forces, of which the most important was an all-day pitched battle at Las Canitas on 7 April in which a mixed force of Marines and Guardias stormed a succession of five fortified positions guarding the stronghold of Dios Olivorio, one of the most troublesome bandit leaders. Unfortunately, Olivorio got away, although his band sustained more than 40 casualties. Subsequently, by way of recompense, another of the major leaders, Vicentico, surrendered outside of Seybo with 180 of his followers. Vicentico's surrender resulted from an extraordinary act of courage and diplomacy on the part of First Sergeant William West. West made his way, accompanied only by an interpreter, to the bandit camp and persuaded Vicentico to meet Lieutenant Colonel G. C. Thorpe, with whom, on 3 July 1917, surrender of the entire band was negotiated. The state of relative peace which had been arrived at by mid-1917 was largely the result of Vicentico's surrender and of the energetic patrolling under the hard-driving Lieutenant Colonel "Hiking Hiram" Bearss. Under Bearss's personal leadership, Marine patrols—many of them not hiking at all but mounted—combed the mountains and fields of Seybo and Macoris, the two easternmost provinces, where banditry centered. Another important bandit surrender (the result of Bearss's work) was that of the leader, Chacha. In addition, ever since first arriving, the Marines had concentrated on a drive to collect and control the large quantities of small arms adrift in the country: as noted earlier, by 1917 some 53,000 stand of arms had been collected and confiscated.

On 1 July 1917, the 2d Brigade numbered 68 officers and 1,932 enlisted men. It was mainly composed of the 3d and 4th Regiments, which, respectively, occupied the northern and southern areas, whose boundary ran east-west along the Cordillera Central.

As 1918 began, banditry was again on the increase, especially in the east. To cope with it the brigade was still mainly on its own, since the Guardia was as yet only half organized. During the year—a year of relentless patrolling through inhospitable terrain fairly crawling with bandits—the Marines had 44 major contacts or ambushes and many more brushes with hostile Dominicans. The Marine combat casualties in 1918 of five killed and 13 wounded give little indication of the physical strain, the bone-deep fatigue, the fires of malaria and dengue, and the frustration of the campaign.

Among the most noteworthy engagements during that year was the attack on 19 January, after a long mountain march, on Olivorio's new stronghold on Mount Colorado. Unfortunately, Olivorio again had excellent advance information, and, although his camp was overrun and destroyed and a few bandits picked up, the leader stayed well ahead of his pursuers.

Hato Mayor, in Seybo Province, was virtually a battlefield; five of the 44 major contacts occurred in or about the village. One ambush, on 24 July, nearly resulted in the extinction of a combined Marine and Guardia patrol led by Captain Charles F. Merkel, a German-born former enlisted man. As Merkel's outfit was making camp in a draw, bandits hit them from three sides. Only by a series of uphill rushes to regain the high ground did the patrol get clear, suffering three casualties but inflicting ten.

Three weeks later, on 13 August, Hato Mayor was the scene of another ambush. A four-man mounted patrol, led by Corporal Bascome Breeden, was set upon by a large bandit force while crossing a stream. Despite heroic resistance, three of the Marines, including the patrol leader, were shot or cut down by machetes. Only Private Thomas J. Rushforth remained, and, although badly chopped and sliced by a machete rush, he managed to stand off the bandits, retrieve his mount, and gallop free under intense fire. In friendly hands at last, Rushforth was found to have at least four wounds; his horse was shot twice.

Only two days after Private Rushforth's hairbreadth escape, a patrol in bivouac near Hato Mayor was jumped during the evening meal. Again, as in the case of Captain Merkel's patrol, a vigorous counterattack in all directions dispersed the bandits. One enlisted Marine was wounded.

As the year waned, so, for the time being, did banditry, at least the vocational as distinct from the political kind. Taking advantage of this momentary lull, General Pendleton was able to lay down his heavy burdens as 2d Brigade Commander and as intermittent Military Governor. In his stead, on 21 October 1918, came Brigadier General Ben H. Fuller, one of the early Naval Academy Marine officers, who was destined in a few years to become 15th Commandant of the Marine Corps.

UPSURGE OF BANDITRY, 1919

The real problem in bringing peace and stability to Santo Domingo was that, like many of the Haitian elite, most of the dominant class had little stomach for the kind of peace and stability that the United States felt was essential. Regrettable as it may seem, there was no applause for the increased school enrollment, vigorous sanitation, road programs, and, particularly, honest finance—a most unwelcome innovation which disturbed existing politico-economic patterns and caused real hardship in certain established strata of the country.

Thus, the well-intended actions of the U. S. occupation, where not more actively opposed, were viewed with the suspicion and hostility that is the lot of do-gooders, whether individual or national. This perennial Dominican state of mind created an ideal climate for political banditry, even though this was often hard to distinguish, as a practical matter, from plain thuggery.

In 1919, such "political" crimes began a steady increase.

This far-from-cheerful news was received by the United States government at a time when relief could be seen ahead from the wartime demobilization, and it was decided to swell the ranks of the 2d Brigade by sending an additional regiment, the 15th Marines, with a squadron of aviation. This outfit, probably the first Marine air-infantry force ever organized, reached Santo Domingo on 8 March 1919. The aviation unit had originally been the first division of Squadron D, 1st Marine Aviation Force, in France; in Santo Domingo it was called "1st Air Squadron."

The 15th Marines, commanded by Colonel James C. Breckinridge, an officer of polish, resolution, and intellect, landed at San Pedro de Macoris in the heart of the eastern bandit country, where more troops were badly needed. With the units already there, the brigade now had more than a hundred officers and 2,500 enlisted men.

As soon as the 15th Regiment was well ashore, a third area, the eastern district, was established. This district included the main trouble zone south of Samana Bay on the eastern tip of the island. During 1919, there were 50 major contacts and at least a hundred lesser skirmishes. Despite the increased tempo of patrolling, only three Marines were killed (two of them officers) and four wounded.

The advent of aviation considerably streamlined the campaign in eastern Santo Domingo. The six Jennies of the 1st Air Squadron, based on a sugar plantation near Consuelo, served as the eyes of Colonel Breckinridge's patrols, and, like the squadron across the border in Haiti, carried mail, supplies, and sick and wounded. Moreover, both squadrons experimented with the new kind of bombing in which the pilot dove toward his target from a 45-degree angle and released his bomb on pull-out at about 250 feet.

In addition to such experiments, the 1st Squadron flew many combat sorties in 1919, and aviation thereby began to carve the initials "USMC" on the bandits of Santo Domingo. The first air attack on bandits took place near Meta de la Palma on 23 July 1919, within days of the Ostermann-Sanderson air-ground ambush of Benoit Batraville in Haiti.

FINAL PACIFICATION AND WITHDRAWAL

Toward the end of 1920, it was decided that the occupation of Santo Domingo could not continue, and that the best determinant would be restoration of general peace coupled with creation of a Guardia Nacional capable of standing on its own feet.

To bring about the first objective, final pacification, Colonel W. C. Harllee, now in command of the 15th Regiment in the turbulent eastern district, hit upon a drastic but effective measure. After blocking off bandit-infested areas, troops and Guardias rounded up virtually every male for a series of mass line-ups in which carefully hidden informers picked out known bandits. These line-ups were often conducted in the open at night under floodlights while the informers were stationed in darkened tents. After five months of the "cordon system," nine successful roundups had been carried out, and more than 600 courtroom convictions for banditry resulted. Following this crackdown, the cordons were discontinued because of the resentment aroused by such methods among those who were innocent. General Lee, the Military Governor, then proclaimed a two months' period of amnesty during which bandits were encouraged to surrender, and, simultaneously, five special anti-bandit groups were trained from among Dominicans who had suffered at bandit hands. At the end of the amnesty, intensive and highly successful patrolling resumed against the few remaining bandits in the field. With cordons, amnesty, and patrols, the pressure was too much, and, at the end of May 1922, when the final amnesty period ended, Santo Domingo was truly, and for the first time, pacified.

Simultaneously the Guardia Nacional (which was renamed "Policia Nacional" to disabuse Dominican leaders who were still hoping to make it into a banana army rather than a true national constabulary) showed a marked increase in efficiency and scope of operations. From 1922 on, as would be the case later in Haiti, there was a progressive Dominicanization of the Policia, which, under the efficient and popular leadership of Colonel Richard M. Cutts, began taking over various interior garrisons from the 2d Brigade. In August 1922, its mission completed, the 15th Regiment was disbanded, as was the 3d. Then the 1st Marine Regiment (which had only just disbanded at Quantico) was recommissioned in Santo Domingo and absorbed the officers and men of the 15th. This left the 2d Brigade with two regiments, 1st and 4th Marines, and the 1st Air Squadron. Brigadier General Harry Lee, the brigade commander and last Military Governor of Santo Domingo, now was concerned mainly with an efficient and economical windup of United States affairs.

In July 1924, the aviation squadron returned to Quantico. On 18 July, the 1st Regiment was redesignated 3d Battalion, 6th Marines, and sailed for home. In August, the 4th Marines sailed for San Diego, long the beloved home port of "Uncle Joe" Pendleton who, retired only two months earlier, was at the landing to greet his old regiment. On 16 September 1924, the rear echelon of the 2d Brigade, a single company, slung arms and filed aboard ship at Santo Domingo City. The occupation of the Dominican Republic was over.

" ...IF ATTACKED, SHOOT AND SHOOT TO KILL"

One of the most stirring orders ever received by U. S. Marines was issued on 11 November 1921 by Secretary of the Navy Edwin Denby, himself a devoted Marine of World War I and the only former Marine ever to become

Secretary of the Navy. The nation was in the grip of a crime wave high-lighted by armed robberies of the U. S. Mail. Four days before "Ned" Denby penned his letter of instruction, President Harding had directed that the Marine Corps "protect the mails from depredations by robbers and bandits." Fifty-three officers and 2,200 enlisted men were already on watch in post offices, railway mail cars, and postal trucks throughout the country. Edwin Denby, who needed no ghost writer, sent this letter:[15]

To the Men of the Mail Guard:

I am proud that my old Corps has been chosen for a duty so honorable as that of protecting the United States mail. I am very anxious that you shall successfully accomplish your mission. It is not going to be easy work. It will be dangerous and generally tiresome. You know how to do it. Be sure you do it well. I know you will neither fear nor shirk any duty, however hazardous or exacting.

This particular work will lack the excitement and glamor of war duty, but it will be no less important. It has the same element of service to the country.

I look with proud confidence to you to show now the qualities that have made the Corps so well beloved by our fellow citizens.

You must be brave, as you always are. You must be constantly alert. You must, when on guard duty, keep your weapons in hand and, if attacked, shoot and shoot to kill. There is no compromise in this battle with the bandits.

If two Marines, guarding a mail car, are suddenly covered by a mail robber, neither must hold up his hands, but both must begin shooting at once. One may be killed, but the other will get the robber and save the mail. When our men go in as guards over mail, that mail must be delivered or there must be a Marine dead at the post of duty.

To be sure of success, every Marine on this duty must be watchful as a cat, hour after hour, night after night, week after week. No Marine must drink a drop of intoxicating liquor. Every Marine must be most careful with whom he associates and what his occupations are off duty. There may be many tricks tried to get you, and you must not be tricked. Look out for women. Never discuss the details of your duty with outsiders. Never give up to another the trust you are charged with.

Never forget that the honor of the Corps is in your keeping. You have been given a great trust. I am confident you will prove that it has not been misplaced.

I am proud of you and believe in you with all my heart.

Mail robberies came to an abrupt halt within days after the deployment of Marine guards was complete; in fact, not a single robber dared to try his luck against the Marines, and not a single piece of mail was lost to a robber during the succeeding four months while Marines stood watch.

In October 1926, there was a recurrence of armed robbery of the U. S. Mail, and the Postmaster General asked for 2,500 officers and men of the Corps. They were promptly provided. Mail robberies again ceased with equal promptness.

LEJEUNE'S "NEW MARINE CORPS"

From what has just been recounted of the expeditions and campaigns which immediately followed World War I, it could be supposed that Marine Corps life and routine had resumed in 1919 on exactly the same basis as that which was interrupted by the war. In fact, nothing could be further from the truth.

Lejeune understood this fact well, even though many other Marines did not. General Lejeune was not only a field soldier of high ability, and a beloved leader, but also a Marine of prescient, active intelligence. To the new Major General Commandant it seemed clear that, despite the fighting triumphs of World War I, the Marine Corps, popular and admired though it was, needed a mission all its own. This realization was reinforced by Lejeune's conclusion that the Marines' immediate role as lightly armed forces of pacification and occupation—"colonial infantry" in the military terminology of Europe—could not go on forever, that time was running out.

In the advance base and expeditionary studies which had preceded the war, Lejeune and his brilliant juniors found an answer. The real, the perennial mission of the Marine Corps, they reasoned, was *readiness*. Readiness was the single common denominator which ran through every Marine Corps expedition of the 20th century and most Marine operations in the 19th. Readiness was certainly a unique mission since the United States did not have a ready standing army in 1920, and for that matter rarely had, the accepted missions of the Army being those of routine garrison and of maintaining a cadre for wartime mobilization.

In 1920, for a maritime nation sooner or later facing a contest for mastery of the world's greatest ocean, readiness meant one thing in particular: the ability to project expeditions overseas to seize and secure advance bases. In other words, readiness in 1920 particularly meant amphibious readiness (which in turn meant amphibious capability). This was something toward which Marines had been groping when World War I interrupted them.

Starting in 1920, several developments progressed hand-in-hand with the Navy's recognition of Japan as the next enemy. These were: reorganization of the Advance Base Force for new purposes; creation of Marine Corps Schools at Quantico; and initial amphibious planning by Marine Corps Headquarters. These led eventually into a series of landing exercises in the

1920s and to the development of special, if primitive, landing force equipment.

One of General Lejeune's first steps after getting his new job under control was to remove the Advance Base Force, or what was left of it, from Philadelphia to Quantico. Truly this was the end of an era, though few realized it; the days when League Island Navy Yard had been the mother of expeditions were over.

Lejeune's immediate thoughts on the new Advance Base Force (it would be 1922 before it was redesignated "East Coast Expeditionary Force") stemmed from the somewhat rosier personnel picture of 1920 than that of future years. There would be two brigades—an infantry brigade (5th and 6th Marines) and a mixed brigade of the 1st Marines (signal battalion, engineer battalion, searchlight battalion, antiaircraft battalion) and 10th Marines (artillery). In addition, the "Marine Flying Field" at Miami having been decommissioned, two "expeditionary squadrons" of aviation (Squadron F: 12 Jennies, three kite balloons; Squadron D: six Jennies, two balloons) were organized. Meanwhile, work was pressed on Marine flying fields at Quantico and Parris Island—the latter, the Commandant proudly told the Secretary of the Navy, "capable of landing the largest and fastest planes."[16] Unhappily, the Commandant's hopes were shortly to be dashed; Admiral R. E. Coontz, the Chief of Naval Operations, intervened to inactivate the Parris Island field in 1921. But Quantico flourished.

In 1920, Quantico had two schools: Officers' Training School, a formalization of the "officers' training camp," a war baby, which had displaced the School of Application; and Officers' Infantry School, one of General Barnett's last creations. The purpose of the latter institution was to impart badly needed professional refreshment to some of the more mature officers, who had been precipitated, by progress in the art of war, into technical and tactical responsibilities at which the field officers of the 1890s would have blanched. General Lejeune, who had commanded Quantico just before his elevation to the commandancy, consolidated both courses into a single institution, the Marine Corps Schools. During 1921, the Schools provided three courses at Quantico: Field Officers' Course, Company Officers' Course, and Basic Course. In late 1924, the Basic School was moved to the Philadelphia Navy Yard, occupying the barracks built before the war for the old Advance Base Force.[17] The mold was now set for the Marine Corps schooling system for years to come.

But General Lejeune did not stop with establishment of Marine Corps

Schools. Being himself a top graduate of the Army War College, he not only hustled picked officers into that institution, into the Command and General Staff School at Fort Leavenworth, and into the Naval War College (where a few Marines had already gone before the war), but, beginning in 1921, into all the Army's excellent branch schools at Benning, Sill, Monroe, Riley, Edgewood Arsenal, and elsewhere. This would guarantee that no foe of the Corps could ever accuse it of ignorance or incapacity in the latest techniques and doctrines of the combined arms. The point was important. Within two years, across the Atlantic, the Royal Marines, ancient comrades and for many years virtually a parallel organization to the U. S. Marine Corps, were to be forcibly stripped of their own combined arms in a "budgetary" cutback which abolished the Royal Marine Artillery—an intentionally crippling attack based on the sophism that a Marine Corps equipped and organized for effective action "duplicates" an army.

To meet the greater staff responsibilities posed by a Corps with an authorized strength of 27,400 (which, in 1920, before the budget ax fell, seemed momentarily attainable) and to direct the wide range of postwar progress, Marine Corps Headquarters clearly needed a shot in the arm. Headquarters still faithfully followed the organization set up by the 1817 Peace Establishment Act (and would continue to do so for some years more); something more like a modern military staff was called for in order to co-ordinate training, prepare war plans, and supervise operations. Until 1920, this need had been met by use of the Major General Commandant's three aides as an executive staff, and by General Lauchheimer, Adjutant and Inspector since 1912, who had, as a partial result of his influence over Barnett, compassed many training responsibilities within his firm grasp. In July 1919, Lauchheimer was felled by apoplexy; early in 1920 he died.

Meanwhile, General Lejeune had moved to set up a "Planning Section" at Headquarters, directly under the Assistant to the Commandant, now his trusted friend and ally, Neville. Shortly after, on 20 November 1920, the new section was redesignated as the Division of Operations and Training and given a general of its own: Logan M. Feland, a Kentuckian who had entered the Corps in the post-Spanish war expansion of 1899. Feland, keen and intelligent, organized the division into three sections: military education, intelligence, and organization. Some months before, though not part of Operations and Training, the Historical Section was also established.

Among the officers assigned to the new division was Lieutenant Colonel Earl H. Ellis, who had been a marked man in the Corps for nearly a decade.

"Pete" Ellis's brilliant imagination had made him a leader among the advance base thinkers of the prewar period. In 1912 he made a reconnaissance of Culebra to establish the concept for the winter maneuvers of 1914. A year later he prepared a series of highly classified lectures on the subject of naval bases, in which he analyzed the problems which the United States would encounter in a war with Japan. This war, he forecast, would depend largely on a struggle for outlying bases, most of which the United States did not have. In 1920, after having served both as General Barnett's aide (while Lejeune was assistant commandant) and as adjutant of the 4th Marine Brigade throughout its hardest fighting, Ellis again had an opportunity to think about the Pacific.

While everyone's attention had been focused on Europe and the Atlantic, Japan, on pretext of her long-standing alliance with Britain, had waged a private war of conquest in the Pacific. At the peace table in Versailles, Japan claimed and received (because she already had them) the greater part of Germany's erstwhile colonies in the Far East and Pacific. By one stroke of the pen, Japan had pushed her forward outposts halfway across the Pacific to Hawaii. Among Japan's gains were the Marianas (except United States-held Guam), the Marshalls, the Carolines, and the Palaus. Suddenly, the Philippines, our own advance base complex in the Far East, were walled off by a belt of positions which commanded the Central Pacific.

As already related, the Navy had quickly grasped the strategic significance of Japan's acquisitions. In 1920, the Office of Naval Intelligence prepared a general forecast, in conceptual terms, of a transpacific war against Japan, and various agencies within the Navy Department were directed to work up a portfolio of war plans to implement this concept. The Marine Corps' share in the working up of the "Orange Plan," as it ultimately came to be known, was a study of required advance base operations—a study which seems largely to have owed its existence to "Pete" Ellis. Having persuaded the planners that such a study must be made, Ellis proceeded to make it. Operations Plan 712, "Advanced Base Operations in Micronesia," approved by the Commandant on 23 July 1921, was the result.

As a starting premise for his 50,000-word plan, Ellis predicted that Japan would attack first; then, in his words:[18]

... it will be necessary for us to project our fleet and landing forces across the Pacific and wage war in Japanese waters. To effect this requires that we have sufficient bases to support the fleet, both during its projection and afterwards.

Ellis's "War Portfolio" outlined much of the Pacific war to come and forecast with remarkable prevision the role which the Marine Corps would play. The United States would have to seize bases all the way across the Pacific, and mainly in the Marshalls, the Carolines, and the Palaus. This would require new weapons and new techniques—reef-crossing vehicles, torpedo planes (brain child of the Marines' ancient foes, Admirals Fullam and Bradley Fiske), especially designed landing craft, and fleets of assault shipping. To seize Eniwetok (one of Ellis's objectives) would, he estimated, call for a strongly reinforced brigade of two infantry regiments; this was exactly the organization which did the job in 1944. The war which Ellis forecast was a war of advanced bases and ready forces—in a word, a war for Marines:[19]

To effect [an amphibious landing] in the face of enemy resistance requires careful training and preparation to say the least; and this along Marine lines. It is not enough that the troops be skilled infantrymen or artillerymen of high morale; they must be skilled watermen and jungle-men who know it can be done—Marines with Marine training.

Operations Plan 712 was not only Earl Ellis's monument; it was his epitaph. In 1923, having been granted a year's leave for unspecified foreign travel, he died mysteriously at the hands of the Japanese while paying a "tourist" visit to Japan's newly acquired Palau Islands.

There were other voices, however; Colonel Dunlap (who was soon to give his life in a heroic attempt to rescue a French civilian during a landslide) prepared an analysis of the British fiasco at Gallipoli. Using the Dardanelles as chapter and verse, Dunlap delineated the problems which would have to be tackled before landing operations could succeed. General Lejeune hammered at the point. "The primary and most important mission of modern Marines is to act as an accompanying landing force for the Fleet in naval warfare," he wrote.[20] Again, addressing the Naval War College in 1923 he preached:[21]

. . . on both flanks of a fleet crossing the Pacific are numerous islands suitable for utilization by an enemy for radio stations, aviation, submarine, or destroyer bases. All should be mopped up as progress is made. . . . The presence of an expeditionary force with the fleet would add greatly to the striking power of the Commander-in-Chief of the fleet. . . . The maintenance, equipping, and training of its expeditionary force so that it will be in instant readiness to support the Fleet in the event of war, I deem to be the most important Marine Corps duty in time of peace.

FIRST AMPHIBIOUS EFFORTS, 1922–29

The newspapers of the early 1920s gave some publicity to the series of land maneuvers conducted by a force known to the public as "the Quantico

Marines." In October 1921, these Marines (their official designation was, of course, the Advance Base Force) held field exercises at the Wilderness battlefield in Virginia. With Smedley Butler on one side and General Lejeune on the other, President Harding, accompanied by Secretary Denby, spent two days inspecting the Marines and watching their doings. Similarly, next year, the whole force hiked from Quantico, via Washington and the White House grounds, to Gettysburg, just in time to re-enact Pickett's charge on its 59th anniversary. This military epic was witnessed, as the Commandant reported, by "the Chief Executive of the Nation, the governors of three States, and a host of distinguished guests." The Marines' camp on the Gettysburg field included "a splendid field house containing five rooms and a bath, christened 'The Canvas White House,' for the President and Mrs. Harding."[22] In 1923, the Expeditionary Force hike led into the Shenandoah Valley, where the cadets of the Virginia Military Institute obligingly provided a grey-clad force for the re-enactment of the Battle of New Market. Finally, in 1924, the featured event was the Battle of Antietam, at Sharpsburg, Maryland, where thousands of spectators applauded amid the smoke and volleys of blank ammunition.

All this, of course, was magnificent, but it was hardly war. General Lejeune undoubtedly realized this. General Butler probably did. In any case, it served a useful purpose in exercising the troops and in reminding the public that it had a Marine Expeditionary Force.

Quite overshadowed by the maneuvers just mentioned, other less publicized but far more important exercises were being conducted by the Marine Expeditionary Force.

During the first four months of 1922 a reinforced "expeditionary battalion" from Quantico—really a primitive battalion landing team—conducted landing exercises at Guantanamo Bay and Culebra. In March 1923, there was a small amphibious exercise at Panama by a detachment of Marines; and, the following summer, another battalion exercise took place on the beaches of Cape Cod. Repeating Earl Ellis's reconnaissance of a decade earlier, Major Holland M. Smith, the first Marine to be assigned to the Joint Planning Committee of the Joint Board of the Army and Navy, was sent in 1923 to the West Indies to find suitable training areas for amphibious exercises. Major Smith quickly recognized that Culebra and the eastern end of Vieques (another island off Puerto Rico's eastern tip) were ideal, and concluded rental agreements which were destined to remain in force for years to come. As in the case of Ellis's trip, Major Smith's was also a necessary preliminary to large-scale maneuvers planned for the succeeding year.

The maneuvers of January and February 1924 were conceived on a broad scale, involving not only the Marine Expeditionary Force, but the Atlantic Fleet and Army forces in the Canal Zone as well. While the 10th Marines and other supporting units of the Marine brigade landed at Culebra and proceeded to organize it as a defended base (in the tradition of the 1902 and 1914 exercises), the 5th Regiment conducted an assault landing at Panama as part of the Fleet's "attack" on the Canal. Immediately afterward, the assault regiment re-embarked and, on 1 February, landed again, this time at Culebra.

Neither landing was any model of amphibious technique, but if it is true that the real purpose of maneuvers is to allow mistakes to be made and recognized, then the 1924 Fleet Problems III and IV were well worth while because almost every possible mistake occurred. At least that was the view of Brigadier General Eli K. Cole, who now commanded the Expeditionary Force; almost everyone else thought so, too, including the naval attack force commander. One noteworthy experiment, however, was the test of two special landing craft—the first such ever to be used by United States forces in modern times, and thus the precursors of craft undreamed of in 1924. Troop Barge "A," the brain child of General Cole, was a twin-engined 50-footer with armor protection for troops and crew. Ponderous as the thing was (it gave boat officers and coxswains—not to speak of embarked Marines—many an extra grey hair by nearly sinking alongside the transport), Troop Barge "A" embodied features which in more practical form would become standard 20 years later. Another equally radical contraption was a boxlike amphibious tank mounting a 75-mm. gun designed by Mr. Walter Christie (whose tank suspension, employed in this as in other designs, was soon to be purchased by the Soviet Union after the U. S. government failed to accept it). The Christie amphibian had been under test in the Potomac at Quantico since mid-1923, but proved unequal to seagoing conditions at Culebra. It would be 15 years before the need already recognized in 1923 would be met, again at Quantico, by the first amphibian tractor.

In 1925, a joint Army-Navy war game was held on Oahu in the Hawaiian Islands. This was a highly theoretical exercise with little practical value to anybody, except the 1,500 Marine officers and men who successfully simulated a 42,000-man Marine landing force. The amphibious planning was effected by a device which would be employed again. In the fall of 1924 the normal curriculum of Marine Corps Schools had been suspended, and instructors and students had become the landing force staff for the maneuvers, which had been executed on 15 April. This was Quantico's first amphibious command-post exercise, and probably the first such in United States history.

During the next seven years, expeditionary service would absorb the energy and manpower of the Corps, and there would be no more maneuvers until 1932. Nevertheless, 1927 represented another landmark. In that year, the Joint Army and Navy Board produced *Joint Action, Army and Navy,* a highly significant publication, many of whose tenets still govern modern joint operations. In the 1927 edition, there appeared for the first time official affirmation of the special amphibious responsibilities of the Marine Corps. For the conduct of naval campaigns, the Marine Corps would:

. . . provide and maintain forces for land operations in support of the Fleet for the initial seizure and defense of advanced bases and for such limited auxiliary land operations as are essential to the prosecution of the naval campaign.

Here was language which crudely foreshadowed that of the National Security Act 20 years later. Moreover, ruled the Joint Board, even in major invasions where the Army might provide the bulk of the landing force, Marines would:[23]

. . . perform the same functions as the Army, and because of their constant association with naval units will be given special training in the conduct of landing operations.

Still another step forward, in 1929, shortly before stepping down from the commandancy, General Lejeune convened a Marine Corps Boat Board whose job was to study the problems of landing craft design. A product of the Boat Board was the 45-foot artillery lighter, a square-built ark without power, which, with stern ramps, was to be eased backward onto the beach and, when unloaded, towed clear. In addition, based on Board designs, the Navy built two motor troop lighters—referred to as "beetle boats"—an armored 50-footer and a 40-footer without armor. These were tested at Quantico and Norfolk and retained at Quantico for some years.

TROUBLE IN NICARAGUA

While much larger Marine forces had been enforcing law, order, and progress in Cuba, Haiti, and Santo Domingo, the Legation Guard at Managua, Nicaragua, only four officers and 101 enlisted men, had since

1913 fulfilled a remarkably tranquilizing role in a remarkably unstable country. In August 1925, despite real misgiving by Managua's foreign colony and even by some Nicaraguan leaders, the State Department withdrew this token symbol and left Nicaragua to her own devices. Within less than three months, on 24 October, General Emiliano Chamorro, head of the Conservatives, seized La Loma, the fortified hill which commands Managua, and, by the beginning of the new year, had purged the government of his Liberal opponents.

In early May 1926, with arms provided from Mexico, the Liberals struck back. Revolt flared along the entire east coast of Nicaragua.

To protect the lives of Americans and extensive American and foreign property in and about Bluefields, principal east coast town, the old 3,200-ton cruiser *Cleveland* was ordered to neutralize the place to forces of both factions. On 7 May 1926, under the *Cleveland's* 5-inch guns, motor sailers made for shore with colors flying and boat-guns mounted, and khaki-clad Marines in field hats and leggings took over Bluefields. A month later, when the coast quieted momentarily, they withdrew. But by August the USS *Galveston's* Marines had the job to do over again, and Bluefields was once more at peace. Subsequently, the squadron flagship, USS *Rochester* (which, as the *New York*, had transported Waller's battalion in the Philippine Insurrection), took over the vigil at Bluefields, landing her Marines under a tall captain, John Thomason, who later reminisced:[24]

... a splendid weapon, this guard: 103 Marines, 80 rifles, 2 machine guns, and the 37-mm. gun for landing force; it was an organization proved and competent and regarded with schooled respect by more than one frustrated Latin-American *junta*.

With American diplomats prodding them, the warring leaders agreed to a conference on 10 October at Corinto on the west coast. The USS *Denver*, another relic cruiser, came along with her Marines, at the request of all parties, just to ensure fair play. Nevertheless, civil war resumed as usual, and, at year's end, with the Liberal cause prospering on Mexican arms and popular sympathy, the United States found the situation deadlocked, despite its desire to keep the *de jure* Conservative government in power. Moreover, as a practical matter, not all the Marines in the Special Service Squadron, a collection of aged cruisers and gunboats beating up and down the Central American coasts, were enough to maintain neutralized zones along the east coast, where trouble was worse and where more foreign interest was concentrated. To meet the crisis, the Navy asked for and got the 2d Bat-

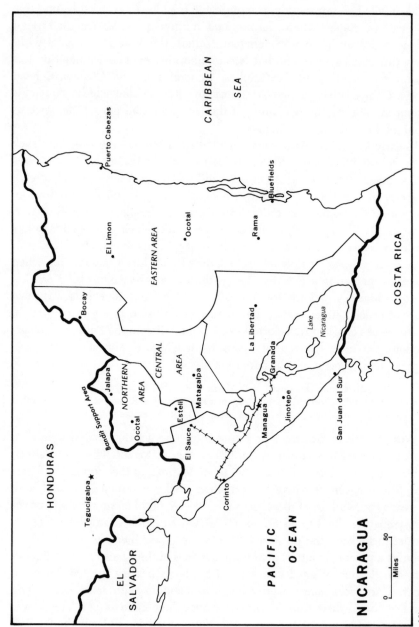

Nicaragua

talion, 5th Marines, which providentially was at Guantanamo Bay. On 10 January 1927, Lieutenant Colonel James J. Meade and the battalion arrived at Bluefields, in the USS *Argonne,* and in a week had prevented a battle brewing upriver at Rama, where a Conservative army built around one old French 180-mm. cannon and seven Lewis guns was squaring off with the Liberals. So pacifying was the effect of the battalion that Meade withdrew on 18 January, leaving one company at Bluefields, and hastened with the remainder of the unit to the west coast of Nicaragua via the Panama Canal.

While the 2d Battalion, 5th Marines, had been en route to Nicaragua from Guantanamo, the focus of revolution had shifted west; the U. S. policy of neutralizing any place on the east coast that was worth fighting for had, in its way, accomplished results. Managua shivered, and the *Galveston,* crowding on every one of her rated 16.4 knots, made for Corinto to send her landing force up to the capital and re-establish the Legation Guard. The landing force arrived at Managua on 6 January. Three weeks later, the 2d Battalion, 5th Marines, after completing their Bluefields operation, had followed to Managua via the railroad from Corinto which Pendleton and Butler had conquered in 1912.

No sooner was Meade's battalion at Managua than the Liberals cut the railroad at Chinandega, outside Corinto, and swarmed through Matagalpa Province, stopping long enough to put a ragged fusillade through the official car of the First Secretary of the U. S. Legation, who was attempting to determine firsthand the extent of the revoluion.

This last, in particular, was not to be brooked. Rear Admiral Julian L. Latimer, Commander Special Service Squadron, on 9 February ordered the entire railroad neutralized, and called for more Marines. On 26 February the first reinforcements arrived from San Diego—Observation Squadron 1, reinforced by a rifle company. This detachment, under Major Ross E. ("Rusty") Rowell, later to become the first Marine aviator to wear stars, debarked at Corinto and hauled their six DHs up to Managua on flatcars. Nine days later, direct from Quantico's Post Dock, aboard the transport USS *Henderson,* came the remainder of the 5th Regiment, with 2d Brigade Headquarters commanded by Brigadier General Logan Feland. Counting all ships' landing forces ashore, plus a battalion from the Scouting Force (detachments from the *Texas, Florida,* and *Arkansas),* there were now some two thousand Marines in Nicaragua distributed in 14 different towns. The Nicaraguan affair had become an expedition.

STIMSON MEDIATES

The United States had two strong reasons for desiring peace and stability in Nicaragua. One was its proximity to the Canal Zone, jugular vein of American strategic interest in the Caribbean. The second was our commitment, self-assumed during Teddy Roosevelt's "Big Stick" days, that the United States, while enforcing a hands-off rule against European nations with Latin-American interests, would in turn assure the protection of those interests, together with our own. This was why the Nicaraguan civil war gave such concern to the State Department and why the Marine brigade had landed.

At almost the same time as the *Henderson* was standing down the Potomac, President Calvin Coolidge was conferring with a trusted advisor, the once and future Secretary of War, Henry L. Stimson, often addressed as "Colonel" by virtue of World War I service. The Nicaraguan mess must somehow be cleared up; would Colonel Stimson go down there as the President's special representative and work out some solution to end the civil war and set the country on its feet? Stimson's answer, of course, was yes.

In mid-April 1927, Colonel Stimson reached Nicaragua. The situation, as he found it, has been well described by his biographer:[25]

Three things speedily became clear. First, the civil war was hopelessly stalemated; both sides were incapable of effective offensive action; the Conservative superiority in numbers was matched by the superior military skill of the Liberal general. If the war continued, neither side could win and all Nicaragua must be the loser. Second, the bulk of the people, including even the active Liberals and Conservatives, were heartily sick of war. . . . Third, most Nicaraguans, on both sides, would be happy to see the war ended by a promise of mediation and good offices from the United States, and, by "good offices," they meant American supervision of a new national election.

The high point of the Stimson mission came on 4 May at Tipitapa, a few miles outside of Managua. Here, under protection of Marines, the leaders of both factions—Adolfo Diaz, the Conservative, and José María Moncada, the Liberal—met with Colonel Stimson. Moncada's presence was in itself a demonstration of confidence in the Americans. He had been sought out by a patrol headed by Major Marion B. Humphrey, and, trusting his life to the Marines, had consented to leave his own lines and enter those of his enemies in order to meet with Stimson.

From a political viewpoint, the meeting was a brilliant success. Diaz and Moncada quickly came to terms which did each credit. Diaz and the Conservatives were to remain in office until 1928. Meanwhile, the Marine brigade was to disarm both armies and assume responsibility for public order, while commencing the organization and training of a native constabulary, the Guardia Nacional. In 1928, there were to be American-supervised, free elections with secret balloting. Thereafter, the United States would support the elected government and maintain order until the Guardia could take over.

From the standpoint of the 2d Marine Brigade, the Peace of Tipitapa was a very large bite indeed. The United States—or more precisely, the Marines —now stood committed to unspecified, but obviously not small, pacification operations in an enormous unmapped jungle twice the size of Haiti, demoralized by civil war and swarming with armed deserters and professional bandits.

But this was still in the future. For the present, with honest co-operation from both sides, the 5th Regiment collected the weapons of the two armies—14,704 assorted rifles, 309 machine guns, and almost six million rounds of ammunition. The reports fail to mention what happened to the 180-mm. cannon at Rama. Within ten days after the peace, while the 5th Marines manned a neutral cordon, both the Liberal and Conservative armies disbanded, and Colonel Stimson went home well pleased. On 19 May, however, heading in the opposite direction, came the 11th Marines (Colonel R. C. Berkeley) and Observation Squadron 4, the former shaken together from remnants at Quantico and Charleston, and from the 1st Brigade in Haiti. These units brought the 2d Brigade up to 181 officers and 2,800 enlisted men, so that it could cope effectively with any possible disorder. More than 45 local garrisons were promptly established, and, seemingly, a bad situation had been relieved. At any rate, that was what Colonel Stimson thought, and, with more immediate effect on the course of operations, so did General Feland. Considerable reduction in the 2d Brigade strength might be undertaken, he opined, within a few weeks once things settled down.

. . . BEFORE THE STORM

Whatever the situation in Nicaragua really was, as distinct from what it seemed to be, the Marine Corps was, at the moment, in dire need of every Marine who could shoulder a rifle. This was because of the China expedition which had most inconveniently been called away in May 1927 to cope with an explosive situation in the Far East. There is no question but that the conflicting, heavy demand for troops in China exerted pressure to reduce the 2d Brigade to the minimum as soon as possible.

This was undertaken immediately. In June 1927, before the 11th Marines had stacked arms, a thousand officers and men were withdrawn from Nicaragua. On 6 September, the 11th Regiment left the country for disbandment, and Observation Squadron 1 merged with Observation Squadron 4 to form Observation 7 (VO-7M). This left the 2d Brigade a very thin brigade indeed—just the 5th Marines and VO-7M. Meanwhile, on 24 August 1927, Colonel Louis M. Gulick succeeded Feland as the cutback proceeded.

Steps were therefore quickly taken to start organizing and training the new Guardia, which, it was hoped, could soon take over policing of the areas in the north with the greatest trouble-potential. Here, too, was a somewhat rosy expectation which events contrived to blight. The Guardia was to have a strength of a thousand men and some 60 officers, of whom about 35 were to be Marines. Following two temporary commandants, the first permanent *Jefe Director*—Brigadier General (Lieutenant Colonel, USMC) Elias R. Beadle—was appointed on 12 July 1927. Once again, miscalculation secured a foothold: the Jefe Director was destined to get, and to remain, consistently out of step with the policies and objectives of the 2d Brigade during the trying months to come.

That these months might be trying was soon foreshadowed. At one o'clock in the morning on 16 May 1927, just 12 days after the Peace of Tipitapa, a covey of some 200 bandit marauders swept through the town of La Paz Centro, shooting and looting, as was the custom of the country. Outside town were camped the Marine detachments of the *Arkansas* and *Florida*, protecting the railroad. When the alarm was raised, Captain Richard B. Buchanan, the detachment commander, had "Call to Arms" sounded and moved out with a platoon. As General Lejeune later related:[26]

Buchanan did a very gallant thing. He went right into that town in the dead of night, and the town was full of those people [bandits]. They were looting the stores and houses; and he was killed by a shot from a window.

Buchanan's second-in-command, Second Lieutenant Clarence J. Chappell, promptly took command and pressed the attack while the mud town zinged with bullets. After a two-hour fight in which another Marine was killed and two more wounded, the bandits cleared out, leaving 14 dead. Captain

Buchanan was the first Marine officer to be killed in the Nicaraguan campaign.

Ten days later at Chinandega, which was still in ashes from an earlier Liberal attack, word came that one "General" Cabulla, a bandit of Liberal affiliation, was terrorizing the vicinity. Again the townspeople sent to the nearby Marine camp for help. Hearing that Cabulla was to be found at El Viejo, not far away, the detachment commander, Captain William P. Richards, took two men with him and set out. As Richards entered the house of a lady who was reportedly entertaining Cabulla, the bandit leader reached under the bed for a pistol, while the aroused hostess swung a machete. Unfortunately for Cabulla, he drew on the wrong man; Richards, a National Match pistol shot, had him faded, and, seconds later, Cabulla's career was ended.[27]

ENTER AUGUSTO SANDINO

While the contending factions turned in their arms during May 1927, one minor leader among the Liberals thought differently and, with 150 armed followers, vanished into the jungle. This man, Augusto "Cesar" (originally "Calderon") Sandino by name, had led a checkered life. As a young blade in 1916 he shot a fellow townsman of San Rafael in northern Nicaragua and sought exile in Mexico, then seething with revolution. Here, working in the Tampico oil fields, he made revolutionary contacts which were later to prove extremely useful. In 1926, things cooled off sufficiently in Nicaragua for him to return, via Guatemala, and go to work briefly as a clerk in an American-owned gold mine at San Albino. The owner later remarked, "He was a fair clerk and was a very forcible and cruel person."[28] To this General Lejeune added, "He is very vain; he has ability; he is ambitious. He would rather be the leader of a band up there in the mountains than be working in the mines as a clerk."[29]

"Up there in the mountains" lies Ocotal, capital of Nueva Segovia Province, Sandino's home country. On 1 July 1927, Ocotal was garrisoned by a 37-man Marine detachment under Captain Gilbert D. Hatfield and 47 guardias under Lieutenant Grover C. Darnall. The Marines occupied a stoutly built adobe barracks, on the town plaza, with a walled compound; the guardias had barracks of their own across the plaza. Receiving a report that Sandino, the missing Liberal leader, was armed and nearby, Captain Hatfield sent word out that it was high time to come in and surrender.

During the night of 16 July, Sandino came in, but not to surrender. Beginning at nightfall of the 15th, small bands of Sandino's forces—800 men in all with eight assorted machine guns, he later claimed—drifted into Ocotal.

Certain bandits, by Sandino's order, carried extra rifles and ammunition to arm sympathizers in the town. More than a hundred habitants of Liberal persuasion responded. The telegraph wires were cut. A detail carrying mining dynamite approached the crude airstrip outside Ocotal, with orders to blow up any Marine planes that might be there (none were). Machine guns and automatic rifles were stealthily sited to cover the plaza and Marine barracks. Altogether, it was a workmanlike plan which Sandino had set down with Latin flourish in a written operation order. His object, he proclaimed, was to "drink *Yanqui* blood."[30]

At 0115 the Marine sentry in front of the barracks saw a suspicious movement and challenged. His answer was a burst of rifle fire; seconds later a machine gun cut loose. Within three minutes both the Marine barracks and Guardia headquarters were under fire from all directions. Under this fusillade, the field music sounded "Call to Arms," which some might have thought a needless formality, and the defenders, who had been sleeping on their arms, sprang to general quarters.

For almost two hours a fire-fight raged. Then the shooting slackened, and Sandino's bugles sounded recall. An hour later, a second attack commenced. This, too, was beaten off, but steady firing continued until 0810. Once again the Nicaraguans checked fire. This time a flag of truce came forward to the Marine barracks. With supreme impudence, Sandino complimented Captain Hatfield on his "brave fight," said he knew the Marines were short of water (they were not, in fact), and demanded their surrender within the hour. Hatfield reported:[31]

My reply was that Marines did not know how to surrender and that water or no water we would stick it out until killed or captured, and that firing would be resumed as soon as the [truce] flag bearer had turned the nearest corner.

At that moment, when Hatfield was telling Sandino's envoy where to go, a section of DH-4s, piloted by Lieutenant Hayne D. ("Cuckoo") Boyden and Marine Gunner Michael Wodarczyk, was warming up at Managua for the routine morning patrol over the northern area. At 1010, as the two planes chugged over Ocotal, it was apparent that something was wrong. While "Mike" Wodarczyk launched a strafing run on some obviously hostile natives below, Lieutenant Boyden proceeded to land his airplane on the deserted airstrip, collared a frightened townsman, and learned what was afoot. Wodarczyk, meanwhile, had confirmed his fears by sighting a panel displayed inside the Marine compound, "Being attacked by Sandino." Boyden took off in a flurry of rifle fire and rejoined Wodarczyk. Both pilots expended all their ammunition in strafing attacks and high-tailed it to get support from Managua.

At 1230, Major Rowell, squadron commander of Observation 1, stormed out of Managua with every operational airplane on the field—five DH-4s—each armed with four 25-pound bombs and every round of machine gun ammunition that could be belted. Despite foul weather, they made it to Ocotal by 1435. In Rowell's words:[32]

I led off the attack and dived out of column from 1,500 feet, pulling out at about 600. Later, we ended up by diving in from 1,000 and pulling out at about 300. Since the enemy had not been subjected to any form of bombing attack, other than the dynamite charges thrown from the Laird-Swallows by the [two-plane] Nicaraguan Air Force, they had no fear of us . . . we were able to inflict damage which was out of all proportion to what they might have suffered had they taken cover.

This was the first combat dive-bombing attack in the history of war. It was a sensational success. Another aviation officer reported:[33]

After the second pass of the planes, the enemy began pouring out of the town and ran wildly to cover, horses were dispersed, and in general there was a wild scramble. This afforded an excellent target for the planes with their machine guns, and bombs were reserved for large groups.

After 45 minutes of this, the DH-4s began to run low on gas and ordnance and headed for base. The battle of Ocotal was over, and the Marines and guardias warily mopped up the battered town while daylight lasted. Approximately 300 bandits and sympathizing townspeople had been killed, about two-thirds by Rowell's dive-bombing—"practically every Liberal family in town being in mourning," commented Captain Hatfield.[34] One Marine was killed, and four Marines and guardias wounded.

This crushing, dramatic—and, to be truthful, unexpected—victory over Sandino on his first major operation had the unfortunate effect of persuading even the most knowing that the bandit leader would never be heard from again. That this was not so, soon became apparent.

The village of Telpaneca is about ten miles southeast of Ocotal. It was garrisoned in September 1927 by a detachment of 21 Marines and 25 guardias, under Guardia Captain (First Lieutenant, USMC) Herbert S. Keimling.

On the foggy night of 18-19 September—just two months and three days after the attack on Ocotal, and at the same hour, one o'clock in the morning—Sandino struck at Telpaneca. As described by a private in the garrison, the affair opened with a bang:[35]

> The first thing that woke us up was a hand-made bomb which exploded in the rear of our quarters. The first rifle shot was fired in the storeroom, where the cooks and messmen were asleep. The first shot had hit Pvt Russell who was sleeping near the front door. This same shot went through his bed and through mine, missing me by a few inches. Pvt Russell, after he was wounded, jumped up and grabbed his rifle and fired three shots and was shot again, right near the heart. He laid down his rifle and went to his bed to lay down and die, which he did in about three or four minutes. . . .

With an intense burst of fire from three submachine guns, the bandits—led by "General" Salgado, a survivor of Ocotal—whooped down, throwing hand grenades and homemade dynamite bombs. Two fierce rushes of riflemen and machete-men swirled up to the front door of the Marine barracks, which here, as at Ocotal, was the main objective. "Vivo Sandino . . . Muera los Estados Unidos . . . Este por Marinos . . ." yelled the 200 outlaws, while the Marines' lone Lewis gun cut them down in the plaza. More dynamite bombs were pitched, this time into the rear of the Guardia barracks; here, *Raso* (Guardia private) Pedro Saballas fielded one and heaved it back with the fuze still burning. Meanwhile, between rushes—showing the Marine Corps touch—the Guardia cook laid aside his rifle and served hot coffee from the bullet-riddled galley stove.

At 0230 the fog began to break, but the outlaws continued their attack, shifting their submachine guns from sector to sector, finally concentrating in the rear of the barracks where a Browning automatic rifle held them at bay. "All night long," related one Marine, "you could hear Lieutenant Keimling give out orders, exposing himself to the enemy, finding out where the snipers were . . . on the job just as any Marine officer would do, if not better."[36]

After 0300, while the fog continued to lift, the defenders saw the bandits beginning to drag off their dead and wounded, estimated at 50, and—this was significant, but then not appreciated—retiring to the eastward. By daybreak, at 0500, with two Marines killed and one guardia badly wounded, all was quiet. The enlisted narrator summed things up:

> This fight was sure a hard one on us men, but we stood it through, and sure would have loved to see them stay for awhile after it got light so we could have showed Sandino our marksmanship.

"WILD BEASTS OF THE MOUNTAINS"

The Ocotal and Telpaneca attacks, which should have convinced anyone that Sandino was operating a going concern with really dangerous possibilities, had a somewhat ineffectual sequel. This was a temporary step-up in local patrolling in Nueva Segovia, but seemingly no apprehension was felt by the brigade commander that he had far too little to control the situation. Moreover, Beadle, the Guardia commandant, with support from the Nicaraguan government, insisted on withholding the bulk of the Guardia Nacional as a rural police force for the peaceful areas, leaving the undermanned Marine brigade to shift for itself in the north.

Meanwhile, on 8 October 1927, there occurred an aircraft crash which was to result in a major campaign.

At about ten in the morning, while on the daily reconnaissance patrol over Nueva Segovia, the 02B-1 (a metal-fuselage version of the old DH) of Second Lieutenant Earl A. Thomas coughed and quit about five miles north of the remote town of Quilali, which had been abandoned by its inhabitants because of bandit depredations. Minutes later, the airplane rammed into the jungled sides of a razor-backed ridge, Sapotillal, destined to be a name of ill omen for Marines.

While Lieutenant Thomas and his observer, Sergeant Frank E. Dowdell, shook themselves out of the wreck unhurt, Thomas's wingman, Marine Gunner Wodarczyk, dipped low, dropped them a map marked with their position, and headed for Ocotal, the nearest airstrip with a friendly garrison. Lieutenant Thomas and Sergeant Dowdell were never again seen alive by our forces. Bandit defectors later revealed that they were followed by a band of 15 outlaws, whom they fought off with their pistols, killing five. Then, they coerced two natives into guiding them toward Jicaro, where there was a small Marine outpost. On the trail, one native attacked them with his machete and cut Lieutenant Thomas seriously; Dowdell shot this native, but the other bolted and brought word to the bandits, some 40 of whom intercepted the two aviators. After their ammunition was used up, they were captured and, according to photographs which Sandino circulated to Honduran and Mexican newspapers, were tortured and hanged. A vivid and only thinly disguised fictional reconstruction of the ordeal of Thomas and Dowdell, "Air Patrol," was written shortly afterward by John Thomason and may be found in *Marines and Others*.

In this oil painting Marine infantry and artillery storm Fort Ch'ojijin, Kangwha Island, Korea, on the lower Salee River, 10 June 1871. Artist: Sergeant John Clymer, USMC.

John Philip Sousa's Band at the St. Louis Exposition, 1893.

Marines bivouacing in the hills of Olongapo, Philippine Islands. The scene is typical of the activities of the Marines during the early days of the occupation in the early 1900s.

Marines fighting insurgents in the Philippine Islands, 1901.

Marines in China, 1905.

Banana War Marine, in a pain ing used as a cover of *Leathe neck*, October 1960. He was lean, leathery, and level eyed He patrolled Nicaragua's swamps for weeks at a time. Being a Marine, he rode whenever possible, using a single mounting stirrup becau his animal was too small for ordinary stirrups. Artist: Colo Donald L. Dickson, USMC.

Major Smedley D. Butler's Marines from Panama brought with them the Benet-Mercie guns for use in Nicaragua against the rebellious uprising in 1912.

Horse Marines in action. This unusual photograph shows infantry and cavalry contingents of the U.S. Marine Corps in action.

By 1130 on the morning of Thomas's crash, Gunner Wodarczyk had dropped word to the Marines at Jicaro, and, 45 minutes later, the outpost commander, First Lieutenant George J. O'Shea, had a rescue patrol on the trail. This group included a squad of Marines, ten guardias, and a surgeon, Lieutenant John B. O'Neill, USN.

Next morning, having covered 22 miles since noon the day before, O'Shea was at the approximate location of the wreck. To the eye, Sapotillal Ridge seemed empty and quiet, and the point moved cautiously forward.[37]

We were 100 yards up when the advance guard was fired on from the trail ahead. We halted, took the best cover available and returned the fire. The hill was occupied by about 200 bandits, who seemed to be well armed and had plenty of ammunition. . . . We began to receive heavy fire from a hill to our right and rear, distant about 100 yards. About ten dynamite bombs were thrown close to us, this time from above. Men above us were yelling to those on the other hill to fire lower, and, on the other hill, they were directing them to drop dynamite bombs on us.

It was a classic ambush; the bandits had known a rescue patrol must come and were waiting. With at least a hundred enemy in his rear, O'Shea determined to press forward. The impetus of the Marines' attack took them through. Momentarily they were clear, but only momentarily; coming down the trail dead ahead were about 75 additional bandits, apparently a reserve group. In the head-on collision there was a burst of confused fighting in which Dr. O'Neill, armed with a dead man's rifle, "did great work."[38] Under a shower of grenades, the bandit reinforcements wavered, then retreated to the next hill. Again beset from the rear, O'Shea pulled his 14 survivors into the thick brush off the trail and retreated down a stream bed. Miraculously, the outlaws missed him, and, after a 30-mile stumble by compass through dense jungle, the patrol reached Jicaro just before midnight the next evening, 10 October.

Until the air crash and O'Shea's ambush, operations had been largely defensive, almost static in fact. Now, however, the idea began to penetrate that Sandino's "Wild Beasts of the Mountains"—as he styled them—would require sustained offensive action. Rumor circulated through Nicaragua that the bandits had a secret base; no man knew exactly where. General Lejeune stated in 1928 that the Marines had been unable to locate it until air patrols did so in November.[39] If correct, Lejeune's statement was a serious reflection against brigade intelligence, since, as early as 15 June, Major H. C. Pierce had reported:[40]

Following information obtained relative to Sandino's camp, etc., from inhabitants:

Sandino's headquarters located at Cerro Chipotes [sic], a high mountain about nine miles to the northeast of Quilali. . . . Camp reported to be at top of mountain with one trail leading from it to Quilali. . . . Two routes from Cerro Chipotes are reported, one to Honduras and the other to the eastward via the Coco River. . . .

Moreover, shortly after the Ocotal attack, a Marine and Guardia patrol, led by an officer who was somewhat of a student of classic war, had actually passed within striking distance of Chipote, which the native guide described. The second-in-command, Captain V. F. Bleasdale, promptly volunteered to take part of the patrol and go there. "I will never divide my force in the presence of the enemy," pronounced the patrol leader, and that was that.[41] Before long, quite a few members of brigade headquarters found themselves wishing that the officer in question had been less inclined to think like Baron Jomini and more inclined to listen to Captain Bleasdale.

At any rate, after the bandit attacks on Ocotal and Telpaneca, and the O'Shea ambush, the necessity of reaching Sandino's base and of bringing him to bay became evident. More immediately, however, nobody had yet been able to reach the wreckage of Lieutenant Thomas's airplane, let alone find any trace of Thomas or Sergeant Dowdell. To attend to these matters, two patrols were launched in a pincer advance on Sapotillal, one (25 Marines and 40 guardias under First Lieutenant Moses J. Gould) moving north from Matagalpa, the other, under Lieutenant C. J. Chappell, following O'Shea's route south from Jicaro. Both were to rendezvous at the site of the plane crash, an order which markedly complicated juncture. Chappell arrived first, on 26 October, and was immediately hit by an aggressive force of some 175 bandits who surrounded him on Sapotillal Ridge and held his patrol in a defensive position until "Mose" Gould came up two days later and, aided by air support, put the bandits to flight. Then—at length— the wrecked airplane was found by Guardia Captain (Second Lieutenant, USMC) R. E. Hogaboom, who shinned up a tree and located the wreck with his old EE field glasses. There were no traces of the two aviators. On the way back to Jicaro, the combined patrols had a pitched battle with another bandit group estimated to contain 250 men. Sixty Sandinistas were killed and wounded; one Marine and one guardia were killed, while another Marine was wounded. One moment of unintended comic relief came while Chappell was surrounded and fighting for his life on Sapotillal Ridge: a supporting aircraft zoomed low and dropped him a copy of his orders to flight training, for which he had previously applied. Any delay in execution was to count as leave.

The upshot of all these fights was the growing realization that the country around Quilali and Sapotillal Ridge was alive with bandits, and that any force entering this area was apt to find itself in trouble. Presumably, in turn, this was regarded by Sandino as a sensitive neighborhood. Adding up everything then known, including information from a number of Sandino's orders which had been found on enemy dead, intelligence (apparently still overlooking Major Pierce's report) concluded that the mysterious Chipote must be somewhere nearby.

On 23 November, after a systematic air search, Major Rowell found Chipote. As described by General Lejeune, who flew over it himself during the subsequent campaign:[42]

> It was a well fortified mountain, with a great many trenches, and they had machine-guns there. They had fields of fire cleared, and they had constructed shacks at each defensive position for the shelter of their men, and on top of the mountain were quite a number of these shacks they had built, some for storehouses, apparently, and some for dwelling places.

Chipote—"La Fortaleza," Sandino sometimes called it, and with good reason—lay about seven miles northeast of Sapotillal Ridge, which was undoubtedly a forward outpost position. Now it was clear why the Telpaneca raiders had retired east: La Fortaleza was 15 miles eastward as the crow flies. Moreover, it was just 26 miles from the frontier of Honduras, where Sandino had friends.

DECEMBER DISASTERS

Now that he knew where Chipote was, Colonel Gulick apparently felt that his troubles were over. If so, he continued to underestimate the staying power, technical proficiency, numerical strength, and base of support which enabled Sandino, a professional revolutionist with international connections, to remain in business. Despite the increasingly ugly tempo of bandit activity since mid-summer, and this in the face of what should have been major setbacks for Sandino, no steps had yet been taken to reinforce the half-demobilized Marine brigade or to get the Guardia Nacional, mainly committed to policing the populated centers of the country, into the campaign as a major force. What was worse, except from the casualty reports, nobody in Washington had yet been made aware that there was real trouble in Nicaragua.

The events of December 1927 would shortly advertise the situation as it in fact existed.

On 19 December, two columns were again sent out into the bandit area with the mission of setting up a base at Quilali and, then, of capturing and destroying La Fortaleza. One, headed by Captain Richard Livingston, set out from Jinotega with 115 officers and men; the other, under First Lieutenant Merton A. Richal, included 40 Marines and 20 guardias, advancing from Telpaneca. It was then believed that Sandino had anywhere from 200 to 500 men. He had, in fact, more than a thousand.

At 0930, 30 December, while the Livingston column toiled forward along abominable trails about a mile south of Quilali beside the Jicaro River, a storm of rifle and machine gun fire, punctuated by the thud of dynamite bombs, burst from both sides of the defile and ahead. Captain Livingston fell wounded in the first volley, and Lieutenant Gould, a stalwart throughout the campaign, assumed command.

The bandits, afterward estimated at 400, were entrenched in foxholes, with regular parapets, on rising ground parallel to the trail. A machine gun and clump of riflemen were firing rapidly from a position across the river. Another machine gun ahead was intended to enfilade the trail, but, Marines thanked God, had been improperly laid and mostly cut vines to the side.

Despite heavy casualties in the first fire, the Marines got their own machine guns into action, while a flanking party of riflemen worked around the end of the bandits' long line of foxholes. As this group began to roll up the enemy line, the outlaws broke and retired. The fight ended as suddenly as it began.

Short as it had been, the ambush hurt. Five Marines and two guardias were killed. Twenty-three Marines and two guardias were wounded, eight seriously. Under Lieutenant Gould, the column collected its dead and wounded, and made its way into Quilali to await junction with the Richal patrol.

Less than four hours afterward, Sandino struck his first blow at the column from Telpaneca. At 1255 a group of some 50 bandits opened rifle and pistol fire on Richal's point at an awkward spot where the trail was steep and narrow. There was a 20-minute fire-fight in which one Marine was seriously wounded, and three bandit dead were counted. Then the patrol resumed its advance.

Next day, almost exactly 24 hours later, Lieutenant Richal's column reached Sapotillal Ridge; Quilali was six miles away. At a trail junction known as Las Cruces, no distance from where Lieutenant O'Shea's little patrol had nearly been annihilated two months before, the bandits hit hard. With a strength of at least 350 and several machine guns, they not only opened fire, but actually charged the Marine advance guard, momentarily forcing them back and—a grievous loss—killing Guardia Lieutenant (First Sergeant, USMC) Thomas G. Bruce, one of the heroes of Ocotal, where he had won the Navy Cross. The bandits dragged off Bruce's body, mutilated it, and stripped it of his gear; Sandino later boasted that he carried Bruce's field glasses.

Lieutenant Richal, aided by Gunnery Sergeant Edward G. Brown, built up a base of fire with a 37-mm. gun, a Stokes mortar, and a machine gun. While getting the machine gun into action, Richal was shot in the head by a bullet which took out his left eye and went through his nose, missing the right eye by a hairsbreadth. With one officer now dead and the other seriously wounded, Gunnery Sergeant Brown took command and launched an attack which ultimately gained Las Cruces hill, a commanding knoll from which the bandits had originally charged. Here, completely surrounded, with one dead and four wounded, the patrol grimly dug in to fight it out. Fortunately, they had a field radio set with which they could raise Quilali. Gould immediately sent out a relief party of 43 Marines, commanded by First Lieutenant Robert G. Hunt.

Had it not been for air support, there is no telling how the affair might have ended. Marine air patrols established cover for the Richal group on 1 January. Next day, they repeated the performance until, at 1415, Hunt's reinforcements arrived, and, with continual air cover, the beleaguered patrol struggled in to Quilali, which the bandits promptly surrounded.

The situation was now critical. The badly mauled force at Quilali had 30 wounded, 11 seriously, including the two original patrol commanders. The senior officer present was a lieutenant. Sandino had them surrounded, under fire, and greatly outnumbered.

After surveying Quilali from the air, Major Rowell concluded that an airplane might, just might, land in the town's grass-grown main street (actually a trail leading up the mountain ravine in which Quilali is located), providing certain houses were demolished. Since, in Lejeune's phrase,[43] the town was nothing but "an aggregation of shacks" and abandoned by its inhabitants for fear of Sandino's depredations, demolitions presented no problem. Engineer tools were dropped, and, while the Quilali garrison set to work under fire on a kind of airstrip, the aviation mechanics at Managua rigged an O2U-1 biplane with an old-type DH landing gear, which the pilots considered best for such a field. By 6 January, Quilali's main street was a fire-swept, chuckholed airfield 100 feet wide and 500 feet long. All that was needed was a pilot with sufficient intrepidity to try it out. First Lieutenant Christian F. Schilt volunteered. As the O2U-1 had no brakes, he would have to rely on Marines to hang onto the wings and keep him from nosing over into the deep ravine which yawned menacingly at the upwind end of the street.

In the three days, 6-8 January 1928, Lieutenant Schilt made ten flights into Quilali. He brought in a relief commander, Captain Roger W. Peard, and 1,400 pounds of emergency medical supplies and provisions. Beginning with Lieutenant Richal, the most seriously wounded, Schilt flew out 18 casualties, most of whom would not have survived evacuation by mule-back. On the eighth landing, the O2U's tail-skid assembly collapsed; on the next, the center section struts bent badly. But one more trip had to be made, and somehow Schilt did it. On this, as in the preceding nine landings and takeoffs, there was continuous enemy fire. For this superb airmanship and for equally superb heroism, Schilt was awarded the Medal of Honor. As General Lejeune said afterward, "That act of Lieutenant Schilt's is one of the most skillful and daring that I have any knowledge of."[44]

Quilali was relieved—but what now? Sandino had clearly inflicted a defeat—a series of defeats, in fact—which was only stopped short of a disaster by the discipline and fighting qualities of individual Marines and guardias, and by the repeated intervention of aviation. From La Fortaleza, the bandit leader, profiting by repeated underestimates on the part of the United States forces, could well afford to be pleased with the state of affairs.

Meanwhile, Captain Peard, in accordance with new plans, grimly led the Quilali force back to San Albino, a mining town far better suited for a base of operations, and here, on 11 January, Major Archibald Young arrived with 60 more Marines and orders to resume operations against El Chipote.

THE END OF EL CHIPOTE

Dismay engulfed Washington after word arrived of the reverses sustained in December. Orders flew for immediate reactivation of the 11th Marines, to be commanded by Colonel R. H. Dunlap, one of the best available. All Marines in the Special Service Squadron (about 300) were landed and attached to the 2d Brigade; several Marine guards from ships of the Battle Force were added. More aviation, including three trimotor Fokkers, the first transport planes ever assigned to the Marine Corps, reinforced

Major Rowell's shoestring outfit. Colonel Gulick was relieved as brigade commander by Brigadier General Feland, who, despite poor health, arrived at Corinto on 15 January with the leading elements of the 11th Regiment. Accompanying Feland was the Major General Commandant, who, in typical Lejeune style, came along to see for himself. By the end of January, the strength of the 2d Brigade had skyrocketed to 2,700 officers and men.

Feland's first step was to reorganize the country into three operating areas —northern, southern, and eastern. The northern area, hot potato for the moment, he assigned to Colonel Dunlap and the 11th Regiment. To the eastern area, where unwelcome signs of renewed banditry were making an appearance, he assigned an aviation detachment of four Loening OL-8 amphibians.

While this build-up took place, the force under Major Young at San Albino Mines concentrated for the final drive against La Fortaleza. Young now had a battalion of four companies—16th, 20th, 45th, and a Guardia company, with a detachment of the 8th (machine gun). And while the cruisers bearing the first reinforcements for the brigade were breasting their way north from Panama to Corinto, Major Rowell launched an all-out—four-plane—air offensive against El Chipote. As Lejeune later testified:[45]

On the 14th of January El Chipote was bombed. The aviators approached it from the clouds, 5,000 feet up, and they came down at the rate of about 200 miles an hour, vertically, so they could drop their bombs accurately . . . it was a very successful bombing operation.

For an hour, using 50-pound fragmentation bombs, white phosphorus hand grenades, and machine guns, Major Rowell and three other pilots (Lieutenants Weir and Lamson-Scribner, and Gunnery Sergeant Munsch) worked over La Fortaleza. Their approach was signaled by the bandits by two rockets, and the airplanes received heavy machine gun and rifle fire during most of the attack. Several of Sandino's barracks and storehouses were hit, and Rowell reported about 45 dead, which could be counted from the air—an indication of the still leisurely pace of aerial warfare.

Under cover of this diversion, Major Young advanced from San Albino and captured, without casualties, a main bandit outpost atop San Jeronimo Mountain, which overlooked San Albino Mines from a distance of only two miles and covered all trails leading toward Chipote.

Five days later (19 January), Young's columns converged on Sandino's stronghold, meeting steady but not strong resistance. It was hoped that the entire bandit force could be encircled and cut off, but this was not to be.

Except for a few stragglers, the bandits made good their escape. Even so, it was a close call. On 26 January, when the 20th Company reached the very top of Chipote, First Lieutenant Howard N. Kenyon, in command, found cooking fires smoking, a freshly butchered beef hanging in the kitchen, and a still limp, undressed chicken by the fireplace in what a prisoner identified as the quarters of "General" Salgado. Fresh tracks led in all directions into the bush. Captured papers showed that Sandino had been there as late as the 20th of the month.

Before returning to San Albino, the Marines destroyed all buildings and supplies, and staked out various small ambushes, which garnered a handful of prisoners. On 28 January, Major Young withdrew via Quilali, where he found that Sandinistas, who were definitely air-minded by now, had done their best to return his favors by digging holes and pits all through Schilt's airstrip.

Sandino's forces evidently were still in the field, and they thus continued to be the main objective of the Marine brigade.

PACIFICATION OF THE NORTHERN AREA

To make the northern area too hot for Sandino and his bandits, General Feland and Colonel Dunlap continued intensive patrolling and established additional garrisons, so that practically every town in Nueva Segovia was safe. Sandino's home town, San Rafael del Norte, was occupied. Patrols began to travel at night, going off the trails into ambush positions by day, a practice which shook the bandits. As a measure not only of the serious state of affairs, but of Feland's energy, there were 28 clashes with bandits in the three months between 15 January and 18 April 1928; during the preceding six months, there had been only 36.

Although rooted out of La Fortaleza, Sandino was far from benched. After a brief respite in Honduras, he re-entered Nicaragua and made straight for the coffee district about Jinotega and Matagalpa, where the rich planters crossed themselves and prayed for protection.

At 1330, 27 February, an empty pack-train which had been on circuit to various outposts, was on the march between Yali and Condega, its home base. The 95-mule train, herded along by 22 native *muleros*, was escorted by 35 Marines and one Navy pharmacist's mate, under command of First Lieutenant Edward F. O'Day.

As O'Day's column toiled and jingled along an open stretch of country near the town of Bromaderos, with a high ridge and a crude native lava wall to the right, they were hit by a fierce burst of fire, accompanied by a shower of dynamite bombs, along the entire right from behind the wall, and from front and rear. The mules stampeded, and the Marines, rallied by Lieutenant O'Day and Sergeant Isham, his leading NCO, formed a firing line along a lower ridge to the left, facing the bandits across the trail.

After an hour of heavy firing and skirmishing, the bandits, more than 600 strong, charged the Marine position in a regular skirmish line, covered by bursts of fire from at least four machine guns. Despite their superiority in numbers, they were thrown back to the trail, where they regrouped, and, under cover of their machine guns, pillaged what they could find in the welter of dead and leaderless animals. Just before nightfall they attacked again; again they were stopped by Marine rifle fire. And again they fell back and resumed continuous small arms fire on the beleaguered platoon of Marines.

Meanwhile, although Salgado, the bandit leader, did not know it, O'Day's get-away man, a corporal from the battalion intelligence section, had made contact with Condega, and the 57th Company, 2d Battalion, 11th Marines, commanded by Captain William K. MacNulty, was on the way. Among MacNulty's NCOs was a young corporal, James P. Berkeley, destined 30 years later to be a major general.

As day broke, the 57th Company established contact with O'Day and attacked the bandits' right flank, supported by a machine gun. At first the outlaws fired back, but by eight o'clock they had retired, and the field remained in the hands of the Marines, five of whom died—three of machete wounds—and eight of whom were wounded. Thus ended the Bromaderos fight, which Sandino subsequently described to a confidant as his most important battle in 1928.

Under steady pressure throughout the northern area, Sandino's forces began to dissipate and operate defensively, continuing depredations against natives, but avoiding combat with Marines. Another result of changed conditions in the north was that, as will be seen, the focus of bandit operations shifted in mid-1928 to eastern Nicaragua. One exception to this general improvement was the action on 13 May—really a collision of forces—in which Captain Robert S. Hunter, leading a patrol northeast of Santa Cruz, was fatally wounded while siting a machine gun against a strong bandit group.

By mid-summer, more than 1,600 bandits had turned in themselves and their weapons (at $10 per rifle), taking advantage of the amnesty which still prevailed. This was a measure not only of the temporary decline of bandit fortunes, but also of the strength Sandino had had when he was riding high.

TROUBLE IN THE EAST

The eastern area (Major Harold H. Utley) was composed of swamp, jungle, banana plantations, mahogany forest, and occasional gold mines. Its highways were rivers; its inhabitants, mainly peaceable Mosquito Indians. The interior country which separates it from western Nicaragua is among the most difficult and remote in Central America. It was into these fastnesses that the campaign in Nueva Segovia forced Sandino's bands. The first warning of this came when Sandino made a sweep of the gold-mining region, raiding and looting two principal mines—La Luz and Neptune, about a hundred miles inland of Puerto Cabezas, where Utley had his headquarters.

To confine and compress the bandits, pressure from the east was needed. A principal agent for effecting this pressure was a short, red-haired, icy-eyed captain, Merritt A. ("Red Mike") Edson.

Two posts, Bocay, on the Coco River, and Cuvali, in mining country, defined the farthest line held by Marine garrisons from the eastern area. These had been established by Edson, CO of the *Denver's* Marine guard, and by Captain Henry D. Linscott (both destined to become general officers).

In mid-July 1928, aviation reported a sizable concentration of bandits far up the Coco River at Poteca, which seemed, from the air, to be an outlaw headquarters, perhaps that of Sandino himself. Although Poteca was 400 miles upstream from the sea and was generally held to be inaccessible, Edson proposed a river expedition in native dugouts. The idea was approved —nobody else had anything better—and, with 46 men, Edson set out.

Boats capsized (intentionally, with the help of native boatmen, Edson soon realized), supplies were lost in the swift jungle river, men faltered with malaria, food ran short, and the patrol would have starved but for air-drops. Nothing like this had been experienced by Marines since the march across Samar. But "Red Mike" pressed on. And on 7 August, foreshadowing by 14 years exactly Edson's assault on Tulagi, the patrol hit and deftly out-flanked Sandino's main outpost, 60 miles above Bocay, where one Marine was killed and three wounded, and ten bandits died. The bandits, who were led by Simon Jiron, one of Sandino's original leaders in the Ocotal attack, had a 60-man ambush laid with machine guns, but a too-itchy trigger finger betrayed them prematurely. Ten days later, "Red Mike" reached Wamblam, just downstream from Poteca, to find that Sandino had fled, leaving most of his stores (and one man, a "colonel") behind. Sandino's supplies were a godsend for the patrol, whose uniforms were falling off and who had, in many cases, not even been able to shave for almost a month.

After Edson had established a permanent garrison at Poteca, General Feland commented, still finding it difficult to believe:[46]

From the standpoint of difficulty, danger, isolation from friendly ground troops, and accomplishments, this small expedition is without parallel in the hard work done by this Brigade.

NICARAGUA'S 1928 ELECTION AND ITS CONSEQUENCES

In November 1928, Nicaragua had its first free and peaceful national election. The resultant change of administration to the winning Liberal party, headed by General José María Moncada, was the first peaceful and constitutional change of party government in the history of the country. This truly remarkable event resulted from the agreements reached at Tipitapa and from the United States-supervised electoral machinery set up under Brigadier General Frank R. McCoy, USA, a distinguished officer with long political and diplomatic experience. The chairmen of the 432 electoral precincts throughout the country were—at the request of leaders of both parties—enlisted men of the Marine Corps or Navy, while the Guardia Nacional and the 2d Brigade provided protection for polling places and ballots. In the words of Dr. Harold W. Dodds, technical adviser to the electoral commission and later president of Princeton University:[47]

These measures were so successful that registration and voting in the remote departments were heavier than in 1924, the only year in which conditions had previously approached a free election. For this the Marines and Guardia deserve great credit. Their task was more difficult than anyone unfamiliar with jungle territory and the operation of bandit bands can readily appreciate.

Following this tour de force and the compressing of Sandino's forces into the wastes and jungles of the interior, he fled, in June 1929, via Honduras, to Mexico, then and for years after the principal center of Communist influence in Latin America. This hegira reduced banditry to the occupational level which had been endemic in Nicaragua for many years.

One immediate consequence of President Moncada's ascendancy was a new policy regarding employment of the Guardia Nacional. Beadle was relieved in March 1929 by Colonel Douglas C. McDougal, who, with the backing of Moncada and cheers from the brigade, immediately began committing more Guardia units to antibandit operations, in which they showed skill and competence. One reason for the effectiveness of the guardias was that they possessed the sanctions and compulsions of police power over the inhabitants, which Marines did not, and could thus dig far deeper into the civilian base, such as it was, that supported Sandino's terrorism.

With the long-overdue full commitment of the Guardia as a fighting force, it became possible to withdraw Marine garrisons from some posts and reduce the brigade strength. General Feland was succeeded on 18 April 1929 by Brigadier General Dion Williams. In August 1929, the 11th Regiment was detached from the 2d Brigade, and on the 31st disbanded while en route to Quantico. The total strength of the Marine brigade then approximated two thousand. All but ten posts in the once-hot northern area were turned over to the Guardia. This commitment of the Guardia imposed new strains and temptations on some of its frailer members. There were, in all, ten mutinies or individual outbreaks in detachments of the Guardia Nacional between the end of 1927 and mid-1932. Five Marines, seconded to the Guardia as officers, were murdered or killed defending themselves in these affrays. But the bulk of the Guardia proved steady, loyal, and effective.

SANDINO RETURNS

While the Guardia Nacional continued the campaign against bandits, the Marines, following the pattern of Haiti and Santo Domingo, were gradually concentrated in reserve, and the native forces took over offensive duties in the field. Marine aviation continued to support all field operations, whether Marine or Guardia. In April 1930, all Marine detachments were pulled out of the eastern area. A year later the entire brigade was concentrated at Managua and Corinto, leaving the country to the Guardia Nacional, now commanded by Guardia Major General (Lieutenant Colonel, USMC) Calvin B. Matthews, like his predecessor, McDougal, one of the Corps' finest shots. In his command, General Matthews had 267 officers and 2,240 enlisted men, while the Marine brigade was cut back to 1,000 officers and men.

Despite this fundamental improvement, which made the situation of the Marine brigade more realistic and more tenable, banditry was by no means dead. In May 1930, financed by world-wide leftist contributions—including a sizable sum from New York City, where *The Nation,* a magazine of the left (pursuing the same line as during the caco revolt in Haiti), spread un-

truths highly favorable to Sandino and inimical to the Marine Corps—
Sandino returned from Yucatan and resumed practice in the northern area.
By coincidence, no doubt, on the first day of the month in which he took
the field again (May Day 1930), a Communist-attended meeting was held in
Union Square, Manhattan, for the purpose of raising funds to buy arms for
Sandino. Significantly, his main sponsor and partisan in the United States
continued to be the All-American Anti-Imperialist League, a fellow-travel-
ing organization formed and directed by Communists.

By the end of 1931, the Guardia had chalked up 141 bandit contacts.
Moreover, on 19 June 1930, near Jinotega, Sandino and 600 bandits had been
hit by an air-strike, led by Captain B. F. Johnson, in which Sandino was
badly hurt. This strike was part of a co-ordinated air-ground operation and
marked the last major contact between Marine forces and any sizable
group of bandits during the Nicaraguan campaign. Earlier, had it not been
for strict obedience to orders on the part of Major Rowell, not only Sandino,
but *The Nation's* correspondent with Sandino (Carleton Beals, an American
in the enemy's camp), might well have been killed. Rowell, on armed reconnaissance, discovered Sandino's main force bivouacked in San Rafael del
Norte. Rather than execute an attack on a town containing civilians, Rowell
—in accordance with General Feland's policy—forebore to strike and merely
made a nonfiring pass. As Major Rowell commented dryly later:[48]

It so happened that the radical news writer, Mr. Beals, was present in the act of in-
terviewing Sandino at the very moment the planes arrived. At a later date, I met Mr.
Beals and urged that he include this incident, in which he was spared the danger of
losing his life, among the list of "atrocities" he was known to be seeking for publication.
However, he found it convenient to omit this incident from the published account of
his interview [with Sandino].

In November 1931 and early in the new year, Sandino, now recovered,
again accumulated foreign arms from Honduras and Mexico, and was able
to bring his forces up to more than a thousand strong for a brief campaign
in the Departments of Leon and Chinandega. Again the Guardia reacted
energetically and, in 1932, after 160 contacts, shattered the bandit organization.

PULLER'S PATROL

To say that the Guardia Nacional had 160 contacts in 1932 is only to note
a statistic. Guardia Company "M" (for "Mobile") based on Jinotega, was
anything but a statistic. With Guardia Captain (First Lieutenant, USMC)

Lewis B. "Chesty" Puller in command, seconded by Guardia Lieutenant (Gunnery Sergeant, USMC) William A. Lee, Company M carried the war to the bandits in a series of patrols seldom surpassed in the history of the Corps. Foremost among these was Puller's patrol into the mountains northeast of Jinotega.

One day early in September 1932, when Captain Puller was reconnoitering north of Jinotega, he stumbled across a trail he had never known existed and which did not connect with any known trail. It was 15 feet wide, newly cut, and obviously well maintained. Equally obvious to Puller was the fact that this trail, which pointed straight toward uninhabited fastnesses, was the bandits' means of descending unobserved from the wilds of the upper Coco River, east of El Chipote, into the populated area surrounding Jinotega.

On 20 September, at the head of his 40-man company, with 18 pack animals, "Chesty" Puller and Lieutenant Lee struck out of Jinotega for the secret trail. On the fourth day out, more than 40 miles from Jinotega, scouts found a well-prepared bandit camp (unoccupied), then another, and another. That day, the patrol rooted out and leveled 18 empty bandit camps along 12 miles of trail. Next day, during a 16-mile march of the kind that made Puller's company the terror of bandits, nine more camps were found and destroyed. So far, despite every sign of bandits, including evidence that scouts were tracking the patrol, not a living man had been seen.

On the following morning, 26 September, as the patrol crossed a stream, Agua Carta, 75 miles out of Jinotega, rifle fire, mingled briefly with the chatter of automatic weapons, burst from the jungle on the right of the trail. The guardias, keen and aggressive, counterattacked, and the bandits melted into the brush. Puller estimated that the brief ambush came from 80 men, with at least two machine guns, trying mainly to pick off the officers.

Across the ridge, over another stream, up a long narrow draw with ridges on both sides, the patrol moved silently ahead. As the point advanced, Captain Puller, second man in column, dove for the ground; so did the point. As they dropped, a bandit automatic rifle blasted on full automatic and, with its first burst, literally truncated the man behind Puller, drenching the captain with a sheet of blood. The whole ridge to the right exploded with dynamite bombs, musketry, hand and rifle grenades, and fire from at least seven machine guns or automatic rifles. Three guardias fell wounded. So did Lieutenant Lee, hit twice and unable to slash the patrol's Lewis gun loose from its pack mule.

Up the slope the guardias began to fight their way under intense fire. Exerting all his strength, Lee managed to get at the Lewis gun and bring it into action. Then more bandits opened fire from the opposite ridge, now the patrol's rear. This brought the total number of bandits to over 150. Finally, the guardias topped the right-hand ridge, faced about, and raked the opposite high ground with musketry and rifle grenades. The bandit firing slackened and ceased. After more than an hour's desperate fighting, the patrol was safe. Better still, they had won. Sixteen dead bandits were found, plus bloody traces of many more wounded.

His own wounded forced Captain Puller to turn back. Even burdened by these, the patrol covered seven miles—"You can never stop, you've got to keep going, when you're carrying wounded on the trail," said Puller.[49] That night one Guardia died and, like the other who had been killed in the main ambush at Agua Carta, was buried in a hidden grave. Four days later, after two more futile ambushes which only further lacerated the bandits, Puller's patrol emerged from the jungle at Jinotega. In ten days they had marched more than 150 miles, fought four battles, destroyed 30 bandit camps, killed 30 bandits, by count, and probably many more. Lieutenant Lee was promptly flown to Managua. "In the days of wooden ships," reported Puller, himself a man of iron, "Lee would have been an iron man."[50] For this epic patrol, Captain Puller was awarded his second Navy Cross, and Lee his third—until the Second World War, the highest number of Navy Crosses ever won by a single individual. Lee's fame as a Navy Cross holder spread far, but evidently was not quite universal. In China in 1939, shortly after reporting for duty, he was questioned by his commanding officer, "Lee, isn't that a Navy Cross I see you're wearing?"

"No, Sir," replied Lee, "that's three of them."[51]

"... A JOB WELL DONE"

Within less than three months, Puller and Lee were again in combat. In the last serious fight of the year, on the day after Christmas 1932, 250 bandits waylaid a train at Punta de Rieles on the new El Sauce-Leon line. After an hour's spirited fighting, the bandits retired minus 63 saddled riding animals. Three out of Puller's 60 guardias on the train were killed; but so were 31 bandits.

Meanwhile, the Marine brigade successfully and peacefully supervised the elections of 1930 and 1932, interrupted by the earthquake and fire of

March 1931, which nearly leveled Managua. The rescue and relief efforts by Marines won the gratitude of Nicaraguans throughout the country.

In April 1931, while Managua was still picking itself up, Colonel Stimson, now Secretary of State under Herbert Hoover, announced that the United States government would no longer undertake general protection of our nationals throughout the interior of Nicaragua; also that the time for withdrawal of the Marine brigade was approaching. Eighteen months later, with another honest election completed, even though banditry was definitely not suppressed, the new non-intervention policy demanded that the United States terminate military occupation of Nicaragua. In so doing, the Americans would leave Nicaragua an efficient Guardia Nacional, a national system of communications, numerous airfields, and many other improvements unheard of before the 2d Marine Brigade's arrival almost six years before. In the words of Secretary Stimson:[52]

The Marines had come to save lives in the civil war; they had remained to disarm the contenders, chase bandits, and hold an election, and they left behind in the end a country peaceful and independent. It was a job well done.

Indeed, on balance, it was, and Brigadier General R. C. Berkeley, the last brigade commander, could feel pride as his flag was hauled down in Managua on 2 January 1933. Little more than a year later, on 22 February 1934, Augusto C. Sandino was lured to Managua and finally shot by members of the Guardia Nacional under orders from the Jefe Director, Colonel Anastasio ("Tacho") Somoza. At the end, the bandit leader, who had himself committed or directed many such summary proceedings, quailed; his nerve faltered and he had trouble controlling his bladder.[53]

LESSONS OF NICARAGUA

The Nicaraguan campaign was both Alpha and Omega in many more senses than most Marines who fought in it then realized.

Nicaragua was the last of the Caribbean expeditions which had been the Marines' stock-in-trade since Panama in 1885. It was also the last paternal-interventionist military operation in which United States forces landed to stabilize, pacify, and, if possible, improve a small, backward country. Years later the mark of Nicaragua would remain on the Corps through the requirement that every second lieutenant must complete a course in Spanish—"bull-cart Spanish" to the old-timers—and through the strong emphasis on small-war tactics and techniques which marked the Corps of the 1930s.

Nicaragua also gave the Marine Corps its last serious fighting until World War II. There is no doubt that the hard campaigning, the perpetual stretching of insufficient means, and the tenacity of the enemy did much to maintain the professional temper of the Corps between the two world wars. Forty-seven Marines and 75 guardias were killed in action or died of wounds; 89 more died from other causes, including malaria, aircraft accidents, and other mishaps; 67 Marines and 122 guardias were wounded in action. Considering the ferocity of the bandits, the totals seem small enough.

But if Nicaragua was the last in a long line of banana wars, it confronted Marines with two innovations of 20th century warfare, neither very clearly recognized by participants in the campaign and each, paradoxically, tending to cancel out the effects of the other.

Augusto Sandino was the first opponent of his kind to be encountered by U. S. Marines—a modern-style guerrilla demagogue, internationally supported, schooled and fostered by the Communist-oriented Mexican left, waging a ruthless politico-military campaign by methods which demonstrably owed much to Lenin's sharp precepts on the techniques of revolution. This is not to say that Sandino himself was a Communist, or would have so recognized himself. Yet, it now seems clear that much of Sandino's support abroad had roots in world communism, and it is a fact that, since his death, he has been securely enshrined in the Latin-American Communist hagiography. Coincidence hardly accounts for the naming (in 1927 when Sandino was still barely identified by United States forces in Nicaragua) of a "Sandino Division" in the Russian-advised Nanking army during the Chinese civil war. Or for the chorus of hallelujahs from 1928 on by prominent foreign writers of the left, such as Henri Barbusse and Romain Rolland; these and others hailed Sandino—who was in truth an unscrupulous, bloody-handed slave of ambition—as a "George Washington." Or for the fund-raising drives in Lower Manhattan which amassed contributions to buy arms with which Sandino terrorized his fellow countrymen and killed U. S. Marines. Such phenomena as these—and Carleton Beals's grossly partisan articles for *The Nation* datelined in the camp of enemies of United States troops—came under the abused heading of "liberalism" in the 1920s. The 1960s had another word for it.

Thus, Sandino was in every respect a wholly new phenomenon for the Marine Corps and the United States, and very much a man of the new century. Unlike Haiti's Charlemagne Péralte or the fiery bandits of Santo Domingo, Sandino was no local primitive on an island who could be isolated by control of the sea and removed from power by systematic police action. In his articulacy, his talent for agitation, his international connections, his exploitation of the press, his deft intrigue, his cynical disregard of political commitments, his vanishing powers across "neutral" frontiers, Sandino is far more readily recognizable in the 1960s than in the 1920s.

If the Marine expeditionary forces in Nicaragua, insufficient as they really were for the task during the entire campaign, had been equipped and supported only with the simple weapons and techniques of Haiti and Santo Domingo, the results would have been even less satisfactory than they were. Fortunately, this was not the case. The second wholly new factor which distinguished the Nicaraguan campaign from its forerunners was that it was the first air-ground war in history. One who early recognized the impact of air support on the tedious campaign was Admiral Latimer, commanding the Special Service Squadron, who reported to the Navy Department:[54]

No report of the military operations in the past year in Nicaragua would be complete without reference to the valuable work done by the aviation detachment. It is believed that these men, under the able leadership of Major Rowell, have written new pages in the history of aviation, and the record of their achievements is one long succession of brilliant exploits. The pilots have flown over a wild and mountainous country in all kinds of weather, where no facilities for landing exist, and they have daily risked their lives in carrying out the tasks assigned to them. They have established themselves as a very important part and integral part of the organization and are now regarded as one of the most valuable assets of the brigade.

Most of the things done by Marine aviation in Nicaragua had been done or experimented with before. But never before had they been done simultaneously and routinely, and never before had combat and logistic air support been woven into the fabric of a campaign as it was by the 2d Marine Brigade between 1927 and 1932.

Taking mid-1928 as typical, the statistics for the preceding year give a measure of aviation's contribution to the campaign:[55]

Eighty-four attacks on bandit forces (including the first dive-bombing attack in history).

Ammunition expended in action: 300 bombs, more than 30,000 rounds.

Sorties hit by ground fire: 82.

Passengers and cargo hauled: more than 1,500 people (including casualties and sick) and 900,000 pounds. Accident rate: zero.

Airfields built: Managua, Ocotal, Esteli, Apali, Jalapa, Puerto Cabezas, Jinotega, Somotillo, El Sauce, Leon, Quilali, Limay, Condega, Jugalpa,

Corinto, Somoto, Telpaneca, and Granada. Typical construction incentive for native labor on one field (Condega): a bonus issue of canned sardines, never a popular item in the tropical field ration; Corporal J. P. Berkeley noted that the total cost of the completed airfield was $900 in pay plus God knows how many cases of sardines.

Miscellaneous services: aerial mapping and photography, meteorology, daily message and mail drops and pickups throughout the country, and long-range radio communications for the brigade.

Technical advances: substitution of the original (biplane) Vought Corsair (O2U) for the World War DeHavilland (DH); advent of metal fuselages (duraluminum); first transport planes in Marine Corps history (Fokker trimotor); brakes on landing gear (". . . hailed with joy by all pilots"); trials of the OP-1 autogiro, an exasperating contraption which was the first rotary-wing aircraft in the Marine Corps, and, with its two Navy sisters, the first such in the United States Armed Forces.

Later on aviation outdid itself in logistic support. In a single week in August 1928 Marine planes lifted 68,614 pounds of cargo. Nine weeks later the squadrons flew 209 sorties in one week (the score for a single year, 1930, was more than 5,000 sorties amounting to 5,900 hours). One of the longest remembered logistic missions of the year was executed for the express bene-fit of a hulking second lieutenant, Wilburt S. Brown, justly nicknamed "Bigfoot." When his shoes gave out on him in the northern area, a replace-ment pair was flown up from Managua: one shoe per airplane. The second airplane, however, was delayed several days by weather; when Lieutenant Brown finally got his other shoe, he was literally barefoot and not amused by aviation humor.

The year in which the last banana war ended, 1933, was the year in which the Fleet Marine Force began. The Marines who sailed home from Corinto were the cadres of the FMF. Only a few months later, when the last Marines left Haiti, the role of the Marine Corps as colonial infantry came to a close. Ahead lay campaigns and battles undreamed of by all but a few. Thus Nicaragua, final campaign of the old Marine Corps, set the stage for the new.

CHINA MARINES

While events in Nicaragua were at pressure peak, the Chinese civil war of 1927 threatened to become another Boxer Uprising. In the struggle between the originally Soviet-supported Cantonese armies and the northern armies under Marshal Chang Tso-Lin, battle lines swayed across the country, and China's historic antiforeignism lashed out at all westerners.

In February 1927, Cantonese troops menaced Shanghai, fat with wealth and foreign concessions. These troops were led by one Chiang Kai-shek, "who," reported the *Marine Corps Gazette,* "is the leader of the so-called Nanking party and is also a very able military commander."

Early in February, by sweeping up Marines from Guam, Cavite, and the Asiatic Fleet, a provisional battalion of 20 officers and 455 enlisted men, under Major Julian P. Willcox, was concentrated and landed at Shanghai. Within two weeks, responding to calls for help, the 4th Marines arrived from San Diego with 66 officers and 1,162 enlisted, commanded by Colonel C. S. ("Jumbo") Hill. Even so, serious disorders and attacks on foreigners continued.

In March, despite the pinch for Marines both in Nicaragua and at home for mail guards, General Lejeune concluded that the China forces must be built up to a brigade and that Smedley Butler was the man to do it. Thereafter, as might have been expected, things happened quickly.

By 25 March, General Butler, with his 3d Brigade staff, was in Shanghai, and the 6th Marines, disbanded since October 1925, were shaken together from East Coast navy yards for duty in the Far East under Colonel Harold C. Snyder. With the 6th Regiment went the 1st Battalion, 10th Marines (75-mm. guns—the ones Barnett could never get to France), engineers, tanks, and an aviation force which was augmented by the lonely little Marine squadron which had been stationed on Guam since March 1921. The aviation units were commanded by Lieutenant Colonel Thomas C. Turner, the driving force of Marine aviation in the 1920s, who was later killed in Haiti.

Shortly after the 6th Marines reached Shanghai in May, the trouble center shifted north, and Butler moved all units except the 4th Marines to Tientsin, where they could protect the line of communications to the American Legation at Peking. For the 4th Marines, this was the beginning of 14 years as "the China Marines" of Shanghai's International Settlement.

In Tientsin, the 3d Brigade's duty soon settled down to watchful waiting with little if any shooting, although the political situation was more than delicate. Old China hand that he was, Butler established a routine of drills, exercises, demonstrations, and gymkhanas, all designed to bring the brigade to a fine polish and simultaneously to show the flag most conspicuously. In this he made particular use of his aviation, still a novelty among all forces in China, native or western. One non-Marine pilot attached at his own request to the Marine squadrons was an Army Air Corps officer then on duty in China, First Lieutenant Thomas D. White, who would, while Chief of Staff of the Air Force years later, therefore wear the Marine Corps Expeditionary ribbon.

As recounted by the historian of Marine aviation, Robert Sherrod, one of General Butler's Tientsin demonstrations had a special climax:[56]

> During an exhibition of stunting. Captain James T. Moore zoomed over the crowds, went into a spectacular climbing roll, lost both wings off his plane and parachuted into a moat in front of the stands. "Trust Smedley," a lady spectator commented. "He always puts on a wonderful show."

By early 1929, China had quieted sufficiently to permit return of the 3d Brigade to the States, leaving the protection of U. S. interests to a strengthened 4th Marines, to the 15th Infantry detachment at Tientsin, and to the Peking Embassy Guard which, complete with its mounted detachment of true "Horse Marines," was practically a battalion task force in strength and capabilities. In the 1932 Sino-Japanese incident at Shanghai, the 4th Marines—reinforced by the 31st Infantry from the Philippines and by some 400 additional Marines from elsewhere—protected the American sector of the International Settlement until trouble had passed. Five years later, during the renewed fighting about Shanghai in late summer 1937, the 2d Marine Brigade, under Brigadier General John C. Beaumont—"Johnny Beau" to his officers and men—was moved posthaste from San Diego to the Far East. It was on this move, reputedly because the post-exchange supplies of the 6th Regiment inadvertently included several thousand candy bars but only one case of soap, that the regiment acquired its unsought nickname, "The Pogey-Bait 6th."

By early 1938 the fighting had again moved elsewhere, and the brigade returned home. At the same time (March 1938), the 15th Infantry was withdrawn from its long-time garrison duty in Tientsin, and a detachment of 230 Marines from Peking took over. This change not only marked the end of the Army's service in China, but also the end of almost two decades of unremitting efforts on the part of the War Department to overcome the State Department's insistence on an independent Marine Legation Guard in Peking, and to bring under the Army "the command of all American troops in China, Army and Marines...."[57]

While the shadows lengthened over the Orient, the detachments in Peking and Tientsin, some 500 in all, faced crisis after crisis. They were still at their posts as World War II engulfed the Pacific.

AT HOME

In February 1929, the House Committee on Appropriations completed its hearing on the Marine Corps budget for the forthcoming year; the Major General Commandant, homely, lion-chested, gnarled and tough as teak, brightened the room with one of his warm smiles. As the hearing started to break up, a member addressed the Chairman:[58]

MR. FRENCH: There is one observation I would like to make: At the time, Mr. Chairman, when General Lejeune was before our sub-committee a few weeks ago, we were not aware that he would not be with us the coming year. I just want to say this for the Record: that he has been the Major General Commandant of the Marine Corps for the entire period of six years that I have been Chairman of the Naval Appropriations Sub-Committee, and during that period he has won the absolute confidence of the members of that committee. He has done that through his intense earnestness, his untiring zeal, his fine integrity, and his most wonderful efficiency. . . .

MR. WOOD: So say we all, General.

A month later, on 4 March 1929, John Archer Lejeune, 13th Commandant, stepped aside, leaving behind him a record until then equaled only by Archibald Henderson.

Lejeune's nine years were years of nominal peace during which more Marines served longer overseas on expeditionary duty than at any time previously. They were years of stringent retrenchment marked by signal progress; of refurbished traditions as steppingstones for the future; of transition illumined by steadfastness. By any comparison, Lejeune's achievements were outstanding:

A modern system of officer education based on Marine Corps Schools, supplemented by rounded use of Army, Navy, and foreign military institutions.

Concentration of the Corps into East and West Coast Expeditionary Forces, coupled with rationalization of the Marine Corps mission in terms of amphibious readiness.

A flexible, broad-based system of officer procurement which would survive Lejeune by many decades. Beginning with May 1921, and every year thereafter, selected colleges were asked to nominate outstanding ROTC graduates for Marine commissions; in June of the same year, 55 meritorious young NCOs assembled for grueling observation and elimination at Eighth and Eye (17 were commissioned a year later); an increased annual increment of Naval Academy graduates into the Corps was firmly established.

A thrifty determination to make-do on scanty means, which years later would still keep the Marine Corps a byword for military economy (in 1925, and occasionally again, Lejeune astounded Congress by voluntarily returning unspent money—a feat which not only rocked Capitol Hill at the time, but made the legislative paths of future Marine budgeteers smooth for years to come).

Two permanent expeditionary-force posts, Quantico and San Diego. In 1928, General Lejeune got $2,205,000, an enormous amount in those days of large-size dollars, to build a new Quantico complete with brick barracks, officers' apartments, an industrial complex, and its own air station, for which the Navy's Bureau of Aeronautics somehow found itself paying generously. The new facilities alleviated one problem described by Lejeune in his 1924 Annual Report:

Our largest Marine Corps post, situated at Quantico, Va., is confronted with a serious situation in that the small town of Quantico, which is surrounded by the post, is an insanitary place and an abode of bootleggers and other undesirable persons.

Once the new base was in operation in 1929, Smedley Butler, the commanding general, established a *cordon sanitaire* and kept all Quantico town out of bounds until a reluctant campaign of self-improvement ameliorated the worst conditions, whereupon the general lifted his interdict and led the post band on a parade down the main street.

A world-wide system of free correspondence training, the Marine Corps Institute, which afforded Marines and even their dependents, means to advance their education wherever they might be. (The MCI, first such institution in the Armed Services by nearly a quarter of a century, was organized with General Barnett's approval on 2 February 1920, mightily sparked by Smedley Butler and Lieutenant Colonel W. C. Harllee, but it survived and took hold under Lejeune.) The matriculation of one distinguished MCI alumnus is recorded in the following letter:[59]

The Assistant Secretary of the Navy
Washington

2 June 1920

Dear Colonel Harllee:

Many thanks for sending me the textbooks. My daughter and I are going to get busy on them this summer and I am proud to be a student in your university.

Always sincerely yours,

Franklin D. Roosevelt.

A conscious recognition and codification of the traditions of the Corps (formal recognition, in 1921, of scarlet and gold as the official colors of the Corps; formal celebration of the Marine Corps Birthday; official copyright of "The Marines' Hymn" in its final version). The text of the *Marine Corps Manual* article published throughout the Corps every 10th of November, and the instructions for its publication, were written out by Lejeune himself over coffee after breakfast on a dining car during an inspection trip in 1921.[60]

Lejeune's successor as Major General Commandant was Major General Wendell C. Neville, who had been Lejeune's comrade and faithful friend for almost 40 years. Still a stentor, Neville quickly caused the Commandant's office to gain a new nickname: "The Cave of the Winds." But "Buck" Neville's days were numbered. Ill health dogged him, and, a year after his appointment, following a stroke in March 1930, he took to his bed for the last time. On 8 July he died while still in office, and, with his passing, the era of Lejeune truly passed into history.

TWO NEW COMMANDANTS, FULLER AND RUSSELL

General Neville's death confronted the Hoover administration with a most unwelcome problem. This problem could be summed up in six words—what to do about Smedley Butler?

In 1930, Major General Smedley Darlington Butler was not only the senior general in the Marine Corps, but, at the age of 48, the youngest officer ever to become a major general and at least a decade younger than his immediate juniors and competitors for the vacancy as Major General Commandant. His combat record, including two Medals of Honor, was one of the most illustrious in the history of American arms. On the other hand, Butler was personally disliked by both President Hoover and Secretary of the Navy Charles Francis Adams. "Disliked" is perhaps not the word for their feeling toward Butler—to say that he was "obnoxious" to them comes nearer the truth. By a combination of forthrightness and indiscretion, seasoned by an inborn genius for publicity, Smedley Butler had become a nationally controversial figure during the "Roaring Twenties." Almost anything Butler said or did, right or wrong, could be calculated to exacerbate the President and his stiff-necked New England Secretary of the Navy (who chilled an inspection of Quantico by lecturing General Butler on "your damned follies").[61]

To compound the Butler problem and render him *persona non grata* to the Navy was Butler's outspoken and oft-spoken dislike for the Naval Academy and its graduates, especially admirals.

If fire-eating Smedley Butler could be said to have had an antithesis among his fellow generals, Brigadier General Ben H. ("Uncle Ben") Fuller would have been that man, soft in speech, kindly, white-haired, avuncular (60 years old), and a Naval Academy graduate. "Uncle Ben" had served as Assistant to the Commandant during Lejeune's last year and all of Neville's commandancy. At one time, General Fuller had been senior to Butler, but had been passed by for his star during World War I.

President Hoover chose the obvious solution. On 9 July 1930, he elevated General Fuller to the commandancy, thus not only restoring Fuller's earlier seniority but passing over both major generals (Butler and Feland) and two brigadiers (Harry Lee and Russell). Within the next year, Smedley Butler, stormy petrel to the last, retired from the Corps after an attempt by President Hoover to court-martial him for a characteristically outright blast at Mussolini. The charges backfired, and Butler was restored from arrest. He promptly retired to the tune of a searing magazine article, "To Hell with the Admirals!"[62] a valediction which no doubt gratified a lifetime ambition that had been long suppressed, if only partially.

Even with Smedley Butler out of the way, President Hoover had no particular reason to count himself among the many friends of the Marine Corps. Neither had General Douglas MacArthur, Chief of Staff of the Army, to whom, understandably, the Marines represented competition for funds and manpower which the attenuated Army of the 1930s wanted badly.

The 1931 enlisted strength of the Corps was 18,000. For fiscal 1932, the Bureau of the Budget reduced this to 17,500, and, in fiscal 1933 (beginning in July 1932), to 15,343. In December 1932, Mr. Hoover called for a further cutback to 13,600, which, General Fuller asserted, would require closing down Parris Island and virtual disbandment of the already skeletonized expeditionary forces. As the Commandant stated:[63]

The Marine Corps fails to understand why it has been marked for reduction in this manner, since other arms of the service have not been so reduced. It is understood that the Budget estimates do not provide for any reduction in the enlisted strength of either the Army or the Navy. . . .

In his second sentence above, General Fuller had indeed put his finger on the nub of the situation. To place President Hoover's proposal in perspective, the administration's aggregate recommendations for "economy" cuts in military manpower for fiscal years 1931-34 were as follows:

Army: none (0.0 per cent)
Navy: 5.6 per cent
Marines: 24.4 per cent (4,400 officers and men)

While President Hoover (whose memoirs entirely avoid the matter) long afterward denied that his Marine Corps cuts were "directed to abolition of any agency,"[64] it was the informed opinion of Marine Corps Headquarters and of Marine friends in Congress that the President's extreme zeal for intrinsically small fiscal savings at the expense of crippling cuts to the Marine Corps was in fact the administration's prelude to abolition of the Corps, or its transfer into the Army. It was further reported that General MacArthur was strongly urging such a course of action.

The press, the public, and Congress reacted sharply. General Harbord (by then retired and chairman of the board of the Radio Corporation of America) went on the air over a nation-wide hookup to defend the Corps whose 4th Brigade he had led at Belleau Wood. Congressional support was quickly mobilized by two outspoken Representatives, Fiorello H. LaGuardia and Melvin J. Maas. Close behind were the Naval Affairs Chairmen of both houses, Representative Carl Vinson (long a Marine friend) and Senator Frederick Hale. In February 1933, while the White House still staggered under the counterattack, both the House Naval Affairs Committee and the Appropriations Committee voted down the Hoover cut and held the Corps to its existing strength of 15,343. Representative William Augustus Ayres, Chairman of the Naval Appropriations Subcommittee, spoke for Congress when he stated:[65]

We have been approached at every turn regarding this proposal to reduce the enlisted strength of the Marine Corps. I have yet to hear a single advocate of it.

After this excitement, the remainder of General Fuller's commandancy was quiet. In February 1933, when "Uncle Ben" had only a year to serve before mandatory retirement at age 64, Brigadier General Russell was brought to Headquarters as Assistant to the Commandant, and quickly began to make his presence felt by such steps as formation of the Fleet Marine Force, a development which we shall examine separately.

On 28 February 1934, with almost 49 years' service as a Marine, General Fuller retired as 15th Commandant, and Major General John H. Russell succeeded him. Although Russell, at 61, was almost as old on assuming the commandancy as John Harris had been, his brief tour was eventful and fruitful.

The Marine Corps which was entrusted to General Russell was, for the first time in a generation, virtually free (the China forces excepted) from its mission as colonial infantry. As Lejeune had foreseen 15 years earlier, the days of pacification and occupation duty as a Marine Corps staple had come to an end. To the new Major General Commandant this situation presented opportunities and challenges. Unlike his predecessors, Russell had almost the whole Corps, uncommitted, at his disposal.

General Russell's first step was characteristic. Finding Congress at long last amenable, he pushed through in May 1934 perilously overdue legislation to junk the antique seniority system by which all Marine officers (except generals) were promoted, and substitute a selection system modeled on the Navy pattern. This reform, which every Commandant had tried to effect since 1916, was one of General Lejeune's few failures in the legislative arena. Commencing in 1935, Russell's law brought a much-needed officer shake-up of monumental proportions. Deadwood (mainly former NCOs of World War vintage whose capacities in senior grades had proved unequal to their valor in France) was forced out. Officers who survived this attrition found themselves promoted with bewildering speed after years of stagnation. Still others were rearranged in seniority. In a sense, it was Russell's last word over the Neville Board which had overridden his recommendations of 1920.

As the son of a rear admiral (who had been wounded in one of the most desperate cutting-out expeditions of the Civil War), Russell appropriately strengthened the Corps' ties with the Navy, and the number of ships' detachments was increased from 39 to 47 during his tour. More important, as will be seen, was his sponsorship of the Fleet Marine Force.

Another of Russell's major improvements was in the Marine Corps Reserve. Although the Reserve dated from 1916, it played no significant part in World War I and nearly died in the early 1920s as a result of fiscal starvation. Following the Naval Reserve Act of 1925 (which for the first time permitted organized units with pay), training programs were instituted, and units sprang up. This prosperity was short-lived, however, for the depression years of 1929-33 found the Reserve broke again. During the lean years which preceded Russell's appointment, most Reserve units drilled and trained without pay—even bought their own uniforms—and thus loyally saved the Reserve from oblivion.

It was 1935 before General Russell finally got the Marine Corps Reserve on its own feet. That year saw these important developments:

Resumption of drill pay and appropriations to support an organized and volunteer Reserve (line and aviation) which at year's end totaled 9,061 officers and men.

Complete reorganization of the previous top-heavy and unwieldy Reserve organization into 13 battalions in key cities.

Inauguration of the Platoon Leaders' Class, a highly successful system of officer-candidate training for college undergraduates, conducted entirely in summer months, which was destined to provide a steady input of well trained and carefully selected young reserve officers.

Dawn of a Reserve pilot program for Marine Corps aviation, an extra dividend of the Naval Aviation Cadet Act of April 1935. This law, incidentally, created a new Marine rank: aviation cadet.

Aviation, moreover, took an obvious step up in the world when, on 5 June 1935, the Aviation Section was divorced from the Division of Operations and Training, Marine Corps Headquarters. In April of the following year, the Section became the Division of Aviation, and the Officer-in-Charge (Colonel Rowell) was designated Director of Marine Corps Aviation. Whether (in long-term hindsight) the divorce of aviation functions from operations and training of the Corps as a whole made for a better Headquarters could be argued, but the change certainly reflected Marine Corps air-mindedness.

In summary, it may well be said that, if Lejeune made the Corps secure and gave it orientation after the World War, Russell laid the essential foundations for much of its effectiveness in the war which was to come. When, in November 1936, General Russell turned 64 and retired after 42 years in the Corps, he could look back on solid achievement to the last. Characteristically, he wasted no time looking back—during the next ten years he wrote a military column in the daily press and published numerous professional articles.

The new Major General Commandant, Thomas Holcomb, could thank his predecessor for important work well done.

AMPHIBIOUS AWAKENING, 1931–39

Ten years had elapsed since Earl Ellis had completed his "War Portfolio" at Headquarters Marine Corps. Ellis was long in his grave, but his spirit still lived.

At Quantico, where Brigadier General R. C. Berkeley commanded Marine Corps Schools in early 1931, a committee made up of three Marine majors (Charles D. Barrett, Lyle H. Miller, and Pedro A. del Valle) and one naval officer (Lieutenant Walter C. Ansel) was at work on a manual which, though never published, was nonetheless historic. *Marine Corps Landing Operations*, the treatise was entitled: it was the first United States military text specifically devoted to the technique of modern amphibious warfare, and it was to be ready by June 1932.[66]

Meanwhile, there were stirrings elsewhere. In December 1931, a so-called "Floating Battalion" (an infantry battalion and a battery of artillery) embarked aboard the two old battleships *Arkansas* and *Wyoming* for maneuvers in the Caribbean. Within a month, a somewhat similar force, made up of 700 Marines, with a regimental headquarters, took part in the February 1932 Joint Army-Navy Exercise on Oahu—"with Japan actually in mind," remembered General Holland Smith.[67]

> But what a dismal exhibition! I realized that we had a great deal to learn before we approached anything like efficiency in amphibious warfare. The Marines landed in ships' boats which were unsuitable for crossing reefs and riding the surf. It was obvious that our elementary need was more efficient landing craft, a retractable type that could get in and out of the surf. Moreover, we didn't have sufficient boats to get enough men ashore at one time . . . the suppositional enemy would have wiped us out in a few minutes. The Oahu operation revealed our total lack of equipment for such an undertaking, our inadequate training, and the lack of coordination between the assault forces and the simulated naval gunfire and air protection.

But even while the Marines thrashed in Oahu's surf and Navy coxswains refused to beach motor-sailers for fear of scratching the paintwork, the staff and students at Marine Corps Schools were doing basic research which would pave the way for great advances soon to come. Throughout the academic year 1932-33, all hands concentrated on a complete historical analysis of the Dardanelles campaign. Continuing to use the Gallipoli fiasco as a post-mortem specimen, staff and students at Quantico painstakingly dissected the major problem of landing operations into component problems and set out to find means to correct the errors which hindsight and history made only too plain.

Still another noteworthy development of that thoughtful year was Marine Corps Schools Advance Base Problem I—an academic demonstration prepared by Quantico for the Naval War College, in which a team of picked instructors presented the steps necessary for the planning and amphibious assault by United States forces of a real objective. The thing caught on instantly—it was no theorizing—and, from that year on, Quantico's Advance Base Problem Team presented a new problem annually (sample: the recapture of Guam from the Japanese), at first only to the Naval War College, later to the other service schools, too.

Quantico, however, did not have a monopoly on amphibious thinking during 1932-33. On 12 January 1933 the Joint Army and Navy Board produced a set of principles, *Joint Overseas Expeditions.* This work—the only American doctrinal writing on amphibious warfare by any non-Marine agency before 1941—dealt briefly, broadly, and soundly with its subject. Many of the tenets found their way into subsequent doctrine. Moreover, this little pamphlet served as a point of departure for a much more fundamental study soon to come.

On 14 November 1933, at the orders of General Russell, then Acting Commandant, classes at Marine Corps Schools were again discontinued, this time to produce "rules and doctrines covering landing operations." The Joint Board pamphlet was to serve as a guide, though not an inflexible one. In fact, the students, who again formed committees to study various aspects of the landing operation, were directed to adhere to the Joint Board view except when convinced that the Board was wrong and the Marine Corps was right. Since they now had available the unpublished 1931 text, *Marine Corps Landing Operations,* the work moved quickly. Their first draft was completed in January 1934; its title was *Tentative Manual for Landing Operations.*

General Russell's reason for abrupt suspension of classroom work at Quantico was not mere whim. Ever since August 1933 he had been in correspondence with the Chief of Naval Operations on a project dear to his heart (bear in mind that Russell, not easily distracted from an idea, had been plugging away ever since 1916 on the need for systematic derivation of a "General Mission" for the Marine Corps). As Acting Commandant, Russell had made one of the most far-reaching recommendations ever to be put forward regarding the Marine Corps:[68]

. . . that the Marine Corps should have a striking force, well equipped, well armed, and highly trained, working as a unit of the Fleet under the direct orders of the Commander-in-Chief . . . [and] that this force be included in the Fleet organization as an integral part thereof, subject to the orders, for tactical employment, of the Commander-in-Chief U. S. Fleet.

This new force (which would replace the East and West Coast Expeditionary Forces), General Russell said should be called either the "Fleet Base Defense Force" or more simply, the "Fleet Marine Force." Fortunately, the Chief of Naval Operations plumped for the latter; and so the FMF was born.

The troops which General Russell had immediately at hand for the new Fleet Marine Force, though more than any predecessor had had for years, were few enough. Moreover, the Cuban revolution in 1933 momentarily drained away officers and men whom Russell had earmarked for the FMF.

The 7th Regiment, shaken together in September 1933 from East Coast Marine barracks and station ships for service in Cuba (where it never had to land), was the last Marine expeditionary regiment ever to be assembled in the time-honored way and packed aboard a battleship (*Wyoming*) and a transport (*Antares*). Henceforth, it would be the Fleet Marine Force.

In approving General Russell's brain child, the Chief of Naval Operations asked him to draw up a Navy Department General Order covering the "command and administrative relations" between the Fleet and the Fleet Marine Force. General Order 241, issued by the Secretary of the Navy on 7 December 1933, exactly eight years before Pearl Harbor, was the result—a charter for the Fleet Marine Force:

1. The Force of Marines maintained by the Major General Commandant in a state of readiness for operations with the Fleet is hereby designated as Fleet Marine Force (F.M.F.), and as such shall constitute a part of the organization of the United States Fleet and be included in the operating force plan for each fiscal year.

2. The Fleet Marine Force shall consist of such units as may be designated by the Major General Commandant and shall be maintained at such strength as is warranted by the general personnel situation of the Marine Corps.

3. The Fleet Marine Force shall be available to the Commander-in-Chief for operations with the Fleet or for exercises either afloat or ashore in connection with Fleet problems. The Commander-in-Chief shall make timely recommendations to the Chief of Naval Operations regarding such service in order that the necessary arrangements may be made.

4. The Commander-in-Chief shall exercise command of the Fleet Marine Force when embarked on board vessels of the Fleet or when engaged in Fleet exercises, either afloat or ashore. When otherwise engaged, command shall be directed by the Major General Commandant.

5. The Major General Commandant shall detail the Commanding General of the Fleet Marine Force and maintain an appropriate staff for him.

6. The Commanding General, Fleet Marine Force, shall report by letter to the Commander-in-Chief, United States Fleet, for duty in connection with the employment of the Fleet Marine Force. At least once each year, and at such times as may be considered desirable by the Commander-in-Chief, the Commanding General, Fleet Marine Force, with appropriate members of his staff shall be ordered to report to the Commander-in-Chief for conference.

Russell's order, with its emphasis on readiness, its clear delineation of command lines, and its careful reservation to the Major General Commandant of necessary command prerogatives, was a model. Marine Corps Order 66, General Russell's implementing order, followed next day. Between the two, the FMF's foundations were well laid. Five days later, the Marine Corps Expeditionary Force Staff became "Headquarters, F.M.F.," and on 11 January 1934 the 7th Regiment, last vestige of the old order, became the harbinger of the new when its battalions were designated as units of the Fleet Marine Force.

While Headquarters Marine Corps was shaping the Fleet Marine Force, the *Tentative Manual for Landing Operations* was being hastily mimeographed at Quantico and assembled in the canvas-backed official binders of the day. Taking Gallipoli both as a horrible example and as a point of departure, this "pioneer work of the most daring and imaginative sort," as a pair of historians have described it,[69] set forth:

A philosophy of amphibious command relations.

A modern concept and technique for a controlled ship-to-shore movement.

Notions of ship-to-shore communications.

Doctrines for air and naval gunfire support.

Fundamentals of embarkation and combat loading of transports.

Fundamentals of shore party organization.

As an adjunct to the Schools and to the Fleet Marine Force, still another agency was needed: one which could begin systematic work on the materiel problems of amphibious warfare. In late 1933 the Marine Corps Equipment Board was established at Quantico, the first U. S. military body whose efforts were devoted to the test and development of materiel for landing operations and expeditionary service. Only five years later, the Equipment Board was destined to justify itself many times over when its members decided to initiate military trials of an ungainly swamp-craft, the Roebling "Alligator," which, under its military title of amphibian tractor (LVT) would revolutionize the science of beach assault.

Thus, by the beginning of 1934 the Marine Corps had in being a school and a viable doctrine for amphibious warfare; a materiel development agency for the same purpose; and field forces which were to test both ideas and hardware many times over during the years ahead.

On 19 February 1934, a primitive battalion landing team from San Diego became the very first FMF unit to engage in U. S. Fleet maneuvers, and, from that time forward, the Fleet Marine Force took part in each annual Fleet Problem, conducting landings at San Clemente (a rock-bound island southwest of San Pedro, California), in the Hawaiian Islands, and at Midway Atoll (which from 1904 to 1908 had been garrisoned by one officer and 20 Marines—a desolate station which the recruiters of the day often forgot to mention).

In the Atlantic, commencing with Fleet Landing Exercise 1 (19 January— 13 March 1935), annual landing exercises were held at Culebra and Vieques.

Naval gunfire support, close air support, ship-to-shore communications, odd-looking landing craft, night landings, attempts at reef-crossing, all had their part as Marines and Navy explored the new medium of warfare. Briefly, in 1936 and 1938, Army units (30th and 18th Infantry) joined in. Unfortunately, when invited to do so again in 1939, General George C. Marshall, Army Chief of Staff, decided that the thing was "impracticable,"[70] and the Army washed its hands of landing exercises until 1941. Even then, according to Admiral King, "Marshall did not seem particularly cordial to the suggestion."[71]

During the years from 1935 to 1941 a procession of experimental landing craft underwent trials at Quantico, Cape May, Norfolk, and Culebra. These included assault boats of Cape Cod dory design, rubber rafts, ramped self-propelled tank lighters and artillery lighters, and, from 1936 on, a fast transport, the World War I four-pipe destroyer *Manley* eviscerated of one fireroom so as to be able to carry 120 Marines. Most important of all, by 1940 there came the first amphibian tractors (including one which bellied down magnificently in mud flats below Quantico, stranding a load of senior officers to the delight of irreverent junior officers and enlisted men). Although Marine interest in amphibian vehicles was anything but new, the LVT had entered the scene as a result of a *Life* magazine article which appeared just as General Little, commander of the Fleet Marine Force, was working out plans for the 1937 Hawaiian landing exercises with Rear Admiral E. C. Kalbfus. This article, describing the Roebling vehicle, caught the admiral's eye, and he in turn showed it to General Little. Recognizing a good thing, the general sent the clipping to HQMC and the Equipment Board, and the amphibian tractor eventually resulted.[72]

Meanwhile, in 1939 there began a memorable tug-of-war between Andrew Jackson Higgins, genius boatbuilder and all-around expediter from New Orleans, and the hierarchy of the Navy's Bureau of Ships, about who could design the best landing craft. Higgins clearly had the better of them in everything but rank. Even so he (and his enthusiastic Marine backers, notably including Brigadier General Holland Smith) very nearly lost out in face of the Bureau's stubborn preference for its own designs. The last word came with some asperity in 1942 from Senator Harry S. Truman's War Investigating Committee:[73]

It is clear that the Bureau of Ships, for reasons known only to itself, stubbornly persisted for over five years in clinging to an unseaworthy tank lighter design of its own. . . . The Bureau's action has caused not only a waste of time but has caused the needless expenditure of over $7,000,000 for a total of 225 Bureau lighters which do not meet the needs of the Armed Forces.

The rest is history. Higgins-designed landing craft (originally built in response to the Marine Corps Equipment Board, which, though stone-broke, had been in touch with Higgins since 1934) hit every beach from Guadalcanal to Normandy.

While the minuscule Fleet Marine Force was learning its lessons and the impecunious Equipment Board was window-shopping for boats, the Schools were hewing out doctrine. In 1938, the thoroughly refined *Tentative Landing Operations Manual* was adopted officially by the Navy under title of *Landing Operations Doctrine, U. S. Navy (FTP 167)*. In 1941, more than seven years after Marine Corps Schools had prepared it, the very same text (even with the original USMC illustrations still in it, as General Marshall wrote in the promulgating note), appeared within U. S. Army covers, as *Army Field Manual 31-5, Landing Operations on Hostile Shores*. This was the first publication ever issued by the Army on amphibious warfare. Indeed, *Army Field Service Regulations* of 1939 made no mention whatever of amphibious operations, while the somewhat hastily revised edition of May 1941 simply murmured: ". . . doctrines pertaining to . . . landing operations on hostile shores are discussed in other manuals," of which, unhappily, there were not yet any in existence.

GIRDING FOR WAR

On 1 September 1939, German *Panzer* units, supported by Stuka dive-bombers, swirled eastward into Poland; two days later Prime Minister Neville Chamberlain broadcast to the world that Hitler had refused England's final ultimatum. World War II had commenced.

On 3 September 1939, the strength of the Marine Corps (to be known within less than a decade and thenceforward as "the old Marine Corps") was 19,701 officers and enlisted men. The Corps was well disciplined, thoroughly trained, and professionally progressive, and its officers, who had been sifted since 1934 by General Russell's selection system, were generally capable. Moreover, the golden harvest of high-caliber junior officers recruited from top graduates of civilian colleges since 1935 gave the Corps a superb base for expansion of its officer corps. The new Major General Commandant, Thomas Holcomb, who had succeeded General Russell in 1936, was vigorous, practical, and highly thought of personally not only within the Corps, but, quite as important, throughout the Navy Department and in the White House. As one of Lejeune's bright young captains of 1916, "Tommy" Holcomb had won the friendship of Assistant Secretary of the Navy Franklin Roosevelt, and in later years President Roosevelt, recalling his early stewardship over Marine Corps affairs, sometimes would open a remark to General Holcomb with the phrase, "We Marines."

A week after Hitler marched, the President proclaimed a state of limited national emergency, and, at the same time, increased the strength of the Navy to 191,000 and the Marine Corps to 25,000. This increase was received with mixed feelings, since many officers and NCOs felt that it would dilute the quality of the Corps inacceptably. For General Holcomb it represented the knock of opportunity.

During the years after 1937, when isolationism ran rampant and defense —not offense—was good politics, the Marine Corps, offensive arm par excellence, found it difficult to share in the increasingly liberal naval appropriations of the period. Admiral William D. Leahy, the Chief of Naval Operations, told Holcomb that the Marines should think up some way to make themselves look defensive. General Holcomb, mindful of Leahy's big naval construction program, shot back, "If you can convince Congress that a battleship is a defensive weapon, I ought to be able to do it with Marines."

With President Roosevelt's declaration of limited emergency, Holcomb's time came. He walked into Admiral Leahy's office with a plan for modest expansion of the two Marine brigades at Quantico and San Diego, and for seven large new units for advance base service, to be called *defense* battalions. The admiral's ordinarily forbidding countenance dissolved into a grin. "Wonderful," he replied, "That's what I call real war planning."[74]

In the strategic context of 1939, the defense battalion program which had been contrived by General Holcomb and Colonel C. D. Barrett, long one of the Corps' most imaginative thinkers, made excellent military sense in addition to being first-rate politics. These units, of which there were eventually to be 19, were simply up-to-date versions of the technical regiment in the old Advance Base Force: three antiaircraft gun batteries (with 3-inch guns), three seacoast batteries (Navy 5-inchers on the 1914 advance base platforms), ground and antiaircraft machine gun batteries for beach and airfield defense, and a team of artificers, ordnancemen, and such other talent as required to make the outfit self-sufficient on a coral atoll. Every one of its thousand-odd specialists carried his rifle and was ready to fight as infantry. This remarkable concentration of firepower, which had zero tactical mobility but could be flung across an ocean on 48 hours' notice, perennially amazed onlookers by its compactness. Strategically, the battalions were to pick up exactly where the Advance Base Force left off two decades earlier. Since in 1939 the United States faced a war to control two oceans with a one-ocean navy and not even enough forward bases for that, the defense battalions afforded a logical means to complement the Fleet in holding the springboards for ultimate offensive operations while denying them, for the time being, to the enemy.

With the initial 1939 expansion came the first reservists, 114 junior officers, the first dividends of the Platoon Leaders' Class, who volunteered for mobilization. Within a year, on 15 October 1940, general mobilization orders followed for the entire Organized Marine Reserve—236 officers and 5,009 enlisted men. Despite local pride and misgivings in the various "home-town" battalions, General Holcomb disbanded each as it arrived at the mobilization point; from there on, the mobilized reservists were just individual Marine replacements headed for the regular units of the Corps. The decision, a hard one, was important, for it proved from the start that there was no room in the Corps for more than one kind of Marine. Once mobilization was complete, General Holcomb directed that the "R" be dropped from reservists' designations. As far as he was concerned, all hands were "USMC."

In the fall of 1940, as the Reserves were called to the colors, the 1st Marine Brigade left Quantico for Guantanamo Bay. Nobody realized it then, but the FMF would never again return to base in Quantico, save briefly the next summer. Like Philadelphia, Quantico had had its day as an expeditionary base. Unlike Philadelphia, however, the Potomac River base had a long future ahead as the home of the Schools, intellectual power plant of the Corps.

In the West Indies, the 1st Brigade trained and trained. On 1 February 1941, while at sea, en route to Fleet Landing Exercise 7 (FLEX-7) at Culebra, the brigade, mightily strengthened by another infantry regiment (the 7th Marines, organized on 1 January 1941), became the 1st Marine Division. "Howling Mad" Smith was in command. On the same day, out west, the 2d Marine Brigade became the 2d Marine Division. General Barnett's vision of an entire Marine division had become reality 23 years later. (Amusingly, the birth of the divisions required the blessing of the Judge Advocate General of the Navy—someone demanded that he search the statutes to be sure it was legal for Marines to have an outfit as big as a division; he did; it was.)

After FLEX-7, in May 1941, the 1st Division went to Parris Island and, momentarily, to Quantico. On 1 March 1941, the third of the division's infantry regiments, the 1st Marines, had been formed in Cuba. Meanwhile, on the West Coast, the 8th and 2d Marines (in that order) had come to life again to join the 6th Regiment in the 2d Division. On rugged San Clemente, defense battalions sweated their guns into position while units of the 2d Division simulated an attacking force. Ashore, led on foot by their hefty regimental commander, the 8th Marines went on a two-week hike reminiscent of Smedley Butler's marches with the Quantico Marines.

During the winter maneuvers of 1941 at Culebra, something new was added when two infantry battalions of the Army's 1st Division were given their first amphibious lessons. Later that year, in June, the First Joint Training Force was formed, consisting of the 1st Marine Division and 1st Marine Air Group (trainers) and the 1st Infantry Division (trainees). All troops in JTF-1 were commanded by Major General H. M. Smith and a joint staff; once trained, the force was intended to become a two-division expeditionary corps for the expanding Atlantic Fleet. Extensive maneuvers (even including the newly organized Marine parachutists) took place in the summer of 1941 at Onslow Beach, North Carolina (adjacent to the Marine Barracks, New River, which had been selected in mid-1940 as the new East Coast expeditionary base). Then the joint training force became Amphibious Corps Atlantic Fleet (ACAF). Its staff, many of whom were destined to follow the fortunes of General Smith throughout the war to come, included some of the finest amphibious talent in the Armed Forces. Overlooked at the time, and since by military historians, was the fact that this staff, under a Marine Corps commander, was very likely the first formally organized joint staff in the history of American arms. Two of the "Gs" (assistant chiefs of staff) were Army, while naval officers filled billets on the special staff, and both Army and Navy assistants were distributed through the entire organization. That such professional cross-fertilization often proved an eye opener to those involved may be judged by the following report later sent to the War Department by one of the Army colonels assigned to the joint staff:[75]

I am of the opinion that the average Naval officer has no conception of amphibious warfare. His idea being to lay offshore, slap a brigade of Marines on the beach, and impatiently await their return aboard ship. During recent maneuvers, I was surprised to find out that in only rare instances, a Naval officer of field grade observed land operations. I am positive the average Naval officer has no conception of land operations, nor of the training or equipment necessary for such operations.

Following the pattern set by JTF-1, the 2d Marine Division on the West

Coast was similarly formed into a corps—Amphibious Corps Pacific Fleet (ACPF)—into which was absorbed for initial training the Army's 3d Infantry Division. With the 9th Infantry Division, subsequently trained by the 1st Marine Division, the 1st and 3d Infantry Divisions were the first three Army divisions ever to receive amphibious training. They also comprised the U. S. assault landing force for the North African landings in 1942. In addition to these three divisions, Marines were later to provide amphibious training for four more from the Army, the 7th, 77th, 81st, and 96th. Thus, out of the Army's eventual 28 amphibiously trained divisions in World War II, seven learned their business from Marines.

The high-pressure expansion of the Corps was reflected in mounting gains in strength. By mid-1940 there were 26,568 officers and men in uniform. A year later there were 53,886. By December 1941 the Marine Corps numbered 70,425, which was within 4,000 of its previous all-time peak in World War I. Most of these increases went to the FMF, at least after Franklin Roosevelt's 1941 chit to Secretary of the Navy Frank Knox, which read:[76]

I am still concerned over the widespread scattering of the Marines into small groups in hundreds of places. I think Tommy Holcomb ought to make a No. 1 priority effort from now on to build up his Expeditionary Force.

F.D.R.

With the build-up of the "Expeditionary Force" came enlargement of the Marine Corps' physical plant. On the East Coast, as we have seen, the New River area, later to become Camp Lejeune, was selected as the main base for expeditionary ground forces and was first occupied at "Tent Camp 1," a foreboding name to its alumni, in September 1941. Nearby, along the Neuse River, construction gangs hewed, dredged, and filled on an airbase complex, Cherry Point, the first new Marine Corps airfield in the continental United States since Quantico (1922). On 1 December 1941 the still half-finished base was designated a Marine Corps Air Station and opened for business under command of Lieutenant Colonel Thomas J. Cushman.

Down the coast, Parris Island strained at the seams with a stream of recruits who were habitually greeted by earlier arrivals with the ominous chorus of "You'll be sorry!" So they were at first, but afterward most were prouder of it than of any other achievement in their lives. To seaward of "P.I.," on Hilton Head (where Marines had landed in 1861) a succession of defense battalions (3d, 4th, and 5th) put in as rugged field duty at Camp McDougal as ever they would in Iceland or the far Pacific. In August 1940, Parris Island was nearly blown and washed away by a 100-knot hurricane and tidal wave, but recruit training never slackened; Quantico took over as a temporary boot camp, and Parris Island emerged from its ruins, tougher than ever. (When the rifle range reopened at Parris Island, a veteran shooter of some standing, Thomas Holcomb, fired the first round at 200 yards, offhand; it was a pinwheel 5.)

Outside San Diego, on the arid, cactus-spiked flats of Kearny Mesa, where the 2d Brigade had conducted field training since 1934, carpenters kicked aside the rattlesnakes to build temporary barracks and messhalls at what was first named Camp Holcomb, but, in June 1940, redesignated Camp Elliott. On Oahu the disused airstrip at Ewa Mooring Mast (so called because it had been intended as a Navy dirigible base) received its first airplanes from the 2d Marine Air Group which, in January 1941, was deployed forward from San Diego.

In still another field the Marine Corps made its way. Beginning in the summer of 1940, after the fall of France, President Roosevelt began the practice of holding informal meetings, usually every week, with General Marshall, the Army Chief of Staff, Admiral Harold Stark, Chief of Naval Operations, and General Holcomb, representing the Marine Corps. From this informal group, as well as from the more formal, less frequent meetings of the Joint Army-Navy Board, germinated the Joint Chiefs of Staff.[77]

"WE'RE SHOVING RIGHT OFF AGAIN ..."

As the storm clouds deepened, units of the Fleet Marine Force, stormy petrels as ever, headed beyond the seas.

On 31 May 1940, advance elements of the 3d Defense Battalion landed at Midway Atoll and began construction of the defenses which helped to turn back the Japanese almost exactly two years later. In March 1941, Palmyra and Johnston Islands, lonely specks of coral southwest of the Hawaiian group, were occupied by detachments of the 1st Defense Battalion, another of whose detachments in August 1941 commenced a race against time and the Japanese to fortify Wake. After landing on 18 March 1941 at Pago Pago, American Samoa, a hybrid defense battalion, the 7th, installed old Navy 6-inch pedestal guns and ships' 3-inch antiaircraft guns while the Marine-trained Fita-Fita Guard (and, after its organization in August 1941, the 1st Samoan Battalion, Marine Corps Reserve) provided infantry support.[78] Though nobody took time to reflect on the fact, this was the first deployment of the FMF into the southern hemisphere. Marine Barracks complements at

Subic Bay, Luzon, and Dutch Harbor, Alaska, also mounted and manned naval guns in addition to their ordinary security duties.

In January 1941, the 4th Defense Battalion moved from Parris Island to garrison and defend Guantanamo Bay. Within four months, the newly organized 1st Marine Division, reinforced by a regiment from the 2d Division, was alerted for expeditionary service in the Atlantic. Britain, with her back to the wall, asked the United States in February 1941 to assume responsibility for the defense of the Azores. The Army, hamstrung by a Congressional prohibition on sending draftees overseas, reported that it could not provide any troops for this purpose until the following September at the earliest. Therefore, President Roosevelt directed that a force of Marines be employed.

As senior regiment in the 2d Division, the 6th Marines were loaded aboard transports on 31 May and shipped out from San Diego for Charleston Navy Yard, thence to join the 1st Division. While the "Pogey-Bait 6th" was coasting down the long west side of Central America, the international situation flip-flopped. Due to the failure of Hitler's negotiations with his fellow dictator, Francisco Franco, danger to the Azores slackened. But Iceland, strategic key to the North Atlantic, remained in mortal peril, as both Winston Churchill (whose troops had been there since May 1940) and the Icelanders themselves realized. With British prompting, Iceland asked the United States for help.

On 10 June, five days before the 6th Regiment was to reach Charleston, it was decided that a provisional brigade, composed of the 6th Marines and 5th Defense Battalion, then at Parris Island, should be sent to Iceland. Between 15 and 22 June the brigade shook itself together at Charleston Navy Yard and loaded winter gear. On the latter date it sailed and on 7 July it arrived in Reykjavik. The rapidity of this movement, combined with short-notice inclusion among the transports of a number of chartered merchant-men sailing under "flags of convenience," afforded embarked Marines experiences destined to make the voyage long remembered, as witness this account by one officer:[79]

Dog-tired from loading the last of several ships we tumbled aboard late in the evening prior to sailing for Iceland. We were half-awakened the following morning by the irregular word being passed: "Now hear this, all the ship's officers, it is seven a.m. Get-up! Get-up!"

This somewhat prepared us for the still unforgettable word passed as we left Charleston and turned to port, heeling to starboard, to set course for Argentia, Newfoundland, viz: "Now hear this, all passengers on the weather deck—lay over to the port side on the double, hang onto the rails, and stay there! *The ship is turning over!*"

The newly appointed chief engineer was experiencing ballasting difficulties in the open ocean. In the excitement occasioned, the *Orizaba* dipped the starboard rails, then recovered, but not until the inexperienced chief engineer had flushed the fresh water lines with diesel oil. The only fresh water thereafter consisted of the dwindling supplies from individual canteens, diligently refilled at Argentia by all.

In any event, the 1st Provisional Marine Brigade's arrival probably tipped the scales and saved Iceland—an example of what a small but immediately ready force can accomplish. There was no combat for the brigade except one in the arena of inter-Service command relations. The original directive for occupation of Iceland provided that United States forces there would be commanded by the senior officer present, whether Marine, Army, or Navy. As the time approached for Army units to go, General Marshall quietly prepared a draft executive order (without letting the Commandant of the Marine Corps know about it) by which the President would forthwith transfer the Marine brigade in Iceland to the command of the U. S. Army. On 3 September, General Marshall presented his draft to the White House. Next day, for the first time, General Holcomb found out what was afoot and (in his own words, "sore as a goat"[80]) wrote a strong protest to Marshall: after all, Iceland was a Fleet base, maintained for naval purposes and sustained by the Atlantic Fleet. Ignoring Holcomb's letter, Marshall addressed an informal reply instead to the Chief of Naval Operations, Admiral Stark. The admiral, good-hearted and anxious to avoid a row with General Marshall, even at the cost of a few Marine prerogatives, acceded without a fight, and, with the Secretary of the Navy's acquiescence, President Roosevelt signed General Marshall's executive order on 22 September. A week later, Brigadier General Marston, commanding the 1st Provisional Marine Brigade, reported for duty to the senior Army officer in Iceland, a newly arrived (and promoted) major general. The latter then published a general order announcing that he had assumed command of the Marine Corps. The brigade remained under the War Department until 8 March 1942, and Hitler never got to Iceland.

THE AGE OF THOMASON

Being a Marine, I have tried to set forth simple tales without comment. It is unnecessary to write what I think of my own people, nor would it be, perhaps, in the best taste. . . .[81]

The writer of the foregoing sentence was Captain John W. Thomason, Jr., a regular Marine officer from 1917 to 1944 who enjoyed the distinction, un-

A self-portrait of John W. Thomason, Jr., then a captain, holding office hours on a recalcitrant private in Peitaiho, North China, in 1932. The sergeant of the guard is the prosecuting witness. This drawing has never before been published.

usual for a man of his calling, of being also one of America's foremost illustrators and one of the most pungent writers of his period. Because he was first and foremost a Marine, not a civilian, he mostly drew and described U. S. Marines. In so doing, he gave to American art and letters the ways, speech, and *esprit* of the United States Marine Corps just as Frederic Remington, a generation earlier, portrayed and thus perpetuated the Indian-fighting regular Army of the frontier. Thomason, it could well be said, in many ways identified Marines to the public of his day, and even to themselves.

For most Marines and for many others of the 1920s and 1930s, the years between World War I and Pearl Harbor were the age of John Thomason, an era of Marine Corps history, customs, habits, and uniforms, destined to be recorded and made vivid through the eye and pen of the Corps' greatest chronicler.

The externals of John Thomason's Marine Corps were little changed from those of the previous 30 years. Uniforms after the World War remained similar to those worn before. Khaki and greens were considered to be, and were worn as, field uniforms; uniform regulations asserted that blues were a normal duty uniform. For dirty work—motor transport, shipping and receiving, and such—there were shapeless blue dungaree overalls. Navy-type canvas leggings were worn over trousers tightly rolled; it was an art of the seasoned Marine to get into his leggings before a parade or inspection without so much as a wrinkle over the kneecap. In 1928, the system of uniforms sustained one shock: the standing-collar blouse was abolished for service uniforms, and roll-collar greens and khaki were substituted.

Nine years later, an even greater jolt hit the Corps, when a serious proposal was advanced to abolish the prized standing-collar blue blouse and substitute a high-school cadet model with white shirt and roll collar. This move gained such momentum (inside Marine Corps Headquarters) that General Holcomb thought it advisable to poll the entire officer corps on the question. The results of this poll: standing collar, 11 to 1.

Another result: in the Major General Commandant's morning mail, an official letter, postmarked Quantico, in due form and technically correct save for one vital omission, the identity of the sender. Subject: comments on sample models of proposed roll-collar blues (then on display at Quantico).

1. It is recommended that the sample roll-collar blue uniforms be returned to the Quartermaster Depot of Supplies, Philadelphia, and that the dummies be sent to Headquarters Marine Corps for duty.[82]

There were, of course, a few other uniform changes: all leather was standardized in 1935 in dark-brown cordovan color; the garrison cap came into use (originally restricted to aviation units, it later became the FMF service headgear); and, precursors of war, field shoes and green utility clothing became regulation, dating, respectively, from 1940 and late 1941.

Shortly after the end of World War I, in 1919, displaying on its ribbon the scarlet and gold colors of the Corps, the Marine Corps Expeditionary Medal was adopted to recognize Marine landings or shore operations for which no other campaign medal was authorized.

The weapons of the Corps were, until the late 1930s, essentially those of the World War. Foremost among these was the '03 rifle, the perennial Springfield, issued to each Marine at boot camp, to live and die with him throughout the Corps. But even the Springfield faced retirement in 1941, when, after two years of stringent and somewhat disapproving trials, the Marine Corps (with some prodding from President Roosevelt) concluded that the new Garand semiautomatic rifle, the M1, was, as finally modified by the Army to overcome defects disclosed in Marine Corps trials, suitable for Marines. Naturally, as the Fleet Marine Force became a force of combined arms, so the weapons and equipment of the Marine Corps branched out. In came the first modern tanks, little turretless four-tonners. (General Holland Smith later remarked that the tanks' armor was so thin you could dent it with a claw hammer.) Army 75-mm. pack howitzers, originally designed for mountain warfare, became the standard light artillery of the Marine Corps because of the ease with which the squat little piece could be broken down into manageable loads for embarkation and landing. With the defense battalions came Navy 5-inch guns, Army 3-inch AA guns, and antiaircraft searchlights and sound locators. Motor transport burgeoned: in 1937 the highest numbered truck in the Corps was #274 in a consecutive series since World War I; within seven years the series would reach five figures.

The Marines in the ranks (superbly portrayed in one of John Thomason's best stories, "The Marine and the Emerald Sweeps") were largely a long-service, competent, experienced group led by senior NCOs who frequently had had service in World War I or, in many cases, as Guardia or Gendarmerie officers in the Caribbean. Two familiar types were the so-called "Polish gunnery sergeants"—a broken-English breed mainly recruited from durable Central European immigrants with soldiering experience in the old country—and the enlisted Naval Aviation Pilots, known colloquially as "NAPs." The latter, both in pay and qualifications the elite enlisted men of Marine aviation, were originally given wings without going through Pensacola; later they got the same flight training as officer pilots and served as a means to augment the number of Marine pilots (there were 100 in 1929) without exceeding the stringent officer personnel ceilings of the 1920s.

The enlisted rank structure of the Corps, though not the rank titles, was assimilated to that of the Army in 1922 as a result of legislation which provided seven pay grades for both Services. General Lejeune thereupon established the following pay grades and ranks:

		Per month
1st Grade:	Sergeant major; quartermaster sergeant	$74
2d Grade:	First sergeant; gunnery sergeant	$53
3d Grade:	Staff sergeant (added in 1923)	$45
4th Grade:	Sergeant	$45
5th Grade:	Corporal	$37
6th Grade:	Private first class	$35
7th Grade:	Private; drummer; trumpeter	$30 or $21

This structure assumed many characteristics of the Christmas tree as the weapons and organization of the Corps became more complex, thus necessitating more specialists for whom additional families of titles were required. Among the ratings introduced (or reintroduced) up to World War II were: master technical sergeant, drum major, paymaster sergeant; technical sergeant, supply sergeant; platoon sergeant; chief cook; field cook, field music corporal; field music (in place of drummer and trumpeter). To reward technical skills not requiring the leadership qualities of noncommissioned rank, nonrated specialists were given extra "specialist pay" without promotion, while any enlisted Marine could increase his monthly pay by $3 to $5 through qualifying as sharpshooter or expert rifleman, a mighty incentive to proficiency in arms which survived the war only to fall a casualty to the administrative turmoil produced by unification.

Until General Russell pushed through the selection system, officer promotion remained slow; periods of 12 to 15 years' service as a lieutenant were not uncommon. A Naval Academy jibe of the early 1930s was the farewell given by a new ensign to a classmate who elected the Marine Corps, "I'll see you in 20 years when we're both captains." Yet, the standing of the Corps at Annapolis increased. In 1890, when Lejeune was commissioned, the Naval Academy academic board recommended against his assignment to the Marine Corps because, in his words, "I stood too high in the class to be assigned to the Marine Corps."[83] For years thereafter, when Academy graduates were allowed to enter the Corps, they came mostly from the low men in each class; moreover, until 1916, when finally suppressed by Josephus Daniels, it was a Service custom that failing or delinquent midshipmen might be offered Marine commissions after discharge from the Academy. In the 1920s and early 1930s, any qualified midshipman who volunteered for the Marine Corps was permitted, within established quotas, to be commissioned without regard to class standing. By the late 1930s, the number of outstanding Annapolis graduates who were electing the Marine Corps so alarmed the naval authorities that a rule was adopted whereby Marine appointments from Annapolis had to be filled in a proportionate distribution from top, bottom, and middle of the group. This, at length, was an arithmetically fair procedure, but it would never have been thought of had not the Marine Corps asserted so strong an appeal.

Another testimonial to Marine quality had quietly been accorded in 1929, when, for President Hoover's summer camp, newly established at Rapidan, Virginia, the Marine Corps was directed to provide the guard detachment—a task which was logically assumed by the barracks at Eighth and Eye. Six years later, when President Roosevelt opened his "little White House" at Warm Springs, Georgia, he called for a Marine guard, which, like the Rapidan detachment, came from Eighth and Eye.

Following World War I, for the first time in Marine Corps history there were organized welfare and morale activities (although "morale" was considered a whining sort of word throughout a Corps which thought in terms of *esprit*). In 1927, a Marine Corps football team, "The Big Team," won a national championship by defeating an all-Army team, 14-0, thus inaugurating a decade of big (and enormously successful) athletics which many thought had some beneficial effect on recruiting and on *esprit,* but which also tended to fix in segments of the public mind the somewhat misfocused image of the typical Marine as a man with a size 17 collar and a size 5 hat. A more directly beneficial (and lasting) addition to the Corps was the Marine Corps Institute, already mentioned, by which thousands of Marines completed or improved their education—a selling point which became increasingly important as the general caliber of recruits progressively improved after the post-World War slump. Another welcome addition to the life of the enlisted Marine was the *Leatherneck,* a Marines' magazine, which was founded as a post newspaper in Quantico in November 1917. It was converted to its later format in 1925, and is still going strong.

On 17 May 1922, Captain William H. Santelmann, the Leader of the Marine Band (and father of a future leader destined to be as highly respected as his father), began projecting the Marine Corps to the country in still another way, when a detail of seven Marine Band musicians began weekly radio broadcasts over Station NOF, the pioneer broadcasting station operated experimentally as an adjunct to the Naval Research Laboratory at Bellevue, in the District of Columbia. These were the first regular musical programs to be broadcast by radio anywhere in the United States.

Headquarters Marine Corps, though not quite the family affair of earlier years, was still small and informal during the 1920s and 1930s. Located in part of one wing of "Main Navy," at 19th Street and Constitution Avenue (then B Street, N.W.), the headquarters retained many features of older times. One officer (Brigadier General H. C. Haines) served as Adjutant and Inspector for 14 years (1920-34); another (Brigadier General George C. Richards) was Paymaster for 27 years ending in 1936. Backbone of the minute civilian force, headed by Chief Clerk Noble J. Wilson (who was to remain on the job until 1958) were nine devoted former Marinettes of the World War who stayed on to become secretaries, and in some cases supervisors, for years to come. Even redesignation in 1939 of the Division of Operations and Training as Division of Plans and Policies (promptly dubbed "Pots and Pans") didn't change much. But 1941, which brought so many other alterations to an expanding Corps, also lifted Headquarters out of Main Navy onto a Virginia hilltop beside Arlington Cemetery. For the first time since July 1800, Marine Corps Headquarters, now in the new Arlington Annex of the Navy Department, was located outside the District of Columbia. From this Headquarters, the Marine Corps was destined to fight not only two major wars, but also a continuing struggle at home for its survival as a useful fighting force.

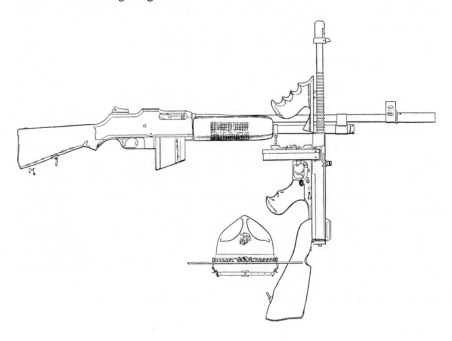

7 ... IN MANY A STRIFE *1941-1944*

No-one can say that the Marines have ever
failed to do their duty in handsome fashion.
—MAJOR GENERAL JOHNSON HAGOOD, USA

A*FTER A BRIGHT* clear daybreak, a Japanese task force consisting of six carriers, two battleships, and three cruisers, escorted by nine destroyers, headed into the wind 230 miles north of Oahu. HIJMS *Akagi*, flagship, flew the "Z" signal originally made by Admiral Togo in 1905, as he led his fleet against the Russians in Tsu-Shima Strait:

The rise or fall of the Empire depends upon this battle. . . .

The date was 7 December 1941, the hour 0600.

One minute later the carriers began to launch aircraft: 49 horizontal bombers, 40 torpedo planes, 51 dive bombers, 36 fighters. An hour later, 171 more bombers and fighters followed in a second wave.

At Pearl Harbor Navy Yard, destination of the Japanese planes, lay eight United States battleships, eight cruisers, and an assortment of smaller ships (including the oldest destroyer in the Navy, USS *Allen*, a 1916 veteran antedating even the venerable flush-decked four-pipers). Ashore, in addition to Marine Air Group 21 (MAG-21) at Ewa and the Marine Barracks, there was an assortment of Marine units: 3d Defense Battalion; 4th Defense Battalion (which had arrived from Cuba just six days earlier); rear echelon of the 1st Defense Battalion, most of whose units were at Wake, Johnston and Palmyra; and the 2d Engineer Battalion. The engineers, borrowed from the 2d Division, were hacking a staging area out of canefields beside Salt Lake, overlooking the Navy Yard; in later years "Salt Lake Camp" would be familiar to almost every Marine in the Pacific as Camp Catlin.

Of course none of the Marines at Pearl Harbor that morning realized that the minutes after 0600 were the passing moments of a death watch—the death watch of the prewar United States Fleet and of a considerable part of the prewar Marine Corps, too.

There are events in the story of nations [wrote Cecil Woodham-Smith] which cut their history in two. Nothing is ever the same again. On the one side, lies the former world, lost, vanished, never to be restored—and on the other a new and strange world, utterly unlike, perhaps to be lamented.[1]

Such an event occurred at 0755, 7 December 1941, when Japanese dive bombers and torpedo planes smashed down on Pearl Harbor. At almost the same instant, other attacking planes hit Army and Navy air bases on Oahu.

At Ewa, the Officer of the Day, emerging from the messhall after breakfast, saw torpedo planes low along the coast skimming past Barber's Point toward Pearl. An aircraft recognition shark, he spotted them as Japanese. As he ran for the guardhouse to sound the alarm, 21 Zero fighters with red meatballs glowing against their off-grey fuselages scourged MAG-21's flight line with incendiary, explosive, and armor-piercing bullets. In 20 minutes of repeated passes, while individual Marines, armed only with rifles and pistols, vainly fired back from the open, nine Grumman F4F Wildcats (the newest fighter planes of the Marine Corps) and 18 dive bombers were shot to pieces and burning. By the time the air group commander, Lieutenant Colonel Claude A. ("Sheriff") Larkin, reached the base (he was held up—and hit— by a strafing Zero that made a pass at his car on the road), 33 airplanes were gone, and a second attack, by more Zeroes and by "Val" dive bombers, was in progress. A third attack, this time by 15 Zeroes, met more resistance; ordnancemen had broken out spare machine guns and ground crews were manning rear-cockpit guns in some of the riddled dive bombers. They got one Zero and hit several others. Describing the events of the morning, Major General R. C. Mangrum, then a squadron commander, reminisced:[2]

I don't know what the time interval was between these attacks, but between the first and second was long enough for me to get from our house at Ewa Beach into my pants and out to the field in time to see my planes destroyed in most expert fashion. . . . And I got a bullet through my erstwhile best Saturday morning inspection pants—but without touching me!

Miraculously, only four Marines were killed at Ewa, but the aircraft loss was virtually complete. Only one airplane, a transport, was still flyable.

In the Navy Yard, where death and catastrophe rained down on the Battle Force, discipline remained unshaken. At the Marine Barracks, guard personnel manned battle stations, security posts, and fire engines. The 3d Defense

Battalion's antiaircraft machine gunners went into action from the barracks parade ground, while property sergeants smashed open crates of helmets and skimmed them out to the troops. Within moments, machine guns manned by the main gate guard (Company A, Marine Barracks) caught a low-flying Zero which, as remembered by one participant, S. R. Shaw (now brigadier general):[3]

. . . on fire with the pilot visibly bleeding, windscreen back, brushed the big monkey-pod tree under which my wife was standing in the yard of our quarters as it glided to a crash at Hospital Point.

During the first minute of the attack, a Japanese torpedo hit the USS *Arizona* on the port bow. Seconds later an armor-piercing bomb smashed through to No. 2 Turret's 14-inch magazine. With a blast that broke windows ashore and even stalled automobiles, the old battleship blew sky-high. Her foremast crashed down; Major Alan Shapley, on duty in Sky Forward, was pitched at least a hundred feet through the air and came to in the water. One of the most durable officers in the Corps, Major Shapley swam clear, to Ford Island, and rescued two shipmates on the way.

Another durable and steadfast Marine was the sentry on watch on the caisson of No. 1 Drydock, who, in obedience to the 5th General Order for Sentinels ("To quit my post only when properly relieved . . ."), stuck to his post under Japanese attacks while the destroyers *Cassin* and *Downes*, exploding and aflame, toppled into each other almost within arm's length. Miraculously, he survived the resulting inferno and, having been on watch since four in the morning, finally telephoned the guardhouse that evening, wanting to know just when they were going to post his relief.[4]

At Camp Catlin, Marines of the 4th Defense and 2d Engineer Battalions were shaken out of their bunks by a low-flying strafer pursued by an even lower trail of bursting flak from some AA battery. The Officer of the Day promptly issued his first (and unimpeachably correct) order of the war: "Sound Call to Arms!" As the bugle blared, Marines poured into battery streets and fell in with rifles, belts, and bayonets. Moments later, one 3-inch antiaircraft battery was ordered down into the Navy Yard and went into position on Kuahua Island just across the channel from the *Arizona*, now a pyre racked by flame and new explosions. Movement of the guns along Kamehameha Highway was hindered by strafers, one of which made sport of Honolulu fire engines, which were zigging and zagging toward the Navy Yard.

By 0945 it was over. Two thousand four hundred and three officers and men were dead or missing in action; 1,178 were wounded. Of these, 112 killed and missing were Marines (mainly from the ships' detachments) and at least 64 more were wounded.[5] While a soft Hawaiian breeze rippled cane-fields on the slopes above Pearl Harbor, dismay and anger reigned amid the wreckage. Yet retrospection reveals that there was nothing to be ashamed of. In the words of the executive officer of the *West Virginia,* probably the hardest hit ship that survived:[6]

Throughout the action, there was never the slightest sign of faltering or of cowardice. The actions of the officers and men were wholly commendable; their spirit was marvelous; there was no panic, no shirking nor flinching, and words fail in attempting to describe the truly magnificent display of courage, discipline, and devotion to duty of all.

THE OUTER ISLANDS

Simultaneously with their hammer-stroke at Pearl Harbor, the Japanese attacked other United States islands manned by Marines. Midway, Johnston, and Palmyra, the strategic outposts of the Hawaiian Islands, were subjected to hit-and-run naval bombardment. Guam, the Philippines (where the 4th Marines had just arrived from Shanghai), and Wake were seriously attacked.

Johnston and Palmyra, both garrisoned by detachments from the 1st Defense Battalion, each received a few rounds from enemy submarines. Neither side sustained any casualties. The raid on Midway, by destroyers *Ushio* and *Sazanami,* was somewhat more serious. In a 23-minute action, the Japanese shelled the atoll, killing two Marines and wounding ten. The 6th Defense Battalion's 5-inch and 3-inch guns replied, scoring hits but no kills.

One casualty of the night was First Lieutenant George H. Cannon, who, although mortally injured by a shell which went directly through the air-port of a concrete communication center, stuck to his post, refused evacuation, and directed re-establishment of communications. After being carried out under protest, he died. For his devotion to duty, Lieutenant Cannon became the first Marine to win the Medal of Honor in World War II.

One of the first reactions to the Japanese attack was to reinforce Midway with additional base-defense troops (from the 3d and 4th Defense Battalions) and aviation. In so doing, VMSB-231, commanded by Major C. J. Chappell, Jr., flew all 17 of its SB2U dive bombers directly from Pearl Harbor to Midway (1,137 miles), the longest single-engine mass flight ever made up to that time. Later on, Midway served as target for passing bombardment by Japanese submarines on their way to and from the eastern Pacific. Three times during the winter of 1942, Midway was shelled; each time, the two defense battalions were ready and replied.

Guam, encircled by enemy bases in the Carolines and Marianas, was a sitting duck, an expected sacrifice to Congress' refusal to fortify the island during the late 1930s. The island garrison, armed with nothing heavier than four .30-caliber machine guns, comprised 153 Marines, reinforced by the 80-man Insular Guard, native Chamorros officered by Marine NCOs.

Promptly on the morning of 8 December (east longitude), Japanese planes from Saipan swooped down and sank the Guam "Navy" (USS *Penguin*, minesweeper; an old tanker; and two patrol craft). They then proceeded to attack the Marine Barracks on Orote Peninsula, and for two days they bombed and strafed the helpless island.

Just before dawn on 10 December, 400 men of the Japanese Naval Guard Force—"Jap Marines" in the common parlance of the Pacific war but actually sailors organized for base defense and amphibious fighting—swarmed across Dungcas Beach, above Agana, under the guns of a heavy cruiser, and made for the town. Meanwhile, some 5,500 Japanese soldiers landed unopposed at Tumon Bay, at Merizo on Guam's southern extremity, and at Talofofo Bay on the east coast.

At 0515, the Naval Guard Force skirmishers hit resistance by Marines and Insular Guards deployed in Agana. The result was inevitable; after a brief fight for honor's sake, the Naval Governor, Captain G. J. McMillin, USN, ordered firing ceased, and the Colors came down.

At a cost of four Marines killed and 12 wounded, the first territory of the United States had fallen to Japan, and its prisoners were quickly herded into bitter custody.

THE DEFENSE OF WAKE

Since the Japanese Fourth Fleet includes transports, and troops with equipment specially suited for landing operations, it appears not unlikely that one of the initial operations of the Japanese may be directed against Wake. If Wake be defended, then for the Japanese to reduce it would require extended operations of their naval forces in an area where we might be able to get at them; thus affording us an opportunity to get at naval forces with naval forces. We should try, by every possible means, to get the Japanese to expose naval units. In order to do this, we must provide objectives that require such exposure.

So wrote Admiral Husband E. Kimmel in April 1941.[7] The letter was prophetic, its logic was characteristic of the man, and it got action.

In August 1941, the first available force, five officers and 173 men from

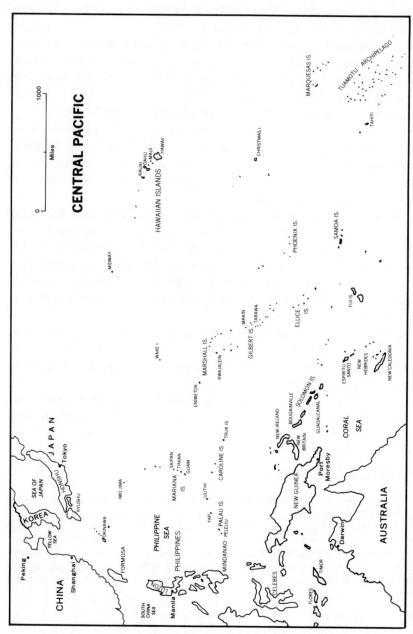

Central Pacific

the 1st Defense Battalion, landed on Wake and immediately set to constructing defenses intended eventually for the full battalion. In November, more Marines arrived, commanded by a taciturn major, James P. S. Devereux, who had preceded them a fortnight earlier. A month later, on 4 December 1941, flown from the USS *Enterprise* onto the half-completed air base, came Marine Fighting Squadron 211 (VMF-211), led by Major Paul A. Putnam. The squadron's ground echelon had been there since mid-November, but even so the field was barely able to receive the 12 new Grumman Wildcats—pretty up-to-date airplanes in the eyes of Marine aviators long accustomed to doing their work with the leavings of more fortunate Navy squadrons.

As of 6 December 1941, the ground defenses of Wake amounted to the full armament of the 1st Defense Battalion (six 5-inch seacoast guns, 12 3-inch AA guns, searchlights, and machine guns). Unhappily, there were less than half the Marines required to man them: 15 officers and 373 enlisted men instead of 43 officers and 939 enlisted, the full strength of the battalion. This meant that one 3-inch battery was entirely without gun crews, and that the other two would man only three of their four guns. Less than half the men were on hand to man the machine guns already emplaced. The primitive radar sets earmarked for Wake were still parked behind the barracks at Pearl Harbor, awaiting shipboard space, and the island had no sound-locators, the pre-radar horns which, with a fair wind, a slow target, and a highly skilled operator, could sometimes track an airplane. VMF-211 was just learning how to operate brand-new aircraft which, beautiful as they were, had no armor, no self-sealing tanks, and racks which didn't match the local model of bombs. But Wake's general readiness was excellent. All hands were thoroughly trained, spirits were high, and the Marines of the defense battalion and fighting squadron were ready to fight with every weapon they had.

At 0650, 8 December (east longitude) an uncoded radio transmission cut through from Oahu—Pearl Harbor was under attack. Major Devereux immediately sounded "Call to Arms"; by 0730 all positions were manned, service ammunition broken out, and an officers' conference held. Alas, at noon, while eight of VMF-211's 12 fighters, back from patrol, were refueling, 36 Japanese bombers droned toward Wake from Roi in the Marshalls. Emerging from a rain-squall with no warning (Wake had no radar), the enemy dropped a close pattern of bombs and strafed the airfield. Despite prompt and dense 3-inch AA fire, no enemy planes were brought down. By contrast, seven out of the eight new Grummans were blasted into junk. The squadron's 25,000-gallon aviation gasoline tank went up in flames; 23 Marines were dead or mortally injured, and 11 were wounded. Two pilots and half of VMF-211's ground crewmen were killed, and the squadron's scanty stock of tools and spares incinerated in a burning tent. Within a few hours, after the dead had been stowed in an empty reefer until graves could be hewn from the coral, there began the ceaseless scavenging of burned-out wreckage for salvageable tools and parts which could keep Wake's remaining fighters flying. As the Japanese bombers headed home for Roi, one diarist recorded:[8]

The pilots in every one of the planes were grinning widely. Everyone wiggled his wings to signify *Banzai*.

Next day there were fewer banzais. At 1145, methodical to a fault, the

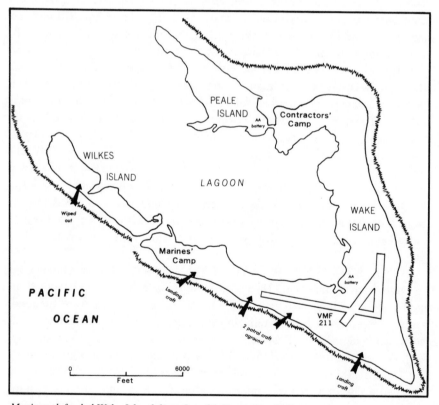

Marines defended Wake Island from 8 to 23 December 1941

bombers again arrived from the south. But this time VMF-211 was in the air and waiting, and the antiaircraft batteries were manned and ready. As the Grummans slashed at the rear of the tight Japanese vee, the 3-inch guns began to bark. One bomber flamed into a spin under the guns of Second Lieutenant David D. Kliewer and Technical Sergeant William J. Hamilton (a veteran enlisted pilot), while the 3-inch, seconds later, scored their first kill. Although bomb damage to Wake was again grave, postwar enemy records note that 14 bombers sustained flak damage.

On the 10th, the pattern was repeated. Once again the antiaircraft slammed away; once again the Marine fighters—all four—caught the Japanese as they came in; once again kills were scored.

At 0300 next morning, Wake's lookouts reported ships offshore. The report was accurate: under Rear Admiral Sadamichi Kajioka, flying his flag in the light cruiser *Yubari*, were two more light cruisers, six destroyers, two destroyer-transports (with the landing force), and two medium transports (with garrison troops embarked). The landing force, numbering 450, was to take the airfield and Wilkes Island, the southwest tip of the atoll. "We expected to have a rough time . . ." mused Admiral Kajioka's chief of staff during a postwar interrogation.[9] They did.

While the Japanese closed the island to begin bombardment and boating at dawn, Major Devereux issued strict orders to hold fire and for no aircraft to take off until the batteries opened. At 0500, the *Yubari* commenced her first firing run, followed by the other two cruisers. For 75 minutes, while the enemy leisurely shelled and imperceptibly closed the south coast of Wake, the Marines hugged their revetments. At 0615, when the cruisers and destroyers were only 4,500 yards offshore, Major Devereux quietly ordered, "Commence firing."

The two south-shore 5-inch batteries (Battery A on Wake proper and Battery L on Wilkes Island) cracked out almost simultaneously; they had been tracking their targets almost an hour. Battery A's first salvo was an over. First Lieutenant Clarence A. Barninger, the fresh-faced, smiling battery commander, spotted down 500. As he reported:[10]

Both shells entered her port side about amidships just above the water line. The ship immediately belched smoke and steam through the side, and her speed diminished. At 7,000 yards two more hit her in about the same place, but slightly aft of the first two. Her whole side was now engulfed in smoke and steam. . . . At this time the destroyer which had accompanied the cruiser came in at high speed and tried to sweep between us to lay smoke, but a shell, an over, aft of the cruiser, struck the forecastle of the destroyer. . . .

While the *Yubari* and her consort were absorbing their knocks, Battery L was getting in its own. The opening salvo was aimed at the *Hayate,* leading a division of destroyers. At 0652, just after the third salvo from the long-barreled 5-inchers, the *Hayate* was swallowed up in a violent explosion, and, as the smoke and spray blew clear, the Marine gunners could see that their target had broken in two and was sinking rapidly. Two minutes later she was gone, the first Japanese surface warship to be sunk in World War II, and the first consequential war loss sustained by the Japanese Navy since the Russo-Japanese War.

For a moment, all hands stared. Then a platoon sergeant broke the spell[11] —"Knock it off, you bastards, and get back on the guns. What do you think this is—a ball game?" and Battery L shifted onto the next destroyer in column, the *Oite.* She too was hit, but turned away, smoking and making smoke, and fled. The next and only target still in the battery's field of fire was the transport division. Again the leading ship was hulled; then the transports, too, swung clear and made off into the smoke of the retiring destroyers. Now one of the light cruisers closed to 9,000 yards. For a few moments, she swapped salvoes with the Marine battery and then, just after sustaining a hit aft, she too broke off action and turned tail.

As this duel was in progress, the third 5-inch battery (Battery B, on Peale Island) finally got targets—the other enemy destroyer division. Hits again, but not so promptly: the Japanese held course and shot one of the two Marine guns out of action, after which they reversed course. It was 0710, and no more targets remained in range. Major Devereux ordered cease firing.

Now was exactly the instant for VMF-211. All four of the remaining planes had taken off as ordered when the surface action began. Major Putnam led the flight, followed by his three most experienced pilots, Captains Henry T. Elrod, Herbert C. Freuler, and Frank C. Tharin. Each airplane was armed with two 100-pound bombs.

Thirty miles southwest of Wake, the Marine fighters caught up with Admiral Kajioka. In a tempest of flak, Elrod and Tharin bombed and strafed the cruisers *Tatsuta* and *Tenryu,* scoring on topside torpedo batteries (on *Tenryu*) and radio shack (on *Tatsuta*). Captain Freuler singled out the transport *Kongo Maru* which he hit on the fantail, touching off a gasoline fire.

As each fighter expended its brace of bombs, the pilot headed for base, rearmed, and went out again. At 0731, during the final sorties, after a pass by Captain Elrod, a Japanese destroyer blew up with a tremendous explosion. This was the *Kisaragi* which had unwisely been deck loaded with depth charges. She was the last kill of the day (and a frustration almost too much to bear for Second Lieutenant John F. Kinney, a relief pilot who was just pushing over for his first bombing run when she blew up in his face).

On Wake jubilation mingled with excitement and canteen cups full of black coffee. Two enemy ships were sunk, eight more had been hit, and postwar investigations of records indicate from five to seven hundred Japanese dead—all at the cost of four Marines wounded and the loss of one plane (Freuler's) which crash landed with its engine shot through and through by flak.

Most important, U. S. Marine gunners and aviators had accomplished a feat never again to be equaled by either side in World War II: the defeat of an amphibious assault.

THE ORDEAL OF WAKE, 11–22 DECEMBER 1941

On 13 December the battered Japanese task force limped into Kwajalein. Here Rear Admiral Kuninori Marushige ticked off the failure factors:

Vigorous seacoast artillery defense,
Fighter opposition,
Foul weather,
Insufficient Japanese forces and means.

The Wake invasion force's wounds were impressive: two destroyers sunk; all three cruisers damaged; three more destroyers and one destroyer-transport badly roughed up; one transport burned out. None of the damaged ships, however, were beyond repair, and on the next try the Japanese would know better. Meanwhile, until reinforcements arrived and repairs were completed, milk-run bombing would serve to soften the Marines. With more troops (from Saipan) and carrier air, Wake should present fewer difficulties.

At the same time as the Japanese were licking their wounds, Marines of the 4th Defense Battalion at Pearl Harbor were working against time, loading the USS *Tangier*, a seaplane tender, with everything Wake lacked: radar, an extra 3-inch AA battery, another 5-inch battery, replacement fire-control gear for all weapons on Wake, beach mines, wire, grenades, aviation spares. At sea, racing from San Diego for Pearl, was the USS *Saratoga*, the aircraft carrier which for years held the world's speed record between the West

Coast and Honolulu. Aboard the "Sara" was Marine Fighting Squadron 221, commanded by Major Verne J. McCaul, earmarked to reinforce what was left of VMF-211. As soon as the "Sara" could reach Pearl and refuel, the *Tangier*, in company with the carrier, escorted by a task force of three heavy cruisers (*Astoria, Minneapolis,* and *San Francisco*), nine destroyers, and a tanker (the venerable 12-knot *Neches*), would sortie for Wake. With resolution and expedition, Wake might yet be relieved.

These plans were for the time being unknown to Major Devereux and Commander Winfield Scott Cunningham, the Navy island commander; Wake's codes had been shredded into an oil drum and sautéed in burning aviation gas. But it was well known to Devereux and Cunningham that the defense was gradually fraying. Daily air raids—the main one about midday by shore-based bombers, the second at dusk by flying boats—whittled away at the airfield and at the batteries.

Every raid was stoutly opposed, not only by the antiaircraft batteries (". . . the defense guns were very accurate,"[12] a Japanese officer commented after the war), but, most of all, by VMF-211. This squadron after 8 December never mustered more than five airplanes, usually less. Its effectiveness was not only a tribute to the airmanship and guts of Major Putnam and his pilots, but the extraordinary feats of the squadron's engineering section, Second Lieutenant Kinney, Technical Sergeant Hamilton, and Aviation Machinist's Mate 1st Class James F. Hesson, USN, who had been "borrowed" from the island commander. Major Putnam reported:[13]

These three, with the assistance of volunteers among the civilians, did a truly remarkable and almost magical job. With almost no tools and a complete lack of normal equipment, they performed all types of repair and replacement work. They changed engines and propellers from one airplane to another, and even completely built up new engines and propellers from scrap parts salvaged from wrecks. They replaced minor parts and assemblies, and repaired damage to fuselages and wings and landing gear; all this in spite of the fact that they were working with new types with which they had had no previous experience and were without instruction manuals of any kind.

That "they changed engines from one airplane to another" was the understatement of the campaign; on 14 December, when the tail of one of the two momentarily effective Grummans was hit square and set afire by a bomb, the three sprinted for the flaming airplane and accomplished the unbelievable feat of stripping the undamaged engine from the burning fuselage and dragging it clear.

On 17 December, seemingly under the impression that Wake's base-development program was going ahead without interrupton, the 14th Naval

District staff at Pearl Harbor asked for a progress report on dredging in the lagoon and for a specific date by which certain projects would be completed.

Prefacing his reply with information on the day's latest air raid (by eight flying boats from Wotje in the Marshalls), the island commander then summarized the facts of life. Half his trucks and engineering equipment were destroyed; most of his diesel oil and commercial explosives had gone up; his garage and blacksmith and machine shops had been burnt out or blasted; and the morale of the 1,200 contract workmen was mostly bad. If Pearl Harbor wanted deadlines met, they had better, concluded Commander Cunningham, do something about the Japanese.

The 20th of December was noteworthy for two reasons: (1) the weather was so bad that it prevented the Japanese raids; and (2) a Navy PBY, practically immune to foul weather, beat its way in and landed in the lagoon, bearing news of the plans and actions of the relief force which had left Pearl Harbor on 15 December and could be expected off Wake on the morning of the 23d. After this message had been delivered, an ensign in the patrol bomber's crew picked up his flight bag and asked for a car to take him to the Pan American Airways hotel. He was almost two weeks late; the hotel had burned down on 8 December.

Next morning the PBY turned over its engines and took off laden with reports and messages in the hands of one officer returning under orders, Major Walter L. J. Bayler, who thereby went down in history as "the last man off Wake."

Within less than two hours—at 0850, 21 December—29 Japanese Navy attack bombers, covered by 18 Zero fighters, lashed down through the overcast and strafed all battery positions. These planes from the aircraft carriers *Soryu* and *Hiryu*, both veterans of the Pearl Harbor attack, brought bad news for Wake: the presence of carrier air meant that the enemy high command wanted Wake badly and soon.

On 22 December, two Grummans were still in commission and out on combat air patrol, flown by Captain Freuler and Second Lieutenant Carl R. Davidson. In mid-morning, at 12,000 feet, Davidson spotted 39 carrier planes coming in from the north. He and Freuler attacked.

Confronted by six Zekes, Freuler in his patched-up F4F-3 unhesitatingly dived at the enemy fighters and got one on the first pass. Flipping his plane into an opposite approach, he lit into another Zero, which exploded so close that a curtain of flame and fragments seared the Grumman. Freuler's plane was badly scorched, manifold pressure dropped, and the controls reacted sluggishly. Just then, looking back toward Wake, Freuler got a last view of Davidson in action against the dive bombers; behind him a Zero was lining up for a run. Davidson was never seen again. Then a Zero got on Freuler's tail and fired a long burst. With bullet wounds in his back and shoulder, Freuler pushed over into a steep dive and dragged his shattered, airplane into Wake for a crash landing. In the words of Lieutenant Kinney, whose shoestring maintenance had kept VMF-211 flying for 15 days, "This left us with no airplanes."[14] Marine Fighting Squadron 211, now including less than 20 officers and men, thereupon reported to the defense battalion as infantry.

While these events were taking place, Wake's relief expedition was plodding west at a speed of advance held below 12 knots by the wheezing engines of the old *Neches*. This was the first westward sally of the war, and the waters beyond sight of Oahu seemed very lonely waters indeed. All hands in the relief force (including this writer) chafed as the grimness of Wake's plight became known. Plans for rapid landing and immediate entrance into combat were discussed and settled. Troops and supplies would have to be lightered ashore; if vitally injured, the *Tangier* would be run aground to ensure delivery of her cargo.

On the morning of 22 December, at the very time when Japanese carrier planes were downing VMF-211's last two airplanes, the relief force was only 515 miles from Wake. Although the fuel supply of his destroyers was adequate, Rear Admiral Frank Jack Fletcher, commanding the task force, felt it might be slim if serious action developed, and, rather than pressing on, as Nelson would have done (". . . always fuelling" was Samuel Eliot Morison's verdict on Fletcher), he commenced to fuel destroyers, steaming north, not west, on a track which brought the force no nearer the objective all day. That night he again turned west. At 0800, 23 December, while Commander Cunningham was ordering Major Devereux to arrange the surrender of Wake, Fletcher was but 425 miles away.

During the uneasy night of 22-23 December, the planners at Pearl knew only too well how close the race was, and that Fletcher was losing. At 0250, Wake had radioed "Enemy apparently landing." Two hours later, another report: "The enemy is on the island. The issue is in doubt."[15] So, too, it was in CinCPac's headquarters above Pearl Harbor on Makalapa, but not for much longer. At 0811, Hawaiian time, Admiral William S. Pye, temporarily in command of the Pacific Fleet, ordered Fletcher to pull back. The latter complied promptly.

Aboard the *Tangier* and *Saratoga* reactions varied from astonishment to shame and anger. Some staff officers pleaded with Admiral Fletcher to disregard his orders and make a dash in to Wake. What neither Fletcher nor they knew was that, while a powerful U. S. task force was within 425 miles of Wake, four new enemy heavy cruisers were patrolling east of Wake, separated by hundreds of miles from escorts or air support, a naked target for the *Saratoga's* airmen and the American cruisers' guns. Nor did they know that the Japanese amphibious task force was clustered about Wake with no apparent measures for security against air or surface attack. Had all this been known, the story of Wake might have been very different and the United States might have had a dearly needed victory.

But it was not known, and Admiral Fletcher, who might have relieved Wake, turned away from the enemy and retired on Midway.

THE FALL OF WAKE

Intermittent, gusty rain-squalls ushered in the black early morning of 23 December, adding their clamor and discomfort to the steady boom of the surf. Behind the cover of this foul weather, Admiral Kajioka's task force advanced on Wake. Because of the previous difficulties in landing, the admiral planned to put most of his Special Naval Landing Force, now numbering about 1,000, aboard two old destroyer-transports, *Patrol Craft 32* and *Patrol Craft 33*, and run them ashore on the reef. Other troops would go ashore in landing craft.

With a reverberating crunch the two patrol craft mounted the reef in a smother of breakers and foam. Two barges scraped bottom as they approached the reef.

Suddenly a pink tracer-stream penciled from the beach of Wilkes Island, and .50-caliber slugs ripped through the gunwales of one barge. A searchlight flared on. Out of the darkness, near the airstrip, a single 3-inch gun, emplaced as an antiboat weapon, cracked and flashed. In swift sequence, 14 rounds punched into *Patrol Craft 33*, which was just debarking her troops. Seconds later, the ship burst into flame, her magazine exploded, and the whole landing area, swarming with Japanese assault troops, was illuminated. "The scene was too beautiful to be a battlefield," lyrically reported a Japanese combat correspondent.[16]

But other troops were well ashore in several places. Having no infantry reserve, the 1st Defense Battalion and VMF-211 had to fight where they stood. VMF-211, commanded by Major Putnam and Captain Elrod, formed a horseshoe of riflemen around the lone 3-inch antiboat gun and were still there hours later. "This is as far as we go" was Putnam's final order to his squadron. They stayed.

"Wilkes Island," stated a Japanese report,[17] "was the scene of a fierce and desperate battle." Indeed it was. After a Japanese company, numbering 100 men, had landed and by sheer momentum overrun the gun positions of Battery F (3-inch antiaircraft), Captain Wesley McC. Platt, senior officer on the island, succeeded first in confining them to their beachhead, and then counterattacked with a dozen of his total of 70 men spread out in isolated defense posts along the beach. Other Marines, 25 in number, pushed in from another front, and the Japanese panicked. The 37 Marines killed four officers and 90 enlisted men and captured two wounded. The landing was annihilated. "In general," concluded a Japanese Navy critique, "that part of the operation was not successful."[18]

Unfortunately, most of the other enemy operations did succeed. By the first hour after dawn, the Japanese had about a thousand infantry ashore on Wake Island alone, where some 201 Marines were stationed, about half as 5-inch and 3-inch gun crews. With the coming of day, the assault was supported by ships' gunfire from 17 ships offshore and by carrier dive-bombing attacks.

At 0700, with his command post under attack and long out of communication with the defenders on Wilkes, whose victory was not known, Major Devereux reported to Commander Cunningham how serious the situation was. Did Cunningham know of any friendly forces near at hand? With a negative reply, the naval officer authorized Devereux to make arrangements for surrender, and, at 0800, accompanied by a field music and bearing a white flag tied to a swab handle, Major Devereux walked southward down the shore road to deliver Wake to the enemy.

The island was surrendered 15 days after the first attack; it was 11 hours after the initial landing before Wilkes, the last strong point, yielded in accordance with orders. The Marines on Wake sustained 20 per cent casualties (81 officers and men killed or wounded). The Japanese losses throughout the attacks on Wake probably exceeded 1,000. U. S. forces on Wake had caused the loss of four enemy warships and appreciable damage to eight more. Twenty-one aircraft were brought down by Marine fighters or flak. According to Japanese reports from Roi, 51 other planes sustained damage from Wake's antiaircraft guns.

With this record as a basis, Major Putnam's final report, which left the island on 21 December, could truthfully state:

All hands have behaved splendidly and held up in a manner of which the Marine Corps may well tell.

At home, in his State of the Union Message on 6 January 1942, President Roosevelt told Congress and the American people:

There were only some four hundred United States Marines who, in the heroic and historic defense of Wake Island, inflicted such great losses on the enemy. Some of these men were killed in action and others are now prisoners of war. When the survivors of that great fight are liberated and restored to their homes, they will learn that a hundred and thirty million of their fellow citizens have been inspired to render their own full share of service and sacrifice.

General Holcomb had a somewhat more pungent comment. During a press conference at which several newsmen, mindful of the Clark Field and Hong Kong debacles, contrasted the Marines' unyielding defense of Wake, the Major General Commandant bristled, "What the hell did you expect, anyway?"[19]

BATAAN-CORREGIDOR: DIRGE FOR THE 4TH MARINES

The 4th Regiment ended its 14 years of Shanghai duty in style. The regiment, which had intentionally been allowed to drop down to only 804 officers and men under Colonel Samuel L. Howard, swung down Bubbling Well Road onto the Bund with drums beating and Colors flying: a brave show, but it fooled nobody, the Japanese especially. On 27-28 November 1941, the regiment's two thin battalions sailed in two merchantmen, the *President Harrison* and *President Madison,* hastily diverted from their normal runs. Three days later the Marines debarked at Olongapo on Subic Bay in the Philippines.

When the Japanese wiped out the U. S. Far East Air Force on the ground at Clark Field—a still not completely explained surprise which came almost ten hours after word of the Pearl Harbor attack had reached General MacArthur in Manila—the 4th Marines were at Olongapo, shaking down for field service which the regiment hoped would be in defense of Bataan Peninsula. By nightfall that day (8 December, east longitude date), the complement of Marine Barracks, Olongapo, was absorbed into the 4th Regiment to permit the two battalions to be "triangularized" into three-company, three-platoon units.

On 10 December, in accordance with plan, the U. S. Asiatic Fleet (a fleet in name only) retired south from Philippine waters. On the same day, the Japanese landed practically unopposed at two points in north Luzon. Two days later another enemy force, this time totally unopposed, secured Legaspi on southern Luzon. The pincers were poised.

Meanwhile, however, Japanese pincers had already closed on several hundred Marine officers and men who might have powerfully reinforced the 4th Marines. Off the China coast a Japanese cruiser overhauled and captured the *President Harrison* in passage to North China to evacuate the Marine detachments from Peking and Tientsin.

The intended port of embarkation for these troops, some 500 in all, was Chinwangtao, where Chief Marine Gunner Lee, last seen in Nicaragua winning his third Navy Cross, was posted with a 20-man detachment at Camp Holcomb, the rifle range. Out hunting early on the morning of 8 December, Lee got word of the Pearl Harbor attack and raced back to camp through cordons of Japanese who were closing in. While Second Lieutenant R. M. Huizenga, who had arrived from the dock area, parleyed with Japanese officers, Lee and his men, all seasoned regulars, broke out crated ammunition, machine guns, and a few BARs and submachine guns, steaming them free of cosmoline under ponchos in the showers. With the Japanese still looking on respectfully, Lee organized a perimeter amid the crates and boxcars, and only orders not to resist, received from Tientsin, prevented the detachment from selling their lives. Subsequently, this detachment, together with the officers and men at Tientsin and Peking, surrendered as ordered and went into captivity.

On 20 December 1941, as the Japanese Fourteenth Army was making its main landings at Lingayen Gulf, Luzon, General Douglas MacArthur requested that "the powerful, veteran 4th Marines"[20] be assigned to operational control of the Army. Admiral Thomas C. Hart, Commander in Chief Asiatic Fleet, immediately acceded. Colonel Howard reported to MacArthur and, after a cordial welcome, was told that the 4th Regiment was to proceed to Corregidor and take over the beach defenses.

Lizard-shaped Corregidor Island was the main island in the defenses of Manila Bay. There were, in addition, three other heavily fortified islands in the mouth of the bay. In terms of World War I, before the days of modern aircraft, the harbor defenses of Manila Bay readily merited their popular description as "the Gibraltar of the Far East." Nonetheless, in addition to their vulnerability to air attack (which could not be remedied because of the 1922 treaty with Japan), the forts in Manila Bay had another—and fatal —weakness. They were dominated by a precipitous mainland peninsula, Bataan, which overlooked Manila Bay. Bataan was the back door to Corregidor.

During the 4th Regiment's three weeks at Olongapo, Colonel Howard reconnoitered the Bataan Peninsula, anticipating that his regiment might defend its vulnerable seaward beaches. This suggestion was brushed aside by MacArthur's chief of staff, Major General R. K. Sutherland, and the 4th Marines were sent immediately to Corregidor.[21]

On New Year's Day 1942, the 4th Regiment absorbed its last Marine reinforcements. The 1st Separate Battalion, a special antiaircraft unit at Marine Barracks, Cavite Navy Yard, became the 3d Battalion, 4th Marines. With this addition, plus survivors of broken units from the other Services, the 4th Marines were destined to go down fighting. The strength of the regiment on Corregidor (less 138 officers and men assigned to the other three islands) was now 66 officers and 1,364 enlisted Marines.

Aside from minor antiaircraft actions by the machine guns and fixed Navy 3-inch guns of the 1st Separate Battalion, the first and only Marine fighting on Bataan took place in a confused action between 23 and 27 January. A Japanese amphibious envelopment landed about 300 infantry, with supporting artillery, on Longoskawayan Point, about a mile and a half west of Mariveles section base and five miles below General MacArthur's headquarters. Inland, separated from the enemy landing area only by a long ridge parallel to the coast, ran the main supply route to Bataan's front lines.

Shortly before this landing, a provisional naval battalion, under Commander F. J. Bridget, had been organized for the local defense of the Mariveles area. This unit, including elements of Batteries A and C, 3d Battalion, 4th Marines, altogether about 200 half-trained sailors and some 75 Marines, was committed against the Japanese and skirmished doggedly to hold the ridge between the enemy and the main supply route. The highly improvised American fire support during this action included 12-inch coast artillery mortar concentrations, a battery of Army 75-mm. guns, two Philippine Army 2.95-inch mountain guns, an 81-mm. mortar section and machine gun platoon sent by the 4th Marines from Corregidor, and 3-inch naval gunfire support from the old minesweeper *Quail*. Neither side made much headway until a jungle-trained battalion of the 57th Infantry (Philippine Scouts) arrived and got the situation under control. During the fighting, the sailors, wearing dyed whites reminiscent of Veracruz, dumfounded the Japanese, one of whom noted in his diary:[22]

Today we have encountered a new kind of enemy. They come walking to the front yelling, "Hey Mac, where the hell are you?" They are completely without fear.

Slightly comic-opera though the Longoskawayan fight was, the Japanese landing posed a real threat, and, without prompt initial action by the few Marines and sailors from Mariveles, would have made further trouble for hard-pressed Bataan.

After Longoskawayan, the Marines were withdrawn from Mariveles to join the rest of the 4th Regiment on "The Rock." Here, as the agony of Bataan drew to its close in April, Colonel Howard labored mightily to organize and reinforce the beach defenses of Corregidor. Despite their urgency, these labors passed anonymously. Not only did communiques omit any reference to the presence of a Marine regiment in the Philippines, but, inexplicably, the only American unit on Bataan-Corregidor to which General MacArthur failed to award the Army's Distinguished Unit Citation was the 4th Marines. This omission was promptly rectified by Lieutenant General Jonathan M. Wainwright, USA, when he took over command following MacArthur's ordered withdrawal to Australia.

Even as the last refugees trickled across from Bataan on 9 April, Japanese siege artillery, 240-mm. howitzers and 300-mm. mortars, ran up their observation balloons from Bataan and commenced registration on "The Rock." The siege of Corregidor had begun.

All through April the Japanese guns and planes pounded away. United States batteries and beach defenses, pinpointed from the heights of Bataan, were beaten into silence. As Corregidor's beach defense unit, the 4th Regiment accumulated a desperate but honorable flotsam of officers and men from other Services—841 Navy survivors; 679 from the Army and Philippine Scouts; 931 other Philippine troops. On 1 May 1942, the regiment numbered 3,891 officers and men.[23] Part of these men were added as supernumeraries to the three regular battalions, while some, mainly from the Mariveles "Naval Battalion," were grouped under a headquarters of six Marine officers and NCOs as a provisional 4th Battalion, which was set aside as an island reserve.

On 29 April, birthday of Emperor Hirohito, the Japanese siege batteries fired a merciless salute of 10,000 rounds. On 5 May, with only four days' water left on Corregidor, they put down 16,000 rounds. Among the few United States batteries left were the two Navy-type 14-inch turrets on Fort

Drum, the "concrete battleship." The other batteries, chiefly disappearing guns in open-topped emplacements, were easy marks for the relentless Japanese gunners and aerial bombardiers. Ten per cent of the Marines of the 4th Regiment were already dead or wounded. In the words of Hanson Baldwin:[24]

> Most of the beach defenses—the barbed wire, the foxholes—were wiped out. Nearly all the beach defense guns were destroyed, and all of the Rock's great batteries were silenced—the mortars, the 12-inch rifles, the 8- and 10-inch disappearing guns, the 155s. The star shells were burned, the searchlights—except for one or two—were wrecked; of the AA guns a few remained, but the fire-control instruments were destroyed.

At 2300, 5 May, while the moon shone bright, Corregidor's defenders heard the roar of motors from across the channel. Enemy landing craft were chugging across the narrow waters from Cabcaben, on Bataan. All three regular battalions of the 4th Marines manned their fixed defenses, while the 4th, the hastily organized provisional battalion, was concentrated in reserve.

The initial enemy landings, contrary to plan, were carried by the current up toward the easternmost tip (the "tail of the lizard") of Corregidor. Here, at 2330, two battalions of the Japanese 61st Infantry made their way ashore under heavy fire. The weapons and ammunition which the defenders had held out for the final fight now went into the action along the entire north shore of Corregidor—"a spectacle," reported one Japanese, "that confounded the imagination, surpassing in grim horror anything we had ever seen before."

Company A, 4th Marines, had a mile-long sector covering the north shore of Corregidor east of Malinta Hill. Despite the slaughter offshore, the Japanese assault battalion knifed through the thin beach positions and made for the high ground in the rear, a hogback along the spine of the island. Here was Battery Denver, an Army AA position whose guns were to be depressed for antiboat and antitank fire to support Company A. When no support came from Battery Denver, Marines investigated and found it had been abandoned. Japanese infantry were already taking possession. Once across the island, they brushed aside Company D's defensive line west of Battery Denver, and began a series of attacks toward Malinta Hill. Meanwhile other landings came in, also to the east.

At 0200 Colonel Howard committed Companies O and P, a 250-man demi-battalion made up mainly of Marines from Headquarters and Service Companies of the regiment, commanded by Major Max W. Schaeffer.

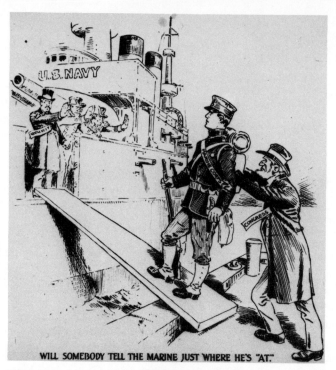

"Will Somebody Tell the Marines," World War I.

Devil Dog sign displayed at Columbus Circle, New York City, World War I.

37mm Howitzer crew from headquarters company, 6th Marines, in action against German positions.

Marines bury their first German dead, Post Command, Moscou, Verdun Front, France, 4 April 1918.

CUNNINGHAM JUST BEFORE THE CRASH. FIRST ATTEMPT
EVER MADE TO CATAPULT PLANE FROM WARSHIP
UNDERWWAY. CATAPULT FAILED TO FUNCTION PROPERLY

Upper portion of photo shows Lieutenant Alfred A. Cunningham, USMC, the first Marine Corps pilot, catapulting from the moving warship, USS *Carolina*, in 1916. Lieutenant Cunningham was the first Corps pilot to accomplish this feat. The lower photo shows the aircraft after it plunged into the sea when the catapult failed.

Italian decoration of the Second Division in Germany, December 16, 1919 by Major General John A. Lejune, USMC.

U.S. Fifth Marines with antiaircraft guns, Mancucourt, France, 1918.

Marines in combat, Santo Domingo.

Schaeffer's orders were to counterattack eastward and attempt to restore the situation in the east (1st Battalion) sector. Before dawn this force launched three separate counterattacks against the Battery Denver position, but eventually spent itself without success and at high cost. Among the heroes of the final attack were Sergeant Major John H. Sweeney and Quartermaster Sergeant John E. Haskin, long-time friends and messmates in the old Corps, who fell within moments of each other while assaulting a Japanese machine gun nest on the slope of Denver Hill.

By 0430 the time had come for Colonel Howard to commit his last reserve. The provisional 4th Battalion, though bravely and competently led by Major Francis H. Williams, was—in words of one of its officers[25]—"a group of 500 sailors with 500 rifles—nothing more." These men were ordered to counterattack through intense shelling and retake Battery Denver. The 2d and 3d Battalions, far more capable of such a task, were tied to beach defenses elsewhere.

At 0600, Williams launched his attack. All glory to the sailors: they kept attacking while they could still stand, but it was Fort Fisher all over again. By 0800, although staggered by the "bold and obstinate counterattack," the Japanese knew they could hold Battery Denver, while Williams knew that his battalion was spent. Within two hours, Japanese tanks were ashore, and the end had come. With more than a thousand wounded lying helpless in the Malinta tunnels, General Wainwright decided to surrender at noon. Captain Golland Lee Clark, a tall young Marine just five years out of Philadelphia Basic School, was ordered to make his way to the enemy with a white flag and a field music to sound the parley. While Captain Clark marched erect and straight into the Japanese lines, coded orders went out to all units to cease resistance at noon: "Execute *Pontiac* . . . Execute *Pontiac*. . . ." As on Wake, Marines began smashing their rifles.

Shaken by tears, Colonel Howard ordered the adjutant to burn the 4th Regiment's Colors and Battle Standard. Then he turned to his executive officer, Colonel Donald Curtis, and blurted, "My God . . . and I had to be the first Marine officer ever to surrender a regiment."[26]

MOBILIZATION AND DEPLOYMENT, 1942

While the far-flung units already overseas strove to hold their thin lines or at least sell themselves dear, mobilization and deployment of home forces began.

The first dispatch sent by the new Commander in Chief U. S. Fleet in Washington (Admiral Ernest J. King) to the new Commander in Chief Pacific Fleet at Pearl Harbor (Admiral Chester W. Nimitz) told Nimitz to cover and hold the Hawaii-Midway line; and to maintain communications between the West Coast of the United States and Australia, chiefly by securing the line between Hawaii and Samoa.

Marine aviation and defense battalions were already deeply engaged in "Ernie" King's first task. To accomplish the second, the 2d Marine Brigade, shaped around the 8th Marines and a battalion of the 10th Marines, was carved out of the already depleted 2d Marine Division. On 6 January 1942 the first United States expeditionary force of World War II, the 2d Brigade, commanded by Brigadier General Henry L. Larsen, sailed from San Diego for American Samoa. While the brigade was en route, a Japanese submarine shelled Tutuila, an event which made the brigade's arrival on 23 January (together with another defense battalion, the 2d) seem all the more timely, especially to the lonely 7th Defense Battalion. Within a few months, in early April, Marine Air Group 13 arrived and balanced out the defense force whose aviation resources until then had consisted of two J2F Grumman "Ducks."

By 18 February Admiral King had arrived at further conclusions. In a memorandum for General Marshall, he wrote:[27]

. . . it will be necessary, as rapidly as possible, for the United States to occupy several additional islands in the central and southwestern Pacific. The purpose will be to establish a system of groups of islands, whose air contingents will provide mutual support, and which would offer security for the operations of our naval forces and sea communications. The island of greatest immediate importance appears to be Efate in the New Hebrides. . . .

On 2 March, after Marshall, by no means convinced, had asked for more details, the admiral shot back a characteristically incisive reply, which, in the words of King's biographer, Walter Whitehill, "anticipated the course the South Pacific war was to take for the next two years."

Admiral King wrote:[28]

The general scheme or concept of operations is not only to protect the line of communications with Australia, but, in so doing, set up "strong points" from which a step-by-step general advance can be made through the New Hebrides, Solomons, and the Bismarck Archipelago. It is to be expected that such a step-by-step general advance will draw Japanese forces to oppose it, thus relieving pressure in other parts of the Pacific. . . .

When the advance to the northwest begins, it is expected to use amphibious troops (chiefly from the Amphibious Corps, Pacific Fleet) to seize and occupy "strong points" under cover of appropriate naval and air forces. The amphibious troops should be relieved by garrison troops as soon as practicable in order that the advance may be continued. . . . The question of the availability of the Marines has been explored, and it appears likely that they are best employed in the amphibious operations and in other advanced work. It would appear that the total Army requirements for the contemplated occupation and advance will not require more than two, perhaps three, Army divisions.

The immediate task was to secure the New Hebrides, an obscure collection of islands previously notable only for cannibalism, virulent malaria, and their unique condominium government by Great Britain and France. For this, the 4th Defense Battalion, until then earmarked for the Tonga Islands, was selected. This battalion, accompanied by base personnel from MAG-24 (for the airstrip which was to be built), landed at Vila, Efate, on 29 March, and found itself holding the only United States position between Japan and New Caledonia. This isolation was underscored a month later when the Japanese landed without opposition at Tulagi, 700 miles north, and, like the Marines in the New Hebrides, began building an airfield on the adjacent island of Guadalcanal.

Despite frightening casualties from malaria (60 per cent of the force came down within the first 60 days), the Efate airstrip was ready to receive fighters by 30 April; on 28 May, a mixed force of Marines, newly organized Seabees, and Army National Guardsmen pushed north from Efate to Espiritu Santo Island and established what later became the greatest base in the South Pacific. Meanwhile, in late May, the stub-winged Grummans of VMF-212, commanded by Major Harold W. ("Joe") Bauer, flew to Efate from Tontouta air base in New Caledonia. Two months later (28 July) Espiritu Santo's airstrip opened. Until the Guadalcanal landings in August, this scanty force— a defense battalion and a fighter squadron, reinforced by some Army troops —was the ultimate projection of America's power in the race to win the South Pacific.

While the planners planned and the first expeditions deployed, the Marines not yet in the war zones trained.

Under Major General Holland Smith, the Amphibious Corps Atlantic Fleet not only continued to give the Army amphibious lessons, but polished the 1st Marine Division, which was preparing to move out. Its last joint exercise with the Army took place inside Chesapeake Bay (to avoid German submarines) in January 1942. One final action by General Smith (at the instigation of his naval gunfire officer, Major Donald M. Weller) had farreaching consequences: this was to persuade the Navy to purchase Bloodsworth Island, a half-awash Chesapeake islet, for a shore bombardment range in order to qualify fire-support ships and naval gunfire spotters. Thus did Bloodsworth become the first full-time amphibious gunnery range ever established.

On the West Coast, the 132,000-acre Santa Margarita Ranch, located north of San Diego, was purchased on 10 March 1942 as a new Marine Corps base to be named for "Uncle Joe" Pendleton. The site was jointly commissioned by President Roosevelt and Mrs. Pendleton, who had survived her husband. "It is a tribute to Uncle Joe—and deserved!" said the President, taking Mrs. Pendleton's hands in his after they had raised the Colors together.

On 9 April 1942, General Joseph T. McNarney, USA, acting Army Chief of Staff, signed a memorandum to Admiral King which was destined to influence the entire participation of the Marine Corps in World War II:[29]

. . . Army amphibious operations will probably be merely the spearhead of a prolonged, heavy, land operation. This is the type of task for which Army division and higher organization is definitely pointed. . . . In the Pacific, offensive operations for the next year or more promise to comprise a series of landing operations from shipboard to small islands with relatively minor forces. This is the type of amphibious warfare for which the Marines have apparently been specially organized. . . . It might be wise to recognize these differences and to separate our amphibious training efforts by concentrating on an Army Amphibious Corps in the Atlantic and a Marine Amphibious Force in the Pacific.

Two weeks later, the Joint Planners, acting on this suggestion, agreed that Army divisions only would be employed in the Atlantic, while Marine divisions would be deployed to the Pacific. This decision, soon ratified by the Joint Chiefs of Staff, had the effect, even if unintended, of accomplishing the general staff's World War I objective of keeping Marines out of France. It also had, at least in General McNarney's note, echoes of the Army view that, while Marines might be suitable for small operations, they had little place in anything bigger.[30]

MARINES AT MIDWAY

Before dawn on 4 June 1942, the Japanese Fleet approached Midway Atoll in two groups, a striking force built around four carriers and an occupation force of amphibious troops in transports. At 0430, 108 fighters and dive bombers took off from their carriers to attack Midway.

The Midway Defense Force had been heavily reinforced since late April, when crypto-intercepts revealed Japanese plans to assault the atoll. The 6th Defense Battalion, almost doubled in size, now included 3-inch, 5-inch, and

7-inch seacoast batteries, plus the greater part of the 3d Defense Battalion. For ground defense there were four infantry companies.

Marine Air Group 22, based on Eastern Island, had a fighting squadron (VMF-221) under Major Floyd B. Parks and a squadron of dive bombers (VMSB-241) under Major Lofton R. Henderson. VMF-221 was equipped mainly with Brewster F2A fighters; "a perfect dud in combat,"[31] later commented Colonel Gregory Boyington, who had had sad experience with them in the Flying Tigers; the dive-bomber squadron was a little better off but not much. They had some Douglas SBD-2s, modern enough but more than canceled by a large complement of fabric-covered antiques, Vought SB2U-3s. Senior Marine officer on Midway was Colonel Harold D. Shannon, in command of the defense battalion; Lieutenant Colonel Ira E. Kimes had MAG-22.

Beginning at 0616, about 30 miles northwest of Midway, VMF-221 valiantly tried to intercept the Japanese bombers, which were screened by Zeroes. In the first attack, nine out of 12 attacking Marine fighters were shot down; in the second, six out of 13 were lost. In the words of a pilot who came through, the Brewsters ". . . looked like they were tied to a string while the Zeroes made passes at them."[32] But the wrack of VMF-221 was not in vain: 32 Japanese bombers never reached Midway.

Fifteen minutes later the remaining enemy attack planes, in two waves, now 18 and 22 strong, respectively, came within gun range, and the defense battalions took over. Although the Japanese plastered Midway's two islands, causing heavy structural damage and large fires, all antiaircraft batteries fired continuously, destroying 10 or more of the attackers. The Japanese report on this phase of the action winced at the Marines' "vicious antiaircraft fire."[33]

Meanwhile, VMSB-241 struck the Japanese carriers and their supporting battleships 150 miles northwest of Midway. One group, the SBDs, attacked the carrier *Akagi,* unfortunately without sinking (and probably without even hitting) her, although eight out of 16 SBDs were lost to fighters and flak. A second group, the old SB2Us, came under heavy fighter attack and had no choice but to go after the battleship *Haruna,* which was the only target at hand. Nothing better than near misses can be claimed, and three SB2Us were the cost.

Next morning, Marine air got in its final blows—a strike against two enemy cruisers limping westward after serious collision damage. Captain Richard E. Fleming, leading a flight of SB2Us, was hit by flak during his dive, and, with his plane already afire, flew it into the after turret of the cruiser *Mikuma,* an act for which he won, posthumously, the Medal of Honor. "He was very brave," commented a Japanese admiral who saw the attack.[34]

At a cost of 48 killed and 39 wounded, Marine air and ground did their best to defend Midway. MAG-22 destroyed at least 43 enemy fighters and bombers, and the defense battalions shot down 10 or more in addition. Of course, the Marine operations just described, while important in such a history as this, were wholly secondary to simultaneous events in the much larger picture of Fleet operations. At the cost of one carrier (USS *Yorktown*) and a destroyer, the Pacific Fleet had inflicted a defeat from which the Japanese Navy never fully recovered. All four enemy carriers, with their full complement of nearly 300 first-line aircraft, as well as a heavy cruiser, had been sunk by American carrier air. Midway was a victory of superior intelligence and superior co-ordination, and a turning point in the war. After Midway the Japanese would never again enjoy the margin of superiority they had during the war's first six months.

One by-product of the unequal battle above Midway by obsolete Marine aircraft against modern enemies was a bit of direct action by Lieutenant Colonel "Sheriff" Larkin: he "gave Jim Roosevelt [a Marine reserve officer] a folder of the action on Midway to take to his Dad." According to Major Roosevelt, the folder was duly delivered at the White House, and "resulted in considerable improvement in the situation shortly thereafter."[35]

OPERATION WATCHTOWER

By virtually destroying Japan's carrier air, the Navy's great victory at Midway had created a magnificent opportunity to turn the tide in the Pacific. Among many who sensed this opportunity, none knew better what must be done—or what tools existed to do it at once—than Admiral King. The tools, and the only tools, were the victorious carriers of the Pacific Fleet and the 1st Marine Division. Their job was to launch an offensive against the southern Solomons.

As the Joint Chiefs of Staff reappraised the situation after Midway, King hammered home the need for prompt action. During late June, still prodding Marshall (who at length assented to the operation but wanted to do it with Army troops, or, if with Marines, under MacArthur's command), King emphasized that the only available fighting forces would be Navy and

Marines, and so should be the command. Almost brutally, he pointed out the incapacity of MacArthur's Southwest Pacific command to make any contribution to an attack on the lower Solomons, and ended by telling Marshall:[36]

I think it is important that this [operation] be done even if no support of Army forces in the South West Pacific area is made available.

To prove that he meant what he was saying, the admiral had already (on 25 June) told subordinates to begin planning for a Navy-Marine operation to recapture Tulagi "and adjacent areas." JCS approval would follow eventually, he asserted. On 2 July it did, but only after King had set the wheels moving unilaterally. One final reclama came from General MacArthur (and from his Navy opposite number in the South Pacific, Vice Admiral Robert L. Ghormley), who believed the forces at hand were inadequate. The JCS overruled them, but ultimately did allow one precious week's extension of time before the attack: D-day was 7 August 1942. Operation Watchtower was the code name.

Only a few weeks before, on 19 May, the 1st Marine Division had sailed from Norfolk for New Zealand. The division's 7th Regiment, with the 1st Battalion, 11th Marines, had been peeled off in March, with the 8th Defense Battalion, to form the 3d Brigade, which was rushed to garrison Western Samoa. The new division commander, Major General A. A. Vandegrift, expected to have six months' training in New Zealand and go to war in 1943. On 26 June, while part of his division was still at sea, Vandegrift (who had been in New Zealand for just 12 days) got the surprise of his life—Admiral King's initial orders for Watchtower, which arrived at Admiral Ghormley's headquarters in Auckland most appropriately while General Vandegrift and several of his principal staff officers were in the act of a courtesy call on the admiral.

Of the million-and-one things which had to be done simultaneously, three immediately stood out: collect intelligence so a plan could be written; unload the noncombat-loaded shipping and then reload it for combat; and plan and execute a rehearsal.

The tactical plan for Watchtower—which was almost finished before the naval attack force commander, Rear Admiral Richmond K. Turner, reported—called for the capture of Tulagi and nearby islands by three battalions, while the remainder of the 1st Division landed on Guadalcanal and secured the airfield which the Japanese were completing. This plan was based on scraps of information obtained here, there, and everywhere, from traders, planters, and shipmasters; the newest chart dated from 1908, and the resultant tactical map of the Guadalcanal landing area was little more than a mimeographed field sketch.

On 26 July, just before rehearsals at Fiji, General Vandegrift learned two highly disturbing facts: first, that Vice Admiral Frank Jack Fletcher, who had earlier missed his chance to relieve Wake and would command the carrier support for the landings, intended to withdraw his flattops (and thus all air support) from the area two days after the landings, even though unloading the transports would take at least four days; second, that the 2d Marines (which Admiral King had attached to the 1st Division in lieu of the absent 7th Regiment) were to be withheld by the amphibious force commander, Rear Admiral Turner, for future operations (which never came off). Hardly cheered by these discoveries, General Vandegrift was even less encouraged by the rehearsals, which he later dismissed as "a complete bust."[37]

"Bust" or not, the Marines sailed from Fiji at nightfall, 31 July, in the first American offensive operation of World War II. The long road back had commenced.

TULAGI AND GAVUTU-TANAMBOGO

At 0240 on the morning of 7 August 1942, Transport Group Yoke, carrying the Tulagi assault force, sheered away from the main body of the attack force and made for the north side of Sealark Channel, which separates Guadalcanal and Tulagi. Landing Group Yoke, commanded by Brigadier General William H. Rupertus, consisted of the 1st Raider Battalion (Lieutenant Colonel Merritt A. Edson); 2d Battalion, 5th Marines (Lieutenant Colonel Harold E. Rosecrans); 1st Parachute Battalion (Major Robert H. Williams); and 1st Battalion, 2d Marines (Lieutenant Colonel Robert E. Hill). The first two battalions were to assault Tulagi; the parachutists were to seize the adjacent islets, Gavutu and Tanambogo; and Hill's battalion, after reconnoitering and securing key features of Florida Island, was to be the local reserve.

Almost miraculously, or so it seemed, the final approach of the American task force was completely undetected. Only at 0614, when the first naval gunfire and air-strikes crashed onto enemy positions, did the Japanese wake up to what was afoot. By then it was too late. Fighters and dive bombers

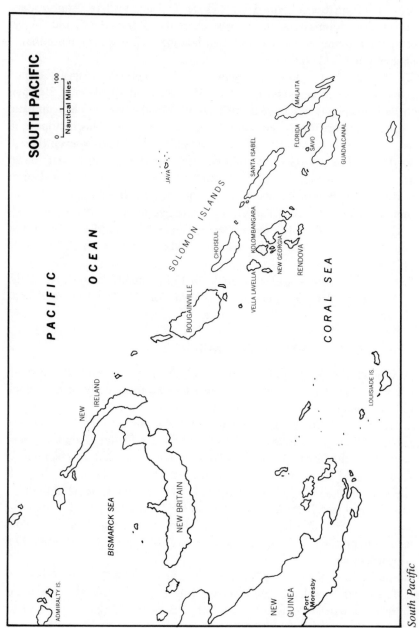

South Pacific

from the USS *Wasp* hit previously located AA positions and wiped out a cluster of Zero float-plane fighters which the Japanese had based on Tulagi Harbor. "We will defend to the last man," was the last radio message sent by the defenders before they smashed their transmitters.[38]

At 0800, covered by 5-inch gunfire from the cruiser *San Juan* and the destroyers *Monssen* and *Buchanan,* "Red Mike" Edson's raiders waded ashore on Tulagi, crossed the cemetery, and swung right to advance along the spine of the heavily wooded island. Later, the 2d Battalion, 5th Marines, landed. For three hours no serious opposition developed. Then, just before noon, Tulagi's 500 defenders (mainly 3d Kure Special Landing Force and naval aviators and ground crews) showed fight. Two hills, Hill 208 and 281, held up the raiders during the afternoon. The former was cleared after an hour's sharp infighting, but Hill 281 required a co-ordinated attack and a 280-round attack preparation by the *San Juan's* 5-inchers. This probably was the first call-fire naval gunfire support mission by a U. S. ship in World War II.[39] By nightfall, Edson had secured all but the east end of Tulagi, and pinned down the remaining defenders in a deep ravine lined with coral caves—an ominous portent of things to come throughout the war.

Equally portentous were the enemy's operations after dark. "The first night on Tulagi," wrote Major John L. Zimmerman, "set the pattern for many nights in the Pacific War."[40] There were four attacks during the night, interspersed with continual individual infiltration. But the raiders held their positions, and next day, together with elements of the 2d Battalion, 5th Marines, worked their way through the caves.

Caves were still a novelty at this stage of the war, but the Marines learned quickly. Bundles of dynamite lashed to poles blew coral chunks into the air and sealed Japanese underground. One overenthusiastic captain miscalculated his charge: the dynamite not only blasted a cave entrance but blew his pants right off.

The recapture of Tulagi was now accomplished. General Rupertus established headquarters in a comfortable cottage, formerly the British Residency.

Gavutu and Tanambogo, lying about a mile east of Tulagi, were a pair of conical coral islands linked by a 1,000-yard causeway. As the site of the seaplane base and main radio station, they were of military importance and were garrisoned by 1,000 Japanese, half of whom were laborers or artisans. The disparate strength of this garrison in relation to that of Tulagi was one of several important facts which the pell-mell collection of intelligence had skipped. As a result, the job of taking both islands was assigned to the 351-

man 1st Parachute Battalion. In retrospect, it is no surprise that the parachute troops (sans parachutes) found themselves in for a rough time.

On the heels of a brisk beach neutralization (280 5-inch rounds in four minutes, or one round per gun every 12 seconds) from the *San Juan* and an air-strike from the *Wasp's* SBDs, and without benefit of surprise—the time of landing was set as four hours after H-hour for Tulagi—the parachutists hit the east shore of Gavutu. Intense fire from coral caves swept the beach; from Tanambogo, long-range enfilading bursts played on the boat lanes. Within 20 minutes, the Parachute Battalion commander, Major Robert H. Williams, was wounded, and the assault had bogged down, mainly because of effective fire from Tanambogo. The last available local reserve in the Yoke Group, Company B, 2d Marines, was committed in an abortive attempt to take Tanambogo singlehanded. This failed.

Although General Rupertus' exaggerated report (from offshore) of 50 to 60 per cent casualties among the parachutists overplayed the situation considerably, the assault was getting nowhere, and the night on Gavutu was uneasy. Next morning, at 0730, the 3d Battalion, 2d Marines, released from division reserve, landed on Gavutu, and, with its attached regimental weapons and tanks, secured the battered island. That afternoon, this battalion got a firm foothold on Tanambogo with a landing supported by an attack across the causeway. After another night of infiltrations, with support from artillery, naval gunfire, and—indiscriminately on both sides—from badly briefed dive bombers, Tanambogo finally fell. Twenty-three prisoners were taken, and 70 enemy were believed to have made their way from all three islands to neighboring Florida, where most were ultimately hunted down. Otherwise, as would occur so often in future, the Japanese casualties were total. One hundred eight Marines were dead, and 140 more were wounded. For this price, in three days of sometimes bitter fighting, Tulagi Harbor now belonged to the Marine Corps.

GUADALCANAL: INITIAL DEPLOYMENTS AND DISASTER

Guadalcanal, a foreboding amalgam of mountains, jungle, swamp, and sword grass, was garrisoned on 7 August 1942 by some 2,230 Japanese, of whom about 1,700 were naval construction troops. This total was less than half the strength which July's frantic intelligence effort had toted up. The Japanese airfield on Lunga Point, soon to be named Henderson Field, was nearly completed on 6 August, 80 per cent, to be exact. As a reward for progress, the Japanese engineers got extra sake that night.

Since the presumed 5,000 defenders were concentrated around the airstrip, General Vandegrift, anxious to "hit them where they ain't," had chosen a beach five miles east of Lunga Point. All the 1st Marine Division, except the forces set aside for Tulagi Harbor, was to land over Red Beach and strike out for the airfield, likewise securing a key eminence known as "Grassy Knoll" (which in fact wasn't captured until after Christmas).

H-hour for the landing was 0910. The ship-to-shore movement to Red

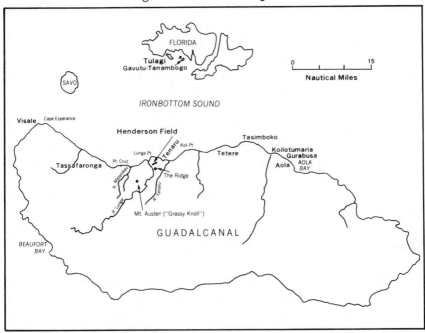

Battle of Guadalcanal, 10 August 1942 to 8 February 1943

Beach from Transport Group X-Ray was made in Andrew Jackson Higgins' LCPs, LCPRs, and LCMs, on the heels of a bombardment by the cruisers *Quincy, Vincennes,* and *Astoria,* and the SBDs of the carriers *Saratoga* and *Enterprise.* At 0913, Colonel Leroy P. Hunt's 5th Marines (less 2d Battalion, on Tulagi) scrambled ashore. To the surprise of many and the undoubted relief of all, there was no opposition. Fifty minutes later, Colonel Clifton B. Cates—who had driven German infantry out of Bouresches in 1918—had leading elements of the 1st Regiment on the beach. Still no enemy.

In the jungle and in the coastal palm groves, the troops thrashed toward the airfield, and supplies began to pile up on the beach. The Navy, anxious to speed unloading, was pushing gear ashore faster than it could be handled by the 310-man shore party, whose size was completely inadequate. Although two unwelcome afternoon interruptions by 27 twin-engined Japanese bombers and 16 Aichi 99 dive bombers failed to hurt the transports, the situation on the beach got worse and worse. Naval officers, unsympathetic to General Vandegrift's overriding need to keep his troops immediately in hand for the fight which was momentarily anticipated, blamed the Marines. The Marines, in turn, blamed the Navy for glutting the beaches by ordering general unloading without bothering to find out if the landing force could handle it. By three o'clock the next morning, all unloading had to be stopped to permit the beach chaos to unscramble itself.

August 8th saw the 1st Division in possession of Lunga Point and the airfield. The Grassy Knoll (Mount Austen) proved, on the ground as distinct from the map, to be too far away to secure immediately, and was not occupied. Except for another air raid (which turned the transport *George F. Elliott* into a blazing hulk), the Japanese had not yet reacted, although five to eight enemy ships, including cruisers, had been reported in an area 350 to 600 miles northwest of, and heading for, Guadalcanal.

That night the Guadalcanal operation came to an abrupt turning point. Admiral Fletcher, who had worried unduly about his fueling problems during the attempted relief of Wake, signaled that, because of aircraft losses (21 out of his 99 fighters) and fuel shortage, he had to withdraw the carriers. Without waiting for permission to do so, he then retired southward, leaving the amphibious force fully exposed. Postwar evidence fails to support Fletcher's concern over fuel (according to their logbooks, his carriers had 17 days' fuel left). Guadalcanal's Marines and the amphibious shipping, still half unloaded, were left with no air cover at all. Admiral Turner, understandably worried over what Japanese air could do to his ships, decided to pull out, unloaded or not. The Marines would just have to fight their battle with what they had ashore. This stunning information was communicated to Vandegrift at a conference aboard Turner's flagship, the transport *McCawley*. In the words of an officer who was present:[41]

Vandegrift told Turner that we were all right on Guadalcanal, but that he would have to know more about the situation on Tulagi before concurring in the withdrawal of the transports. Turner said, "I thought you would want to check, so I have *Southard* standing by to take you over." Vandegrift, Peyton (Turner's chief of staff), Linscott, and Thomas boarded *Southard*, which headed for Tulagi.

A few minutes after General Vandegrift boarded the old destroyer-minesweeper, all hell broke loose. The sky brightened right overhead with arching tracers; the horizon exploded in gun flashes and, shortly, in ominous pyramids of flame. Nevertheless, the general and his party completed their conference and arrangements at Tulagi as planned, returning at daylight to concur in Turner's decision. Not until then did they learn that disaster had compounded itself. A Japanese task force had fallen upon our cruiser screen east of Savo Island in the waters between Guadalcanal and Florida. In a half hour's slaughterous night action, four fine cruisers—*Vincennes*, *Quincy*, *Astoria*, and HMAS *Canberra*—were surprised, eviscerated, and destroyed by a Japanese striking force led by Rear Admiral Gunichi Mikawa. Other than one 8-inch salvo from the *Quincy*, which she got off in her death agony scoring a hit on Mikawa's flag bridge, the damage inflicted by our ships on the enemy was negligible. The U. S. Navy had sustained a defeat second only to Pearl Harbor; at a single stroke, a third of the heavy cruisers in the Pacific Fleet, and 1,024 officers and men, were wiped out. If Guadalcanal was to be held, the Marines would have to do it, alone.

"CAN THE MARINES HOLD IT?"

After the Savo Island debacle, Sealark Channel, between Guadalcanal and Tulagi, was christened "Ironbottom Sound." By the afternoon of 9 August, Ironbottom Sound—at least on the surface—was empty of United States ships. No friendly aircraft were in the air. The 1st Marine Division had been left on its own. In the words of Hanson Baldwin, as they appeared in the *New York Times*, "It is as if the Marines held Jones Beach, and the rest of Long Island were loosely dominated by the enemy."[42] In a pessimistic letter to General Marshall, Major General Millard F. Harmon, USA, the Army commander in the South Pacific, observed gloomily:[43]

The thing that impresses me more than anything else in connection with the Solomons action is that we are not prepared to follow up. We have seized a strategic position. . . . Can the Marines hold it? There is considerable room for doubt.

If there was doubt in the mind of General Vandegrift, or of his fighting operations officer, Colonel G. C. Thomas (who had been a platoon sergeant at Belleau Wood), it didn't show. With his back to the empty Sound, "Jerry" Thomas issued the general's first orders: Get the airfield finished. . . . Get the supplies off the beach and dispersed into dumps. . . . Establish a perimeter around the airfield. . . . Dig in.

Counting noses on Guadalcanal, the so-called division was a force built around five (not the normal nine) rifle battalions; total strength, about 10,000. There were 6,075 more on Tulagi. In his hurry to vacate this danger- ous area, Admiral Turner had carried off headquarters and regimental weap- ons of the 2d Marines and part of the 3d Battalion, 10th Marines, all told, about a thousand more. These, without General Vandegrift's knowledge or sanction, were dumped ashore at Espiritu Santo with Turner's orders "to re- inforce the garrison there."[44] It would be 9 October before Vandegrift could pry back these badly needed troops.

As important as the nose count, or perhaps even more so, was to check the supplies which the division had after the transports shoved off. There was enough ammunition. Sandbags, entrenching tools, and barbed wire were short (only 18 spools of wire got ashore). There were no land mines at all. Practically all the 1st Engineer Battalion's equipment, apparently thought by the Navy to represent frills, had been carried away in the USS *Fomalhaut*. (One bulldozer, one only, got ashore; it became part of the margin of ultimate victory.) Fortunately, some battered Japanese engineering equipment was taken. This, too, helped turn the tide. There was so little food that, even with large stocks of captured enemy rations, the ration was cut to two meals a day. As for rations, the following comment gives the feel of those days:[45]

Fish and rice, fish and rice, fish and rice. And black coffee without sugar, flat candy, dehydrated potatoes, cabbage and carrots. We finished off the meals with a Jap cigarette, using pasteboard holders provided with each pack so that the acid in the cheap paper wouldn't give us lip sores. Sometimes the Jap diet was broken by a plate of beans, canned salmon, or a slab of beef from a Lever Brothers cow.

While Guadalcanal Marines wondered what to do next, the Japanese Army had its worries, too. Astonishing to relate, their Navy had omitted to tell them of Tulagi's seizure in May or of the airfield abuilding on Guadalcanal, until the whole venture was publicized by Vandegrift. The first Army reac- tion was to divert a reinforced infantry battalion, the Ichiki Detachment, originally formed to capture Midway, to retake Guadalcanal. This 900-man unit was supposed to land on 18 August and sweep a Marine division into the sea, an operation which Vice Admiral Raizo Tanaka, one of the enemy's best, later likened to "a housefly's attacking a giant tortoise."[46]

Reports thus began to come in of Japanese activity east of the perimeter now occupied by the 1st Division. To probe these, part of Company A, 1st Marines, was formed into a patrol on 19 August under a stocky young captain, Charles H. Brush, Jr. About noon, as Brush's people pressed on (in hope of making their midday halt near a fruit grove reported ahead), the point froze and signaled, "Enemy in sight." Four Japanese officers and 30 enlisted men were strolling down the trail. Brush's swift attack overwhelmed them; 31 were killed, and three got away. Typically careless with documents, the Japanese carried interesting papers. As Brush remarked:[47]

With a complete lack of knowledge of Japanese on my part, the maps the Japanese had of our positions were so clear as to startle me.

Brush's ambush partly avenged the loss, a week earlier, of a 25-man patrol led by Lieutenant Colonel Frank Goettge, division intelligence officer, which had been all but wiped out west of the perimeter.

Obviously an attack was brewing. This was confirmed by radio intelligence and by another more exotic source, the native scouts of the British Solomon Islands Constabulary. They were led by Captain W. F. M. Clemens, the strapping, bemoustached British district officer, who had serenely emerged from a jungle hide-out when the Marines landed on Guadalcanal.

With all this talk of fighting, it seemed high time to get some planes onto the airfield. The 1st Engineer Battalion, making-do with the dinky Japanese equipment, had the strip ready for business on the 12th, but, despite a previous promise to Vandegrift by Turner, that he would have shore-based air by 11 August, none was in sight. On 15 August, however, four small, fast transports (converted from old four-pipe destroyers) darted up to Guadalcanal bearing a Navy aviation base unit (Cub-1) shepherded forward by a Marine aviator, Major Charles H. ("Fog") Hayes. With 400 drums of aviation gas, 282 assorted bombs, and a roll of fuel-straining chamois under his arm, Major Hayes and his sailors set about making the field habitable to airplanes. Henderson Field, they christened it, in honor of Major Lofton R. Henderson, of VMSB-241, who was widely believed in those days to have crashed his stricken dive bomber onto a Japanese cruiser at Midway (actually, although bravely killed in action, Henderson did no such thing).

On 19 August, while Captain Brush was mowing down the advance guard of the Ichiki Detachment (for such they were), the USS *Long Island* (first in the large family of "jeep" carriers) was approaching Guadalcanal with the forward headquarters of MAG-23, commanded by Lieutenant Colonel C. L. Fike, and two Marine squadrons: VMSB-232 (12 SBDs, Major Richard C. Mangrum) and VMF-223 (19 F4Fs, Captain John L. Smith). Next afternoon, while some Marines cheered and a few even wept, "Dick" Mangrum and John Smith pancaked their airplanes on Henderson Field, and Marine aviation entered the battle for Guadalcanal.

That night was uneasy. Listening posts out forward of the Ilu River (which, because of bad maps, everyone on Guadalcanal called "the Tenaru") began to fall back with enemy patrols on their heels. Along the Ilu, held by Lieutenant Colonel Edwin A. Pollock's 2d Battalion, 1st Marines, there was a disturbance about midnight: a native, bleeding from stab-wounds in his chest and throat, staggered into the Marines' lines with word of 250 Japanese out front. This was Sergeant Major Vouza, retired from the Solomons Constabulary, who had been "interrogated" with a samurai sword and left in the bush to die—a premature action by the Japanese, as the brave old man then got up and made a day's march west to the Marines' perimeter and got there simultaneously with the Ichiki Detachment (for which he received the George Medal and Silver Star).

Hardly had Vouza's warning been received when musketry began to rattle and green flares went up. The first enemy thrust was a head-on attack across the sandspit mouth of the Ilu. Colonel Cates wrote shortly afterward:[48]

They were walking right in the edge of the surf and got tangled up in some barb wire that we had salvaged from fences. They started jabbering so our bunch let go with everything they had. They immediately rushed our positions, and it was a grand mess for a few minutes. After driving them from our positions they [sic] took refuge right in the edge of the surf underneath a three-foot bank and there they stayed about 50 yards from our line. By that time their main force closed in and tried to advance down the narrow sand spit; naturally the slaughter was terrific. The rest of the main body had deployed on the east side of the river—about 100 yards from our lines—and a beautiful fire-fight continued for many hours. They were well equipped with mortars, 70-mm. cannon, flamethrowers, and heavy machine guns. Our first artillery concentration hit right on the bunch along the beach, so they withdrew about 200 yards and started digging. For some unknown reason, I shifted the artillery—remember that it was dark as pitch—to that exact spot, and there the poor devils stayed until next day when I maneuvered a battalion around their rear and cut them off.

That battalion (1st Battalion, 1st Marines, Lieutenant Colonel Lenard B. Cresswell) swung across the Ilu upstream from the fight, and swept down on Colonel Ichiki, compressing his ill-fated unit against the curtain of fire from across the stream. Meanwhile, from overhead the newly arrived fighters slashed down. That afternoon, while Marine light tanks mopped up huddled enemy groups along the sandspit, Ichiki—known among the Japanese for "magnificent leadership and indomitable fighting spirit"[49]—burned his colors and shot himself. Fifteen of his men, all wounded, survived to be captured, and a handful got away into the jungle. Thirty-four Marines were killed, and 75 wounded (mostly from the 2d Battalion). Admiral Tanaka commented:[50]

This episode made it abundantly clear that infantrymen armed with rifles and bayonets have no chance against an enemy equipped with heavy modern arms. This tragedy should have taught us the hopelessness of "bamboo-spear" tactics.

Colonel Cates's verdict was even more succinct:[51]

In my opinion it boils down to this. The Japs are excellent individual soldiers, but their headwork is very poor. They have gotten away with murder so many times, maybe they think that it only takes a small force to lick a big one. Well, they got badly fooled once anyway.

THE MAKIN RAID

While Colonel Ichiki's ill-fated battalion was landing on Guadalcanal, two companies of the 2d Raider Battalion, under Lieutenant Colonel Evans F. Carlson, were in action more than a thousand miles northeast, in a submarine-launched raid on Makin Island in the Gilberts.

This unit, "Carlson's Raiders"—not to be confused with the 1st Raider Battalion, "Edson's Raiders"—had been organized and trained under exceedingly unorthodox conditions by its commander (an acquaintance of Franklin Roosevelt), who, after resigning from the Corps in the 1930s, had spent some time as an observer with the Chinese Communist forces in North China. Despite General Holcomb's even less than lukewarm assent to Carlson's methods, the latter's philosophy of military training, epitomized by the Chinese phrase, *Gung Ho* ("Pull Together"), had found influential support in Washington and was perforce accepted by the Marine Corps (at least, for this battalion).

In a confused landing from the *Argonaut* and *Nautilus,* the 222-man force made its way ashore on 17 August, only to lose surprise because of the accidental discharge of a rifle. Once on the beach, against 83 Japanese, the raiders fought a tactically muddled action which did the unit little credit (despite outstanding leadership by Major James Roosevelt, the battalion executive officer). The raiders won, but only after many errors, and re-embarkation through a vicious surf further disorganized the force, so much so that nine men were left behind. Later, when the Japanese reoccupied Makin and set about fortifying it in earnest (an unintended sequel to this raid),[52] these men were taken and beheaded. Thirty Marines were killed in action or thus captured.

All in all, the Makin raid ("a piece of folly," wrote General Holland Smith)[53] signally failed to distract the Japanese from the struggle in the Solomons. Its only possible effect, as mentioned, was to bring about heavy reinforcement of the atoll (which 15 months later had to be taken for good by an Army regiment). In addition, among the few who learned the full story, the operation served to place a chill on the raider program. Although all raider units, including this battalion, were destined to perform good fighting in the months ahead, the raider concept, perhaps unfairly, never quite lived down Makin, and *Gung Ho* acquired an unintended derisive connotation.

THE JAPANESE REACT

The first important dividend of the Guadalcanal landings was the Japanese decision to commit the Seventeenth Army under Lieutenant General Harukichi Hyakutake to recapture the island. This force, with headquarters at Rabaul, was to have spearheaded the enemy drive across New Guinea to take Port Moresby from General MacArthur, and would undoubtedly have done so but for the 1st Marine Division. For its new task, however, Hyakutake's army was maldeployed and short of shipping.

After the Ichiki Detachment's unsuccessful curtain-raiser, the Kawaguchi Brigade, a 6,000-man force, and about 1,000 men of the 5th Yokosuka Special Naval Landing Force, were ordered south posthaste. As soon as possible, the Seventeenth Army's two remaining infantry divisions would be sent forward. Getting them there was up to Admiral Tanaka, whose destroyers and transports soon won their nickname, "The Tokyo Express."

To support Tanaka's first convoy carrying the Yokosuka SNLF, the Japanese Combined Fleet, including three carriers, three battleships, and eleven cruisers, swept down from Truk. On 24 August parts of this force collided with planes of the *Enterprise* and *Saratoga* in what was later named the battle of the Eastern Solomons. One enemy carrier, *Ryujo*, was sunk, and the *Enterprise* was wounded but not fatally. The effect of this battle on Guadalcanal was three-fold:

John L. Smith's fighters got their first big bite of the war, when the Grummans of VMF-223 jumped a large formation of bombers and fighters headed for Guadalcanal. Here, the Marines learned for the first time what a good fighter they had: six of the previously "invincible" Zeros and ten bombers flamed in. "A Zero can't take two seconds' fire from a Grumman," reported one pilot, "and a Grumman can sometimes take 15 minutes' fire from a Zero."[54]

Eleven SBDs from the damaged *Enterprise* (remnants of Scouting 5 and 6, commanded by Lieutenant T. F. Caldwell, Jr., USN) headed for Henderson Field and based there, attached to Mangrum's squadron, for almost a month— "the best Marines I ever saw who wore bell-bottomed trousers," Mangrum commented afterward.[55] This and several subsequent carrier mishaps with similar results evoked a wry aside from General Rowell, "What saved Guadalcanal was the loss of so many carriers."[56]

Guadalcanal dive bombers caught up with Admiral Tanaka on the morning of 25 August. Led by Mangrum, the Marine and Navy SBDs plastered the enemy flagship, knocking the admiral momentarily unconscious, and, even more important, sinking the transport *Kinryu Maru*, with most of the Yokosuka SNLF aboard. "We were caught napping," ruefully wrote Tanaka. "It would be folly to land the remainder of this battered force on Guadalcanal," he added, and turned back. As he did so, the destroyer *Mutsuki* had the unusual ill fortune to be hit by a B-17 and thus became the first Japanese combatant ship to be sunk by horizontal bombing in World War II.

Within five days after Guadalcanal's respite thus won, aviation reinforcements made it up to "Cactus" (the island's apt code-name): VMF-224 (Major R. E. Galer) and VMSB-231, which was commanded during most of the subsequent campaign by a veteran of Midway, Captain Elmer ("Iron Man") Glidden. These, with the *Enterprise's* invaluable SBDs and a handful of almost useless Army Air Force P-400s, brought Henderson Field's strength up to 64 aircraft. Improperly designed and unsuitably equipped as the Army squadron's P-400s were, its pilots soon won the Marines' hearts by their attitude and by their bombing and strafing attacks on Japanese ground forces (which was all the low-ceiling pursuit planes were good for)—"They were good and willing boys," said General Thomas.[57]

Almost as important as the aviation reinforcements just mentioned, on 1 September came a detachment of the 6th Naval Construction Battalion, 392 Seabees and two bulldozers, bringing the total of the latter on Guadalcanal up to three. What greeted the new arrivals was well described by Robert Sherrod:[58]

Living conditions were appalling. Pilots had to fight and fly all day on a diet of dehydrated potatoes, Spam, or cold hash—and sometimes Japanese rice. . . . Sleeping in a mud-floored tent was constantly interrupted by Japanese cruiser planes ("Louie the Louse" or "Washing Machine Charlie") which flew around murdering sleep and dropping occasional bombs, or by destroyers or submarines which stood offshore and lobbed shells at Henderson Field. When a man could get away for a bath in the Lunga River, the only time he could take his clothes off, he frequently found there wasn't any soap. If he didn't catch malaria from the Anopheles mosquitoes which swarmed into his foxhole, he was almost certain to get dysentery that tormented his bowels. . . .

Into all this—with gusto—on 3 September came Brigadier General Roy Geiger, commanding the 1st Marine Air Wing. Leaving wing headquarters on Espiritu Santo, Geiger established his forward command post in a Japanese shanty, "the Pagoda," within a couple of hundred yards of the field on Guadalcanal, where bullets and bombs were flying.

Two days later came still another welcome visitor: the first regular air transport run into Henderson Field, by an R4D (known to the Army as the C-47 and to civilians as the DC-3) of Marine Air Group 25, loaded with pogey-bait and cigarettes; on the return trip, wounded went out, the first air evacuation of wounded Marines since Nicaragua. The next trip brought in ammunition and aviation gas, and took out more casualties. This was the genesis of the famed South Pacific Combat Air Transport Command (SCAT) organized around MAG-25 and commanded by Lieutenant Colonel P. K. Smith. Before the end of the campaign, they hauled 2,879 wounded and untold tons of supplies.

There was work aplenty for all the aviation that could fly from or onto Henderson Field. Although the "Cactus Air Force" shot down 56 enemy planes (at a cost of 11) during the first ten days' operations, Rabaul got 63 more fighters and bombers on 1 September. Every noon—"Tokyo time," men called it—in came a heavy raid. Japanese barges full of reinforcements were swarming down every night and even by day, though this last was something they soon learned not to do. And Henderson Field, in its own way, was as formidable an opponent as the enemy:[59]

. . . a bowl of black dust which fouled airplane engines, or . . . a quagmire of black mud which made the takeoff resemble nothing more than a fly trying to rise from a runway of molasses.

THE BATTLE OF THE RIDGE

As early as 21 August, right after the battle of the Tenaru, General Vandegrift realized that every available Marine would be needed on Guadalcanal; that day he moved the 2d Battalion, 5th Marines, across from Tulagi. Ten days later the 1st Raider Battalion (Edson's) and the Parachute Battalion followed. Meanwhile, signs multiplied of an alarming enemy buildup east and south of the perimeter. Martin Clemens' scouts reported a concentration of several hundred Japanese, with large stocks of supplies, at Tasimboko, on the coast about 20 miles east of Lunga Point. It was decided to attack this group with an amphibious raid.

On 8 September, Colonel Edson landed his 1st Raiders, then the Parachute Battalion, and attacked Tasimboko under covering fire from the World War I 4-inchers of destroyer transports *Manley* and *McKean,* and a six-plane air strike. At first the attack went easily, then slowed. By mid-morning, Edson realized that his 850-man force was fighting nearly 1,000 enemy equipped with artillery. Edson pressed the attack, called in air, and launched a flanking group under his executive officer, Lieutenant Colonel Samuel B. Griffith.

When Griffith's people entered Tasimboko after a rapid thrust through the jungle, the Japanese retired, leaving 27 dead and many supplies: a battery of 75-mm. cannon, several 47-mm. antitank guns, more than 500,000 rounds of small-arms ammunition, land mines, and a poncho full of assorted documents—an intelligence bonanza—scooped up by correspondent "Dick" Tregaskis. As the Marines destroyed what they couldn't carry, it became clear that Tasimboko had been a main base for a large force, most of which had faded into the jungle. In Edson's clipped, husky summation, "That bunch at Tasimboko was no motley of 400 Japs, but two or three thousand well-organized soldiers. . . ."[60]

How right Colonel Edson was, would soon be confirmed by Major General Kiyotake Kawaguchi, the base supply echelon of whose heavily reinforced brigade had been hit by the raid. Moving since 2 September, by trails cut through the jungle, Kawaguchi was concentrating for an all-out attack against the perimeter.

To bolster the southern front, until then sketchily manned by detachments from the pioneers, artillery, amphibian tractor, and other division troops, the Raider Battalion, with the parachutists still attached, moved out into the jungle along a grass-covered ridge which dominated the approaches to Henderson Field, a mile north. This was initially described as a "rest area" (something the Raiders amply deserved), but meant something quite different to Edson, who urged Vandegrift to occupy the position. "When we got back to the Lunga and they sent us out toward the Ridge, I was firmly convinced we were in the path of the next Jap attack," he said.[61]

All day on 12 September the raiders and parachutists dug in along the ridge, while Edson and Griffith confirmed by reconnaissance what they already suspected—that Nips were gathering thick in the jungle to the east and south. That night at 2100, an enemy plane dropped a flare over Henderson Field. In answer, naval gunfire began coming in from three enemy destroyers and a cruiser in Ironbottom Sound, and a flare soared out of the jungle in front of the ridge.

On the heels of this flare, Kawaguchi launched his first probing attack down the right bank of the Lunga River, which paralleled the line of the ridge. The raiders held. Accustomed to victories in Borneo and the Philippines, the 3,450 assault troops screamed down twice more onto Edson's right. The thin line of Marines recoiled onto the spurs of the ridge and held there until day. At dawn, Edson counterattacked, but the Japanese were too strong to budge. All day the raiders dug in, forming a holding line to the rear of existing front lines. Four air raids, including one by 42 planes (of which 16 were shot down), lashed the perimeter. Beginning just after nightfall, Kawaguchi struck again, with his main effort squarely against Edson's center, and a fierce supporting attack against the already battered right. At 2130 and again at 2200, two more attacks came down the center again and against the parachutists on the left. As Edson pulled his men back to their final positions, the 105-mm. howitzers of the 5th Battalion, 11th Marines (the heaviest field artillery in the division), crashed down. In the grim dark, Edson, equally grim, was everywhere. To a group of aimless stragglers, he snarled, "The only thing those people have that you haven't got is guts."[62]

All night Kawaguchi's battalions clawed at the ridge. All night they were torn to pieces by the accurate close-in defensive concentrations of Colonel del Valle's 11th Marines, by Edson's heavy Brownings, and by grenade-throwing riflemen. Each time the Japanese attacked they announced it with a red flare, and down came the Marine artillery.[63] Elsewhere, two other secondary attacks hit the perimeter; both were turned back. Toward dawn, after a group of Japanese had actually penetrated to General Vandegrift's command post, where they, too, died, the division's lone reserve, the 2d Battalion, 5th Marines, was fed forward into Edson's lines. And the lines held.

By dawn's early light, the battle had petered out. More than 600 enemy dead strewed the ridge; according to Japanese records, some 1,500 were killed or died of wounds as the shattered brigade stumbled back through the malarious jungle. Forty Marines were killed or missing, and 103 were wounded. For the intrepidity and resolution he so abundantly displayed that night, Colonel Edson received the Medal of Honor; so did Major Kenneth D. Bailey, one of the raider company commanders, soon to die in action on the Matanikau. "I hope," said Edson softly, soon after this most crucial battle, "the Japs will have some respect for American fighting men. I certainly have learned respect for the Japs. . . . They're good, all right. But I think we're better."[64]

REACHING OUT TO THE MATANIKAU

On 18 September, General Vandegrift received his first major reinforcement. The 7th Marines, long held in Samoa, nearly diverted to MacArthur, and even more nearly misapplied by Admiral Turner to the Ndeni operation which so intrigued him (this was a plan to build an airfield on Ndeni, a malarial island in the Santa Cruz group east of the southern Solomons), finally came home to the 1st Division. Getting them to Guadalcanal proved an ordeal for the Navy; the carrier *Wasp* was torpedoed thrice when the convoy ran into a submarine pack and had to be sunk by our own forces; the new battleship *North Carolina* was also torpedoed and temporarily out of the fight, as was the destroyer *O'Brien*, for good. But the 7th Regiment's convoy got through: 4,262 reinforcements as yet not blooded but highly trained, 147 vehicles, 1,000 tons of rations, ten units of fire, 3,823 drums of aviation gas, and engineer equipment; altogether, a bonanza. As a dividend, came also a steady stream of Navy carrier planes and pilots from crippled or sunken CVs; these enabled Geiger to keep 50 or more aircraft flying in the Cactus Air Force.

With 19,200 ground Marines on Guadalcanal and 1,014 under Geiger, General Vandegrift could reorganize his perimeter and move out to meet the Japanese rather than fighting them on his own five-yard line. His first concern lay to the west, along the Matanikau River, where intelligence suggested that the Japanese were concentrating and reinforcing.

Lieutenant Colonel Lewis B. Puller, veteran of Nicaragua and the caco wars, made the first thrust, a battalion-strength combat patrol deep in the jungle to the Matanikau headwaters. On 24 September, spotting rice-fires on Mount Austen, he fell on an enemy bivouac. Reinforced after the fight, Puller pressed on toward the mouth of the Matanikau, where it was planned that the 1st Raiders, moving along the coast, would meet him.

On 27 September, three battalions—Puller's 1st Battalion, 7th Marines, the 2nd Battalion, 5th Marines, and the Raiders—concentrated at the appointed place after a heavy fire-fight with Japanese forces across the river. Due to co-ordination troubles (and stout enemy resistance), the attack across the river went badly. Colonel Griffith, now the Raiders' CO, was hit in the shoulder by a Jap sharpshooter ("Good shot!" he exclaimed as he staggered and fell). To outflank the frowning line of enemy positions on the bluffs west of the Matanikau, part of the 1st Battalion, 7th Marines, was shuttled beyond Point Cruz by landing craft in an amphibious envelopment. This, too, ran into trouble: after pushing rapidly inland, the force found itself cut off from the beach and beleaguered by strong Japanese opposition. The commanding officer and executive officer of the detachment were, respectively, killed and wounded. Ammunition was low, and radios failed.

Aloft, a cruising Marine SBD pilot saw the situation and called for aid. Colonel Puller made his way aboard the USS *Ballard*, a seaplane tender converted from an old four-stack destroyer, which was supporting the force, and, with a train of landing craft, got her in position to help. In the tradition of Sergeant Quick at Guantanamo Bay, Sergeant R. D. Raysbrook stood up under heavy Japanese fire and semaphored fire commands to the *Ballard*, whose guns blasted a path to the beach. But enemy machine guns on Point Cruz concentrated viciously on the rescue craft, and they would have been driven off but for Signalman 1st Class Douglas A. Munro, USCG. Engaging the Japanese with machine guns in his own Higgins boat, Munro herded the other landing craft in, while Lieutenant Dale M. Leslie, the SBD pilot, made repeated strafing runs. As the Marines, with all wounded and weapons, were evacuated from the beach, Signalman Munro was killed, but not before he had bravely accomplished his mission. He was posthumously awarded the Medal of Honor. Two Navy coxswains, Sergeant Raysbrook, and Platoon Sergeant A. P. Malinowski, Jr. (who singlehandedly covered the withdrawal of his company with a BAR), received Navy Crosses. In summing up what was a defeat, though not a disaster, "Sammy" Griffith later remarked:[65]

. . . we had most faulty intelligence of Japanese strength and dispositions. No orders would have ever been given for a battalion to go up to Kokumbona and patrol from there had there been any realization that there were several thousand Japanese between the Matanikau and Kokumbona. Faulty intelligence was the cause of the whole breakdown.

Shortly after this unfortunate action, which cost the 1st Division 60 killed and 100 wounded, further Japanese reinforcements reached Guadalcanal. Not only the Sendai Division, a crack outfit under Lieutenant General Masao Maruyama, but a regiment of 150-mm. howitzers were now ashore. With these weapons, much the heaviest artillery ashore on either side, the enemy had the range and hitting power to shell the perimeter from position-areas far beyond General Vandegrift's reach. General Maruyama, a man who thought of all the details, even included in his operation plan instructions for the receipt of General Vandegrift's surrender:[66]

After the enemy commander has transacted the terms of the first item [blanket capitulation], he shall be accompanied by a necessary number of side guards and interpreters, head toward the mouth of the Matanikau River by way of the coastal road, and agree to the terms of surrender to the commander of our force.

To edge the 150-mm. howitzers (promptly nicknamed "Pistol Pete") back out of range of Henderson Field, General Vandegrift decided to make another push beyond the Matanikau. His plan, except in scale (it was larger), was a thought-out version of the previous operation. This time, moving out on 7 October, the 5th Marines advanced along the coast and (using the attached 1st Raiders) pinned down a stubborn enemy force holding the right bank of the Matanikau. Meanwhile, the 7th Marines, with Colonel William J. Whaling's scout-sniper group attached, made a deep envelopment inland before wheeling north toward Ironbottom Sound along the enemy side of the Matanikau. Simultaneously, the Raiders, in a desperate, small action at dusk on 8 October, erased the Japanese bridgehead. The operations that day of the 2d Battalion, 7th Marines, were recorded by John Hersey, then a young correspondent five years out of Yale, in what has become a minor classic in the literature of World War II, *Into the Valley*.

In the enveloping force it was Colonel Puller who drew blood. On 9 October, as his battalion neared the sea, he came on a large Japanese force in a deep valley with a steep ridge at their backs. Puller called for artillery and put all his mortars into the valley. As the enemy scrambled up the slope to escape the rain of shells, Puller's riflemen and machine guns sent them tumbling back down again into the inferno. The slaughter kept up until the mortar ammunition was gone. One of the few Japanese survivors, an officer, recorded in his diary that 690 men were killed in this episode alone.

Aside from this spectacular kill, the operation enabled General Vandegrift to establish an outpost line from the mouth of the Matanikau inland to cover the two principal crossings. At a cost of 65 killed and 125 wounded, the three days' marching and fighting were well worth while.

THE JAPANESE STRIKE BACK

Despite the successful ending of the Matanikau actions, General Vandegrift could hardly relax. The Japanese continued to build up their strength by nightly Tokyo Express, and the United States still lacked the margin, both on Guadalcanal and afloat, to ram home a decision. To give General Vandegrift more help, Admiral Turner was finally directed to forget about Ndeni and concentrate on supporting Guadalcanal. The 164th Infantry, an Army National Guard regiment on New Caledonia, was ordered forward to Cactus. In covering this important convoy, the hard-pressed Navy got into a hot night action, the Battle of Cape Esperance, in which, on 11 October, a Japanese cruiser and destroyer were sunk, and practically every other enemy ship took something of a beating—all at the cost of one American destroyer (USS *Duncan*). Next day, Marine and Navy SBDs from

Henderson Field, led by Lieutenant Colonel Albert D. Cooley, commanding the newly arrived MAG-14 which was in process of relieving MAG-23, caught and sank two surviving enemy destroyers, *Natsugumo* and *Murakumo*.

The 164th Infantry, 2,850 strapping Minnesota and Dakota lumberjacks, got ashore, the first (and highly welcome) Army reinforcements, not counting the handful of P-400s, for a command which had already evacuated 800 battle casualties and hospitalized 1,960 with malaria. A considerably less welcome arrival on Guadalcanal about this time was General Hyakutake, who came to take personal charge of events soon to shape up.

The day the soldiers arrived (13 October) developed ominously with a surprise air raid at noon, which played hell with Henderson Field and prevented effective interception of a second raid which followed soon after. During the afternoon General Hyakutake's 150-mm. howitzers began steady interdiction and harassment of the field, a maddening methodical process, from positions in Kokumbona safely out of range of anything the Marines had. But that night topped all previous nights. For 97 minutes, under aircraft flares, the battleships *Haruna* and *Kongo* shelled Henderson Field with 918 rounds of 14-inch—one screaming high-velocity 1,500-pound shell every six seconds for the better part of two eternal hours. As one participant, Admiral Tanaka, wrote:

The whole spectacle [made] the Ryogoku fireworks display seem like mere child's play. The night's pitch dark was transformed by fire into the brightness of day.

After the battleships finally went home, night bombers and "Pistol Pete" took over, and, when day broke, the defenders, sleepless and shaken, found the field all chaos and destruction, aviation gas burned or blown up, and 48 airplanes (including 35 precious SBDs) shot.

Under continued artillery fire and still another air raid at noon, Henderson Field was out of action; worse (if possible) Guadalcanal was practically out of aviation gas. By transferring the remaining fighters to "The Cow Pasture," a grass alternate fighter strip, and by draining the tanks of two lamed B-17s caught by naval gunfire, General Geiger got a few fighters up in time to intercept the day's second air raid, and downed nine bombers and three Zeroes.

Under cover of another gun-strike, this time, two heavy cruisers which put 752 8-inch projectiles onto Henderson Field, the Tokyo Express continued to deliver General Maruyama's division to the island, all through the night of 14 October. Next morning, the Japanese didn't even bother to withdraw their transport but just continued unloading at Tassafaronga, as if Ironbottom Sound were Tokyo Bay. By 1000 General Geiger got 12 SBDs flyable, scrounged enough gas to get them airborne, and began to hammer the transports. B-17s flew up from Santo to hit them, and the brave but ineffectual Army P-400 fighters turned-to nobly as light bombers. Grumman fighters strafed. General Geiger's own pilot, Major Jack R. Cram, slung torpedoes onto the General's PBY5A (the *Blue Goose*) and, as all torpedo planes were knocked out, made the only such attack of the day. Harried by Zeroes, the rugged old amphibian smoked and strained its way back just in time to make the field, while a Grumman of VMF-121 picked off a Zero which tried to shoot the *Blue Goose* out of the landing circle.

The fruits of this convulsive effort were most gratifying: three large transports burned out and beached, and the remainder in flight. Even so, the Japanese had landed another 4,500 troops. And that night (early morning, 16 October) came still another naval shelling: 1,100 rounds of 8-inch and 5-inch (mostly the former, unfortunately). Aside from all-around battering, loss of sleep, alarm, and despondency, this bombardment further reduced Geiger's aircraft inventory. Three days earlier he had had 90 planes; now he had 34, including only nine F4Fs.

The sole available fighter reinforcements, Lieutenant Colonel Bauer's VMF-212, flew up from Efate. As Bauer, almost out of gas after the long hop, was about to land, a dive bomber raid came in. Almost by reflex, "Joe" Bauer pulled up his landing gear, closed flaps, and roared alone into the enemy formation. Before he finally had to land, he had gotten four Val dive bombers, a feat which won him a Medal of Honor that became posthumous a month later, when he went down at sea and was never seen again.

Since early September, Japanese engineers had hewn a hidden trail from Kokumbona south into the deep jungle and across cliffs and precipices for a distance of 35 miles, where it ended within striking distance of Edson's Ridge. Over this dank trail, on 16 October, General Maruyama's troops staggered out in single file, each man carrying one artillery or mortar round lashed to his pack. Five thousand six hundred enemy infantry—eight battalions—were to hit Vandegrift's southern perimeter on 18 October, while another 2,900, with tank support, would roll up the Matanikau positions. Then, Maruyama would retake Henderson Field and carry out the details of General Vandegrift's surrender as previously planned.

While the Japanese slithered and tugged through the jungle, things were happening elsewhere. In Noumea, Vice Admiral William F. Halsey, arriving on what he thought was an inspection tour, received dispatch orders to relieve his classmate, Admiral Ghormley, as ComSoPac. "The critical situation requires a more aggressive commander," said Nimitz.[67] Halsey was such a man.

At home, during a press conference on 19 October, a reporter asked Secretary of the Navy Knox if the Marines could hang on to Guadalcanal. "I certainly hope so," was the best answer he could give.[68]

Meanwhile, despite the fact that General Maruyama, way behind schedule, was nowhere near his jump-off position, the Matanikau force under General Tadashi Sumiyoshi began a series of gingerly attacks, with a lot of artillery preparation and tank probes but little push. In four days' action, these tactics cost him nine tanks, and, particularly from the howitzers of the 11th Marines, on 22 October, the virtual annihilation of an infantry battalion massed for a night attack.

During this uneasy time, as General Vandegrift and his staff tried to account for the rest of Maruyama's force, which seemingly had vanished into the jungle, President Roosevelt, concerned for his Marines, penned a handwritten memorandum to the Joint Chiefs of Staff on 24 October:[69]

My anxiety about the Southwest [sic] Pacific is to make sure that every possible weapon gets into that area to hold Guadalcanal. And that having held it in this crisis that munitions and planes and crews are on the way to take advantage of our success. . . .

That same night, half a world away from 1600 Pennsylvania Avenue, General Maruyama finally got his regiments (one, the 29th Infantry, Sendai's crack outfit) into position south of the Ridge. They were not wholly undetected: during the afternoon a Japanese officer was seen in the jungle's edge with a pair of binoculars studying the Ridge, and a Marine patrol observed "many rice-fires" smoking up the Lunga Valley in the jungle beyond Lieutenant Colonel Puller's 1st Battalion, 7th Marines, who were all the U. S. Marines facing Maruyama's two regiments.

At 0300, amid a drenching rain that had begun at nightfall, the Japanese attacked.

For 30 minutes the first attack beat down into the face of Puller's prepared concentrations and final protective lines. Then it slackened. While the division reserve battalion, from the nearby 164th Infantry, began to feed small units into Colonel Puller's positions, the Japanese regrouped and came back against the Ridge. Fighting his fight on Edson's Ridge in Edson's style, Puller received word from one company commander that ammunition was about gone. "You got bayonets, haven't you?" he barked.[70] Sergeant John Basilone—"Manila John" to his men—had a machine gun section that fired 26,000 rounds before daybreak and managed singlehandedly to break up a Jap infiltration while "the ground just rattled." The Medal of Honor was his reward.

Next morning—the troops spoke of it later as "Dugout Sunday"—with the airstrips nothing but bottomless muck, Japanese planes and ships had things their way. On the ground, "Pistol Pete" dropped a round on Henderson Field every ten minutes. Enemy destroyers swept into Ironbottom Sound and sank the USS *Seminole*, fleet tug, while small craft scurried. Only when the 3d Defense Battalion's sharp-tongued old 5-inch guns caught HIJMS *Akatsuki* within range and put three shells into her, did they withdraw. When Fighter 1 finally dried, Geiger got a chance to intercept the Japanese raids and push the Zeroes away from Guadalcanal. In the process —a process which by nightfall cost the Japanese 22 planes (not to speak of four bagged by the 3d Defense)—Captain Joseph J. Foss, later to become Governor of South Dakota, shot down four Zeroes, his second four in three days. Foss received the Medal of Honor.

That night (25 October) General Maruyama committed his reserve in another series of headlong, stupid frontal attacks on the bolstered lines of Puller's battalion and the 164th Infantry. All through the dark, enemy groups staggered forward to be blown back by blasts of firepower, such as the three rounds of 37-mm. canister from Puller's left, which slaughtered an entire Japanese weapons company caught in close column almost under the gun's muzzle.

Further west, pushed hastily forward onto a bare ridge to cover the south end of the Marines' line along the Matanikau, the 2d Battalion, 7th Marines (Lieutenant Colonel H. H. Hanneken, last seen bringing down Charlemagne Péralte in Haiti, 1919) had a desperate night. With the better part of a regiment, the Japanese struck and struck again at the lines of Company F, 7th Marines. By daybreak the Japanese were on the ridge, fighting from American foxholes. Rallying 17 cooks, messmen, communicators, and company runners, the battalion executive officer, Major Odell M. Conoley, stormed the ridge with a shower of grenades, and, in the morning light, retook the position. Boxed in by mortar barrages, he held it.

With this fight as the finale, the enemy's strongest attack against General Vandegrift had failed. Strewn about the perimeter and in the jungle, more than 3,500 Japanese lay dead, including at least one general and the

COs of both regiments which had assaulted Puller's positions on the Ridge. Less than a tenth of that number of Americans had fallen. Even so, Geiger was now down to 30 airplanes.

On 26 October, as Maruyama's shattered division recoiled from the perimeter, Admiral Halsey launched his slim task forces against the strong Japanese fleet which had been hovering northeast of Guadalcanal, waiting for Maruyama to make the kill. "Attack, repeat attack," was Halsey's final signal and earnest to the weary Marines that the South Pacific Navy was in fighting hands. In the resulting Battle of the Santa Cruz Islands, the Navy scored a bloody standoff. Against the loss of the carrier *Hornet* and major damage to other valuable ships, could be counted seriously immobilizing injury to two enemy carriers. In this battle of time and resources, they might as well have been sunk.

One sinking, 24 hours earlier, at Espiritu Santo, even if not due to enemy action, dealt a sore blow to Guadalcanal. Here, the careless merchant crew of the Army transport *President Coolidge* ran her right into a United States minefield. As the ship went down, she took with her the first new "Long Tom" 155-mm. guns in the South Pacific; "Pistol Pete" had gained a reprieve through an American fumble.

DECISION IN NOVEMBER

By the end of October, the weary, malaria-riddled, and still unknowingly victorious Marines on Guadalcanal had begun to sing a ditty to the tune of the British "Bless 'Em All":

> They sent for the Army to come to Tulagi,
> But General MacArthur said, "No!"
> He gave as his reason, it wasn't the season—
> And besides, there was no U.S.O.

Whether this was exactly fair to General MacArthur (who was also in need of troops from home) is beside the point. It did highlight a widespread feeling on Guadalcanal that the Marines of the 1st Division and 1st Wing had about done their share—as indeed they had—and that, as Admiral King had earlier laid down, it was high time for someone else to relieve the Marines for future offensive operations. This point of view was vividly expressed in another set of verses familiar to South Pacific Marines, "Our Fighting Men."

Did they but know it, relief and reinforcements were on the way. As a result of the President's personal intervention, the 25th Infantry Division was headed for the Solomons, and so were the 8th Marines from Samoa, portions of the 5th and 9th Defense Battalions, two companies of the 2d Raiders pried loose from Admiral Turner's grip, and a welcome assortment of Army and Navy supporting units. Marine Air Group 11 (Lieutenant Colonel William O. Brice) landed at Tontouta on 30 October, and its squadrons were soon on Henderson Field. This brought the Marine aviation strength at Cactus to 1,557 officers and men, with 191 other aviation personnel from the Army and Navy; appropriately, on 15 November, Henderson Field was officially designated a Marine air base, which it always had been anyway.

Meanwhile, as he had been trying to do ever since September, General Vandegrift again set out to expand his perimeter. On 1 November, Colonel Edson launched an imposing group, comprised of the 5th Marines, 2d Marines (less 3d Battalion), Whaling Group, and 3d Battalion, 7th Marines, toward Kokumbona. Tactically, the push closely resembled the previous Matanikau offensives, and, four days after jumpoff, the 2d Marines, with a battalion of the 164th Infantry attached, attained a defensible outpost line a mile west of Point Cruz. On the point itself, the 5th Marines penned a Japanese battalion. For three days, the enemy held, but, on 3 November, the 5th Marines crushed them in a co-ordinated assault, killing some 300 and capturing many weapons.

While Edson was fighting to the west, Colonel Hanneken and the 2d Battalion, 7th Marines, probed east toward Koli Point, where Japanese were reported concentrating. The reports were accurate; Admiral Yamamoto had urged General Hyakutake to build up forces on both sides of the perimeter, and the Tokyo Express was speeding down six destroyers with a regiment of infantry to be landed east of Koli Point.

On the night of 2 November, the enemy 230th Infantry landed east of Hanneken's bivouac at the mouth of the Metapona River. This was bad, not only because of the Japanese strength, but doubly so because the Marines' radios had been rained out by a soaking downpour, making it impossible for Hanneken to raise the perimeter before afternoon. Meanwhile, he retired toward Koli Point. Here, once the radios got working again, help came along the coast by boat on 4 November, in the form of Colonel Puller and the 1st Battalion, 7th Marines. At the same time the 164th Infantry moved inland, parallel to the coast, with a view to striking north, as had been done several times west of the perimeter.

Once joined, and with the regimental command group to co-ordinate them (not to mention General Rupertus, at last over from Tulagi), the two battalions pushed east on 6 November, while the 164th swung toward the coast. Next day, the combined force waited (in vain) for an expected Japanese landing east of Koli which, due to a change of plans, never came off. Then, having located the enemy still further east, astride the mouth of the Gavaga River, on 8 November both regiments closed in. During this process two noteworthy casualties were sustained: the indomitable Puller was benched under protest with what he described as "a fanny full of 'scrapnel,'" and General Rupertus came down with dengue fever. Command passed to Brigadier General Edmund B. Sebree, USA, who had come north from Noumea to make ready for the impending arrival of the Americal Division, the 164th's parent unit. On 9-10 November, the Japanese pocket was surrounded, at least for the moment. Hard fighting ensued as the enemy tried, and tried again, to break out. Finally, on the night of 11 November, pushing through a hole in the lines of the 2d Battalion, 164th Infantry (whose CO was forthwith relieved), the preponderance of the enemy got away. Even so, about 450 Japanese were killed.

Amid all this confusion on both flanks of the perimeter, Admiral Turner, a hard man to convince, had insisted, Vandegrift and the Marines be damned, on going ahead with organizing a separate force to build an airfield at Aola Bay, 40 miles from Lunga. This fruitless scheme (which had to be abandoned a few weeks later) absorbed, among other troops, the 2d Raiders. Now came their chance: at General Vandegrift's request, the Raiders were detached to harry the Japanese who had walked through the 164th Infantry on the Gavaga.

What resulted was one of the great combat patrols in the history of the Corps. Between 8 November and 4 December, the 2d Raider Battalion, handled with great skill by Carlson, marched 150 miles (ultimately circumnavigating the perimeter), killed 488 enemy in more than a dozen fights and ambushes, and gathered invaluable intelligence. The Raiders' casualties were but 16 dead and 18 wounded.

A month earlier, the Japanese had, in the words of one of their ablest planners (Captain Toshikazu Ohmae, IJN), concluded that "the situation was becoming very serious."[71] A major reinforcement of Guadalcanal, to be covered by the Combined Fleet, was planned for November. Ironically, both the Japanese reinforcement convoy and one bringing forward the 182d U. S. Infantry headed for Guadalcanal almost simultaneously. Both were strongly screened. The collision of these forces on the night of 12-13 November resulted in "one of the most furious sea battles ever fought,"[72] a 24-minute action in which the heavy cruiser *San Francisco* all but sank the Japanese battleship *Hiei* in a 3,000-yard slugging match—United States 8-inch against enemy 14-inch—that cost the lives of two American admirals (Norman Scott and Daniel Callaghan). Two United States light cruisers (*Atlanta* and *Juneau*) and four destroyers died; by a miracle, the *San Francisco* survived. The Japanese, frustrated in a planned bombardment, lost two destroyers that night, and, next day, the *Hiei* went to the depths of Iron-bottom Sound, helped by torpedoes and bombs from VMSB-131. As soon as the facts of this heroic engagement (which was named, officially, the Battle of Guadalcanal) reached the Marines on Lunga Point, Colonel Thomas drafted a heartfelt message which General Vandegrift sent to the Navy. It ended, ". . . to them the men of Cactus lift their battered helmets in deepest admiration."[73]

Despite this fierce fighting, two Japanese cruisers battered Henderson Field that night with some 1,000 rounds of 8-inch, a shelling which inflicted far less loss than might have been expected. This became painfully apparent to the enemy after day broke on 14 November.

Dawn searches from Henderson Field located the retiring bombardment force. Wounded by an immediate torpedo attack, the heavy cruiser *Kinugasa* was sunk later in the day by Navy planes; two other cruisers and a destroyer were damaged. But the great catch of the 14th took place about noon, when 42 dive bombers and torpedo planes, Marine and Navy, flew out from Henderson Field to begin work on 11 transports steaming down the Slot. Commanded by Admiral Tanaka, they were bearing more than 10,000 troops. All afternoon, with even the Flying Fortresses scoring hits, everything that could fly bit into Tanaka's convoy. Admiral Tanaka had good reason never to forget that afternoon:[74]

. . . every hit raising clouds of smoke and fire and transports burst into flame and take the sickening list that spells their doom. Attackers depart, smoke screens lift and reveal the tragic scene of men jumping overboard from burning, sinking ships. . . .

By sundown seven of his 11 had gone down in flames. That night Tanaka resolutely rammed the remaining four ships, all battered, onto the beach near Tassafaronga. Four thousand shaken soldiers made it ashore with 260 cases of ammunition and 1,500 bags of rice.

As a finale that same night of 14-15 November, came a violent battleship duel, one of only four such during the entire war. Here, the *South Dakota* (heavily damaged) and the *Washington* sank a Japanese battleship, the *Kirishima*, which, with two heavy cruisers, was headed down to shell Henderson Field again.

Thus ended three days of naval battle which decided the campaign of Guadalcanal. Many weeks of fighting ashore lay ahead, but the tide had turned. As Admiral Halsey later wrote:[75]

> If our ships and planes had been routed in this battle, if we had lost it, our troops on Guadalcanal would have been trapped as were our troops on Bataan. We could not have reinforced them or relieved them. . . . Unobstructed, the enemy would have driven south, cut our supply lines to New Zealand and Australia, and enveloped them.

General Vandegrift was brief and blunt: "If the surface Navy continues to perform as they have since Admiral Halsey took over, then this place is safe for democracy."[76]

"THE JAPANESE NEVER AGAIN ADVANCED"

On 9 December 1942, with the Army's Americal Division and a good part of the 2d Marine Division on Guadalcanal, General Vandegrift turned over command to Major General Alexander M. Patch, USA, and the exhausted, victorious Marines of the 1st Division began embarking for Australia. Many men were too weak to make it up the cargo nets. Their gear and clothing were torn and scanty. The only personal possession, noted the division quartermasters with pride, that most had kept through thick and thin were their Marine Corps emblems.

As the 1st Division departed, the 25th Infantry Division began to arrive. And on 4 January 1943 came the 6th Marines and an advance command echelon of the 2d Division under Brigadier General Alphonse De Carre (Major General John Marston, the division commander, was not allowed to accompany his troops to Guadalcanal because he ranked General Patch, the senior Army officer present). Coincident with this, all troops on Guadalcanal were combined under the XIV Corps, U.S. Army, headed by Patch.

In turning Cactus over to General Patch, General Vandegrift was also able to bequeath freedom from the tactical thrall of Admiral Turner, whose desire to run military operations ashore had so often vexed and frustrated the hard-pressed Marines. During a late October visit to Guadalcanal, General Holcomb had convinced Admiral Halsey that the landing force commander must enjoy parallel (not subordinate) relations with the naval amphibious commander, and that Vandegrift's subordination to Turner during a long land campaign was unsound and unreasonable. Halsey then embodied these conclusions in a dispatch to Admiral King, which General Holcomb jealously shepherded through the intermediate higher headquarters, as he made his way back to Washington. King approved, and thus was born the historic principle of parallel command which is central to American amphibious doctrine.

The remainder of the Guadalcanal campaign fell into two phases: breeching and reducing the Japanese line which ran inland from the Matanikau to Mount Austen (that "Grassy Knoll" which was to have been secured on the first day); then, a steady push along the coast to Cape Esperance. While these operations were in progress, the Japanese belatedly decided to cut their losses and withdraw, a difficult and delicate business which would require weeks to consummate.

On 13 January, while Army units attacked the inland positions, the 2d Division advanced along the coast from Point Cruz. Going was slow as the Japanese resisted on each of the steep ridges that lay athwart the zone. But the deep valleys perpendicular to the coast were ideal target areas for naval gunfire, and the 10th Marines had with them the first two of an amphibious breed soon to become well known: naval gunfire liaison officers, one of whom, Lieutenant (jg) Alfred E. Moon, USNR, would see service with Marine assault troops at Tarawa, Kwajalein, Saipan, Tinian, and Iwo Jima. With primitive shore fire-control parties from the Marine artillery, assisted by Marine bombardment liaison officers aboard destroyers bearing such Marine names as *Nicholas* and *O'Bannon*, both close and deep supporting fires eased the advance. "A very heartening sight and sound to all the troops ashore," commented Major F. P. ("Toots") Henderson, one of the pioneer naval gunfire officers.[77] Another presumably heartening sight was seen by the 8th Marines on 15 January, when, for the first time in the Pacific war, Marines used flame-throwers to burn out three bunkers with crisply efficient results.

For the final push to Cape Esperance, terminal of the Tokyo Express, General Patch grouped two Army regiments (147th and 182d Infantry) with the 6th Marines, under the 2d Division staff. This military amalgam was referred to as the "CAM" ("Composite Army/Marine") Division. On 26 January, the XIV Corps "became engaged in the nearest thing to a pursuit that the South Pacific ever saw,"[78] and, within hours after the last living Japanese had been skillfully extricated from Guadalcanal, Army troops secured Cape Esperance on 9 February 1943.

The box score for this crucial, desperate campaign included 1,504 Marines killed and 2,619 wounded. Even though the Japanese Navy managed to get 13,000 troops off Guadalcanal, more than 24,000 Japanese were killed there or died of disease. Each side lost 24 combatant ships. Marine aviation, which flew 2,117 sorties from Cactus, lost 118 planes but shot down 427. Most of these were from the cream of Japan's naval aviation, and their loss was felt throughout the rest of the war.

That Guadalcanal, the first offensive, was a great turning point, was easier to recognize in hindsight than at the time. But the Japanese so recognized it. "After Guadalcanal . . ." said Captain Ohmae, "I felt we could not win."[79] Victory at Guadalcanal, the point of maximum extension and conflict by both the United States and Japan, represented a twofold triumph, a triumph of readiness and a triumph of effort. Without the existence of the ready Fleet Marine Force, the United States could not have launched the Watchtower offensive; without the superb effort of all hands, Marines, Navy, and finally, Army, which outweighed only by ounces the fierce effort of the Japanese, Guadalcanal could not have been won.

For the Marine Corps, Guadalcanal had the significance of another Belleau Wood. As at Belleau Wood, which, in Clemenceau's words, "saved Paris," Guadalcanal's Marines and sailors prevented the collapse of the South Pacific theater. Like Belleau Wood, Guadalcanal was a first effort against a new and supposedly invincible enemy. In each case, the fighting qualities of the individual Marine provided the margin of victory. Guadalcanal, however, had a new significance for the Marine Corps. Bitter, desperate, and crucial as were the ground actions, those in the air were equally so. In fact, in this decisive battle, the main effort was in the air (mainly by Marine aviators), and the role of the 1st Marine Division was to secure a base from which aviation could operate. That the division steadfastly did so finally assured the success of the campaign.

No better epitome of the Guadalcanal campaign has been written than that by General Vandegrift, in his special preface to the official monograph:[80]

We struck at Guadalcanal to halt the advance of the Japanese. We did not know how strong he was, nor did we know his plans. We knew only that he was moving down the island chain and that he had to be stopped.

We were as well trained and as well armed as time and our peacetime experience allowed us to be. We needed combat to tell us how effective our training, our doctrines, and our weapons had been.

We tested them against the enemy, and we found that they worked. From that moment in 1942, the tide turned, and the Japanese never again advanced.

THE CENTRAL SOLOMONS

The ultimate objective of our South Pacific offensive (for such, after Guadalcanal, it had become) was Rabaul. This meant a succession of hard pushes up the ladder of the Solomons. With the 1st and 2d Marine Divisions recuperating from Guadalcanal, the role of Marines in the initial advance into the Central Solomons was marginal. But before the campaign was over they were missed.

In the first move north, even before Guadalcanal was completely secured, the 3d Raiders, with elements of the 10th and 11th Defense Battalions, landed surprisingly unopposed on Pavuvu and Banika Islands in the Russells. MAG-21 followed as soon as an airstrip could be put down. During February and March 1943, amphibious reconnaissance patrols, provided by the 1st Raider Battalion, worked north into New Georgia, Kolombangara, and Vangunu.

Among the half-dozen landings planned for the capture of New Georgia in the summer of 1943, ground Marines took part in three: Segi-Viru; Rendova-Munda; and Rice Anchorage-Enogai. Marine aviation (2d Marine Air Wing, under Brigadier General Francis P. Mulcahy) provided most of the air support for the whole campaign.

The first landing, speeded up to prevent capture of an intrepid Australian coastwatcher by encircling Japanese, brought the 4th Raider Battalion, less two companies, to Segi in western New Georgia on 21 June. As soon as an Army unit could take over the security mission, the Raiders, under Lieutenant Colonel Michael S. Currin, took off on 27 June to capture the Japanese-held harbor of Viru, 11 miles away through dense jungle and mangrove swamp. Four days later, after a grueling march with Japanese patrols nipping at their heels, the Raiders, divided into two storming parties, seized the two points, Tetemara and Tombi, forming the entrance to Viru Harbor, in brisk fighting that cost 28 Marine casualties. But the Japanese had 61 killed and 100 wounded, and United States naval vessels were unloading in Viru by the afternoon of 1 July.

The main objective of the New Georgia campaign—an Army show—was Munda airfield, which the Japanese are said to have built under a camouflage of palm-tree tops held aloft by cables while the trunks were cut clear. The first step in capturing Munda was to land on neighboring Rendova. In this group, mainly Army, the 9th Defense Battalion (Lieutenant Colonel William

J. Scheyer) had the job of providing antiaircraft defense and, equally important, of setting up its two batteries of new 155-mm. Long Toms to shell the airfield and support the Army's advance on Munda itself. Not until 5 August

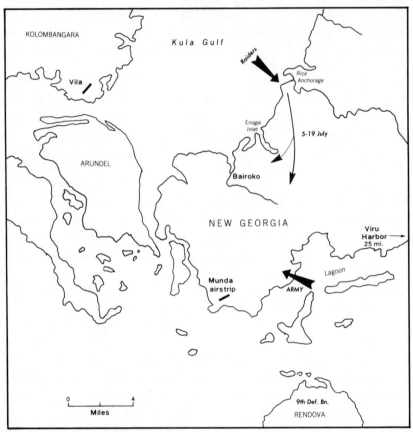

Operations in New Georgia, July 1943

(seven weeks after landing) was Munda taken; throughout, the 9th—and, later, the 11th—Defense provided fire support and shot down planes. In addition, Marine tanks provided much of the push in this feeble and fumbling advance. ("When I look back," wrote Admiral Halsey of this operation,[81] "the smoke of charred reputations still makes me cough.") At the end of August, the trusty Long Toms were shifted to the north shore of New Georgia, and pounded Vila airfield, on Kolombangara, just as they had Munda.

The major and most arduous Marine ground action on New Georgia, however, was the two weeks' campaign by the 1st Raider Regiment at Enogai and Bairoko. The mission of Colonel H. B. ("Harry the Horse") Liversedge, commanding the regiment (with two Army battalions attached), was to land at Rice Anchorage, on the northwest shore of New Georgia, and prevent the Japanese from reinforcing Munda overland. This mission required the capture of the neighboring harbors of Enogai and Bairoko.

The 1st Raider Battalion, under Lieutenant Colonel Griffith, restored from his wound, executed one of the war's few U. S. night landings at Rice Anchorage on 5 July, and set out for Enogai through rain and vile New Georgia jungle. Of one part of this march, "Sammy" Griffith recalled:[82]

It is probably less than three-quarters of a mile (as the crow flies) from Giza Giza to the Tamakau, but, as one Raider said when I foolishly called this fact to his attention, "That may be, Colonel, but we ain't crows."

On 9 July, after repelling a Japanese attack en route, the raider battalion hit the enemy outposts defending Enogai. Next day, in a determined attack through mangrove roots and huge banyan trees shattered by bombing (including one which chose the occasion to topple onto Griffith's CP), the raiders took the village, killing 350 enemy and capturing four 140-mm. guns which had posed a hazard to United States destroyers and PT boats in the lower reaches of Kula Gulf.

Bairoko, the next objective, proved too tough a nut to crack, even though Liversedge was reinforced by the 4th Raider Battalion. All day on 20 July, with no flame-throwers and nothing heavier than 60-mm. mortars, two raider battalions and an Army infantry battalion ground to a halt before a well-defended, bunkered line mounting heavy automatic weapons, supported by 90-mm. mortars. With an inexcusable miscarriage of air support and 236 casualties, Liversedge's forces had to fall back on Enogai. Ultimately, Bairoko was evacuated by the Japanese and occupied by Army units without opposition.

The last Marine participation in the Central Solomons operations was by the 4th Defense Battalion, one of the most put-upon, yet most capable, of that hard-worked and frustrated species. On 15 August, supporting an Army landing force covered from the air by VMF-123 and VMF-124, the 4th Defense landed on Vella Lavella and, by the end of September, claimed

42 enemy aircraft shot down during 121 raids. Said the Army commander, Major General Robert B. McClure, "This operation was my first experience with the Marine defense battalions, a very superior organization indeed ... a superior job."[83]

OPERATION CHERRYBLOSSOM

The Guadalcanal bard (a captain in Edson's raiders), who in 1942 penned the verses of "Our Fighting Men," proved in less than a year that he was a strategist, too. His last stanza read:

> We can take it, said a Raider. It won't be long
> 'Til the Admiral bellers, and we'll shove on;
> And a little while later, we'll be landing again,
> To make Bougainville safe—
> For *Our Fighting Men!*

By September 1943, with a prod from General MacArthur, Admiral Halsey's planners were contemplating just that. In June, the 12th Defense Battalion, together with Army troops, had already secured a base on Woodlark Island, in the Trobriands. To neutralize Rabaul, bases had to be seized from which U. S. fighters and dive bombers could get there and back. Given the radius of 1943's single-engine airplanes, this meant somewhere on Bougainville.

On the southern end of this forbidding jungle island, the Japanese had a major complex of airfields and defending troops. To bypass these, Admiral Halsey decided to land midway up the west coast, at Empress Augusta Bay, and build an airfield at Cape Torokina. This area was outposted by 270 Japanese, remote from reinforcements. To distract the enemy, a diversionary raid—"a series of short right jabs . . . to conceal the power of the left hook to his midriff at Empress Augusta Bay"[84]—was planned to hit neighboring Choiseul Island just before the Bougainville landing. D-day was 1 November 1943. The operation was code-named "Cherryblossom."

Cherryblossom was blessed from the beginning with a capable and co-operative command team. Rear Admiral T. S. Wilkinson, a thoughtful and notably reasonable officer, had superseded Turner; Major General C. D. Barrett, the brilliant amphibious thinker of the thirties, had taken over command of the I Marine Amphibious Corps ("IMAC") in Noumea after relief of his predecessor at Admiral Halsey's request. Barrett's command, alas, was short (he died as a result of an accident in October 1943), but his successor, in turn, was none other than General Vandegrift, hastily recalled to the South Pacific to fill the gap. The result, as one historian put it, was "that the Bougainville operation resembled that of Guadalcanal—minus most of the errors."[85]

The 3d Marine Division, which had been activated on 16 September 1942, was to execute the Bougainville landing as the principal ground component of IMAC. Its regiments were the 3d, 9th, and 21st (all infantry), the 12th (artillery), and the 19th (a composite unit which included engineers, pio-

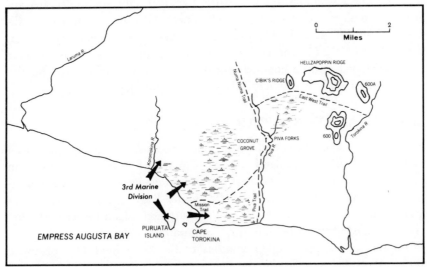

Landing at Cape Torokina, Bougainville, 1 November 1943

neers, and a Seabee battalion). After securing the Torokina perimeter, which was to embrace an air base, the Marine amphibious corps was to be relieved promptly by its Army counterpart, the XIV Corps.

The "series of short right jabs" represented by the raid on Choiseul was the brain child of a brilliant young major, J. C. Murray. As the basis for a raid to confuse and unbalance the Japanese, it was his idea to use all the intelligence assembled while Choiseul had been a candidate for the main landing. The attack was to be delivered by the 2d Parachute Battalion (operating as usual in the South Pacific without parachutes). "I desire an immediate and credible appearance of a large force," said General Vandegrift to Lieutenant Colonel V. H. ("Brute") Krulak, the parachutists' CO.[86] The task, which was enthusiastically executed, could not have fallen into more capable hands.

During the night of 27-28 October, the 725-man force landed at Voza on the southwest shore of Choiseul. After a series of reconnaissance patrols, the battalion captured and gutted the Japanese barge base at Sangigai on 30 October, killing 72 enemy and purposely chasing survivors into the jungle to spread the news. Meanwhile, a company patrol raided and shelled with mortars another Japanese staging base 25 miles away on Choiseul Bay. As the Japanese swarmed in angry reaction, Krulak, everywhere at once despite a wound sustained in the Sangigai fight, ambushed the approaches to Voza and prepared a well-mined perimeter to cover his withdrawal. This took place by night on 3 November. A success in every respect, the raid cost only 11 Marine dead and 14 wounded. As a bonus, an alert parachutist picked up a complete set of Japanese minefield charts for the Shortlands area, which Admiral Halsey received with joy.

BEACHHEAD ON BOUGAINVILLE

The 3d Division, which, under Major General Allen H. Turnage, had been training hard in New Zealand, was to land with two regiments up (from left to right, 9th and 3d Marines). While these secured a shallow beachhead between surf and swamp, the 2d Raider Regiment, attached, was to seize Puruata Island offshore and push a battalion inland to block Mission Trail, the most likely route for enemy counterattack.

Despite zealous prior representations to the Navy by IMAC planners, the naval gunfire support for the landing was inadequate in concept and execution: unqualified and improperly stationed fire-support destroyers put salvo after salvo into the water offshore while the Japanese beach defenses shot landing craft to bits and disorganized the ship-to-shore movement. Fortunately, six Marine air squadrons did much better (well that they did—it was the last time until 1945 that Marine aviation was able to support a Marine landing).

Even so, the lone Japanese infantry company, with its 18 pillboxes and one casemated 75-mm. gun, put up a notable fight, which the distressingly amateur and scanty fire support could have obviated. Four landing craft were sunk and ten were damaged by direct hits, and the beaches themselves were raked by well-aimed rifle and machine gun fire. The man who, almost alone, reversed the situation was Sergeant Robert A. Owens, Company A, 3d Marines. Seeing his comrades killed as they closed in on the 75-mm. gun, Owens charged the casemate, plunged inside through the fire-port as the crew tried to load and fire, and swept the surviving Japanese out through the rear exit, where Owens fell dead of multiple wounds. For this brave attack Owens received the Medal of Honor posthumously.

Fortunately for the landing force, Sergeant Owens's aggressiveness and spirit were not unique that day. The 3d Division had been thoroughly trained in small-unit and individual tactics, and the leadership of lieutenants and junior NCOs soon brought order to the beaches and to Puruata Island, where the Raiders had a full day of fighting through the thick brush. One cause of disorder not attributable to the enemy, however, was the heavy surf, which, on the 9th Marines' beaches alone, broached and stranded 86 landing craft.

By nightfall, after 182 casualties and a day which had included smart and rapid unloading (a matter of understandable concern to General Vandegrift, considering his experiences on Guadalcanal), all units held their sodden, swampy objectives. Moreover—and this was a matter of equal credit to Navy and Marines alike—despite a 120-plane raid from Rabaul, a record 14,000 troops and 6,200 tons of supply and equipment were ashore. This meant that the transports could leave in a hurry and head south to hustle up the 21st Regiment and the leading elements of the Army's 37th Infantry Division.

That night, while the 3d Division braced itself for a counterlanding, strong elements of the Japanese Eighth Fleet thundered down toward Empress Augusta Bay. Here, just after midnight, Rear Admiral A. S. Merrill, with a weaker but resolutely fought force of light cruisers and destroyers, intercepted superbly. The Japanese lost a cruiser and a destroyer, with heavy damage to three other ships. The enemy transports and counterlanding force streaked for home, while a hard-charging destroyer division commander, Captain Arleigh A. Burke, scourged the retiring Japanese on their way in the first of his many friendly assists to the Marine Corps in war and peace.

BOUGAINVILLE SECURED

Aside from air raids, which were plentiful since Rabaul was only 210 miles away, the first Japanese reaction after the battle of Empress Augusta Bay was a dawn counterlanding by a 475-man battalion on the west flank of the 3d Division perimeter. This force had come down from Rabaul in destroyers and landed undetected just outside the American perimeter. It was attacked on 7 November, first by the 3d Battalion, 9th Marines, then by the 1st Battalion, 3d Marines. After a confused action in swamp and thick jungle, with pockets of Japanese isolated by Marines and Marines isolated by Japanese, the *coup de grâce* came from a heavy and skillfully placed artillery preparation by the 12th Marines (under the beloved Colonel John Bushrod Wilson), which, on the morning of 8 November, caught and killed about 300 enemy. Thus ended what became known as the battle of Koromakina Lagoon; 377 Japanese were dead, while Marine casualties totaled 47.

The day after this Japanese defeat, command of the I Marine Amphibious Corps, and thus of Bougainville, passed from General Vandegrift to Major General Roy S. Geiger, last seen commanding the air defense of Guadalcanal in its most desperate hours. General Geiger thus became one of the few practicing airmen (like Field Marshal Kesselring on the other side of the war) ever to assume and retain tactical command of major ground operations. Geiger, who had been flying since 1916, was characterized (accurately) by *Time* Magazine (22 November 1943) after he took command, in the following sentence: "Thick-set, poker-faced, chilly-eyed General Geiger is another Marine's Marine."

The Japanese on Bougainville nearest to the Torokina perimeter were the 23d Infantry with some attached artillery. Their approach to the area was the only approach anyone could use, the Numa Numa or Piva Trail which runs on a narrow strip of relatively solid ground amid swamps beside the Piva River as it ebbs toward the bay. This trail had been outposted by the 2d Raider Regiment on D-day, and, by 5 November, the raiders' trail-block began to get pressure from the Japanese. For the next 12 days the main offensive action of the 3d Division was a series of fights to push the 23d Infantry back up this trail and clear of the perimeter. The troops involved (all under tactical command of the 9th Marines' CO, Colonel Edward A. Craig) were initially from the 3d Raider Battalion, then the 1st and 2d Battalions, 9th Marines, and finally from the 2d Battalion, 21st Marines. Altogether, there were five battalion- or company-scale actions on 9, 13, 14, and 17 November. Fought in waist-deep mud, in dense jungle, and finally in an inland coconut grove, the "Piva Actions" (as the official monograph lumps them) ended with the Japanese still full of fight despite 540 killed. They had been shoved up the Piva Trail onto the so-called East-West Trail in an area of jungle and craggy, vine-entangled foothills, from which their ejection and extermination were to pose extreme difficulties. Marine casualties in the Piva actions amounted to 39 killed and 71 wounded.

The junction of Piva Trail with East-West Trail occurs in an area known as "Piva Forks" because of a large swamp formed by the east and west forks of the Piva River. Here, between 19 and 24 November, the 3d Marines (Colonel George W. McHenry) clashed six times with the 23d Infantry in the battles of Piva Forks and of Cibik's Ridge (the latter named for the officer whose platoon seized and held one of the first bits of high ground encountered in the campaign). The final attack on well-organized Japanese coconut-log bunkers and pillboxes in the Piva swamp was preceded by the heaviest artillery preparations so far fired during the war for a Marine attack: seven battalions of artillery (12th Marines reinforced by three Army battalions) shot 5,760 rounds in 23 minutes. Results were excellent. By dark the 3d Marines had overrun the enemy positions and held a line facing east astride the East-West Trail.

During this steady expansion of the perimeter eastward and inland, the 37th Infantry Division had arrived and, without significant opposition, had taken over and advanced the west sector of the perimeter. Seabees, too, had been working on the Torokina airstrip, which was "opened" unexpectedly on 24 November by a limping Marine SBD damaged in an air-strike up the line.

Marine planes, however, were not the only ones which came regularly to Cape Torokina. In mid-November there were 15 known enemy airfields within 250 miles of Empress Augusta Bay, and during the month there were 90 alerts, 22 of which materialized in the form of major raids. This gave ample work for the 90-mm. guns of the 3d Defense Battalion (Lieutenant Colonel Edward H. Forney), which was destined to stay on Bougainville longer than any other Marine ground unit, until June 1944.

While the 3d Division gathered itself for the final action of the campaign, the 1st Parachute Battalion walked into considerable trouble, when, on 27 November at the outset of an amphibious raid, it landed inadvertently in the middle of a superior Japanese force at Koiari, 10 miles east of Cape Torokina. The surprise was mutual: a Japanese officer waded out to meet the raiders' landing craft and gave them a chatty hail—his last words. But the battalion was soon surrounded and hard pressed by a stronger force. Only by the aid of three destroyers and a battery of 155-mm. guns firing from the perimeter 16,000 yards away, was the battalion evacuated after dark with 17 killed and 93 wounded. The senior destroyer ("a sharp shooting ship,"[87] reported the Corps naval gunfire officer) was the USS *Fullam* —the first time on record anyone of that name had ever come to help the Marines. The gunfire officer said:[88]

The FOs, the 155 battery, and the ships all did marvelous jobs, as never a round fell within our own lines. Even greater testimony to the effectiveness of their fires was the fact that the Japs were meek and quiet during the entire withdrawal operation, despite the heavy concentrations of fire they had delivered on the previous attempts to get the boats in to the beach. The FOs were in the last boat to shove off the beach. Before signing off with "CSMO," they gave a final spot and asked to keep the fire going while they made the run to the boats and got out to sea.

The final expansion of the Corps beachhead took place in December, and entailed the capture of three stubbornly held and cunningly organized hills between Cibik's Ridge and the Torokina River. Here—on "Hellzapoppin Ridge," Hill 600, and Hill 600A—the 23d Infantry made its final stand from 12 to 23 December. To reduce these three positions and drive the remaining Japanese east of the Torokina was the task of the 21st Marines, under Colonel Evans O. Ames. The capture of Hellzapoppin Ridge on 18 December was signalized by one of the earliest and most tactically precise close air strikes executed by Marines in World War II. After artillery and even mortars had been unable to get effective fire into the enemy positions, VMTB-134 (Major A. C. Robertson), under ground control from the front lines, attacked with six TBFs which dropped forty-eight 100-pound bombs within 75 yards of the 21st Marines' front, while the regimental executive officer, Lieutenant Colonel A. H. Butler, rode along with the flight leader to help out. On 23 December, when relief of the 3d Division by Army units had already started, Hill 600A fell, and the Bougainville operation, insofar as all Marines except the 3d Defense Battalion were concerned, was over. The cost of Bougainville was 423 dead Marines and 1,418 wounded.

CLOSE AIR SUPPORT ON BOUGAINVILLE

The episode at Hellzapoppin Ridge should not be overlooked. The combination of Marine aviation supporting Marines on the ground, joined by effective radio communications and controlled from the front lines, was no on-the-spot improvisation.

Although there had been jury-rigged, prearranged air strikes on Guadalcanal (some even involving depth charges as bombs), effective close air support never developed, nor did subsequent air support ventures in the undistinguished New Georgia campaign provide much encouragement.

When the 3d Division was going into commission, however, the division air officer, Lieutenant Colonel John T. L. D. Gabbert, set about a serious study of ways to make close air support effective. Using himself as a guinea pig (crouching without shelter in an open field while different weight bombs were detonated statically at measured distances), Gabbert arrived empirically at the now classic "yard-a-pound" factor for close support; that is, you can safely drop a 100-pound bomb 100 yards from friendly troops in the open. Moreover, he organized division air-liaison parties headed by Marine dive bomber pilots borrowed from the 1st Wing. These people, with suitable field radios (the best Gabbert could get, anyway) were to live with the supported troops and control Marine air from the front lines. Had the Japs used white phosphorus mortar shells on New Georgia to confuse our attempts to mark targets with white smoke grenades? Gabbert stocked his air-liaison parties with a whole spectrum of different colored smokes. Finally, when the thing was worked out, he convoked an air support school attended by every infantry operations officer in the division.

The result was inevitable. When the 3d Marine Division went into its first battle, a modern doctrine for Marine close air support had been evolved, and all hands had confidence that it would really work. That it did was first proven in combat—most appropriately on 10 November, 168th Birthday of the Corps—when 12 TBFs from VMTB-143 and VMTB-223 dropped 144 100-pound bombs on Piva Village within 120 yards of the front lines of the 2d Battalion, 9th Marines. The results were highly successful: with the 9th Marines on their heels, the Japanese retired from their positions, leaving 40 dead behind. On nine more occasions during Operation Cherryblossom, the division called for tactical air support against targets closer than 500 yards. Only once (13 December) did a bomb light in friendly lines.

Marine close air support, sired in the jungle of Nicaragua, was thus born anew in the jungle of Bougainville.

GENERAL HOLCOMB RETIRES

After General Vandegrift turned over Bougainville to Geiger, he resumed his interrupted journey to Washington, where General Holcomb, after seven years as Commandant, was preparing to retire. As he recalled years later:[89]

I had been Commandant for seven years and I had never permitted any Marine officer above 64 to remain on active duty; so, to be consistent, I had to apply for retirement . . . and recommended the appointment of General Vandegrift as my successor.

Reluctantly, President Roosevelt acceded to the retirement of his old friend, but, according to Holcomb, with a reservation:[90]

I would like to explain that the President always, in conversation with me, associated himself with the Marine Corps. When he was Assistant Secretary he had specific charge of the Marine Corps and always referred to the association as "we Marines." So he said, "You know, the first thing you know we are going to be left out of things. We are not represented on the Joint Chiefs of Staff . . . and if you would like to be a member, I want you to be one, because we Marines are going to be left out, the first thing you know, if we are not represented."

General Holcomb's reply foreshadowed the outcome: "Mr. President, naturally I would like it very much. I don't know how the Joint Chiefs of Staff would feel about it." He soon found out (and so did President Roosevelt) that Admiral King, convinced believer in separate but not necessarily equal facilities for Marines, seconded by General Marshall, strongly opposed any such idea. Stubborn and annoyed though Roosevelt was, the matter was not worth a breach with his chiefs of staff, and it was with some relief all around that General Holcomb finally accepted an appointment as Minister to South Africa.[91]

Member of the JCS or not, General Holcomb could look back on a historic commandancy.

The Marine Corps, which had numbered some 18,000 when he became commandant, was, on the last day of 1943, 391,620 strong.

Women Reservists (13,201 of them on 31 December 1943) were now in the Corps; "WRs," they were simply called. Alone among the Services, the Marine Corps eschewed cute nicknames for its women. The coming of women into the Marine Corps did not win approval in all quarters. On the day in February 1943 when the women's program was approved, General Holcomb related, Archibald Henderson's picture crashed to the floor in the Commandant's House.

A radical innovation and sign of the times in 1943 was the acceptance of Negroes for enlistment in the Corps. They were initially organized into two colored defense battalions (51st and 52d) and in service units of the Fleet Marine Force, but within a decade were destined to be fully integrated throughout the Corps.

For the first time since 1919 the Marine Corps again included draftees. As in World War I, this was no free choice—there was no dearth of volunteers—but rather an imposition on the Corps. Nonetheless, on 5 December 1942, when voluntary enlistments from men 18 or over were terminated for all Services, the Marine Corps had no option. Acceptance of conscripts meant an immediate reduction in physical and mental standards for recruits, and forced acceptance by the Marine Corps of men who would never previously have been considered fit to be Marines.

The imperative demands of an enormously enlarged Corps had brought about a vast training effort. The Basic School in Philadelphia disbanded in July 1942, and its organization was swallowed up in the Reserve Officer Courses and Officer Candidate Courses running full blast in Quantico. Likewise, the peacetime Senior and Junior Courses at Marine Corps Schools were superseded by the high-pressure Command and Staff Course and the Air-Infantry Course. To meet the predicted requirements for pilots, large numbers of naval aviation cadets (more than 2,100 between March 1942 and March 1943) were hastily commissioned as second lieutenants with no basic Marine training or indoctrination whatever. This left the Corps, for the first time in many years, not only with a 240 per cent increase in pilots, but with an appreciable number of junior officers who, however much they wanted to be Marines, were neither trained nor qualified for even the most elementary general military requirements of their rank. That this undesirable situation continued even after experienced Marine officers had recognized it, was largely due to unwillingness in the Naval Air Training Command at Pensacola to meet obvious and legitimate needs of the Marine Corps.[92]

Throughout the Corps, temporary buildings had sprung up right and left. In the fall of 1942, some 50,000 more acres of training area were added to the Quantico reservation. This accretion was named the Guadalcanal Area. On the West Coast both a Replacement Training Command and a Troop Training Unit were organized. The latter agency was charged with supervision of landing force training for organized units (mainly Army) in amphibious operations.

When General Holcomb stepped down, four Marine Divisions, four air wings, and 19 defense battalions were in being, together with a numerous family of supporting and service units. Although far from being (or ever wanting to be) the "second land army" for which it would later be assailed by foes of the Corps, the Marine Corps, under Holcomb's leadership, had become a powerful, balanced force of combined arms including aviation. On retirement, Thomas Holcomb received his fourth star and thus became the first full general in the history of the Corps—a well-deserved reward.

NORTH TO NEW BRITAIN

The Bismarck Archipelago squarely blocked General MacArthur's push north and west via New Guinea into the Philippines. To breach this barrier and hook left along the New Guinea coast it would be necessary to control Vitiaz and Dampier Straits, which separate New Guinea and New Britain. To effect this, in turn, required establishment of United States forces in western New Britain, where, at Cape Gloucester, the Japanese 65th Brigade, an aggregation of odd lots, had 9,501 troops and one major airdrome.

For the capture of Cape Gloucester, MacArthur had the 1st Marine Division, now commanded by General Rupertus. After a long-remembered eight months of recuperation at Melbourne, Australia, the Guadalcanal veterans were again fighting fit. Operation Dexterity would project them, on the day after Christmas 1943, into jungle worse and wetter than Guadalcanal had ever been. As a Marine historian and veteran of the campaign described New Britain:[93]

In the memory of the men who fought there, American, Australian, and Japanese, it will remain one of the evil spots of this world.

From the Marine division's viewpoint, planning for the Gloucester operation was complicated by an attempt on the part of Lieutenant General Walter Kreuger's Sixth Army (the higher headquarters under which the division was placed) to dictate an unsound scheme of maneuver. This conflict came dramatically to a head on 14 December 1943 during a visit by General MacArthur. When the general asked the 1st Division staff how the division liked the plan, Colonel E. A. Pollock, division operations officer, in the words of the official history:[94]

... took the bit in his teeth and, ignoring both of his immediate superiors, told the area commander bluntly that the Marines did not like any part of it.

Following the conference, which ended on a somewhat strained note, the Army planners (apparently on MacArthur's orders) conceded the principal points at issue, and the 1st Division got its way, which was to eliminate a highly questionable Normandy-style assault by paratroopers and concentrate, rather than disperse, the striking power of the Marine division in a simpler scheme of maneuver.

The landing at Cape Gloucester on 26 December was lightly but effectively supported by gunfire from a handful of cruisers and destroyers, and by bombers from Major General George C. Kenney's Fifth Army Air Force. One novel feature of the fire-support effort was the presence of two rocket LCI-gunboats, a development of the LCI-gunboats first seen in the Treasury Islands in October 1943. Another novelty, provided by the Fifth Air Force, over Marine objections, was an aerial smoke concentration which was supposed to screen the landing, but which, as had been foreseen by Colonel Pollock, mainly served to blind and confuse landing-craft coxswains. Since the landing turned out to be practically unopposed (the first casualty on D-day was a man killed by a falling tree), even the modest support which was available proved sufficient, and the purblind ship-to-shore movement had no adverse effect except on tempers. Surprise, at any rate, had been achieved.

What did exert adverse effect immediately and on no small scale was the terrain of the landing area inland from the shallow beaches. Labeled "Damp Flat" on the maps, this proved to be jungle swamp forest (" 'damp' up to your neck," cracked a Marine), treacherous muck and tangled vegetation.

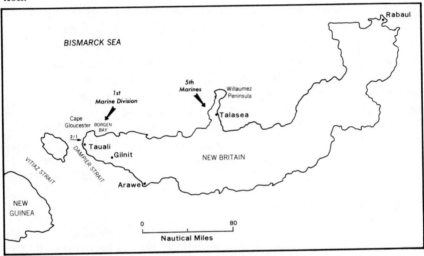

New Britain Operations, December 1943-January 1944

As the 7th Marines, in assault under Colonel Julian N. Frisbie, secured the initial beachhead, including the key terrain feature, Target Hill, Colonel Whaling landed his 1st Marines in trace and swung right, through the abominable swamp, toward Gloucester airdrome.

Despite a night counterattack by a Japanese infantry battalion, which the 2d Battalion, 7th Marines, stood off resolutely, the division pushed ahead. On 28 December (a day when 16 inches of rain were recorded), the 3d Battalion, 1st Marines, encountered and disposed of an enemy strong point less than a mile short of the airfield. Next day, after the 5th Marines (Colonel John T. Selden) had landed from reserve, the 1st Battalion, 1st Marines, supported by tanks, swarmed across the easternmost of Gloucester's airstrips, while at the same time the 5th Regiment hit the center of the airfield and pushed toward its western edge. On the 30th, the Japanese, who had prudently retired to high ground south of the field, launched a counter-attack. By noon this final effort had spent itself at small cost to the 1st and 5th Regiments, and Cape Gloucester airdrome belonged to the Marine Corps.

While the main landings were sloshing ahead, a separate battalion task force built around the 2d Battalion, 1st Marines, commanded by Lieutenant Colonel J. M. Masters, Sr., landed near Tauali, on the opposite side of Cape Gloucester, 12 miles distant as the crow flies but tactically remote from the division. Code-named Task Force "Stoneface" (reportedly an allusion to Colonel Masters' renowned poker face), this force had the job of sealing off the main coastal trail which led south from Cape Gloucester and thus prevent-ing the escape of retreating enemy. Although none such were immediately encountered, Japanese troops were in the area, and, during a black down-pour before dawn on 30 December, they hurled themselves at Stoneface's perimeter. The result was an intense, confused action which lasted until day-light, when the attack ebbed and most of the attackers were dead. This ended serious opposition in this vicinity, and after ten days of patrolling, Colonel Masters linked up with the main body of the division at Gloucester airdrome, thus efficiently concluding that phase of the campaign.

"...CAREFUL, BRAVE FIGHTERS"

Although the main objective had been achieved, the relative lack of op-position gave evidence that the Japanese could not yet be written off. The best intelligence suggested that General Matsuda, the enemy commander, had concentrated his remaining forces in the vicinity of Borgen Bay, a short distance from the invasion beaches, where a commanding elevation, Hill 660, lay little more than a mile south of Target Hill. To cover that jungle mile and seize Hill 660 would require two weeks of strenuous campaigning, with nature, as usual, the more forbidding enemy.

On New Year's Day 1944, Brigadier General Lemuel C. Shepherd, Jr., the assistant division commander, launched an independent force, built around the 7th Regiment and 3d Battalion, 5th Marines, south toward Borgen Bay through the unpenetrated jungle. Together with the usual supporting and service units, General Shepherd's force included an artillery group (1st and 4th Battalions, 11th Marines) under a fellow Virginian, Lieutenant Colonel R. B. ("Marse Robert") Luckey.

The push to Borgen Bay entailed three hard fights, all of which were made infinitely more difficult by endless rain and by dense swamp and jungle that hid defenders from attackers, though each might be only a few feet from the other.

The first Japanese stand took place along a narrow stream ("Suicide Creek," the troops called it) with steep banks which defied infantry attack and prevented approach by tanks. For two days a stalemate held until the 17th Marines (division engineers under Colonel H. E. Rosecrans) bulldozed a causeway which allowed the new Sherman tanks, a welcome novelty in the Marine Corps, to shoulder their way across. Close behind came the 3d Battalions of both the 5th and 7th Marines. The surviving Japanese melted back into the jungle.

The second battle, which lasted two days, 9-10 January, was the most difficult and decisive of the campaign. On Aogiri Ridge, a key terrain feature which the jungle hid completely until the 3d Battalion, 5th Marines, walked into it, the Japanese had constructed 37 mutually supporting bunkers interlocked by tunnels throughout the ridge. Their purpose in defending here was to protect their main supply route running inland from Borgen Bay to Magairapua, site of General Matsuda's headquarters.

At the end of the first day, despite unstinting effort, the attack had gotten virtually nowhere. Lieutenant Colonel Lewis W. Walt, the new battalion commander (who had just replaced Lieutenant Colonel D. S. McDougal, wounded a few days before), realized that his tenuous hold on the ridge might slip. To "Lew" Walt, raised in Edson's hard school, this was unthinkable. One 37-mm. gun, with its lethal stock of canister, was available. As his regimental commander recounted:[95]

> Walt called for volunteers; there were none forthcoming. He then grabbed the 37 himself and attempted to push it up the ridge. . . . Immediately on seeing their new battalion commander and his orderly on the gun, Walt had plenty of volunteers.

Yard by yard the gun was advanced. Every few paces, Walt laid the piece and loosed a blast of canister. As his gunners were killed or wounded beside him, other Marines pushed forward. Just as night fell they reached the crest; here, within ten yards of enemy positions, the 3d Battalion dug in. Five times between 0115 and dawn, the Japanese counterattacked furiously. Five times the 5th Marines refused to budge. At the last, the enemy battalion commander and two of his officers burst through to the command post of the Marines only to be killed, before Walt could shoot them down, by a providential short round from the 11th Marines.

The Japanese attacks during the morning of 10 January expended the final reserves (two battalions) available to General Matsuda. Even so, Hill 660, the only enemy position which could still command the landing area, remained in Japanese hands. To capture this slimy, moss-and-jungle-crusted crag, General Shepherd turned to the 3d Battalion, 7th Marines, commanded by Lieutenant Colonel Henry W. Buse. Buse, in turn, was supported by a provisional aggregation of tanks, half-tracks, infantry weapons, and a couple of rifle platoons, grouped about the Weapons Company, 7th Marines, led by an indomitable old-timer, Captain Joseph E. Buckley.

After two days of probing, much of it uphill on all fours under Japanese fire, Buse led his exhausted men to the top of Hill 660 in an explosive rush just as night fell on 14 January. In the words of two combat correspondents:[96]

The boys were tired, wet to the skin, and going on nerve alone. Not even Colonel Buse could explain it, but spontaneously those bedraggled and bedeviled Marines rose and charged that vertical face of rock and clay. . . . That night we camped on the crest of Hill 660.

The expected banzai counterattack came during the hours before dawn on 16 January. Like so many previous attacks against the lines of the 1st Marine Division, this, too, failed.

With the capture of Hill 660, the Cape Gloucester phase of the New Britain campaign was over. Gloucester airdrome (which proved of little value after all) was secure, and a Marine-held perimeter covered the west side of Dampier Strait. Of the men who had achieved this result, an Army general staff observer reported:[97]

The Marines are careful, brave fighters. . . . With combat experience, Army personnel will be just as good. These men are in splendid physical condition and were spoiling for a fight. They were like hunters, boring in relentlessly and apparently without fear. I never heard a wounded Marine moan. The aid men, unarmed, were right up in the front lines getting the wounded. Fire discipline was excellent.

FINAL OPERATIONS ON NEW BRITAIN

Although General Shepherd's hard push to Borgen Bay marked the last and almost the only heavy fighting during the New Britain campaign, extensive operations, including much patrolling and one regimental shore-to-shore movement, marked the 1st Division's final months on the island.

The patrols conducted on western New Britain during January and February 1944 had two main objectives. The first was to locate General Matsuda's headquarters somewhere in the interior and to find out where and how the Japanese were withdrawing. This information was obtained by a series of company and battalion patrols from the 1st and 5th Marines, which not only explored the interior of western New Britain, but, in the case of Colonel Selden's 5th Marines, leapfrogged by battalions more than 60 miles along the north coast in a series of amphibious attempts to cut off the retiring enemy. In order to co-ordinate the extensive patrolling required southward throughout the roadless interior, Colonel Puller was placed in over-all command of all such patrols.

The second patrol objective—to bisect New Britain from north to south and return—eventually resulted in the largest (384-man) Marine patrol during World War II (or probably in the history of the Corps). This column duly qualified as a patrol because, in the words of its leader, Lieutenant Colonel Puller, "Everything's on two feet." Between 30 January and 18 February, this body, task organized for the purpose and named "the Gilnit Patrol," from its objective in the south, accomplished the secondary mission of the Marine division, to insure that western New Britain was clear of Japanese forces.

Once it had been determined that General Matsuda was withdrawing eastward toward Rabaul via the north coast of New Britain, it was logical to try to intercept him by an over-water envelopment to secure the Willaumez Peninsula. This 25-mile promontory is 120 miles east of Cape Gloucester; at its base the terrain bottlenecks practically all known escape routes toward Rabaul. As the 5th Marines had already leapfrogged as far east as Iboki, 60 miles from Gloucester, in Colonel Selden's attempts to catch Matsuda, this regiment, with reinforcing units, was directed to land midway up the west side of the Willaumez Peninsula, drive across, seize Talasea airfield, a one-horse (or, as it literally turned out after capture, a one-plane) Japanese airstrip, and patrol southward. The regiment had five days to plan and mount out for a 6 March D-day. In keeping with the impromptu nature of the operation, the amphibious lift and fire support were very impromptu indeed: 57 Army-manned landing craft, a handful of Navy LCTs, and, for "naval gunfire," if beach targets presented themselves, four Sherman tanks jury-rigged to fire from LCMs.

Despite haste, landing-craft breakdowns, guess-and-by-God night navigation over the 57-mile approach, and the absence of air support promised by the Fifth Air Force, an assault wave of Marine amphibian tractors crunched ashore at Volupai beach from the Navy LCTs, and the 1st Battalion, 5th

Marines, established a beachhead through which the 2d Battalion struck out for Talasea. Well-fed, aggressive Japanese defenders put up a respectable fight which constituted the most severe if not the only appreciable beach opposition encountered by the 1st Division in the campaign. Three days later, after a running series of small actions with the retiring Japanese, mainly on the part of the 2d Battalion, 5th Marines, Talasea was secure. Colonel O. P. Smith, the new regimental commander, who on 1 March had inherited Colonel Selden's job when the latter became division chief of staff, thereupon established his command post at a nearby mission, and the 5th Regiment settled down to a few weeks of active patrolling (which bagged 150 prisoners) and luxurious baths in the peninsula's hot springs.

THE END OF THE CAMPAIGN

The end of the New Britain campaign, which cost the Marine Corps 310 killed and 1,083 wounded, as well as untold hardships, also marked the end of the 1st Marine Division's long sojourn under General MacArthur. Finally despairing of any other means of getting the Marines back to naval command for the great operations impending in the Central Pacific, Admiral Nimitz appealed to Washington, and, in this instance, General MacArthur complied with the decision. His valediction for the Marines was characteristic. The general said to a Marine officer:[98]

You know, in Central Pacific, the 1st Marine Division will be just another one of six Marine divisions. If it stayed here, it would be *my* Marine division.

Nonetheless, on 28 April 1944, the 1st Marine Division was relieved by the Army's 40th Infantry Division, and the Marines, instead of sailing for Australia, as all hands hoped, went from wet and dismal New Britain to an almost equally wet and dismal base camp, Pavuvu in the Russell Islands. In the tone of proud self-pity which occasionally marks the postwar literature of this division, its history, *The Old Breed*, muses (pretty aptly insofar as Pavuvu was concerned), "Nothing was ever too bad for the 1st Marine Division."

The New Britain campaign was the last jungle operation by a Marine division in World War II, and surely it was the ultimate of its kind. But there are other noteworthy aspects of this miserable campaign. It was, for example, the only Marine amphibious operation in World War II not supported by naval or Marine aviation. Undaunted, however, the 1st Division organized its own liaison aircraft squadron manned by Marines with past flying experience (but no wings or flight pay), using scrounged Army L-4s and L-5s.

Another anomaly of the operation was the division's use of Army Engineer Special Brigade landing craft. At the moment, the Marines were glad enough to get any kind of landing craft and thought highly of much of the support they thus received. The Navy, more correctly taking the long view, regarded the Army's venture into large-scale operation of landing craft as an improper incursion by another Service into purely naval functions.

Finally, New Britain was the last occasion until Korea when a Marine division served directly under Army command. Occasionally the relationship was trying, though more so at the outset when inexperienced superiors sometimes tried to set their ideas against the veterans of Guadalcanal. In the long run, however, it worked well enough, especially under Douglas MacArthur, who must be given credit for considerable insight into the psychology of Marines, an insight which was to be manifest six years later when the 1st Marine Division again came under his command.

"IN A ROWBOAT AT RABAUL . . ."

At the other end of New Britain lay Rabaul. With its capacious, volcano-ringed harbor, its five airfields, its hundreds of Japanese aircraft, its 90,000 defenders, Rabaul was the capstone of the enemy position in the South Pacific. As such, together with Kavieng on adjacent New Ireland, Rabaul was the steadfast objective of our long push up the Solomons chain. That push, from its origin in the New Hebrides and Guadalcanal, was a series of amphibious operations in conjunction with shore-based air. These operations logically devolved upon Marine aviation, shore based and, until the advent of the Corsair, short legged. "Without anyone intending it quite that way," wrote Robert Sherrod, "Marine aviation became an air force for the South Pacific."[99]

Aircraft Solomons (AirSols), a joint command, waged the aerial war against Rabaul. Three of its seven commanders were Marines. One of its respected non-Marine commanders was Major General Nathan F. Twining, USA. During the months when AirSols assaulted Rabaul head-on, Major General R. J. Mitchell, USMC, had the command. Out of 84 shore-based squadrons, which between 1942 and 1945 hammered Rabaul, 33 were Marine; and they were at it longest and hardest, from Bougainville until the end of the war.

In addition to their stock-in-trade, single-engine carrier-type airplanes, the Marines of AirSols flew twin-engine PBJs (named B-25 "Mitchells" by the AAF, no relation to Marine General Mitchell); they even flew four-engine PB4Ys (B-24 "Liberators," two of which, on 4 February 1944, took the first U. S. aerial photos of Truk). Most of all, they flew the F4U, the "Corsair," the gull-winged "U-Bird" which ultimately became the trade-mark of Marine aviation and which many said was the finest fighter in the Pacific war.

One special field in which Marine aviators led the way in the Pacific was in night fighters. As early as 1941, seven senior Marine pilots were sent to England to train with the Royal Air Force, and one thing they learned was an appreciation of the importance of being able to shoot down enemy bombers at night. After a good deal of salesmanship (Marine Corps Headquarters had already shown its interest in the idea by programming the first Marine night-fighter squadron for early 1945), one squadron, VMF(N)-531, was organized in November 1942. The commanding officer, and father of the art as it developed (with many headaches), was Lieutenant Colonel F. H. Schwable, son of an old-time Marine officer of the early 1900s. Commencing in September 1943, Schwable's squadron finally went to work, based in the Russells:[100]

. . . in an airplane [the jury-rigged PV-1] that is admittedly makeshift for the job, with guns that may or may not all fire and with instruments that are difficult to read and radar that so far has an average of one out of three working. . . .

Nonetheless, working with specially trained Marine controllers on the ground, by June 1944, when relieved by a successor, this pioneer squadron was credited with 12 night kills, four by Schwable; it was his frustration to be ordered out of combat, over protest, with only one plane to go before becoming the Pacific's first night-fighter ace.

Southwest Pacific air—General Kenney's oft-publicized Fifth Air Force—had bombed Rabaul from time to time since the Japanese took it in January 1942; this effort, stepped up to its peak in the month between 12 October and 11 November 1943, had been co-ordinated with the Bougainville landing. As soon as Marine fighters could begin flying out of Torokina, AirSols took over on the heels of two carrier strikes which found Rabaul still alive (more than 300 operational aircraft) and kicking.

Beginning on 17 December 1943, AirSols tackled the massed fighters of Rabaul. The officer who led the first sweep and who continued to do so with virtuoso airmanship until shot down in January, was Major Gregory ("Pappy") Boyington. One of the most flamboyant and belligerent pilots in the history of the Marine Corps, Boyington was also among the best. His final score of 28 enemy kills in air combat made him the top Marine ace of World War II and won him the Medal of Honor. Happily this one wasn't posthumous; after going down off Rabaul, he was picked up by a Japanese submarine, and, though mistreated for the rest of the war, characteristically he survived.

On 19 February the Japanese made their final strong stand against Air-Sols. Fifty enemy fighters swarmed up to resist 145 U. S. fighters and attack-planes. Twenty-three defenders were shot down; and, on the following day, the Japanese withdrew from Rabaul everything that could fly, sending the planes north to Truk.

Meanwhile, to complete the ring of bases around Rabaul and Kavieng, the Green Islands were secured by New Zealand troops in February, under cover of Marine air, and became a base for Schwable's night-fighters. When, to everyone's relief, a planned assault on grim Kavieng was canceled, Emirau, in the St. Matthias Islands due north, was occupied instead. The landing force at Emirau, under Brigadier General A. H. Noble, was shaped around the new 4th Marines, recommissioned at length after Corregidor and composed mainly of officers and men from the raider units, which had been disbanded.

Logically, with the Japanese shot out of the air over Rabaul and with the beautiful harbor choked with sunken hulks, it might be supposed that the campaign against Rabaul had ended. Unfortunately for Marine aviation, this did not prove to be the case. When AirSols was disestablished in June 1944, the Marines were merely transferred to the Southwest Pacific under a new label, AirNorSols (Aircraft, Northern Solomons), and, whether they liked it or not, were kept at the task of pounding Rabaul's ruins until the end of the war.

In the Rabaul air offensive, Marine aviation flew 14,718 sorties, twice as many as were flown by any other air arm in the campaign—Army, Navy, Australian, or New Zealand. Marine aviators dropped 7,142 tons of bombs. By the most conservative method of estimation, they shot down at least 200 enemy planes during the two-month showdown which began in December 1943. In a masterpiece of understatement, the U. S. Strategic Bombing Survey later noted, "The attacks on Rabaul . . . were continued longer and in greater volume than required."[101] From this intense preoccupation with broken-backed Rabaul grew ennui, frustration, legend, and even song:

If the engine conks out now,
We'll come down from forty thou'
And we'll end up in a rowboat at Rabaul,
In a rowboat at Rabaul. . . .

On the other hand, ennui or no, Rabaul was the final act in the liquidation of the South Pacific theater and in the liquidation of Japan's highest quality combat aviation, too. To quote Sherrod again:[102]

It was in the Solomons, starting with Guadalcanal, that Marine aviation made one of its most important contributions to the winning of the war against Japan: the major role in the destruction of the best elements of the enemy's Naval Air Force, which was superior in quality to his Army Air Force.

Of that hemorrhage of the quality of Japanese naval air in the Solomons, the Strategic Bombing Survey concluded, "The Japanese never fully recovered from this disaster, the effects of which influenced all subsequent campaigns."

THE CORPS SCENE, 1942–44

World War II was the first war in which Marines used in their own right the entire panoply of the combined arms: Marine air, Marine artillery, Marine armor, Marine engineers, Marine antiaircraft battalions, and Marine coast defense battalions. In World War I, the 4th Brigade had enjoyed the support of these arms, but never in Marine hands. In terms of weapons and equipment, the Marine Corps had fully come of age by 1943.

In addition to the conventional spectrum of weapons and tactics into which the Corps entered full scale, there were original developments as well: close air support, for example (Bougainville); first use of the amphibian tractor (Guadalcanal); mobile base-defense units (Wake, Midway, Guadalcanal).

The last of these, however, represented a final culmination of Marine thinking which dated back to 1901. By 1944, the 19 defense battalions had played their part and had begun to disband or convert into antiaircraft artillery battalions (which were simply defense battalions minus their ground and seacoast defense units). The base-defenders' exit from the scene was not without honor and credit to the Corps, however: between 1941 and 1943, Marine seacoast batteries, armed mainly with Navy 5-inch guns, engaged, sank, or damaged more enemy ships than the U. S. Coast Artillery throughout its entire history.

But the Marine Corps had projects which were odd, as well as original. As a result of Secretary Knox's fascination by the German assault on Crete with parachutists and gliders (an assault which secretly convinced the Germans never to use either en masse again), the Marine Corps was ordered to form units of both. These decisions and the resulting programs overlooked both the uselessness of gliders anywhere in the Pacific and the limited value of parachutists. Marine parachute units did get to war and fought valiantly, though they never jumped in combat; the glider program was canceled in 1943. Still another washout was the barrage balloon effort. In all, five squadrons were organized and served in the South Pacific. In mid-1943, having trapped no enemy planes, they were disbanded.

In 1942, General Holcomb approved a significant change in "The Marines' Hymn"; in the time-honored line, "We have fought our country's battles on the land and on the sea," was substituted ". . . in the air, on land, on sea." General Lejeune, who had established the original official version of the hymn, and done so much for aviation, too, died on 21 November 1942.

In the same year a Marine tradition passed into momentary eclipse. As a result of an act-first-think-later edict by the Navy Department, officers of the Navy and Marine Corps were urged to contribute their swords to the nation's scrap-metal drive. The few Marines who were foolish or insensible enough to comply had ample cause to regret their haste when the Mameluke sword was quickly restored by General Vandegrift after the war's end. Close on the heels of the sword's departure came that of the Sam Browne belt. Still another casualty was the field hat. The old slouch hat, which had sheltered American Marines ever since the Spanish-American War, gave way to stamped-cardboard sun helmets, which the troops soon nicknamed "elephant hats."

But the major change in the Marine family of uniforms was the retirement of khaki from its time-honored status as a field uniform to garrison duty. Although the 4th Marines, some troops on Guadalcanal, and some of the senior defense battalions fought in khaki, the green utility clothing, or "dungarees," adopted in 1942, became the combat uniform of Marines. With the new dungarees came the shapeless utility cap, an unsightly nuisance destined to plague the Corps for years to come. Still another change in headgear was the new steel helmet, more practical and better protection than World War I's "tin helmets" in which Marines fought the early actions of 1941-42. To put a proper Marine imprint on the new helmet came the camouflaged cloth helmet-cover, worn by Marines but by no other Service; often seen in the most desperate fighting in the Pacific, this simple cloth cover came to distinguish and symbolize the assault Marine for years to come, until plagiarized by others.

In the field of administration, the opening half of World War II was a series of changes, improvisations, and patchwork as the Corps tried to adapt its simple administrative system, which had worked so neatly for 18,000 Marines, to a Corps 20 times as large. Company administration went by the board; instead, personnel matters were handled at battalion level or higher. In the place of an officer corps which prided itself on administrative nicety, the new wartime Marine officers had to think first and always of combat techniques. To fill the vacuum, soon arose a stratum of specialized administrators, "administrative Brahmins," they were later sardonically dubbed. So complex and fast-changing became the ground rules that an unofficial pocketbook, Hooper's *First Sergeant's Guide,* once a slim leaflet, outgrew the *Marine Corps Manual* in bulk and frequently in authority.

With an immense War Department dominating what was now called "the zone of the interior" or just "the ZI," and with common sources of personnel input as a result of the draft, the Marine Corps began to feel the first chill harbingers of unification. For example, a frequent cause of friction at barroom level was a 1943 joint agreement between the War and Navy Departments allowing military police or shore patrols to exercise cross-Service jurisdiction. In practice, this mostly meant stateside Army MPs asserting authority over lone Marines and sailors, a novelty which the average Marine found unwelcome.

Another and far more serious area of War Department influence over the Marine Corps developed in the field of manpower planning and procurement. Beginning in August 1942, the President referred military manpower decisions to the Joint Chiefs of Staff for recommendation; hitherto, taking the case of the Marine Corps, he had personally approved Marine personnel ceilings as presented to him by the Secretary of the Navy on recommendation of the Commandant. The new procedure meant that the Army, in the person of two of the four Joint Chiefs, now for the first time had a voice in Marine manpower decisions, and in a forum where the Marine Corps had no voice. In 1943, a JCS committee (the so-called "Maddox Committee"), originally convened to re-examine Army manpower requirements, turned its guns on the Marine Corps, when Army members charged that the Marine Corps was becoming a ground force comparable to and in duplication of the Army. The issue of Service roles and missions having been raised, it did not easily die. A second committee was convened to consider this question, with primary relation to manpower requirements. Here again, Army representatives belabored the alleged Marine Corps duplication of the Army —though, considering the Army's world-wide commitment to amphibious battles, in strict logic it might have been said that the reverse was the case. At any rate, the Army line then and thereafter in JCS manpower deliberations was that the Marine Corps, *ipso facto,* was a "wasteful duplication" of the Army; and, in the committee in question, Army representatives made a determined attempt to hold the Marine Corps to its 1943 strength of 360,215, with a troop base of four (not six) divisions, the latter a proposal which was destined to reappear in 1948.[103]

In Marine Corps Headquarters the organization created by the Peace Establishment Act of 1817 at length gave way, at least in part. On 1 May 1943, the Adjutant and Inspector's Department was abolished, and, in its stead, was created the Personnel Department. The last A&I, in a direct line running back 126 years, was Brigadier General L. W. T. Waller, Jr. Under the lightning hand of Brigadier General Gerald C. Thomas, brought back from the South Pacific with General Vandegrift, the Division of Plans and Policies now became the vital core of Headquarters.

But the Headquarters itself sometimes got scant consideration from Admiral King's hard-driving, ruthless administration as Chief of Naval Operations. Under a wartime executive order, King asserted and mainly got jurisdiction over Marine Corps Headquarters, as well as the bureaus and offices of the Navy Department, an encroachment which pleased General Holcomb not at all. On one occasion in 1942, when identification cards were new, a Marine sentry on watch at "Main Navy" detained Admiral King for some minutes (in strict compliance with orders) until the fuming admiral produced his ID card. When King complained to Holcomb, the Major General Commandant sent for the sentry in person—and promoted him to corporal.

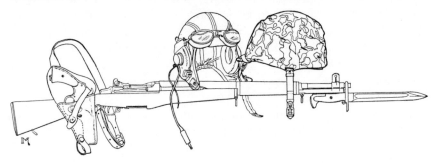

8 UNCOMMON VALOR *1943-1945*

. . . Uncommon valor was a common virtue.
—FLEET ADMIRAL C. W. NIMITZ

EARLY in 1943, when Guadalcanal had been won, the strategic views of Admiral King ran as follows:[1]

The region offering us the greatest freedom of offensive action appeared to be the Central Pacific. A major offensive there, as visualized by King, would jeopardize Japanese lines of communication, present a possibility for major combat with the Japanese fleet, provide bases from which to bomb the Japanese home islands, and permit the neutralization and occupation of outlying Japanese positions. It would lead directly to the Marianas Islands which, for many years, King had regarded as the key to the western Pacific. Indeed, since the beginning of the war, King had repeatedly emphasized to Marshall his conviction of the unique strategical importance of these islands, but Marshall would not see it King's way. In any operation in the Central Pacific King hoped to use Marines as the landing force.

In addition to the reservations of General Marshall, King faced continuing disagreement from two other widely separated quarters: General MacArthur, who regarded any advance toward Japan except via the Philippines as strategically sacrilegious; and the British Chiefs of Staff, who often seemed to consider the Pacific war an irrelevant diversion for the American Navy (". . . their false strategy,"[2] gnashed Lord Alanbrooke). Thus, as the long-range strategy of the war began to take shape, it was necessary to decide how much effort could be set aside for the Pacific from the beat-Hitler-first requirement (enough to "maintain and extend unremitting pressure against Japan,"[3] said King). Then it was necessary to settle whether the road to Tokyo was to lead only through Manila, or whether the United States forces were to advance in two mutually supporting columns, the second across the Central Pacific.

As early as the Casablanca conference attended by President Roosevelt and Prime Minister Churchill and the Combined Chiefs of Staff (January

1943), an offensive in the Central Pacific was accepted in principle. At the Trident conference (Washington, May 1943), the seizure of the Marshalls and Carolines was included in the strategic objectives approved for 1943-44. Since the Gilbert Islands provided natural steppingstones between the most advanced United States positions in the Ellice group and the Marshalls, the Joint Chiefs of Staff then directed Admiral Nimitz to plan the capture of a foothold in the Gilberts by 1 December 1943, as a preliminary to the Marshalls assault. The Quadrant conference, held at Quebec in mid-August by Roosevelt, Churchill, and the military chiefs, ratified this decision, and, among other strategic objectives for 1943-44, decided upon seizure of positions in the Gilberts, the Marshalls, the Palaus, and the Marianas. These decisions came very close to a reversion to the U. S. Navy's long-studied prewar Orange Plan, which owed so much to the strategic insight of "Pete" Ellis. General MacArthur's dissent—that such a Central Pacific thrust would be "time-consuming and expensive"[4]—was overruled, though not for good.

The strategic concept which underlay the decision to push across the Central Pacific was to use carrier air to isolate each objective while Marines took it. This strategy marked a long advance from the initial tenet of the South and Southwest Pacific (which persisted in the European theater throughout the war), that each succeeding amphibious objective had to be within range of friendly shore-based aviation. By giant strides the U. S. Navy and Marine Corps now set out to apply "unremitting pressure against Japan."

THE V AMPHIBIOUS CORPS

The instrument Admiral Nimitz intended to use was the newly created Central Pacific Force, which was soon to become the Fifth Fleet headed by Vice Admiral Raymond A. Spruance, the victor at Midway. Under Spruance came Rear Admiral Marc Mitscher's carrier task force, Rear Admiral Richmond Kelly Turner's Fifth Amphibious Force (whose job was to land troops and support them), and Major General Holland Smith's V Amphibious Corps.

Originally, Nimitz and his staff (who in May 1942 had judged that a single Marine raider battalion might retake Guadalcanal and Tulagi from the Japanese) doubted whether a corps headquarters would be needed to command and plan landing force operations against the small islands of Micronesia. As the complexities and difficulties of amphibious assault sank in, however, Nimitz quickly recognized the requirement for full-scale, high-level landing-force participation in the campaign which lay ahead. Writing with characteristic frankness to General Holcomb in June 1943, Nimitz avowed:[5]

> . . . I now frankly confess that if I ever entertained doubts that a corps commander was necessary, I am *now* not only fully convinced of his necessity—but am sure he should be the best man you can dig up.

Such a man was Holland M. Smith.

Two months later, on 25 August 1943, General Holcomb redesignated Headquarters, Amphibious Corps Pacific Fleet, commanded by General Smith, as Headquarters V Amphibious Corps, and transferred it from San Diego to Pearl Harbor for duty with the Central Pacific Force. In an aside as he signed General Smith's orders, Holcomb reportedly observed to one of his staff, "He's the only general I've got who can shout louder than any admiral."

The corps staff which General Smith brought to Pearl Harbor, although designated by a new title, was one of the most experienced in the Armed Forces at that time, dating back as a going joint staff to its original 1941 entity as Headquarters Amphibious Corps Atlantic Fleet. Its most recent responsibility had been the amphibious training of the Army's 7th Infantry Division for the Attu landings of May 1943, and of a joint Army-Canadian force for the "assault" on Kiska (which General Smith repeatedly predicted would be found abandoned, and was).[6]

General Smith's Navy opposite number, Admiral Turner, brought to the new partnership hard-won wisdom from the Solomons. Wrote General Smith:[7]

> On first meeting he suggests the exacting schoolmaster, almost courtly in courtesy. He is precise, affable, in an academic manner, and you are tempted, in the first five minutes of acquaintance, to make the snap judgment that he is a quiet, softly philosophic man. Nothing could be farther from the truth. Kelly Turner is aggressive, a mass of energy, and a relentless task master. The punctilious exterior hides a terrific determination. He can be plain ornery. He wasn't called "Terrible Turner" without reason.

In combination—often, if not always, a stormy combination—Smith and Turner were destined to wage and win the greatest amphibious campaigns in the history of war.

OPERATION GALVANIC

> The Gilbert Islands [stated Admiral King] are a group of coral atolls lying athwart the equator. . . . Their location is of great strategic significance because they are north and

west of other islands in our possession and immediately south and east of important Japanese bases in the Carolines and Marshalls.[8]

As a springboard for the Marshalls, the Gilberts were essential, if only to provide bases for shore-based photographic strikes on which future intelligence planning had to depend. To photograph the Gilberts (which had been British until 1942), the 5th Defense Battalion, under Lieutenant Colonel G. F. Good, Jr., had secured Funafuti in the Ellice Islands, on 2 October 1942. From Funafuti, of whose occupancy the Japanese remained unaware until the spring of 1943, United States bombers and photo-planes probed the Gilberts.

The original plans of Admiral Nimitz called for seizure of Tarawa Atoll and of Nauru, a cliff-fringed phosphate island in the Gilberts. After a model of Nauru's frowning cliffs and defenses had been shown the planners, it was decided to substitute Makin, which the 2d Raider Battalion had attacked in 1942. Makin was a much easier target than Nauru or Betio, the principal island in Tarawa Atoll.

Tarawa Atoll is a triangular necklace of flat coral islands, 18 miles long on its longest side. Betio Island is about two miles long and never more than a half mile wide. It lies at the southwest corner of the atoll and adjoins the entrance from the open sea into Tarawa's lagoon. In 1943 Betio was sheltered by palms and pandanus; its highest natural elevation is ten feet above sea level. Most significant of all, the entire island is ringed by a coral reef. In the words of Admiral Nimitz:[9]

> The ideal defensive barrier has always been the one that could not be demolished, which held up assaulting forces under the unobstructed fire of the defenders and past which it was impossible to run, crawl, dig, climb, or sail. The barrier reef fulfills these conditions to the letter.

The defenders of Betio numbered 4,836 Japanese naval troops, of whom 2,619 were first-line Special Naval Landing Force men. Their commander was Rear Admiral Meichi Shibasaki, who was destined to be killed in action on 21 November 1943. The defense system for Betio was so thoroughly constructed that Admiral Shibasaki reportedly said that the Americans could never capture the island in a million years. Offshore between beach and reef were mines, barbed wire, and concrete antiboat obstacles sited to canalize attackers into fire-lanes of weapons ashore. Surrounding the island was a coconut-log barricade, really a retaining wall three to five feet high. There were 14 coast-defense guns ranging from 5.5-inch to 8-inch, the latter having been taken from the British at Singapore. Twenty-five field guns

U.S. Marines near the Dominican Republic during the Battle of Guayacanac, 1916.

Turning of the Tide depicts the Marines in hand to hand combat with the Germans for possession of the now-famous Belleau Woods.

Second Division Marines in Belleau Woods, World War I, 1918 by artist
Sergeant Tom Lovell, USMCR.

Brigadier General Charles A. Doyen, Major Holland M. Smith, and
Lieutenant Robertson in snow.

U.S. Marines in France, World War I.

American and Naval officers rendering a salute to Allied troops parading in Vladivostok, Russia, 1918.

Landing party composed of infantrymen of the Philippine Constabulary and Marines from the USS *Sacramento* going ashore against the Colorums at Socorro, Bucas Grande, Philippine Islands, 24 January 1924.

Crew of the USS *Pittsburgh* and U.S. Marines mustered on the fantail of the vessel during change of Command, Shanghai, China, 1927–28.

were emplaced in covered positions, and 14 tanks mounting 37-mm. guns were dug in for static defense. Betio's 16 antiaircraft guns were all dual purpose, several being the big Navy 127-mm. model. The backbone of the beach defenses were 106 pillboxes mostly mounting 13-mm. machine guns. All structures, shelters, and magazines surrounding the airfield were heavily bomb proofed and many were built of reinforced concrete. The whole system—which in all included more than 200 coast-defense, AA, or antiboat

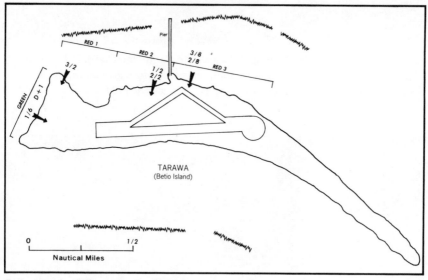

Betio Assault, Gilbert Islands, 20-21 November 1943

guns—had been under intensive construction ever since September 1942 following the ill-advised Makin raid.

Two unanswered questions troubled the Marine and Navy planners: Would the Japanese fleet sortie and direct a major naval attack against the amphibious task force (or Joint Expeditionary Force, as it was then called)? Would there be enough water over Betio's reef on the day in November and at the time of day suitable for landing to permit landing craft (LCVPs) to get across?

The first consideration, that of the enemy fleet, dictated that the landings at both Makin and Betio should be begun and completed with utmost speed to avoid exposing our own ships—including those most vulnerable, the loaded transports—to a Japanese counterstroke. This ruled out pre-D-day bombardment, and also the Marine proposal that artillery be landed a day early on unoccupied Bairiki Island, next to Betio, to soften the defenses and support the assault.

The second question, that of the tide and the reef, immediately caused the Marine planners to insist that the leading assault waves land in amphibian tractors, which could both swim and negotiate the reef. Only 125 could be scraped up, just enough for the first three waves, together with a small reserve for logistics. The following waves, needed to maintain the momentum of attack, would have to be boated, and, if grounded on the reef, would have to be ready to wade the remaining 500 yards in chest-deep water under Japanese fire. Every effort was made to accumulate accurate tidal data. The basic chart of the Gilberts was almost a century old. Gilberts residents and shipmasters contributed what they could, but this was partially contradictory. The most that could be said was that the preponderance of evidence indicated that there would be five feet of water over the reef on the morning of D-day (20 November 1943), but there was a disturbing minority view that a local phenomenon, called "a dodging tide," might well knock all calculations into a cocked hat. This was what was destined to happen.

The forces allocated for Operation Galvanic were the 2d Marine Division (Major General Julian C. Smith), which had had seven months' recuperation in New Zealand, and one Army regiment, the 165th Infantry, which was to secure Makin. In addition, the V Amphibious Corps Reconnaissance Company was to land on unoccupied Apamama, another of the Gilberts. The 6th Marines were set aside as landing force reserve for the operation; this meant that General Julian Smith would have to attack Tarawa with only two-thirds of his division and could not get the 6th Regiment without clearance from Admiral Turner and General Holland Smith.

Since the north or lagoon shore of Betio Island was less heavily defended and since the lagoon waters were sheltered, landings were to be made on that side, with the 2d Regiment (Colonel David M. Shoup), reinforced by one battalion of the 8th, in the assault. The fire support plan was one of the most ambitious conceived up to this time. In addition to both shore-based and carrier air bombings before D-day, four battleships, two heavy cruisers, three light cruisers, and nine destroyers were to support the assault, over which Rear Admiral Harry Hill was the naval attack force commander and General Julian Smith's counterpart afloat. Co-ordinating with the ships' bombardment, carrier planes were to bomb and strafe the beaches from dawn until just before H-hour. Over 3,000 tons of shells and bombs were allocated for prelanding bombardment.

Altogether, a most impressive plan. Even so, the 2d Division's chief of staff, Colonel Edson, expressed reservations in his quiet, steely way:[10]

> We cannot count on heavy naval and air bombardment to kill all the Japs on Tarawa, or even a large proportion of them. Neither can we count on taking Tarawa, small as it is, in a few hours. . . . I think it may take a little longer. These Nips are surprising people.

In a curious inversion of Admiral Shibasaki's boast, an American admiral (Rear Admiral H. F. Kingman) waved aside any such pessimism. At the final briefing before Betio, he pronounced:[11]

> We do not intend to neutralize it, we do not intend to destroy it. Gentlemen, we will obliterate it.

To which Julian Smith, normally soft-spoken and unassuming, rose to reply:[12]

> Even though you Navy officers do come in to about a thousand yards, I remind you that you have a little armor. I want you to know that Marines are crossing the beach with bayonets, and the only armor they'll have is a khaki shirt.

"WE HAVE NOTHING LEFT TO LAND . . ."

At 0441 on 20 November 1943, as the transports and fire support ships took station off Tarawa Atoll, a red star cluster soared up over the silent island. Moments later the 8-inch battery on the west end of the island began dropping shells in the transport area. The battle for Betio had begun.

The *Colorado* and *Maryland*, followed by the other heavy ships, returned fire. The *Maryland*, closing to within 5,000 yards of the beach, fired 42 rounds of 16-inch which blew the battery to kingdom come in a sheet of flame. For an hour the battleships and cruisers pounded away, then checked fire to let the planes come in (a half hour late). After the strike the bombardment resumed, while the boat waves formed and destroyers and control vessels picked their way into the lagoon. Betio was masked by a dense cloud of smoke and haze punctuated by bright red fires. To the Marines in the amphibian tractors it seemed as if nothing could be left alive.

At 0803 it was evident that the leading waves were behind schedule. H-hour was delayed twice, first to 0845, then to 0900. After leaving the line of departure the amtracs came under ineffective fire from 75-mm. air-burst and a few machine guns. At 0854, just six minutes before the scheduled time for H-hour, both the control vessel and air observers reported that the leading waves were still 15 minutes behind. In spite of this information, Admiral Hill ordered naval gunfire ceased, as originally planned, at 0855 (H-5). During the next 15 minutes, as a result of this early lift of fire, the unprotected tractors closed the beach without support. Shortly after the bombardment lifted, the Japanese opened fire. By 0910, when the first Marines gained Red Beach 1, a deadly crescendo of machine gun, mortar, and artillery fire was lashing the water. The first battalion which landed sustained about 10 per cent casualties before reaching the beach, while succeeding battalions lost about 20 per cent of their strength in the water. On the reef, landing craft grounded, and Marines commenced to breast their way forward. Robert Sherrod recalled the long walk in:[13]

No sooner had we hit the water than the Japanese machine guns really opened up. There must have been five or six of these machine guns concentrating their fire on us—there was no nearer target in the water at the time. I don't believe there was one of the 15 men who wouldn't have sold his chances for an additional twenty-five dollars added to his life-insurance policy. It was painfully slow, wading in such deep water. And we had 700 yards to walk slowly into this machine gun fire, looming into larger targets as we rose onto higher ground.

On Red Beach 3, where the destroyer *Ringgold,* inside the lagoon, had kept on firing until the very last moment, Major H. P. ("Jim") Crowe got his 2d Battalion, 8th Marines, ashore relatively intact. Approaching Red 2, Lieutenant Colonel H. R. Amey, commanding 2d Battalion, 2d Marines, was killed in the water by a burst of machine gun fire. Lieutenant Colonel W. I. Jordan, an observer from the newly organized 4th Marine Division, immediately assumed command and continued in. At 1030 Colonel Shoup and the 2d Regiment command group made their way ashore in the shelter of the long pier that jutted out between Red 2 and Red 3. A radio report came in that the 3d Battalion, 2d Marines, was hung on the reef off Red 1 and taking heavy casualties. Shoup ordered the battalion commander to land them over Red 2. The reply came back, "We have nothing left to land."[14]

Despite this bleak report, part of the 3d Battalion, 2d Marines, together with flotsam from other units, had made it ashore on the far right side of Red 1 (the extreme west tip of Betio), where Major Michael P. Ryan, senior officer present, assumed command. In Ryan's jury-rigged group were two Sherman tanks, the only ones left out of six which had started for the beach. Ryan immediately commenced pushing south along the west shore of the island, taking the Green beach defenses in flank as he went.

By midday, General Julian Smith had committed all reserves, except one remaining landing team (1st Battalion, 8th Marines). Therefore, it was essential to secure the 6th Marines, still held out as over-all reserve by Admiral Turner and General Holland Smith. At 1331, the 2d Division commander asked for the 6th Regiment; while awaiting the reply, Julian Smith organized his remaining artillerymen, motor transport men, and other headquarters specialists into a provisional infantry battalion which it was his intention to land and lead in person if other reserves were denied. Shortly afterward, the 6th Marines were released to division.

As evening approached, three battalions held a shallow, boxlike perimeter about the base of the long pier. Major Ryan's improvised force had a solid hold on the western tip of Betio. Casualties were heavy (1,500 dead and wounded, estimated General Smith); all types of supplies were low. The beaches were still fire-swept and clogged with dead, debris, and wounded waiting to be evacuated. Five 75-mm. pack howitzers from the 1st Battalion, 10th Marines, were ashore on Red 2 and preparing for action. A handful of medium tanks were still operable. Communications, depending on drenched, battered, unreliable radios, were tenuous. If Admiral Shibasaki could counterattack after dark, he might well break through and destroy Colonel Shoup's perimeter.

"WE ARE WINNING . . ."

Shibasaki's situation during the night was not as bright as Marines crouched between the water's edge and the log barricades imagined. He had lost control of his units mainly because the intense bombardment, relatively haphazard though it was, had destroyed his communications. Therefore, whatever his desires, the admiral was unable to launch a counter-attack, and the night passed quietly.

As soon as day broke the battle resumed its ferocity. The 1st Battalion, 8th Marines, attempting to reinforce the beachhead, took heavy casualties between reef and beach. Meanwhile, in order to split the defense, Colonel Shoup ordered the attack pressed southward across the airstrip. In an aside to Sherrod, who was at his command post, Shoup remarked,[15] "We are in a mighty tight spot." Up forward with his 2d Battalion, 8th Marines, "Jim" Crowe, a moustached old-timer with service dating back to World War I, bellowed, "You'll never get the Purple Heart a-laying there in those fox-holes, men!"

But again, the situation on the western edge of Betio was encouraging. In mid-morning, using one naval gunfire spotter who was with him and whose radio still worked, Major Ryan got in communication with a destroyer. Supported by her 5-inch guns and his two tanks, he attacked south, and, shortly after noon, had cleared the entire west shore. Now the 6th Marines could land to attack along the south shore of the island. Later on, as the 1st Battalion, 6th Marines, worked their way onto Green Beach, Colonel Edson joined Shoup ashore and assumed command, thus freeing the latter to fight his own regiment (despite a wound), while Edson co-ordinated all action ashore. Shoup's final situation-report to General Smith at the end of the day summed up the state of affairs:[16]

. . . Casualties many; percentage dead not known; combat efficiency: we are winning.

Shoup

THE END OF THE BATTLE

Our weapons have been destroyed, and from now on everyone is attempting a final charge. . . . May Japan exist for ten thousand years![17]

Shortly after this final message went out to Tokyo from Betio early on 22 November, General Smith moved his command post ashore. The day's fighting took the form of a hammering push along the south shore's heavy defenses by Major W. K. Jones's 1st Battalion, 6th Marines, and of an attempt to clean out the final resistance on western Betio, a strong point between Red Beaches 1 and 2. That night Marines held a line across Betio, facing east, about a mile from the far end.

Commencing at 1930, the Japanese launched three desperate attacks against the 1st Battalion, 6th Marines. The last assault, at 0400, was their "final charge." Despite continued pounding by the 10th Marines' howitzers and by destroyers offshore, the enemy surged forward to be stopped time and again by Jones's men. When day broke, 325 Japanese dead were counted. The failure of these attacks marked the end of the defenders' capability to hold, and, by midday, the 3d Battalion, 6th Marines, had reached the east tip of Betio. After inviting Admiral Hill and his chief of staff to come ashore and see what the battlefield looked like, General Julian Smith announced at 1330, 23 November, that organized resistance was at an end. After 76 hours of bitter combat, Betio was in the hands of the 2d

Marine Division, of whom 990 were dead, and 2,391 were wounded. All but 17 of the Japanese defenders were killed.

Among hundreds of heroes, two stood out: First Lieutenant W. D. Hawkins, whom a veteran of Tarawa unhesitatingly described as "the bravest man I have ever known";[18] and Colonel Shoup, who, more than any single man, held the beachhead. Both received Medals of Honor; Hawkins' was posthumous.

Although Tarawa was a magnificent victory, the public and many military people who should have known better cried out in shock. To expend 3,381 casualties in 76 hours seemed a fearful price for a small coral island. Both the inevitability and the necessity of the battle were lost sight of.

Tarawa, the first true amphibious assault in modern times, was inevitable. Tarawa was by necessity a head-on assault from the sea, delivered and supported by the fleet: as General Vandegrift later said, ". . . assault from beginning to end."[19] That such assaults would have to be made had been recognized and predicted ever since the days of Earl Ellis, but Tarawa was the first time that theory had been translated into practice. As a Marine historian, Captain J. R. Stockman, wrote:[20]

There had to be a Tarawa. This was the inevitable point at which untried doctrine was at length tried in the crucible of battle. The lessons learned at Tarawa had to be learned somewhere in the course of the war, and it now seems providential that they were learned as early and at no greater cost than was involved.

There were many important lessons. The one which stood out in highest relief was the capability of the amphibian tractor as an assault vehicle. It will never be known exactly how many Marines were killed in that terrible advance from the reef to the beach, but it is certain that, with enough LVTs to sustain the momentum of the attack, this loss would have been greatly reduced. In the amphibian tractor, product of the Marine Corps Equipment Board, Betio proved that we now had a reef- and beach-crossing troop carrier capable of meeting the tests ahead.

Of hardly less significance were the findings in the field of fire support. Both the concept of the naval gunfire plan and its execution are open to severe criticism. The destructive effects of long-range, area bombardment by warships had been grossly overestimated. After Tarawa, it was clear that ships would have to close and destroy individual beach defenses and batteries, one by one. The 15 minutes which elapsed between Admiral Hill's check-fire and the landing of the first wave had allowed the defenders to recover; in future, regardless of preplanned timings, fires had to be kept on the beaches until the assault waves were virtually there.

Air support at Tarawa was inadequate, poorly planned, poorly timed, and ineptly executed. General Holland Smith immediately asked the Navy to allocate carrier decks to a Marine air wing which could properly support future landings. This request was turned down for the time being, but Navy pilots received far better training for close support after Tarawa.

Communications had to be improved. The Betio assault was dogged by messages sent but never received, and by field radio gear which proved unequal to battle conditions. The communications setup of a battleship (Hill's flagship) was inadequate to the complexity of a landing operation; specially designed amphibious command ships, such as had already been used in the Mediterranean, were the answer.

The ship-to-shore movement needed to be more flexible so that it could adjust to events on the beach. The flow of supply shoreward had to be subject to landing force control and responsive to the needs of battle, not merely to the objective of getting ships unloaded and away (this was a problem dating back to Guadalcanal).

Each of these lessons was crucial, and each would be quickly applied in operations to come.

For the Marine Corps, Tarawa, like Guadalcanal, was a milestone. Once and for all, Betio proved the validity and the soundness of the Marine Corps' prewar amphibious doctrine. Just as there could not have been a Guadalcanal without the Marine Corps, so there could not have been a Tarawa. But behind the contributions of readiness, doctrine, and capability stood the individual Marine. This was recognized, in a moment of insight, by *Time* Magazine:[21]

Last week some 2,000 or 3,000 United States Marines, most of them now dead or wounded, gave the nation a name to stand beside those of Concord Bridge, the *Bon Homme Richard*, the Alamo, Little Big Horn, and Belleau Wood. The name was Tarawa.

MOPPING UP THE GILBERTS

Almost 200 Japanese had to be killed or captured in outposts elsewhere on Tarawa Atoll. On 27 November, after patrolling the length of the atoll, the 2d Battalion, 6th Marines (Lieutenant Colonel R. L. Murray) compressed all of them into a single body which staged a last stand on Buariki Island. After a sharp fight, which cost the battalion 32 killed and 59 wounded, the Japanese were annihilated.

In addition to Tarawa Atoll, there were two other objectives in the Gilberts: Makin and Apamama. As previously noted, Makin was assigned to the

27th Infantry Division (less detachments) and was executed by that head-quarters, under Major General Ralph C. Smith, USA, using a 6,472-man landing force shaped around the 165th Infantry (reinforced). Since Makin was nearer the Marshalls and thus nearer the enemy threat, Admiral Turner accompanied the Makin force, and so, perforce, did Holland Smith. Except for General Holland Smith's presence, and some of his staff, the Makin landing, executed on 20 November, the same day as Betio, was an Army operation. On 23 November, four days after the landing, Makin's 284 Special Naval Landing Force defenders were finally subdued and the island declared secure.

Apamama was initially scouted by the V Amphibious Corps Reconnaissance Company under Captain J. L. Jones, brother of Major W. K. Jones then commanding the 1st Battalion, 6th Marines, on Betio. The Reconnaissance Company landed from the submarine *Nautilus* on 21 November, finally located and got the best of a platoon of Japanese on 24 November, and secured the island on the 25th. Next day, the 3d Battalion, 6th Marines, and the 8th Defense Battalion arrived to establish the atoll's defenses and start construction of an airfield.

Finally, to make sure there were no enemy coast-watchers or outposts adjacent to Tarawa, the 2d Division's reconnaissance company (Company D, 2d Tank Battalion) searched three neighboring atolls, Abaiang, Marakei, and Maiana, on 30 November and 1 December. No Japanese were found.

On completion of these subsidiary operations, the Gilberts were securely in American hands, and only a few weeks remained before the next move: an attack on the Marshalls.

OPERATION FLINTLOCK

All during the planning and execution of the Gilberts operation, preparations were going forward for a larger, far more complicated, and—most feared—even more costly operation. Operation "Flintlock," the invasion of the Marshalls, had been planned ever since mid-1943, and, at higher levels, the work was almost completed when the 2d Marine Division took Tarawa. "The battle for Tarawa," wrote Marine historians,[22] "constituted the turning point of plans and preparations for Flintlock."

On 6 December 1943, following General Holland Smith's recommendation that the Marshalls scheme be re-examined, Admiral Nimitz assembled his top subordinates and presented them with a bombshell: earlier objectives should be abandoned and past plans junked. The new objective which Nimitz boldly proposed was Kwajalein, the world's largest lagoon, located deep inside the hard outer crust of defended islands which were the original targets. Kwajalein would be simpler to take than the earlier objectives; once captured, it would be a better base, and it was the strategic heart of the Marshalls. After they recovered from their surprise ("I, for one, was startled,"[23] recalled Admiral Turner), the planners acceded. A few days later, with JCS approval, Nimitz announced the new plan. The

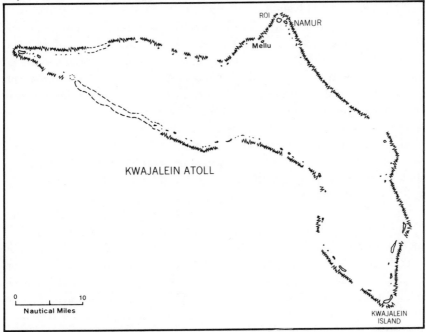

Kwajalein Atoll, Marshall Islands

V Amphibious Corps would land simultaneously on Kwajalein Island, at the south end of the lagoon, and on Roi-Namur, in the north. In addition, a small force of soldiers would secure unoccupied Majuro Atoll as a supporting base. After various postponements, the D-day finally selected was 31 January 1944, which barely allowed time enough to complete preparations.

Meanwhile, all hands made a concentrated effort to take advantage of the lessons so abruptly learned at Betio. Typical of this effort was Admiral Turner's blunt report, "Lessons Learned at Tarawa." This penetrating study, mainly of mistakes, was responsible for and foreshadowed many of the successful innovations which were to appear in the Marshalls.

One particularly important development, among many, was establishment, under control of the V Amphibious Corps, of an air and shore bombardment range on Kahoolawe Island, Hawaii. There, Marine and Navy gunnery officers began the painstaking training of carrier pilots and each fire-support ship in accurate methods intended to pinpoint and destroy individual beach defenses and batteries. A reproduction of a section of Betio's beach defenses provided targets.[24]

Kwajalein and Roi-Namur (the latter a pair of adjacent islets joined by a causeway) are typical Central Pacific coral islands forming part of Kwajalein Atoll. Each commands a deep-water entrance into the lagoon, and, in 1943, each had a Japanese air base and defending garrison. Since the capture of Kwajalein Island was assigned by General Smith to an Army force, the 7th Infantry Division under Major General C. H. Corlett, USA, whereas Roi-Namur went to the new 4th Marine Division (Major General Harry Schmidt), we shall focus on the latter.

Although not fully realized at the time, the defenses of both Kwajalein and Roi-Namur were not nearly as strong or as well developed as those on Betio or in the outer Marshalls. Here was a dividend of Nimitz's decision to strike the center rather than the edges. There were, nevertheless, 3,000 defenders, all Japanese Navy aviation or base-defense troops, on Roi-Namur. The defenses themselves included two coast-defense batteries each containing two twin-mount 5.5-inch dual-purpose naval guns, plus two 37-mm. antiaircraft guns. There were, in addition, 28 twin-mount 20-mm. and 13-mm. machine guns of the kind that had been so deadly at Tarawa, and 19 beach pillboxes mounting 7.7-mm. machine guns. Except for four massive concrete blockhouses, there was a general lack of heavy underground construction. Barbed wire and good grade concrete were not available, because American submarines were sinking or damaging two out of every three cargo ships carrying such essential cargoes. On the lagoon face of the islands, there were no underwater obstacles or mines, and beach defenses were weak.

Taking full advantage of the lessons of Tarawa, the general plan for the seizure of Roi-Namur was evolved. After two days of heavy, deliberate pounding of the main objectives by precision naval gunfire and air, adjacent lightly held islets would be secured, and the 4th Division's artillery (the 14th Marines, Colonel Louis G. DeHaven) would land. Next day, supported by overwhelming naval gunfire, artillery, and air, one regiment, the 23d Marines, would assault Roi, while the other, the 24th, landed on Namur. All assault landings were to be from inside the lagoon, in amphibian tractors, which, as a result of Tarawa, were being run off the assembly lines at a rate of 500 a month.

The naval attack force, headed by a newcomer to the Pacific campaign, Rear Admiral R. L. Conolly, included three old battleships, three escort carriers for close-support air, five cruisers, and 19 destroyers. Among the innovations presented by Admiral Conolly's force were: USS *Appalachian*, one of the new specially designed headquarters ships; LCI-gunboats, such as had been tried out in the Treasury Islands and at New Britain; and naval swimmers organized for the discovery and destruction of beach obstacles, the underwater demolition teams, or UDTs, as they soon were known. Admiral Conolly had played an outstanding role in the capture of Sicily and was destined to be respected and admired by all Marines with whom he served. Unfortunately his amphibious group, particularly the transport and landing ship officers and men, were green and unskilled. For an inexperienced naval force to land an inexperienced division was asking for headaches.

One problem which vexed General Smith was a succession of attempts to subordinate the V Amphibious Corps to Admiral Turner, a matter which had already been settled (in the other direction) by Admiral King's 1942 decision that the landing force and naval amphibious commanders should occupy parallel status. When Nimitz in August 1943 had placed Smith's headquarters under Turner, King had countermanded the order within 48 hours. A month later, Turner had proposed to Admiral Spruance that he, Turner ("who always had suppressed ambitions to be a General," growled Smith[25]), should be given control over training the V Amphibious Corps for future operations. Spruance had turned down the suggestion, but, within a month, when the command organization for Galvanic had appeared from the mimeograph machines, General Smith's headquarters had been missing, and the troops of the V Amphibious Corps had been parceled out under Navy commanders. Once again, as only he could, "Howling Mad" Smith had protested and had won his point. Finally, after the same thing had recurred in the Flintlock plan, Admiral Nimitz had imposed a final compromise: (1) during plans and training, landing force and naval commanders would be coequal; (2) during operations, the naval commander would have over-all operational control; but (3) when ready to do so, the landing force commander would land and assume full control of fighting ashore. This was not exactly what General Smith had wanted, but it could be lived with.

But V Amphibious Corps came under attack from another quarter as well. On 27 December, Lieutenant General R. C. Richardson, USA, senior Army commander in the Central Pacific, delivered a private memorandum to Admiral Nimitz. Richardson reminded Nimitz that he had questioned all along the wisdom of employing a Marine headquarters to command amphibious troops in the operations ahead. He suggested instead that Nimitz request the assignment of an Army corps headquarters to replace that of Holland Smith (whose individual competence he questioned), adding (in a refrain familiar to Marines) that Marine officers did not possess the requisite experience and training for the duties of a corps staff and that the V Amphibious Corps staff was "inexperienced and untrained."[26]

Nimitz, always neutral in inter-Service matters, simply forwarded Richardson's memorandum to Admiral King, who, in concert with General Vandegrift, made short work of it. Richardson, however, was destined to be heard from again.

D-DAY OPERATIONS, ROI-NAMUR

Although the main object was quite simple—namely, to place four battalions of artillery on islets from which they could support the forthcoming assault—the operations required on D-day as preliminaries to the capture of Roi and Namur were highly complicated. Units of the 25th Marines under Colonel S. C. Cumming, plus the division scout company, had to make five separate landings to secure the entrance to the lagoon and six islands commanding the approaches to Roi and Namur. The 14th Marines, whose howitzers had to support the morrow's assault on Roi-Namur, and all the myriad supporting units (including more than a battalion of amphibian tractors and the new gun-carrying armored amphibians) were grouped with the 25th Marines under the assistant division commander, Brigadier General J. L. Underhill. Underhill's group included as many amtracs as the entire 2d Division had had at Tarawa only ten weeks earlier. The 4th Division as a whole had 240 LVTs and 75 armored amphibians.

During the preceding 48 hours the Navy had poured thousands of tons of shells onto the Marshalls in a crushing but deliberate and carefully aimed bombardment (by the end of D-day the tonnage was 6,919). Repeated attacks by carrier and shore-based air had destroyed Roi's once powerful 24th Air Flotilla, and thus had partially avenged Wake. All these measures reflected Admiral Turner's determination to capitalize upon the lessons of Tarawa.

With such resources and support, the principal problems encountered on D-day came from the inherent complications of the plan and the inexperience of all concerned, especially the landing ship and amphibian tractor crews. The intricately phased movement of the tractors into the lagoon broke down when the primary control vessel, a destroyer, had to abandon her duties in order to provide covering fire for minesweepers, leaving the LVTs leaderless. Communications were abominable. The early model, low freeboard amtracs had power pumps with no manual auxiliary for use when gas was low or gone, and refueling boats failed to show up as ordered inside the lagoon. To worsen the situation, LST skippers refused to refuel or even salvage sinking tractors, on the jurisdictional grounds that they had been originally launched from other ships.

Nevertheless, all five landings were made somehow. During the forenoon the 1st Battalion, 25th Marines, secured Mellu and Ennuebing Islands, southwest of Roi, to the tune of carrier air support, naval gunfire, and rockets from the new LCI-gunboats. Of the 35 Japanese who outposted the two islands, 30 were killed, and five dazed prisoners were taken. In mid-afternoon, following strenuous efforts to assemble and organize enough amtracs to make the landings, the 2d Battalion, 25th Marines, captured Ennubirr and Obella Islands, southeast of Namur. On Ennubirr, where the Japanese main radio station was located, an enemy platoon put up a fight: 24 Japanese were killed at a cost of seven Marine casualties. While this action was in progress, the 3d Battalion, 25th Marines, landed on Ennumennet, just north of Ennubirr, where ten enemy were killed. The final operation of the day was the capture of Ennugarret Island, immediately adjacent to Namur itself, by an attack from Ennumennet. This task was complicated; twilight was falling and only four operable LVTs remained to Lieutenant Colonel J. M. Chambers, commanding the 3d Battalion. Nonetheless, by compressing 120 men into his first and only wave, Chambers, no man to abandon a mission, managed to establish a beachhead while the defenders withdrew to Namur.

During this day when little went according to plan, except the final results, the Navy continued to pound Roi and Namur. Huge fires and magazine explosions punctuated the deliberate drumbeat of bombardment. Whatever happened, Admiral Conolly was exerting every effort to prepare the main objectives and to ease the next day's assault. In the process, Conolly acquired a nickname. Dissatisfied with the positioning of the USS *Maryland* for her bombardment duties, the admiral ordered, "Move really close in."[27] From that moment forward, he was "Close-In" Conolly and a marked man among Marines.

THE CAPTURE OF ROI AND NAMUR

The stage was set, to an extent, for the capture of Roi and Namur on the following day, 1 February. Colonel Louis Jones's 23d Marines, on the left, were to seize Roi, which was almost all airfield, while Colonel F. A. Hart, commanding the 24th Marines, would assault Namur on which the Japanese had most of their supply installations including—as the 24th Marines would

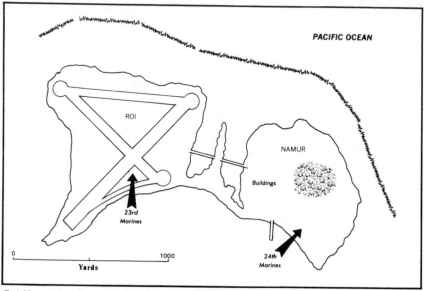

Roi-Namur Landings, Marshall Islands, 1 February 1944

soon discover—huge quantities of ammunition and explosives. The 23d Marines were to land in as yet uncommitted LVTs from the 4th Amphibian Tractor Battalion; the 24th would have to depend on the depleted remainder of the amtracs used the day before to secure the outlying islands. Trying to tidy up the previous day's legacy of confusion, Admiral Conolly and General Schmidt postponed the hour of landing until 1100 in order to permit the assault regiments to find tractors and embark and form up.

At the appointed hour, the 23d Marines, embarked by a fresh tractor battalion, were ready to go. The 24th, despite efforts since daylight, still were unable to marshal enough amtracs for the assault.

Never one to wait long, Colonel Jones chafed impatiently. Moments after

W-hour he demanded to be released, and the control vessel acceded. The 23d Marines churned toward Roi, while the 24th milled desperately.

Moving in close on the heels of ships' gunfire, rockets, and strafing aircraft, which loosed a final string of eighteen 2,000-pound bombs along the beach when the leading wave was only 500 yards offshore, the 23d Marines encountered virtually no opposition on the beach. Every enemy pillbox was destroyed or neutralized. The few living Japanese in sight were dazed and groggy. As the Marines surged forward across the debris-strewn airfield, Colonel Jones radioed to General Schmidt: "This is a pip X no opposition. . . ."[28] And so it proved. Although the whole day was consumed in getting the regiment across the island in an orderly fashion and in mopping up confused enemy survivors, there was no organized resistance. By nightfall, Roi was secure and safe, except for several trigger-happy outbursts among the 23d Marines. The landing had cost only 86 casualties.

Out of 110 amtracs originally allocated for their landing on Namur, the 24th Marines could only round up 62, but, as Colonel Jones headed for Roi, the leading waves of the 24th Marines attacked, too.

On Namur the bombardment had done its work as well as it had on Roi. Here, however, the clutter of debris, fallen buildings, and vegetation made co-ordination more difficult and aided the few active Japanese in their defense. Even so, the attack worked forward in good style. Then, at 1305, occurred one of the memorable mishaps of the Pacific war. Mopping up a large concrete blockhouse, an assault team of the 2d Battalion, 24th Marines, hurled a satchel charge inside. Seconds later there was an explosion which shook the entire island. The blockhouse had been chock full of torpedo warheads. On station above the beaches, a 4th Division air observer, Major C. F. Duchein, felt the shock, saw the explosion, and radioed, "Great God Almighty! The whole damn island's blown up!"[29] From a mushroom cloud that towered thousands of feet skyward, rained huge concrete chunks, a few unexploded warheads, and all manner of other debris. One company suffered 57 casualties from this explosion alone; the 2d Battalion as a whole counted 120 including its commanding officer (who refused to be evacuated). For the moment the battalion was virtually out of the fight.

Profiting by the stunning explosion, the Japanese, who were already about as disorganized as possible, began to resist more stubbornly, and, instead of pushing across Namur in a few hours, like the 23d Marines on Roi, the 24th encountered more of a fight. By nightfall (when General Schmidt had landed and set up his command post on the beach), two-thirds of the island had been taken. In the darkness, occasionally lightened by Navy star shells, small groups of Japanese attempted to infiltrate, but, save for one determined attack at dawn, which required tank support to stop, achieved nothing. Next morning, with tanks and half-tracks, the 24th Marines launched a co-ordinated sweep which reached Namur's extremity at noon; two hours later the island was declared secured, and the 15th Defense Battalion (Colonel F. B. Loomis) slowly began the tedious job of organizing and digging in.

The score in casualties made Roi-Namur the counterfoil to Betio. One hundred ninety-five Marines were killed and 545 wounded—less than one-quarter of the cost of Tarawa. From the Japanese garrison, 3,472 were buried, and 91 prisoners were shipped back to Pearl. Among the Marine dead were Private First Class Stephen Hopkins, son of Harry Hopkins, President Roosevelt's confidant and special assistant, and Lieutenant Colonel Aquilla J. Dyess, shot down in the forefront of his battalion's final assault on Namur. For his bravery and leadership, Dyess received a posthumous Medal of Honor.

Of the Namur assault in particular, Colonel Walter Rogers, General Schmidt's incisive, energetic chief of staff, had this to say:[30]

> The attack was seriously hampered by the failure of the tractors to get to the line of departure on time. I think the 24th Marines would have overrun Namur during the first hour or two if their assault troops had all landed as originally planned.

As a last word on this confused, complicated, and highly successful operation, Admiral Conolly simply observed, ". . . the plans were made to work, and that is the final test of a command and its organization."[31]

ENIWETOK—EXTRA DIVIDEND

The rapid and effective seizure of Roi-Namur and of Kwajalein (which Army troops secured on 4 February) whetted the planners' appetites for more. According to Admiral Spruance:[32]

> The Kwajalein operation went through so quickly and with such small losses that Admiral Nimitz sent me a radio asking my recommendation on going ahead as soon as possible with the capture of Eniwetok. . . .

The same idea, that of employing the joint expeditionary force reserve which had not been needed at Kwajalein for the capture of Eniwetok, had already occurred independently to Holland Smith. Accordingly, when Admiral Turner broached Nimitz's suggestion, the general simply reached into his desk and produced a plan whereby the V Amphibious Corps reserve, 22d Marines and 106th Infantry (less 2d Battalion), would be grouped under Brigadier General T. E. Watson to seize Eniwetok Atoll. Admiral Hill, who had commanded the attack force at Tarawa, was designated as General Watson's opposite number. D-day was 17 February, less than three weeks after the original landings in the Marshalls.

Three principal islands had to be taken in order to control the atoll and its magnificent lagoon: Engebi, at the northern end, containing an airfield, and Eniwetok and Parry Islands, at the southern end, commanding the wide channel entrance. Aside from a small security detachment and base development personnel, the atoll was not garrisoned by the Japanese until early January 1944, when 2,586 troops of the 1st Amphibious Brigade (Army) arrived from Manchuria. Therefore the brigade's organic weapons, including a few tanks, plus two fixed Navy 120-mm. guns on Engebi, constituted the entire defensive armament of the atoll, a welcome change from Tarawa and Kwajalein. Although the Japanese immediately began an energetic program of field fortifications, including some concrete pillboxes, their efforts were doomed to be overtaken by events.

Already pummeled by carrier air-strikes, the islands were to receive more of the same, and, beginning with the arrival of Admiral Hill's group, three old battleships and three heavy cruisers would provide the main fire support for the assault. As at Roi-Namur, artillery would be established on offshore islets to support the assault. Engebi, thought to be the most strongly held, was to be taken first, by the 22d Marines; then would follow, in order, Eniwetok and Parry, assigned to the 106th Infantry. The 10th Defense Battalion (Lieutenant Colonel Wallace O. Thompson) would then take over. For the 22d Marines, who had been garrisoning Western Samoa since mid-1942,[33] this was to be a maiden operation. Under Colonel John T. ("Johnny") Walker, the regiment had been trained to a fine edge. For the 106th Infantry also, Operation "Catchpole" (the code-name for Eniwetok) was the first. All told, General Watson's group totaled 10,376, of whom 5,820 were Marines. Although properly a strong brigade in organization and supporting troops, nobody took time to designate it as such: "Tactical Group 1" was all the title the force ever had. Since only a fortnight elapsed between General Watson's first news of the operation and D-day itself, the hard-pressed planners had no time for niceties.

At daylight on 17 February Admiral Hill's ships and planes began bombarding Engebi and the other islands, while minesweepers, working with secret Japanese charts captured by a Marine reconnaissance unit on Kwajalein,[34] cleared a channel into the lagoon. By early afternoon, following a 20-mile run up toward Engebi, Hill had put the V Amphibious Corps Reconnais-

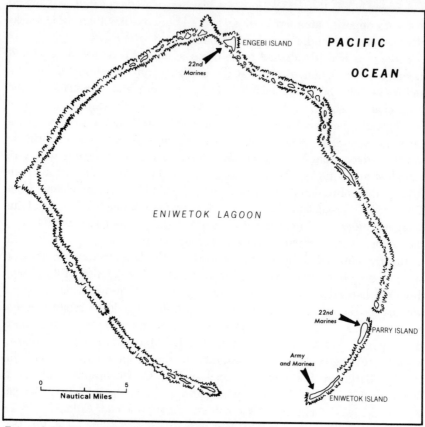

Eniwetok Landings, Marshall Islands, February 1944

sance Company ashore on two unoccupied neighboring islets, and the Marine and Army light artillery battalions were on their way in. When night fell, they had registered and began making night hideous for the 1,200 defenders of Engebi.

Next morning, reinforced by a company of medium tanks and supported by a two-hour naval bombardment, the 22d Marines landed on Engebi's lagoon shore. The ship-to-shore movement was executed smartly and precisely by Army LVTs of the 708th Amphibian Tank Battalion, a competent and experienced unit whose performance considerably outshone the green amtrac battalions at Roi-Namur. With two battalions in assault and the third mopping up behind them, the 22d Marines attacked straight across the island. Although the advance was rapid and spirited, the mopping up was tough because of the enemy "spider-hole" emplacements—central holes with radiating tunnels running out to well-camouflaged rifle pits. Even so, by 1450, Engebi was officially declared secure, although appreciable mopping up and a highly unsettled night remained ahead.

During the afternoon of D-day General Watson's intelligence officer reported bad news: captured documents showed that there were at least 800 Japanese, previously undisclosed, dug in on Eniwetok and Parry. There were, in fact, 908 enemy on the former, and 1,347 on the latter.

The capture of Eniwetok Island by the 106th Infantry, ultimately reinforced by the 3d Battalion, 22d Marines, consumed three days commencing 19 February. As it turned out, the Marine battalion, acting in lieu of the 106th Infantry's missing 2d Battalion, became involved in the hardest fighting and, in the words of the official history, "bore the brunt of the operation."[35] While Eniwetok was being slowly taken, artillery was landed so as to be able to support the final landing, that on Parry, located northeast of Eniwetok.

Displeased by the slowness with which Eniwetok had been secured, General Watson decided to substitute the 22d Marines for the 106th Infantry in the landings on Parry, now set for the morning of George Washington's 212th birthday. During the preceding days, Admiral Hill's ships pounded Parry with more than 900 tons of naval gunfire, about four times as much as had been accorded to Eniwetok. Moreover, the Marine pack howitzer battalion was moved down to Japtan Island, an unoccupied spit north of Parry, from which the attack could be supported. To give the tired 22d a reserve, General Watson ordered the 10th Defense Battalion to organize a 500-man provisional infantry battalion, a measure that cheered the hearts of the base-defenders.

Promptly at 0900 on 22 February, the 22d Marines made their landing. One battalion, the 2d, attacked straight to the front and secured the north end of Parry Island. The 1st Battalion, despite having been landed 300 yards south of its assigned beaches (and thus encountering some "friendly" naval gunfire), likewise crossed the island and wheeled right to sweep southward. Behind the two assault battalions came the 3d, which also wheeled right beside the 1st. At 1300, the 1st and 3d Battalions jumped off. Though the Japanese attempted no counterattack or maneuver, they fought hard; at one time, their mortar and machine gun fire even forced the USS *Pennsylvania* to shift station. After overrunning the main enemy center of resistance, in the zone of the 3d Battalion, 22d Marines, the attackers pushed rapidly ahead despite enemy minefields. By evening all but the 400-yard tip of Parry was in the hands of the 22d Marines, and the island was declared taken. General Watson, not generous with his compliments, thereupon radioed Colonel Walker:[36]

Well done, Johnny. My sincere congratulations to the 22d Marines and their supporting units. You have done a magnificent job.

And so they had. With only a fortnight's notice and few specific preparations for the job in hand, the 22d had, in their first campaign, stormed two well-defended islands manned by veteran enemy troops from the Manchurian ("Kwantung") army, and had played a stellar role in the capture of a third. At a cost of 254 dead and 555 wounded, the 22d Marines, assisted by the Army, had fought and won a battle foreseen 23 years earlier by Earl Ellis, and in so doing had advanced the strategic timetable of the war by almost half a year.[37]

LESSONS OF THE MARSHALLS CAMPAIGN

The most important lesson of the Marshalls was that the Navy and Marine Corps, using doctrines and techniques stemming directly from those of Quantico in the mid-1930s, had learned how to conduct a true amphibious assault, starting from zero at the water's edge, yet in the end overwhelming any possible defense. This knowledge, gained at Tarawa, enabled all objectives in the Marshalls to be won with fewer casualties, Army and Marine, than one Marine division had sustained on Betio.

In the Marshalls there were important technical advances. Naval gunfire support, sparked by the V Amphibious Corps training exercises at Kahoolawe, came into its own as an arm of overwhelming power and, when properly wielded by trained ships and shore fire-control parties, one of amazing precision. The LCI-gunboats were employed in mass for each assault. Naval star shells for the first time relieved the darkness of the battlefield each night. In the field of air support, rocket-carrying aircraft made their appearance to strafe beaches and knock out pinpoint targets.

A highly effective system of tactical air observation by Marine observers was introduced (in the face of reservations by the Navy) by the 4th Marine Division. Underwater demolition teams (one of which included a future Assistant Secretary of the Navy, John T. Koehler) swam ashore to reconnoiter and clear assault beaches and their approaches. Specially designed command ships provided mobile headquarters and communication centers for the control and co-ordination of the assault. The ship-to-shore movement, heart of the amphibious attack, had been mastered; amphibian tractors (a direct development of Quantico) carried assault troops across reefs and beaches while amphibian trucks, or DUKWs, sired by the Office of Scientific Research and Development and procured as an Army item, provided logistic support.

Finally, in the all-important field of communications, a new type of unit, the clumsily named Joint Assault Signal Company (or JASCO), had been added. In the JASCO were grouped all the specialized communication teams needed to control naval gunfire and air support and for the regulation of the ship-to-shore movement. This unit provided a nerve system for the assault, so that the immense support potential of the Fleet could be flexibly and effectively applied on the beach.

As a result of the Marshalls campaign the Marine Corps had a fourth experienced division, and, in the 22d Marines with their reinforcing artillery, tanks, and supporting units, the nucleus of another. Despite General Richardson's disparagement, Holland Smith's headquarters had proved its mettle in planning and in training large forces for complex, strongly opposed operations. Even though Admiral King, while promoting both Spruance and Turner after the Marshalls, resisted a third star for General Smith or any other Marine in the Pacific, Secretary Knox overruled him,[38] and the V Amphibious Corps now had a lieutenant general.

AVIATION PROBLEMS

By 1944, Marine aviation had come a long way since the great days of Guadalcanal, but mostly in the wrong direction. In mid-1944 the Corps had five aircraft wings, comprising 126 squadrons and 112,626 officers and men, of whom 10,457 were pilots. Despite its size and quality, this enormous force—six times as large as the whole 1939 Marine Corps—had practically nothing to do. Slogging to and from Rabaul was, in the current phrase, merely "kicking the corpse around"; in the Gilberts and the Marshalls, the

4th Wing, depressingly entitled 4th Marine Base Defense Air Wing, was occupied in the pedestrian chore of keeping bypassed islands neutralized. This service involved such drudgery as dropping diesel oil to pollute truck gardens, and unsung attacks on AA batteries which only existed to shoot back at Marine dive bombers on their daily trudge.

The truth is that, for a variety of reasons, aviation had become virtually separated from the line[39] and from the mainstream of naval aviation as well. Marine aircraft had not been made available to support Marine ground troops or a Marine amphibious operation since Bougainville; in the Central Pacific, under the aggressive leadership of Captain R. F. Whitehead, USN, amphibious air support had become a Navy monopoly in which the presence of Marines was totally lacking and, some said, unwelcome. With the assent of some senior aviators, as Robert Sherrod points out, "A new generation of Marine pilots matured without ever knowing the deck of a carrier."[40] Neither did this new generation know Basic School, nor the ground training heretofore considered essential for all Marine officers, ground or aviation. At Marine Corps Headquarters, ever since the Director of Aviation had been given the additional title as Assistant Commandant (Air), there had been a marked tendency to separate the administration of the Corps into two spheres, ground and air. In the field, Marine Air Wings Pacific (MAWPac), the senior aviation headquarters in the Pacific, located at Ewa, which General Rowell had commanded since 1941, was out of touch with its nominal superior, CinCPac, and had no relationship at all with General Holland Smith's headquarters, which before long was to become Fleet Marine Force Pacific (FMFPac). General Geiger, who would surely have recognized and equally surely have attacked these problems, was thoroughly occupied as a corps commander. In 1939, after Fleet Landing Exercise 5, he had said, "the primary reason for the Marine Corps having airplanes is their use in close support of ground units."[41] The central problem of Marine aviation in 1944 was that this dictum—dogma, it should have been—had been largely forgotten by too many Marines, ground as well as air.

To get Marine flyers out of the rear areas, away from the milk-runs—more important, in General Thomas's blunt phrase, "to get Marine aviation back into the Marine Corps"[42]—General Vandegrift and his Director of Aviation, Brigadier General Louis E. Woods, set about to attain what had been proposed ever since 1926, and by Holland Smith as recently as the Gilberts post-mortems—to have aircraft carriers specifically assigned to carry Marine aviation units for support of amphibious landings. This move was calculated to enable Marine aviators to resume a place in the forefront of the war and to do so in support of the rest of the Corps.

The proposal which Generals Vandegrift, Thomas, and Woods put forward was to eliminate some 15 squadrons and increase the number of planes in the remaining ones (which pleased Admiral King, who had been grumbling about the size of Marine aviation); to put Marine air groups aboard eight escort carriers organized into two Marine Air Support Groups (MASG) for amphibious operations; and to convert MAWPac into Aircraft, FMFPac, thus answerable to General Smith, and to assign a senior Marine aviation planner to Admiral Nimitz's headquarters. Incident to these changes, which were duly accepted by the Navy and put into effect in the latter half of 1944, General Rowell was relieved by Major General Francis P. Mulcahy, who thereby became the first commanding general, AirFMFPac.

Insofar as the field organization of Marine aviation was concerned, this program established enduring precedents and relationships. One problem which was not solved, however, was the divided organization of Marine Corps headquarters, a condition destined to create difficulties and anomalies for some time to come.

OPERATION FORAGER

As we have seen, it was the unwavering conviction of Admiral King, which the JCS sustained, that the Mariana Islands were the key to the Central Pacific because they dominated the lines of communication of Japan's "Inner South Seas Empire." The capture of the Marianas, King believed, would provide bases from which the Pacific Fleet could attack the enemy's sea-air communications and strike with equal ease at the Palaus, the Philippines, Formosa, or China. Moreover, as proved to be the case, Admiral King felt that a thrust at such a sensitive area would bring out the Japanese Navy for a major fleet action. In pressing this point of view (which was opposed to the end by General MacArthur and, to a lesser degree at first, by General Marshall),[48] King found unexpected support from General Henry H. Arnold of the Army Air Force, who wanted to base his new B-29 "Superfortresses" in the Marianas for the bombardment of Japan. The upshot was a JCS directive issued on 12 March 1944 which, in addition to canceling the no longer necessary Kavieng and Rabaul assaults, directed Nimitz to seize the southern Marianas commencing on 15 June 1944.

It was an irony characteristic of war that, having finally mastered the problem of attacking coral atolls, Admiral Turner and General Smith were now compelled to focus their efforts on a new and much more difficult type of objective.

The greater Marianas—Guam, Saipan, and Tinian—are rugged, mountainous, wooded (though less so in the case of Tinian), and, in terms of previous Central Pacific objectives, large (Guam is more than 30 miles long, Saipan about 14). Coral reefs, almost unbroken, ring each, and compound the difficulty of assault. By mid-1944 all three, together with several lesser islands, were strongly garrisoned by a total of some 60,000 Japanese. A thousand miles from the nearest American base, they constituted the most remote and formidable overseas targets until then encountered by United States forces during the war against Japan.

For Operation "Forager"—the conquest of Saipan, Tinian, and Guam, in that order—Admiral Spruance's Fifth Fleet, aggregating more than 800 ships, was to land and support three Marine divisions, two Army divisions, and a reinforced Marine brigade. The Joint Expeditionary Force came under Vice Admiral Turner, while the Expeditionary Troops, comprising all the landing and garrison forces, were commanded by Lieutenant General Holland Smith. General Smith had two other hats as well: command of Northern Troops and Landing Force, charged with the capture of Saipan and then of Tinian; and Administrative Command, V Amphibious Corps, a rear headquarters at Pearl Harbor, responsible for administrative and logistic functions in support of all ground Marine units in the Pacific. This last organization was ultimately to grow into Headquarters, Fleet Marine Force Pacific. To exercise his three commands, General Smith had three separate staffs made up of officers from headquarters, V Amphibious Corps. The fourth and last major landing force headquarters for the Forager operation was Southern Troops and Landing Force, under General Geiger, for the assault on Guam. This was the III Amphibious Corps headquarters, as IMAC had been redesignated.

PLANS AND PREPARATIONS, SAIPAN

General Smith's Northern Troops and Landing Force (NTLF) staff,[44] headed by Brigadier General G. B. Erskine, had to plan an operation which, in the words of one of the war's most ably written histories was:[45]

. . . primarily amphibious in the purest sense of the word. That is to say, it was initially a large-scale assault on a hostile shore carried out by specially trained troops who were embarked from distant overseas bases and lifted to their destination by combat-loaded ships.

To execute this assault, were assigned the 2d and 4th Marine Divisions (the former now commanded by Major General Watson, newly promoted after Eniwetok). As a common reserve for either the Northern or Southern Landing Force, General Smith had the 27th Infantry Division, portions of which had served at Makin and Eniwetok. The 77th Infantry Division, in the Hawaiian Islands, on 20 days' notice, served as a strategic reserve.

In sharp contrast to the 19,000 enemy which Pearl Harbor intelligence planners predicted, there were 29,662 Japanese on Saipan. Three-quarters of the defenders were army: 43d Division, 47th Independent Mixed Brigade (a regimental combat team with extra artillery), a tank regiment, an antiaircraft regiment, two engineer regiments, and many smaller units. Lieutenant General Yoshitsugu Saito commanded. The naval defense forces were concentrated in one area, about Tanapag Harbor, Saipan's port, and were commanded by Admiral Nagumo, who had led the attack on Pearl Harbor. Although numbers of heavy fixed guns, some as large as 8-inch, were on the island, many were not emplaced, primarily due to the lack of proper materials, sent to the bottom by American submarines. As a result, the defenders had to rely on earthworks, caves, and trenches as their principal fortifications. In the rugged, mountainous, overgrown terrain, which facilitated camouflage and permitted maneuver, however, there was far less need for heavy defense works. Even so, as of D-day, the Japanese had emplaced four short-barreled 8-inch guns, eight 6-inch, nine 5.5-inch, eight 5-inch dual purpose, and several concrete blockhouses, pillboxes, and ammunition bunkers. In addition, there were three airfields: Aslito, the main air base, on southern Saipan; an off-wind strip at Charan Kanoa on the west shore; and Marpi Point field, a small strip in the extreme north.

Saipan was divided into several defense sectors radiating approximately from Mount Tapotchau, the 1,554-foot crag which commands the island. The mass of General Saito's field artillery, his tank regiment, and one infantry regiment in general reserve were centrally located east of Tapotchau and Mount Fina Susu, another key terrain feature. In conformity with the tactical doctrine which the Japanese employed with uniform lack of success almost to the end of the war, Saito's plan was to "demolish the enemy landing units at the water's edge."[46]

The American plan called for intense air operations against Saipan and Tinian on 11 and 12 June, followed on the 13th by a day's long-range bombardment from the seven new fast battleships which ordinarily roved with the carrier task forces. Next day four old battleships and five cruisers, trained and proven in shore bombardment ever since the Gilberts, would arrive and take over. On 15 June, the two Marine divisions would land abreast on the west side of Saipan, 2d Division on the left, 4th Division on the right. Up north, above Tanapag Harbor, the floating reserve units of NTLF would stage a demonstration which, it was hoped, would fool the enemy. The immediate objective of the landings was seizure of an initial line far enough inland to preclude Japanese direct fire being placed on the beaches. To do this rapidly, more than 700 amphibian tractors, including the new 75-mm. gun-carrying armored amphibians, had the job of pushing the first waves about a mile inland before debarking—a bold plan which, unfortunately, failed in the event.

A serious ammunition explosion at Pearl Harbor sank six LSTs, but en route to Saipan, the spirits of many were high and confident, buoyed by the successes at Kwajalein and Eniwetok. Displaying his usual foresight, Brigadier General Edson, now second-in-command of the 2d Division, tersely said, "This one isn't going to be easy."[47] Aboard Admiral Turner's flagship, the USS *Rocky Mount*, General Smith gave a more categoric opinion:[48]

We are through with the flat atolls now. We learned how to pulverize atolls, but now we are up against mountains and caves where the Japs can dig in. A week from today there will be a lot of dead Marines.

THE SAIPAN ASSAULT

The morning of 15 June 1944 dawned bright and clear. While four battleships, eight cruisers, and seven destroyers took station and commenced firing close aboard the Charan Kanoa beaches, four regiments of Marines—from left to right, the 6th, 8th, 23d and 25th—boated in amphibian tractors for the run in. Preceding the first waves, at least as far as the reef, were 24 LCI-gunboats. From there in, covered by strafing aircraft, the armored amphibians would lead. The Marines, veterans of Tarawa and the Marshalls, were experienced and resolute; the supporting naval forces under Admirals Turner and Hill were equally experienced and capable. For four days previously, Saipan had been bombarded by air and naval gunfire. Seemingly, everything that could be done had been done. After executing his signal, "Land the landing force," Admiral Turner set H-hour at 0840.

On the way in, the gunboats raked the beaches ahead with 40-mm., and the fire-support ships stepped up their salvoes. The *Indianapolis* and *Birmingham* hammered Afetna Point, which separated the divisions' beaches, with 8-inch and 6-inch. To the south, the *Tennessee* pounded Agingan Point, flanking the 4th Division's assault. Short of the reef the gunboats turned clear, and the armored amphibians opened fire. A pall of smoke and dust masked the low ridges which formed a saucer in rear of the beaches.

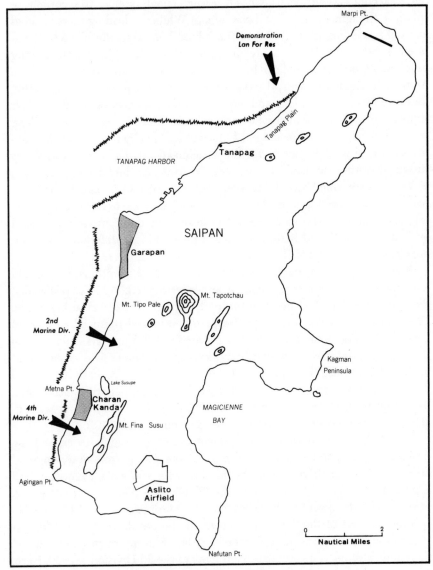

Landings on Saipan, Mariana Islands, 15 June 1944

As the first LVTs bellied over the coral, the reef seemed to explode in a torrent of Japanese mortar and artillery fire. Reports differ as to how many tractors were hit, but there is no difference of opinion that the fire was intense, accurate, and persistent. Observers afloat, seeing the curtain of splashes, thought the reef had been mined. While the leading waves landed and debarked—mostly far short of the inland line originally planned—long-range grazing fire from enemy machine guns pelted the gently sloping beaches. Pinned to a shallow beachhead and flanked by vicious fire from Afetna and Agingan Points, the assault companies found themselves fighting for every inch. Calls for help and requests for additional naval gunfire and air support, as well as aerial surveillance to locate the sources of the shelling, went out over all nets, but not until Marines had finally reached D-day's objective line (two days later) was the beachhead relatively safe. Casualties sustained during the landing far exceeded 2,000; in the 2d Division alone, 553 men were killed and 1,022 wounded. Out of 68 armored amphibians which led in the 6th and 8th Marines, 31 were sunk or disabled. Five of the original infantry battalion commanders in the two divisions were wounded on D-day, while the 2d Battalion, 6th Marines, had four different commanding officers before nightfall.

What had gone wrong? In one sentence, General Smith said, "We did not soften up the enemy sufficiently before we landed."[49] More specifically, the fast battleships had done an inexpert, haphazard day's shooting on the 13th, and the D-day air and gunfire plan overlooked the need to blanket possible position areas from which field artillery and mortars could fire on the ship-to-shore movement and beachhead (it was Saito's field artillery east of Mount Fina Susu that did most of the damage). This fire, in turn, wreaked such a toll among the shore fire-control and tactical air-control parties that, during much of D-day, the most powerful fleet in the history of war was unable to provide effective support for the 2d and 4th Divisions.

June 16th and 17th were mainly devoted to the struggle to expand the beachhead to a point which would prevent the enemy from observing and firing into it from short range. On the left, where Mounts Tapotchau and Tipo Pale dominated the advance, the 2d Division had the hardest going. Strong night attacks hit both the 8th and 6th Marines on 15 and 16 June, respectively. That of the 16th (more correctly, before dawn on the 17th) involved the first large-scale tank attack against Marines during the war: 44 light and medium tanks struck the left flank of the 2d Division at 0330. Here, in the glare of 5-inch star shells, Company B, 6th Marines, stood its ground with grenades and bazookas, while enemy tanks cruised among the foxholes, and three destroyers and the USS *California* hammered the oncoming attackers. Off to the side, Colonel J. P. Risely, commanding the 6th Marines, sat on a stump and calmly smoked a cigar as he watched. When day broke at last the 6th Marines were still there, and so were 31 derelict hulks from the enemy's 9th Tank Regiment.

Meanwhile, important events had been taking place on the larger stage. As Admiral King had hoped, the Japanese fleet was coming out. Accordingly, after his usual painstaking analysis, Admiral Spruance conferred with Smith and Turner on 16 June, and arrived at the following decisions: (1) To cancel the Guam landings, scheduled for 18 June; (2) to land the 27th Infantry Division on Saipan and shift the Guam forces into reserve for Saipan; (3) after nightfall on 17 June, when the Fifth Fleet had sortied to meet the Japanese, to withdraw the amphibious shipping eastward while sending the old fire-support battleships into a covering position west of Saipan. Except for a few supporting destroyers and escort carriers, this would leave the V Amphibious Corps in a lonely position on Saipan, but, unlike Fletcher's precipitate withdrawal from Guadalcanal, was obviously the correct reaction to the enemy threat.

Although the Fleet, perforce, was absent, the situation ashore had improved. Holland Smith had landed and opened his command post at Charan Kanoa[50] and with the arrival ashore of most of the 27th Division on the night of 17-18 June, virtually all NTLF reserves were on the beach and available (the Marine reserve regiments, the 2d and 24th, had been committed on D-day). Moreover, after fierce initial resistance, the Japanese were beginning to feel the strain. On the night of 18 June, though far from licked insofar as any front line Marines could discern, the enemy headquarters burned its secret papers, and a message went back to Tokyo: "By becoming the bulwark of the Pacific with 10,000 deaths we hope to requite the Imperial favor."[51]

That same day, while the 2d Division held its pivot position on the left, the 23d, 24th, and 25th Marines pushed abreast across the canefields toward Magicienne Bay on Saipan's east side, where the Japanese had most feared initial landings. Somewhat less rapidly,[52] on the right of the 4th Division, the 165th Infantry secured Aslito Airfield with no opposition, while the 105th Infantry extended the 27th Division's front further right to the cliffs and caves of the south shore. By the 19th, the island was completely bisected, with a remnant of the Japanese force compressed into Nafutan Point at the extreme southern tip; this area, reportedly containing about 500 enemy,[53] was assigned to the 2d Battalion, 105th Infantry, to clean out. Although a 27th Division unit, this battalion was placed under corps control for this mission. Later, Major General Ralph Smith, the Army division commander, requested that the entire 105th Infantry be given this job, and General Holland Smith acceded.

The following two days were devoted to completion of the corps pivot movement in preparation for a sustained drive up the north-south axis of Saipan. The 2d Division continued to hold fast on the left while the 4th, having reached the far side of the island, swung north. On 20 June, the 25th Marines, under Colonel M. J. Batchelder, captured Hill 500, an eminence honeycombed with caves and tunnels, which had originally been the command post of the 47th Brigade commander, Colonel Oka, thought by some to have been the same Oka who had commanded a regiment during the Matanikau actions on Guadalcanal.

While the Marine divisions formed for the northward attack, the 27th Division landed its remaining regiment, the 106th Infantry, continued mopping up the corps rear, and slowly compressed the remaining enemy trapped on Nafutan Point. Meanwhile, the Navy had scored great successes: on 19 June, a massive air attack on Spruance's fleet, made by virtually the entire combat strength of Japanese carrier aviation, was destroyed by Task Force 58 off Guam, with 346 enemy planes shot down as against 30 American losses.[54] This sweeping victory, known among naval aviators as the "Marianas Turkey Shoot," enabled Admiral Spruance to thrust confidently toward the enemy fleet. On the afternoon of 20 June, at the very maximum range of our aircraft, Spruance made contact with the carriers of Vice Admiral Jisaburo Ozawa's Mobile Fleet, the main striking force of the Japanese Navy. In all, counting submarine attacks on the fringe of battle, the Japanese lost three carriers, *Taiho, Shokaku,* and *Hiyo.* A hundred United States planes failed to return, many having run out of fuel driving home the attack. Though he had won one of the great naval victories of the war, Spruance was immediately criticized by some hotheads for not forgetting the Marianas operation and chasing away after Ozawa's fleet. The Marines on Saipan, who were never out of his thoughts, had good cause to think otherwise.

THE ATTACK NORTHWARD

After the Battle of the Philippine Sea, as Spruance's victory was called, the fleet returned to Saipan, and the enemy defenders realized that Ozawa had not been able to turn the tide. In the words of a Japanese historian, "The garrison on the Mariana Islands resembled fish caught in a casting net."[55]

Now the V Amphibious Corps was in line facing north, 2d Division on the left, still marking time ("We are having a hard time holding these boys back," commented Colonel Shoup[56]), 4th Division on the right. By 22 June, the 2d Division's turn had come. Attacking north into "a nightmare of sheer cliffs and precipitous hills,"[57] the 6th and the 8th Marines (Colonel C. R. Wallace) not only captured Mount Tipo Pale, but began the grueling advance up Tapotchau, key terrain feature of Saipan. On the right, the 4th Division forged ahead through the broken, craggy, cave-riddled shores of Magicienne Bay. Theirs was a battle of flame thrower, pole-charge, grenade, and bulldozer. At corps headquarters, General Holland Smith warned the 27th Division to prepare to go into line next day between the two Marine divisions, leaving a battalion of the 105th Infantry and some tanks to finish the slow mop-up of Nafutan Point.

On the morrow, with 18 battalions of artillery in support, plus the air and the naval gunfire which the Japanese so dreaded ("officers and men lived in deadly fear of it," wrote Colonel Hayashi[58]), the three divisions attacked. The day began badly because the 27th Division, in the center, was seriously late, 55 minutes, in jumping off. Moreover, once under way, the division ran into heavy resistance against which the left assault regiment scored no advance whatsoever, while the right regiment made only 400 yards. Because the Marine divisions on both sides couldn't entirely hold back, the corps front began to assume a concave "U" shape. Nevertheless, the 2d Battalion, 23d Marines, captured Hill 600 through a shower of enemy grenades. "It was all you could do to climb it, let alone fight up it," said Lieutenant Colonel E. J. Dillon, the battalion commander.[59]

While the 23d Regiment mastered Hill 600 and tried to maintain contact with the bogged-down 165th Infantry, the 24th Marines bit into the base of Kagman Peninsula, and the 2d Division continued its determined struggle toward Tapotchau. To round out the problems of the 27th Division, the 2d Battalion, 105th Infantry, instead of attacking Nafutan Point at daybreak as ordered, waited until 1400 and then got nowhere. In addition, this battalion became the center of a staff muddle: both NTLF headquarters and the 27th Division issued it orders, a matter which Holland Smith's staff considered an infringement of the corps commander's prerogative.

At the end of the day General Holland Smith could no longer hide his concern over the 27th Division's showing. In a conference with Major General Sanderford Jarman, USA, senior Army officer on Saipan and prospective island commander, the Marine general asked Jarman to go to General Ralph Smith in an effort to get the 27th Division moving. Jarman assented, and, in his words:[60]

I talked to General [Ralph] Smith and explained the situation as I saw it and that I felt from reports from the Corps Commander that his division was not carrying its full share. He immediately replied that such was true; that he was in no way satisfied with what his regimental commanders had done during the day . . . and stated that if he didn't take his division forward tomorrow he should be relieved.

On 24 June, both the 2d and 4th Divisions scored good advances in the east and west. The 2d Marines, under Colonel W. J. Stuart, pushed forward into the outskirts of Garapan, Saipan's principal town, while the 8th Regiment, reinforced by the 1st Battalion, 29th Marines (whose presence and special role will be explained) pushed onto the southern slopes of Tapotchau. For the 10th Marines the early hours of the 24th were punctuated by Japanese counterbattery fire, one concentration of which lit squarely on the regimental fire-direction center, killing the regimental executive officer (Lieutenant Colonel R. E. Forsyth) and wounding both the intelligence and operations officers. The 1st Battalion's fire-direction center took over control of the regiment, and support continued without interruption. The 6th Marines also lost their executive officer, Lieutenant Colonel K. F. McCleod, killed in the front lines by a sniper forward of Mount Tipo Pale.

On the left, the 4th Division fanned eastward onto the Kagman Peninsula. In the center, however, neither the 106th Infantry nor the 165th made the advance for which Ralph Smith had hoped. In fact, the 27th Division, still stymied by the stout Japanese defense of what the soldiers called "Death Valley," made no substantial advance at all. Neither did the battalion on Nafutan Point. This was too much for Holland Smith. That afternoon, after securing the approval both of Admiral Turner and of Admiral Spruance, he relieved the 27th Division's commander. "Ralph Smith has shown that he lacks aggressive spirit," he said, "and his division is slowing down our advance. He should be relieved."[61] General Jarman was temporarily given command of the Army division until the arrival, some days later, of a replacement, Major General G. W. Griner, USA. Of conditions which he found within the 27th Division during his week in command, General Jarman reported to Army superiors:[62]

Based on my observation of the 27th Division for a few days, I have noted certain things that give me some concern. They are, first, a lack of offensive spirit on the part of the troops. A battalion will run into one machine gun and be held up for several hours. When they get any kind of minor resistance they immediately open up with everything they have that can fire in the general direction from which they are being fired upon. Second, at night if a patrol comes in around their bivouac area they immediately telephone in and state they are under a counter attack and want to fall back to some other position. Third, I found that troops would work all day to capture well-earned terrain and at night would fall back a distance varying from 400 to 800 and sometimes 1,000 yards to organize a perimeter of defense. . . .

Major General Ralph Smith was one of five Army general officers relieved in combat during the Pacific war, but the only one relieved by a Marine Corps officer. This circumstance, combined with future substandard performance on the part of the 27th Division, and an apparently deliberate inflammation of the matter by a newspaper chain contributed to the subsequent generation of a bitter inter-Service controversy which will be noted later.

Meanwhile, as the 27th Division attempted to solve its problems under new leadership, two important gains were scored. On the right, the 4th Division swept across the Kagman Peninsula in a fine attack, while, on the left, the 2d Division finally captured Mount Tapotchau.

This decisive achievement on the left was mainly the work of the 1st Battalion, 29th Marines, under Lieutenant Colonel R. M. Tompkins, ably supported by the 3d Battalion, 8th Marines. Tompkins' battalion had been attached to the 2d Division for a special mission which was canceled late in the planning phase of Forager; it had, however, been retained as a tenth rifle battalion in the division for the duration of the campaign. On 25 June its presence paid off, when, making brilliant use of smoke to cover a complicated maneuver, Tompkins disengaged two of his companies from contact with enemy to the front and led them in person up a precipitous flanking route to the very top of Tapotchau, which the Japanese had left temporarily unoccupied. One of Tompkins' officers later wrote:[63]

Three requisites are necessary to the bold execution of such an undertaking. The battalion commander must have imagination; he must be willing to gamble; he must know the enemy and the terrain over which the action is to take place. Of these three, the latter is the most important; it will determine the odds in the gamble. Lt. Col. Tompkins had all of these requisites and more.

The taking of Tapotchau was the turning point of the Saipan battle. Although much hard fighting lay ahead, the situation was now grimly clear to General Saito. In a dispatch to Tokyo, he reported, "There is no hope for victory. . . . "[64]

SAIPAN SECURED

With Tapotchau and Kagman Peninsula in the hands of the V Amphibious Corps, the enemy were firmly compressed into northern Saipan, and, for a change, the attackers could observe all the Japanese rear area rather than vice versa. The price of this progress, as of 28 June, underscored how fierce the struggle had been: 2,116 Marines killed and missing, and 246 Army killed and missing; 6,377 Marines wounded, and 1,023 soldiers wounded. Grand total for less than two weeks' fighting: 9,762 Americans killed, wounded, and missing.

The operations until 1 July were mainly preparatory for the final phase of the battle. For the 27th Division this meant catching up with the 4th Division; this result was finally accomplished by a series of bypassing maneuvers, so that "Death Valley" could be mopped up at leisure while the advance continued. The 4th Division tidied up the Kagman Peninsula, soon to become the site of a U. S. airstrip, and the 2d Division worked its way down the north slopes of Tapotchau. General Saito, at the same time, established a "final line" across the island, running from Tanapag Village on the west coast through Hill 221 (Radar Hill), a central eminence. Still hoping for some miraculous intervention, Saito kept his engineers slaving each night on Marpi Point field, so that Japanese air could somehow reverse the situation.

Nafutan Point, however, still held out, and the 2d Battalion, 105th Infantry, despite sharp prods from corps headquarters (the sharpest: relief of the battalion commander), was little further ahead than before. On 24 June, to quote General Griner's later verdict, ". . . a fainthearted attack was made. The means were available for complete success had a determined attack been made."[65] The remaining Japanese, commanded by a Captain Sasaki, were not fainthearted. On the night of 26-27 June, Sasaki marched his 500 survivors "in column of twos," Holland Smith reported wrathfully,[66] right through the 105th's lines and over the unfortunate battalion's command post. Two hours later, Sasaki struck Aslito Airfield and began setting

United States aircraft afire, while aviators of VMO-4 and Seabees rallied a defense. At about the same time, the 25th Marines, in reserve bivouac on Hill 500, and the 14th Marines, pounding away on their schedule of night fires, were attacked. The 2d Battalion, 14th Marines, promptly took up their rifles and BARs, and, at a loss of 33 casualties, killed 143 Japanese before they could resume duty as cannoneers. In all, the 14th and 25th Regiments and the Seabees and VMO-4 killed about 500 enemy in this unforeseen melee. At any rate, though, the Nafutan Point problem had, in a way, solved itself.

On 1 July, the Saipan battle entered its final stage. The 2d Division pushed forward in a sustained drive that, in three days, captured the riddled debris of Garapan and brought Tanapag Harbor into U. S. hands. This permitted the division to be "pinched out" as the island narrowed, so that the 4th and 27th Divisions could continue abreast, with the 2d in NTLF reserve. Both the 27th and 4th Divisions likewise pushed ahead, and, in fitting celebration of Independence Day, cracked General Saito's "final line."

The continued compression of the defenders made it obvious to General Smith that a final banzai charge could be expected. On 2 July, he issued orders to all units to take special precautions against such attacks and to leave no gaps in front lines at night. As the advance continued, on 6 July he paid a special visit to General Griner to warn him that the 27th Division might receive a banzai that night down Tanapag Plain.[67]

Next morning at 0445, General Smith's prediction came true. More than 2,500 Japanese, short of weapons, food, and everything but courage, surged down on the loosely tied-in battalions of the 105th Infantry. Despite all prior warnings, a 500-yard gap lay wide open between the 1st and 2d Battalions (which were bivouacked together) and the 3d Battalion.[68] This gap the enemy found and hit, overrunning and surrounding the two unwary battalions on the plain (the 3d was to the right on higher ground). The desperate fighting which followed only too literally resembled Custer's last stand: one Army battalion commander, already wounded, was killed in his command post manning a machine gun (for which he was awarded the Medal of Honor). During this holocaust the regiment's 3d Battalion, only marginally involved, stayed put and made no effort to rescue their comrades who were being massacred. In rear of the 105th Infantry, the charge swept onto the 3d Battalion, 10th Marines. Here the Marine artillerymen cut fuzes down to muzzle-burst (4/10 second) and fired their howitzers point blank into the enemy; blew the turret off the attackers' lone tank; then seized rifles, pistols, and BARs and held their ground as infantry. Among the battalion's 136 casualties was its commanding officer, Major W. L. Crouch, killed at his guns. "The Japs came at us four abreast," said one cannoneer. "We fired 105s into the ground 50 feet in front of us."[69] Surrounding the Marine positions, reported a correspondent, "The whole area seemed to be a mass of stinking bodies, spilled guts, and brains."[70]

As day broke, the remnants of the two Army battalions formed a perimeter on the shore at Tanapag Village, where, 15 hours later, after being shelled mistakenly by their own artillery and after an attempt by the 106th Infantry to relieve them had turned back 300 yards short of their position, they were finally evacuated by amphibian tractors. Between them the two units had suffered 668 casualties in one of the most overwhelming banzai charges of the Pacific war.

As prelude to this fierce attack, General Saito, too fatigued and broken to take part in the charge itself, gathered his staff for "a farewell feast" of sake and canned crabmeat. Then, in the words of one of the staff:[71]

Cleaning off a spot on the rock himself, Saito sat down. Facing the misty East, saying "Tenno Haika! Banzai!" [Long live the Emperor!] he drew his own blood with his own sword, and then his adjutant shot him in the head with a pistol.

A day later, in a cave not far from the scene of Saito's death, Admiral Nagumo, who had launched the attack on Pearl Harbor, put his pistol to his head and shot himself.

As soon as the 27th Division had restored its shattered lines, General Smith relieved it with the 2d Marine Division, which had been briefly in corps reserve, and the two Marine divisions advanced rapidly. On 9 July the 4th Division overran Marpi Point, and, after one of the hardest struggles of the war, Saipan was declared secured. In this instance the word may have been somewhat stretched; the crags and limestone caves and matted brush continued to yield hold-out Japanese for months to come. Furthermore, the mop-up of 11-12 July at Marpi Point was rendered almost unendurably pathetic by mass suicides of Saipan's civilians, who preferred to drown themselves and their babies rather than face American capture that Japanese propaganda had taught them to fear.

Saipan cost the United States 16,525 casualties, of whom 3,426 were killed in action. Of the total casualties, 12,934 were Marines. But Saipan, the first B-29 base in the Pacific, was worth far more. When told of the loss of Saipan, Admiral Nagano, the Supreme Naval Advisor to Emperor Hirohito, replied,

"Hell is on us."[72] Another Japanese admiral said, "Our war was lost with the loss of Saipan. I feel it was a decisive battle."[73] So did General Holland Smith, who wrote:[74]

I have always considered Saipan the decisive battle of the Pacific offensive. Creasy, establishing the criterion for his *Battles,* defined decisive as an event which varied the world drama in all its subsequent scenes. Saipan was decisive because it varied the Pacific drama in all its subsequent scenes.

THE SAIPAN CONTROVERSY

On 12 July, before fighting had stopped, General Richardson, Admiral Nimitz's Army commander, was on Saipan with blood in his eye. Eight days earlier, without consulting Nimitz, he had convened a board, headed by Lieutenant General S. B. Buckner, USA, to investigate "the summary relief and displacement" of Ralph Smith,[75] an awkward if not a provocative step which would put Richardson in the position of passing judgment on the actions and decisions of senior Navy and Marine officers neither under his command nor in any way answerable to him. When the convening of the Buckner Board later came to Admiral King's attention, he promptly (and correctly) characterized it as "improper and prejudicial to inter-Service relations."[76]

Once on Saipan, Richardson bypassed corps headquarters and went directly to that of the 27th Division, where he reviewed the troops and distributed decorations, needless to say without the concurrence of Holland Smith, under whose command the Army division still was. Then, Richardson supervised the taking of testimony for the Buckner Board.[77] This done, he called on Holland Smith (whom Spruance, aware of the explosion that was building up, had pledged "to suffer in silence," no easy task for "Howling Mad"). In the presence of General Harry Schmidt, General Richardson berated both Holland Smith and the Marine Corps. In an electric atmosphere, on an island whose conquest, largely by Marines, marked one of the greatest victories of American arms, Richardson asserted, "You and your commanders aren't as well qualified to lead large bodies of troops as general officers in the Army. We've had more experience in handling troops than you've had, and yet you dare remove one of my generals! You Marines are nothing but a bunch of beach runners anyway. What do you know about land warfare?"[78]

When Richardson had finished, he went to see Admiral Turner, who was under no such pledge of forebearance as Smith. News of the general's activities had preceded him aboard the *Rocky Mount*, the admiral's flagship, where Turner was waiting. The latter reported:[79]

> I informed General Richardson that I am still in command for the Joint Expeditionary Force, and requested to be informed as to his authority for exercising command functions on shore on Saipan. Lieutenant General Richardson replied that he was here by oral direction of the Commander in Chief [Nimitz], but declined to exhibit any authority nor to state the terms of his orders. He also declined to admit that he was in any manner accountable to me while visiting this command. The purposes of the questions asked were, first, to ascertain if the Commander in Chief had actually authorized Lieutenant General Richardson to conduct an investigation of the combat performance of either Army or Marine Corps troops; and, second, if such authority had not been given, then to afford protection to the Commanding General, Expeditionary Troops [Smith] against irregular interference in the discharge of his duties.

While all this was going on, a San Francisco newspaper led off in editorial demands that supreme command in the Pacific be entrusted to the Army, under General MacArthur's leadership, citing allegedly excessive casualties on Saipan under Marine command and claiming that Ralph Smith had been relieved because he advocated more deliberate, less costly tactics.

In the face of this attack, much of it viciously slanted against Holland Smith and the Marine Corps, Admiral Nimitz chose to remain silent. He likewise took no action on Admiral Turner's official complaint against Richardson, which Spruance, in full agreement with Turner, had forwarded to Pearl Harbor. When the Buckner Board brought in its expected finding, that Ralph Smith's relief by Holland Smith had been unjustified, Nimitz merely referred it to the latter and to Turner for comment, which was duly rendered. Shortly afterward, in forwarding to Washington Admiral Spruance's report on the conquest of the Marianas, Admiral Nimitz, more than ever anxious to dampen the controversy, actually deleted from Spruance's original, in India ink, comments which reflected on the 27th Division.[80] Nonetheless, in October 1944, when General Richardson complained to the admiral about a *Time* Magazine article which presented Holland Smith's, Turner's, and Spruance's (and the Marines') side of the Saipan affair, Nimitz immediately wrote Admiral King that he was "in complete accord with . . . Lt. Gen. Richardson"[81] and recommended that the author of the *Time* article be identified and his credentials as a correspondent be revoked. This Admiral King disapproved. Then he declared in a memorandum for General Marshall:[82]

> I share in Admiral Nimitz's desire that the personnel of the 27th Division be not unjustly criticized because the relief of Major General R. C. Smith was found to be necessary. However, I am still more concerned as to the implications of the investigation conducted by the Board convened by General Richardson . . . [who] should have known

that the investigation would inevitably involve joint command questions that were not within his province. Furthermore, I note that the record of the Board includes intemperate attacks on the personal character and professional competence of Lieutenant General Holland M. Smith, who was given no opportunity to hear the charges against him, or to testify, or to present evidence. General Richardson's unilateral handling of this problem of joint command by an ex parte investigation was, in my opinion, improper and prejudicial to inter-Service relations.

King's thunderclap ended the controversy, as well it might, until September 1948, when partisans of the 27th Division (with the acquiescence of the War Department) reopened the matter, but without altering the verdict of responsible historians which, summarized, runs along the following lines:

Despite the popular title of the controversy as "Smith vs. Smith," personalities had little if anything to do with the affair (Holland Smith spoke highly in his memoirs of Ralph Smith as an individual). Neither was there any fundamental gulf between Marine and Army tactics, though on Saipan there was unquestionably considerable disparity in execution between the Army and Marine divisions.

The affair never would have taken place if the 27th Division's combat performance had not been below the standards set by the other divisions of the V Amphibious Corps. Such performance had, in fact, been foreshadowed by the dilatory work of the regiments of the division at Makin and Eniwetok. Subsequently, on Okinawa, the 27th Division was withdrawn from the front lines on the decision of an Army corps commander.

Much of the inter-Service animus of the controversy stemmed from General Richardson's conviction, expressed as early as 1943 (in conversation and in his "eyes-only" memorandum of 27 December to Admiral Nimitz), that the Marine Corps should be debarred from high command in the Pacific, and that General Holland Smith, in any case, was unqualified—a view not supported by Smith's unbroken record of victories. Richardson (who never won a victory in his career), with an assist from certain newspapers, was seemingly determined to convert the affair into an inter-Service controversy which would embarrass the Marine Corps, and largely succeeded in doing so.

From the viewpoint of the Marine Corps, the Saipan controversy was wholly regrettable and was a source of needless rancor in postwar years. Like the alleged (and unfounded) Belleau Wood "publicity grab" in 1918, it was seized upon as "proof" of Marine intransigency and unfairness toward other Services. It is historically important and has been discussed in detail because of the vast amount of misinformation which has grown up around it and because it unfortunately clouded relations between the Marine Corps and the Army for some years afterward.[83]

TINIAN—"THE PERFECT AMPHIBIOUS OPERATION"

Tinian, only three miles across the water from Saipan, is very different from its northern neighbor. Where Saipan is rugged and frowning, Tinian is symmetrical, neat, and green. It has two elevations: Lasso in the north center, called "mountain" by courtesy, and Hill 580 in the south. Otherwise the cane-covered terrain is gentle and rolling. Like Saipan, Tinian is ringed by sharp coral cliffs, but more so; there are only three beach areas (two in

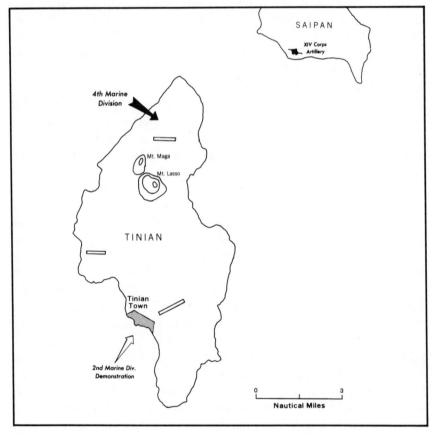

Tinian Landing, Mariana Islands, 24 July 1944

448

the northwestern corner of the island and one at Tinian Town) of which but one, by the standards of 1944, would have been thought suitable for landings. Tinian Town, in the southwest, commanding the main beach, was a flimsy counterpart of Charan Kanoa: an administrative village built around a sugar mill and a wharf.

Because Saipan and Tinian compose a defensive locality subject to mutual observation and within range of each other's guns, and because Tinian in 1944 had three airfields and one more building, its capture was an essential corollary to that of Saipan.

To protect Tinian's sheer cliffs the Japanese had a powerful system of coastal batteries; three captured British 6-inch guns, ten 140-mm. guns in three positions, ten more 4.7-inch dual-purpose guns, five 76-mm. dual-purpose, and six 75-mm. AA guns. In addition, there were 30 twin-mount 25-mm. AA machine guns, a vicious weapon capable of cutting swathes in ground units. Most of the foregoing were manned by the 4,110 Navy defense and base forces. The Japanese Army garrison of Tinian consisted of four rifle battalions, one light artillery battalion, a tank company, and the usual supporting units. The CO was Colonel Kiyochi Ogata. Including his 5,052 troops, the defenders totaled 9,162.

Ogata's defense plan was logical and typical of Japanese tactics. Inside the ring of coast artillery, he divided the island into sectors, each with a local garrison, while two of his rifle battalions and the tank company were held out as a mobile reserve in the vicinity of Mount Lasso. Because the Tinian Town beaches seemed the only ones that any sensible attacker could use, the overwhelming weight of beach defense was concentrated there. Covering the two northwest beaches—one only 60 yards wide, the other 160—were a few machine guns, one or two antiboat guns, and no mines. While the battle for Saipan ground forward, Ogata did what he could to improve his defenses, which were strong; but, like all the Marianas defenders, he was seriously handicapped because his supplies of concrete, reinforcing steel, and other construction material, had been cut to a trickle by United States submarines.

While Colonel Ogata worked on his fortifications, American artillery on Saipan began a systematic program of wrecking them. Under Brigadier General A. M. Harper, USA, able commander of the Army's XXIV Corps Artillery (lent to the V Amphibious Corps for the Forager operation[84]), every field artillery battalion on Saipan, heavier than the 75-mm. pack howitzers, was grouped. With General Harper's four battalions, this made 13.

Between fire missions on Saipan, all these battalions went to work on the north half of Tinian. For the southern half of that island, precision naval air took over, and, throughout the island wherever there were targets which defied air or artillery, naval gunfire had the ultimate responsibility. This methodical bombardment, co-ordinated and largely conceived by Major J. L. Stewart, a hardy perennial of the V Corps G-3 section, put 32,107 rounds of artillery onto Tinian at a rate of more than a round a minute for the 15 days preceding the landing. An exciting development for both sides (though in different ways) was the debut in July of napalm, a fearsome mixture of jellied fuel oil and gasoline dropped by close-support aircraft in large fire-bombs.

As Marine and Army artillery and the ships and aircraft of the Fifth Fleet went about their work of locating and destroying all the defenses of Tinian, the attackers organized and planned. On 12 July, General Smith, on assuming command of the new Fleet Marine Force Pacific, passed command of the V Corps, and thus of NTLF, to General Harry Schmidt, who was in turn succeeded in command of the 4th Division by Major General Clifton B. Cates. Rear Admiral Harry Hill (who had commanded the naval forces at Tarawa and Eniwetok) was to command the Tinian attack force. The 2d and 4th Marine Divisions were to land on Tinian, and the 27th Division would remain on Saipan in reserve.

But the great question was, where to land? The obvious beaches, at Tinian Town, were heavily fortified. As Holland Smith said to Admiral Turner, "If we go ashore at Tinian Town, we'll have another Tarawa."[85] Despite the fact that the landing of one division in assault ordinarily demanded more than a mile of beaches, the planners felt that the tiny, almost undefended northern beaches offered conclusive advantages: avoidance of the Tinian Town defenses; opportunity to employ Saipan's artillery to support a landing on north Tinian; rapid capture of Ushi Point Airfield; tactical surprise; a three-mile shore-to-shore hop from Saipan which, among other things, meant that supplies could be entrucked on Saipan and rolled off on Tinian. After a growling show of reluctance put on for the occasion, Turner (who had privately reached the same conclusions) agreed: land the 4th Marine Division, swiftly followed by the 2d, over Beach White 1 (60 yards wide) and White 2 (160 yards). It was unheard of, but all hands set to work to make the thing succeed. The assault was set for 24 July (J-day).

In the resultant landing plan, the 4th Division was arrayed in a column of great depth and striking power. With all the 2d Division's tanks attached, to add a swift armored punch, General Cates planned to land the 24th Marines in column of battalions over the left, 60-yard White 1, while the 25th Regiment landed two battalions abreast over White 2. To prevent the slightest, fatal delay on either beach, the 4th Division shore party was doubled in size so that each tiny beach would have the shore party normal for an entire division. No artillery heavier than pack howitzers was to go to Tinian; while thirteen 105-mm. and 155-mm. battalions thundered from Saipan, the four 75-mm. battalions of the two Marine divisions would be grouped for the crossing. Riflemen would leave packs behind: the load was restricted to weapons, ammunition, poncho, a spoon, and a bottle of mosquito repellent. Every serviceable amphibian tractor in V Corps (533 vehicles) was put at the disposal of General Cates. Meanwhile, Navy frogmen and Marine amphibious reconnaissance swimmers stealthily covered every inch of the beaches and approaches, looking for defenses, obstacles, and mines. General Cates and his regimental, battalion, and even company commanders, were repeatedly flown over their objectives for a look-see.

During the final two days before J-day, the preparatory fires reached crescendo. Three battleships, two heavy cruisers, three light cruisers, and 16 destroyers ringed Tinian with flame, pouring nearly eleven thousand 5-inch or heavier projectiles onto the island during J-minus one and J-day. Support aircraft disgorged bombs and napalm, while General Harper's 156 cannon hammered north Tinian.

When J-day dawned, the defenders of the Tinian Town beaches saw a battleship, two cruisers, and fire-support destroyers screening a large force of transports which were debarking U. S. Marines off the southern beaches. This was Admiral Hill's demonstration force; the troops were the 2d Division. The demonstration was beautifully executed, with loaded LCVPs coming within 2,000 yards of the beaches, and the Japanese opened fire with everything in the book including the three 6-inch guns, which promptly pumped 22 rounds into the old *Colorado* and six more into destroyer *Norman Scott*, killing her captain and inflicting 307 casualties on both ships.

While the demonstration occupied Colonel Ogata, the attack force formed to the north. Its main fire support came from two more battleships and three cruisers and the barrage rockets of 30 LCI-gunboats. The spearhead of this whole effort was three companies of Marine riflemen, landing in 24 amphibian tractors. On the speed and smoothness of their attack the outcome depended.

The landing succeeded beautifully. After a quick fight with a group of local defenders on White 1, the 24th Marines' assault company moved clear smartly. On White 2 a last-minute infestation of mines, plus potholes and coral heads, slowed progress more than the enemy. Once ashore, said one officer, "it was a cake walk."[86]

By nightfall, all three infantry regiments of the 4th Division and the four pack howitzer battalions were ashore and in business. At a cost of 15 killed and 225 wounded, 15,614 Marines had landed and secured all planned objectives and were braced for Ogata's counterattack. This came, as expected, during the first night. Three times—left, center, and right—the Japanese surged in with all they had. Company A, 24th Marines, piled up 476 enemy dead and, at the end, was down to 30 men, but their line held. In the center the attack hit the boundary between the 24th and 25th Marines, and one charge pushed through to the artillery in rear. While two batteries of the 2d Battalion, 14th Marines, continued their fire mission, the third held off the enemy with a curtain of .50 caliber machine-gun fire which "tore the Japanese to pieces."[87] The last attack included tanks. In the shadowy light of Navy star shells, the 23d Marines opened fire with half-tracks, bazookas, and antitank guns. An observer reported:[88]

The three lead tanks broke through our wall of fire. One began to glow blood-red, turned crazily on its tracks, and careened into a ditch. A second, mortally wounded, turned its machine gun on its tormentors, firing into the ditches in a last desperate effort to fight its way free. One hundred yards more and it stopped dead in its tracks. The third tried frantically to turn and then retreat, but our men closed in, literally blasting it apart. Bazookas knocked out the fourth tank with a direct hit which killed the driver. The rest of the crew piled out the turret, screaming. The fifth tank, completely surrounded, attempted to flee. Bazookas made short work of it. Another hit set it afire, and its crew was cremated.

As the flaming tanks lighted the scene, the close-ranked Japanese infantry was mowed down. Next morning, 1,241 dead enemy were counted in and in front of the 4th Division's lines. In the words of General Cates, this one fierce fight "broke the Japs' back."[89]

Indeed it had. While the 2d Division landed and went into line on the left, the 4th expanded the beachhead without serious opposition and prepared to take Mount Lasso. Both Generals Cates and Watson landed on the 25th. Next day the 25th Marines, hardly opposed, overran Lasso, and the 2d Division reached the east coast, scarcely stopping as they crossed Ushi Point Airfield, later to become historic as the starting point of the atom bomb's trip to Hiroshima.

So it went for a week. As the uncommitted units of Ogata's regiment withdrew south, the two Marine divisions, making full use of tanks in the flat canefields, and supported on both flanks by the Fleet, scored daily gains of three and four thousand yards. Except for the rain and the humidity, the advance—especially after Saipan—seemed like a field exercise. On 30 July, Tinian Town was overrun, abandoned by all but a single confused Japanese. By the 31st the Japanese were compressed into the bottom tip of Tinian, where nature provided a last cliff-walled redoubt. Here, during a night melee, two battalions of the 8th Marines clung to the cliff face and its edge while the enemy made unceasing attempts to push them off. At daybreak, when the Marines were still there, the end was in sight. By mid-afternoon, 1 August, except for enemy groups holed up in the rugged southern coast, all Tinian was in the hands of the V Amphibious Corps, and General Schmidt, whom Admiral Turner had given two weeks to take Tinian, delivered it in nine days.

Through tactical surprise, superb amphibious reconnaissance, overwhelming firepower, and expert planning, the Tinian operation succeeded magnificently. Its cost was without precedent in any comparable landing assault during the war: 328 killed, 1,571 wounded. This was less than D-day's casualties on Saipan. Among the dead, however, were two battalion commanders, one from the infantry (Lieutenant Colonel John Easley, who had survived a wound on Saipan), the other an artilleryman (Lieutenant Colonel Harry J. Zimmer). Still another casualty was Sergeant Peter B. Saltonstall, son of a member of the Senate Naval Affairs Committee. Battles are never easy on those who get hit.

"In my opinion," said Admiral Spruance, "the Tinian operation was probably the most brilliantly conceived and executed amphibious operation in World War II."[90] And to Holland Smith, known as a perfectionist, "Tinian was the perfect amphibious operation in the Pacific War."[91]

THE RETURN TO GUAM

The recapture of Guam had been a long-standing exercise at Quantico, but before the days of the amtrac. Thus the prewar "Guam Problem," though useful as background, was automatically superseded the day the Marine Corps got an assault vehicle capable of crossing reefs. For the Marines' return to Guam in 1944, a new plan was needed.

Guam is not unlike Saipan, but bigger and with much more jungle and no canefields. The south half is rugged and mountainous (highest elevation: 1,334 feet); the north half is rolling and jungle covered, with two smaller elevations, Mount Santa Rosa and Mount Barrigada, the latter more of a ridge. The east coast of Guam is coral cliff broken by a few bays and stream mouths. On the west lies Apra Harbor in the shelter of Orote Peninsula, site of the old Marine Barracks. North and south of Orote, which divides the coast into two sectors, are beaches backed by ridges and eventually by the mountains. The natives of Guam, the Chamorros, were and are likeable, loyal, and well disposed to the United States.

Since the capture of Guam in 1941, the Japanese had gradually built up their strength and defenses as the war moved closer. By the summer of 1944 they had, in aggregate, more than an infantry division on the island, mainly from the famed Kwantung Army, plus a large naval base and defense force. All told, the garrison rounded out at 19,000. Guam's coast defenses were formidable: nineteen 8-inch guns, eight 6-inch, twenty-two 5-inch, and six 3-inch. In addition to the dual-purpose 5-inch guns, there were eight 75-mm. AA guns. The army units on Guam had 81 pieces of field artillery, 86 anti-tank guns, and two tank companies. Although Guam could and later did accommodate many more airfields, the Japanese had only two: one on Orote Peninsula beside the old Marine Barracks; the other beyond Agaña, the principal town and island capital. Lieutenant General Takeshi Takashina, who had the 29th Division, the major army unit on Guam, commanded the defenses as a whole.

Like his fellow island commanders, General Takashina had felt the pinch of American submarines, and his supply of construction materials was low and unbalanced. Using what he had or could improvise, he gave highest priorities to creation of a well-organized system of beach defenses along Guam's west coast ranging from Tumon Bay (north of Agaña) to Facpi Point, south of Orote. To defend these landing areas and match fortification priorities, he concentrated his troops to cover the west coast.

One pinch which he did not feel, however, was for whiskey; Guam, as Marines were soon to learn, was stocked with oceans of synthetic Japanese Sun-Tory "Scotch" and with only less generous stores of sake and good Asahi beer.

The plan for Operation "Stevedore" (Guam's code-name) called for two landings on the west coast: one north of Orote on the Asan beaches by the 3d Marine Division, up from the South Pacific; the other south of Orote at

Agat, by the 1st Provisional Marine Brigade, which had been created on 22 March 1944 by the addition of the 4th Marines and one of the 12th Marines' pack howitzer battalions to the 22d Marines (reinforced). Brigadier General Lemuel Shepherd, fresh from New Britain, had the new brigade. The Commander Southern Troops and Landing Force was General Geiger, whose headquarters, redesignated III Amphibious Corps on 15 April, had been slated for the Kavieng assault until it was canceled. Geiger's naval opposite number was more than welcome to the Marines: he was none other than Admiral Conolly. Early in the planning, he looked General Geiger in the eye and said, "My aim is to get the troops ashore standing up. You tell me what you want done to accomplish this, and we'll do it."[92]

Fortunately for all concerned—except the embarked troops who were destined to sweat out seven weeks aboard ship between Guadalcanal, the mounting area, and Guam—the long delay between 18 June, the original date for Guam, and 21 July, the final one, gave Admiral Conolly all the time he needed. Shaken by the initial casualties on Saipan, Admirals Turner and Conolly and Generals Smith and Geiger determined that Guam would receive the most devastating preliminary bombardment in the history of the war. Conolly, skilled and versed in such work from his experience at Roi-Namur, immediately programmed a series of carrier strikes co-ordinated, from 8 July on, with daily bombardment by a division of heavy cruisers. Six days later, Conolly himself arrived aboard the command-ship *Appalachian,* whose crew he delighted by closing to 3,500 yards offshore and forthwith ordering them to join the bombardment with both of her 5-inch guns ("*Appalachian,* ably supported by other elements of the Fleet, this day bombarded Guam,"[93] he reported solemnly to Admiral Nimitz). In addition to the *Appalachian's* firepower, Conolly also brought that of the *Colorado,* whose deep-throated 16-inch guns were soon joined by those of still more battleships and cruisers. More important, however, with Conolly came Geiger, and, for the next week, the two commanders and their staffs teamed in a systematic effort to knock out every known enemy defense on Guam. A master target file was established; every day, as intelligence accumulated, new targets appeared. Every day's bombardment by air and naval gunfire crossed off others. Daily photo-reconnaissance flights verified results, as Marine naval gunfire officers, Navy gunnery officers, air staff officers, and corps artillery officers worked together to pick Guam clean. "On this island, no matter where one goes, the shells follow," bewailed a Japanese diarist.[94] Well he might: during the 13-day preliminary bombardment the Navy fired 6,258 of the 14- and 16-inch shells, 3,862 rounds of 8-inch, 2,430 of 6-inch, and 16,214 of 5-inch. Colonel Takeda, the senior surviving enemy officer on Guam, reported that by 21 July (W-day) all coast defense guns in the open, half of those in caves, and about half of all defensive installations inshore of the landing beaches had been destroyed. In addition, he noted, "there were scattered outbreaks of serious loss of spirit."[95]

Commencing 14 July, an underwater demolition team spent three nights reconnoitering both the Asan and Agat beaches. Then, with two more UDTs, a systematic program for destruction of beach obstacles began. By midnight of the last day before the landing, Navy swimmers had blown up 940 separate obstacles and garnished the 3d Division's beach with a large sign, "Welcome Marines."

GUAM LANDINGS

On the morning of 21 July the two landing groups formed offshore. While the amphibian tractors roared and churned and control vessels jockeyed forward to mark boat lanes and lines of departure, ships and aircraft stepped up their attacks to a final crescendo: W-day's plans for Guam called for 1,494 rounds of 14- and 16-inch, 1,332 of 8-inch, and 15,560 of 5- and 6-inch. After a hundred torpedo planes and fighters bombed and strafed, LCI-gunboats dumped 9,072 rockets onto the beaches, and then, as the naval gunfire rolled inexorably inland and to the flanks, the armored amphibians charged ashore firing.

The 3d Division landed between two "Devil's horns," Adelup and Asan Points. Inland from these the ground rose in a natural amphitheater, with steep bluffs (Chonito Cliff) frowning down on the 3d Marines (Colonel W. C. Hall) on the left, and even steeper ones directly ahead of Colonel A. H. ("Tex") Butler's 21st Marines. On the right, the 9th Regiment, under Colonel E. A. Craig, had more jungle but less climbing: their most important job was to push to the south toward General Shepherd's beachhead below Orote. The initial enemy reaction was light: sporadic mortar fire which, as the day went on, thickened into heavy shelling from behind the encircling ridges. But by noon one battery of the 12th Marines (Colonel John Bushrod

Wilson) was ashore and firing, and, within four hours, the entire regiment was in the fight. The 14th Defense Battalion (Lieutenant Colonel W. F. Parks) had also landed in part and, in the absence of enemy aircraft or warships, was firing general support missions for the division with its AA

Landings at Guam, Mariana Islands, 21 July 1944

457

weapons. That night General Turnage had his command post ashore, and his division had a precarious, because somewhat overextended, hold on a beachhead two miles across and a mile deep. The day's casualties totaled 697.

General Shepherd landed his brigade on the Agat beaches with the 22d Marines, under Colonel M. F. Schneider, on the left, and the 4th Marines (Shapley) on the right. As a reserve for the 1st Brigade, General Geiger had attached an Army regiment, the 305th Infantry from the 77th Infantry Division, in III Amphibious Corps reserve. Enemy resistance, primarily from two antiboat guns in an overlooked concrete blockhouse on Gaan Point, was vicious. Twenty-four LVTs were hit or blown up by mines, and both regiments encountered heavy machine gun and mortar fire at the beach. As the Marines pushed inland, however, they worked clear of the beaten zones, and, by nightfall, the 1st Brigade, at a cost of 350 casualties, held its objectives and was braced for an active night. Characteristically, General Shepherd, carrying his prized Haitian coco-macaque stick, had landed early and was established in a command post on Gaan Point.

The first serious counterattack came that night as expected. While smaller probes pushed at the 3d Division, the enemy's 38th Infantry launched three strong attacks against the brigade. Two of these (one including tanks) hit the 4th Marines; the third came in at Agat Village on the 22d Marines' left flank. All were repelled in a night of hard fighting, the net result of which was the end of the 38th Infantry.

THE CAPTURE OF OROTE PENINSULA

Until the two landings could link up, operations on Guam were perforce divided into two separate efforts—that of the 3d Division to break out of the Asan amphitheater, and the 1st Brigade's reduction of Orote Peninsula, which was the prerequisite to link-up.

The first step for the brigade was to get on top of Mount Alifan, which dominated the 4th Marines' zone and much of the brigade beachhead. While the 305th Infantry filled the center of the brigade's expanding front, the 4th Regiment attacked uphill through thick jungle that even the Japanese had not thought vulnerable to penetration. That afternoon, having dropped gas masks (the first throwaway in every landing), packs, and every ounce of extra gear, the 1st Battalion, 4th Marines, finally puffed to the top.

With Alifan secure, General Shepherd's next step was to land another regiment of the 77th Division which could take over the 4th Marines' lines so that the Marine regiments could swing left for the assault on Orote Peninsula. With two regiments ashore, the 77th Division then went into line on the Marine brigade's right, while the 9th Defense Battalion (Lieutenant Colonel A. E. O'Neil) took over the beach and AA defense of the southern perimeter. By nightfall on 24 July, the brigade, attacking through swamp, had gotten across the neck of the peninsula and bottled up more than 3,000 Japanese Naval Guard troops, the main enemy force left in the south.

Next night, after a fruitless attempt to evacuate the peninsula by landing barges, which were destroyed by artillery and naval gunfire, the Japanese nerved themselves on sake and synthetic Scotch for a banzai breakout. Through the splash of a rainstorm, the 4th and 22d Marines could hear the enemy preparations which, said one Marine, "sounded like New Year's Eve in the Zoo."[96] At about 2230, the inflamed Japanese streamed up from the swamp into the lines of the 22d Marines. Corps, brigade, and 77th Division artillery, plus every infantry weapon that could shoot, hammered the massed Japanese attack. After a hand-to-hand struggle by the 3d Battalion, 22d Marines, the onslaught ebbed, only to be followed, shortly before midnight, by another furious surge which again was stemmed by the weight of close-in firepower. Finally, at 0130, the enemy made a last try. Yet, when this was spent, as with every other banzai, the Marine lines were unbroken. Much credit for the repulses goes to the artillery, which fired some 26,000 rounds onto Orote Peninsula between midnight and 0300. General Shepherd later wrote:[97]

At daylight over 400 enemy dead lay in front of our lines. I personally counted them (as best I could) myself. Within the lines there were many instances when I observed Japanese and Marines lying side by side, which was mute evidence of the violence of the last assault.

For three days, after a prompt morning jump-off on 26 July, which the banzai failed to delay, the 1st Marine Brigade pushed ahead through thick minefields, mangrove swamp, and well-organized enemy defenses. On the afternoon of 27 July, the 22d Marines could look down on the ruins of Marine Barracks, Guam; next day they took it.

As the 22d worked along the north side of the peninsula, the 4th Marines, whose zone now included the lion's share, hammered at the final enemy defense line sited, appropriately enough, astride the old Marine Barracks rifle range. Here, many pillboxes and other emplacements had to be reduced before the attack could advance, and it was in the approaches to this line that the 4th Regiment lost its executive officer, Lieutenant Colonel Samuel D. Puller, shot by a sniper. By massing all the brigade tanks and borrowing some from General Bruce, the 77th Division commander, General Shepherd gave Colonel Shapley the means to breach the rifle-range line on the afternoon of 28 July. On the following morning the brigade swept up the length of Orote airfield against disorganized Japanese remnants, and, at four that afternoon, a 4th Marines patrol reached the end of the peninsula. Orote was now secure.

An important formality remained: at 1530, 29 July, two years and 230 days after the fall of Guam, while Generals Holland Smith, Geiger, and Shepherd, and Admiral Spruance, watched, an honor guard of the 22d Marines presented arms still warm from fighting and hoisted the Colors on the Marine Barracks flagpole.

That same afternoon, the first of MAG-21's people came ashore to establish the group, commanded by Colonel Peter P. Schrider, on the Orote field. On 4 August, for the first time since 1931 (when the Marine squadron on Guam was withdrawn), Marine aviation returned to the island, where the group stayed for the rest of the war as part of the Pacific Fleet's shore-based air garrisons in the forward area.[98]

GUAM SECURED

While the 1st Brigade and the 77th Division were taking southern Guam, the 3d Marine Division was fighting an equally important and far more frustrating battle in the Asan amphitheater, which Samuel Eliot Morison, who saw both, described as "a miniature Salerno."[99] Here, terrain was an even more intractable foe than the Japanese. Moreover, with all three regiments in line and the 9th Marines reaching wide to the right in their effort to link up with the brigade, General Turnage's 9,000-yard front was stretched thin and backed by only one battalion in division reserve.

The 100-foot cliffs confronting the 21st Marines ("that a trained cliff climber with line and spikes would have a hard time getting up,"[100] said Colonel Butler) had been scaled under fire on W-day by the 2d Battalion. Thereafter, the 21st clung to its precarious hold, against counterattack and infiltration by night, and mortar and artillery fire around the clock. Every 24 hours, 14,500 pounds of ammunition, water, and food had to be gotten up somehow, and the wounded had to be brought down. To solve this problem, the 19th Marines (the division engineers, under Lieutenant Colonel

R. E. Fojt) rigged a wire trolley from the fire-swept cliff edge to its base; in a Navy basket stretcher, supplies were hauled up, and casualties swayed back.

For the 3d Marines, the uphill fight over Chonito Cliffs, with the Fonte Plateau looming ahead, went slowly indeed. In fact, as postwar intelligence studies revealed, General Takashina was making his main defense in this area, and the 3d Regiment was up against a substantial part of the enemy 29th Division in the position defense of a natural fortress. After four days' tug-of-war on this line, Takashina decided that the only way to deal with the 3d Division was a massive counterattack. Unlike the spree on Orote, this was carefully planned as a co-ordinated night attack on a two-regiment front, supported by reserves concentrated from as far away as Tumon and Pago Bays (near Finegayan and Yona, respectively). Seven battalions, totaling at least 4,000 effectives, stealthily concentrated for an attempt to push the 3d Marine Division into the sea.

At 0400, 26 July, after hours of increasing enemy pressure in the form of local probes and heavy mortar and artillery concentrations, the storm broke. On the 21st Marines' cliff top, a Japanese battalion swarmed down, shouting, "Wake up and die, Marine!" (to which one rifleman shouted back, "Come on in, you bastards, and we'll see who dies!").[101] Another battalion smashed into a lightly held gap on the right boundary of the 21st Marines and headed for the division support areas and the beach. In the 3d Marines' zone the blow fell hardest on the 2d Battalion, 9th Marines, which had been attached to the 3d Regiment to replace its worn-out 1st Battalion. Here, on the slopes of Fonte Hill, with riflemen finally down to two clips per man and mortars down to six rounds per tube, the battalion fought a desperate battle. The tide of battle barely turned when a tank platoon arrived, laden with ammunition. A human factor in turning the tide was a burly company commander, Captain Louis H. Wilson, Jr., who, although wounded three times, fought his company all night against seven attacks, rescued a wounded Marine under Japanese fire, and never gave an inch—a feat which won him the Medal of Honor.

As other enemy units hit hard all along the 3d Division's front, the division support areas became a battlefield. Engineers, shore party, motor transport battalion, and hospital patients fit to grab a rifle, all formed secondary defense lines and mounted local counterattacks. The 12th Marines, notably the 2d Battalion (Lieutenant Colonel D. M. Weller), had to continue urgent fire missions with reduced gun-crews while other cannoneers repelled enemy suicide charges and showers of grenades. When a Japanese infantry battalion got in rear of the 3d Battalion, 21st Marines, the battalion CO, Lieutenant Colonel W. H. Duplantis, buried his cipher device and fought on.[102]

When day broke, it was apparent that the enemy attack, resolute and well planned as it was, had failed. The 3d Division Marines, who mopped up after the heaviest and best organized counterattack of the Pacific war, had no way of knowing that they had not only killed 3,500 Japanese, but, more important, had virtually destroyed General Takashina's capability for further organized defense of Guam.

Following the great night battle, the 3d Division was able to push forward to the force beachhead line, securing, at long last, Fonte Hill and Mount Chachao (adjoining Mount Alutom, also taken), and joining up with the 77th Division on Mount Tenjo. One casualty during these operations was the commanding officer, 2d Battalion, 3d Marines, Lieutenant Colonel Hector de Zayas, who was killed by an enemy rifleman on 26 July. On 28 July, while directing the retirement of his forces from the Fonte Plateau, General Takashina was killed. With III Amphibious Corps headquarters ashore and with his divisions linked up and moving, General Geiger could now conclude Guam as a corps battle.

Wheeling both the 3d and 77th Divisions for a push to the north, Geiger pressed the retreating enemy. As the Japanese tried to organize Mount Santa Rosa for a final defense, III Corps called for five days' intensive naval gunfire bombardment and air strikes against this position. After suffering heavy casualties, the Japanese were forced to abandon it without a fight before our troops even reached the position. Although there were several sharp local actions, like that of the 9th Marines at Finegayan, the northward advance assumed many characteristics of a race between the two divisions to see who would get to the end of Guam first. Toward the last, as the island broadened, General Geiger committed the 1st Brigade on the 3d Division's left, and the battle ended on 10 August, with the III Corps at Ritidian Point after the many remaining Japanese melted into caves and jungle from which they resisted sporadically until 10 December 1945, when the final clash took place (the last two Jap soldiers on Guam yielded in May 1960).

Landing force casualties for the Guam campaign were 1,350 killed and 6,450 wounded, or 7,800 in all, of whom 6,964 were Marines. When we consider that Guam and Saipan were of similar size and terrain, had similar defense systems, and that the combatant strength of Guam's garrison was close to that of Saipan, the contrast in American casualties—7,800 to 16,525 —is as striking as that between Roi-Namur and Tarawa. The relatively light casualties and rapid seizure of Guam must be attributed to the postponement of the original landings and the resultant unprecedented scope and effectiveness of the pre-W-day bombardment by Admiral Conolly. As General Geiger stated in his action report, "The success of this operation with comparatively few losses is largely attributable to this preparation."[103]

One other noteworthy aspect of the Guam operation was the high degree of inter-Service co-operation manifested by all participants. Not only did Admiral Conolly do a typically capable job of landing and supporting the landing force, but the close and effective relationship between the 77th Division (whose commander, Major General A. D. Bruce, USA, had served under Lejeune in France) and all Marine formations left nothing to be desired.

LESSONS OF THE MARIANAS

The conquest of the Marianas provided the first occasion on which a Marine headquarters exercised command above the level of corps. Holland Smith's Expeditionary Troops, composed of nearly six divisions, was in fact a field army and was the largest single command ever held by a Marine headquarters in the field, although General Geiger (but not his headquarters) later assumed command of the Tenth Army on Okinawa after the death of the Army commander. As we have seen, General Smith's exercise of this command was never accorded clear title by the Army, and an aftermath of the Marianas campaign, though never reduced to writing, was a tacit understanding at CinCPac and higher levels that Army divisions would not again be placed under Marine higher command, and that the ceiling of Marine tactical command in the field would be the corps. The decision, despite General Smith's vigorous contrary efforts, that the new FMFPac headquarters was to be purely administrative and never tactical, reflected this understanding, to which the Marine Corps naturally was not a party.[104]

Among the combat lessons which stood out was the importance of naval gunfire support, when properly delivered by trained ships and experienced gunnery staffs. "The might of naval bombardment was so terrific," wrote an enemy senior officer, "that Japanese officers and men lived in terror of it."[105] Close air support continued to be throttled by inadequate communications and by the absence of Marine aviators in the supporting Navy squadrons and controlling staffs. One bit of progress was registered, however; under the urging of General Geiger's air officer, the well-trained air liaison parties of the 3d Marine Division were allowed by the Navy to control—not merely advise and ask for—certain front line air strikes. Both Geiger and Holland Smith meanwhile reiterated previous recommendations that Marine aviation be allowed back into the close-support game. This time their pleas were heeded.

One tactical development of immense importance was the success in combat of a new organization for the Marine rifle squad, pioneered in the raider battalions and subsequently developed for official adoption by a Quantico board headed by Colonel S. B. Griffith. Throughout early 1944, this basic fighting element of the FMF was reorganized in all divisions so as to be subdivided into three "fire teams." Each of these four-man groups was built around a corporal team-leader and an automatic rifle. This reorganization not only trebled the automatic firepower of the squad, but strengthened and decentralized its tactical leadership. The result, first noted in reports on the Marianas, and uniformly in later battles, was a notable gain in the aggressiveness and hitting power of Marine infantry.[106]

OPERATION STALEMATE

In an arc that swings southwest from the Marianas to the southern Philippines, the Palau Islands lie about midway, some 500 miles east of Mindanao. Thus in 1944 they constituted an important and heavily defended position on Japan's inner defense line, as well as a flanking base from which MacArthur's northward thrust toward Leyte could be hit. In March 1944, Admiral Nimitz issued instructions for an operation against the Palaus to be executed in September. The code-name, oft praised in hindsight for its aptness, was "Stalemate."

The Stalemate planning was dogged from the outset by a series of changes in objectives, troops, and command organization. What emerged at the end was a two-division operation to be under General Geiger and III Amphibious Corps Headquarters. The 1st Marine Division, after an exhausting time of "rest and rehabilitation" in the Russell Islands, was to capture Peleliu, a main island in the southern Palaus, while the 81st Infantry Division would secure Angaur, south of Peleliu. Because III Amphibious Corps was highly occupied with the Guam campaign and because of more extensive operations which were canceled, much of the planning for the Palau assault was supervised by a provisional higher headquarters commanded by Major General Julian C. Smith, who had led the 2d Division at Tarawa.

The terrain of Peleliu, the Marines' objective, was an ominous mixture of Tarawa and Saipan. Its size (six miles by two) lay halfway between, while its low, flat southern half and beaches dense with obstacles and mines, enclosed a large, well-built air base. Rising abruptly behind the airfield and dominating all Peleliu was a long precipitous ridge, the Umurbrogol, honeycombed with coral-limestone caves and masked in jungle growth. A coral reef, sometimes backed with mangrove swamp, encircled the entire island. These naturally inhospitable features had been underscored in every possible way by Japanese energy and ingenuity, and, more particularly, by a naval construction unit, staffed by sappers and miners, whose specialty was caves and tunnels. After the battle, 500 such caves and tunnels remained sufficiently intact to be counted. Most were tiered with bays, laterals, and alternate entrances. Some were six stories deep, with exits and fire-ports on all levels. Entrances were traversed and steeply dipped to keep out blast, flame, and direct fire, while many gun-ports had sliding steel doors. Later, when battle was joined, the USS *Portland* fired five 8-inch salvos, without effect, at a gun so emplaced. "You can put all the steel in Pittsburgh onto that thing and not get it," was the gunnery officer's comment.[107]

Based on a trove of documents taken on Saipan, Marine planners knew that there were 10,700 Japanese on Peleliu, divided about evenly between Army and Navy. The backbone of the Army force (taken from the 14th Division, one of Japan's best and oldest) consisted of five infantry battalions with supporting artillery and tanks. The Navy component had the usual mixture of base and construction troops together with a tenacious, hard-fighting Naval Guard Force. The plan of Colonel Kunio Nakagawa, who, despite the presence of other senior officers, commanded the tactical defense of Peleliu, was based on a thoroughly realistic concept arrived at by Lieutenant General Inoue, over-all commander in the Palaus: dig deep, hold fire during preliminary operations, counterattack and infiltrate when advantageous (but no banzais), and hold the Umurbrogol to the last.

The scheme of maneuver selected by General Rupertus, who still had the 1st Marine Division, was to land all three of his infantry regiments abreast over five wide beaches on the southwest shore of Peleliu. The 5th Marines, under Colonel H. D. ("Bucky") Harris, were to go in the center and surge across the airfield. On the right, Colonel Hanneken's 7th Regiment (less one battalion held out as division reserve) was to nip off the island's southern tip. On the left, Colonel Puller, with the 1st Marines, drew the hardest job of all —wheel left and attack up the long axis of the menacing Umurbrogol. Both Generals Geiger and Julian Smith wanted to attach an Army regiment from the 81st Division as the 1st Division's reserve, but, for reasons which are still obscure, General Rupertus would have none of it.

Rupertus' naval counterpart was Rear Admiral George H. Fort. In the attack force were five old battleships, eight cruisers, and 14 destroyers. This imposing group suffered, however, from ammunition shortages (resulting from expenditures on Guam) and, most of all, from lack of an experienced shore bombardment gunnery staff. This naval deficiency was compounded by the fact that General Rupertus had no naval gunfire officer on his staff.[108]

The 1st Division was handicapped in other ways. Despite its peerless *esprit* and *expertise* in jungle warfare, the division was without experience in atoll or cave fighting, much of its equipment was worn or nonstandard (as a result of long isolation from the rest of the Marine Corps) and the Pavuvu area in the Russell Islands was totally unsuitable either for the rehabilitation or the extensive retraining which the situation demanded. As one 1st Division Marine grunted, "If they give us a battle star for Cape Gloucester, they ought to give us a couple for this dump."[109]

On 12 September, three days before the landing, the fire support ships and planes from four escort carriers began to bombard Peleliu. Because most of the important targets were deep underground or hidden by jungle, because of skimpy aerial photo coverage during planning, and because of lack of experienced supervision, this bombardment has been correctly described as "the least adequate for its purpose of any in the Pacific."[110] This inadequacy was, of course, not realized by the fire support group commander, who on D-minus one reported, with monumental optimism, that everything of importance had been destroyed, and that he had run out of targets. There were other optimists, however: at the critique following the final rehearsal, General Rupertus announced with characteristic self-assurance, "We're going to have some casualties, but let me assure you this is going to be a short one, a quickie. Rough but fast. We'll be through in three days. It might take only two."[111]

In the same mood, on D-day the captain of the transport carrying 1st

Regiment headquarters asked Colonel Puller as he started to debark, "Coming back for supper?"

"Why?" replied Puller.

"Everything's done over there. You'll walk in."

"If you think it's that easy," shot back Puller, "why don't you come on the beach at five o'clock, have supper with me, and pick up a few souvenirs?"[112]

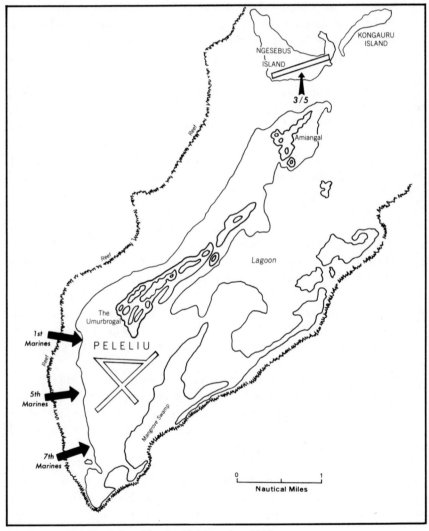

Landings at Peleliu, Palau Islands, 15 September 1944

PELELIU: INITIAL ASSAULT

Superficially speaking, the final preliminaries for the 1st Marine Division's assault on Colonel Nakagawa's beaches seemed to be exactly those which had preceded successful past landings against stiff resistance. Underwater demolition swimmers reported the reef clear. After daybreak on 15 September, naval gunfire, laced by air strikes, rose to crescendo. Rocket and mortar gunboats formed up to precede the armored amphibians and the amtracs. In the dead, humid air, a smoke screen lingered on the beaches and presumably masked any surviving defenses.

Yet when the amphibian tractors crossed the reef, almost as at Saipan, mortar and artillery fire began to crash down. Closer in, from each flank, antiboat guns picked off LVTs (26 in all), and machine gun bursts combed the wading riflemen.

In hindsight, we can see that, for all its sound and fury, the 1,406 tons of D-day bombardment accomplished little. Lack of effective direction and target intelligence squandered much of this fire amid sand and mangrove, while, amazingly, the deadly flanking terrain (such as the tiny unnamed island beside the 7th Marines' boat lanes) remained unneutralized. From here on it would be up to the riflemen.

On the right the 7th Marines walked into a hornets' nest of unscathed pillboxes, minefields, a blockhouse, and antiboat guns which enfiladed the beach. Amid the turmoil and debris of burning LVTs and DUKWs, the leading battalion commander, Major E. H. Hurst (who was fresh from indoctrinating Women Marines on a New England campus), kept his head, imperturbably reorganized his assault from the cover of an antitank ditch, and pushed forward.

In the center, where resistance was less heavy and the flanking fire diluted, the 5th Marines advanced across the southern part of the airfield in fine style. By nightfall, despite the loss of both the CO and executive officer of one assault battalion, the 5th had thrust across the entire island and established itself firmly for next day.

But the 1st Regiment, on the left, had the hardest going of all. A coral ridge, pierced by caves and studded with pillboxes, undetected in preassault air photos, lay square behind the regiment's beaches. On its left, a fortified bastion jutted out from the shore. In the words of Captain George

P. Hunt, whose Company K had the job of anchoring the regiment's (and thus the division's) left flank:[113]

The Point, rising 30 feet above the water's edge, was of solid, jagged coral, a rocky mass of sharp pinnacles, deep crevasses, tremendous boulders. Pillboxes, reinforced with steel and concrete, had been dug or blasted in the base of the perpendicular drop to the beach. Others, with coral and concrete piled six feet on top, were constructed above, and spider holes were blasted around them for protecting infantry. It surpassed by far anything we had conceived of when we studied the aerial photographs.

The reduction of this position cost Captain Hunt two-thirds of his company, and, once established with 30 survivors in the burned-out Japanese defenses, he was cut off by fierce counterattacks. At sometime during the succeeding 30-hour battle to hold the point, word reached Colonel Puller that Hunt had just beaten off another attack, was low on ammunition, and was down to 18 men. "That's fine," said Puller. "Tell him to keep pushing." Subsequently, as a tactics instructor at Quantico, with a well-earned Navy Cross, Captain Hunt produced a full-scale replica of the defenses of his point, which served for years afterward in the "Assault of a Fortified Position" demonstration familiar to every graduate of Marine Corps Schools.

During the afternoon, Colonel Nakagawa launched his first counterattack. This was no banzai charge. It was a co-ordinated tank-infantry thrust across the north leg of the airfield close to the boundary between the 1st and 5th Marines. The Japanese light tanks—really only tankettes—were met by a torrent of fire from everything that could shoot. Marine Shermans which could eat them alive, joined with bazookas, antitank guns, even pack howitzers and a passing Navy dive bomber. While the enemy tanks cruised (briefly) inside Marine lines, riflemen stood fast and went to work on the Japanese infantry. Almost as suddenly as it started, the attack was over. All but two of Nakagawa's tanks were crumpled and derelict; the infantry had withdrawn. Other lesser counterattacks followed; all were repelled.

As night fell, the 1st Division held (precariously) less than half of what General Rupertus had planned to take on D-day. Nevertheless, much of the artillery was ashore. Tanks had landed promptly. Brigadier General O. P. Smith, the assistant division commander, had landed an advance command post and had a firm grip on the battle. Although General Rupertus had hastily thrown in the division reconnaissance company to be frittered away as infantry replacements, he had been dissuaded from premature commitment of his one reserve battalion. The day's cost was 210 killed and 901 wounded. Almost half of these casualties had befallen the 1st Marines, but, in the best Puller tradition, the regimental commander reported that night, "Ready to resume the attack at 0800."[114]

The succeeding week will never be forgotten by any Marine who served on Peleliu. While the 7th Marines methodically reduced the teeming defenses on the south end of the island and the 5th Marines overran the airfield and all northeast Peleliu, the 1st Regiment, with one battalion from the 7th, battered head-on at the Umurbrogol hill mass. Here the problem of Peleliu—"a horrible place," said *Time* Magazine[115]—became clear; here such ominous cave-ridden terrain as the Horseshoe, Death Valley, the Five Sisters, the Five Brothers, and Walt Ridge became known and named.

The first attack on Walt Ridge on 19 September typified many others. Jumping off with 90 men, Captain Everett P. Pope led Company C, 1st Marines, across a fire-swept causeway through swamp, under intense fire from what later was called the Horseshoe. When his two tanks skidded into the muck he pushed on with a rush that got the company atop a bare hill to the front. But the hill wasn't a hill—it was a long ridge exposed to intense flanking fire from another ridge to the left and completely swept by axial fire from further ahead. In the coral, no man could dig in. As night fell, the company was down to its captain and 15 men. All night, against repeated Japanese surges and continual machine gun and mortar fire, the handful held. In the final enemy charge before dawn, when ammunition was gone, Captain Pope led his people in throwing chunks of coral at the attackers. Finally the remnant squad-size "company" was ordered down from the terrible ridge. Two weeks were to elapse before the Marines scaled and held it again. By his valor and intrepidity that night, Captain Pope won the Medal of Honor.

After a week of such fighting the 1st Marines were finished. With 1,749 killed and wounded (56 per cent is the statistic), the regiment was no longer an effective unit. It was relieved by the remaining two battalions of the 7th Regiment, who continued the deadly grind.

To General Geiger it was incomprehensible that General Rupertus should continue to fight such a battle without fresh troops and virtually no reserve. Even so—for the moment—he kept his own council. In the words of Geiger's operations officer:[116]

The Corps Commander [Geiger] was disinclined to impose any particular line of action on the Division Commander [Rupertus], although more than once he had felt the urge to do so.

Nonetheless, on 20 September General Geiger's patience wore thin. At the 1st Division command post he sat down with Rupertus.

During the course of the discussion General Geiger stated that he thought that the 1st Marines should be relieved and that he was considering moving an Army RCT over to replace them. At this, General Rupertus became greatly alarmed and requested that no such action be taken, stating that he was sure he could secure the island in another day or two [organized resistance actually ended 68 days later]. The upshot of it was that General Geiger directed the Division Commander to prepare plans for embarkation of the 1st Marines for evacuation and further stated that he would immediately take steps to attach an RCT of the 81st Division to the 1st Marine Division.[117]

Thus it came about that the 321st Infantry (which had just taken part in the three-day capture of Angaur) joined the 1st Marine Division, while the battered 1st Regiment limped aboard ship for Pavuvu. "We're not a regiment," the division's history quoted one Marine as he left Peleliu, "we're the *survivors* of a regiment."[118]

"THE MEN ARE VERY TIRED"

Ravines, which on the map and photographs appeared to be steep-sided, actually had sheer cliffs for sides, some of them 50 to 100 feet high. With nothing else on your mind but to cover the distance between two points, walking was difficult. . . . There were dozens of caves and pillboxes worked into the noses of the ridges and up the ravines. It was very difficult to find blind spots as the caves and pillboxes were mutually supporting.

So wrote General O. P. Smith, in his journal,[119] of the terrain which had to be taken before Peleliu could be considered secure. Looking at the still unconquered Umurbrogol after two weeks of fighting, a 7th Marines battalion commander simply said, "The men are very tired."[120]

With the fresh and capable 321st Infantry available, the situation began looking up. The soldiers' first job was to advance north up the west road, skirting the Umurbrogol mass, while a battalion of the 7th Marines covered their inboard flank. Once at the upper end of the terrible jumble, the 321st swung east, cross-island, while the 5th Marines, quickly reassembled on 25 September from the northeastern peninsulas, continued through to the northern extremity of Peleliu.

In the north the 5th Regiment fought a campaign of its own. A separate hill mass, Amiangal, only less formidable than the Umurbrogol because it was accessible and smaller, was riddled with masterpieces of the sapper's art. This massif had to be reduced. On 28 September, the 3d Battalion, 5th Marines (Major J. H. Gustafson), executed a miniature landing assault on

Ngesebus Island, which lies a half mile off Peleliu's north end. The Ngesebus attack was probably the most strongly supported small amphibious assault of the war; the battalion was supported by a battleship, a cruiser, two destroyers, the massed division and corps artillery, a company of armored amphibians, a tank company, and—best of all, thought many Marines—the Corsairs of VMF-114, which had touched down on Peleliu's battered field two days before. This was the first time since Bougainville that a Marine landing had received any, let alone 100 per cent, support from Marine aviation. The whole show came off beautifully. The 463 defenders were overwhelmed, and the 3d Battalion lost only 28 men. The most important result was that Japanese reinforcements could no longer work their way down from the northern Palaus onto Peleliu via Ngesebus.

The Japanese defenders were now wholly confined to the Umurbrogol pocket, which was surrounded by the 7th Marines and a provisional infantry battalion from the 11th Marines and the 1st Pioneer Battalion. In recognition that, for all original purposes of the operation, Peleliu was secure, Admiral Fort so declared on 30 September. Even so, eight weeks of hard fighting lay ahead.

As noted above, Marine aviation had taken over the Peleliu base, which on 12 October became a Marine island command like Guam and Tinian. Marine Air Group 11, under Colonel Caleb T. ("Zeke") Bailey, brought three fighting and one torpedo-bombing squadron up from the nether South Pacific. From then on, during the long siege of the Umurbrogol, the Peleliu Corsairs rendered daily close support to the 1st and 81st Divisions on napalm and bombing runs without even bothering to raise their landing gear. In addition, the transport planes of VMR-952 took over air logistics for the struggle. One notable airlift: 4,500 extra pounds of hydrogen to replenish the flame throwers of the 1st Marine Division which had been exhausted against Peleliu's unheard-of caves.

Shortly before aviation's arrival on Peleliu, MAG-45 (first under Colonel F. M. June, then under Colonel R. C. Mangrum) took over the air defense of the newly acquired fleet anchorage at Peleliu's neighboring atoll, Ulithi. Although Japanese air attacked only once (11 March 1945), the mission, that of defending a fleet advance base, was, however humdrum, highly appropriate for Marine aviation.

On 5 October the 5th Marines relieved the spent 7th Marines on the cordon around the Umurbrogol pocket. Despite three weeks' hard fighting, the 5th was still fit for 11 days more. Toward the end, one of the regiment's ablest battalion commanders paid tribute to his men: "Every Marine fighting in those hills is an expert. If he wasn't, he wouldn't be alive."[121] In a spontaneous gesture toward those experts, the ship's company of the USS *Mount McKinley* sent ashore every one of their 500-case allowance of recreation beer—an act of generosity not soon forgotten in a war where cans of beer were like golden ingots.

By mid-October the Umurbrogol pocket had been compressed by about one-third, and the 1st Marine Division was finished. General Geiger therefore arranged to have the 81st Division take over the wearying siege. On 16 October, a month after the initial landing, command of the Umurbrogol operation passed to the CO, 321st Infantry; four days later the 1st Marine Division was relieved. The last unit of the division in action against the Japanese was Major E. H. Hurst's 3d Battalion, 7th Marines. It was not until 25 November that the pocket was finally overrun by the 81st Division, and not until 1955 that the last Japanese came out of the caves and surrendered.

Marine casualties on Peleliu came to 1,252 killed and 6,526 wounded; for the Army, the score was 208 and 1,185, respectively. The grand total, 9,171, was almost as high in ratio of American casualties to enemy defenders as Iwo Jima's all-time 1.25-for-1 figure. The operation was a heart-breaker in every sense, the more so as many postwar students have joined Admiral Halsey (who attempted to have it called off beforehand) in his view that seizure of Peleliu was unnecessary for MacArthur's invasion of the Philippines. Another admiral who took part in the campaign, J. B. Oldendorf, later mused:[122]

If military leaders were gifted with the same accuracy of foresight that they are with hindsight, undoubtedly the assault and capture of the Palaus would never have been attempted.

MARINES IN THE PHILIPPINES

While the divisions and brigade which had conquered the Marianas and Peleliu took a breather in "rest" camps—2d and 3d Divisions mopping up Guam and Saipan; 4th Division really resting on Maui; 1st Division back at Pavuvu; 1st Brigade on Guadalcanal—a mixed assortment of ground and aviation units supported General MacArthur's long-heralded return to the Philippines.

In the Leyte landings during October 1944, the V Amphibious Corps

Artillery, under Brigadier General T. E. Bourke, "joined the Army" as artillery for XXIV Corps. This attachment was a swap for the XXIV Corps Artillery which had been lent to General Holland Smith for the Marianas. General Bourke's force (excluding attached Army units) consisted of a headquarters battery, a DUKW company, the 5th 155-mm. Howitzer Battalion, the 11th 155-mm. Gun Battalion, and the air liaison parties of the 2d and 3d Marine Divisions—the last in order to assist the Army in controlling naval air support. The entire aggregation totaled 1,528 Marines.

The first Marines to land on Leyte went in on 21 October 1944, just across the channel from Basey on Samar, where, on 24 October 1901, Waller had landed his two companies for the arduous campaign on Samar. From October until 11 December, the Marine artillerymen fought through the Leyte campaign, including support for the 7th Infantry Division's muddy battle for Ormoc. Just before the end of the campaign the Japanese parachuted an assault force at Buri airfield, inshore of Leyte Gulf. Among a motley of mechanics and AA gunners, the senior officer present was Captain E. S. Roane, Jr., commanding the V Corps Artillery air section, based at Buri. With the 30 Marines in his detachment, Captain Roane organized a spirited ground defense against almost 500 Japanese, and, as other troops fell back, some rallied on Roane's perimeter. With some 175 soldiers and a couple of rescued AA guns, Roane held his position for two days until an Army infantry battalion arrived and took over. Three days later (11 December) the campaign ended for V Corps Artillery.

For Marine aviation, the Philippines campaign began on 25 October 1944 at Tacloban airfield, where General Mitchell, commanding the 1st Marine Air Wing (AirNorSols), was up from the Solomons as an observer. During the Leyte Gulf battle many Navy planes from sunken or damaged carriers made for Tacloban, then only half complete. Realizing that they were heading for an unfinished section of strip, General Mitchell, a veteran carrier pilot, grabbed a pair of signal flags and took station as landing signal officer at the end of the field, safely guiding in 40 out of 67 emergency landings.

General Mitchell's presence in the Philippines was the result of Marine aviation's mid-war hunt for work. Under General Kenney and the Far East Air Force, most of the 1st Marine Air Wing was being kept behind in the Solomons in unemployment. As Admiral Halsey put it:[123]

. . . when Kenney was not keeping it [the 1st Marine Air Wing] idle, he was assigning it to missions far below its capacity.

Besides being a fine friend of the Marine Corps, Admiral Halsey was no man to see combat muscle wasting away. Shortly before General Mitchell had talked his way up to "observe" the initial Philippine operations, Admiral Halsey went directly to General MacArthur and "called these Marines to his attention."[124]

Within less than a month, one of Mitchell's fighter groups (MAG-12, Colonel William A. Willis), plus a much-needed night fighter squadron (VMF(N)-541), was under orders to be at Tacloban, the muddiest field on Leyte, on 3 December. Two days later the night fighters made their first kill: an Oscar fighter. MAG-12, meanwhile, went to work on enemy troop convoys, fighters, and protection for our own shipping. Except that they also had trains to shoot up, it was like Guadalcanal, but without Guadalcanal's urgency. As a side line, the Marine fighters took on support for the Army landings at Ormoc (7 December) and Mindoro, a week later. When the Leyte operation ended after Christmas 1944, the five Marine squadrons had destroyed 63 enemy aircraft, sunk 7 destroyers, 17 transports and cargo ships, and damaged at least 12 more. MAG-12 received an Army unit citation, and, in releasing the night fighters, commanded by Lieutenant Colonel P. D. Lambrecht, General MacArthur signaled: "Your night fighter squadron has performed magnificently repeat magnificently."[125]

While Marine fighters were enjoying themselves over Leyte and Samar, the 1st Wing's seven dive-bombing squadrons were preparing for support of the Army's forthcoming invasion of Luzon. Two groups of SBDs were to be sent forward, MAG-24 (Colonel Lyle H. Meyer) and MAG-32 (Colonel C. C. Jerome). By virtue of seniority (he was General Mitchell's chief of staff, too), "Jerry" Jerome assumed command of the force.

The first thing that was apparent was that neither the Army nor even the Navy yet had a close air-support doctrine really tailored to the needs of the front-line customer, although the Navy's was widely recognized (even by a few Army Air Force officers)[126] as better. The salient defect in both, it was clear to Marines, was jealous refusal to allow direct control of air strikes by the troops being supported. Such control had been fundamental in the 3d Marine Division's arrangements on Bougainville. Unfortunately, Marine aviation had been excluded from air support shortly afterward, and the Bougainville doctrine was not accepted by anyone else.

In preparation for Luzon, therefore, a MAG-24 officer, Lieutenant Colonel Keith B. McCutcheon (who had gone through Basic School as a student of "Chesty" Puller), was given the job of shaping and then teaching a proper

A 50-foot armored motor lighter emerging from water for land attack in Nicaragua, 1927.

Marines use motorcycles for transportation. From a series by Palmer, 1928.

An airplane in Nicaragua. From a series by Palmer, 1928.

"Howlin' Mad" views the wreckage—Marine Lieutenant General Holland M. Smith, commander of the expeditionary troops in the Iwo Jima operation, and his chief of staff, Colonel S. Brown, survey the bogged-down, surf-battered wreckage that marks the landings of the Leathernecks on the Japanese bastion. The soft volcanic sands of the beach stalled heavy equipment, making the vehicles vulnerable to enemy artillery and mortar fire.

A lone Marine covers the flank of the patrol. From this vantage point, the enemy had a clear view of the Marines landing on Iwo Jima.

Marine patrol with Japanese prisoner captured in Japanese hospital.

Marines crouch on the beach as Japanese land mines knock out a couple of their tanks. Moving Marines keep low, to duck sniper fire. One of the tanks burns in the background.

First flag on Guam on boat hook mast.

doctrine to be used in the forthcoming campaign. Because of wide divergency between Marine thoughts on the subject and the prevailing Army Air Force doctrine, it was recognized that Marine air liaison parties would have to work with the supported Army troops. Therefore the 1st Wing obtained six veteran air liaison officers from the 4th Division (one of whom, Captain F. R. B. ("Frisco") Godolphin, a classics professor by calling, was destined to be Dean of Princeton College within less than three years). Around these officers working at Torokina air base (Bougainville again) was organized a group of air liaison parties similar to those in the Marine divisions, but with a better doctrine to go on.

The point of departure of this doctrine might have been written by General Geiger himself:[127]

Close support aviation is only an additional weapon to be employed at the discretion of the ground commander. . . . Close support should be immediately available and should be carried out deliberately, accurately, and in coordination with the other assigned units.

The Sixth Army's landing at Lingayen Gulf, Luzon, took place on 9 January 1945. Exactly two weeks later, Colonel Jerome had a field carved out of dry rice paddies at Mangaldan, outside Dagupan, and the Marine air groups arrived. In accordance with Fifth Air Force orders, Colonel Jerome was designated Air Base Commander, Mangaldan, and Commander, Marine Air Groups, Dagupan—"MAGsDagupan," for all practical purposes, a dive-bomber wing. This meant, as Jerome later pointed out, that the job of running MAG-32 devolved on his second-in-command, Colonel J. L. Smith, Guadalcanal ace and Medal of Honor man, who had finally succeeded in breaking loose from stateside duty and was back at war. In aggregate, MAGsDagupan totaled 168 aging Douglas dive bombers, 472 officers, and 3,047 enlisted Marines.

The first important mission assigned to MAGsDagupan came on 31 January. The day before, General MacArthur had ordered the 1st Cavalry Division: "Go to Manila. Go around the Nips, bounce off the Nips, but go to Manila."[128] For the headlong thrust, the Marines were to maintain nine dive bombers on station over the cavalry column as it forged south along Luzon Highway 5. During the 66-hour dash that began on 1 February, Marine aviators covered the open left flank of the cavalry division, and slashed a path for its advance. Brigadier General William C. Chase, USA, whose 1st Brigade led the division, kept his Marine air liaison jeep beside him from beginning to end. As the yellow-legs entered Manila, General Chase said, "I have never seen such able, close, and accurate close support as the Marine flyers are giving us."[129] Major General Verne D. Mudge, USA, the division commander, enthused even more:[130]

> I can say without reservation that the Marine dive-bomber outfits are among the most flexible I have seen in this war. They will try anything, and from my experience with them I have found that anything they try usually pans out. The dive bombers of the 1st Marine Air Wing have kept the enemy on the run. They have kept him underground and enabled troops to move up with greater speed. I cannot say enough in praise of these dive bomber pilots and their gunners. . . .

Once the cavalrymen became engaged in the subsequent hard fighting to reduce central Manila, the Marine aviators jury-rigged a homemade airstrip on Quezon Boulevard and flew dive-bomber strikes from a city street.

In addition to their support for the cavalry, MAGsDagupan quickly won the confidence (over initial misgivings) of other Army divisions and were soon flying strikes all over central Luzon. One such, on 9 February 1945 by VMSB-341, worked over enemy-held Corregidor in partial repayment for the ordeal of the old 4th Marines. Before the end of the campaign, 1st Wing SBDs supported all ten Army divisions in Luzon, as well as the North Luzon guerrilla force headed by hold-out U. S. Army officers who had escaped from Bataan. To work with the latter, a Marine air liaison party was landed inside guerrilla lines by LCT and controlled 186 strikes under jungle conditions harking back to Nicaragua.

On 14 April 1945, MAG-24 SBDs flew the last Marine mission on Luzon, in support of the 37th Infantry Division, originally based on Bougainville and once (1943) part of IMAC under General Geiger. During 11 weeks in the campaign, MAGsDagupan flew 8,842 sorties, fired a million and a half bullets, and dropped 19,167 bombs. While they constituted only 13 per cent of all Luzon-based aircraft during this period, they flew 49.7 per cent of all sorties.

During the Luzon campaign, plans were afoot for reconquest of the southern Philippines—Cebu, Panay, Mindanao, and Palawan—by the Eighth Army. After their virtuoso showing, both the Leyte and Samar fighter groups (MAGs 12 and 14) and the Luzon dive-bomber groups were assigned to this operation, which began on 8 March 1945. All groups except MAG-14 (Colonel Zebulon C. Hopkins) were to be under Colonel Jerome as Marine Air Groups, Zamboanga—"MAGsZam." MAG-14, being based at Guiuan on southern Samar, could support operations on Cebu and Panay without moving.

To support the Eighth Army's mostly unopposed 52 landings in this campaign, Marine flyers operated from three fields on Mindanao: Dipolog, a guerrilla-held grass strip on the north coast; San Roque field at Zamboanga, renamed Moret Field for Lieutenant Colonel Paul Moret, killed in 1943; and Titcomb Field at Malabang (named for Captain John A. Titcomb, a valiant air liaison officer killed in action on North Luzon). In front of the operations shack at Moret Field, the well-shot-up tail of a Zero fighter proclaimed the truth of an adjacent sign: "They Have No Tails in Zamboanga."

The most active Marine support in the southern Philippines was at Cebu, all over Mindanao, and on Jolo. At the last named, MAG-32's five-day bombardment of Mount Daho, an ancient Moro stronghold in the hands of a Japanese battalion, enabled the 41st Infantry Division to take the place without a casualty. In the Zamboanga landing and campaign (March 1945), all air operations were commanded by Colonel Jerome and executed by MAGsZam, now comprising almost 300 aircraft (all Marine except for an Army P-61 night-fighter detachment and some Navy search and rescue PBYs). This was the only campaign in World War II in which all air operations came under Marine command.

But there was one casualty of the Philippines campaign: the SBD itself. This truly dauntless little dive bomber, which Marine aviators had been flying since 1940, was at last declared outmoded. In July 1945, as the Philippines campaign neared its end, the last two SBD squadrons in the Marine Corps (MAG-24's VMSB-133 and 241) were decommissioned.

When the war ended, MAGsZam were helping the Army to mop-up and were getting ready for the invasion of Japan. Lieutenant General R. L. Eichelberger, USA, who commanded the Eighth Army, gave the Marine aviators a handsome send-off:[131]

> The value of close support for ground troops as provided by these Marine fliers cannot be measured in words, and there is not enough that can be said for their aerial barrages. . . .

IWO JIMA

After the capture of bases in the Marianas, the first order of business was to prepare for the long-heralded air offensive against the Empire by Army Air Force "Superfortresses." The first raid on Tokyo from Saipan (by XXI Bomber Command) was staged on 24 November, four and a half months after the island had been secured. Before long it became apparent to anyone who talked to the B-29 crews that Japanese fighters and flak were chew-

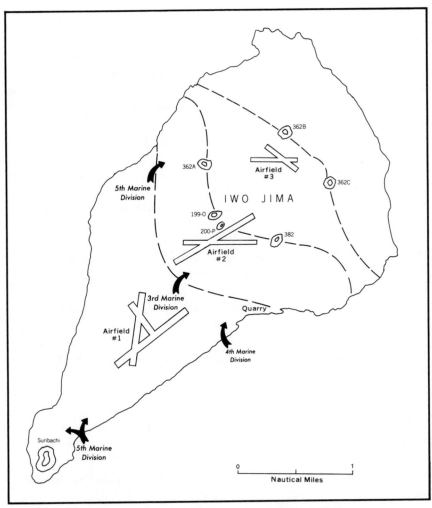

Battle for Iwo Jima, Volcano Islands, 19 February to 15 March 1945

ing the big bombers to pieces, that casualties were high, that morale was poor, and that the long-range attacks by high·level bombers without fighter escorts were, despite the dogmas of Mitchell and Douhet, not doing very well. In the words of Army Air Force Major General Curtis LeMay, "This outfit [the B-29s in the Marianas] had been getting a lot of publicity without having accomplished a hell of a lot in bombing results."[132]

One reason for this state of affairs was enemy occupancy of Iwo Jima, a small island midway between the Marianas and Japan, about 650 miles south of Tokyo. Radars on Iwo gave metropolitan Japan two clear hours' warning on every B-29 raid. Iwo's fighters (the island had two large air-fields and a third one building) harried the incoming bombers and slashed at the homeward-bound cripples. Moreover, Iwo served as a staging base for Japanese raids on the Marianas. In American hands the situation would be reversed: Iwo-based fighters could protect the bombers; Iwo would be a haven for the cripples; by refueling at Iwo, each B-29 could carry more bombs.

As early as July 1944, General Arnold, Chief of the AAF, had recognized the importance of Iwo Jima and had urged its seizure to the Joint Planners in Washington. Soon after, Lieutenant General Harmon, commanding Army Air Forces in the Pacific, similarly pressed Admiral Nimitz. The admiral acceded and so recommended to Admiral King and the JCS. The decision was arrived at in October: the Navy and the Marines would capture Iwo Jima to support the Air Force. D-day was to be 19 February 1945. "Detachment" was the code-name of the operation.

Iwo Jima is a barren, volcanic island about eight square miles in area. At one end rises an extinct volcanic crater, Suribachi Yama, 556 feet high, joined to the island by a narrow strip of ridge so that from the air one gets the impression of the head and slender neck of a venomous snake. From the base of Suribachi the island widens and rises to a jumbled northern plateau ringed with cliffs. Except for two stretches of beach, on each side of the widening neck, no feasible landing areas exist. Coarse, black volcanic sand covers much of the island; under that and on the plateau lies rock through whose fissures rise steam and sulphurous fumes from still warm volcanic entrails. In the phrase of a Marine who fought there,[133] "Not worth fifty cents at a sheriff's sale." One of the few surviving Japanese defenders added:[134]

It had been written on the geographical book as only an island of sulphur, no water, no sparrow, and no swallow.

The defenses of Iwo Jima were in all probability the most elaborate in construction, the most numerous in density, and the best integrated of any in the Pacific, if not in all World War II. Altogether, there were more than 730 major defense installations, including 120 guns larger than 75-mm., 130 howitzers, 90 large mortars and rocket launchers (including a dozen 320-mm. mortars and numerous launchers for 550-pound rockets), 69 antitank guns, more than two hundred 20-mm. or 25-mm. machine guns, and 24 tanks. The eastern beach defenses alone included 201 major installations, among which were 21 massive blockhouses with five-foot concrete walls, 91 pillboxes, and 32 covered artillery emplacements. Coast defense emplacements, mainly for 6-inch and 4.7-inch guns, blockhouses, and covered artillery emplacements were built with reinforced concrete walls and overheads ranging from three to five feet thick; some had 50 feet of earthen cover. Like Peleliu, the island was honeycombed with many-storied, concrete-lined caves interconnected by at least 13,000 yards of tunnels. This tiny island, all fortress, was defended by more than 21,000 veteran troops under Lieutenant General Tadamichi Kuribayashi, onetime commander of the Imperial Guard in Tokyo, "whose partly protruding belly," reported Radio Tokyo, "is packed full of strong fighting spirit." Holland Smith's opinion of the man was short but conclusive: "Of all our adversaries in the Pacific, Kuribayashi was the most redoubtable."[135] After the battle, another Marine officer said, "Let's hope the Japs don't have any more like him."[136]

The two Harrys of Tinian, General Schmidt and Admiral Hill, were to assault Iwo Jima. Superimposed over the landing force and attack force headquarters of Schmidt and Hill were those of the two past grand masters, Holland Smith and Kelly Turner, who would exercise over-all command of the operation from afloat.[137]

The scheme of maneuver adopted by the V Amphibious Corps was rigidly dictated by the terrain. Of the possible beaches, those on the east shore, though flanked by Suribachi on the left and by 100-foot cliffs and a yawning quarry on the right, were better than anything else to be had. Schmidt's plan was to land with two divisions abreast, the 4th Division under Major General Clifton B. Cates on the right, and the 5th Marine Division (a newcomer, commissioned on Armistice Day 1943) under Major General Keller E. Rockey on the left. Backing up the assault, in reserve this time, would be the 3d Division, now in the hands of Holland Smith's former chief of staff, General Erskine, known to his people as "The Big 'E' " or, sometimes, "The Flame Thrower."

BEFORE D-DAY

It was immediately clear to Generals Smith and Schmidt and their planners that Iwo Jima was the roughest proposition which had confronted any Marine landing force in World War II. This being so, after a careful study

of the island and its defenses (". . . much the best such analysis ever submitted to this command," remarked Admiral Turner[138]) the two Marine generals asked for ten days' heavy and searching bombardment, Guam style.
They got three; anything longer was not considered strategically compatible
with the carrier strike on Tokyo which was to coincide with the Iwo landings. As a sop, arrangements were made for Air Force B-24s and B-29s to
bomb Iwo Jima every day during the six weeks preceding commencement
of the naval bombardment. This high-level bombing through clouds, it was
optimistically predicted by Admiral Spruance, would equal the results of
an extra day or more of intensive naval bombardment. Neither General
Smith nor General Schmidt was in the least satisfied. That the Tokyo carrier
strikes, which were supposed to support the Iwo operation but in the event
had few if any military results, should have deprived the assault forces of a
fourth day of preliminary bombardment was a costly irony and an example
of a subsidiary operation overriding the primary mission. "We may expect
casualties far beyond any heretofore suffered in the Central Pacific," predicted Holland Smith.[139]

While the Air Force bombed, the Japanese built. At the beginning of the
72-day succession of daily air raids, the aerial photographs showed 450
major defenses; six weeks later, on D-minus 3-day, the known total had
grown to 730, including an ominous 131 per cent increase in the number of
coast defense and dual-purpose AA guns.

The three-day preliminary bombardment of Iwo Jima was to be executed
by six battleships and five cruisers firing 14,000 14-inch and 8-inch shells
to an accompaniment of precision carrier air strikes. Taking advantage of
the costly lessons learned at Peleliu, this bombardment and all preliminary
operations before the landing were to be directed by a separate amphibious
staff under Rear Admiral W. H. P. Blandy, one of the ablest gunnery officers
in the Navy. An advance group of Marine officers headed by Lieutenant
Colonel Donald Weller, foremost authority in the Corps on naval gunfire
support, was attached to Blandy's staff to make certain that the bombardment, limited though it was, would be most effective.

On 16 February 1945, D-minus 3, Admiral Blandy's advance force arrived off Iwo Jima. Blandy's primary mission on that day was destruction of
coast defense and AA guns which could keep the ships and aircraft of the
joint expeditionary force at arm's length. Dank mist and rain rendered visibility very poor, and the firing (". . . a slow, careful probing for almost in-
visible targets,"[140] wrote a correspondent) was repeatedly interrupted be-

cause neither ships' spotters nor air spotters could find their targets. But even when visibility permitted, storms of flak kept the spotting planes so high that target identification was well-nigh impossible. John P. Marquand, who was aboard one of the battleships, related:

> Our task force was like a group of big-game hunters surrounding a slightly wounded but dangerous animal. They were approaching him slowly and respectfully, endeavoring to gauge his strength and at the same time trying to tempt him into action.

As might have been expected, the results of the day's firing were extremely disappointing. Foul weather and enemy antiaircraft had, in effect, canceled one of the three precious days of preliminary bombardment over which the planners had debated so hotly.[141] Only 17 targets were destroyed. This left more than 700 to go.

The bombardment on D-minus 2 was mainly shaped to support the beach reconnaissance by Navy and Marine frogmen. Visibility had now turned excellent, and ship and air spotters could see what they were shooting at. So could the Japanese. At 0935 the heavy cruiser *Pensacola*, on bombardment station, took six 6-inch hits from a cliffside battery on the northwest shore, which hulled and set her afire, killing or wounding 115 men. After an otherwise uneventful morning (during which 61 targets were destroyed or badly damaged), a dramatic turn of events took place off the eastern beaches.

Apparently under the impression that the landing had begun, Japanese gunners opened intense well-aimed rapid fire, from hitherto completely undisclosed flanking batteries, on the landing craft and on the LCI-gunboats supporting the underwater swimmers. Within a matter of minutes all 12 LCIs had taken hits, mainly from 6-inch batteries at the base of Suribachi and imbedded deep in the face of the quarry on the right flank. Nine LCIs were soon out of action; of 720 officers and men aboard the 12 little ships, 170 were killed or wounded during 45 minutes' hot action that would have done honor to John Paul Jones.

Only one more day remained before the landing.

Because of the hidden firepower that the Japanese had revealed, Colonel Weller urged Admiral Blandy to scrap previous bombardment schedules for D-minus 1 and devote all remaining heavy ammunition and firepower to the single urgent task of destroying the fearsome defenses that commanded the beaches. Blandy acceded and massed four battleships offshore, within rifle-shot of the enemy batteries, for a day of pounding seldom equaled in the annals of amphibious warfare.

By nightfall the situation was considerably more encouraging. Out of the

201 important targets in the main landing area, 115 were destroyed or seriously hurt. Eleven coast defense guns, 22 of the 33 5-inch dual-purpose guns that could bear on the landing, 16 out of 20 big blockhouses, and 48 out of 93 pillboxes were destroyed or heavily damaged. As a result of this necessary concentration on the beach defenses, the rest of the island had been only lightly covered, and untouched artillery, rocket, and mortar positions still existed in great numbers throughout the remainder of Iwo Jima. Another day of preliminary bombardment, using the additional ammunition and firepower of the two new battleships which Admiral Spruance had diverted from the Iwo bombardment group at the last minute (see footnote 141), would at least have permitted full expenditure of ammunition allowed (the three days' bombardment having proven insufficient to do so) and would certainly have taken out many enemy defenses clear of the beaches, the assaulting of which claimed many Marine lives. Nevertheless, as General Schmidt later wrote, ". . . it was the destruction of those masked batteries by ships' gunfire which enabled our D-day landing to succeed."[142]

The large number of defenses on Iwo Jima could not conceivably have been destroyed within the allotment of time, ships, and ammunition. The bombardment by thoroughly trained ships and carrier aircraft under expert supervision was, in itself, highly effective. It illustrated the high point which precision naval bombardment had attained since the groping days of Tarawa. Undoubtedly, however, longer bombardment before D-day would have materially shortened the battle and saved many lives.

While Blandy was working over Iwo, the joint expeditionary force, 800 ships in all, was en route to the objective. Aboard the USS *Eldorado*, Admiral Turner's flagship, along with General Holland Smith, was James Forrestal, Secretary of the Navy. At the final conference, he spoke a few words:[143]

This next target, Iwo Jima, like Tarawa, leaves very little choice except to take it by force of arms, by character, and courage. . . . My hat is off to the Marines. I think my feeling about them is best expressed by Major General Julian Smith in a letter written to his wife after Tarawa: "I can never again see a United States Marine without experiencing a feeling of reverence."

When Holland Smith's turn came, after predicting 15,000 casualties, he closed on a note of determination:[144]

We have taken such losses before, and if we have to we can do it again. The Navy brought us here, and we have never yet had to swim ashore. The Navy has never let us suffer from lack of food, water, or ammunition. Sometimes it has been close. . . . In Admiral Turner we have full confidence—we would rather go to sea with him in command than any other admiral under whom we have served. We have never failed, and I don't believe we shall fail here. It's a tough proposition. That's the reason we're here.

"EIGHT SQUARE MILES OF HELL"

Anyone who has been there can shut his eyes and see the place again. It never looked more aesthetically ugly than on D-day morning, or more completely Japanese. Its silhouette was like a sea monster, with the little dead volcano for the head, and the beach area for the neck, and all the rest of it, with its scrubby brown cliffs for the body. It had the minute, fussy compactness of those miniature Japanese gardens. Its stones and rocks were like those contorted, wind-scoured, water-worn boulders which the Japanese love to collect as landscape decorations.[145]

Final preparations for the landing on Iwo Jima incorporated all the lessons learned throughout our march across the Pacific. Seven battleships, eight cruisers, and nine destroyers, together with 40 gunboats and rocket craft, took station at daybreak, 19 February, and commenced the heaviest prelanding bombardment in the history of war: more than 5,000 tons of everything from 16-inch shells to 5-inch rockets were to be hurled onto Iwo Jima before noon on D-day. In the air, 48 carrier planes, led by Lieutenant Colonel William F. Millington, and VMF-124 flying from the USS *Essex*, raked the beaches with napalm, rockets, and machine guns; aboard the *Eldorado*, Landing Force Air Support Control Unit One, commanded by Colonel V. E. Megee, co-ordinated the strikes. At long last Marine planes were supporting Marines again and were flying off carriers.[146]

While Iwo Jima shuddered under a pall of smoke and debris, twenty thousand 5-inch rockets hissed toward the island from the rocket-ships, and the amtracs churned resolutely toward the terraced black beaches. The assault regiments, from left to right, were: 28th Marines (Colonel H. B. Liversedge); 27th Marines (Colonel T. A. Wornham); 23d Marines (Colonel W. W. Wensinger); and 25th Marines (Colonel J. R. Lanigan). In reserve, from the 4th and 5th Divisions, were the 24th Marines (Colonel W. I. Jordan) and 26th Marines (Colonel C. B. Graham), while the 21st Marines, up from Guam, commanded by Colonel H. J. Withers, was the forward element of the 3d Division. In contemplating his division's line-up for the assault, General Cates reflected on the grueling fight ahead of the 25th Marines and mused, "If I knew the name of the man on the extreme right of the right-hand squad of the right-hand company of the 25th Marines, I'd recommend him for a medal."[147]

As the first waves touched down—on time to the minute—it was apparent that, whatever lay ahead, the beach neutralization had done its work. Except on the extreme right where the 3d Battalion, 25th Marines, immediately encountered trouble, resistance during the first hour was moderate. Later in the day, after the naval gunfire lifted, mortar and artillery fire began to hit the beaches with an intensity that boded ill.

The 5th Division's immediate job was to knife its way across the narrow neck of Iwo, face south, and capture Mount Suribachi from whose top enemy observation posts called down fire on the eastern beaches. An hour and a half after landing, men of Company B, 28th Marines, aided by tanks landed early and expertly, had fought through a half mile of battered defenses and were on the west shore. Other battalions of the 28th were facing south for the climb up the fire-swept mountain, while the USS *Santa Fe* steadily pounded 6-inch shells into the base of the volcano, only 200 yards clear of the Marines' left flank. To the right of the 28th Marines, the 27th pushed across the lower end of Airfield No. 1 and covered the rear of the attack on Suribachi.

The 4th Division's fight was uphill in every sense, both by terrain and opposition. Intense fire from everything in the book, but mortars especially, poured down from the right flank and ahead. The 15-foot sand terraces stopped tanks and armored amphibians, while riflemen floundered in the coarse black sand (". . . like trying to fight in a bin of loose wheat,"[148] said the division's history). As the day wore on, shelling of the beaches intensified, and landing craft and shore parties took heavy casualties. Heavy surf broached boats and swamped vehicles. Of the rapidly mounting casualties, Robert Sherrod, on the beach with the assault waves as usual, reported:[149]

Whether the dead were Japs or Americans, they had one thing in common; they had died with the greatest possible violence. Nowhere in the Pacific war had I seen such badly mangled bodies. Many were cut squarely in half. Legs and arms lay 50 feet away from any body. In one spot on the sand, far from the nearest cluster of dead, I saw a string of guts 15 feet long. Only legs were easy to identify; they were Jap if wrapped in khaki puttees, American if covered by canvas leggings. The smell of burning flesh was heavy in some areas.

Among the dead was Gunnery Sergeant "Manila John" Basilone, who had won the Medal of Honor at Guadalcanal. A fighter to the last, he had just cleaned out a blockhouse when a mortar burst cut him down.

There was no counterattack the first night. The six regiments ashore, with two tank battalions and gunners of the 13th and 14th Marines, had a well tied-in line and expected the worst. But Kuribayashi was too disorganized after the day's pounding to mount a push. Moreover, during the night, Navy mortar-boats (specially rigged LCIs) dumped more than 10,000 rounds of 4.2-inch high-explosive into the Japanese rear areas, mostly in the 4th Division's zone. So once again, in spite of the enemy's worst, a Marine landing force was ashore to stay, at a cost of 566 killed and 1,755 wounded during the first day's fight.

The first things to be done were three in number: capture Suribachi; pivot the rest of the corps to the right for the main attack up the backbone of Iwo; and then get hold of the high ground between the two airfields, which was alive with minefields and mutually supporting pillboxes.

On 23 February, after a vertical assault (upward, not downward), the 2d Battalion, 28th Marines, gained the peak of Suribachi and broke out a small set of Colors; soon afterward an unknown Marine scrounged a larger flag from the USS LST-779, and an Associated Press photographer, Joe Rosenthal, snapped a picture which would take its place in the pictorial annals of our country beside "The Spirit of '76" and "Washington Crossing the Delaware." As Secretary Forrestal looked up from the beach and saw the brave scrap of color, he said to General Smith, "The raising of that flag on Suribachi means a Marine Corps for the next 500 years."[150]

While the 28th Regiment fought its separate war in the south and the 25th Marines held the pivot, Colonel Wornham swung the 27th wide up the west beaches for long gains that brought the corps front into line as planned. In the center, however, Colonel Wensinger's 23d Marines were nearly spent in their fight to get over the top of Airfield No. 1 and onto the abrupt, well-fortified terrace that separated it from Airfield No. 2. It was high time for fresh troops, and, on 21 February the 21st Marines were ordered in. For the moment the regiment was attached to the 4th Division; its job was to pass through the 23d and break through to the second airfield. Three days later and less than a thousand yards ahead, Company K, 21st Marines, won its way across the naked, fire-swept junction of the runways on Airfield No. 2 and clung to a toehold on the opposite side, while the 24th Marines on their right assaulted "The Amphitheater," a forbidding bowl ringed with caves and pillboxes.

On 24 February, the 3d Marine Division entered the battle as an entity in its own right. General Erskine landed his command post; he was given back the 21st Marines; and, with only the 3d Regiment missing (held afloat as expeditionary troops reserve), he assumed the corps main effort, driving up the center through General Kuribayashi's iron belt of cross-island defenses. On the same day, General Schmidt landed, and the deployment of the V Amphibious Corps was complete. Eighty-two thousand United States Marines were ashore on Iwo Jima.

"IT TAKES COURAGE . . ."

At Tarawa, Saipan, and Tinian, I saw Marines killed and wounded in a shocking manner, but I saw nothing like the ghastliness that hung over the Iwo beachhead. Nothing any of us had ever known could compare with the utter anguish, frustration, and constant inner battle to maintain some semblance of sanity. . . .[151]

So wrote a wounded lieutenant in the 4th Division. A major in the 3d Division recalled later that the place looked like Doré's illustrations for the *Inferno*. A sergeant said, "Here, everything is beach, and you just can't get off it."[152]

The seemingly endless battle for Iwo Jima assumed an almost stylized pattern—attack up the center to take the high ground and break through the successive cross-island lines, combined with bitter fighting along the bare coastal flanks. In this scheme of things the 3d Division spearheaded the corps advance, while the 4th and 5th Divisions ground their way savagely along, always receiving fire from uphill and always under enemy observation.

After the 21st Marines crossed Airfield No. 2 on 24 February, the object of the next three days' fighting (by the 9th Marines) was capture of two hills, 199-O and 200-P, tiered and tunneled inside, with 25-mm. AA machine guns nested outside to sweep the airfield and its approaches. These were manned by some of the best troops Kuribayashi had: the Special Naval Landing Force with the anchor and chrysanthemum on their helmets. On 27 February, the capture of 199-"Oboe" by Lieutenant Colonel Robert E. Cushman's 2d Battalion, 9th Marines (the veterans of Fonte Hill), together with a good advance by the 1st Battalion, finally cracked the main defense line and put the corps in position for an important advance. While General Erskine smashed at the center, Generals Cates and Rockey were up against heartbreaking obstacles. Hill 382, a precipitous rockpile crowned by the wreckage of a radar and studded with antitank guns, was the scene of attack after attack by the 4th Division; finally, on 28 February, Colonel Wensinger, deep voiced, eagle eyed, and tenacious, worked the 23d Marines completely around the malevolent hill, and that was that. General Rockey's problem was an even worse protuberance—Hill 362-A, a menacing butte which jutted out from the northwest shoulder of Iwo and commanded the entire west shore and therefore the 5th Division's entire zone. This was tunneled like Amiangal on Peleliu; when high-explosive shells were fired into cave-mouths on 362-A, smoke emerged from other caves many yards away. But on 2 March, after the 27th Marines had done their best, the 28th finished the job, and Hill 362-A was secure.

Meanwhile, the 3d Division had broken loose. On 1 March, thrusting the 21st Marines forward with the aid of a thunderous preparation by corps artillery, a battleship, and a heavy cruiser, the "Big 'E'" scored an 800-yard advance to Motoyama Village and into the desolate valley which had served as Kuribayashi's support area. To reinforce this breakthrough, General Schmidt ordered General Rockey to make his main effort on the right along the 3d Division boundary. By 3 March, the 3d Division was separated from the sea, 1200 yards ahead, by only one final ridge-line, and a week more of hard fighting.

During the first week in March, the Iwo Jima battle seemed truly without end. The experienced units which had landed and fought their way over two-thirds of the hateful island had suffered terrible casualties. Replacements diluted the drive and skill which had brought the V Amphibious Corps so near, yet seemingly so far, from the end. In the words of Major I. R. Kriendler, the 3d Division's G-1, "They get killed the day they go into battle."[153] While this tragedy was going on, General Schmidt repeatedly asked that the 3d Marines, still held afloat in reserve, be landed. One fresh regiment of experienced Marines, he was convinced (along with everyone else ashore) would, at this stage, shorten the battle by a week or more. But General Smith and Admiral Turner refused to see it his way. And on 5 March, while green replacements were dying as they entered the lines, the veteran 3d Regiment was returned to Guam.

That same day, General Schmidt ordered a day's breather. The attack halted, while bone-weary rifle units pulled themselves together for the final effort, and artillery and naval gunfire pounded away at Kuribayashi's last defense line.

Among the weariest of all on Iwo were the 4th Division. From the outset the 4th had faced the slowest going and the most consistently miserable terrain. South of Hill 382 and the Amphitheater, there was another intractable eminence, crowned by a blockhouse, Turkey Knob. Beyond all these lay a blasted wilderness of crags, caves, buttes, and canyons. The 4th Division's ordeal was well described by one of its officers, quoted in the division history:[154]

It takes courage to stay at the front on Iwo Jima. It takes something which we can't tag or classify to push out ahead of those lines, against an unseen enemy who has survived two months of shell and shock, who lives beneath the rocks of the island, an enemy capable of suddenly appearing on your flanks or even at your rear, and of disappearing back into his hole. It takes courage for officers to send their men ahead, when many they've known since the Division came into existence have already gone. It takes courage to crawl ahead, 100 yards a day, and get up the next morning, count losses, and do it again. But that's the only way it can be done.

On 6 March, despite an artillery preparation of 22,500 rounds from the 12th, 13th, and 14th Marines, and from the corps artillery, progress was scarcely better than before. Only the tank-dozers and fire-breathing armored flame throwers seemed able to bite into Iwo's caves and crags.

This exhausting stalemate, with only one more ridge-line to go, spurred General Erskine to a stratagem he had long cherished—a night attack to overrun the third of Iwo Jima's stubborn Hills 362 (362-C), now the toughest remaining obstacle between the 3d Division and the sea. At 0500, 7 March, amid mist and rain squalls, the 3d Battalion, 9th Marines, under Lieutenant Colonel H. C. Boehm, attacked in complete silence on compass bearing, with no artillery preparation and no naval star shells. Bayonets and flame throwers were the only weapons used until daylight. Before the sleeping Japanese came to, Boehm's men had crossed more than 250 yards thick with caves and pillboxes and captured a key supporting position, Hill 331. After daybreak, as the groggy Japanese awoke and began to fight, Boehm pressed ahead against fierce opposition which was too late to stop the battalion. By 1400, the 9th Marines were atop 362-C looking down (still from some distance) at the sea. Two days after this first Marine night attack in World War II, a patrol from the 21st Marines reached the shore itself. To prove that Iwo Jima was indeed split lengthwise, the patrol leader filled a canteen with sea water and sent it back to General Erskine tagged, "For inspection, not consumption."

As the battle at length began to draw to its close, Iwo Jima was already an air base. The first United States plane to land (a Navy TBM which was forthwith abandoned by its pilot under enemy small-arms fire) had been reclaimed by the 3d Division's acquisitive air officer and was making regular spotting flights from Airfield No. 1, along with the Grasshoppers of the division observation squadrons. Air logistics by three Marine transport squadrons proved a godsend. When enemy shelling struck a dump and blew up most of the American 81-mm. shells on the island, mortar ammunition was air dropped and later flown in by the ton from the Marianas. At least as important, stateside mail was actually delivered to the front lines on 1 March—a record for the war and a tribute to toiling Navy mail clerks from San Francisco westward. But the best small-scale logistic lift during the battle was by VMF-225; when eight of its Corsairs flew up from Agaña to escort Admiral Nimitz on his visit to Iwo, each pilot brought two bottles of bourbon for the 3d Division, surely a high point in the annals of the air-ground team. On 4 March, the first wounded B-29 lurched onto Airfield No. 1, which had just been reopened under new management by the 2d Separate Engineer Battalion. Soon after, Marine Torpedo-Bombing Squadron 242 arrived. To protect the B-29s over the Empire, the Air Force VII Fighter Group flew in. These airmen quickly won the friendship of the battered Marine divisions by taking on close-support missions in fine style with their P-51s under control of Marine air liaison parties and Colonel Megee's LFASCU.

On 16 March, the 3d Division reduced its last and most fiercely contested pocket of resistance. That same day, to help the 5th Division (which fought longer, took more ground, and took more casualties than any division on Iwo), the 21st Marines swept rapidly to Kitano Point, the north tip of the island. General Erskine thereupon announced the end of organized resistance for the 3d Division. While this was going on, the 4th Division finally overran the desperately defended command post of Major General Sadasue Senda, Kuribayashi's infantry commander, and General Cates's hard battle was over, too. For General Rockey there remained nine more days of bitter though local fighting by the 28th Marines to capture a cave-lined gorge reminiscent of the heart of Peleliu's Umurbrogol. Here, in a monster bunker, General Kuribayashi (whom Emperor Hirohito promoted to full general almost but not quite posthumously) had his final headquarters. On 24 March, the Iwo Jima radio, which throughout the struggle had reported events to Chichi Jima and thence to Tokyo, came up on net for the last time: "All officers and men on Chichi Jima, farewell. . . ."[155] The rest was silence.

Iwo Jima cost the V Amphibious Corps 25,851 casualties, of whom 5,931 were killed. Among the killed and wounded were 738 Navy doctors and hospital corpsmen whose courage, skill, and tenderness can never be forgotten by the Marine Corps. Five rifle battalion commanders (Lieutenant

Colonels Ralph Haas, H. U. Mustain, T. M. Trotti, J. A. Butler, and C. W. Johnson) were killed at the head of their men; fourteen were wounded, including Lieutenant Colonel J. M. Chambers of the 3d Battalion, 25th Marines, whose desperate leadership in the initial assault won him the Medal of Honor. Of the more than 20,000 Japanese defenders, 216 prisoners were taken, and most of the rest died; thus about 1.25 Marines became casualties for every enemy defender—a grim ratio never equaled before or since in the history of the Corps. The final justification for these casualties appears in the terse observation of General Marshall, no Marine Corps fan, that the seizure of Iwo was "of vital importance to the air assault on Japan."[156] More graphically, the Air Force official history adds up the score: by the end of the war, 2,251 B-29s carrying 24,761 crewmen made safe emergency landings on Iwo's fields.[157]

"The capture of Iwo is the classic amphibious assault of recorded history," is the verdict of Princeton University's team that studied the amphibious operations of the war.[158] That it was. It was also the largest Marine Corps battle in the history of American arms. In the V Amphibious Corps as it fought on Iwo Jima, Harry Schmidt commanded the largest force of Marines ever to take the field. "It is fortunate," wrote Admiral Spruance in his action report, "that less seasoned or less resolute troops were not committed."[159] Speaking of those troops, Nimitz coined a phrase not soon forgotten—"Uncommon valor was a common virtue."[160]

OPERATION ICEBERG

Okinawa, an island 70 times the size of Iwo Jima, lies 325 miles south of Japan and 450 miles east of the China coast. First visited by Marines under Commodore Perry in 1853, it is a key position for control of the China Sea and for operations toward China or Japan. In 1945, Okinawa was the point at which the high road and the low road of the Pacific war finally intersected—the ultimate westward terminus, short of Japan itself, of Nimitz's drive across the Central Pacific, and a northward projection of MacArthur's advance on Tokyo via New Guinea and the Philippines.

The capture of Okinawa and adjacent small islands, called Operation "Iceberg," was decided upon as a substitute for taking Formosa, a plan which had been long entertained. Big enough, with excellent naval anchorages and airfield sites, but appreciably smaller than Formosa and considerably nearer the Empire, Okinawa was finally judged the better bet.

Okinawa is 60 miles long, running more or less north-south, and varies in width from two to 18 miles. Its terrain is wooded and mountainous in the north, and rolling and densely farmed in the south. The Ishikawa Isthmus, Okinawa's wasp waist, separates the two regions. Although the island is ringed by a coral reef—no longer a great problem by 1945—there are numerous feasible landing beaches on both sides. The weather is temperate, but very humid and rainy, a fact which became all too apparent when Marines returned to Okinawa 92 years after Commodore Perry's brief visit.

After a slow start, the Japanese accelerated defense preparations on Okinawa. In 1944, 32d Army Headquarters was created, under Lieutenant General Mitsuru Ushijima, a capable and well-thought-of officer, to organize

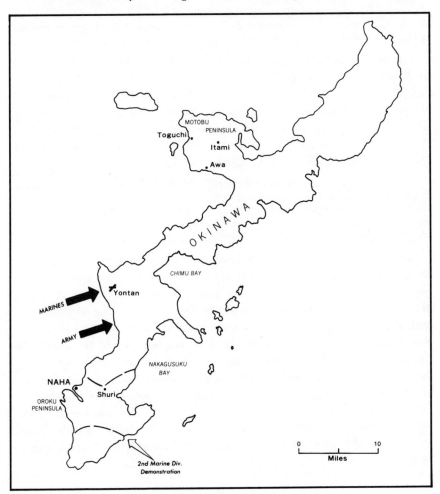

Battle for Okinawa, 1 April to 21 June 1945

the defenses and to command the major units on the island. These were two infantry divisions (24th and 62d), a strong brigade, a tank regiment, and all manner of artillery—field, coast defense, AA, and heavy mortar units of the type encountered on Iwo. Horse, foot, and guns, the 32d Army and Okinawa's naval base force totaled well over 100,000.

General Ushijima's defense plan was based on a new concept which the ruthless persuasion of war had at length driven home to the Japanese Army. He was not going to try to destroy the landing force on the beach. In a final report from Iwo Jima, General Kuribayashi had underscored this thought:[161]

However firm and stout pillboxes you may build at the beach, they will be destroyed by bombardment of main armament of the battleships. Power of the American warships and aircraft makes every landing possible to whatever beachhead they like.

Whether Ushijima ever saw this observation, he had arrived at similar conclusions by early 1945. Despite the existence of strong, well-integrated beach defenses on Okinawa, the general decided to withdraw inland, not to oppose an attack on the beaches, and to hold fire at the outset of any landing. This radical concept—which freely conceded the capability of the U. S. Navy and Marine Corps to land anywhere they pleased, regardless of opposition—was expressed in Ushijima's "Battle Instructions":[162]

Generally speaking, we must make it our basic principle to allow the enemy to land in full. Until he penetrates our position and loses his freedom of movement inside our most effective system of fire-power and until he can be lured into a position where he cannot receive cover and support from naval gunfire and aerial bombardment, we must patiently and prudently hold our fire. Then, leaping into action, we shall destroy the enemy.

Based on this thought, General Ushijima concentrated his main forces in the southern third of the island and set about constructing a series of cross-island defense lines in great depth. These, he correctly reasoned, would have to be taken by frontal attack at great cost, with maximum delay, and with minimum support from the enormous firepower of the Fleet. Elsewhere, except on Motobu Peninsula, a defensible area in the north, the Japanese left only token forces. General Ushijima's command post was located in tunnels under ancient Shuri Castle, onetime home of the Regents of Okinawa and squarely centered in rear of his main line of resistance.

In complete ignorance of their opponent's radical, logical defense strategy, the American planners prepared for a typical beach assault, bigger than anything before but not much different from Saipan or Guam, except in its king size.

The expeditionary troops headquarters for Iceberg was Tenth Army, commanded by Lieutenant General Simon Bolivar Buckner, USA; thus, Okinawa was to be the first major landing operation under Admiral Nimitz (except for Attu in the Aleutians in May 1943) in which a Marine did not have the top troop command. Under Buckner were two corps, the III Amphibious Corps, still commanded by Geiger, and the Army's XXIV Corps, under Major General John R. Hodge, USA. As usual, the top naval amphibious commander was Admiral Turner, who by 1945 was practically irreplaceable. The attack force commander charged with landing and supporting Geiger's corps was Rear Admiral L. F. Reifsnider, tall, courtly, and kindly. In addition to the troops in the two corps, General Buckner had several other important organizations under him: a division-sized demonstration force (2d Marine Division); the 77th Infantry Division, to be used for capture of certain islands offshore of Okinawa; the 27th Infantry Division, in army reserve; and the Tactical Air Force, Tenth Army, which was mainly the 2d Marine Air Wing, commanded by Major General F. P. Mulcahy, until shortly before, commanding general, AirFMFPac. All shore-based aviation was to come under General Mulcahy, whose biggest job, in the face of the kamikaze suicide planes of the Japanese, first seen in the Philippines, was air defense. All told, Tenth Army came up to 183,000 troops, of whom more than 80,000 were Marines. Admiral Spruance's Fifth Fleet mustered 1,457 ships.

The tactical plan for the capture of Okinawa involved a week of elaborate preliminary operations before L-day, Easter Sunday, 1 April. First the 77th Division, reinforced by the Fleet Marine Force reconnaissance battalion, would seize a fleet anchorage and advance base in the Kerama Retto, a group of islands 30 miles west of Okinawa. Thereafter would follow the most ambitious preliminary bombardment in the history of the war. Ironically, in view of Ushijima's decision not to use his beach defenses, which the intelligence experts had failed to divine, this week of fruitless pre-D-day bombardment was one of the factors which had caused Navy planners to turn down Holland Smith's plea for even one more day of bombardment for Iwo Jima, where it was desperately needed.

On the day before the landing, Army 155-mm. "Long Toms" would be established on offshore islands within supporting distance of the beaches. Then, on L-day, the two corps would land abreast at Hagushi on the west side of the island close to Yontan and Kadena, two of the largest airfields. After cutting across the island, the III Amphibious Corps would wheel left and clean out northern Okinawa, while the XXIV Corps, consisting of the 7th and 96th Infantry Divisions, would turn south and head for Shuri Castle and Naha, Okinawa's principal city. During all this, the 2d Marine Division, in reserve afloat, would stage a feint at landing off beaches in the far south of the island, which had been selected as alternates if for any reason the main landing beaches should prove unfeasible.

Throughout the planning there was an undercurrent of comment and rumor that, in this largest Pacific amphibious operation, the lion's share of the fighting would go to XXIV Corps in the south, while the Marines would be mopping up in the north; and that the 27th Division was slated to receive a Presidential Unit Citation as an "amend" for Saipan (a step which General Marshall had indeed hinted to Admiral King).[163] None of these developments materialized, but they indicated that the Saipan controversy had by no means been digested. Fortunately, even though he had headed General Richardson's "Buckner Board," General Buckner was to prove himself too large a man to countenance such pettiness.

Geiger's scheme of maneuver for III Amphibious Corps was keyed to the corps' supporting role, whereby the Marines would assist the main effort made by XXIV Corps. Of the III Corps' two divisions, the 1st (now commanded by Major General P. A. del Valle) would land on the right, and on the left the 6th Division (organized from General Shepherd's brigade on 7 September 1944) would cover both corps and Army left flank. In addition, the 6th Division had the immediate job of taking Yontan Airfield. The corps reserve was the new 29th Marines, commanded by Colonel V. F. Bleasdale, last Marine regiment to be formed in the States, and the new division's third regiment. The line-up of III Corps assault regiments from right to left was: 5th Marines, 7th Marines, 4th Marines, and 22d Marines.

All pre-L-day operations went ahead as planned. The Kerama Retto landings took place successfully on 26 March, but with one ominous event: just after daylight that morning a Japanese aircraft smashed into the destroyer *Kimberley* knocking out five guns and inflicting 54 casualties. Succeeding suicide attacks damaged four more ships. The kamikaze drive to destroy the U. S. Fleet had commenced.

III CORPS LANDING AND INITIAL OPERATIONS

General Ushijima's refusal to defend his beaches converted the Tenth Army's landings into the war's greatest anticlimax. There had been nothing like it since the Kiska hoax in 1943, when the Japanese permitted the Americans to bombard and assault a deserted Aleutian island. The selection of April Fools' Day for the landing was more appropriate than the planners could have conceived.

While XXIV Corps wheeled south, the 1st Marine Division pushed across the island against little or sometimes no opposition, and the 6th headed up Okinawa. General Shepherd had the job of sweeping the northern end of the island, and, more important, of locating and destroying the enemy force which intelligence reported on Motobu Peninsula, a protuberance from the northwest coast. There, some two thousand Japanese had a well-organized defense system in an area the size of Saipan. Like Saipan, the peninsula was dominated by a 1,200-foot mountain, Yae Take.

On 12 April, the 29th Marines pushed onto the peninsula and promptly hit opposition whose tenacity and extent made it clear that Motobu was no regiment-sized bite. General Shepherd pulled in the 4th Marines and commenced a viselike compression—not an ordinary envelopment—of Yae Take, with the 4th Regiment attacking the forward face while the 29th, pushing in exactly the opposite direction, assaulted the rear. On the 16th, after three days' arduous sparring against an enemy who used the rugged, forested ground skillfully and whose artillery was a bane to the 6th Division, the 4th Marines were in position for the final assault. The 1st Battalion, the same unit that had puffed up Mount Alifan on Guam, had a similar climb on Yae Take and a hard fight at the top. "That 1,200-foot hill looked like Pike's Peak," said an officer of the 4th Regiment. Next day the two regiments linked up and commenced a northward sweep which completed the capture of the peninsula.

The week on Motobu—a campaign within a campaign, like the Talasea show on New Britain, but larger and harder fought—was characterized by tactical originality, aggressiveness, and maximum use of every kind of supporting fire that was available. While the 15th Marines, under Colonel R. B. Luckey, dueled with the well-fought Japanese artillery, the 6th Division resorted to support from armored amphibians, air, and naval gunfire. To Admiral Reifsnider, whose ships supported the division, General Shepherd radioed: "The effectiveness of your gunfire support was measured by the large number of Japanese encountered. Dead ones."[164] The aviators distributed their favors impartially—during a front line visit, General Geiger, of all people, was pinned down in a ditch by "friendly" strafing.

Except for General Shepherd's operations, the first month on Okinawa was uneventful for the III Amphibious Corps. While the Army moved south to fight the decisive battle, the two Marine divisions patrolled, mopped up, and chased guerrillas. On 27 April, General Buckner lifted the 1st Division out of III Corps and parceled it out to XXIV Corps as a reserve, leaving General Geiger with a one-division corps. Even earlier the 11th Marines had been detached from the 1st Division and were reinforcing the fires of the 7th and 96th Division artillery; at the head of his regiment, Colonel "Bigfoot" Brown, he whose shoes required the special airlift in Nicaragua, grandly reported to the XXIV Corps artillery commander as "liaison officer" and was soon in the thick of what was shaping up as an artilleryman's battle.

INTO THE LINES

After a taste of Ushijima's medicine, General Hodge, the XXIV Corps commander, wrote in mid-April, "It is going to be really tough. . . . I see no way to get the Japanese out except blast them out yard by yard."[165]

With three divisions in line, XXIV Corps was finding the going slow and hard. On the west, the understrength 27th Division, which had been committed on 9 April, was stalled. To get a firmer grip on the battle, General Buckner decided to assign the 27th Division to duties in the rear as island garrison troops and to replace it by a Marine division. On 1 May, the 1st Marine Division took over, and, after a week of steady fighting, including the repulse of a Japanese counterlanding, General Geiger was ordered to assume command of the 1st Division zone and bring down the 6th Division on the seaward, right flank of III Corps' new zone. Henceforth until the end, the battle was to be fought by the two corps in line—III Corps on the right, XXIV Corps on the left. (The 2d Marine Division, meantime, had been returned to Saipan to prepare for the invasion of Japan.)

At this time the Okinawa battle had been going on five weeks and was nowhere near won. The Navy, whose ships offshore were taking a fearful pasting from the stream of kamikaze attacks, had good reason to chafe under the "yard-by-yard" tactics of the Tenth Army, and much pressure, some even in the press, was exerted to try to influence the army command to use one or both Marine divisions (or the 2d Division in reserve on Saipan) for an amphibious end-run to outflank Ushijima's fixed lines.[166] Despite sharp prods from Admiral Turner, General Buckner remained obdurate, however, and III Amphibious Corps was kept in the line to fight a land battle by the rules of land warfare.

The significance of this decision was not overlooked by an able war correspondent on the scene, the *New York Herald-Tribune's* Homer Bigart:[167]

> There were two ways of employing the Marine 3d Amphibious Corps after its speedy cleanup of northern Okinawa. It could be landed behind the Japanese lines in the south, or it could add power to the frontal assault on the Shuri line. Our tactics were ultra-conservative. Instead of an end run, we persisted in frontal attacks.

Correspondent Bigart was not the only one who had raised the question of an amphibious flanking movement by the Marines. During an April visit to Okinawa with General Thomas, General Vandegrift had urged such a course of action on Admiral Nimitz and General Buckner, only to be told that the suggested landing area—the beaches which Buckner's staff had selected as alternate beaches for the main landing—were not feasible. In Army councils, General Bruce, the 77th Division's capable and aggressive commander, made the same proposal for his own division, which had learned its amphibious lessons under Geiger at Guam, but this was also turned down.[168]

What faced General Geiger was the Shuri line—General Ushijima's main battle position, a deep belt of densely fortified hills, minefields, caves, defended hillside burial vaults—and Japs. For the 1st Division, this meant the attack and capture of Dakeshi Ridge, and south of it, another even more formidable eminence, Wana Ridge. While Dakeshi Ridge was the key terrain feature in the corps zone, the 6th Division confronted the western anchor of the Shuri line—a trio of mutually supporting hills named Sugar Loaf, Horseshoe, and Half Moon.

On 12 May, under Colonel E. W. Snedeker, who had relieved Colonel Hanneken after Peleliu, the 7th Marines got to the top of Dakeshi and stayed there. Ahead lay Dakeshi Town, Wana Ridge, and Wana Draw, a death-trap approach to Shuri. A week later, still besieging Wana, the 7th Marines were relieved by the 1st Regiment (Colonel A. T. Mason); in nine days' hot action the 7th Regiment had suffered 1,249 casualties. As the 1st Marines took over the heartbreaking assault, still another formidable enemy turned against them: "General Mud." The late spring rains set in without respite and grounded everything on wheels and almost everything on tracks. Even jeeps and bulldozers foundered, while artillerymen served pieces trunnion-deep in water. Front line supply was by human pack trains that slithered through the muck.

While the 1st Division pressed slowly toward Shuri, the 6th Division advanced along the coast. The division's debut on 10 May was an assault river crossing right out of the field manuals, by the 22d Marines over a footbridge thrown across the Asa Kawa ("Kawa" means "river") by the 6th Engineer Battalion. Despite enemy fire, the bridge stayed in long enough for assault companies to get over in a predawn rush; later, when enemy demolition men blew up both themselves and the bridge, amtracs filled in for a day until the engineers got in a Bailey bridge across which tanks rolled triumphantly.

On 12 May, the 22d Marines first encountered Sugar Loaf. Six days' hard fighting and another regiment, the 29th, now under Colonel Whaling, were required before the battered hill was in Marine hands. Also required was such courage as that displayed by Major H. A. Courtney, Jr., executive officer of the 2d Battalion, 22d Marines, who with 40 Marines held the top of Sugar Loaf for almost a whole night until he was cut down by an enemy grenade while leading a desperate counterattack. His last words were, "Keep coming!" His reward was the Medal of Honor.

From 18 May until the 23d, General Shepherd pressed forward from Sugar Loaf. Using a fresh regiment, Colonel Shapley's 4th, and forcing another river crossing, the Asato, the 6th Division reached the northern outskirts of Naha, principal port on the west coast.

Ushijima's forces in the Shuri line were now in serious trouble. Sugar Loaf and its supporting hills had fallen. The 1st Division was probing at Shuri itself. Worse still, the 96th Infantry Division, on the other side of the island, had captured Conical Hill, a key position near Yonabaru. The loss of this hill convinced General Ushijima that it was time to fall back to lines farther south and thus prolong the battle to the utmost.

Perhaps as a cover for the enemy retirement, 24 May was marked by a storm of kamikazes that the Navy estimated at more than 150. Nine ships, mostly on radar picket duty, were hit; two were sunk. That night came a Japanese airborne landing on Yontan Airfield, which had been captured by U. S. forces on L-day. Here the 1st Marine Antiaircraft Group, four AA battalions, commanded by Colonel K. W. ("Shorty") Benner, a veteran basedefender, came into its glory. Under the blast of the group's 90-mm. and 40-mm. guns, only one of the enemy transport planes made the field intact; even so, its battered cargo of demolition men, who were ultimately killed by aviation personnel, destroyed nine aircraft and damaged 29, including the transport of Major General J. T. Moore, CG, AirFMFPac, who had arrived that morning on business from Pearl. Shortly afterward, mindful of the night's fireworks, wags of the 2d Marine Wing put up a sign beside Operations—"Welcome to Yontan. Every Night a Fourth of July."

About noon on 26 May, the 1st Marine Division sensed the novel impression of slightly slackening resistance at Shuri; on division request the old battleship *New York* launched her floatplane spotter for a look around. What he saw was a gunnery officer's dream: the roads south of Shuri jammed with retreating troops and vehicles. Within 13 minutes the cruiser *New Orleans*, which was in close range (*New York* was well out but frantically closing) had a nine-gun 8-inch salvo on the way, followed by as many more as the sweating turret-crews could ram and fire. Other ships raced in without command, launching planes, sharing spotters, and pouring out salvos. Muddy fields and foul weather be damned, the 2d Wing sent off 50 Corsairs to join the fray. The day's slaughter left the roads blocked with wrecked tanks, shattered trucks, and corpses. Even so, leaving a die-hard rear guard to hold the line, General Ushijima deftly completed his retirement 11 miles south to the Kiyamu Peninsula, while the mud-bound Tenth Army thrashed in frustration. One outfit was still able to move, however. On 29 May, Company A, 5th Marines, with General del Valle's approval, angled into the zone of the 77th Division, which was still held up in front of Shuri Castle, and raised the 1st Division's Colors over Ushijima's late stronghold.

MARINE AVIATION IN THE OKINAWA CAMPAIGN

For Marine aviation, Okinawa was the biggest, most all-around, and in some respects the most important operation of the war. More than 12,000 officers and men from Marine aviation (about 12 times the number of aviation personnel on Guadalcanal) fought at Okinawa in 22 shore-based squadrons, 10 carrier squadrons, an air-warning group, and a miscellany of headquarters and service units.

Most but not all of this effort came under General Mulcahy's Tactical Air Force (TAF), which, before the campaign ended, also included several Army squadrons. The backbone of TAF was the 2d Marine Air Wing, ultimately composed of four groups, MAGs 31, 33, 22, and 14. In addition, a fifth group, MAG-43, commanded and controlled four air-warning squadrons, plus some Army signal air-warning and fighter control detachments. Outside TAF were the Marine fighting squadrons aboard the fast carriers *Bennington* and *Bunker Hill*, the squadrons aboard two Marine CVEs that finally got into the war (*Block Island* and *Gilbert Islands*), and the four Grasshopper observation squadrons working with III Amphibious Corps. The nerve centers that controlled all this aviation were two: Air Defense Command, under Brigadier General W. J. Wallace, whose job was to stand off kamikazes, and Landing Force Air Support Control Units (LFASCU), commanded by Colonel Megee, who had pioneered the idea so effectively on Iwo Jima. The Tenth Army had a Marine LFASCU, under Colonel A. R. Kier, while III Corps and XXIV Corps each had one, too, commanded respectively by Colonel K. H. Weir and Lieutenant Colonel K. D. Kerby.

Because of Ushijima's tactics, General Mulcahy received the unexpected gift of two immediately operational airfields, Yontan and Kadena. The first units to fly off them were the III Corps Grasshoppers, but, within a week after L-day, Colonel J. C. ("Tobey") Munn's Corsairs of MAG-31 were ashore at Yontan and in business. MAG-31's first kill at Okinawa took place as planes were being flown off the escort carriers that had ferried them to Okinawa: a kamikaze made straight for one CVE (USS *Sitkoh Bay*), and five Corsairs shot him to pieces 50 feet short of their former home. Two days later Colonel Ward E. Dickey led in MAG-33 to Kadena, which brought the total of Marine aircraft on Okinawa inside the first ten days to well over 200.

At the outset (and at the end, too) the big job was kamikazes. The first great kamikaze blitz—355 suiciders—came on 6 April, one day too early for the shore-based Marines, but just in time for the Marine squadrons with the fast carriers, who shot down 17. Of the 355 Japanese, 22 got past fighters and flak and hit 22 ships, of which three were sunk. The next big attack, 185 strong, came on 12 April, while enemy gunners ashore tried to neutralize Kadena and Yontan (mud grounded more planes than artillery, however). Again the carrier fighters got the lion's share—51 this time for the four Marine squadrons (VMF-112 and 123 in the *Bennington*, and VMF-221 and 451 in the *Bunker Hill*). On 16 April, 165 kamikazes slashed at the Fleet, mostly against the brave and battered radar picket ships which outposted Okinawa to give warning of enemy air. One such, the USS *Laffey*, was hit by five suicide attacks only to be saved from destruction by 12 Corsairs from VMF-441. "Marines to the rescue. Just like Hollywood," noted Lieutenant Commander Frank Manson, one surviving officer who managed to keep his sense of humor.[169] The captain of the USS *Hugh W. Hadley*, hit four times in a later attack and then screened by VMF-323, said afterwards, "I am willing to take my ship to the shores of Japan if I could have these Marines with me."[170]

One naval officer who was less enthusiastic about the advent of Marine air on the scene was Rear Admiral C. T. Durgin, who commanded all escort carriers (including the Marine CVEs) at Okinawa. Despite the mid-1944 agreement between General Vandegrift and Admirals Nimitz and King that the Marine air support groups aboard the CVEs were to be used specifically for close support, Admiral Durgin put his blind eye to the telescope and kept the Marine squadrons of the *Block Island* and *Gilbert Islands* away from close support duties for 74 of Okinawa's 82 days of battle. To make matters perfectly clear, agreement or no agreement, as to how he felt about Marine CVE aviators supporting their comrades ashore, the admiral subsequently wrote Admiral King a scorcher which ended:[171]

. . . this command sees at the present writing no reason for such assignments and has no intention of allowing it to occur.

Although Admiral Durgin's stand obstructed employment of Marine aviation in its logical role and effectively prevented an adequate combat test of the Marine CVE concept, about 40 per cent of all direct support strikes on Okinawa were flown by Marines. The results were as good as could be expected against Ushijima's subterranean warriors; all supporting arms, even though employed throughout the campaign with unprecedented volume and high efficiency, recorded equal frustration.

As the Okinawa battle dragged on, reinforcing aviation units came in. MAG-22, under Colonel D. W. Torrey, which had been exiled on Midway since 1942, arrived in May and based on Ie Shima, an outlying island captured by the 77th Infantry Division. A month later, Colonel E. A. Montgomery brought up MAG-14 from Samar. With these reinforcements, TAF finished the Okinawa battle and the air battle in the Ryukyus, which continued until the war's end. When the curtain descended, Marine pilots had accounted for 506 enemy aircraft.

THE END OF THE LAST BATTLE

Although the bulk of the Ushijima's army fell back to the southern tip of Okinawa for a last stand, the naval garrison, commanded by Rear Admiral Minoru Ota, hung onto Oroku Peninsula, which, not unlike Motobu in the north, juts out from the west shore of Okinawa, south of Naha. Oroku contained a large airfield, but, more important at this stage of the campaign, it flanked the advance of the Tenth Army and could not be ignored. While General del Valle's muddy veterans slogged south, supplied by air-drop because the roads were completely out, General Shepherd received orders to take Oroku. Instead of beating the 6th Division's head against the base of the peninsula, which was strongly held, an amphibious assault against the tip was decided upon.

With five days to plan, the division staff, spark-plugged by Lieutenant Colonel V. H. Krulak, the G-3, whipped up a shore-to-shore movement in column of regiments, the 4th Marines leading. In a driving rain on the grey dawn of 4 June, anniversary of Midway, supported by a battleship, two cruisers, a destroyer, and 15 battalions of artillery, Colonel Shapley landed his regiment from LVTs and LCTs and pushed rapidly inland with the 29th Marines following and fanning left into line beside the 4th. As the regiments advanced against scattering opposition, the 6th Engineer Battalion threw a Bailey bridge across from Naha—the longest bridge built by Marine engineers during the war—and the 6th Signal Company outdid itself by running telephone cable from the division command post across the estuary in rubber boats, using the mast of a sunken ship as a pole. Meanwhile, the 22d Marines sealed the landward base of Oroku to prevent the Japanese from spilling out against the 1st Division. Once again General Shepherd was using the maneuver of compression which had worked so well on Motobu. In ten days' steady fighting slowed by mud and minefields, the 6th Division pushed the Japanese into a corner and thence into oblivion. More than 4,000 enemy were killed at a cost of 1,608 Marine killed and wounded. Admiral Ota, who had successfully defended Bairoko in New Georgia against the 1st Raiders in 1943, directed the fight from an underground CP complete with electricity and running water. His last message to Ushijima was: "Enemy tanks are attacking our headquarters cave. The Naval Base Force is dying gloriously."[172] Then the admiral killed himself.

The Oroku battle, like that on Motobu, was separate and distinct and tactically refreshing. The use of the Marine amphibious capability to attack Admiral Ota from the rear was the only instance during the Okinawa campaign when the III Amphibious Corps was allowed to exploit its ability to outflank by sea.

While the 6th Division was fighting amphibiously, the 1st Division, which now had the coastal flank, solved its logistic problem by opening up a beach south of the Oroku Peninsula at the town of Itoman and receiving its "beans and bullets" by sea. In the fight to take Itoman, the assault battalion commander mounted himself in a 75-mm. armored amphibian from which he both directed and supported the fight from offshore.

Ahead of the 1st Division lay what the division's history described as "a very nasty layout." A steep ridge, Kunishi, lay square athwart the division zone, fronted by a half mile of flat open fields and rice paddies. It was held in force. Even with the superb division tank battalion doing its utmost, the 7th Marines, commanded by Colonel E. W. Snedeker, were unable to get across those fire-swept flats. After a last effort by daylight on 11 June, Colonel Snedeker decided to try a night attack. It worked. Two companies got across before daybreak. All day, battered by counterattack and cut off by Japanese fire onto the flats, the two companies held. Next night, Colonel Snedeker advanced again; this time the whole regiment got onto the ridge. Then, for four days, with Marines on top and Japanese inside, a fierce battle raged. The 1st Tank Battalion lost 21 tanks. Supplies came by air, and wounded stayed forward on the ridge.

On 17 June, while the Kunishi fight neared its close, the 6th Division resumed its right-flank position for a final attack across ridges toward the sea. Next day, under Colonel C. R. Wallace, the 8th Regiment (of the 2d Division), brought back from Saipan, relieved the weary 7th Marines and attacked southward with the vigor of a fresh outfit. As General Buckner watched the 8th Marines push forward, an enemy shell hit the observation post, wounding the general in the chest. Ten minutes later he was dead. General Geiger thereupon assumed command of the Tenth Army, becoming the first Marine to command a field army, and the only American aviator ever to do so. Less than an hour before Buckner's death, the 22d Marines lost their regimental commander, Colonel H. C. Roberts. Colonel Roberts, an officer of great courage, had won the Navy Cross and the Distinguished Service Cross as a hospital corpsman at Belleau Wood in 1918. He held a second Navy Cross for service in the Coco River expedition in 1928[173] and had just been awarded a third Navy Cross for heroism on Okinawa.

Three nights later, General Ushijima, who had fought so hard a fight, committed hara-kiri beside his chief of staff. Some hours earlier, on 21 June, General Geiger declared organized resistance to an end, and Okinawa, the last battle, was over.

During Okinawa's 82 days the Marine Corps, including ships' detachments and aviation, lost 3,440 killed and 15,487 wounded. In addition, 547 Navy doctors and hospital corpsmen became casualties in their struggle to save others. The Fleet—which stayed off Okinawa despite all the shore-based air of the Japanese Empire—paid a terrible price for the slow progress of the campaign: 36 ships sunk and 368 damaged, and 4,907 officers and seamen down to Davy Jones's locker—more losses than Pearl Harbor and more dead than either the Marines or the Army ashore. "Certain high Navy officers here," wrote columnist David Lawrence from Washington, "feel that a major mistake was made in handling the Okinawa campaign." Then he went on to pose a series of questions to be debated as long as the operation is remembered:[174]

Did the Army officers who handled the campaign adopt a slow course? Were there other landing places that could have been used? Why were the Marine Corps generals, who had had far greater experience in handling amphibious operations, not given an opportunity to carry on another type of campaign that might, perhaps, have meant larger land casualties at the outset, but in the end a quicker all-around result for the armed forces as a whole?

THE END OF THE WAR

The end of the war, on 10 August 1945 when the Japanese sued for peace, came as an anticlimax to most of the combat troops in the Pacific. Both amphibious corps were gathering their strength for the forthcoming invasion of Japan, which, atom bombs or not, the combined forces of sea power had already rendered unnecessary. During the weeks after the surrender, most Marines prepared themselves for demobilization or for occupation duty as the case might be. When the surrender document was signed on 2 September aboard the USS *Missouri* in Tokyo Bay, General Geiger, among many U. S. Army, U. S. Navy and foreign senior officers, represented the U. S. Marine Corps. Alone though he was (General Holland Smith having been transferred home in July 1945), he stood for an unbroken series of victories in desperate battles, for 80 Medals of Honor won by men of his Corps, and for 86,940 dead and wounded United States Marines.

THE CORPS SCENE

Although the natural focus of attention rested throughout the war on the Marine divisions and the Pacific arena, Marines served elsewhere and performed many other duties ranging from diplomatic couriers (a service provided by Eighth and Eye) to cloak-and-dagger work with the OSS. Selected officers dropped by parachute, served with the Chetniks in Jugoslavia, with the French and Belgian *Résistance,* and with guerrillas in North China. Others ranged the China coast in piratical armed junks, preying on Japanese coastwise traffic, landing arms and agents, and relaying information. Eleven thousand officers and men served in ships' detachments with the Fleet in both hemispheres. More than 20 officers, mostly aviators, served with the British forces in Europe and the Middle East for varying tours as observers or planning advisors. One who survived, Brigadier General Lewie G. Merritt, had the curious distinction of being the first and only Marine pilot to be shot down by the Luftwaffe—in 1942, near Bardia in North Africa.

Colonel H. D. Campbell advised Lord Mountbatten on the air plan for the Dieppe raid, while Lieutenant Colonel R. O. Bare helped plan and served in the Normandy landings. Captain J. H. Magruder III acted as liaison officer between the British Navy (Flag-Officer, Holland) and Field Marshal Montgomery's 21 Army Group in the crossings of the Maas and Rhine rivers and the liberation of the Netherlands. A defense battalion, the 13th, commanded by Colonel R. M. Cutts, Jr., manned the defenses of Guantanamo Bay until 1944, thus becoming the sole Fleet Marine Force unit to serve in the Atlantic theater after 1942. The 13th Defense Battalion's lonely aviation counterpart was VMS-3, based at Bourne Field, St. Thomas, Virgin Islands, until 1944. This squadron, which, as VO-9M, had come directly from Haiti in 1934, not only stayed overseas longer (1919-1944) than any other unit in the Marine Corps, but was the only Marine aviation unit stationed in the Atlantic after 1941. The only Marine Barracks in the European theater, at Londonderry, Ireland, organized in 1942, distinguished itself by forming its own bagpipe band, which won acclaim (and many piping contests) among the dour Orangemen of North Ireland.

One special category of Marines—brought into being by Brigadier General R. L. Denig, the Corps' first Director of Public Relations—was that of combat correspondent. The combat correspondents—Marines first and reporters and photographers second—were former newsmen and writers enlisted into the Corps, fully trained for combat, and then sent to fighting units of the FMF. Their reporting equaled the most vivid and authentic in World War II, and their instant success caused the system to be copied by the Army. The duty was not easy: on Iwo Jima, six combat correspondents and two public information officers were killed, while 14 correspondents were wounded. Out of a 1945 total of only 256 officers and men assigned to public relations duties in the 485,000-man Corps (which belies loose assertions about the extent of Marine publicity operations), the foregoing casualties in only one battle—almost ten per cent—are impressive.

At home, as the war rolled on, the Marine Corps became a huge replacement training establishment. The last FMF unit to be organized in the States, the 29th Marines, left Camp Lejeune in 1944. Thereafter, the output of the supporting establishment was mainly comprised of replacement drafts processed out of Camp Lejeune (where a cluster of technical schools grew up) and Camp Pendleton's Training and Replacement Command. But replacements weren't the only trainees: beginning in 1943, officers of the Royal Netherlands *Korps Mariniers,* second in seniority by only a year to the

British Marines, began training at Quantico as a preliminary to reorganization of their corps in exile. By 1944 several hundred Dutch enlisted Marines had been assembled in the States from the West Indies and from those who had escaped the German or Japanese invaders. Using this group as a cadre, the Dutch government arranged to have the U. S. Marine Corps undertake the organization, training, and equipment of a Netherlands Marine Brigade at Camp Lejeune. Before the war's end, several thousand Dutch Marines completed the program, and as a result the postwar *Korps Mariniers* bears an abiding resemblance to the U. S. Marine Corps, as well as a comradeship which is warmly reciprocated.

When General Vandegrift took over Marine Corps Headquarters in 1944, a statement widely attributed to the new management—"There are only two kinds of Marines: those who have been overseas and those who are going"—became policy. As a result, it proved almost impossible for a man to wear the globe and anchor without heading for the Pacific. By the end of the war, 98 per cent of all officers and 89 per cent of all enlisted Marines (from a Corps whose top strength reached 484,631) could proudly claim to have served overseas and mostly in combat, a record not even approached by any of the other Services.

Like all wars, World War II was a killer of traditions. The 1937 *Uniform Regulations* simply went by the board, and, for the last two years of the war, the Corps operated without an effective compilation of such regulations, their place being taken by a hastily prepared interim directive which embodied several careless mistakes and unnecessary lapses from the high standards and traditions of the past. A more fundamental lapse was the separation of the Marine from his rifle. Until the war, the rifle issued to each Marine on first enlistment stayed with him until he died, retired, or made sergeant major; under pressure of wartime supply exigencies, rifles became organizational property like tent pins and mess gear. The Marine Corps Good Conduct Medal, whose high standards had made it a hard-earned prize for the finest enlisted men, was, together with the Navy Good Conduct Medal, appreciably downgraded as a result of hints that long-standing Navy and Marine criteria were disproportionately high in comparison to those for the recently instituted (1941) Army Good Conduct Medal.

Doomed by the war but not killed until a year afterward was the prolifery of enlisted ranks which had gradually flowered since 1922. The enormous spectrum of specialization needed for 1945's Fleet Marine Force had already brought about the so-called "SSN" system whereby every military specialty was identified by a number capable of being digested and regurgitated by IBM machine. Once adopted, this system rendered unnecessary the wide and often picturesque range of NCO ranks which, at the war's end, were as follows:

1st Grade: Sergeant major; first sergeant; master gunnery sergeant; master technical sergeant; quartermaster sergeant; paymaster sergeant.

2d Grade: Gunnery sergeant; technical sergeant; supply sergeant; drum major.

3d Grade: Platoon sergeant; staff sergeant; chief cook.

4th Grade: Sergeant; field music sergeant; field cook.

5th Grade: Corporal; field music corporal; assistant cook.

6th Grade: Private first class; field music first class.

7th Grade: Private; field music.

Another war casualty was the time-honored system of "specialist pay" whereby technically qualified enlisted men received extra pay instead of NCO ratings, which were reserved only for leaders; faced by unparalleled demands for technical skills, the Corps junked specialist pay and promoted everyone.

More damaging, however, than any loss of tradition was the loss of a great and loyal friend: when President Roosevelt died in 1945 the Marine Corps lost a supporter whose enthusiasm and pride in the Corps never wavered. With his death ended an era of smooth sailing and warm regard for the Marine Corps (and for the Navy, too) within the executive branch of the government.

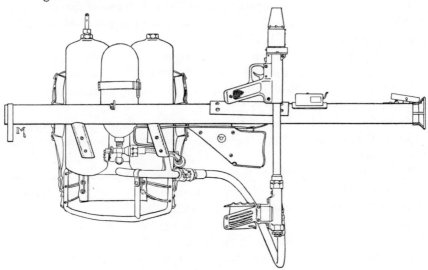

9 FIVE YEARS OF CHALLENGE *1945-1950*

We have pride in ourselves and in our past, but we do not rest our case on any presumed ground of gratitude owing us from the nation. The bended knee is not a tradition of our Corps.
—GENERAL A. A. VANDEGRIFT, 6 MAY 1946

*T*HE TASKS and problems which faced the Marine Corps immediately after the war were as follows:

To demobilize a Corps of five hundred thousand officers and men and "get the boys home" under pressure of a wave of home-town hysteria that temporarily crippled our foreign policy and is embarrassing to remember.

To maintain efficient occupation forces, two or three divisions strong, in North China and Japan. This was a task next to incompatible with the pell-mell demobilization of 1945-46.

To shape the organization and select the right people for a postwar regular Marine Corps about five times the size of the 1939 Corps (in 1945, Congress had established 107,000 officers and men as the authorized peacetime strength of the Corps).

To confront ill-defined but disturbing pressures for extensive reorganization of the defense establishment which boded nothing but trouble for the Marine Corps.

To respond professionally to the chorus of doubts and unanswered questions inspired by the advent of the atom bomb, especially prophecies that "there would never be another amphibious landing."

None of the foregoing problems and challenges could be attacked in academic calm or in the isolation of the laboratory. Business had to go on as usual. This chapter shows a new Marine Corps—for assuredly Pearl Harbor was the dividing point between the "Old Corps" and the new—in a new and distracting national and governmental environment, attempting to carry on with its duties and "do that which is right."

DEPLOYMENT AND DEMOBILIZATION

When the war ended, the V Amphibious Corps, still commanded by General Schmidt, was completing preparations for the invasion of Kyushu, southernmost of the Japanese home islands. Thus the corps headquarters and two divisions, the 2d (Major General L. P. Hunt) and 5th, now under Major General T. E. Bourke, were immediately sent to occupy southern Japan.[1] Air support for the corps came from the 2d Wing, with MAG-31 based at Yokosuka. Corps headquarters was at Sasebo, site of one of Japan's most important navy yards, while the 2d Division camped amid the ashes of Nagasaki. Routine occupation operations and demilitarization of the Japanese forces proceeded efficiently and uneventfully. In defeat the Japanese were as co-operative as they had been unyielding in battle.

By December 1945, the 5th Division was released for disbandment; next month corps headquarters went home, and, in June 1946, the 2d Marine Division sailed from Japan for Camp Lejeune to become one of the two peacetime divisions of the postwar Marine Corps and the first division assigned to the newly created Fleet Marine Force Atlantic.

The III Amphibious Corps, commanded by Major General Rockey after General Geiger succeeded Holland Smith at FMFPac, instead of invading the Tokyo Plain, went to North China, arriving on 30 September. The nominal mission of the corps, 47,000 strong, was to accept the surrender of Japanese forces there; its even more important mission was to stabilize this strategic area and prevent its fall either to Russia or to Chinese Communists. Corps headquarters, 1st Wing headquarters, and the 1st Division went to Tientsin, with one regiment up to Peking and a battalion at Chinwangtao; the 6th Division landed on the Shantung Peninsula, with headquarters at Tsingtao, and the 1st Wing provided air support. Without realizing that they were performing the last China duty for years to come, the troops, willingly tutored by the old China hands, rapidly set about becoming new China hands.

Meanwhile, demobilization rushed ahead. In November 1945, the 4th Division disbanded; in December the 3d followed suit, while the 5th lasted a month longer. In April 1946, the 6th Division, reduced in size but still at

Tsingtao, became the 3d Marine Brigade. Elsewhere, while enlisted men and officers of other Services rioted and held demobilization mass meetings from Manila to Oahu, the Marine Corps in general demobilized with discipline and dignity.[2]

At home, as noted above, it was decided that the Atlantic Fleet would have its Fleet Marine Force, too. The peacetime Corps would, it was hoped, number two divisions, a brigade, and two wings. Amid the demobilization turmoil, Headquarters set about selecting regular officers from the best qualified reservists who applied. At the same time, a number of regular officers whose war records had not measured up were quietly retired. Little by little the postwar Corps took shape.

THE CHALLENGE OF BIKINI

After the two bombs exploded at Bikini in July 1946, General Geiger returned to Pearl Harbor and wrote General Vandegrift about what he had seen. His letter concluded:[3]

Under the assumption that atomic bombs can be produced in large quantities, that they can be used in mass attacks against an enemy objective, and that our probable future enemy will be in possession of this weapon, it is my opinion that a complete review and study of our concept of amphibious operations will have to be made. It is quite evident that a small number of atomic bombs could destroy an expeditionary force as now organized, embarked, and landed. . . . It is trusted that Marine Corps Headquarters will consider this a very serious and urgent matter and will use its most competent officers in finding a solution to develop the technique of conducting amphibious operations in the atomic age.

Within six months Geiger was dead, but his letter served as a tocsin. General Vandegrift responded in kind—"The sense of urgency Lieutenant General Geiger expresses is the feeling of the Marine Corps"[4]—and passed the problem to a blue-ribbon panel headed by General Shepherd, who had just returned from China to become Assistant Commandant of the Corps. Among General Shepherd's subordinates were Colonel Merrill B. Twining, one of the ablest and most imaginative thinkers in the Corps, and Colonel E. C. Dyer, an aviation officer of extensive technical attainment. Quantico, naturally, was the scene of deliberation.

At this stage of the game, Marine Corps Schools were in intellectual ferment. Staffed by war-tested officers whose overriding concern was to take stock of the immense experiences just past, Quantico was ripe for such a project. The Advance Base Problem Team was being reactivated under the professional hand of Colonel R. E. Hogaboom; an edition of slim, blue-bound manuals, the *PHIB* series so-called, were reducing Marine-developed wartime techniques to print; and a team from Quantico and Washington had just completed, under the cryptic naval title, *USF-63*, a landmark compilation of amphibious doctrine for the postwar Navy and Marine Corps. Among many who were active in all this, the names of Twining and Hogaboom, and of Lieutenant Colonels Weller, Krulak, Shaw, Hittle, and J. C. Murray stand out.

After three months' intense study of the problem that Bikini had presented to General Geiger, the special board reached its conclusions and sent them forward on 16 December 1946 to General Vandegrift:[5]

Under atomic attack, the World War II amphibious assault was finished. Normandy (more a ferrying operation than a true oceanic amphibious assault in any case) and Okinawa would never be repeated.

Wide dispersion and great rapidity had to be attained in future assaults but without loss of control, flexibility, or concentrated striking power at the critical point. Parachutists, gliders, transport planes—all the much-glamorized airborne machinery—were no more use than landing craft, were airdrome-bound, and were many times more vulnerable on the ground or in the air.

Transport submarines to a limited extent, large flying boats capable of beaching ("Flying LSTs"), and, above all, carrier-based helicopters, presented the only viable possibilities for amphibious attack in an atomic war. The Marine Corps should forthwith press for development of transport seaplanes and assault helicopters, and should immediately organize a helicopter experimental squadron. Marine Corps Schools should start work on a doctrine for helicopter landing operations.

In Krulak's view the report voiced:[6]

. . . a prospective military philosophy. It consists of thinking in terms of the next war instead of the last. This means starting with ideas, when you have nothing more tangible, and developing them into the concepts, procedures, and weapons of the future.

Even though the top capacity of any helicopter then flying was the pilot and two Marines, General Vandegrift approved the special board's report within 72 hours. By December 1947, Marine Helicopter Experimental Squadron One (HMX-1) was in business at Quantico air station.

It was 1933 all over again.

"... THE FATE OF THE MARINE CORPS
LIES SOLELY AND ENTIRELY WITH THE CONGRESS"

On the beach at Iwo Jima, James Forrestal said that the Marine Corps had earned its future for the next 500 years. Within 15 months the Corps was in mortal peril.

Back in November 1943, General Marshall had signed a memorandum which had profound if indirect implications for the Marine Corps. This was a proposal that the Air Corps be separated from the Army and that the Armed Services then be merged under a single Department of War, with a single chief of staff and an armed forces general staff. Although this memorandum was never directly acted on, it was the first of a series of defense reorganization proposals of the next 18 years. Adding impetus to the movement, which by 1945 had become a continuous operation (as Secretary Forrestal noted,[7] "... through the organization of public opinion by the War Department"), was the fact that Marshall's ideas coincided closely with those held by the new President, Harry S. Truman, whose long association with the Army had made him as much its champion as President Roosevelt had been of the Navy and Marines. "When Roosevelt was here," he reportedly said of the White House,[8] "this place was like a damned wardroom. As long as I'm here, the admirals will never get in again." And they never did.

After some initial confusion (which was never shared by Admiral King) the Navy came to realize that adoption of Marshall's ideas—which by late 1945 had been officially presented to the press and Congress by a War Department spokesman, Lieutenant General J. L. Collins—meant the end of the Naval Establishment and all it had stood for since 1798. More importantly, many thought, the "Collins Plan" represented a move in the very flush of victory to discard the Anglo-American system of high command and strategic planning, which had just won the greatest war in history.

While the Collins Plan was being debated in the newspapers and on Capitol Hill, a debate with far more direct bearing on the Marine Corps was going on among the members of the Joint Chiefs of Staff. In August 1945, Secretary of the Navy Forrestal presented his Department's plans for the strength and composition of the postwar Navy and Marine Corps. President Truman, who had already disclosed his leanings toward some type of armed forces merger, thereupon asked the Joint Chiefs of Staff to review Secretary

Forrestal's plan in light of the postwar "roles and missions" of all the Services. From the succeeding interchange of views, it became clear that, in the War Department's strongly held concept of the future defense organization, only a negligible place existed for the Marine Corps. The rationale of the new definition was to circumscribe the functions of the Marine Corps to such an extent that, like the British Marines after 1923, its existence in any strength or its possession of effective weapons would be out of the question. In a duet, the Commanding General, Army Air Forces (General Spaatz) and the Army Chief of Staff (General Eisenhower) voiced the War Department's program for the Marine Corps:[9]

That the Marines should hereafter be allowed to fight "only in minor shore combat operations in which the Navy alone is interested."

"That the size of the Marine Corps be limited to small . . . lightly armed units, no larger than a regiment, to protect U. S. interests ashore in foreign countries, and to provide interior guard of naval ships and shore establishments."

That the total strength of the Corps (which had topped 485,000 only a year before) should in future be limited to 60,000 with no expansion in time of war (*i.e.*, abolition of the Marine Corps Reserve).

That Marine units be held below the size requiring the combining of arms (translation: nothing much bigger than machine guns for the Marine Corps).

That Marine aviation be merged without entity into what might be left of naval aviation, or be transferred outright to the Air Force.

That Marines be restricted to the "*waterborne* aspects of amphibious operations" (duty as landing craft crews and beach labor parties).

When the Navy recovered its breath, Admiral Nimitz, the new Chief of Naval Operations, responded that the War Department program was no less than a proposal "to eliminate the Marine Corps as an effective combat force."[10]

The legislative echo of the Collins Plan and of the War Department's Marine Corps proposal was soon heard. In January 1946, a Senate bill (S. 2044) was introduced embodying the substance of the Collins Plan. Insofar as the Corps was concerned, this legislation included authority that would permit the new Secretary of Defense to prescribe by fiat, without congressional check, the roles and missions of the Armed Services. This would remove the Marine Corps from the protection of Congress where it had stood since 1798, and would enable accomplishment of the War Department program by the stroke of a staff officer's pen. The Marine Corps had not faced such a threat (backed by the clear statements of intent by the Army and Air Force chiefs) since Theodore Roosevelt's day. At the same time, a less formal but even more trenchant statement of intent came in a public speech on unification by an outspoken Army general officer spokesman:[11]

As for the Marines, you know what Marines are. They are a small, fouled-up Army talking Navy lingo. We are going to put those Marines in the regular Army and make efficient soldiers out of them.

On 6 May 1946, General Vandegrift, square cut, blue eyed, and soft spoken, wearing his Medal of Honor ribbon, appeared before the Senate Naval Affairs Committee to give his views on S. 2044. In his hand was a prepared statement which owed much to the counsel and pen of Colonel Twining. General Vandegrift said:[12]

Marines have played a significant and useful part in the military structure of this nation since its birth. But despite that fact, passage of the unification legislation as now framed will in all probability spell extinction for the Marine Corps. I express this apprehension because of a series of facts which I feel must now be placed in your hands as an important element in your deliberations. They may be summarized in one simple statement—that the War Department is determined to reduce the Marine Corps to a position of studied military ineffectiveness—and the merger bill in its present form makes this objective readily attainable. . . .

It may be said that the apprehensions which I have just voiced are unnecessarily pessimistic, that the value of the Marine Corps is so obvious that its destruction is unthinkable—its perpetuation a foregone conclusion. Nevertheless, I know that the War Department's intentions with respect to the Marine Corps are well advanced and carefully integrated. . . . And I also know that the structure of the unification bill as it now stands will provide perfect implementation of those designs. . . .

In its capacity as a balance wheel Congress has on five occasions since 1829 reflected the voice of the people in examining and casting aside a motion which would damage or destroy the United States Marine Corps. . . . Now I believe that the cycle has repeated itself again, and that the fate of the Marine Corps lies solely and entirely with the Congress. . . .

The Marine Corps, then, believes that it has earned the right to have its future decided by the legislative body which created it—nothing more. Sentiment is not a valid consideration in determining questions of national security. We have pride in ourselves and in our past, but we do not rest our case on any presumed ground of gratitude owing us from the nation. The bended knee is not a tradition of our Corps. If the Marine as a fighting man has not made a case for himself after 170 years of service, he must go. But I think you will agree with me that he has earned the right to depart with dignity and honor, not by subjugation to the status of uselessness and servility planned for him by the War Department.

The national reaction to General Vandegrift's statement was instantaneous and favorable; that of the White House was equally instantaneous, but in the opposite direction. The Commandant had dealt S. 2044 a body blow, a kick in the groin, some thought, and, when Congress adjourned in August, the merger bill was unacted on.

As General Vandegrift realized, however, the death of S. 2044 was merely a reprieve insofar as the Marine Corps was concerned. Sure enough, in January 1947, another bill, nominally agreed to by all Services, was sent up to the Hill. This bill, too, included the same provisions which would permit administrative reduction of the Marine Corps to nonentity without recourse to Congress. To confirm General Vandegrift's fears, a draft executive order was circulated, which was to be issued by the President on passage of the bill, containing language of the most narrow and limiting character regarding the functions of the Marine Corps. As one widely read Washington columnist, David Lawrence, reported in March 1947, "A program of legislative sabotage is underway to undermine the future of the Marine Corps."[13]

In the face of this emergency, General Vandegrift turned to his most trusted advisors and formed a strategy board for the defense of the Marine Corps. This board, headed by General Edson, from whom it afterward took its name, included such resolute figures as General Thomas and Colonel Twining, as well as a handful of devoted juniors.[14] When an order was promulgated forbidding opposition testimony to the bill on the part of Navy and Marine officers, Edson, with the iron firmness and calm which had won him his Medal of Honor, submitted his request for immediate retirement and headed for Capitol Hill. In trenchant testimony, Edson, hero of the Ridge, took the legislation to pieces as General Vandegrift, under administration pressure, was no longer able to do. Public and congressional opinion rallied to the Marine Corps, the technical issue being whether the unification bill should or should not contain a congressional statement defining the roles and missions of the Marine Corps (as well as similar protective language for naval aviation).

Taking a neutral position, Forrestal noted in his diary on 18 April:[15]

To my mind, I said, the question of whether definition of functions was included in the law or not was of no consequence, but that (a) the Marines felt very strongly that it should be in and (b) the White House felt equally strongly that it should not be in. . . . Senator Saltonstall disagreed, saying that he would like to point out very respectfully that the Marines occupied a unique and singular place in the hearts of the people and that, whether or not Congress did anything about it, the people would.

Despite intense opposition from the proponents of merger (including Rear Admiral Forrest Sherman, Deputy CNO and one of the bill's spokesmen), a strongly sympathetic Congress included a charter for the modern Marine Corps in the legislation as passed.[16]

The salient features of the new law (the National Security Act of 1947) affecting the Marine Corps were as follows:

It reaffirmed the Corps' status as a military service within the Department of the Navy (a bone of contention both before and thereafter, for despite explicit ruling by the Judge Advocate General, groups in both Navy and Army found it convenient to dismiss the Marine Corps as part of, rather than partner of, the Navy).

It provided for the Fleet Marine Forces, both ground and aviation, and inferentially for the Marine Corps Reserve.

It gave the Marine Corps the mission of seizure and defense of advanced bases, as well as land operations incident to naval campaigns.

It gave the Marine Corps primary responsibility for development of amphibious warfare doctrines, tactics, techniques, and equipment employed by landing forces.

It afforded Marine Corps representation on the powerful Joint Staff (one agency the creation of which Edson feared, fought, and failed to stop).

It gave the Marine Corps collateral missions of providing guards for naval shore stations and ships' detachments; and, stemming back to the 1798 and 1834 Marine Corps laws, assigned to the Corps "such other duties as the President may direct."

In sacrificing a brilliant career for what he believed was right, General Edson had attained great results. Through his efforts, through those of a devoted nucleus of former Marines and Marine friends in Congress, and, most of all, through the unwavering support of the American people, the Corps was—for the time being—safe.

MARINES IN NORTH CHINA

In North China, the III Amphibious Corps had occupied four key cities: Peking, Tientsin, Tsingtao, and Chinwangtao. The last, less known than the other three, was the shipping point for the Kailan coal mines whose fuel kept lights burning as far south as Shanghai and whose output was essential to the economic stability of North China. Because of North China's proximity to Manchuria and her economic and agricultural resources, the Chinese Communist Eighth Route Army, located in northern China, was poised to take over North China as the Japanese surrendered, but the presence of the Marines frustrated this. Their mission, though never defined with clarity, certainly was not to fight the Chinese Communist forces, but it was most definitely to establish order (including repatriation of Japanese), open communications, and enable the produce and products of North China to move to market. Behind this, as stated by Secretary Forrestal in November 1945, lay another factor. "There is strong pressure to bring the Americans out of China, particularly the Marines," he wrote. "If we do, we invite a vacuum of anarchy in Manchuria, and it is obvious that into that vacuum ultimately . . . the Russians will flow."[17]

As the winter of 1945-46 set in, III Amphibious Corps was deployed as follows: Peking and Tangku, 5th Marines; Tientsin, corps, 1st Division, and 1st Wing headquarters, and 1st and 11th Marines (with the 11th billeted in the Chinese arsenal that Smedley Butler had helped capture in 1900); Chinwangtao and the intervening railroad, 7th Marines; Tsingtao and environs, 6th Division (soon to be redesignated as 3d Marine Brigade).

At first the Communists merely watched unenthusiastically while Chinese Nationalist units deployed into North China behind the Marines. Then, while General Marshall, drafted by President Truman as Ambassador at Large to China, tried ineffectively to compose the fundamental differences between the two factions, sabotage, roadblocks, sniping, and train wrecking became the order of the day. Marine outposts along the two key rail lines (Tientsin-Peking and Tientsin-Chinwangtao) and Marine train-guards were dangerously exposed, but somehow communications held.

Yet, as Forrestal told President Truman on his return from a flying inspection of the Far East, leaving the Marines so deployed rather than concentrated for offensive action was "a dangerous invitation to trouble."[18] The correctness of this warning was soon proved at Anping (where the Seymour relief column had finally been forced back toward Tientsin in 1900). Here, on 29 July 1946, an 11th Marines convoy en route to Peking encountered a completely unexpected roadblock. As the trucks halted, a burst of rifle and machine gun fire swept the column, and Chinese Communist riflemen attacked in a shower of grenades. The convoy commander was killed in the first volley, and, for four hours, the 40-man escort fought off a series of attacks in which four Marines were killed and 12 wounded. Finally, as the action slackened, the Marines loaded their dead and wounded onto undamaged vehicles and broke clear. A relief force retrieved the remaining trucks and found 12 Communist dead.

In another "incident," aviators forced down inside Communist-controlled territory were held for weeks before return, while, in the same month as the Anping incident, several enlisted Marines on a supply run (for ice for the beer cooler) were ambushed and kidnapped near Liou-Shou-Ying, on the railroad outside Peitaiho. A truce team secured their release.

The last serious action between Marines and the Communists took place on the night of 4-5 April 1947 at Hsin-Ho, the 1st Marine Division's ammunition supply point near Tangku, which was guarded by a small detachment of the 1st Battalion, 5th Marines. Already the object of two lesser attacks, the detachment was hit by some 350 Chinese in a well-planned operation whose object was to obtain ammunition. After attacking the dump perimeter at several widely separated points, the Chinese laid an ambush, including mines, for the relief column which they knew would come. Before finally withdrawing, the Chinese sustained six killed and 25 wounded, but five Marines were killed and 16 were wounded. This action was the most important, and unprovoked, of some 18 attacks against Marines by Chinese Communists between 1945 and 1948 in which ten Marines were killed and 33 wounded.[19]

These were but symptoms of deepening trouble. As the Chinese Nationalists crumbled, the Communists waxed stronger. By the end of 1946, it was clear that General Marshall had failed. By 1948, the one remaining American-occupied position in China was Tsingtao, where the Marines, now commanded by General Thomas, protected a base for the Seventh Fleet. Throughout 1947 and mid-1948, while the Communist cause prospered, pressure increased at home to withdraw the Marines. The decision was made harder by realization that if they once went, there would probably never be another return to China. On 1 November 1948, Mukden, capital of Manchuria, fell, and Admiral Oscar C. Badger, commanding the Seventh Fleet, got a warning order to evacuate dependents from Tsingtao and to plan for withdrawal of the Marines. Within a month, 33 Nationalist divisions, equipped and trained by the U.S. Army, had defected to the Communists. The end was at hand, and on 6 May 1949 the Marines said good-bye to China. "One thing is clear," Forrestal had written, "the Marines were the balance of order in China...."[20]

GENERAL VANDEGRIFT'S RETIREMENT

On the last day of 1947, General Vandegrift's term as Commandant expired. Even had he sought reappointment after his grueling commandancy, it would not have been tendered: memories of his stand on unification were too fresh among the White House staff, where, despite his final mild testimony on the 1947 legislation, he had, after 1946, come to be regarded as a symbol of intransigency. General Vandegrift's successor was General Clifton B. Cates, whose outstanding combat record dated back to Belleau Wood. General Cates had commanded in battle every unit from a platoon to a division, accumulating in the process three Purple Hearts, a Navy Cross, and a Distinguished Service Cross.

The 18th Commandant's tour had included administrative problems and external pressures unheard of in the history of the Corps. General Vandegrift had taken over at flood tide, but had stayed on to face the exasperations of demobilization, an abrupt change in favor at the White House, and two years of attack on the very existence of the Corps itself.

Although General Vandegrift and his advisors (notably General Thomas) did everything in their power to retain or restore the prewar mien and tone of the Corps, the going was uphill. In response to a nation-wide chorus of gripes from demobilized Army veterans, the War Department had convened a board headed by a retired officer, James H. Doolittle, to survey the postwar lot of the enlisted man. The widely publicized recommendations of the Doolittle Board, which in hindsight can only be called mischievous insofar as the regular forces were concerned, called for an almost complete leveling between officers and enlisted men, with a concomitant abandonment of disciplinary traditions proven in peace and war. Saluting was to be "deemphasized"; officer and enlisted uniforms were to be made alike; badges of rank made small and inconspicuous; officer and NCO privileges slashed. From the egalitarian tenor of the Doolittle report, one had impressions of the peasants and workers remolding the Tsarist armies of 1917. Everything was there but political commissars and comrades.

In face of the pressure and publicity of the Doolittle recommendations, to which the War Department largely acceded, the Marine Corps, rightly or not (Marine voices had been notably silent amid the gripers), adopted a service uniform which indeed made it hard to tell an officer from his men, put officer-style pockets onto redesigned enlisted blues, kept NCO chevrons small, and abolished the salty and distinctive enlisted man's barracks cap in favor of a conservative model like that of the officers.

When it became clear that the jumbled enlisted rank structure had to be reduced to postwar simplicity, there was an aberrant impulse to abandon even the traditional Marine names for NCO ranks; one proposal (which nearly carried) was to create the rank of "chief sergeant," followed by "sergeants 1st, 2d, and 3d class." This was only defeated by those who argued that the Corps, voluntarily eroding its own individuality, would present an amenable face to unification by adopting en bloc the Army's NCO rank titles then current. And so it came about that one of the last acts of the outgoing Commandant was to approve for postwar Marines, over misgivings, the Army's titles of master sergeant, technical sergeant, staff sergeant, sergeant, and corporal. That this stroke created a new Corps without gunnery sergeants and abolished rank titles in some cases going back to 1798 (such as quartermaster sergeant) was seemingly overlooked.

In spite of these debits (and in face of opposition from the War Department, which had long begrudged Marines their dress blues), General Vandegrift found the money to get the whole Corps back into blues, no small achievement.

Another hard decision was presented to General Vandegrift after passage of the unification act, when all Services were urged to bring their headquarters into the Pentagon, hitherto a War Department building. Although the Navy Department did so, General Vandegrift preferred the site and view (and better parking) of Arlington Annex, and was able to keep Marine Corps Headquarters on its hilltop, within earshot of the bugles in Arlington.

In summary, General Vandegrift had presided over the Corps in its greatest strength and prosperity (as he had commanded its field forces in one of their greatest campaigns); he had been forced, with little warning, to fight for the existence of the Corps and to see it pushed by external forces in directions no right-minded Marine would have chosen or condoned.

As for General Cates, resolute fighter that he was, the forthcoming years promised fighting enough if the Marine Corps was to be kept intact to fight again.

"THE NEW CONCEPT"

While the pilots of HMX-1 tried out their five new helicopters in early 1948, the staff at Quantico was getting down to the details of what soon became known as "The New Concept"; *i.e.*, a new concept for the execution of an amphibious assault using helicopters as landing craft and aircraft carriers as transports. By the standards of 1948, this was not revolutionary; it was breath-taking.

What the new concept envisaged, in brief, was an assault landing without concern for reefs, beaches, beach defenses, and surf; a landing from the air but free of the inflexibility, tactical disorder, vulnerability, and disorganization of parachute operations; an airborne attack independent of airfields and airheads; a landing force that could be launched from ships widely dispersed and under way miles offshore. At a time when the Marine Corps had only five two-passenger helicopters, Colonel Twining and his juniors worked out loading and embarkation data and landing diagrams for regimental assaults involving 240 machines of characteristics yet unattained, and ten aircraft carriers which the Navy had not yet decided to convert into helicopter assault ships.

The first test of the new concept came at Camp Lejeune in May 1948. For Exercise Packard II, the annual amphibious command post exercise of Marine Corps Schools, HMX-1 embarked aboard the USS *Palau*, a World War II jeep carrier of a type already almost out of date for fixed-wing aircraft. The problem was the landing of a (simulated) regiment. In actuality only 66 officers and men, and the headquarters and communication gear needed for the play of the problem, went ashore. But there were 103 carrier landings; flight-deck procedure was satisfactory. "The operation was entirely successful," reported Colonel Dyer, HMX-1's CO.[21] Theory had become fact. The era of vertical envelopment had arrived.

As 1948 wore on, new machines appeared. The Piasecki HRP-1, then the world's largest helicopter, dubbed "The Flying Banana," was added to Quantico's aircraft inventory. In November came the first published doctrine: Marine Corps Schools' *Employment of Helicopters (Tentative)— PHIB-31* in the "Amphibious Operations" series. Here was 1948's successor to 1934's *Tentative Landing Operations Manual.* Promptly Quantico's instructors took over the new text for their classes, while the schools troops and HMX-1 worked away in repeated exercises and demonstrations for anyone who would watch. One notable spectator, on 15 June 1950, was President Truman, who came to Quantico for a look at Marine capabilities. After watching a simulated helicopter assault, ex-Captain Truman grinned, patted the barrel of a 75-mm. pack howitzer used in the "landing," and, old-time field artilleryman that he was, said, "I like this best."[22]

BACK TO THE WALL

In mid-1948, General Cates said to a newspaper correspondent who had been with him on Guadalcanal:[23]

My biggest worry is to keep the Marine Corps alive. . . . There are lots of people here in Washington who want to prevent that, who want to reduce us to the status of Navy policemen or get rid of us entirely.

In the two years that followed, much occurred to confirm the Commandant's fears and to demonstrate that the Marine Corps was under pressure from many quarters.

During the war, it will be remembered, Admiral King and his staff had to a degree managed to interpose the Chief of Naval Operations between the Commandant and direct access to the Secretary of the Navy, a highly important prerogative. In 1947, while all attention was focused on the unification controversy, a Navy Department reorganization bill (Public Law 432) was enacted, in the words of King's successor, Fleet Admiral Nimitz,[24] "to perpetuate or to continue the functions of the Navy Department as they were found necessary during the war." While the Marine Corps was not mentioned in this legislation nor seriously considered in connection therewith, the language of the law could be construed to imply that the Marine Corps was part of the Navy proper and therefore under command of the CNO, a possibility which disturbed General Vandegrift from the moment when he learned of the bill's introduction. Nonetheless, the Marine Corps made no complaint until, at the eleventh hour before enactment, General Vandegrift (with Admiral Nimitz's support) asked for and obtained from Secretary of the Navy John L. Sullivan, written assurance—a gentlemen's agreement—that the new law was not intended to alter the Commandant's direct responsibility to the Secretary (which, after all, antedated the existence of the Chief of Naval Operations by 117 years), or otherwise alter the historical status of the Marine Corps within the Department of the Navy.[25]

For the moment, under the Sullivan-Vandegrift agreement, relations between Marine Corps Headquarters and CNO remained in harmonious balance. Before long, however, under a new Secretary of the Navy, a new CNO, and a new Secretary of Defense, the Marine Corps was destined to face rebuffs, reductions in strength, and exclusion from high councils when the future of the Corps was at stake.

The first example of such an exclusion came on 11 March 1948. On that date, in an effort to resolve the muffled but seething controversy over Service roles and missions, which had been kept going despite Congress' decisions in the Unification Act, James Forrestal, first Secretary of Defense, gathered the Joint Chiefs of Staff and their aides for a four-day conference in seclusion at Key West, Florida. Among numerous hot items on the agenda, there were few hotter than those dealing with the Marine Corps, whose Commandant was not among those present but was represented by the Chief of Naval Operations, Admiral Louis Denfeld, an obviously unsatisfactory arrangement to the Marine Corps.

Twelve days after the conference, Major General Alfred M. Gruenther of the Army, director of the newly formed Joint Staff, told the press some of the decisions which had been arrived at. Among these were three which adversely affected the Marine Corps:[26]

That future mobilization plans would put a four-division ceiling on the wartime strength of the Corps. Since the Corps had fielded six top-quality divisions in the recent war this seemed intended to hold down the Marine Corps, rather than to make efficient use of mobilization potential. As General Cates quickly pointed out to the Secretary of the Navy:[27]

If the Marine Corps, which maintains two divisions in peacetime, is limited to four divisions in wartime, it would have to expand by a mere 2:1 ratio, whereas the Army, with the equivalent of ten divisions in peacetime and a mobilization goal of 100 divisions, would have to undertake a 10:1 expansion. . . . If the latter ratio is within safe and effective limits of expansion, the former [for the Marine Corps] . . . is certainly indicative of wasted mobilization capabilities. I do not believe that the nation can afford any such waste.

That the Marine Corps would not exercise tactical command of units higher than corps level. This was a perpetuation of the informal limit imposed after Saipan, and an apparent step to insure that the Fleet Marine

Force headquarters with the two fleets would be kept desk bound and precluded from active operations or campaigns.

A final prohibition—meant to imply that Marines merely duplicate the Army—*that "the Marines are not to create a second land army,"*[28] a phrase which, like much of the thought behind the other two limitations, stemmed directly from the "1478" memoranda of 1946.[29]

In vain General Cates protested. Even though Admiral Denfeld afterward said he had no recollection of any understandings limiting the wartime size of the Corps or the headquarters it would field,[30] he was outremembered by the other participants in the conference, and the decisions stuck.

On 28 March 1949, James Forrestal was succeeded by another and very different Secretary of Defense, Louis A. Johnson, a West Virginia lawyer-politician, who, it was soon apparent, had little regard for either the Marine Corps or the Navy. By May, the new Secretary had requested the resignation of Secretary of the Navy Sullivan, and a new Secretary of the Navy was in office. In seeking a successor to John L. Sullivan, the White House staff told one candidate that the next secretary must give advance assurances that he would not oppose eventual abolition of the Marine Corps or transfer of naval aviation to the Air Force.

Secretary Johnson's personnel planning soon made it clear what was intended for the Marine Corps. In 1948, the last year under Forrestal, the Fleet Marine Force was 35,086 strong, with 11 infantry battalions organized into two understrength divisions, and 23 aviation squadrons forming two wings. In the succeeding year, Secretary Johnson cut the FMF to 30,988, a 14 per cent reduction. For fiscal year 1950 (beginning mid-1949) came still another cut, this time by 5 per cent, to 29,415, which finally forced General Cates to reduce the FMF infantry battalions to eight; in the same year came a directive to decommission 11 aircraft squadrons, reducing the number to 12, a 48 per cent drop in Marine aviation's combat strength. When the Korean War intervened in June 1950, the forthcoming year's plans called for a further reduction of the Fleet Marine Force to six battalions and 12 squadrons comprising 23,952 officers and men, a 19 per cent drop for the year, and a 33 per cent aggregate cut during the two calendar years since Johnson had taken office.[31] An indication of the thinking behind these cuts was the refusal of high-level planners, despite repeated protests by General Cates, to recognize in war plans even the existence of the two Marine divisions; in the defense planning of the Johnson era, the standard unit of measure of Marine Corps forces was the infantry battalion landing team, a striking throwback to the "1478" proposals that the Marine Corps organization be limited to "lightly armed units no larger than a regiment."[32]

An even more pointed indication of Secretary Johnson's thinking came to light in the Fleet Marine Force structure imposed by the Secretary of Defense for fiscal year 1951: although by stringent economy, General Cates had been able, in the face of manpower cuts mentioned above, to maintain a total of eight battalion landing teams in the two divisions, Secretary Johnson nonetheless directed that two BLTs be disbanded and the total reduced to six. As General Cates stated:[33]

> It is not merely to be a question of cuts in men and money—although they are severe enough. We are being told in detail—and told by the Department of Defense—*where and how* these cuts are to be made—by striking into the heart of our combat forces. . . . I cannot agree that a cut so pointedly directed at reducing the combat strength of this highly effective organization is an economy.

Lest there be any doubt about the administration's fundamental intentions, Secretary of the Army Kenneth C. Royall testified to a Senate committee in April 1949 that President Truman should, in Royall's verbal counterpoint, "make the Marines part of the Army, or the Army part of the Marines." When asked by Senator Saltonstall if he were advocating that the Secretary of Defense "abolish the Marine Corps and make it part of the Army," Royall replied, "That is exactly what I am proposing."[34]

Marine aviation was in even deeper trouble than was the Line. In mid-April 1949, Secretary Johnson assembled a group of influential Washington correspondents in his office for a private luncheon and revealed that the papers directing transfer of Marine aviation to the Air Force were on his desk. On 26 April, in an off-record speech at the Waldorf-Astoria in New York, he announced that there were "too many Air Forces,"[35] and that he was taking steps to do away with Marine aviation. By the end of April, well-founded rumors had reached such proportions that Chairman Carl Vinson of the House Armed Services Committee took a hand. Sending for Secretary Johnson on 28 April, he laid down the law: Marine aviation would not be abolished or transferred, and any such future steps affecting the Marine Corps would please be referred in advance to Congress before action was taken or predicted. In the manner of a strict old schoolmaster making an errant pupil write out 50 times "I promise not to . . .," Mr. Vinson then obtained the following memorandum from the Secretary:[36]

I have been hearing the rumors about the transfer of Marine and naval aviation to some other branch of the Service.

1. Under the law this cannot be done.

2. It has not been under contemplation, and from time to time numerous statements have been made by me to that effect.

3. There are no such studies being carried on in the National Military Establishment. Furthermore, I want you to know that before any step of this kind would be seriously considered, I should ask permission to discuss the matter before the Committees of both Houses of Congress.

Louis Johnson

POST-WAR STATUS OF THE FMF

While the future existence of the Fleet Marine Force was being challenged, its position within the Navy and Marine Corps scheme of things was in the process of profound modification, to understand which it is necessary to look backward a few years.

In 1917, when President Wilson directed Secretary Daniels to detach a force of Marines for service with the Army, he wrote:

You will direct the Major General Commandant of the Marine Corps to report to the Secretary of War for this duty.

No mention was made of the Chief of Naval Operations in this order, and this instance illustrated the status of Marine operating forces during the period before 1933. In that year, as we have seen, General Russell recommended that an expeditionary force:

. . . be included in the Fleet organization as an integral part thereof, subject to the orders, for tactical employment, of the Commander-in-Chief, U. S. Fleet.

Russell's proposal was accomplished by General Order 241. Under this order the Marine expeditionary force was to be maintained by the Commandant in readiness for operations with the Fleet and was "for tactical employment" to be part of the Fleet, but the Commandant was to designate the units to serve in it, and it was to be under the Commandant's command except when embarked with the Fleet or when engaged in Fleet exercises. That the troops designated for the FMF were operating forces of the Marine Corps (as contrasted to operating forces of the Navy) was never questioned.

By the end of World War II, however, Fleet Marine Force, Pacific, had become a type command of the Pacific Fleet, just as submarines and destroyers were; moreover, all the combatant forces of the Marine Corps were assigned thereto and had been under the command of Fleet commanders continuously for from one to five years. The exceptional circumstance had become the rule. Following the war, no effort was made by Marine Corps Headquarters to detach operating units from the Fleet Marine Force or to establish the Commandant's undivided command over units not engaged in Fleet exercises. When the Atlantic Fleet got its Fleet Marine Force in 1946, command relationships identical with those in the Pacific were adopted. And in 1947, when the Navy informally queried Marine Corps Headquarters to determine whether it was desired to keep General Order 241 on the books as an effective General Order, a heedless staff officer let the matter slip through his fingers.

As, by 1947, there were no combat forces ordinarily under command of the Commandant, the once clear distinction between Marine Corps combat forces and operating forces of the Navy was in danger of disappearing through general use of the term, "the operating forces," to mean the operating forces of the Navy under command of the Chief of Naval Operations as provided for by the 1947 Navy Department reorganization law. More important for the future, in danger of being lost was the principle that Marine Corps forces (*i.e.*, FMF units) *could* be detached from the operating forces of the Navy.

When, as will be related, Admiral Forrest Sherman succeeded Admiral Denfeld as CNO in 1949, the issues which had been temporarily deferred by the gentlemen's agreement among General Vandegrift, Admiral Nimitz, and Secretary Sullivan were quickly precipitated. That Admiral Sherman accorded little weight to the agreement in contrast to his embracing interpretation of Public Law 432 was soon evident. He set about trying to establish the precedent of CNO's military command over the Marine Corps and its Commandant, and from Defense Secretary Johnson he obtained explicit permission "to have a free hand in the interior organization of Marine divisions."[37] He even asserted that every ship's detachment was in effect a Fleet Marine Force unit (and that, vice versa, FMF units were practically no different from ships' detachments)—a throwback to the days before 1903 when sundowning transport commanders asserted military command over Huntington's and Lejeune's battalions. Proceeding along these lines, Admiral Sherman tried during 1949 and early 1950 to interpose the office of CNO between General Cates and the Secretary of the Navy, and to reduce

Marine Corps Headquarters to a technical bureau—like Personnel or Supplies and Accounts—in the Navy Department.

Events were destined, however, to correct this trend.

". . . DENIED VOICE, VOTE, OR INFORMATION"

As an outgrowth of the controversy between the newly hatched Air Force and the Navy which had continued unabated since 1946, the House Armed Services Committee began a series of hearings in October 1949 on the related subjects of Unification and Strategy. Although the purpose of these hearings, among other matters, was to give the Navy its day in court, inter-Service tensions were not markedly dissipated. Following testimony by Admiral Denfeld and by Generals Cates and Vandegrift, ably seconded for aviation by Brigadier General Megee, General Omar Bradley, USA, Chairman of the JCS, delivered a statement which was interpreted by many as a personal attack on Admiral Denfeld and was described by the committee[38] as intentionally slighting to the Marine Corps. As an aside, the general also announced that amphibious operations as then practiced by the Navy and Marines were a dead letter and that there would never be another major amphibious assault.

A week after the close of hearings, Secretary of the Navy Matthews removed Admiral Denfeld from office as a result of his testimony to Congress. Admiral Sherman, the Navy's most extreme advocate of unification, succeeded Denfeld. At the same time, Secretary Matthews considered action against General Cates, but Louis Johnson observed that "it was politically unwise to bring any pressure whatsoever upon the Commandant of the Marine Corps."[39]

Although the burden of testimony during the hearings dealt with the woes of naval aviation, ample evidence came to the Committee that the Marine Corps was also in process of being substantially reduced. Further, despite the safeguards written by Congress into the 1947 security act, this objective was, by 1949, within measurable reach. For fiscal year 1950, General Cates had cut the supporting establishment to the bone in order to keep fighting units intact. Now, as we have seen, he had been told by the Pentagon to cut deeper—to reduce the number of infantry battalions to a point where the Marine division would no longer be an effective fighting force. In a blunt statement on 17 October 1949, General Cates testified that self-defense was "not easy when you lack voice, vote, or information." Continuing, he said:[40]

We do not believe there has been a complete acceptance in all quarters, of that part of the National Security Act relating to the Marine Corps. On the contrary, it appears to us that the power of the budget, the power of coordination, and the power of strategic direction of the armed forces have been used as devices to destroy the operating forces of the Marine Corps. . . . I likewise entertain well warranted fears that it is planned to employ such forces as will remain to us, not on their intended mission but scattered in minor units around the world assigned to duties which ignore their special training and unique offensive capabilities.

Adverting to another matter equally serious and perhaps even more pressing for the moment, General Cates then testified that a virtual freeze had been placed on the amphibious training of the Fleet Marine Force during the forthcoming year. The Chief of Naval Operations had allocated all available amphibious shipping to the Army for a training program of its own, which would culminate in a large non-Marine amphibious maneuver with the Fleet in Puerto Rico.

Under sympathetic questioning by the Committee, General Cates then disclosed that, in April, Secretary Sullivan had asked that the Marine Commandant be allowed to sit in attendance when the Joint Chiefs of Staff took up agenda items dealing with the Marine Corps; Secretary Johnson's reply (relying on Public Law 432) was:[41]

I cannot see any need or justification for giving the Commandant of the Marine Corps a special role which is not accorded to the chiefs of various other arms and services which are considered integral parts of the Army, Navy and Air Force, respectively.

In other words, as General Cates put it elsewhere,[42] ". . . attempting to diminish the Marines, by an administrative device, to a position comparable to the Veterinary Corps or the Bureau of Yards and Docks."

The Commandant's basic thesis, that the top structure of the Defense Department did not afford adequate representation for Marine Corps views in matters of vital concern to the Corps (and to the national security), was accepted by the Armed Services Committee. The committee report, published four months later, recommended that the Commandant of the Marine Corps be made a member of the Joint Chiefs of Staff. Representative Vinson thereupon introduced a bill (H.R. 7580) to this effect.

Representative Vinson's bill was the partial result of certain conclusions which had become clear to advocates of a strong Marine Corps during 1948-

49. These views, which General Cates's testimony amply confirmed, added up to two main points: that if the Corps were to survive, the Commandant must gain access to the level—that is, the JCS—at which the important decisions relative to the Corps were now made (direct access to the Secretary of the Navy, though still important, was no longer enough); and, in view of the series of personnel cuts imposed administratively on the Fleet Marine Force by the Defense Department, some type of manpower floor must be established below which it would be impossible to push the Marine Corps except with the consent of Congress. A move to effect the latter was proposed by Admiral Halsey, always a staunch friend of the Corps, in 1949. Halsey's suggestion was that a legally fixed constant percentage of the defense manpower appropriation each year be assigned to the Marine Corps; six per cent was the admiral's idea at the time, as he put it in a speech, "Six per cent spells security!"

Although neither the Vinson Bill nor Admiral Halsey's six per cent (simultaneously introduced as S. 2177, by four senators and 56 representatives) was acted on by Congress that year, they focused public and congressional attention on the Marine Corps' problems and crystallized a good deal of thinking on what the Corps most needed to remain an effective fighting component of the defense establishment. As 1950 dawned, with nothing apparently ahead but the prospective diminution of the FMF to six battalions and 12 squadrons, an editorial ground swell, initiated by the Hearst chain, stirred on behalf of the Corps. From a rising volume of congressional and White House mail, it was apparent that people were becoming uneasy about the Marine Corps.

THE CORPS SCENE

As might be expected, the years following the war were years of change as the Corps accustomed itself to its larger peacetime strength and to the new environment of the defense establishment.

One noticeable change in the complexion of the Corps was that sea duty, which (except during the two World Wars) had for many years past absorbed about a third of the officers and men in the Corps, now claimed about five per cent. This was not because the number of ships' detachments had decreased, but because the FMF had assumed a position of permanent size and importance as a national force in readiness. When John Harris became Colonel Commandant in 1864, he had had 20 years at sea; in 1909, the eight representative line officers who testified against T.R.'s assault on the Corps had chalked up a total of 73 years' sea duty among them (one, Colonel Paul St. C. Murphy, had served 11 tours afloat). After World War I, while every Marine officer could count on at least one cruise afloat during his career, two was the norm, and three not unusual. By 1950 such expectations no longer existed. Only about a hundred ships' detachment billets existed at any given time for Marine officers, while fewer than three thousand enlisted men could similarly serve. What this dilution of its naval character portended for the Corps could not be clearly discerned in 1950, but it was a factor to be noted and taken into account.

In partial compensation for the decline in sea duty came an innovation. In late 1946, a U. S. Mediterranean Squadron (later the Sixth Fleet) was re-established. With it came and remained a floating battalion of Marines from the 2d Division, rotated half-yearly, showing the flag again off the shores of Tripoli.

Another change that marked the postwar scene was in the composition of the enlisted corps. In the late 1930s, 55 per cent of all enlisted men were privates at the munificent stipend of $20.80 a month. Eighteen per cent more were privates first class, while the remaining 27 per cent were NCOs, predominantly chosen for leadership capabilities. By 1950 the distribution (not to mention the pay) had altered sharply: Only 15 per cent of the enlisted men were privates, 45 per cent were Pfcs, and a whopping 40 per cent were NCOs. What this reflected was the enormous increase in technical requirements for the modern Fleet Marine Force, as well as the abolition of specialist ratings, already noted. The fact that nearly half the Corps wore chevrons willy-nilly, diluted the status and authority of individual noncommissioned officers, while the fact that many promotions had to be made for technical skills rather than leadership caused concern among officers and NCOs alike.

Still another change—and this one most definitely welcome—was the postwar formalization between the State Department and the Marine Corps of previous piecemeal arrangements to use Marines as security guards in American embassies and legations throughout the world. The first guard of this type, six hand-picked noncommissioned officers, had been established in the American Embassy, Moscow, when, in 1934, the United States resumed diplomatic relations with Russia. Since, as one diplomatic historian noted,[43] "Marines have been at home in embassies for generations," the arrangement worked effortlessly, and, under the pressures of the "cold war," was made permanent. As an ultimate result, almost a thousand Marines, mostly noncommissioned officers, were henceforth to stand guard at more than 90 diplomatic posts throughout the world. General Heywood, remembering the controversy over the U. S. Legation guard at Peking, would have been pleased.

A profound change which many believed might undermine the discipline of the Corps was the substitution in 1950 of the Uniform Code of Military Justice for the honored and proven Articles for the Government of the Navy, dating back to the earliest days of the Naval Services. The new code imposed Army-type forms and terminology, oceans of extra paperwork, and elaborate, lawyer-ridden procedures onto a Corps which had prided itself on quick, simple, and severe justice for all offenders. Most missed by commanding officers was their former power to confine intractables on bread and water for a season of reflection.

To make certain that the new Corps was well educated, both Generals Vandegrift and Cates paid much attention to the development of Quantico. The postwar pattern of officer schooling was rigorous and firmly enforced. Basic School was re-established, no longer on the barracks square at the Philadelphia Navy Yard, but at Brown Field, Quantico's original though long superseded air facility. For company officers and junior field officers there was the Junior School, located in the newly constructed Geiger Hall; for the most senior field officers, the Senior Course held sway in Breckinridge Hall, site of the wartime Command and Staff Course initiated in 1943. In early 1950, to emphasize Quantico's dual function as a center both for research and for teaching, Marine Corps Schools was formally divided into two coequal parts: the Marine Corps Educational Center and the Marine Corps Development Center, the latter absorbing the old Equipment Board which had served so well since 1933.

A cherished tradition barely missed the axe when in 1949 Secretary Johnson abruptly prohibited future observances of November 10th as Birthday of the Marine Corps. Such was the immediate reaction throughout the Corps, from General Cates right down, that even Louis Johnson budged to the extent of conceding that there was nothing in the books to keep Marines from celebrating their birthday as a family party, and November 10th was duly observed in 1949 and ever after.

A more private shock was reserved for General Vandegrift when he learned that the Commandant of the Marine Corps was about to be dropped from the select list of top Service officials entitled to a chauffeur and limousine; General Cates was equally shaken to discover in 1949 that the new Defense Department's table of protocol honors omitted the special formalities, gun salutes, and precedence always hitherto specified for the Commandant. Both the limousine and the honors were saved by stiff remonstrance, but the episodes are indicative of the climate of the time.

Headquarters Marine Corps witnessed the final demise of the organization established in 1817, when, on 16 July 1946, the Pay Department and office of the Paymaster were abolished, and when, on the same day, the Quartermaster's Department was more stylishly redesignated the Supply Department and the Quartermaster became the Quartermaster General. The last Paymaster was Major General R. R. Wright, and the last Quartermaster (who carried on almost a decade longer as Quartermaster General) was Major General W. P. T. Hill, famed for one of the longest memories and some of the quickest answers (especially before congressional committees) in the history of the Corps.

As 1947 arrived, General Geiger was fighting for his life at Bethesda; three weeks later, he died, having served his Corps on active duty for 41 years. Less than two months later General Russell died in California, the Fleet Marine Force his monument. For the Marines who survived, the forthcoming decade promised glory, frustration, and challenge.

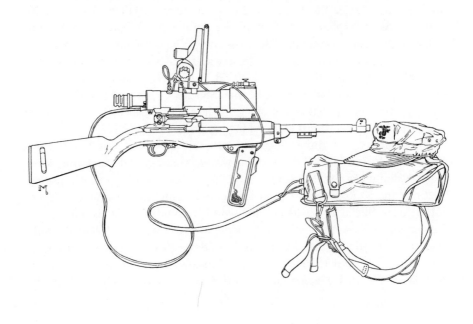

10 ...IN THE SNOW
OF FAR-OFF NORTHERN LANDS *1950-1953*

The Marines were ready to fight; if they had not been,
we might still be fighting in the Pusan perimeter.
—HANSON W. BALDWIN

I N JUNE 1950 the most imminent danger which appeared ahead for the
Marine Corps was another slash in strength: by the 30th of the month the
Corps, which had numbered 78,715 enlisted men a year before, was to be
cut back to 67,025. Fleet Marine Force infantry battalions had already
shrunk to two two-platoon rifle companies; light artillery batteries supposed
to have six howitzers could only man four. The 1st Marine Division at
Pendleton, trained and hard though it was from two years under Graves
B. Erskine, was about the size of a World War II regimental combat team.
Keeping pace with the erosion of the Marine Corps and with General
Bradley's prediction that amphibious warfare was finished, the Navy was
decommissioning transports and junking landing craft.

On Saturday, 24 June, Secretary of State Acheson, put through an
urgent call to President Truman who was at home in Independence, Missouri: Communist North Korean divisions were invading South Korea.
Next day the United Nations Security Council made the Communist breach
of the peace official and called on the world "to render every assistance." As
Russian-made T-34 tanks rolled into Seoul and Yak fighters strafed the railroad yards, President Truman ordered the Seventh Fleet and American air
units in the Far East to help the fast collapsing South Korean army. Three
days later, General MacArthur, United States commander in Tokyo, re-

ported that only American ground troops could prevent complete disaster. The President agreed, and, on 30 June 1950, the Korean Incident became the Korean War.

The morning after President Truman sent the Seventh Fleet into action, General Cates was in conference with Secretary Matthews and Admiral Sherman, urging that the FMF be employed. Their replies were noncommittal. United States ground forces were not yet committed; moreover, there was some sentiment on the Joint Staff during those first days that the Korean "police action" might be a good one to settle without Marines— a new and interesting precedent. General Cates reacted typically. Acting on his own responsibility upon his return to Arlington Annex, he sent the 1st Division a warning order to get ready to go to war.

By 1 July, while ill-prepared and flabby occupation troops from Japan were frantically mounting out for Korea and the North Koreans were advancing southward at will, more interest was shown in the possibility of using Marines. Prodded by General Cates, Admiral Sherman asked for estimates on how long it would take before a Marine force could start for Korea from the West Coast. Armed with this information, Admiral Sherman sent a private message for the eyes of General MacArthur, via Rear Admiral Turner Joy, naval commander in the Far East—for the asking, MacArthur could have a Marine brigade complete with supporting air; did he want it? Faced with mounting catastrophe, MacArthur radioed the JCS for immediate assignment of just such a brigade. When the Joint Chiefs convened to consider the general's request, General Cates showed up uninvited; the situation had become so grave that he was allowed to sit in, and the dispatch of Marines to Korea was promptly approved.

"NO UNIT IN THIS BRIGADE WILL RETREAT"

The 1st Provisional Marine Brigade, the first troops to be sent to Korea from the United States, sailed from San Diego on 14 July, as soon as the Navy could get transports alongside. Composed of the 5th Marines (Lieutenant Colonel R. L. Murray), one battalion of the 11th, MAG-33 (Brigadier General T. J. Cushman) with three fighting squadrons, and supporting troops (including a helicopter detachment), the brigade numbered 6,534 Marines. The brigade commander was Brigadier General Edward A. Craig, who had commanded the 9th Regiment during the Guam campaign and served as Harry Schmidt's G-3 on Iwo Jima.

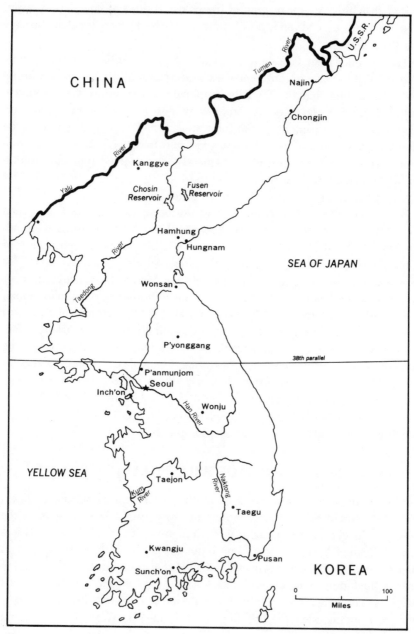

Korea

The measure of General Craig as a commander was made clear in his remarks to the brigade officers just before sailing:[1]

. . . It has been necessary for troops now fighting in Korea to pull back at times, but I am stating now that no unit in this brigade will retreat except on orders from an authority higher than the 1st Marine Brigade. You will never receive an order to retreat from me.

As soon as the transports cleared San Diego, General Craig and his staff flew to Tokyo, via Pearl Harbor. Here, they stopped for a conference with General Shepherd, commanding FMFPac, who had just returned from four days in the Far East. Among much of interest was word that, as a result of General Shepherd's missionary work in Tokyo, General MacArthur favored employment of the Marine brigade as an integral air-ground team.

News of even greater import that General Shepherd brought back with him (and passed to General Cates when they met at Camp Pendleton on 12 July) was that General MacArthur was asking the JCS to assign him the entire 1st Marine Division, at war strength, for an amphibious counterstroke. This development had materialized during a private conference between Generals Shepherd and MacArthur on 10 July. After harking back to the New Britain campaign, when the 1st Division had served him well, General MacArthur rose, pointed the stem of his corncob pipe at the port of Inchon, on the west coast of Korea, and said, "If I only had the 1st Marine Division under my command again, I would land them here and cut the North Korean armies attacking the Pusan perimeter from their logistic support and cause their withdrawal and annihilation."

General Shepherd's reply was prompt—"Why don't you ask for the 1st Marine Division, General?"

"Do you think I can get it?" shot back MacArthur.

General Shepherd then suggested that MacArthur immediately ask the JCS for the division, adding that he (Shepherd) could have it ready, less the RCT already in Korea, by 1 September. It was then agreed that General Shepherd would draw up a dispatch for MacArthur to send to Washington requesting the division. Composing the message in an anteroom presented few difficulties, since General Shepherd had arrived with the draft of just such a recommendation in his pocket, awaiting the propitious moment.[2]

MacArthur's original idea—boldly conceived amid disaster—had been to hold the Marine brigade in Japan until it could be reinforced by the 2d Infantry Division for use in an amphibious attack along the lines he had revealed to General Shepherd. By the time the Marine brigade's transports reached Korea and caught up with General Craig's party, two weeks after sailing, the situation had deteriorated so rapidly that the brigade's first job was to backstop the perimeter around Pusan into which shaken Army and ROK (Republic of Korea) units were already streaming.

On 3 August, within hours after the brigade debarked at Pusan, Marine F4Us from VMF-214 ("The Black Sheep," Boyington's old outfit) aboard the small carrier USS *Sicily* scored first blood in an air strike over Inchon.[3] On 7 August, eight years to the day after the Guadalcanal landing, and 32 since Belleau Wood, the 5th Marines were in hot action, plugging holes in the Pusan perimeter.

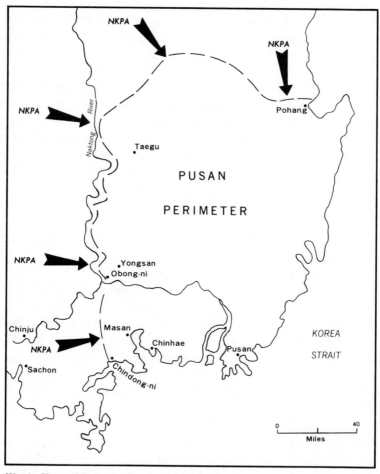

War in Korea–Maximum Communist Advance

The first phase of the brigade's operations was an attack to the southwest beyond Masan. This was the first genuine offensive action that the hard-pressed American forces had been capable of since the start of hostilities. Ironically, the first Marine casualties came from trigger-happy Army troops unaware of their presence, and paradoxically the 11th Marines, who lost a howitzer to sharp enemy counterbattery fire, took more losses on the first day than the infantry. The weather, typical of South Korea in August, was scorching and steamy. Temperatures ranged from 100° to 112°F. Water was at a premium. The terrain was that which had appalled Captain Tilton in 1871—". . . a sort of chopped sea of immense hills and deep ravines lying in every conceivable direction."

During the week that the brigade attacked toward the towns of Sachon and Chinju, the Marines got their first taste of the enemy. They found him spirited, tenacious, well trained, and generously equipped with Russian gear. Used to having the campaign their own way, the North Koreans fought confidently, but reacted with considerable surprise when they found themselves facing troops who gave no ground, hung on to their weapons, and brought in their wounded and dead.

For the first three days, the brigade, with parts of the 5th and 27th Infantry attached, fought to clear Tosan, a key road junction, which controlled the routes toward Sachon and Chinju. Chinju was held in force by North Korean veterans of the Communist armies in China. By 9 August the pressure of the Marine brigade and its air support was too much, and the Reds began to withdraw. Pursuing towards Kosong (on the way to Sachon), the 5th Marines covered ten miles. Next day (the 11th) came a windfall. About noon, as the 11th Marines began shelling Kosong, a North Korean motorized regiment took to the road in haste; while the artillery poured it on, VMF-323, flying from the jeep carrier *Badoeng Strait,* raked the column with rockets and 20-mm. guns. More than 40 vehicles were burned out and most of the remaining hundred or so abandoned, including numerous Russian jeeps with American lend-lease Ford engines.

On 12 August as the brigade forged forward toward Sachon, a hurry-call came in to detach the 3d Battalion, 5th Marines, for a rearward move of 25 miles. Two thousand Communist troops had infiltrated the perimeter, overrun two Army artillery battalions, and blocked the main road to the front. Thus, while the 1st Battalion of the 5th Regiment slugged its way through a hotly fought ambush just short of Sachon, the 3d Battalion attacked simultaneously in the opposite direction on another front 25 miles away. Co-ordination of the day's far-flung fighting was accomplished by helicopter. Both battalions came through in fine style, and the brigade was poised to take Sachon next day.

Unfortunately for the hopes of all hands, Sachon remained untaken by the Marines. At nightfall, General Craig was ordered to pull back post-haste and occupy a new sector, 75 miles northward. A Communist division had pushed across the Naktong River—the Marne of the Pusan perimeter—and, as in 1918, the 5th Marines were being thrown in to turn the tide.

On 15 August, as the Marine rifle companies slogged through Miryang, in what would soon become known as "the Naktong Bulge," a British liaison officer watched them and reported to his headquarters in Tokyo:[4]

I am heartened that the Marine Brigade will move against the Naktong salient to-morrow. They are faced with impossible odds . . . but these Marines have the swagger, confidence, and hardness that must have been in Stonewall Jackson's army. They remind me of the Coldstreams at Dunkerque.

The 4th North Korean (NKPA) Division was across the Naktong in strength near Obong-Ni and pushing the battered 24th U. S. Infantry Division before it. Under operational control of the 24th Division, the Marine brigade's job was to counterattack, liquidate the enemy bridgehead, and regain the river line. The immediate problem was to take a steep ridge (Obong-Ni on the maps, "No-Name Ridge" to the correspondents) which frowned directly across the brigade front and was held by a Communist regiment. Colonel Murray formed the 5th Regiment in column of battalions, 2d Battalion in the lead. The battalion's two thin rifle companies pushed across the open rice fields, bare and fire-swept as the wheat field at Belleau Wood; then, they attacked up the steep ridge. Three times the Marines reached the top; three times they had to pull back. The fourth time, in mid-afternoon, with the help of carrier-based Marine air, they stayed, and what was left of the battalion was relieved by the 1st Battalion, who set their teeth for a stormy night.

Before dusk came the ominous clamor of tanks. Russian T-34s, hitherto spoken of as invulnerable by survivors of the headlong flight south, were counterattacking on the 5th Marines' right. Marines stood to their rocket-launchers and recoilless rifles, while a section of Marine tanks sallied forward. First blood came unexpectedly to a Corsair on station overhead. Spotting the advance, the aircraft swooped down with bombs and rockets, blasting the rearmost tank and scattering its supporting infantry. As the remaining T-34s approached, the Marines stood their ground; when the leading tank was a hundred yards away, the bazooka-men let go, followed by well-aimed rounds from the recoilless rifles and 90-mm. armor-piercing shell from the Marine tanks. One after another the Russian tanks were ripped apart and set afire by the resolute blast of fire. Amid the burning hulks, it became clear that Communist tanks need hold no special terror for troops willing to stand and fight. Nevertheless, the Marines' prowess against the T-34s so impressed General J. Lawton Collins, the Army's Chief of Staff, who was on a flying visit to Korea, that he sought and obtained a memorandum from General Craig as to how the Marines did it.

Following the tank action came a night of repeated infiltrations and, after midnight, a series of hard attacks that all but pushed the 1st Battalion, 5th Marines, off the ridge. As dawn approached and it became evident that the Marines were there to stay, the NKPA division commander issued orders for his rear units to begin retiring across the Naktong. By daylight, as the 3d Battalion, 5th Marines, hooked around the right flank of the ridge to take the next hill, the Communist retreat became a rout. Every airplane that MAG-33 could fly joined in the slaughter; the 11th Marines hammered the river crossings; when night descended again, the air group's night fighter squadron, VFM(N)-513, took over. On the 19th, the only North Koreans left in the Naktong Bulge were dead ones amid the flotsam of a wrecked division. Thirty-four large-caliber artillery pieces were taken by the brigade, including five U.S. Army 105-mm. howitzers recaptured. Enemy casualties exceeded 4,000.

For almost two weeks the Marine brigade was held in reserve as other reinforcements began to arrive and the North Koreans regrouped. Then, on 1 September, the Communists hit the perimeter with all they had, and at the same sore spot. Two days later they were over the Naktong once more, and the 1st Marine Brigade (which was trying to get ready for its part in the forthcoming amphibious operation) was again marching to the sound of the guns. The brunt of the enemy attack into the Naktong Bulge had fallen on the 2d Infantry Division, of which the 4th Marine Brigade had years earlier been a part, and the 5th Marines had the experience of again advancing through the 9th Infantry, this time west of Yongsan instead of in France. Unfortunately, the 9th Infantry was in trouble: having been attacked on 3 September by an NKPA division, they were reeling back as the 5th Regiment breasted its way forward with the 1st and 2d Battalions in line. In the resulting collision, the 9th NKPA Division came out second best, and, after three days' hard fighting, including the destruction of numerous enemy tanks, had been hustled back six miles by the Marines.

Captured Japanese command post on Tarawa.

Tank shields men on Saipan beach.

Semper Fidelis. This Marine, a member of the "Fighting Fourth Marine Division," threatens the enemy even in death on the beach at Iwo Jima. His bayonet fixed and ready for the charge, he was killed by intense enemy sniper fire during the attack.

Mount Surabachi continues to resist. Flames visible are from a burning American vehicle. Time, 8:40 a.m.

Lieutenant General Graves B. Erskine at first command post on Motoyama Airfield #1, Iwo Jima.

At Mindoro, Philippines, Marines of the 3rd Marine Division (Rein.), Fleet Marine Force, Pacific, from Okinawa, Japan, cross a three-strand rope bridge, one of three types of bridges set up by the 1st Pioneer Battalion for Operation Tulungan.

Marine Corps Air Station, El Toro, California. A group shot.

Colonel Robert D. Heinl, Jr., commanding officer, U.S. Marine Detachment, Edinburgh Military Tattoo (Scotland) and Brussels Exposition (Belgium).

With the situation well in hand and with the vital ground overlooking the Naktong again retaken by the brigade, 2d Division troops could safely take over on 5 September to permit the Marines to continue urgent preparations for General MacArthur's amphibious end run.

Thus ended the 1st Marine Brigade's series of hard and well-fought battles to save the Pusan perimeter. As the first reinforcements to sail from home and as the only United States troops in the perimeter who never tasted defeat, General Craig and his Marines could well hold their heads high. The cost had been 902 casualties, of whom 172 were killed. Not a single Marine had allowed himself to be taken prisoner. In 38 days the Marine brigade marched 380 miles and fought three major engagements—each a counterattack—the loss of any one of which would have jeopardized the United Nations position in Korea. Marine Air Group 33 flew 1,511 sorties, 995 of them in close support of Marine or Army ground units; moreover, Marine pilots flew helicopters in combat for the first time in history. Of the Marine air-ground team in the perimeter, one Army regimental commander wrote to Washington:[5]

The Marines on our left were a sight to behold. Not only was their equipment superior or equal to ours, but they had squadrons of air in direct support. They used it like artillery. . . . We just have to have air support like that or we might as well disband the Infantry and join the Marines. . . .

Most of all, though, the Marine brigade's fine performance was an object lesson in another Marine Corps specialty: readiness. Depleted and slashed to the bone though the Corps was in 1950, what little remained was still ready to fight and ready on an instant's notice. The brigade's best tribute was Hanson Baldwin's short sentence in the *New York Times:* "The Marines were ready. . . ."[6]

MOBILIZING THE MARINE CORPS

The Marine brigade which had been flung into Korea was, in the words of a British observer:[7]

. . . well trained and physically toughened, the NCOs were hard, and the officers looked like officers. They wore badges of rank proudly, and the men reacted accordingly. Regimental spirit was tangible. . . .

To form this spearhead of regulars, the 1st Marine Division at Pendleton had been stripped, with only 3,386 officers and men being left behind.

Now it was up to Marine Corps Headquarters to re-form the 1st Division for MacArthur's counterstroke, which, after three successive requests for the entire Marine division, the JCS had finally approved.

To meet other world-wide commitments, plus fielding 24,000 Marines in a war-strength division and 4,000 in an air wing, and then building the 2d Division to war strength, it was obvious that the 70,000-odd men of the peacetime Corps were insufficient. Five days after the brigade sailed, President Truman, with the approval of Congress, ordered mobilization of the Organized Marine Reserve, bringing to the Colors 138 units totaling 33,528 officers and men, many of them experienced Marines from World War II. A hemisphere away in the Mediterranean, the 3d Battalion, 6th Marines, was ordered from duty with the Sixth Fleet and dispatched, via Suez, toward Japan for incorporation into the 1st Division as a battalion of the 7th Marines. At Camp Lejeune, the 2d Division contributed all but its headquarters and a cadre: 6,800 of its Marines were transferred to Pendleton. After this happened, a strategic planner in the Pentagon mopped his brow and said: "The only thing left between us and an emergency in Europe are the Schools Troops at Quantico."[8]

After assuring himself, amid the administrative maelstrom, that his division was formed and embarked, Major General O. P. Smith, the new commander of the 1st Division, arrived in Tokyo on 22 August with a planning group from the division staff. Although D-day was only 24 days off, none of them yet knew D-day or H-hour, and only barely where the landing was to take place. Inchon on the west coast of Korea, the port of Seoul, they learned, was the objective. By landing there General MacArthur intended, as he had explained to General Shepherd, at a single stroke to retake the Korean capital, cut the communications of the North Korean invasion, and relieve the Pusan perimeter. Because of tidal fluctuations (the daily range went as high as 33 feet), 15 September would be the only suitable D-day until mid-October.

It was not until 5 September that the entirely reconstituted 1st Marine Division was in one piece in one place (almost, that is—the brigade was just then leaving the Naktong Bulge behind). Its 7th Regiment, commanded by Colonel H. L. Litzenberg, had been raised by the expedient of re-designating the 6th Marines and concentrating them directly from Camp Lejeune and the Mediterranean. The 1st Regiment, mainly shaken together from reservists and regulars drafted from Marine barracks, had been put together in ten days by Colonel Puller, who had persuaded the Commandant to give him his old regiment after spending $19.00 on commercial telegrams to Headquarters. Finally, on 3 September, quite unexpectedly the Marine division had acquired what eventually was to become a trusted fourth infantry regiment, the 1st Korean Marine Corps (KMC) Regiment. From the moment of attachment, this doughty unit, guided by Marine advisers, patterned itself zealously on the U. S. Marine original, even adopting the globe as its insignia and fighting the good fight in the best Marine style.

At home, even while the division was mounting out for Inchon, the Marine Corps had, through no effort of its own, suddenly become the object of an outpouring of national feeling.

A member of Congress, Representative Gordon L. McDonough of California, one among many who had become increasingly worried over the disregard in which the Marine Corps and its views were held in the Pentagon, wrote President Truman on 21 August, urging that General Cates be accorded a voice in the Joint Chiefs of Staff. This was a step which the President, to put it mildly, did not approve. Mr. Truman, on 29 August, dictated a reply (seen by none of his advisers) which made Marine Corps history:

My dear Congressman McDonough:

I read with a lot of interest your letter in regard to the Marine Corps. For your information the Marine Corps is the Navy's police force and as long as I am President that is what it will remain. They have a propaganda machine that is almost equal to Stalin's.

Nobody desires to belittle the efforts of the Marine Corps but when the Marine Corps goes into the Army it works with and for the Army and that is the way it should be.

I am more than happy to have your expression of interest in this naval military organization. The Chief of Naval Operations is the Chief of Staff of the Navy of which the Marines are a part.

Sincerely yours,

Harry S. Truman.

The story broke on 5 September when a columnist printed both letters. Public reaction was immediate and violent. To add fuel to the fire, the Marine Corps League was holding its annual convention in Washington that week. By five the next afternoon, President Truman sent for General Cates and gave the Marine Corps a Presidential apology:[9]

Dear General Cates:

I sincerely regret the unfortunate choice of language which I used in my letter of August 29 to Congressman McDonough concerning the Marine Corps. . . . I am certain that the Marine Corps itself does not indulge in such propaganda. . . .

The Corps' ability to carry out whatever task may be assigned to it has been splendidly demonstrated many times in our history. It has again been shown by the immediate response of the Marine Corps to a call for duty in Korea. Since Marine ground and air forces have arrived in Korea I have received a daily report of their actions. The country may feel sure that the record of the Marines now fighting there will add new laurels to the already illustrious record of the Marine Corps.

Sincerely yours,

Harry S. Truman.

Although his views on the underlying issue remained uncompromising, the President's straightforward apology and his subsequent disarming personal appearance (on the suggestion of Vice President Alben Barkley and of General Cates) at the Marine Corps League banquet next day went far to quiet the uproar. For the immediate future, the forthcoming landing at Inchon (of which the public would not know for another week) was destined to divert general attention to other aspects of the Marine Corps. For the long run the episode underscored to friends and enemies of the Corps alike the home truth of Senator Saltonstall's remark to Forrestal: ". . . that the Marines occupied a unique and singular place in the hearts of the people."

"THE NAVY AND MARINES HAVE NEVER SHONE MORE BRIGHTLY"

General MacArthur's concept of the Inchon-Seoul operation—and it was his personally in the face of serious doubts and opposition in high quarters, including the Joint Chiefs of Staff—involved four steps: to land amphibiously at Inchon, to capture Seoul, to cut the communications of the North Korean Army, and, using the forces in the Inchon-Seoul area as an anvil, to crush the North Korean Army by a stroke from the advancing Eighth Army. To do the thing with a typical flourish, MacArthur yearned to have Seoul back in friendly hands by 26 September, exactly ninety days after the initial Communist invasion.

"The amphibious landing," General MacArthur wrote in 1956, "is the most powerful tool we have."[10] Unfortunately, as the general also pointed out, as of 1950 the amphibious assault was somewhat out of fashion:[11]

I believe that Generals Bradley and, probably, Collins were fundamentally opposed to amphibious operations as an acceptable technique of modern war. General Bradley some time before publicly had so expressed his professional judgment. . . .

Thus the first task of the Inchon planners was to prove that it could and should be done at all. "It was the prize gem—*if* we could take it," observed one admiral.[12]

Inchon is an oriental city the size of Omaha, separated from Seoul by about 20 miles and by the Han River. Its seaward approaches are difficult to say the least: bottomless mud flats coursed by strong currents and punctuated by precipitous islets surround granite-walled shores without beaches. The tides are worse than at any other port in the Orient. Militarily speaking, the harbor is commanded by Wolmi-Do, a rugged, cave-infested island which is connected to Inchon's dock area by a causeway 600 yards long. Compared to these natural considerations, Inchon's defenses, though appreciable, were of secondary concern. Some 2,200 defenders, not the best troops in the North Korean Army, had an excellent system of caves and emplacements, but mostly failed to occupy them. More than 21,500 enemy troops, many of much better quality, were in the Seoul-Kimpo area, however.

The American organization for the landing was complicated, and unnecessarily so. Superimposed upon the vital working parts, which were the 1st Marine Division (the landing force), under General Smith, and Amphibious Group 1 (the attack force), commanded by Rear Admiral J. H. Doyle, were the X Corps (Major General E. M. Almond, USA) whose amphibious component was the Marine division and its staff (with juncture of command at the amphibious group-division level), and Joint Task Force 7 (an organizational false-face making Seventh Fleet headquarters appear "joint" rather than naval), reporting directly to General MacArthur. Fortunately, as in the case of Guadalcanal, the working plans were completed at working levels by the experts without much opportunity for higher headquarters to become involved except as information addressees.

The plan for the assault, arrived at by the staffs of Amphibious Group 1 and the 1st Marine Division, was a tour de force. "Make up a list of amphibious *don'ts*," reminisced one of Admiral Doyle's capable staff, "and you have an exact description of the Inchon operation."[13] The tides, as has been pointed out, dominated all other considerations. Only second in importance was the need to secure Wolmi-Do—". . . the key to the whole operation," wrote General Smith[14]—as a prerequisite to any further landing at Inchon.

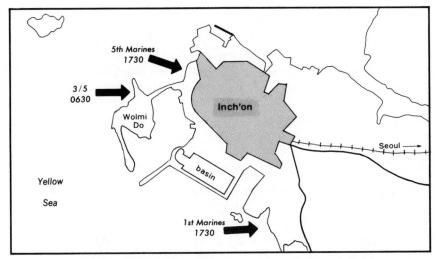

The Inchon Landings, 15 September 1950

But the relationship between the tides and Wolmi-Do was a tricky one. On 15 September, the one feasible day, there would be sufficient water to land soon after daylight, with the next high tide coming just before dark. Let General Smith tell how the planners made the best of the situation:[15]

The Navy was in agreement that Wolmi-Do should be taken out first, as it commanded the waterfront of Inchon, but no solution had been arrived at as to how this could be done before the main landing in the dock area of Inchon. . . . To make a morning landing on Wolmi-Do would, of course, require a night approach by the ships involved. The Navy, from the start, did not consider it feasible to make a night approach through the tortuous and mud-lined channels in the vicinity of Inchon with the slow-moving and unmaneuverable APAs, AKAs, and LSTs. The urgency of the morning landing on Wolmi-Do was pointed out to the Naval Staff and it was finally agreed that it would be possible to make a night approach with DD, APD, and LSD types. These ships were maneuverable, had plenty of power, and were equipped with radar navigational instruments.

The resultant plan, therefore, was to take Wolmi-Do on the morning tide, using the 3d Battalion, 5th Marines, commanded by Lieutenant Colonel R. D. Taplett, with a strong tank force attached, then—and this was nerve-wracking—wait all day for the evening tide and land the remainder of the 1st Division at Inchon with only 99 minutes of daylight to go. "The remainder of the 1st Division" was only the 1st and 5th Marines and supporting troops; the 7th Regiment would not arrive at Inchon until 21 September and was earmarked for the inland operations around Seoul. Following the seizure of Inchon, the 7th Infantry Division (which had fought beside Marines in the Marshalls and Okinawa, and had been brought to strength by adding 8,000 South Korean levies) was to land administratively behind the Marines. The 1st Marine Air Wing (Major General Field Harris) was to provide close support both from the decks of the *Sicily* and the *Badoeng Strait* (known to successive Marine squadrons as "the Bing-Ding") and by the assignment of MAG-33, still under General Cushman, to X Corps as a tactical air command.

Following establishment of the Inchon beachhead by the Marines, the X Corps plan was to capture Kimpo Airfield; clear the south bank of the Han River; cross the Han and capture Seoul and the commanding ground to the north; and, finally, in accordance with General MacArthur's concept, act as the anvil against which the North Korean Army would be crushed by pressure from the south.

While the planners were still engaged in their 23-day sprint, preliminary air-strikes began on 10 September against Wolmi-Do. Appropriately, VMF-214 and VMF-323, the old reliables of the Pusan perimeter, opened the ball. For two more days, Seventh Fleet planes worked over the landing area and vicinity; then, it was naval gunfire's turn. To lure the defenders into disclosing their gun positions on Wolmi-Do, three destroyers closed the island within pistol-shot on 13 September, and, after a half hour's shooting, baited the enemy gunners into action. This was exactly what the four supporting American and British cruisers and orbiting aircraft were waiting for, and the results, for the North Koreans, were disastrous. Two destroyers were hit in the process, but not badly.

Before daylight on D-day, the attack force gingerly eased its way up the channel toward Inchon. Aboard the flagship, USS *Mount McKinley*, in addition to General Smith and Admiral Doyle, were General MacArthur and General Shepherd (whom MacArthur had asked to accompany him as personal adviser on amphibious matters), and a star-studded galaxy of admirals and generals, soon dubbed "VIKs" (Very Important Kibitzers) by the working staffs. At 0545, the fire-support ships opened with everything they had; at 0600, down came Corsairs from the 1st Wing. Then, 15 minutes before touchdown, three rocket ships let go thousands of 5-inch rockets with an awesome whoosh onto Wolmi-Do. Following this build-up, Tap-lett's smartly executed assault was almost anticlimactic in its success. Twenty-five minutes after the first waves hit the beach, up went the Colors atop Radio Hill, key terrain feature on the island. "That's it," said General MacArthur on the command ship's bridge. "Let's get a cup of coffee."[16]

During the intervening hours until 1730, H-hour for the main landings, final preparations and bombardment continued, and carrier aircraft hit everything they could find in a 25-mile circle around Inchon. Then, as the afternoon wore uneasily on with still no counterstroke at the 3d Battalion, 5th Marines, the remainder of the division boated. Once again the shelling was stepped up, once again the rocket ships poured it on, and finally the 1st and 5th Marines headed for their beaches in an ominous twilight of autumn rain and smoke from burning buildings ashore.

The plan was to have the 5th Regiment, landing on the left, take most of the town, while the 1st, coming in wide on the right, swung around to cut off Inchon from Seoul. It succeeded brilliantly, but not effortlessly. Considering everything that might have happened, the regimental commanders had every reason to feel well satisfied at landing their battalions (using scaling ladders and cargo nets to get over the seawalls); attaining planned objectives in the black night, mud, and rain; and getting by with total casualties of 22 killed and 174 wounded. Their reward came in a generous dispatch from the flagship:

> The Navy and Marines have never shone more brightly than this morning.
> —MacArthur

As the division moved out to the force beachhead line next day and General Smith established himself ashore preparatory to the march on Seoul, the world learned that, despite all post-World War II crape-hanging, another successful amphibious operation had been conducted by the U. S. Navy and Marine Corps. Among the many professional comments soon to be heard on the Inchon landing, none went closer to the heart of the matter than a few sentences from Admiral Doyle's action report:[17]

> . . . It is my conviction that the successful assault on Inchon could have been accomplished only by United States Marines. This conviction, I am certain, is shared by everyone who planned, executed or witnessed the assault. My statement is not to be construed as a comparison of the fighting qualities of various units of our armed forces. It simply means that because of their many years of specialized training in amphibious warfare, in conjunction with the Navy, only the United States Marines had the requisite know-how to formulate these plans within the limited time available and to execute these plans flawlessly without additional training or rehearsal. . . . All these facts emphasize the soundness of our national policy in entrusting to the Navy and Marine Corps the specialization in, and the development of, amphibious warfare. Conceivably in the future we may be required to execute many amphibious landings on many fronts.

THE CAPTURE OF SEOUL

On 17 September, two days after Inchon, the 1st Division was poised for its thrust inland. Colonel Murray was to take the 5th Marines, on the left, to Kimpo Airfield, then across the Han and up the right bank into Seoul. Colonel Puller and the 1st Marines were to drive straight ahead along the Inchon-Seoul highway, capturing Yongdung-Po en route, then cross the river and join forces with the 5th Marines in taking the capital. Meanwhile, the 7th Infantry Division would land behind and support the Marine advance.

As the 5th Marines prepared to jump off from their lines of the previous night, the first North Korean counterattack materialized. Six Russian tanks —"caviar cans," the perimeter veterans named them—and 200 enemy infantry plowed unwittingly into the outpost line of the 2d Battalion. In the resultant ambush, all six tanks and practically all the infantry were wiped out, one T-34 tank being destroyed at point-blank range by a 2.36-inch bazooka in the hands of a resolute corporal who knew, according to the book, that his weapon was incapable of destroying a T-34 tank. While the "caviar cans" were still burning and the Marines mopping up, Generals MacArthur, Shepherd, and Smith, accompanied by a train of correspondents, including Miss Marguerite Higgins, drove up for a visit. While General MacArthur had his picture taken against a backdrop of Marines, smoking enemy tanks, and dead North Koreans, Army staff officers chided their 1st Division counterparts on having arranged another typical Marine publicity stunt. They were right: although unarranged, the affair was typical of the Marine Corps, and it got publicity.[18]

By nightfall, the 2d Battalion, 5th Marines, was at Kimpo Airfield. Next day the entire base was secured despite a night counterattack which was repulsed by Company E, 5th Marines. The first airplane to land on the captured field was a Marine helicopter carrying General Shepherd and his G-3, Colonel Krulak. As the general debarked from his helicopter, it was with pride that he found himself within the lines of the battalion (2d Battalion, 5th Marines) in which, beginning in World War I, he had served as platoon leader, company commander, and, finally, on the eve of the Second World War, as battalion commander. Within two days, while the 5th Marines formed for their crossing of the Han, MAG-33 staged into Kimpo and began flying shore-based air support for X Corps.

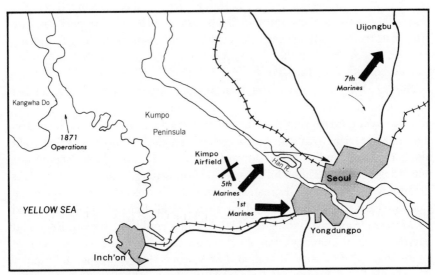

The Capture of Seoul, 20-25 September 1950

The 1st Marines, with a more direct route to the Han, hit more opposition and had to advance more slowly. On 29 September, however, Colonel Puller had his people on the outskirts of Yongdung-Po, where the North Koreans were massed for a stand.

That such was their intention was quickly proven by a furious night counterattack. Before dawn, five tanks led a Red battalion at the 2d Battalion, 1st Marines. Private First Class W. C. Monegan, Jr., a 19-year-old rocket gunner who had already killed his first tank in the 17 September fight, blasted two T-34s at spitting distance. As he aimed in on the next one, a burst of machine gun fire cut him down in the dark, and he died without ever knowing that he had won the Medal of Honor, or that his battalion had stoutly repulsed the enemy.

All day on 21 September the 1st Regiment battered Yongdung-Po with discouragingly small gains, except in one quarter. Company A, 1st Marines, attacking under cover of standing rice, found an undefended street and advanced without opposition into the very heart of town, while the rest of the 1st Marines were fighting in the outskirts. At the junction of their street with the Inchon-Seoul highway, the company commander, a six-foot-four captain named Barrow, set up a defense and proceeded to fight off all comers, including enemy reinforcements streaming along the highway to make trouble for the 2d Battalion, 1st Marines. During the night, some 500 North Koreans and five T-34s attacked the Marine position, but, after five fruitless attacks, which lost them all their tanks and 275 dead, gave up the effort. Then they gave up more: by daybreak the North Koreans had evacuated Yongdung-Po.

The 5th Marines crossed the Han against opposition on 20 September after an amphibious reconnaissance, using amtracs supported by artillery and by naval gunfire from the USS *Rochester's* long-barreled 8-inch guns—a thoroughly Marine way to cross a river. Then the regiment wheeled right along the river and attacked toward the line of hills which marked the outskirts of Seoul. These hills were held in strength, and the tenacious defense which the North Koreans put up indicated clearly that, in the usual Communist tactic, the city would be a battlefield. For four days, supported by Marine air and everything the 11th Marines could fire, the 5th Regiment hammered at the enemy main line of resistance, for such it was. On 24 September, while the 2d Battalion, 5th Marines, fought desperately under its wounded CO, Lieutenant Colonel H. S. Roise, who refused to be evacuated, Colonel Puller led the 1st Regiment across the Han by LVTs into Seoul. Meanwhile, on the day before, the newly arrived 7th Marines also crossed the river, downstream at the 5th Regiment's crossing, and were swinging north of the city to cut off reinforcements. At last, General Smith had his whole division in the battle for Seoul.

Events were closing in on the North Korean People's Army. Not only was the 1st Marine Division pushing into Seoul, but elements of the 7th Division were also fighting in the southern outskirts. Moreover, the effects of the landing were now being felt by the enemy throughout the peninsula. On 23 September the American and South Korean forces in the Pusan perimeter were finally able to register appreciable gains, and it was clear that the Communists were crumbling.

The hardest fighting, through the heart of Seoul, fell to the 1st Marines, who got the brunt of the pressure to take the city in time for the announcement to be made 90 days after the Communist attack. On 25 September, although hard fighting was going on everywhere in town, General Almond concluded that Seoul was in UN hands (mostly) and so announced. This news seemingly failed to get through to the North Koreans manning the street barricades which made every block a fortress, or to those in the north of town who that day encircled and cut off a company of the 7th Marines.

When X Corps assured General Smith on the night of 25 September that the enemy was "fleeing," the only noticeable phenomena in the front lines were hard counterattacks against the 1st and 5th Marines. But by the afternoon of 27 September even the North Korean Communists had had enough, and, as resistance decreased, American Colors began to appear over important buildings throughout Seoul. As the Colors went up all over town, a X Corps staff officer needled Colonel Puller, "Ever since that flag-raising picture on Iwo Jima got published, I'm convinced you Marines would rather carry a flag into battle than a weapon."

"Not a bad idea," Puller replied. "A man with a flag in his pack and the desire to run it up on an enemy position isn't likely to bug out."[19]

On 1 October, to complete the Red defeat and to protect Seoul against renewed incursions, Colonel Litzenberg and the 7th Marines were ordered to secure Uijongbu, an important communications center ten miles north of Seoul. This final move involved three days' surprisingly stiff fighting through a series of defiles before the North Koreans at length broke. On the last day, 3 October, which marked the end of serious combat for a time by the Marine division, General Cates, who had arrived from Washington on an inspection, had the satisfaction of watching the 7th Regiment make a three-mile advance past abandoned enemy dumps and artillery and complete the capture of Uijongbu as ordered.

The war against the North Korean Communists had virtually ended. The cocky, tough, well-trained little Red army which had momentarily humiliated American forces was dispersed and broken. U. S. Marines had cut their communications, nearly all of which passed through or near Seoul, and liberated the South Korean capital; the Eighth Army had pushed out of the Pusan perimeter and made contact with X Corps. The Marines alone had taken 4,692 enemy prisoners, inflicted 13,666 casualties, destroyed 44 tanks without the loss of a single Marine tank, and recaptured quantities of American weapons and equipment abandoned in the initial disasters. Supporting these victories, the 1st Wing flew 2,774 sorties between 7 September and 9 October. The cost in Marine casualties was 2,459, of whom 457 were killed. Six Marines were missing, including two known prisoners —one a ground Marine, the other an aviator; the ground prisoner was the first such in the entire history of the 1st Marine Division, parent unit of the brigade. Once again Marine readiness had enabled the Corps to live up to its "First to Fight" tradition and, more important, to win.

NORTH TO WONSAN

The strategic sequel to the triumph at Inchon and Seoul was another amphibious flanking maneuver, this time a right hook up the east coast into Wonsan, and thence, after many rapid changes in high-level plans and objectives, northwest from the "throat" of Korea toward the Yalu River, frontier of China. The 1st Division and 1st Wing originally had the job of taking Wonsan by assault, but, in General Smith's words, "History just got ahead of us for once"[20]—by the time Wonsan's channels had been cleared of a large and expertly laid Russian minefield, ROK troops were already there, and the 1st Wing had only to fly its Corsairs onto Wonsan Airport. On 26 October, when the 1st Division finally was able to land on Kalma-Pando Peninsula, jutting out into the great bay, the Marines were chagrined to find that Bob Hope and a USO show had arrived ahead of them (by air) and that they were greeted by a large sign reading, "This Beach Is All Yours Thru Courtesy of Mine Squadron Three."

The job that lay ahead of General Smith was one of the largest, geographically, that ever confronted a Marine division. After much soul searching, the JCS had authorized operations north of the 38th parallel and, with reluctance, to the Yalu itself.[21] Pursuant to this decision, as part of the general advance, the 1st Division was assigned a zone of action almost 300 miles in depth and about 50 miles wide, extending from below Wonsan to the Yalu. About the same time, over General Smith's protest, General Almond detached from the division for X Corps use the 7th Motor Transport Battalion, a reinforcing FMF battalion specifically attached to the Marine division to give it the added land-transport capability which Army divisions have and Marine divisions usually do not require. To carry out the missions assigned by X Corps, General Smith gave to the 1st Regiment the job of securing and patrolling the Wonsan area, while the remainder of the division advanced by road and rail to Hamhung, farther north, and prepared to advance to the Yalu.

In the fine clear autumn weather, the blue waters of Yonghung-Man (Wonsan Bay) sparkled brightly and reminded New Englanders of the coast of Maine in early fall. During the Inchon-Seoul campaign, the weather had been, as one officer put it, "hot, dirty, and dusty."[22] Now, 150 miles north and a month later, there was frost in the mornings and thin ice on the paddies. Marines who had scoffed and groaned in San Diego, when heavy cases of winter clothing went aboard ship, now began to ask when the QM was going to issue it.

Although the mood of the troops in Korea was one of relaxation, and all higher headquarters were exuding predictions of the end of hostilities, the 1st Marines soon discovered that the war was not over. One battalion, outposted south of Wonsan at Kojo, was determinedly attacked by part of a North Korean division which was trying to make its way north to Communist China, while the 3d Battalion, 1st Marines, underwent something approaching a siege during two weeks' occupation of Majon-Ni, a road junction between Wonsan and Yangdok, of vital importance in cutting the northward flow of NKPA units and fugitives. Under the canny leadership of Lieutenant Colonel T. L. Ridge, the battalion held a perimeter including the town and a homemade airstrip, reminiscent of Quilali 32 years earlier, while the better part of an enemy division supported by numerous guerrillas did its unsuccessful best to clear the bottleneck. During Ridge's 16-day stay at Majon-Ni, which included November 10th and a birthday cake, the battalion captured 1,395 prisoners and killed 525 enemy. Later, Major General Clark Ruffner, USA, the X Corps Chief of Staff, commented, "The Marines did a masterful job at Majon-Ni. . . ."[23]

ADVANCE TO THE RESERVOIR

To General Smith the idea of having his division stretched out from Wonsan to north of Hamhung (and still further as the advance continued) was far from attractive in the best of circumstances. On 1 November, however, when word came in that Eighth Army units had been hit hard by authentic Chinese Communist Forces (CCF) well south of the Yalu, the general knew it was high time to concentrate, not to disperse. Next day, to bring matters nearer home, a ROK division outside Hamhung captured Chinese prisoners from the 124th CCF Division. Red China had entered the war.

The Marine division's zone of action dog-legged northwest from Hungnam, upward through lofty mountains past the Chosin Reservoir, a manmade lake 75 miles inland, and thence to the Yalu. The only possible route of advance up this zone was the precipitous mountain road which coiled its way through deep passes and along cliff edges from Hamhung to the reservoir. It was General Smith's plan to advance in column of regiments, 7th Marines leading, 5th Marines next, and the 1st to follow along and close up as soon as they could be disengaged in Wonsan.

On 2 November, the 7th Marines passed through the ROK troops outposting Hamhung and struck out for the Yalu. The mood of Colonel Litzenberg ("Litz the Blitz"), as befitted an advance guard commander heading into unknown country with an unknown enemy ahead, was wary and prudent. The regiment and its artillery (3d Battalion, 11th Marines, commanded by Lieutenant Colonel F. F. Parry, a descendant of Colonel-Commandant John Harris) were well closed up. Flank security—a job for a mountain goat once the seacoast plain was behind—was strong and alert. Marine Corsairs scouted ahead and orbited aloft. Occasional light resistance, mainly long-range small arms fire, was brushed aside by artillery and air support.

That night the regiment, bivouacked in a mountainous perimeter south of Sudong (just below Chinhung-Ni), was hit by the 124th CCF Division, three regiments strong. Their orders, in this first contact, were "Kill these Marines as you would snakes in your homes."[24] At midnight, the 1st and 2d Battalions, 7th Marines, holding the hills in the forward half of Litzenberg's perimeter, came under skilled and determined attack. The quilted-coated Chinese who weren't killed kept coming, working their way forward and infiltrating wherever a soft spot showed. Bugles emitted eerie wails, whistles blew, and green pyrotechnics rose and fell. A handful of the few remaining NKPA "caviar cans" added to the pandemonium. While the Marine rifle companies held tight to their hilltops in the perimeter, many Chinese got down into the low meadow along the road where headquarters and weapons units and cannoneers fought private battles all night. But all hands stood fast, and, when day came, the Corsairs and the artillery and the regiment's mass of supporting weapons helped the infantry to clear the perimeter in an all-day mop-up. Two enemy regiments had made the attack; according to captured records, they came off short seven companies between them, with more than a thousand dead.

But the fighting had only begun. Ahead lay the hamlet of Chinhung-Ni, mouth of the tortuous Funchilin Pass, which rises 2,500 feet in eight miles and is the gateway between the coast and the mountain plateaus above. First at Chinhung-Ni, where the 7th Marines, with a fine assist from VMF-312, killed the last five North Korean T-34s, then for two days in the pass, Litzenberg's tightly formed column—really a mobile perimeter—fought its way upward toward Koto-Ri, the town at the upper end of the climb. By 7 November, the 124th Division was spent; that night what was left of the

Chinese broke contact and vanished. Since this seemed too good to be true, Colonel Litzenberg sent out a patrol which covered 25 mountain miles in 26 hours and watched Koto-Ri for almost two hours. The way was clear, and on the morning of November 10th, 175th Birthday of the Corps, the 7th Regiment's advance guard swung into Koto-Ri, a name soon to become historic in the annals of the Marine Corps.

Three days later the 7th Marines reached Hagaru-Ri, a considerable town at the lower end of Chosin Reservoir. Hagaru-Ri had been selected as the division's forward base for the operations ahead, and there the 7th Regiment halted while General Smith endeavored to close up the division and improve his communications.

Halting, closing up, and improving communications to the rear were not much in vogue in Korea at that moment. There was talk of a race to the Yalu—in which the Marine division was not conspicuously out front— and, from General MacArthur himself, of getting the boys home by Christmas. These sentiments were not shared by General Smith, his staff, or his regimental commanders. In bleak mid-November, with winter on in dead earnest, his left flank wide open (it was 80 miles southwestward to the nearest Eighth Army troops), and with obvious evidence that the Chinese Communists were present in strength, General Smith found himself unable to join in the euphoria which pervaded all headquarters from X Corps up. On 15 November he wrote General Cates:[25]

So far our MSR [main supply route] north of Hamhung has not been molested, but there is evidence that this situation will not continue. . . . I do not like the prospect of stringing out a Marine division along a single mountain road for 120 air miles from Hamhung to the border.

While Colonel Litzenberg occupied Hagaru-Ri, General Smith got the 5th Marines up from the coast and distributed their battalions along the MSR. Under Colonel Puller (who had just been selected for brigadier), the 1st Marines were disengaged at Wonsan, after being relieved by the 3d Infantry Division and a ROK regiment, and moved north. The 1st Engineer Battalion, commanded by Lieutenant Colonel J. H. Partridge, went all-out to strengthen and widen the road for armor and heavy trucks, while two vital airstrips were hewn out of the frozen soil, one for transports at Hagaru-Ri and another for light aircraft at Koto-Ri. Every day, ammunition and supplies went forward to dumps being built up at the two towns. As streams froze solid and the roads glazed with ice, the troops burrowed into cold-weather clothing and checked each other for signs of frostbite.

Although the enemy seemed dormant in the X Corps zone, they were opposing the Eighth Army with might and main, and intelligence reports from all sources told of Chinese columns across the Yalu 150,000 strong. To help the Eighth Army, General MacArthur ordered General Almond to swing his X Corps attack left from the Chosin and bore in westward against the Chinese left flank and main supply route. This maneuver would put the Marine division on the cutting edge—sharp, and thin, too—of the new main effort of X Corps. (Other troops in X Corps: 7th Infantry Division on the Marines' right and the I ROK Corps to the right of them.) On 24 November, the 7th Marines pushed west of the reservoir higher still, through Toktong Pass, to Yudam-Ni; two days later, the 5th Marines joined them for the westward thrust. Meanwhile, Puller brought two of his battalions up from the coast; one went to Hagaru-Ri, the other to Koto-Ri. With the exception of one rifle battalion (1st Battalion, 1st Marines) holding the lower end of the Funchilin Pass, and a few smaller units still on their way up the MSR, General Smith had his division concentrated at last and poised for combat. While attack orders were being issued for the next day's jump-off from Yudam-Ni, word came in that the Eighth Army was in trouble: their right-flank corps, a ROK formation, had given way and exposed U. S. Army and Turkish units to a violent flanking attack. Disorganization and panic were reported, and the Eighth Army was falling back. Bad as this news was, General Smith was still unaware of worse: eight Chinese divisions under a veteran Communist general, Sung Shih-lun, were massed in the hills west of Yudam-Ni and along the MSR. Their mission: ". . . to destroy the Marine Division."[26]

YUDAM-NI

The 5th Marines' attack on 27 November was hard fought and gained 2,000 yards. Clearly the Chinese were holding in strength and not withdrawing. That night, with the mercury 20 below zero and the wind howling down from Siberia, General Sung struck. Three divisions attacked the lines of the 5th and 7th Marines at Yudam-Ni, while others cut the MSR between Hagaru-Ri and Yudam-Ni, and between Hagaru-Ri and Koto-Ri. Shortly after, still another Communist force broke the route below Koto-Ri. The 1st Marine Division, concentrated in four tight perimeters, was surrounded by a Chinese army group. Dispersed units of the 7th Infantry Division (one of whose regiments, the lightly opposed 17th Infantry, a week earlier had reached the Yalu at Hyesanjin) in the rear, and to the east of the reservoir, were also hit hard, but paradoxically, in attempting to destroy X Corps, the

Chinese chose to batter themselves against the one American division in Korea which, despite the prevailing overconfidence, was properly concentrated, ready, and prepared for the worst.

The bulk of the fighting power of the 1st Marine Division, two infantry regiments and three battalions of the 11th Marines, was at Yudam-Ni. The division command post, its air-head, and most of its service units, were at Hagaru-Ri, 14 miles away. On 28 November, after recognizing (as X Corps apparently did not yet) the seriousness of the situation, General Smith ordered the 5th Marines to hold their westward attack and the 7th to clear the route between Yudam-Ni and Hagaru-Ri. Next day, when the MSR was still not reopened, the general pulled the 5th Regiment back to Yudam-Ni, with orders to co-ordinate their action with the efforts of the 7th Marines. That night, as disaster rained down on United Nations forces throughout Korea, General Almond attached the beleaguered units of the 7th Infantry Division, in Koto-Ri and north thereof, to the Marine division. Next day, after General Almond had flown to Hagaru-Ri for a personal conference to inform General Smith of his decision to fall back on Hamhung, General Smith took immediate steps to concentrate on Hagaru-Ri.

The absolute essential for concentration of the Marine division, involving extrication of the 5th and 7th Regiments, was to retain control of Toktong Pass, which had been outposted on 27 November by Company F, 7th Marines, commanded by Captain W. E. Barber. The five-day defense of this isolated position, seven lonely miles from Hagaru, against unceasing Communist attacks, ranks as one of the most gallant stands of the Corps and deserves to be numbered with San Jose, Wake, Quilali, and Edson's Ridge.

While holding off the Chinese onslaughts on Yudam-Ni, Colonels Litzenberg and Murray, operating under General Smith's instructions, fought their battle in a sort of junta. As General Smith later wrote:[27]

Having no Assistant Division Commander, only two choices were open to me in the matter of command at Yudam-Ni; turn over command of both RCTs to Colonel Litzenberg who was senior, or depend on the spirit of cooperation of the two RCT commanders. I chose the latter course and I was not disappointed. . . .

The first task for the Yudam-Ni force was to regroup, in accordance with division orders, so that the 7th Marines would clear the way back, while the 5th would execute the disengagement. Lieutenant Colonel R. G. Davis's 1st Battalion, 7th Marines, was accordingly given the mission of advancing alone eight miles across country to reinforce Barber's hard-pressed company and clear Toktong Pass.

After fighting all afternoon, 1 December, to break clear of the perimeter,

Davis led his battalion off the road into the howling darkness. Stretchers were loaded with extra ammunition; each man in the reserve company carried an 81-mm. mortar round in addition to his normal load. Stumbling forward over icy rocks, the leading company guided on the stars. During halts, troops collapsed in their packs "like dominoes,"[28] while two men, delirious with cold and privation, had to be tied up. By 0300, after crossing three mountain ridges and coming within a mile of Captain Barber's perimeter, the battalion halted until daylight, indifferent to scattered Chinese fire. In the dawn, Davis roused his numb Marines and, in radio contact with Barber at last, waited until an air-strike cleared the final advance. With true panache, Barber, commanding from a stretcher despite a wound, offered to send out a patrol to lead the relief battalion onto "Fox Hill," where 82 unwounded Marines out of the original 240 still held their ground. Toktong Pass was secure. Captain Barber received the Medal of Honor for his resolute stand, as did Colonel Davis for his incredible march.

Meanwhile, with the 3d Battalion, 5th Marines, leading, the main body slowly fought its way out. Overhead the aircraft of six Marine squadrons took turns in support; on 3 December alone, 145 close-support sorties were flown. At the pass, Taplett's advance guard joined up with Davis's battalion, and the long column made its way through the all-important defile.

At nightfall, 3 December, they entered Hagaru-Ri. The walking wounded, too many to ride, hobbled behind the jeeps and trucks carrying those too weak or too hurt to stay on their feet. The column, with its wounded and enemy prisoners, had marched and fought 79 hours to cover the 14-mile stretch from Yudam-Ni. All they had left behind were some of the dead, decently buried at Yudam-Ni, and eight howitzers of the 4th Battalion, 11th Marines, pushed off the road when their prime movers ran dry of diesel fuel on the long march. As General Smith reported, when the last elements of the 5th and 7th Marines reached Hagaru-Ri, he was convinced "that the critical part of the operation had been completed."[29]

HAGARU AND KOTO-RI

As soon as the Chinese struck, on the morning of 28 November, General Smith had moved the forward echelon of his command post, himself included, from the safety of Hungnam up to Hagaru-Ri. The only way that he could move, as in so many other instances during this time, was by helicopter, of which the Marine Corps still had the first and only unit in Korea.

Next day, 29 November, as we have seen, X Corps ordered General Smith to try to withdraw the 5th and 7th Marines to Hagaru-Ri, and at the same time attached to the Marine division three Army battalions from the 7th Infantry Division, which were cut off and disintegrating east of the reservoir. On the afternoon of 30 November, General Almond flew to Hagaru-Ri for his conference with General Smith. Fall back, and quickly, were his orders; weapons, equipment, or supplies that stood in the way were to be jettisoned or destroyed. General Smith replied briefly and pointedly that the 1st Marine Division was going to fight its way out as a unit and would bring out its guns and gear.[30]

Meanwhile, Koto-Ri was crowded with a miscellany of Marine and Army troops halted when the Chinese cut the MSR between there and Hagaru-Ri. In addition to the garrison (2d Battalion, 1st Marines, and 1st Marines headquarters), the main fighting elements present were two Marine tank companies, Company G, 1st Marines, on their way from detached service to rejoin the parent 3d Battalion at Hagaru-Ri, and 41 Independent Commando, Royal Marines. The Royal Marine unit commanded by Lieutenant Colonel D. B. Drysdale, RM, had been attached to the Marine division on 20 November as a result of backstage arrangements between General Shepherd and British Marine friends. Thus, for the first time since the Boxer Uprising, British and American Marines were again serving together in combat, and against the same enemy as in 1900.

On 28 November, not only was the MSR cut, but Chinese troops began closing in on Koto-Ri. "That," said Colonel Puller, "simplifies our problem of finding these people and killing them."[31] Next afternoon, when the Chinese attacked, he was as good as his word. With Marine air strikes helping out, the 1st Marines and their transient guests stood off the assault in fine style, and the enemy retired leaving more than 150 dead. Colonel Puller's next task, on General Smith's orders, was to clear the MSR from Koto-Ri into Hagaru-Ri, where the situation was far more serious. There a weakened battalion was trying to hold a four-mile perimeter, and Colonel Puller made haste to try to reopen the road and to send reinforcements as soon as he could. These he grouped into a task force.

Task Force Drysdale, taking its name from the Royal Marines' CO, who was senior, was made up of the British commando, Company G, 1st Marines, an Army infantry company, 29 tanks from the two Marine tank companies, and a long convoy (141 vehicles) of headquarters and service troops and gear. From the moment Drysdale moved out on 29 November, it was clear that the column faced hard going. Late that afternoon, in the winter dusk, about halfway to Hagaru-Ri, the vulnerable truck column was stalled, even though the armor and infantry at its head could still fight on. Colonel Drysdale requested instructions from General Smith: Should they press on, cost what it might, or turn back on Koto-Ri? Given the situation at Hagaru-Ri, the general had only one answer: Drysdale must come ahead with whatever he could bring with him. Into the night, most of 41 Commando, a tank company, and the Marine rifle company fought their way toward Hagaru-Ri, arriving some hours later.

The remainder of the task force, still stalled, amounted to the Army infantry, a few British Marines, and the U. S. Marine clerks, cooks, communicators, MPs, and drivers, who took up their rifles and joined the fight as infantry. Under repeated Chinese attack, the convoy finally broke down into four mixed perimeters, the largest consisting of about 130 men under Major J. N. McLaughlin, the senior surviving officer. Before dawn, with ammunition and grenades expended and after stalling the Chinese as long as possible to permit individual escapes, McLaughlin surrendered for the sake of his wounded. Forty-four Marines were thus taken, 17 of whom later escaped from prison camps. During imprisonment, McLaughlin's steadfast courage and moral leadership helped bring the Marine prisoners through unshaken.

The arrival of Drysdale's reinforcements at Hagaru-Ri was a bonanza to Lieutenant Colonel Ridge, whose depleted 3d Battalion, 1st Marines, was again holding a hard-pressed perimeter against heavy odds. As defense commander for the division's command post and base, Ridge had the job not only of deploying his own battalion and two batteries from the 11th where they would do the most good on the four-mile perimeter, but of organizing the myriad headquarters and service troops to plug the gaps. After dark on 28 November, the Chinese had attacked in division strength. All through the night and into the next day, there was a nip-and-tuck struggle for East Hill, a ridge that commanded Hagaru-Ri and overlooked General Smith's CP. After X Corps (Army) engineers had given way, Major R. R. Myers, Ridge's exec, led a forlorn hope from the final scrapings of the perimeter—Marine engineers, clerks, and gunners, and some Army and ROKs. Although Myers never got the Chinese off East Hill—this task eventually required a regiment almost a week later—his desperate handful contained them, and the perimeter held. In the circumstances, this was well worth the Medal of Honor which he later received.

After a relatively quiet 24 hours, during which Lieutenant Colonel Partridge's engineers continued to hew at the frozen soil under floodlights to finish the airfield, the Chinese division again attacked. Once again much of the fight centered along East Hill, where the enemy was stopped by the 1st Service Battalion, commanded by Lieutenant Colonel C. L. Banks. With Drysdale's reinforcements in hand, Ridge's thin lines again held, and though nobody yet knew it, the worst was over at Hagaru-Ri.

The worst was definitely not over, however, for the Army battalions trapped east of the reservoir. Under repeated Communist attacks and despite Marine air support by day, the three battalions finally disintegrated into unarmed bands of stragglers dragging their way across the frozen reservoir toward Hagaru-Ri. After the first able-bodied soldiers reached the Marine perimeter, Lieutenant Colonel Olin Beall, one of the master raconteurs of the old Corps, organized a rescue force which brought in 319 leaderless, frostbitten, and wounded Army troops from the ice on 2 December, a feat which earned him the Army's Distinguished Service Cross. Of 1,050 soldiers who made it to safety at Hagaru-Ri, 385 were made fit for duty and were rearmed and equipped by the Marines.[32]

"... ATTACKING IN A NEW DIRECTION"

While the division regrouped at Hagaru-Ri, the most pressing problem was evacuation of more than four thousand casualties who had accumulated as a result of the desperate fighting at Yudam-Ni and Hagaru-Ri. Air Force and Marine R4Ds droned in and out of Partridge's 2,900-foot airfield, and even one four-engined Navy R5D, piloted by an old-time aviation pilot, Chief Aviation Electrician's Mate B. J. Miller, made the hair-raising round trip. As space permitted, Marine dead (136 in all) and spare equipment ranging from typewriters to extra weapons was flown out, while more than five hundred Marine replacements were flown in—a fact which flabbergasted Major General W. H. Tunner, USAF, of the Air Force Combat Cargo Command, who flew to Hagaru-Ri expressly to propose an aerial Dunkerque. General Smith replied, in the same tenor as to General Almond, that every Marine capable of fighting would stay for the final break-out, and that only the casualties would travel by air. General Harris, who had moved his wing headquarters and MAG-12 to Yonpo, near Hungnam, was likewise on the job to see that all went well and to plan the big air-support effort ahead.

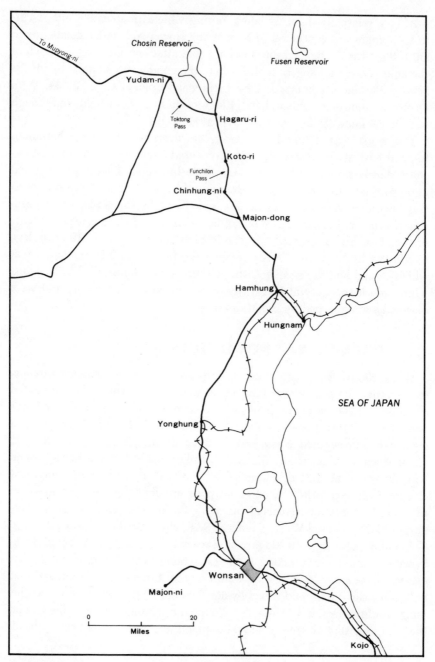

Road Net Leading to the Chosin Reservoir

In a message to Rear Admiral E. C. Ewen, Commander Task Force 77, whose fast carriers were now giving their all-out effort to support the Marines, he said:[33]

The next job is to get them off this hill. I want to be able to cover their flanks and rear one hundred percent, and to blast any major resistance to their front. Can use all the help you can give me until they get down. Tell your pilots they are doing a magnificent job.

It was about this time that General Smith said with literal truth, "We are not retreating. We are just attacking in a different direction."[34]

On 6 December, the 7th Marines led the way out of Hagaru-Ri, first out as they had been first in. As Colonel Litzenberg and the attached division trains fought their way toward Koto-Ri under a watchful umbrella of support air from the 1st Wing and from four fast carriers, Colonel Murray and the 5th Regiment, in addition to holding the perimeter, set out, with 76 aircraft in support, to clear East Hill of the tenacious Chinese who still overlooked Hagaru-Ri and the road to Koto-Ri. Although the hill was carried with surprising ease, the Chinese counterattack that night, by an entire division, against the 1st and 2d Battalions, 5th Marines, was one of the hottest of the war. With good help from an Army tank platoon, the lines held, and the slaughter of massed Communist attackers piled quilted corpses in windrows under the guns of the Marines.

As the 7th Regiment made its way south, hard fighting fell to their direct-support artillery, Parry's 3d Battalion, 11th Marines. During the night of 6-7 December, after earlier brushes, the battalion and adjacent trucks were hit on the road by more than 800 Chinese. In the teeth of the attack, Parry resolutely deployed his cannoneers as infantry, while the battalion's howitzers went into action at point-blank range with muzzle-burst, from positions among stalled and burning trucks.

By nightfall on 7 December, after the 2d Battalion, 5th Marines, had put Hagaru-Ri and its remaining dumps to the torch and served as rear guard for the division's 11-mile column, the first stage was over, and all hands (14,229 United States and British troops) were concentrated in Koto-Ri.

The final obstacle lay ahead. Funchilin Pass was held by Chinese troops whose mission was to prevent the 1st Division from reaching the sea. Midway down the pass, to complicate matters to the utmost, 24 feet of one-way bridge with sheer cliffs rising to the left and sheer cliffs dropping away to the right, had been blown up by the enemy.

General Smith's plan was to attack downward with the 7th Marines, supported by the 5th, while Puller and his two battalions took over the rear guard. At the same time, the 1st Battalion, 1st Marines, still holding Chinhung-Ni at the bottom of the pass, was to attack uphill in the old direction, and capture Hill 1081, the mountain which dominated the defile. To span the crucial 24-foot gap, fortune had provided among the troops at Koto-Ri an Army engineer company specially trained in Treadway bridging. Eight Air Force "Flying Boxcars" from Japan thereupon air-dropped eight 2,500-pound sections of bridge, and the engineers were in business. To prevent a stalled tank from blocking the narrow road, the tanks were to form as the last motor elements in the column. As before, only drivers, relief drivers, radiomen, and wounded were allowed to ride. Every other Marine, regardless of duty or rank, was to march as an infantryman so as to provide maximum fighting strength ready to deploy at any point of attack. And once again General Harris (whose son, Lieutenant Colonel W. F. Harris, had been killed the day before at the head of his battalion on the road to Koto-Ri) massed the Corsairs and night-fighters of the 1st Wing with the Navy's carrier squadrons to cover the last stage of the march to the sea. As O. P. Smith noted:[35]

As the breakout from the Chosin Reservoir area progressed, the optimism in fact became confidence. . . . There were still 11 miles to fight through before we reached Chinhung-Ni, from which point the remaining 35 miles of road to the coast were reasonably free of the enemy. There was still a bridge to be repaired before we could be sure of getting out our equipment. But the men instinctively felt that we were over the hump. During the evening I heard singing coming from a tent near mine, and it was not maudlin singing. I do not know who was doing the singing, but I know it gave me quite a lift. Here was confidence.

While the 7th Marines pushed south on 8 December, the 1st Battalion, 1st Marines, attacked up the pass and along the ice-coated ridges. The day before, the battalion commander had personally patrolled the route with a squad and an artillery forward-observer team; when they saw Hill 1081 and its neighbors alive with unwary Chinamen in the open, the forward observer brought in the entire division artillery together with Army units from below Chinhung-Ni, and one of the great shoots of the war resulted.

During the 8th, the two attacks, north and south, got within six miles of each other. In a temperature of 14 below, the 1st Battalion, 1st Marines, poised for the final push on 1081 and took it in a fine charge just in time for the leading riflemen to see the advance guard of the 7th Marines coming down the road.

Covered by the 1st Battalion, 7th Marines, the Treadway bridge came into position. It fitted. The pass was open, and the 1st Marine Division crossed onward.

There was further fighting below, for the Chinese made final attempts to head off the division by parallel marches through the gorges and ridges, but the fierce cold was too much for many of them. And as the American tanks finally clanked down—one painted, "Only 14 More Shooting Days Until XMAS"—one of the last in column did break down, and those behind were lost. Aside from these tanks, and 117 dead regretfully buried at Koto-Ri, the 1st Marine Division emerged from the mountains tired, proud, and intact, bringing its wounded, its weapons, many of its dead, and a quantity of enemy prisoners. The division entered the staging areas at Hungnam on the sea, where the rear guard closed during the night of 11-12 December. By salvaging abandoned Army trucks found all along the road, Colonel Puller came out with more transport than his regiment had at the beginning of the campaign.

General Smith, who had been visited at Koto-Ri by General Shepherd, on hand as representative of Commander, Naval Forces, Far East, for the amphibious redeployment about to begin, moved down by helicopter to Hungnam. During the reservoir campaign, his division and Marine aviation had taken 4,400 battle casualties (730 killed) and many more from frostbite. For the Chinese the campaign was a disaster: according to intelligence reconstruction, they sustained some 37,500 casualties, including about 25,000 killed in battle or by cold and disease. On their own records, the three Chinese armies which assailed the Marine division were finished at the end of the campaign; indeed, they disappeared from the enemy order of battle and were not identified again for months to come.

Shortly after coming down from the reservoir, General Smith wrote a heartfelt letter of thanks to Field Harris.[36]

During the long reaches of the night and in the snow storms, many a Marine prayed for the coming of day or clearing weather when he knew he would again hear the welcome roar of your planes. . . . Never in its history has Marine aviation given more convincing proof of its indispensable value to ground Marines. A bond of understanding has been established that will never be broken.

From 26 October to 11 December, 3,703 sorties were flown on request and under control of the Marine division. In addition, the Marine helicopters of VMO-6 made aviation history by flying 837 missions during the campaign. Marine and naval aviation, operating and controlled by their own proven doctrines, were the joy and deliverance of the Marine division and the open envy of others. Writing of the Marine air-ground team in a professional journal soon after the campaign, an Army captain suggested:[37]

> Our tactical air arm should spend a few months with the Marines. I don't know what causes the difference, but it is there. The Marine pilots give us the impression that they are breaking their hearts to help us out. . . .

In the history of the Marine Corps, the 1st Division's anabasis is paralleled only by Guadalcanal and then only in part. Each campaign was a lonely ordeal and, in each, faint hearts in the rear wrote off the Marines as lost. But each time, leadership, discipline, self-reliance, and *esprit* carried the day. In the words of a distinguished military historian, S. L. A. Marshall:[38]

> No other operation in the American book of war quite compares with this show by the 1st Marine Division in the perfection of tactical concepts precisely executed, in accuracy of estimation of situation, in leadership at all levels, and in promptness of utilization of all supporting forces.

REDEPLOYMENT AND GUERRILLAS

While X Corps fell back on Hungnam under the guns of the Navy and commenced a seaborne evacuation ("redeployment" was the current euphemism), the Eighth Army, in full retreat and considerable disorganization, broke contact with the enemy and withdrew more than 200 road miles rearward in just over three weeks.

On Christmas Eve 1950, as bleak a Christmas Eve as in 1941, the last ships cleared Hungnam. Admiral Doyle's "amphibious operation in reverse," conducted with General Shepherd at his side, had succeeded magnificently. Thanks to the Navy, the Marine division was safely afloat and so were the other salvaged X Corps units. The Marines' destination was Masan and a camp in the very same bean patch where the 1st Brigade had camped in August. Here, in Eighth Army Reserve, the division received 3,400 replacements and began squaring away its gear for future fighting.

Even after the Eighth Army front finally solidified well below Seoul, danger still existed of a Communist breakthrough in the east and from increasing guerrilla actions against the Eighth Army communications leading north and inland from the east coast port of Pohang. To backstop the line and put an end to the guerrillas, Lieutenant General Matthew B. Ridgway, USA, the new Eighth Army commander (who had served in Nicaragua with the 1928 electoral commission), ordered the Marine division to protect the army's MSR from Pohang northwest to Andong. From 12 January to 15 February 1951, the division patrolled and skirmished with guerrillas from a North Korean division which had gone to ground in the area. With particular help from the helicopters, which proved ideal for guerrilla fighting, the Marines harried and disorganized the guerrilla division into ineffectiveness, while simultaneously giving the replacements a taste of active service. On 15 February, a ROK division took over the job, and the Marine division headed for the front lines again.

"KILLER" AND "RIPPER"

General Ridgway, a fighting soldier who packed part of his gear in a Marine seabag, was determined to get the Eighth Army back into the war and regain the offensive. Within less than a month after his assumption of command following the accidental death of Lieutenant General W. H. Walker in December, American soldiers were advancing. By February General Ridgway had decided on a serious offensive, Operation "Killer," and chosen the Marine division—now in IX Corps—for the main effort. With the possible exception of Okinawa, there had been nothing like this since World War I in France. Once again under the Army, Marines were marching to the front far from the sea (in spite of General Smith's sensible urging that the division be committed with one flank on blue water), preparing to join in a land campaign as they had at Soissons, St. Mihiel, Blanc Mont, and the Argonne.

With General Ridgway on hand to watch, "the most powerful division in Korea"[39] (as he once described it) jumped off on 21 February from positions forward of Wonju, in the very center of the line. General Smith's objective was to capture Hoengsong, eight miles ahead, a supply center and hub of enemy road communications, held by a Chinese division. After an uneventful first day's advance of four miles through broken wooded hills crossed by swift streams—a Korean Argonne—the left assault regiment, the 1st Marines, hit a well-defended hill mass on the 22d, George Washington's Birthday. All day and part of the next, while the 5th Regiment worked forward on the right, the 1st chopped away; Marine tanks rolled through the rubble of Hoengsong on the 24th, and the 5th Marines fought a brisk action with Chinese rear elements trying to hold on to high ground east of town.

That afternoon General Smith received an unexpected new job. The IX Corps commander had just died of a heart attack, and General Ridgway selected the Marine general to take over the corps until an Army general could be brought out from the States. Brigadier General Puller (who had made his number in the Masan bean patch) thereupon assumed command of the Marine division and thereby became still another Marine general who had commanded everything from a platoon to a division in action.

On 1 March, while the Commandant in Washington was exchanging St. David's Day greetings with the Royal Welch Fusiliers, IX Corps resumed the offensive under General Smith. The Marine division's job this time, with 1st and 7th Marines in the attack, was to capture a line of hills which extended square across the division zone due north of Hoengsong. With the 11th Marines' howitzers and rocket-launchers pounding away, tanks and Corsairs led the attack on a well-organized system of bunkers and log barricades. For three days the division slugged ahead through slush and mud, the 7th Regiment encountering the hardest fighting on the division's left. Then, as Marines prepared for a final assault, the Chinese pulled back, and, on 4 March, the two regiments dug in on their objectives.

General Ridgway's next attack, Operation "Ripper," was no less than a push, by IX Corps again, back to the 38th parallel. Once again the 1st Division's zone ran through trackless, wooded country punctuated by mountain peaks. During Ripper's first three weeks, beginning on 7 March, atrocious weather, spring mud, and terrain put up at least as much opposition as the enemy, who was content—for reasons soon to be disclosed—to withdraw without serious fighting. Both the 1st Marines (now commanded by Colonel F. M. McAlister) and the 7th (which had been inherited by Colonel H. R. Nickerson) fought isolated actions, but the Korean Marine Regiment had the hardest fight. The KMCs, who had been reattached to the Marine division, stormed Hill 975 in a battle which lasted all day, 23 March, and did not end until three the next morning. As the operations officer of one of the KMC battalions reported, in his own English, "Our indominatable [sic] spirit which finally recaptured Hill 975 after hand and hand combat will brilliantly decorate our KMC history."[40]

In April, Seoul and Inchon were again in UN hands and the Eighth Army was advancing all across the front. Soon after, the 7th Marines, attached to the 1st Cavalry Division while the Marine division was momentarily in corps reserve, were among the first troops over the 38th parallel. Then, while the intelligence experts speculated anxiously as to just when the Chinese would recoil in counteroffensive, the 1st Division, back in the attack, on 21 April secured Hwachon Reservoir just north of the parallel, another reservoir which Marines would long remember. Appropriately, just at this moment, General O. P. Smith (back in divisional command), who had serenely led the division through so many battles, was preparing to turn over command to Major General G. C. Thomas, who was thereby entering combat in the third major war of a career that began at Belleau Wood.

THE CHINESE COUNTEROFFENSIVE

All during the Eighth Army's steady advance to the 38th parallel, intelligence had clearly shown that the Chinese were preparing a truly massive counterstroke. Despite around-the-clock efforts by Fifth Air Force to interdict the narrow peninsula's few and extremely channelized communications, the Communists had built up to a strength of about 700,000, and the end was nowhere in sight. Therefore the advance of the Marine division, like its advance in November, was wary and carefully "buttoned up."

Well that it was. Before midnight on 22 April the Chinese struck the west and central lines of the Eighth Army in full force. Their objective was simple: to drive the United Nations forces into the sea.

One prong of the enemy attack found a soft spot just left of the Marine division. The adjacent 6th ROK Division, careless of its flanks, had definitely not "buttoned up," and, in General Smith's words, when hit "simply evaporated."[41] During the last two hours of 22 April, the Chinese penetrated almost four miles at this point, caroming off the refused strong points of the 7th Marines on the division left. Before daybreak, the Chinese had opened a gap ten miles wide and ten miles deep. On the Marines' right, which was tied in to the southern arm of Hwachon Reservoir, the Korean Marine Regiment, exposed to equally hard blows, counterattacked and drove the Chinese out of their positions.

As daylight came, the situation maps showed the Marine division standing firm with a heavy tide of Chinese reinforcements washing around its left flank. First, General Smith committed one battalion of his reserve regiment, the 1st Marines, on the left, then the entire regiment. Then, on IX Corps order, the division pulled slightly back, still keeping its right tied to the reservoir and trying to contain the breakthrough by pulling out the 7th Marines and echeloning its battalions to the left rear, back to Chunchon. All day the Marines worked rearward, slowed down by the job of getting out all dead and wounded (mostly by helicopter) before the living and the fit could retire.

The night of 23 April and the following days held hours of hot action, especially for the 1st Regiment, on the angle of the refused, sensitive left. The 3d Battalion, on the extreme tip, found itself surrounded all night and still under heavy attack by mid-morning. To the left rear of the Marines, far back in the abandoned zone of the hapless 6th ROK Division, the British 27 Brigade, as General Smith noted, "did a fine job of stopping the forward thrust of the Chinese."[42] Again IX Corps ordered a daylight retirement, which the Marine division executed mainly without breaking contact with strong enemy forces. By the 26th, however, the crisis was past—for the time being—and IX Corps was saved, largely through the steadfast defense of the Hwachon corridor by the Marines. And that morning, having again brought his division through hard battle which others failed to withstand, General Smith turned over command to General Thomas.

Eighth Army, having by 26 April gradually absorbed the first phase of the offensive and closed ranks again, then withdrew in orderly style to defense lines which had been prepared rearward by thousands of toiling "Yoboes" of the Korean Service Corps. Thus, by 30 April the Marines were established just north of Hongchon, halfway back to Hoengsong, and, by a westward shift of corps boundaries, back again under General Almond in the X Corps.

In mid-May the Chinese resumed their attack with 125,000 troops hurled against ROK units to the east of the 2d Infantry Division, which was on the Marines' right. This time the rupture was even worse: on the 16th, enemy units pushed 30 miles into a re-entrant that threatened to sweep the 2d Division away. On 17 May a fierce assault by a Chinese regiment hit the 3d Battalion, 7th Marines, who turned it back (and took 82 prisoners to boot) with good help from tanks, the 11th Marines, and from MAG-12 and MAG-33. Next day, when it was apparent that the 2d Infantry Division was again in trouble, General Thomas executed a deft maneuver which ended up with the 1st Regiment taking over (and holding) former 2d Division ground, and with the Marine division echeloned to the right and propping up the rear of the Army division, which then faced east, reacting into a gap left by fleeing ROK troops, and held. Then, as the Chinese offensive finally spent itself, the United Nations forces counterattacked.

FROM THE SOYANG TO THE PUNCHBOWL

As far as General Thomas was concerned the first part of the UN counterstroke was more of a pursuit than an attack. The terrain leading back toward Hwachon Reservoir was, as the Marines well knew, terrible, and so were the rain, fog, and bog. Behind a thin screen of sacrificial North Koreans, the Chinese streamed rearward, leaving weapons, supplies, and many prisoners (the Eighth Army took more than 10,000 prisoners during the last week in May, of whom the Marine division contributed a good share). Here was a moment of potential victory. Lieutenant General James Van Fleet, the Eighth Army's new commander rightly observed:[43]

In June 1951, we had them whipped. They were definitely gone. They were in awful shape.

Briefly the Marines were alerted for an amphibious right hook, going in at Kojo up the east coast to outflank the fleeing Chinese, but, despite the eagerness of Generals Thomas and Van Fleet, the idea was vetoed from above, and once again, as on Okinawa, Marine amphibious capability to outflank was shelved in favor of a dry-land, head-on attack.

The Soyang River was the first barrier on the way north. The Marines crossed handily and pushed on until, on 31 May, they were looking down on Yanggu at the east end of much fought-over Hwachon Reservoir. Then, extending still eastward, the Marine division continued the attack on 4 June, moving amid the precipitous east-coast mountains that range south from Wonsan. For ten more days the attack slugged ahead against increasing resistance and many prepared fortifications. Conspicuous for its fine fighting performance was the KMC regiment which General Thomas wisely provided with good Marine officers and NCOs as advisers and instructors. As Colonel Krulak, General Thomas's chief of staff, moralized, "In order to get a return from something, you've got to invest in it."[44]

North of Yanggu the 2d Infantry Division was pulled out of the attack, and the 5th Marines moved to the right to take over their zone. This meant that the Marine division was advancing with all regiments in line, and the supporting arms, especially the 1st Wing's Corsairs, were the main reserve. Unfortunately, the Communists also had supporting arms (a fact which became increasingly evident as the war went on and belied armchair characterizations of the Communists as a thrown-together "peasant army"). During three days' steady pushing from 3 to 6 June, the 1st Regiment reported an average of one round of "incoming" every two minutes around the clock. Moreover, in this precipitous country where the enemy mined the narrow rice-paddy valleys and fortified the heights, the tank, as one senior officer sadly remarked, was "a sick beast."[45] All told, the advance northeast of Yanggu was no bowl of roses, and the casualty lists showed it. For the first ten days in June, the cost of this steady fighting to the Marine division was higher than for any previous full month, though, to be sure, it was for a four-regiment, square division, with all four regiments in action. Neglecting this obvious fact, higher headquarters, who had arrived *in vacuo* at theorizing yardsticks of what constituted acceptable casualties, tended to wring their hands over Marine losses even though the Marines accepted them as the cost of hard fighting. Moreover, the enormous efficacy of the helicopter for rapid evacuation of Marine wounded (and the fact that no wounded Marine in Korea was ever abandoned) counted heavily. As an example, during June 1951, the 1st Regiment took 1,111 casualties, but only 67 failed to survive, a statistic which gladdened the hearts of the Navy's doctors and corpsmen.

The corps objective, which the Marine division gained on 20 June, was a sheer line of mountains looking down into a deep, almost circular valley with similar heights on the other side. This was promptly named the Punchbowl. Here, on X Corps order, the division set to work on a heavily wired, trenched, and mined front line more on the order of 1916 than 1951. There was good reason, however: in June, Communist overtures had been received for truce negotiations, and, although the men in the front lines did not yet realize it, the general trace of the Korean front, in effect, had been politically stabilized two years before the fighting ended. From a tactical point of view, the war at this point became one of position, not maneuver. Moreover, since the Communists had more than 700,000 men in the field, while the combined UN and ROK forces totaled about 450,000, the change was logical. For the Marine division, in any case, a breather was evidently in order, and, for the second time since the Marines had landed in Korea, the division was allowed a few weeks out of combat, commencing in mid-July.

AIR SUPPORT

After the Chosin Reservoir, the Marine air wing regrouped in Japan, and, as the 1st Division re-entered combat in early 1951, so did the wing. There was a difference, however. In the initial operations, at General MacArthur's specific direction, Marine air had properly been ordered to support the Marine ground troops as an air-ground team. By 1951, unfortunately, other counsels prevailed, and, when the wing resumed active work, it was assigned to Fifth Air Force, placed under centralized control, and used in general support of the Eighth Army as a whole.[46] This change was rationalized on the theory that everything that flew should be kept separate, under the

Air Force, from the troops which fought on the ground, whereas the fundamental fighting concept of the Marine Corps is that ground and air are one and indivisible. Obviously, the two doctrines were irreconcilable, and that of the Air Force finally prevailed.

As a concession to the Marine point of view, after a succession of representations by Generals Smith, Harris, and Thomas, the aircraft at a forward airstrip, K-46, were briefly allocated exclusively to the Marine division, but this arrangement soon lapsed. This assignment was welcome while it lasted, but it was only a crumb by comparison to support from the full wing, over which the division had lost control. Moreover, as will be seen, once diverted the Marine air groups received many jobs which neglected their special training and capability in close air support.

The period from June through September 1951 marked an attempt by airpower enthusiasts to test the claim, dating back to Douhet and Mitchell, and often touted during World War II, that, given the chance, aerial interdiction of an enemy's rear could destroy the ability of his army to fight in the front lines. The narrow neck of Korea, with its numerous tunnels, defiles, and mountain roads, and with the Navy controlling the sea on both flanks, seemed an ideal terrain for such an experiment. If it couldn't work in Korea, it wouldn't work anywhere.

Operation "Strangle" was initiated with fanfare on 5 June. Eight key routes were divided by Fifth Air Force among the various air commands in Korea. The 1st Marine Air Wing (commanded by Major General Christian F. Schilt from 25 July on), drew three, along the east coast. During forthcoming months the whole might of United States air power in Korea thundered and swooped, night and day, at the rear-area zone of interdiction, while the front line troops did the best they could with the scant air support which remained. The results were extremely disappointing; as on Iwo Jima, while we bombed, the enemy built. By the end of Operation Strangle (which was allowed to peter out, sans fanfare),[47] the front line forces, resources, and positions of the Communists were many-fold stronger, as a result of their respite, than they had been to begin with. In the words of Vice Admiral J. J. ("Jocko") Clark, one of the Navy's hardest fighting aviators, who commanded the Seventh Fleet, "The interdiction program was a failure. It did *not* interdict."[48]

In late August (while Strangle was still being pursued), further consideration, more serious than in the spring, was given to an amphibious flanking attack on the east coast, to be delivered by the Marine division. Once again, however, despite the enthusiasm which the idea aroused among Marines and with General Van Fleet, too, the proposal came to naught. Soon afterward, the 1st Division was back in line, girding for an offensive to bring the rest of the Punchbowl into American hands. The zone of the attack, which jumped off on 5 September, was probably the most rugged in which the division fought during the Korean War, dominated by precipitous, heavily wooded mountains, and almost unpierced by roads or trails. Having had all summer to dig in, the North Korean defenders, supported by 92 guns whose supply of ammunition had been anything but strangled, contested each hilltop and bunker, and all four regiments had fighting aplenty. In terms of difficulty of terrain and fierceness of enemy resistance, the September battle ranks as one of the three or four foremost campaigns of the war.

In the nature of things, the September offensive was a battle of supporting arms, or should have been. Except, however, for the 11th Marines (who fired as many as 11,000 rounds in one day on a 6,000-yard front), the division's advance was largely the work of its riflemen—first the 7th Marines, then the 1st, and finally the 5th and the KMCs. During 18 days' fighting, General Thomas requested 182 air-strikes and got only 127 from the JOC ("Joint Operations Center," a name of ill fame and ill omen among front line soldiers and Marines, for the top air-control agency); among those he requested, only 24 were delivered within a half hour, and about half of the remainder required more than three hours, while some were delayed six to seven hours. In the 21 September attack by the 1st Regiment (now commanded by Colonel T. A. Wornham) on Hill 854, a particularly bad piece of terrain, the assault troops fought all day with virtually no support until the accidental arrival of four Marine Corsairs on the way home from a Strangle strike with unused bombs to jettison. Looking over the situation after the offensive closed on 24 September, General Thomas officially described the division's air support as "unsatisfactory" and tried to do something about it.[49]

With tacit support from Army superiors, many of whom had become convinced converts to Navy-Marine air-support doctrines during the Korean War, General Thomas asked officially that all close support for the Marine division come from the Marine wing and that the Marine division be assured at least 40 close-support sorties per day while in combat. After much correspondence and many conferences, the request—which was strongly opposed by Major General F. F. Everest, USAF, who commanded the Fifth Air Force—was beaten down. The principal line of argument used against General Thomas was summed up by one staff officer: ". . . they want more than their share—the 1st Marine Division has to understand that it is just one more division in Korea."[50] To this and to other stock arguments General Thomas's account of his reply (during a conference with General Everest) was:[51]

[Everest] gave me the drill about how few aircraft he had and how he can't allot aircraft to every division, etc., etc. I told him that my interest was in this Division; that we brought our own aircraft along to this war; that our officers and men were trained and fought with the expectation of receiving air support; that the others had not ever expected it and that arguments concerning the unfairness of so supporting us would not stand examination.

On that line, the matter rested. Unfortunately, the problem was not one which the Marine Corps, or its representatives in Korea, could influence effectively. It was inherent in the theater command relationships approved by the JCS, behind which lay the dogma of the separation, not the integration, of air and ground. Never, during the rest of the war, did the Marine division get all the air support it needed and felt entitled to, nor wholly by Marine air (though the situation improved somewhat during the last months of the war). On the other hand, the Marine wing, under Major General C. C. Jerome, in time evolved into a virtual tactical air force for the Eighth Army, and was ultimately given the mission, in 1953, of supporting the whole Eighth Army. In so doing, Marine aviation made a notable contribution in demonstrating and furthering the use of really close air support across the whole front.

During late 1952 and 1953 (by which time Major General V. E. Megee had assumed command of the 1st Wing), there were important innovations in equipment and tactics. For instance, the faithful Corsair was replaced by the F9F Panther jet; the photo version of the Corsair was supplanted by the twin-jet F2H Banshee; and the Marine Corps' miscellany of World War II Douglas transports was partly supplanted at last by the more adaptable Fairchild R4Q "Flying Boxcars." Tactics and techniques had to be changed to accommodate the higher speeds and shorter endurance of the new planes to proven concepts of air-ground operations developed with piston-engined aircraft. The jet fighter-bomber proved itself as a more steady and accurate platform for guns, bombs, and rockets than its piston-engined forebears; and the casualty rate for pilots engaged in close-support missions dropped by more than half. Marine jet photo planes, unarmed except for cameras, were sent on solo, deep penetration missions—to the Yalu and beyond—

thumbing their noses at intercepting MIGs. Marine jet night-fighters escorted night raids by Air Force B-29s, whose crews insisted on Marine cover.[52] And finally, "the reliable old AD maulers" of MAG-12, under the veteran command of Colonel R. C. Mangrum, continued to win the affection of Marine and soldier alike as they dumped seemingly endless loads of munitions into the enemy front lines.

GENERAL SHEPHERD BECOMES COMMANDANT

In 1947, when selecting General Vandegrift's successor, President Truman had weighed two names, Cates and Shepherd. As he himself explained, there seemed little to choose between two officers with such distinguished records, so his nod went to the elder and more senior, while a quiet promise went to the junior. By 1951, General Shepherd's turn had come, and, on 1 January 1952, he became 20th Commandant of the Marine Corps.

Aside from the urgencies of war, the last year of General Cates's tour had been eventful.

In late 1950, the defense mobilization program for the Korean War was announced. It provided for an expansion of the Army from 10 to 26 divisions, while the Marine Corps, which had performed so excellently in the field, was to be increased by a single regiment, and the actual strength of the Corps at the end of the forthcoming fiscal year was to be reduced by 28,000.

On 25 January 1951, acting on behalf of 43 other senators, Senator Paul H. Douglas of Illinois (who had been wounded as an officer in the 5th Marines on both Peleliu and Okinawa) introduced a bill to provide that the Marine Corps should consist of four divisions and four air wings, and that the Commandant should be a member of the Joint Chiefs of Staff. Seventy-six members of the House, led by Representative Mike Mansfield, also a former Marine, sponsored an identical bill.

On introducing this legislation, which bore the number S. 677, Senator Douglas stated:[53]

Events over the years show clearly that notwithstanding the clear intent of Congress that this nation have at its disposal an adequate combatant Marine Corps, there are nevertheless forces at work within the Executive Department which have attempted, with considerable success, to destroy the combat effectiveness of the Marine Corps. It would be excellent if this issue could be left to administrative action, but both the past and present experience has shown that this is inadequate if we are to carry out the intent of Congress insofar as the Marine Corps is concerned.

The reasons for this situation are obvious to all. While the Joint Chiefs of Staff are men of fine character and are sincere patriots, the majority of them are fundamentally . . . opposed to the Marine Corps as a combatant organization. Notwithstanding their many expressions of good will toward the Marine Corps they have nevertheless tried to destroy its capability to function on any appreciable scale in combat. . . .

We have in the past attempted to provide for this combatant Marine Corps by expressions of Congressional intent. It is clear that expressions of intent are ineffective. We must have direct Congressional action in the form of law.

The Senate and House hearings on the Douglas-Mansfield Bill, held in April and May 1951, parallel those of January 1909, when, as in 1951-52, Congress devoted its attention to what the Marine Corps was intended to do and be. During hearings, the "force-in-readiness" or expeditionary role of the Marine Corps was emphasized in order to set in proper perspective its other major function, amphibious warfare. It was brought out that the principal role of the Corps in the past had been as an expeditionary force. It was predicted that this would continue in the future. Finally, by analysis of previous JCS actions, it was demonstrated that the Commandant would not ever be consulted on matters affecting the Marine Corps until he gained direct access to the Joint Chiefs of Staff.

The Department of Defense strongly opposed the bill on the ground that the Chief of Naval Operations adequately represented Marine Corps interests in the JCS. All members of the Joint Chiefs testified against the legislation (while the Commandant and every living ex-Commandant supported it), but the principal opposition spokesman was Admiral Sherman, who insisted that CNO commanded the Marine Corps, an assertion which Secretary Matthews contradicted in a dramatic passage during the presentation of his views. Subsequently, the surprise production by the Senate Armed Services Committee of the Sullivan-Nimitz-Vandegrift gentlemen's agreement of 1947 further highlighted the inconsistency of Admiral Sherman's position. A final by-product of the hearings was an exhaustive legal analysis and legislative determination of the status of the Marine Corps as a military service in its own right. As hearings progressed it became obvious that this was one of the central points in issue, and that the bill could not logically pass unless Congress was clear in its mind and intent that the Marine Corps, despite its close and unique partnership with the Navy, was nevertheless a distinct Service. This fact the House Armed Services Committee affirmed in its report:[54]

Actually the Marine Corps is and has always been since its inception a separate service, distinct and apart from the United States Army, United States Navy, and United

States Air Force. Both the United States Navy and United States Marine Corps are under the cognizance of the Secretary of the Navy, but the committee emphasizes the fact that this has no bearing on the autonomy of either service.

The legislation passed the Senate by unanimous consent, and, on 16 May 1952, after a debate studded with praises for the Marine Corps, the House passed it by a vote of 253 to 30. In the final conferences to align the House and Senate versions, the resultant bill emerged with provisions for three, rather than four, standing Marine divisions and air wings and it provided that, with respect to matters of direct concern to the Marine Corps, the Commandant should enjoy coequal status with the members of the JCS. On 28 June 1952, President Truman signed what thereby became Public Law 416, 82d Congress, and General Shepherd became the first Commandant of the Marine Corps to sit with the Joint Chiefs of Staff. Reflecting somewhat earlier on the Marine Corps bill (when its passage first seemed assured), the *New York Times* voiced a general feeling in its columns:[55]

This Congressional action is a direct reaction to: (1) the magnificent record on the ground and in the air of the Marines in Korea; and (2) the persistent attacks upon the Marine Corps by high officials inside and outside the Pentagon during and since the "unification" fight.

The foregoing legislative process had been rather hard on General Cates. Although the initiative for Public Law 416 had been wholly from Capitol Hill, the administration's disapproval could not help but bear strongly on the Commandant, especially since he favored Congress' objectives and had to say so during hearings. Initiation of the legislation brought General Cates's service to a fine finish after four strenuous years of successive reductions and attacks on the Corps, and, at the last, of Marine victories in battle.

EAST AND WEST COAST ISLANDS

While the 1st Marine Division and 1st Wing hammered away on the mainland of Korea, two detached forces of United States and Korean Marines held a fringe of islands off the enemy shore on both coasts. The story of Marine operations from 1951 to 1953 in the east and west coast islands is one of the least known of the war.

During the general withdrawals of December 1950, Rear Admiral Allan E. Smith, commanding the Navy's Korean blockade force, urged that several of North Korea's many offshore islands be held in order to facilitate blockade, provide bases for raiding and intelligence operations, and afford observation posts for naval bombardment and air-strikes. The naval high command agreed, and, in early 1951, defense commands were established for the east and west coast islands. Each force consisted of a U. S. Marine headquarters with subordinate Marine island command groups and attached shore-fire control and communications personnel, and Korean Marine infantry. The west coast command held five islands (Sokto and Chodo, off Chinnampo; Paengyong-Do, Taechong-Do, and Yongpyong-Do, straddling the 38th parallel). The east coast command ranged from Yang-Do, only 120 miles south of Vladivostok, to Wonsan (where seven islands were occupied or outposted, with Yodo as headquarters), to Nando, just north of the "bomb-line." Although both commands were part of the Seventh Fleet, they were manned and administered by Fleet Marine Force Pacific.

Operations on the west coast, under immediate command of the British blockading force, involved relatively little combat. The principal jobs of the west coast forces were support of guerrilla units, protection of the highly important air-warning radars on Chodo, and military government of the thickly populated islands. On the cold and storm-beaten east coast, almost all islands but Nando were under intermittent and sometimes heavy shelling, and two were attacked. There were practically no civil populations, but the islands bulged with intelligence and communications units, and raids, gun-strikes and air-strikes by the Seventh Fleet were the order of the day.

In Wonsan harbor, possession of the inner islands was essential to continuation of the naval investment of this key port and rail and road bottleneck. One of the main jobs of the Wonsan force was operation of Briscoe Field, on Yodo. This was a short, crude airstrip hewn out in June 1952 by Seabees, under Communist shell-fire, to serve as a haven for crippled planes and a base for search and rescue work. As it was the only UN airfield north of the 38th parallel, Briscoe Field was seldom inactive. Between the helicopter station-ship off Wonsan and Briscoe Field, more than 50 downed pilots were brought in or plucked from the bay or snatched from enemy hands after crash landings on the nearby mainland. In this work the Wonsan-based helicopters provided some of the earliest and most convincing experience data on the amount of flak damage which the "choppers" could really stand.

Enemy attacks on the east coast islands were directed against Hwangto-Do, in Wonsan Harbor, and Yang-Do in the far north. The first was a successful Chinese raid on the night of 28 November 1951 against a small detachment of British and Korean Marines. The second was a landing on 19 February 1952 by an enemy battalion, in 30 sampans, in an effort to take Yang-Do. The first three waves made good their landing, and there occurred an all-night battle ashore between the invaders and a Korean Marine company led by the island command detachment of U. S. Marine officers and men, while two American destroyers and a New Zealand frigate intercepted enemy reinforcements. All enemy who got ashore were finally killed or captured. This was the only amphibious repulse on either side during the Korean War. In addition to these two actions, the Wonsan islands sustained numerous heavy bombardments in 1953. As an appropriate finale to the 861-day investment of Wonsan, the last (official) round of the war was fired there—an 8-inch high-capacity shell from the USS *Saint Paul* which landed during the final minute before commencement of the truce.

FINAL OPERATIONS

As the winter of 1951-52 set in on the main line of resistance, the 1st Division settled down on the north side of the Punchbowl with 11 miles of front to hold in some of the bleakest territory in Korea. When November 10th arrived, General Thomas arranged to have every single weapon in the division, from rifles up, fired at high noon in one earth-shaking volley, following which every combat aircraft in the 1st Wing screamed down in a series of front line air-strikes. Shortly before, as another firepower novelty, the division arranged to get long-range naval gunfire support from the battleship *New Jersey's* 16-inch guns, the only naval guns able to reach inshore to the Marine division's sector. After the one-ton shells wreaked devastation in the Communist reverse-slope positions, the enemy troops were told, according to prisoners, that this was American atomic artillery. Throughout the winter such bombardments became standard.

Another practice which the Marine Corps had made standard was mass tactical and logistical employment of helicopters. In September 1951, Helicopter Transport Squadron 161 (HMR-161), commanded by Lieutenant Colonel G. W. Herring, the first such squadron in the Armed Forces, was attached to the division and was quickly set to work. Basing calculations on Quantico's *PHIB-31* and adding empirical corrections as they went along, the chopper squadron was soon performing such feats as transporting the entire combat supply of a fighting battalion into the front lines, or lifting the division reconnaissance company onto a key mountain top under the guns and eyes of the enemy, or moving the 11th Marines' rocket battery up and down the division front for surprise fire, or displacing the division reserve to key points in the vast sector. Before the war ended, HMR-161 flew 18,607 sorties, carrying 60,046 passengers (including almost 10,000 wounded) and 7,554,336 pounds of cargo. Before 1950, as with amphibious assault before World War II, helicopter operations in battle were a theoretical possibility. In Korea, the Marine Corps converted theory into reality.

On 10 January 1952, General Thomas returned to the United States to assume duty as Assistant Commandant. He was relieved by Major General

War in Korea–Stalemate along the Main Line of Resistance

J. T. Selden, another 1st Division veteran of World War II. During the dreary winter of position warfare, General Van Fleet again had the 1st Marine Division work up plans for amphibious "end runs" on both the east and west coasts, and again circumstances intervened. As spring approached, Van Fleet visited General Selden, and said:[56]

> Selden, I can give up as much real estate as necessary on this flank, but I want you to move to the western flank, for there, with my headquarters, President Rhee, and the peace conference going on just north of your new lines, I cannot give up an inch.

Soon afterward, on 23 March, the Marine division was pulled out of line and shifted 180 miles across Korea to the far western end of the line, guarding the vulnerable corridor leading to Seoul and overlooking the Panmunjom truce site. Here, holding a 35-mile front—longer than that of any other division in Korea—the Marines, flanked on the right by another un-yielding unit, the British Commonwealth Division, insured the security of Seoul and anchored the UN left flank.[57] Tactically, the situation was complicated because most of the front lines were forward of the Imjin River, while the division reserve and support areas lay behind it. Moreover, parts of the front were pierced or bordered by two other rivers, the Sachon and the Han.

In these positions the Marine division fought a series of bloody and bitter trench-warfare actions of a type and scale unheard of by Marines since World War I. As described by a volunteer Marine of this period, life in the lines seemed a throwback to 1918:[58]

> The front, or front lines, are rarely referred to as such. "MLR" is used instead. It stands for "main line of resistance." In our case the MLR is a deep trench, from five to seven feet in depth, running along the ridgeline of the hill mass occupied by our platoon. Theoretically, the MLR is a continuous avenue from coast to coast, cutting the peninsula of Korea in half. . . . Our bunkers are situated on the reverse slope of the ridge, out of sight from the enemy trenches. A Yukon stove in each bunker provides heat. . . . It is oil-fed from a five-gallon can which rests on top of the bunker. Candles provide light inside the bunkers. The arrangement of the inside of the shelter—the thick wooden supporting beams, the sandbag walls, the crude wooden table, the photographs of beautiful women nailed to the beams, the rifles, ammunition belts, grenades, the candlelight—reminds one of a set for "What Price Glory."

Culminating in mid-August 1952, bitter fighting, mainly by the 1st Marines, centered about "Bunker Hill," a no-man's land eminence which commanded parts of the MLR, but unfortunately, lay under the guns and observation of Taedok Song, a frowning elevation in Chinese hands. Outpost "Siberia" was also the scene of heavy fighting. On 26-27 October, after Major General Edwin A. Pollock had relieved General Selden (29 August), the 7th Marines, commanded by Colonel T. C. Moore, fought the first of a series of vicious struggles to hold "The Hook." The Hook was a shell-torn, cratered, battered ridge which jutted forward from the MLR and also commanded the vital Imjin River crossings linking the Marine and Commonwealth Division forward areas with their supporting units.

As 1953 came in, fighting centered about such outposts as "Berlin," "East Berlin," and "Hedy," all code-names for bits of terrain possessing tactical advantage in the inconclusive, hard-fought war of raids, bombardments, and ambushes in no-man's land. From 26 to 29 March, the Chinese launched a fierce attack to gain a triangle of key outposts—"Reno," "Carson," and "Vegas," so named by the battalion which established them, because holding them was a gamble. The loss and subsequent recapture of "Vegas" by the 5th Marines, under Colonel Walt, were marked by desperate fighting and by artillery and aerial bombardment of an intensity seldom equaled during the war. Briefly in May—shades of Guadalcanal—the 1st Marine Division was relieved by the 25th Infantry Division. During this period, only the 11th Marines (commanded through the winter by Colonel H. N. Shea) and the division tanks continued in action. As the Marines returned to the MLR for the last time, in June 1953, Major General R. McC. Pate assumed command, thus becoming the last general officer to command the 1st Marine Division in combat in Korea.

By 27 July 1953, the UN truce negotiators (whose backstage Talleyrand was a Marine officer, Colonel J. C. Murray) had dotted the last "i" and crossed the last "t." At 2200 that night, in accordance with the agreement which had been so painfully negotiated, firing ceased. A sergeant in the 1st Marines recalled:[59]

A beautiful full moon hung low on the sky-line like a Chinese lantern. Men appeared along the trench, some of them had shed their helmets and flak jackets. The first sound that we heard was a shrill group of voices, calling from the Chinese positions behind the cemetery on Chogum-Ni. The Chinese were singing. A hundred yards or so down the trench, someone began shouting the Marine Corps Hymn at the top of his lungs. . . .

DEVELOPMENTS AND LESSONS OF KOREA

The Korean War was unforeseen, unpopular, and technically old-fashioned. Nevertheless, it produced many developments of importance as far as the Marine Corps was concerned.

Far and away the most important was the helicopter, which the Marine Corps pioneered, first brought to Korea, and then first used in combat. Of only less importance was another Marine development: practicable lightweight plastic body armor for the assault rifleman, the armored vest, or "flak jacket," as the troops called it. This garment was the product of research and tests at the Field Medical Laboratory at Camp Lejeune and resulted in a startling drop in fatal abdominal and chest wounds; when its success had been demonstrated on Marines, the Army asked for and obtained 63,000 from the Marine Corps. Another Marine "first" was the thermal or "vapor-barrier" boot which, after serious frostbite casualties in the first winter, resulting from inadequate footgear, virtually eliminated frozen feet for both riflemen and Corsair pilots.

Among the war's operational lessons, two stood out. One was underscored by Douglas MacArthur in a single sentence: "The amphibious land-ing is the most powerful tool we have." Since 71 per cent of the globe is covered by oceans, this is likely to remain so, but it was in serious danger of being overlooked by military deep-thinkers after World War II. The second lesson—also a reaffirmation of long-held Marine ideas and experi-ence—was that of the soundness and superiority of Marine and Navy air-support doctrines. In the test of the open market, front line soldiers in Korea, Army or Marine, overwhelmingly preferred the Marine brand of air support, flown by Marine pilots. To provide this air support, the 1st Marine Air Wing flew 127,496 combat sorties (a total considerably in excess of that for all of Marine aviation in World War II) and lost 436 aircraft.

Even more important than either of the foregoing operational lessons was the more profound one that immediately ready, professional expeditionary forces exert an influence out of all proportion to their size at the outset of any war, large or small, near or remote, and that the Marine Corps had once again provided the United States with such a ready fighting force.

One lesson of great importance in terms of the military philosophy of the United States was, however, lost sight of before the end of the war. This lesson was later underscored in an address by Lieutenant General M. B. Twining:[60]

Naval strength, therefore, lies in the aggregate power and capability of the fleet as an entity, rather than in the arithmetical sum of the strength of its several components. This is plainly demonstrated by the naval history of the Korean conflict.

For example, the 1st Marine Division at Inchon in September 1950 was able to ac-complish a major strategic purpose in a few days. This brilliant success was due to many factors in addition to the bravery, skill, and combat discipline of the Division itself. There was the mobility of the fleet which assembled and placed it there. There was the skill of the amphibious forces in coping successfully with tides and hydro-graphic conditions which beggar description. There was the training and know-how of the gunners of the naval fire-support ships covering the exposed and tortuous ap-proach. There was the skill and perception of the carrier pilots who covered the land-ing area, supported Marines on the ground with bomb and rocket, and interdicted the battlefield to the approach of enemy reinforcements. It was the combination of these elements in concert which produced, at Inchon, a strategic reaction exceeding many-fold the cumulative or total capabilities possessed by each element of the fleet acting alone.

We Marines were to become aware of this only too keenly in the days which fol-lowed. The 1st Division became the war horse of the United Nations Forces in Korea, from the Chosin Reservoir to Panmunjom. But it was never to participate again in a great strategic stroke like that at Inchon. The winning combination which had taken Inchon and Seoul had been broken up. The surface ships, operating as a form of floating artillery, bombarded Wonsan and the northern ports for years with no discernible result; the carriers participated with the Air Force in operations against the enemy lines of communication—the 1st Marine Air Wing was separated from its teammate, the 1st Marine Division, thereby destroying the most effective air-ground team the world had ever seen. The Wing was placed under Air Force command and operated as a component of the 5th Air Force. . . .

The fleet, which had performed so brilliantly in September 1950 as a balanced instrument of seapower, had been dispersed by circumstances into separate, relatively ineffective components—of land, sea, and air.

Twenty-six thousand forty-three Marines were killed and wounded in Korea. Of these, 4,262 died. These totals were more than twice as many casualties as the Corps sustained in World War I. Forty-two Marines won Medals of Honor, 28 posthumously. During the Korean War, 7,190 American troops were captured by Communists: only 227 were Marines. The over-all behavior and *esprit* of the handful of Marine prisoners were exemplary. As the Senate Permanent Investigating Subcommittee reported in 1956, after investigating Korean prison camp scandals:

. . . The Marines assisted each other and maintained their military organization within the prison camp. For the most part they took an interest and cared for their fellow Marines who were in difficulty. The existence of a strong discipline, a well-organized chain of *esprit de corps,* and faith are given credit for the very commendable showing of Marine prisoners of war.

Semper Fidelis could therefore still remain the motto of the Corps.

THE CORPS SCENE

The Corps scene during the Korean War was oddly split between the urgent atmosphere of war in the Far East and a stateside environment where business, even much military business, went ahead as usual. While one division and one wing were fighting a major war, two divisions and two wings (the fruits of the Douglas-Mansfield Bill) were perforce pursuing their normal jobs of making themselves ready for trouble as soon as they could. Marine Corps Schools, Camp Pendleton, and El Toro, carried the main burden of training for the war—the Schools for turning out junior officers, and Pendleton and El Toro for preparing and processing the steady flow of replacements for the Far East. By the end of the war, 60 per cent of the Corps had traveled that path and fought in Korea. Conspicuous in Pendleton's cycle was the ordeal of cold-weather training which all ranks below colonel had to undergo at Pickel Meadows in the snow-girt High Sierras; no Marine training was ever tougher or more practical for the purpose.

Under General Shepherd, Marine Corps Headquarters underwent further reorganization. On 7 February 1952, "Pots and Pans," the Division of Plans and Policies, was abolished, and, in its stead, a full-fledged general staff organization was substituted. This departure was necessary to handle efficiently the business of a Corps whose strength exceeded two hundred thousand. Another departure was the creation of the Fiscal Division, a step which deprived the Quartermaster General of his ancient power of the purse. The first Fiscal Director, an iron choice for a tough job, was Brigadier General D. M. Shoup. As a result of Public Law 416, there was created the Plans Branch, a hard-working blue-ribbon unit whose job it was to advise the Commandant regarding his new JCS duties.

In June 1951, a fundamental but almost unnoticed change took place in Marine promotion procedures. Ever since the advent of promotion by selection it had been customary, because of the relatively small number of available active general officers, to fill out senior Marine selection boards with a minority of rear admirals, usually three. In 1950, after Admiral Sherman overruled General Cates's customary suggestion of certain admirals for this duty and substituted an instructed delegation of his own choice, General Cates quietly sought and obtained a change in the law, by which retired Marine general officers might fill such vacancies, and such thereupon became the procedure.

To support the Corps at war strength for the second time in a decade, new posts came into being: Twenty-Nine Palms, a vast artillery training area in the southern California desert; the Marine Corps Supply Center, Albany, Georgia, ultimately destined to be the main East Coast logistic base; and—harking back to 1918—a Marine Corps Air Station at Miami.

11 THINGS PRESENT
AND TO COME *1953-1962*

*It is a notable fact that few men have ever left the Marine Corps without a
feeling of undying loyalty toward it.*
—General A. A. Vandegrift

*J*UST as there had been no victory in Korea, so there was to be no demobilization, or at least no contraction of the Corps comparable to those of
1919 and 1946. Marine reservists who had been among the first to fight, as
well as the draftees whom the Corps had been compelled to take during the
war, were, in the jargon of the Pentagon, "released," and regulars took over.

The deployment of the Fleet Marine Force after Korea reflected the continuing exigencies of the cold war. Most of the 3d Marine Division (reconstituted on 7 January 1952) was permanently stationed on Okinawa, its base
bearing the illustrious name, Camp Smedley D. Butler. Teamed with the
3d Division, the bulk of the 1st Wing, in Japan with headquarters at Atsugi,
provided the air portion of a ready United States expeditionary force in the
Far East. An infantry regiment from the 3d Division and an air group from
the 1st Wing were organized as the 1st Marine Brigade, based at the former Kaneohe naval air station (another new post) on Oahu as a reserve in
the Central Pacific. After 20 dreary months on occupation duty fronting the
demilitarized zone between North and South Korea, the 1st Marine Division was at length relieved and returned to its home station, Camp Pendleton, teamed with the 3d Wing at El Toro. On the East Coast, the 2d
Marine Division and the 2d Wing continued the Atlantic, Caribbean, and
Mediterranean missions they had carried on together since 1946. The
deployment just described was destined to be that of the Marine Corps
for years to come.

ANOTHER COMMANDANT

The commandancy of General Shepherd was one both of achievement and of consolidation. The enactment of Public Law 416 was, in certain respects, the most significant single development of these years. Fortunately, in his new role with the Joint Chiefs of Staff, General Shepherd enjoyed the warm friendship from earlier days of Admiral Arthur Radford, the forceful chairman of the JCS who had fought so hard for the Navy and the Marine Corps during the early days of unification. General Shepherd's friendship with the admiral eased the Marine Corps' debut in a new arena, and helped to establish without difficulty the general pattern of Marine participation in JCS matters.

But while the Marine Corps was finding its voice in the Joint Chiefs of Staff, a fundamental clarification of its role within the Naval Establishment was in progress. As a natural consequence of Public Law 416, the status of the Commandant and of the Marine Corps, in relation both to the Chief of Naval Operations and to the Secretary of the Navy, was closely re-examined. In September 1954, Secretary of the Navy Robert B. Anderson took positive action to insure that the Commandant, like the Chief of Naval Operations, should be a "command assistant" directly responsible to the Secretary and thus to dispel, once and for all, the notion that the Marine Corps and its Commandant were under military command of the CNO. Instead, as Mr. Anderson put it,[1] "They are, in every sense of the word, a team."

General Shepherd's highly successful tour as Commandant ended with 1955. A tribute to his unqualified accomplishment was the decision by his former colleagues, the Joint Chiefs of Staff, to nominate him, upon retirement, as Chairman of the Inter-American Defense Board, the first Marine officer ever to fill this important post, and the first full-time Chairman since the days of World War II.

In 1956, General Randolph McCall Pate, who, after commanding the 1st Marine Division in Korea, had returned to Marine Corps Headquarters as Chief of Staff, succeeded General Shepherd as Commandant. In accordance with a practice which had grown up with regard to the other Service chiefs, the new Commandant was nominated for a term of only two years, despite the fact that the law specifically provided a four-year term for the Commandant of the Marine Corps. Although General Pate was subsequently reappointed for his second two years, the technical illegality of such two-year appointments piqued Congress and was destined to become an issue.

Another matter in which Congress attempted to intervene on behalf of the Corps during General Pate's commandancy was the maintenance of the Marine Corps at a strength sufficient to meet the three-division and three-wing mandate of Public Law 416. Experience had demonstrated that, with the Corps' extensive non-FMF security force commitments at various shore stations and afloat, to maintain the "combat" divisions and air wings specified in the law demanded a 200,000-man Marine Corps. Commencing in 1955, Congress for several years appropriated funds for this strength level (in excess of administration budget recommendations based on plans for a progressively reduced Corps), but was never successful in persuading the Bureau of the Budget to release or expend the money, at least for the purposes for which appropriated. Thus, one major problem of General Pate's administration was an ever-tightening personnel situation. On the other hand, a difficulty which had dogged some earlier Commandants was spared General Pate. With the appointment as Chief of Naval Operations of Admiral Arleigh A. Burke (who was probably more admired among Marine officers than any previous CNO since the creation of that office in 1915), relations between the Commandant and the Chief of Naval Operations attained an all-time high of harmony and mutual understanding.

RIBBON CREEK

Three months and eight days after General Pate became Commandant, the Marine Corps sustained the most serious misadventure in its history. On the evening of 8 April 1956, an overzealous Parris Island drill instructor, who had been drinking while on duty, ordered an unauthorized night march during which six recruits were drowned in Ribbon Creek, a tidal stream in the swamps that border the island. The circumstances of this tragedy focused national attention on the Marine Corps and on its methods of recruit training. Generally conceded to be the most successful in the country for producing discipline, loyalty, and prowess in battle, the Marine Corps system, nevertheless, came under heavy criticism (except from Marines themselves) on the part of those who considered it overexacting or even brutal. In an appearance before the House Armed Services Committee on 1 May, General Pate laid all facts developed by the various official inquiries of the incident before the Committee and promised appropriate remedial action. After his statement, Representative Carl Vinson, Chairman of the Committee, congratulated him in these words:[2]

General Pate, you have reported this morning not only to this Committee, but to the nation. During my 42 years in Congress, this is the first time within my memory that the senior officer of any Armed Service has had the courage to state in public session that his service could be deficient in some respect.

Following the Ribbon Creek episode, changes were introduced into the recruit training methods and organization of the Corps, many of them at the behest of the newly appointed Inspector General of Recruit Training, Major General Shoup, destined in a few years to command the Corps. More drill instructors were added, and all were more carefully screened. Recruit training was lengthened, physical training made far more rigorous, and officer supervision of the whole process increased. Some asserted that these unquestioned improvements were to an extent negated by sternly enforced prohibitions which precluded noncommissioned drill instructors from resorting to forms of direct action which had gradually become accepted as normal. Sharp insight into the problems of a post-Ribbon Creek drill instructor was voiced, after a visit to Parris Island, by Hanson Baldwin of the *New York Times:*[3]

There are 13 pages of "do's" and "don't's" for the DI; most of them "don't's," in an order dated April 22. These put a greater premium upon example, persuasion, psychology and leadership, and downgrade fear as a means of hammering a platoon of rookies into shape. But it also puts much more strain upon the DI. He can still "yammer" at a recruit; he can still "crawl his frame" orally though not with profanity. And he can drill and drill and drill. But he must establish his moral ascendancy over some 75 undisciplined, self-centered young men almost as soon as they get out of their civilian clothes, or else the platoon will run him. . . .

Despite the promptitude and thoroughness with which recruit training was overhauled, Ribbon Creek left a bad taste with the public and, even more so, within the Marine Corps. The episode was highly damaging in that, for the first time in the history of the country, public confidence was shaken, at least momentarily, in the philosophy of the Marine Corps, if not in the Corps itself. On the other hand, the strengthened, morally more intense, thorough recruit training methods which resulted, while placing heavier demands upon the drill instructor, produce Marines as good as those of the old "head-in-the-bucket" era which ended on 8 April 1956.

IN THE FAR EAST

The retention in the Far East of a strong Seventh Fleet, with a Marine division and air wing, was well justified by events.

In February 1955, the Communist Chinese seized the island of Ichiang, thus rendering indefensible the adjacent Tachen Islands, belonging to the Chinese Nationalists. When the Nationalists attempted to evacuate the Tachens, the Communists in turn tried to block the operation and thus trap the Nationalist garrison and inhabitants. To prevent the distinctly possible eruption of general fighting throughout the Formosa Strait area, the Seventh Fleet moved in, landed Marines and naval beach parties, and evacuated some 24,000 civilians and soldiers without further incident in what the *New York Times* described as "the most forthright action against Communism since the Korean War."[4]

Three months later, in response to a call for help from the French and the Vietnamese governments, Seventh Fleet amphibious forces and Marines were sent to North Vietnam to evacuate over 300,000 refugees from the oncoming Communist Viet-Minh. In this operation, 68,000 tons of cargo and 8,000 vehicles were also saved from falling into Red hands.

On 23 August 1958, Communist Chinese shore batteries on Amoy Bay opened on the Kinmen (Big and Little Quemoy) Islands. As the daily volume of "incoming" swelled to 50,000 rounds and Red fighters attacked Nationalist planes over Formosa Strait, it became logical to assume that an attempt to seize the islands was brewing. Such an assault would be the prelude to full-scale attacks on Formosa and the Pescadores. Faced with this ominous possibility, the Seventh Fleet was reinforced and Fleet Marine Force troops were ordered to Formosa and remained there until the threat of invasion had passed.

The succession of events in the Far East from 1955 on underscored a requirement which had already been recognized and met in the Mediterranean—the need for a ready battalion of Marines afloat with the Fleet—and, from 1958 on, the 3d Division maintained such a floating battalion under Commander Seventh Fleet.

In 1959 and again in 1960-61, Communist-inspired civil war broke out in Laos, the landlocked state which provided a buffer between the non-Communist states of southeast Asia and Red China and its puppets. Promptly, troops of the 3d Marine Division deployed southward, and, in the latter crisis, some went ashore in Thailand, with the permission of that government, as part of a Pacific Fleet joint task force commanded by Major General Donald M. Weller. In addition, as conditions worsened in Laos, Marine aviation was called on to provide helicopter units, here, as in other roadless, underdeveloped countries, the universal vehicle and antibandit weapon.

Early in the following year, as Communist guerrillas preyed increasingly on South Vietnam, the U. S. Navy and Marines gave coastal flanking protection for the country's long seaward face—so reminiscent, strategically at least, of the east coast of Korea. While American warships patrolled to prevent seaborne infiltration of enemy groups from North Vietnam, Marine officers and NCOs from the amphibious reconnaissance units of FMF Pacific worked ashore with such native counterguerrilla forces as the "Sea Swallows," an organization of amphibious irregulars dedicated to clearing the southern tip of their country of Communist bandits. During March 1962, in the marshy estuaries of the Camau Peninsula, Marine "observers" accompanied "Sea Swallow" combat patrols and took part in several successful, aggressive actions.

TO THE SHORES OF THE LEVANT

In the autumn of 1956, the cold war grew hot in the Mediterranean after Egypt's seizure of the Suez Canal. To protect American and other civilians being evacuated from Alexandria, the Sixth Fleet's Marine battalion was called on to make the Corps' first Mediterranean landing in 52 years. Between 31 October and 4 November, the 3d Battalion, 2d Marines, supported State Department officials in processing and protecting some 1,500 civilians from 33 different countries, and got them safely aboard Navy transports which had been rushed to the scene. While British and French aircraft bombed and strafed Alexandria, and Egyptian ships and shore batteries wildly fired back, one Marine participant in the landing reminisced:[5]

Sitting in Alexandria harbor was like being in the center of the Rose Bowl, watching the activity about you.

Less than two years later, in July 1958, Lebanon, lying between Israel and pro-Communist Syria, was menaced by a Communist-supported rebellion obviously aimed at toppling the government of pro-Western President Camille Chamoun. Following the fall of the neighboring Iraqi government to a Communist-led *coup d'etat*, President Chamoun appealed to the United States to send troops to uphold his government. Within 30 hours, on 15 July, the 2d Provisional Marine Force, a brigade-scale grouping of battalion landing teams from the 2d, 6th, and 8th Marines, under Brigadier General S. S. Wade, landed at Khalde Beach, Beirut. As seen from the shore, the landing was impressive and well timed:[6]

Precisely at 3 p.m., the first of the landing barges ground ashore. . . . Within a few minutes the battalion was ashore. Then came swarms of jeeps and heavy tanks. Smoothly and quickly the huge ships disgorged their loads and with scarcely a hitch the powerful force rolled into position. . . . [An urchin] shouted at one of the Marine sentries guarding the tanks. "What have you come here for anyway," he asked belligerently, "to start a war?" The sentry, a gawky young Marine who looked as though his uniform and the equipment dangling about him were about to fall from his scrawny shoulders, glowered sternly at the young Lebanese. "We are here at the invitation of the Lebanese government to protect the country's independence," he recited, repeating word for word the briefing officer's formula. Then he added on his own, "And *not* to start a war."

Some days later, an Army airborne force arrived, landing at the Beirut airport which the seaborne Marines had secured, and, as at Veracruz, a more senior Army general assumed command of all troops ashore. Officers with a sense of history could reflect that it had been 55 years since the USS *Brooklyn's* Marines had landed at Beirut during disorders of bygone days, and some 2,000 years since Roman legionaries had bivouacked in the same olive groves that now sheltered men of the Fleet Marine Force.

On 30 September, having secured Beirut and its approaches and having stood by during the peaceful election and inauguration of a new president, the last elements (3d Battalion, 6th Marines) of the American landing force withdrew. General Wade's headquarters returned home, and the Sixth Fleet, with its floating battalion of Marines, resumed its accustomed vigil.

Operation "Bluebat," for such was the code-name for the Lebanon landing, gives cause for reflection.

Nominally, Bluebat was merely a brief test of power in the latter-day "Hundred Years' War" which communism has imposed on the 20th century. Since the Marines' entrance into Lebanon was unopposed, the landing will receive only a brief note in history. That it might have been the beginning of another Korea is overshadowed by the fact that it was not.

Yet the Lebanon operation was a significant move in the real war of limited objectives, as distinct from the hypothetical general war of nuclear terror with which prophets of doom have mesmerized our era. Not all the megaton missiles and intercontinental bombers in existence could have effected the desired result that United States sea power, with a cutting edge of Marines, was able to bring about without firing a shot in anger.

Another paradox presents itself. It was five days after the landing, in full force, of seaborne Marines from 18-knot transports, before the first lightly armed airborne troops reached Lebanon, and that only after delicate and uncertain negotiation, in a tug-of-war against Communist political pressure, for overflight permissions from each country in the path of the transport planes. The airborne brigade's heavily laden seaborne "tail"—which at length gave the air-lifted unit appreciable sustained fighting power—did not begin to arrive until eight days after the initial landing. It would be easy (and unfair) to suggest that the differences in timing between the seaborne and the airborne forces resulted from differences in readiness between the Marines and the paratroopers. In reality a far more fundamental factor was responsible: the inherent ability of maritime expeditionary forces, positioned at sea in international waters and supported by the fighting and staying power of the Fleet, to anticipate trouble and hover indefinitely, if need be, in easy reach of the key point. A century and a half before the Lebanon landing, it was (in Mahan's words) those same "far-distant, storm-beaten ships, upon which the Grand Army never looked [that] stood between it and domination of the world." So, in the 1960s, with their embarked Marine expeditionary forces, the successors of those ships stood off the Levant and wherever else needed throughout the globe, and stand today.

GENERAL SHOUP ASSUMES COMMAND

In 1959, as General Pate's tour as Commandant neared its end, the Secretary of the Navy, in an action not unlike that of Gideon Welles in 1864, reached well down the lineal list to select Major General David M. Shoup as 22d Commandant, bypassing nine more senior general officers in the process. General Shoup was confirmed for a four-year term after the Senate Armed Services Committee had refused to accept the two-year non-statutory nomination originally sent in by the administration. On appointment, he became the third Commandant of the Marine Corps to wear the Medal of Honor and the first Medal of Honor man ever to sit with the Joint Chiefs of Staff.

General Shoup's administration was immediately marked by emphasis on economy, austerity, and merciless pursuit of efficiency. Like General Pate before him, General Shoup was faced with a declining Marine Corps strength, resulting from Defense Department and Bureau of the Budget cuts in the Corps, even when Congress had appropriated funds to maintain increased strengths. Instead of the 27 battalion landing teams of the three Marine divisions in 1956, by 1960 there were but 21. In fiscal year 1960, official testimony before the House Military Appropriations Subcommittee disclosed that the Bureau of the Budget withheld approximately 25 per cent of the Marine Corps' appropriated budget of $202,000,000.[7]

Yet at the same time the Marine Corps, like the Navy, faced with increasing commitments, was compelled to spread itself thin. In 1960, as it became clear that the Caribbean, too, had become another arena of the active struggle against communism, the maintenance of floating units in the West Indies had to be resumed for the first time since the early 1930s. With Cuba's Communist dictator, Fidel Castro, voicing threats ever more stridently, the defense of Guantanamo Bay also resumed its earlier importance for the Fleet Marine Force. And, for the first time in more than a century, with U. S. Navy units regularly cruising African waters in 1961 and 1962, a miniature floating battalion of Marines (actually a reinforced rifle company with a detachment of supporting aviation) was back on the old "African Station," whilom realm of King Ben Crack-O, visiting and exercising at such places as Monrovia, the Canaries, Freetown, Bathurst, and Capetown, then rounding the Cape of Good Hope and returning via Suez. The national response to these and other demands of the cold war in 1961 was a general strengthening of our defenses. Early in the year, President Kennedy authorized a 3,000-man increase for the Marine Corps, followed in short order in the forthcoming defense budget by a buildup to 190,000 enlisted—the first upward strength changes since Korea. Building thriftily on this foundation and by dint of the most strenuous personnel economies, it was possible by 1962 to restore the FMF to its vital strength of 27 battalion landing teams and to raise the manning level of Marine aviation squadrons—some of which had been shrunken by 20 to 30 per cent of authorized strength—to more than 90 per cent.

With this welcome reinforcement and in the face of 1962's world-wide challenges and demands, General Shoup drove the Corps hard, his objective, in his own widely quoted words, "To ensure that our Corps is always ready, willing, and able to carry out efficiently any mission that we may be assigned, and by so doing to continue to merit the trust and confidence of our people."[8]

In late 1961 and early 1962, as charges were being advanced, mainly by irresponsible critics, of undue indifference within the Armed Forces toward communism, and a concurrent failure to indoctrinate troops in anti-Communist theory and information, General Shoup attracted widely favorable national attention by a series of public statements in which he drove home the Marine Corps view—associated historically with all truly professional troops—that it was unnecessary and, at times, even counterproductive to train Marines to hate anyone, even an enemy to be encountered in battle. The job of the Marine Corps, he underscored, was to be ready to fight any enemy, any time, anywhere, whom the President or Congress might designate, and to do so coolly, capably, and in a spirit of professional detachment.

THE CORPS SCENE

Following the end of the Korean War, the Marine Corps scene was marked—especially under Generals Shepherd and Pate—by steady efforts to conserve and foster the tone and traditions of the Corps which had either weakened or lapsed under the impact of two wars and unification. It was no accident, but really a kind of defense mechanism, that the post-Korea Marine Corps saw the return of the field hat (at least for shooters and drill instructors), limited readoption for ceremonial purposes of the pre-1939 infantry drill and the Sam Browne belt, restoration of the traditional ranks of marine gunner, gunnery sergeant, and lance-corporal, and even reinstitution of the pre-Josephus Daniels custom of officers' dinners in mess, the last an inspiration of General Shepherd himself.

Not content with having brought the gunnery sergeant back onto the scene, General Pate in 1957 re-established at Marine Corps Headquarters the post of Sergeant Major of the Marine Corps. The first incumbent in the new line was Sergeant Major William Bestwick. Another act of rescue by General Pate was his preservation of the Marine Corps Expeditionary Medal. By a tour de force of administrative unimagination during the 1930s, it had been decided that, when the existing supply of such medals was disposed of, the medal itself would lapse and be replaced by the Navy Expeditionary Medal. In the nick of time, the Commandant sought a reprieve which Secretary of the Navy Thomas Gates willingly granted, and the most senior of Marine and Navy campaign medals is still with us.

The practice of using Marines for military security duties demanding maximum reliability continued to increase. In addition to the established embassy guard program under the State Department, Marines had guarded the American High Commissioner throughout his tenure in occupied Germany and were employed in a number of domestic posts and sites of special importance, such as the Marine detachment at Camp David, the Maryland mountain camp of the President. In addition, from 1954 on, HMX-1, the Marine helicopter squadron at Quantico, had the responsibility of providing helicopter services for the President and White House staff. This commitment occasionally reached far afield from Quantico, as when a Marine helicopter rescued President Eisenhower's press secretary, James

Hagerty (himself the father of a Marine officer), from a Communist-frenzied Japanese mob during the Tokyo riots of 1960.

On the international military scene, U. S. Marines continued to justify the globe as their emblem: in 1961 and 1962, Fleet Marine Force units conducted practice landings or training exercises in such far-flung spots as Navplion, which had known the fleets and *Epibatae* of Athens; Sardinia and Turkey; Korat, Siam; on the slopes of Fujiyama; Zambales in the Philippines; Cadiz; and Chumunjim on the east coast of Korea. Moreover, the Marine Corps found itself performing foreign training and advisory work reminiscent of the 1920s. In Korea, a Marine advisory group remained after the war, first in Pusan, then Seoul, to continue training the Korean Marines. On Taiwan, a staff of Marine officers and men brought the Chinese Nationalist Marines to a high polish, while individual U. S. Marine advisors were, on request of the countries concerned, assigned to work with the forces of Brazil, Chile, Peru, Argentina, Venezuela, and Colombia. In 1958, the United States acceded to the long-standing request of the Haitian government for a Marine Corps military mission to reorganize and revitalize the Haitian Armed Forces, descendants of the Garde d'Haiti of other days, and, in January 1959, 25 years after the end of the occupation, a detachment of Marine officers and NCOs reopened headquarters on the Champ de Mars in Port-au-Prince. The Marines were back, but this time solely in the capacity of advisors.[9]

On the operational scene, exactly a decade after Colonel Twining and his officers at Quantico had conceived their "new concept" of the helicopter-borne landing, the Navy in 1956 recommissioned the old jeep carrier USS *Thetis Bay* as the first assault helicopter transport, with more advanced and larger such ships soon to follow. To accommodate the modern concept and to make good use of the practical lessons derived from the reality of assault helicopters, new aircraft, new shipping, and new weapons, the Fleet Marine Force was reorganized and restructured in 1956 and 1957. The resulting organization, while still readily recognizable as descended from its predecessors which had served so well in the Pacific war and Korea, was somewhat lighter, far more flexible, and pre-eminently tailored to the new requirements and new challenges of the times.

On the heels of restructuring came new weapons and equipment. In 1962 the FMF turned in its battle-tested M1 rifles, familiar to this generation of Marines as was the Springfield two decades earlier; the M14 7.62-mm. replacement model was issued concurrently with M60 machine guns which superseded the Brownings that had fought in three wars. To avoid any lapse in readiness, the change-over for all units of FMFLant was accomplished in one 24-hour period. For aviation, in addition to ever-advancing new aircraft, there were equally impressive developments: the "expeditionary" short airfield shaped around portable catapults, carrier arresting gear, and other naval aviation techniques adapted for use ashore; the amphibious assault fuel supply system (essentially a collapsible tank farm designed to marry across the beach with Navy tankers afloat); and, before the end of 1962, one squadron per air wing of the massive new GV-1 air transports.

To assure himself that the Headquarters and the administration of the Corps were correspondingly streamlined, General Shoup, no respecter of traditions, began reorganization of Marine Corps Headquarters in 1961. An earlier reorganization casualty (1960) was the Marine Corps Board which, in its day, dating from the commandancy of General Vandegrift, had generated and fostered the "new concept" of amphibious warfare and had provided much of the consistent rationale of the Marine Corps' stand on unification and defense organization problems. Then, in July 1961, in the face of stubborn and finally public opposition from certain of the old-time quartermasters led from the retired list by Major General W. P. T. Hill, the Commandant secured legislation abolishing the separate category of supply officers. Thus at length ended the ancient division, dating from 1798, of Marine officers between Staff and Line.

And finally, on 20 February 1962, the Corps scene enlarged to dimensions yet unforeseeable when Lieutenant Colonel John H. Glenn, Jr., one of the Corps' ablest pilots, chosen from among the best qualified candidates of three Services, successfully conned a space vehicle in three orbits of the earth. After landing in the Atlantic, Glenn was safely plucked from the sea by the destroyer USS *Noa* (later flown by helicopter to the USS *Randolph*), and won renown and glory for the Marine Corps as the first American to encircle the globe in space.

Altogether it was a very large and a very new Marine Corps which Archibald Henderson could have recognized only by its *esprit* and its fighting prowess. These remained the same.

EPILOGUE

As of 1962, with many intervening ups and downs, the Marine Corps had expanded more than tenfold in 24 years. General Shoup's Marine

Corps of 1962 was larger than General Marshall's Army in 1939. Moreover, this order of expansion was no longer the hasty consequence of war or general mobilization. History seemingly had settled that the Marine Corps, along with the other Armed Services, must be large and stay large as long as the 20th century's struggle for world supremacy remained at issue.

The question which 1962 left unanswered to the years ahead was this—to what extent would the effects of bigness ("the curse of bigness," it might be, in Brandeis' phrase) change or dilute the inherent character of the Marine Corps? In other words, could the experience and temper of an eminently efficient and successful small Corps be passed on to the larger successor? Clearly, to transmit that experience and that temper would be the single most important task of every remaining active Marine commissioned or enlisted before 1939—to hand down to those who followed what had been good and unique and distinguishing and traditional in the old Corps.

A second question unanswerable in 1962 was to what extent the trends of American defense organization—leveling, standardizing, monolithic, superadministered, overcentralized, unfriendly to elite units—would leave room for a viable Marine Corps. This question was obviously in the thoughts of a former Assistant Secretary of the Navy, John Nicholas Brown, when in 1951 he said, "In the vast complex of the Department of Defense, the Marine Corps plays a lonely role."[10]

Other questions come to mind. To what extent, if at all, have mid-20th century weaponry and technology rendered the Marines' mode of war obsolete? What is now, or what should be, the status of the Marine Corps in the Armed Forces scheme of things? What are the abiding future functions that the Marine Corps can perform?

Trained men who will stand and fight are never obsolete. It was not the bowman, but the long bow, not the cavalryman, but the horse, which vanished from the scene. Men—the man, the individual who is the Marine Corps symbol and stock in trade—constitute the one element which never changes. Whether the landing force lands by pulling boat, by motor sailer, by diesel-driven barge, or by helicopter, there must still be fighting men to project American maritime power onto the farther shores and the islands in between. The fearsome, untried weapons of today and tomorrow cannot change the fact that only attack—not defense—wins war; nor have these weapons made the Marine and his mode of warfare more or less obsolete than any other trained and disciplined soldier who stands in the forefront of battle.

From the Marine Corps' traditional role as a force in readiness, a rule of thumb may be derived and stated. As the larger Services are reduced between wars, in strength and perforce in readiness and striking capability, the need for a ready Marine Corps goes up. It is no accident that so much of the Marines' fighting and expeditionary service have taken place between formal wars. Far from being obsolete in an era of atomic weapons, the ready expeditionary force, made up of professionals, is the cutting edge of the cold war.

As long as the sea is at our gates, North America will remain the last great island. Her strategy, if she is to win and survive, must be maritime. In the words of one of the Corps' intellectual leaders,[11] the United States must:

> . . . make the sea its ally and not its enemy: use the sea as a friend in conveying its power and influence throughout the world, and not merely as a sterile barrier protecting its shores from the threat of invasion.

That our strategy is immutably maritime becomes clearer each day as we recognize that much which has been briefly labeled "airpower" is a passing phenomenon. Ahead there remain only the two unchanging kinds of warfare, land warfare and naval warfare. America's safety and well-being depend in primary measure upon American ability to control and, even more important, to exploit control of the seas. Thus, maritime warfare is our predominant mode of warfare, and that is where the Marine Corps finds its place, as the nation's ready maritime expeditionary force. This role suits the Marine Corps beyond all others, because of the naval character of the Corps.

The historic partnership and mutual dependence between the Navy and the Marine Corps is as old as the nation and is unique and precious. Nevertheless, as we have seen, frequent attempts have been made—some even originating in and pursued by the Navy—to dissolve this partnership either by outright abolition of the Corps or by transferring it to the Army. During the years immediately preceding 1952, ill-founded talk was spread in high places, mainly by opponents of the Douglas-Mansfield legislation, that the Marine Corps itself was aiming for autonomy, complete and separate.

There could be no greater folly. The Marine Corps has become what it is as a naval service, and a naval service it must remain. Bear in mind that the anchor in our Marine Corps emblem symbolizes the fact that the Marine is a maritime soldier. So were his forebears, the *Epibatae* of Greece and Rome's *milites classiarii*. And the original title of the Royal Marines in

1664 was "The Duke of York and Albany's Maritime Regiment of Foot."

Of greater importance than all that which is past, is the fact that the United States is a maritime nation. The corollary of this fact is a maritime strategy. For Marines the further implication is equally pointed that the Marine Corps, to retain its strategic effectiveness, must likewise retain its character as a maritime Corps. As such it must cherish and strengthen its associations with the Navy. Conversely, the Navy must recognize that the Marine Corps has come of age and that, while drawing upon the strength and resources of American sea power, the Marine Corps also contributes to those resources in abundant and more than equal measure.

Within the foregoing pattern, the future functions of the Corps are clear.

First among them is to be ready to fight any time, anywhere, and to "perform such other duties as the President may direct."

A second Marine function is to serve as a ready amphibious expeditionary force, whether for police action during peace or for the seizure and defense of advance bases in war. Collateral to this function Marines must continue to serve at sea with the Fleet (an essential to retaining the maritime habits of the Corps) and do their share in the Navy's shore establishment.

The final main function of the Corps is to preserve and enhance its professional quality and thereby retain its position in the defense establishment as a professional, elite force, military but not militaristic, an example and a soldierly standard of comparison for all comers.

If the past is truly prologue, then the functions just stated are those which history has determined for the Marine Corps during its long evolution from one battalion of Continental Marines to three divisions and three air wings. To be allowed the means and to be left free to perform these functions well—for "prudent, vigilant pursuit of our own military business," as General Shepherd put it[12]—is all the Corps has ever asked. In the words of another Commandant, General Cates:[13]

> The Marine Corps has no ambition beyond the performance of its duty to its country. Its sole honor stems from that recognition which cannot be denied to a Corps of men who have sought for themselves little more than a life of hardship and the most hazardous assignments in battle.

From 1775 onward, Congress and the American people have looked favorably on the Marine Corps and have enabled it to survive to fight our country's battles in the air, on land, and sea. The future of the Corps lies in their hands.

Here's health to you and to our Corps
Which we are proud to serve;
In many a strife we've fought for life
And never lost our nerve.
If the Army and the Navy
Ever gaze on Heaven's scenes,
They will find the streets are guarded
By United States Marines.

APPENDICES

APPENDIX 1
MARINE CORPS STRENGTHS

THERE are several different ways of stating the strength of a military organization. Each has its special meaning and usefulness to personnel planners, and each differs, for any given year, from another. Every Service, including the Marine Corps, has an authorized strength, which is established by Congress and is in the nature of a permanent ceiling; authorized strength is rarely attained, except in times of war or emergency. The actual ("appropriated") strength of the Marine Corps from year to year depends on the amount of funds appropriated by Congress each year. On a few occasions, it has depended on whether or not an administration in power was willing to release all these funds to the Marine Corps, or in effect impose an executive reduction in the strength of the Corps. Of course, actual strength at any given moment (sometimes called "on-board" strength) varies from month to month with the ebb and flow of deaths, discharges, retirements, and new inputs. In times of peace or stability, fluctuations in actual strength throughout the year are not great, but in active periods, such as those preceding the two World Wars, or in a year of demobilization, often become extreme. For example, the on-board enlisted strength of the Marine Corps on 30 June 1941 (sometimes called the "end-strength" because 30 June marks the end of a fiscal year) was 51,020; five months later, when the Japanese attacked Pearl Harbor, this figure had grown to 66,319. Still another approach is to give an average figure for the entire fiscal year; ordinarily, but not always, this should agree with the appropriated strength.

In earlier times and extending into this century, the foregoing nuances of what the administrators and management experts now describe as "personnel accounting" were unknown to the Marine Corps and to its historians. Thus, in terms of the 1960s, it is sometimes impossible to state exactly what particular type of strength is referred to in early documents or accounts. By consulting the Naval Appropriation Acts over the years, one can arrive at appropriated strengths, while, by poring through successive authorizations by Congress, the changes in ceilings can be reconstructed. However, from 1849 on, the President was given authority, in his discretion, to enlist Marines in lieu of "landsmen" (the old title for ordinary seamen), thus enabling the actual strength of the Corps to be temporarily augmented (as occurred during the Civil War) from Navy manpower allowances.

In light of what has just been explained, the strength table which follows may have the appearance of a crazy quilt and would certainly be so regarded by any G-1 planner. Nevertheless, it includes all significant changes in authorized (*i.e.*, ceiling) strength of the Corps, together with significant fluctuations in actual strength at given times. At certain points, the figures will appear to be at variance with those given in previous histories of the Corps; my sources, unless otherwise stated, have been the Annual Reports of the Commandants, Naval Appropriation Acts, and other acts of Congress. Figures in *italics* represent authorized strengths; those in roman represent actual (on-board) personnel at the given moment.

YEAR	OFFICERS	ENLISTED	REMARKS
1779	124	3,000	Revolutionary War peak; enlisted strength approx. only.
1794	*6*	*306*	Marines authorized for the six frigates of 1794.
1798	*33*	*848*	Initial authorized strength on establishment of the Corps, 11 July 1798.
1799	*40*	*954*	
1803	26	453	Reduction in accordance with executive order from President Jefferson (strength as of 14 Feb.).
1809	*45*	*1,753*	By Feb. 1812, only 38 officers were on active duty.
1814	*93*	*2,622*	War of 1812.
1817	*50*	*865*	Peace Establishment Act.
1829	49	948	
1834	*59*	*1,224*	Strength authorized by 1834 reorganization.
1847	*71*	*2,319*	Mexican War.
1851	67	1,154	
1855	53	1,338	Increased by executive order, in place of landsmen.
1856	53	1,538	Increased by executive order, in place of landsmen.
1857	53	1,778	Increased by executive order, in place of landsmen.
1858	53	2,010	Increased by executive order, in place of landsmen.
1861	*93*	*3,074*	Civil War; actual strength 1 Jan. 1861, 1,892.
"	93	4,074	Increased by executive order, in place of landsmen.
1876	75	2,074	
1878	84	2,000	
1889	77	2,100	
1896	76	2,600	
1898	*119*	*4,713*	Included 43 officers and 1,640 men for Spanish War service only.
1899	*201*	*6,062*	Naval Personnel Bill of 1899.
1902	*201*	*6,812*	

YEAR	OFFICERS	ENLISTED	REMARKS
1903	278	7,532	
1905	278	8,771	
1908	333	9,521	
1912	351	9,921	
1916	381	9,947	
"	649	14,981	National Defense Act, 1916; actual strength, 354 officers and 10,727 enlisted men.
1917	649	17,400	Included newly established warrant officer grades.
"	1,325	30,000	World War I; actual strength, 6 Apr. 1917, 419 officers, 13,000 enlisted men.
1918	4,024	75,500	Actual strength, 11 Nov. 1918, 2,474 officers, 70,489 enlisted men; peak actual strength, 74,788 officers and men.
1920	1,097	27,400	Actual enlisted end-strength, 1920: 16,061.
1921	1,087	21,903	
1927	1,198	18,000	
1933	1,192	15,343	
1939	1,354	18,052	End-strength, 30 June 1939.
"	1,568	25,000	Authorized by executive order, 8 Sept. 1939.
1941	4,106	66,319	7 Dec. 1941.
1943	14,549	391,620	31 Dec. 1943.
1945	37,664	485,113	Actual 1945 and World War II peak.
1947	7,000	100,000	
1949	7,149	78,715	
1950	7,254	67,025	Outbreak of Korean War—on-board strength, 30 June 1950.
1953	18,731	230,488	End of Korean War.
1956	17,809	182,971	
1961	16,132	160,438	End-strength, 30 June 1961.
1962	16,658	172,555	On-board strength, 31 May 1962.

APPENDIX 2
MARINE CORPS ORGANIZATION

SIMPLICITY, flexibility, and maximum fighting power with minimum dead-weight have been the dominant characteristics of Marine Corps organization throughout its history.

During the 18th and 19th centuries, the two basic organizational units of the Corps were the ship's detachment for service afloat and the marine barracks, a depot and security organization associated with a navy yard ashore. A typical seagoing detachment had one or two officers and up to 60 enlisted men, while the strength of a marine barracks was determined by the number of sentry posts required to be manned, plus a margin of casuals and seagoing replacements. A field officer (major or above) normally commanded a marine barracks. Both the ship's detachment and the barracks continued to perform their accustomed functions in 1962 and were little changed in composition or duties from what they had been a century before.

For any serious operations ashore beyond the capabilities of a ship's detachment or seaman landing party, the Marines of early days were formed into extemporized companies with widely varying strengths (50-100 men and one or two officers being typical), two or more of which might form a battalion. Exceptionally, as in Florida or Panama, battalions might in turn be grouped into a temporary regiment or even a brigade, but the strengths of these imposingly titled formations were very small as compared to those in the mid-20th century, and both the battalion and the regiment were *ad hoc* task organizations without permanent identity. Battalions and regiments were, of course, usually commanded by field officers. To illustrate the diversity in size and composition of typical battalions of early days, one has only to consider Waller's battalion in the Boxer Uprising (130 men, two companies), Twiggs's battalion in the Mexican War (334 men, five companies), and Huntington's battalion in the war with Spain (623 men, six companies). From World War I on, the strength, though not the detailed internal organization, of a Marine infantry battalion has remained fairly constant (1,000 or more men in four or five companies).

During General Biddle's commandancy, a system of permanently num-bered companies—each composed of two officers and 100 men—was adopted, and one or more of such companies were permanently assigned to each shore station with a Marine garrison; in addition, certain numbered companies were assigned to the Advance Base Force (see below). At the various posts, men fully eligible and fit for expeditionary service were detailed to the num-bered companies, while short-timers, casuals, and "sick, lame, and lazy" were pooled in what were designated as "barracks detachments."

The first permanently organized tactical units of the Marine Corps were the regiments and technical companies of the Advance Base Force, which came into being during the first decade of the 20th century. These organizations included the crew-served weapons of the day: machine guns, field artillery, and heavier semimobile naval guns. On the outbreak of World War I, the Marine units assigned to the AEF were organized on the Army model, with giant 250-man companies (one platoon of which would have served as a company in the Mexican or Civil Wars) designed to absorb the heavy casual-ties correctly anticipated. The rifle, bayonet, and machine gun were the principal weapons of the World War I Marine.

After World War I, three factors influenced the organizational thinking of the Corps: (1) the continued and increasing presence of more and different weapons and equipment; (2) the prewar composite tradition of the Advance Base Force as a well-rounded entity embodying self-sufficient capabilities; and (3) the amphibious studies and experiments of the 1920s and 1930s. The interaction of these three influences produced the Marine brigade—a self-sufficient, balanced grouping of supporting arms and services around an infantry regiment, in effect a miniature division. This concept, especially adapted to landing operations, sired the later "regimental combat team" (RCT), or, as it was finally called, "regimental landing team" (RLT). Although the basic ground-fighting unit of the Fleet Marine Force in 1962 had become the Marine division, a powerful striking force of combined arms built on three infantry and one artillery regiment, more than 18,000 strong, the brigade concept remained alive, and during both World War II (Eniwetok and Guam) and Korea (Pusan Perimeter) Marine brigades proved their tactical worth. A still further, logical evolution of the brigade, first seen in Korea, was inclusion of appropriate tactical aviation as part of the brigade, which is now standard operational practice in the Marine Corps.

The organization of Marine aviation generally followed that of naval avia-tion, with the squadron, a homogeneous grouping of from 12 to 24 aircraft, as the basic unit. Squadrons were assigned to air groups, and the latter in turn to air wings, both the group and the wing being of flexible organization depending on the missions to be performed. Generally, however, the air wing embodied the spectrum of aviation capabilities required to support a Marine division in combat. A typical wing might include more than three hundred aircraft, ranging from all-weather fighters to transport helicopters, and some 11,000 officers and men.

After the war with Spain, the Navy began the practice of maintaining Marine units called "floating battalions" embarked aboard transports and attached to the Fleet. This distinctive exploitation of the Corps' naval and expeditionary character solidified into standing doctrine with the advent of the cold war in 1946, and, by 1962, it was normal for Fleet Marine Force battalion landing teams (BLT) to be embarked in amphibious shipping and on station in such potentially troubled waters as the Mediterranean, the China Sea, and the Caribbean. An offshoot of the same conditions which made the floating battalion part of Marine Corps doctrine likewise resulted in the late 1950s in an arrangement with the Navy to have Marines provide the entire deck force and air departments (normally seaman functions) of the assault helicopter carriers assigned to base Marine helicopter units. This arrangement—the brain child of Major General D. M. Weller—enabled the Navy to keep more carriers in commission within its manpower ceilings, put substantially increased numbers of Marines at sea (thereby maintaining the naval experience and background of the Corps), and placed Marine airmen afloat to support and conduct Marine air operations. But nothing is new under the sun: precedent for General Weller's idea could be found in the destroyer complements of the Special Service Squadron of the 1920s and 1930s, where, because of the continual need for small landing forces in Central America, each destroyer's deck force was made up of Marines, who formed a landing force when needed and otherwise served as deck hands to work the ship.

As of the mid-20th century, the over-all organization of the Corps had evolved from a collection of ships' detachments and a few marine barracks into the Operating Forces of the Marine Corps (the FMF, the security forces, ships' detachments, and non-FMF units under direct command of the Commandant), and the Marine Corps Supporting Establishment (all the units and bases required to procure, train, and support the Operating Forces). Marine Corps Headquarters continued to preside atop the structure, and the 22d Commandant carried on in the footsteps of his predecessors.

REFERENCES

CHAPTER ONE—*THE OLD CORPS*

1. Extract from Athenian decree of June, 480 B.C., full text in *New York Times*, 5 June 1960.
2. Flavius Vegetius Renatus, *De Re Militarii* ("Military Institutions of the Roman"), Book V, Sec. 7 and 16. Under the Roman empire there were two fleets, each with an attached legion composed of ten cohorts, as well as detachments of *milites classiarii* assigned to the Roman guard-ships on the Danube. According to Vegetius, the uniforms of the *milites classiarii* were "sea-green."
3. King Charles II Order in Council, 28 October 1664, text given in *Britain's Sea Soldiers,* Col C. Field (London 1924), Vol. I, 15. *A List of the Forces of the Sovereigns of Europe,* J. Millan (Paris 1761), assigns the French five seaman-regiments: *Vieille Marine,* 1627; *Royal Vaisseau,* 1635; *Royal Marine,* 1669; *Regiment Amiral,* 1669; *Suisses,* 1719. Vagts, *Landing Operations,* 228—a poor source where Marines are concerned—says these were "to guard ports and provide forces for ships."
4. On 28 May 1775, Col Henry Babcock, of Stonington, Conn., wrote John Hancock: "I should be extremely obliged to you if you would please to lay before the Hon'ble the Continental Congress the following Proposal: that I have leave to raise two Battalions of Marines." For further information on the so-called Nova Scotia project (which apparently lay behind this of-

fer), see "The Committee on Nova Scotia," E. T. Turnbladh, *The Leatherneck,* November 1960.
5. *Journals of the Continental Congress,* 10 November 1775, Vol. III, 348.
6. Quoted on p. 7, *A History of the United States Marine Corps,* Col C. H. Metcalf (New York 1939).
7. This and the quotation in the following paragraph are from Capt Samuel Nicholas letter to an unidentified friend, 10 April 1776, in *The Remembrancer, or Impartial Repository of Public Events,* Part II, 1776, 212-214, text kindly supplied by LtCol P. N. Pierce.
8. Another Marine officer, 2dLt James Hoard Wilson, was killed aboard *Cabot,* one of the other ships in this action, and three enlisted Marines, names unknown, are recorded to have been killed by the same "first broadside" that felled Fitzpatrick.
9. Quoted on p. 146, *John Paul Jones: a Sailor's Biography,* RAdm S. E. Morison (Boston 1959).
10. Alexander Hamilton letter to James McHenry, 17 May 1798. In Library of Congress, Hamilton Papers.
11. James McHenry letter to Samuel Sewall, 9 April 1798, *ASP, Naval Affairs,* I, 34.
12. Naval Committee, House of Representatives, resolution of 22 May 1798, in *American State Papers, Naval Affairs, 1789-1836* (Washington 1834-1861), Vol. I, 56.
13. Full debate, including committee and

Congressional action on the Marine Corps Act, may be found in *Annals of the Congress, 1789-1824* (Washington 1834-1856), 5th Congress, 2d Session, 1784-85, 1835-36, 570-71, 597, 600-01, 1855, 2132, and 3774-76. An excellent legislative history of the act is given in "From 1783 to 1798," Maj E. N. McClellan, *Marine Corps Gazette,* September 1922.

14. Quotations in this paragraph (except for SecNav's remark, from *Naval Documents, Quasi-War with France,* II, 90) are from the Marine Corps Act of 11 July 1798 (1 Stat. 594).

15. The earliest known annual budget for the Marine Corps, that of 1801, totalled $119,825.80. *Naval Documents Related to the United States Wars with the Barbary Powers* (Washington 1939-45), Vol. II, 115.

16. Quoted on p. 81, "Highlights of U. S. Marine Corps Activities in the District of Columbia," J. D. Thacker (Washington 1952).

17. LtCol W. W. Burrows letter to 2dLt Henry Caldwell, 22 September 1800, *Naval Documents, Quasi-War with France,* VI, 374. Col Burrows might well sympathize with Caldwell's grievance since he himself was receiving bitter criticism from Capt Thomas Truxtun, USN, who asserted, "the youngest sea lieutenant in the Navy takes seniority . . . over the oldest Marine officer in service," (a misstatement of Art. 40, *Navy Regulations,* 1775, which in fact said, "All sea officers of the same denomination shall take rank of the officers of the Marines.") and challenged the Commandant's authority to detail Marine officers to duty without prior approval of each ship's captain. In a letter to the Secretary of the Navy, Truxtun, after remarking "the unimportance of the Marine corps, especially in time of peace," growled, "Lieutenant Colonel Burrows takes upon himself too much, and it is time he should be put right." *Naval Documents, Quasi-War with France,* Vol. VII, 187 and 195.

18. Capt Daniel Carmick letter to LtCol W. W. Burrows, 15 October 1802.

19. By Act of 22 April 1800, which, by concurrently abolishing the grade of major in the Marine Corps, caused administrative troubles for some years.

20. The Capitol was not the only security responsibility of the Washington Marine Barracks. On 8 May 1801, the Commandant of the Marine Corps was directed to establish Marine guards from sunset to sunrise over "the departments of State, War, & the Navy." *Naval Documents Related to the Quasi-War Between the United States and France* (Washington 1935-38), Vol. VII, 222.

21. On 3 March 1801 Congress authorized construction of "Eighth and Eye" and appropriated $20,000 for the purpose, which amount, even with generous use of troop labor, proved insufficient.

22. Quoted in *Home of the Commandants,* prepared by Historical Division, HQMC (Washington 1956), 8.

23. On two occasions (February and November) in 1803, members of the House of Representatives proposed further reductions in the Corps and reduction of the Commandant's rank to that of captain. After Burrows' resignation, the Secretary of the Navy put off appointing a successor Commandant, Franklin Wharton, for three weeks until "The motion for abolishing the Office of L^t. Col^o. Commd^t. of the Marine Corps" was rejected by Congress. See *American State Papers, Naval Affairs,* Vol. I, 110-111, and *Naval Documents, Barbary Wars,* Vol. II, 357, and Vol. III, 534.

24. Benjamin Stoddert letter to Capt John Barry, USN, 13 July 1798.

25. This and the quotations by Carmick in the following paragraph are from his letter to an unidentified friend, 12 May 1800, *Naval Documents, Quasi-War with France*, Vol. V, 500. Also see letter Capt Silas Talbot, USN, to Secretary of the Navy, 12 May 1800.

26. At home, throughout the war, the Marine Corps had the job of safeguarding and escorting the numerous French prisoners captured by the Navy and held mainly at Lancaster, Pa., Frederick, Md., New Castle, Del., and Burlington, N.J.

27. All that Jefferson allowed the Corps were ships' detachments, guards of 1 sergeant, 1 corporal, and 15 privates, at Boston, New York, Philadelphia, Washington, and Norfolk Navy Yards, and headquarters personnel in Washington. *Naval Documents, Barbary Wars*, Vol. II, 157. *Naval Documents, Quasi-War with France*, Vol. VII, 269.

28. Eaton, who had served as an officer in the Continental Army, asked for 100 Marines and two field pieces, but all Commodore Barron, of the Mediterranean Squadron, gave him was Lieutenant O'Bannon, a midshipman, and 7 enlisted Marines. The composition of the force, according to Eaton's journal, was as follows: 8 USMC and 1 USN, 25 European "cannoniers," 38 Greek mercenaries, 90 Arabs in Yusuf's suite, a small party of Arab cavalry, and about 200 camel-drivers and muleteers. Yusuf commanded the Arabs, and O'Bannon the "Christians." *Naval Documents, Barbary Wars*, Vol. V, 398.

29. William Eaton letter to Capt Samuel Barron, USN, 29 April 1805, *Naval Documents, Barbary Wars*, Vol. V, 554.

30. *Ibid.* The composition of O'Bannon's storming party was: 8 Marines, 26 Greeks, and a dozen or so "cannoniers"—not more than 50 in all. Much having been made of the fact that only 8 Marines were in Eaton's force, it is fair to point out that they nevertheless numbered about one-fifth of the actual assault force, that the only persons killed in Eaton's entire force were two of the Marines, and that three of the 14 reported serious casualties of the action were Marines. In addition, 2 Marine officers and 67 enlisted men were serving aboard the three ships, *Argus, Hornet*, and *Nautilus*, which took part in the battle.

31. Quoted in "The Marine Band—President's Own," Maj C. W. Hoffman, *Marine Corps Gazette*, November 1950.

32. LtCol Franklin Wharton letter to Capt John Hall, 29 June 1805. Two factors—both beyond Hall's knowledge or control—rendered the mix-up more serious than might be apparent: (1) maintenance of the Marine Band had become a charge against appropriated, rather than non-appropriated, funds in 1804, and enlistment of the additional bandsmen created an illegal over-obligation; and (2) the new Secretary of the Navy, Robert Smith, was a fanatic for economy. To make matters still worse for the unfortunate captain, LtCol Burrows, who had ordered him to obtain the musicians, was dead by the time (September 1805) when Hall and his Sicilians reached the United States. No wonder Hall wrote, ". . . there has been some little difficulty in settling my accounts at the Navy Office respecting the Band I enlisted at Catania."

33. President James Madison, message to Congress, 1 June 1812, *Messages and Papers of the Presidents*.

34. Quoted in pamphlet, *A Masonic Oration on the Death of Brother Wm. S.*

Bush, Lieutenant of Marines (Philadelphia 1812).

35. Maj R. S. Collum, *The History of the U. S. Marine Corps* (New York 1903), 55.

36. On 16 April, after two years of war, Congress finally increased the Corps by 49 officers and 799 enlisted, bringing it to a total strength above 2,700 officers and men. In recommending this increase, Secretary of the Navy William Jones drew attention to "the gallant part this distinguished Corps has acted in all the noble victories which have been achieved, its character for discipline, valor, and patient endurance of the most severe service. . . ." *ASP, Naval Affairs,* Vol. I, 307.

37. Surgeon A. M. Montgomery, USN, letter to Capt J. M. Gamble, 15 July 1813, in *ASP, Naval Affairs,* Vol. II, 96.

38. Capt J. M. Gamble report to the Secretary of the Navy (no date) 1815.

39. Quoted in Collum, *op. cit.,* 53.

40. Secretary of the Navy William Jones report to the President, 30 October 1814.

41. G. R. Gleig, *A Subaltern in America,* quoted in *Poltroons and Patriots,* Glenn Tucker (New York 1954), Vol. II, 534.

42. Commodore Joshua Barney report to the Secretary of the Navy, 28 August 1814.

43. *United States Gazette,* 27 August 1814, and *Federal Republican,* 30 August 1814.

44. Quoted in *Poltroons and Patriots, op. cit.,* II, 548. But W. M. Marine, *The British Invasion of Maryland* (Baltimore 1913), 98, attributes the remark to Cockburn.

45. Quoted in "Commandants of the Marine Corps," LtCol G. D. Gayle, *Marine Corps Gazette,* November 1950.

46. Joint Resolution of Congress, 22 February 1815.

47. Quoted in McClellan, "From 1783 to 1798," *op. cit.*

48. All the foregoing punishments are from *Marine Corps Headquarters Order Book,* 22 August 1803-January 1815. Apparently this stiff discipline produced results, as witness the following quotation from a letter received by LtCol Burrows: "With respect to the Marines I am happy to say that a change for the better has taken place in their conduct. We no longer see them intoxicated as formerly—nor is the neighborhood disturbed with their nocturnal riots and outrages. . . ." *Naval Documents, Barbary Wars,* Vol. II, 400.

49. Quoted in "The Corps' Oldest Post," J. W. Porter, *Marine Corps Gazette,* November 1950.

50. *Navy Regulations,* 1814. Still another time-honored function of the Medical Department (in which Marines apparently received cut-rate attentions) is described in the following order: ". . . the Surgeon of every Ship of War in the Service of the U S—should make a charge to be deducted out of the pay of each Officer Seaman & others on board—for making a perfect Cure of the Veneral disease, the following sums, viz—

"For a Commissioned Officer ten Dollars

"For a Warrant Officer Seven Dollars

"For all & every other description of Officers Seamen ordinary's or others five dollars except Marines who are to pay only three dollars for such Cure—"

Naval Documents, Quasi-War with France, Vol. VII, 127.

51. *Naval Documents, Barbary Wars,* Vol. II, 497.

52. Officers' pay and rations as per Act of 11 July 1798, *op. cit.;* enlisted pay fixed by President in accordance with the Naval Armament Act of 1 July

1797 first appears in Secretary of War's letter, 16 March 1798, *Naval Records, Quasi-War with France*, I, 41.

53. The first Paymaster of the Corps, Lt James Thompson, was not appointed until April 1799. Until then, Maj Burrows performed additional duty as Paymaster, and drew the full extra pay and allowances of the office. *Naval Documents, Quasi-War with France*, Vol. III, 68, and Vol. VII, 150.

54. The original annual clothing allowance of the enlisted Marine (11 September 1798) was: "1 Hat, 2 pr. Woolen overalls, 2 pr. Linen do. 1 Coat, 1 Vest, 1 Stock of black Leather & Clasp, 4 Shirts, 4 pr. Shoes, and 1 Blankett.—" *Naval Documents, Quasi-War with France*, Vol. I, 390.

55. These regulations lasted barely a year, being superseded in late 1805 by another and more detailed set. Secretary of the Navy letter to LtCol Franklin Wharton, with enclosed regulations, in *Naval Documents, Barbary Wars*, Vol. VI, 291.

56. Quoted in "Pig-Tail Marines," LtCol J. H. Magruder III, *Marine Corps Gazette*, February 1956.

CHAPTER TWO—*THE AGE OF ARCHIBALD HENDERSON*

1. Complete proceedings of LtCol Wharton's trial are in *ASP, Naval Affairs*, Vol. I, 503 ff.

2. Proceedings of general court-martial, case of LtCol Anthony Gale, in "Records of General Courts-Martial and Courts of Inquiry, Navy Department, 1799-1867," National Archives. Information on his appeals to Congress for redress may be found in House Naval Affairs Committee report of 27 January 1829, in *ASP, Naval Affairs*, Vol. III, 284.

3. Quoted in Gayle, "Commandants of the Marine Corps," *op. cit.*

4. See report by a special committee on Expenditures in the Navy Department, House of Representatives, 28 February 1821, *ASP, Naval Affairs*, Vol. I, 740. The underlying premise of the proposal was that the Marine Corps was really an aggregation of separate detachments, ashore and afloat, and needed no Corps organization or headquarters functions other than those performed by the Secretary of the Navy.

5. LtCol Archibald Henderson letter to Secretary of the Navy, 27 March 1821.

6. A stirring account of the Quallah Battoo landing is given in the report of Lt Irvine Shubrick, USN, 6 February 1832, in *ASP, Naval Affairs*, Vol. IV, 157.

7. This and the following quotations on the Charlestown mutiny are from Collum, *op. cit.*, 64-65.

8. See Fourth Auditor, Treasury Department, letter to the Secretary of the Navy, 28 May 1829, in *ASP, Naval Affairs*, Vol. III, 581 ff. As an unhappy sequel, the Paymaster of the Corps, Capt J. L. Kuhn, was dismissed in 1832.

9. Master Commandant David Conner letter to Lieutenant Isaac McKeever, USN, 30 January 1830. Considerable background information on the anti-Marine Corps activities of the Navy Commissioners may be found in a memorial transmitted to the Senate and House of Representatives by Bvt LtCol W. H. Freeman, on 15 February 1836, in *ASP, Naval Affairs*, Vol. IV, 835 ff.

10. Enclosures to Secretary of the Navy letter to President of the Senate, 24 March 1830, *ASP, Naval Affairs*, Vol. III, 560 ff.

11. Report by Representative William Drayton, Committee on Military Af-

fairs, quoted in *U. S. Naval Institute Proceedings,* June 1954, 660.

12. The recommendations given here were actually almost a restatement of those made by Secretary of the Navy Southard in his Annual Report for 1827, except for the provisions to abolish the Commandancy and Headquarters, and to have no Marine officer above the rank of captain, all of which were worked out and presented to the Secretary in Capt John Rodgers, USN, letter to Secretary of the Navy, 25 October 1831, printed as an enclosure to the Annual Report of that year.

13. Act of 30 June 1834 (4 Stat. 712).

14. LtCol Archibald Henderson letter to Secretary of the Navy Samuel L. Southard, 18 November 1823, in *ASP, Naval Affairs,* Vol. II, 92.

15. Col Archibald Henderson letter to LtCol R. D. Wainwright, 1 July 1837.

16. Quoted in "California Beachhead—1847," Capt Lewis Myers, *Marine Corps Gazette,* January 1947.

17. Quoted in Metcalf, *op. cit.,* 120.

18. Commodore M. C. Perry report to Secretary of the Navy, 4 July 1847.

19. MajGen Winfield Scott, USA, letter, 27 August 1847, quoted in Collum, *op. cit.,* 97.

20. MajGen J. A. Quitman, USV, report to MajGen Winfield Scott, USA, 29 September 1847.

21. In addition to Quitman's report, *op. cit.,* my account of the Chapultepec assault and its preliminaries is based on the action report by LtCol S. E. Watson to Commanding General, Volunteer (4th) Division, 16 September 1847, and on the mass of firsthand testimony by participants in the battle, given in Proceedings of a General Court-Martial at Marine Barracks, Brooklyn Navy Yard, case of 1stLt J. S. Devlin, 31 August 1852. This case, arising out of a feud between

the accused and Maj J. G. Reynolds, dealt in part with certain circumstances of the Chapultepec action, and adduced lengthy testimony on the subject from surviving officers of the battalion. Among published accounts, the most useful, insofar as the Marine battalion is concerned, is *History of the Mexican War* (Washington 1892), MajGen C. M. Wilcox, late CSA, 452-482. Wilcox, then a regular lieutenant, was General Quitman's aide-de-camp during the battle, and his is by far the best firsthand, professional narrative of the operations of this division, which included the Marine battalion. Also see Winfield Scott's dispatch to Secretary of War, 18 September 1847.

22. Quitman report, 29 September 1847, *op. cit.*

23. Collum, *op. cit.,* 98-99, gives the casualty list of the Marine battalion, by name and by phase of the action in which sustained. An unfortunate aftermath of the battle, mentioned in note 21, *supra,* was a controversy in which 1stLt J. S. Devlin, a former enlisted man of shady reputation, aspersed the conduct of Maj Reynolds, at Chapultepec, first by an anonymous letter in the *Brooklyn Eagle,* 12 July 1852, and later by a pamphlet, both of which disparaged the performance of the Marine battalion in Mexico—the pamphlet being apparently his revenge for the court-martial which dismissed him from the Corps. See pamphlet, *Conclusive Exculpation of the Marine Corps in Mexico,* Bvt Maj J. G. Reynolds (New York 1853), which was Reynolds' rebuttal.

24. Most accounts credit Capt B. S. Roberts, USA, of the Mounted Rifles, with having raised the Colors over the Palacio Nacional since he was Officer-of-the-Day of the guard ordered to do so. 2dLt Nicholson, of the

Marine battalion, was Roberts' Officer-of-the-Guard, however, and actually bent on the flag and ran it up. See 2dLt Thomas Yardley Field letter to Robert Beale, Sergeant-at-Arms of the Senate, 15 March 1848, in Thomas Yardley Field correspondence, HQMC Archives.

25. Pamphlet, *Information in Regard to the United States Marine Corps* (Washington, 1875); Thacker, "Highlights," *op. cit.*, 85.

26. For comprehensive accounts of the California operations, see *Messenger of Destiny*, W. H. Marti (San Francisco 1960), based on Gillespie's unpublished papers, and *The Life of Commodore Robert F. Stockton* (New York 1856). Also see Stockton's dispatches to Secretary of the Navy, 5 February 1847 and 18 February 1848.

27. Capt A. H. Gillespie report to Secretary of the Navy, 16 February 1847.

28. Commodore W. B. Shubrick report to Secretary of the Navy, 21 February 1848.

29. Col W. R. Wendt, "One Fair Corner," *The Leatherneck*, December 1953.

30. Commodore James Armstrong letter to Capt A. H. Foote, USN, 19 November 1856.

31. This and the quotation immediately following are from Commodore Foote's report to Commodore Armstrong, 26 November 1856.

32. *Ibid.* Very likely this occasion marks the first exposure of U. S. Marines to any form of chemical warfare, though the Corps' experience with rockets dates back to Bladensburg.

33. *Ibid.*

34. Quoted in "A Touch of Tradition," LtCol J. H. Magruder III, *Marine Corps Gazette*, November 1959.

35. *Washington Star*, 1 June 1857.

36. *Ibid.*

37. *Ibid.*

38. Obtaining artillery weapons and training from the Army in 1857 marked the culmination of 34 years' effort on the part of Henderson. The first recommendation on this subject, which proposed for the Marine Corps "the double character of marine infantry and marine artillery," appeared in 1823. See Col Archibald Henderson letter to Secretary of the Navy, 22 November 1824, *ASP, Naval Affairs*, Vol. II, 90, forwarding a memorial to Secretary Southard, signed by 25 out of the 49 officers in the Corps, urging such a reorganization, under date of 19 November 1823.

39. As early as 1823, Henderson attempted to set up regular arrangements for commissioning West Pointers into the Marine Corps. As he wrote the Secretary of the Navy, ". . . it but rarely happens that a graduate from West Point is not a gentleman in his deportment, as well as a soldier in his education." Col Archibald Henderson letter to Secretary of the Navy, 23 November 1823, in *ASP, Naval Affairs*, Vol. II, 91.

40. Henderson's 1847 instructions presumably derived, at least in spirit, from the letter of instruction on the same subject issued in 1798, which enjoined, ". . . no indirect Methods are allowable to inveigle Men into the Service of the United States; it is forbidden therefore to inlist any Individual while in a State of Intoxication, or to have him sworn untill twenty four hours after he shall have signed the Inlistment." Secretary of War letter to Lieutenant of Marines, USS *Constellation*, 16 March 1798, in *Naval Documents, Quasi-War with France*, Vol. I, 41.

41. *Ibid.*

42. Quoted in "Leatherneck Salesmen,"

LtCol L. F. Snoddy, *Marine Corps Gazette,* August 1955.

43. Quoted in Hoffman, "The Marine Band," *op. cit.*

44. For a comprehensive review of typical court-martial punishments of the 1820s, see *ASP, Naval Affairs,* Vol. II, 79, 84.

45. See Col Archibald Henderson letter to Secretary of the Navy, 26 September 1827, annexed to Annual Report of Secretary of the Navy for 1827, on the subject of rearming the Corps.

46. Property receipt, Marine Barracks, Brooklyn, signed by Capt W. A. T. Maddox, 6 June 1850.

47. Rt. Hon. W. S. Churchill, *The Grand Alliance* (Boston 1950), 449.

48. The romantic supposition has sometimes been advanced that the "Marine theme" is that of an old Spanish folksong, picked up by Marines while on duty in Mexico in 1847-48. To account for Offenbach's use of the theme, it is pointed out that he reportedly spent some time in Spain and might himself have heard the theme there, using it later in *Geneviève de Brabant.* Although this hypothesis has been asserted—occasionally as outright fact—even in official and semi-official publications and correspondence, it is completely unsupported, so far at least, by any primary evidence whatsoever.

49. Information supplied from family annals by LtCol F. F. Parry, a direct descendant. Col Harris, who apparently had "a green thumb," discovered the beans during a visit to Lima, Peru, while his ship was lying at Callao, and brought some home to Philadelphia.

CHAPTER THREE—*OUR FLAG'S UNFURLED TO EVERY BREEZE*

1. Isaac Toucey letter to Col John Harris, 17 October 1859.

2. Israel Green, "The Capture of John Brown," *North American Review,* December 1885, 564.

3. Col R. E. Lee, USA, surrender ultimatum to John Brown, 18 October 1859, in National Archives.

4. This and the subsequent quotation from Stuart are from his letter to his mother, 31 January 1860, made available through the kindness of Col W. M. Miller and now in Marine Corps Archives, HQMC.

5. *Ibid.*

6. This and preceding quotations from Green are from "The Capture of John Brown," *op. cit.*

7. Col John Harris letter to Secretary of the Navy, 26 July 1861, forwarding Reynolds' action report of 24 July 1861.

8. Flag-Officer S. F. Du Pont report to Secretary of the Navy, 15 November 1861.

9. Petition by the Mayor and City Council, St. Augustine, Florida, to Flag-Officer Du Pont, 25 March 1862.

10. *Diary of Gideon Welles,* ed. by H. K. Beale (New York 1960), entry of 20 August 1862.

11. This and the immediately following quotation from Huntington were supplied from Huntington family papers in the possession of LtCol J. H. Magruder III.

12. *Welles Diary,* 20 August 1862. Other details of the Reynolds case may be found in *Proceedings of a General Court Martial, Washington, D.C., 7 May 1862, in the Case of LtCol Jno. G. Reynolds* (privately published pamphlet in Library of Congress).

13. *Welles Diary,* 13 April 1863.

14. *Ibid.*

15. *Ibid.,* 4 November 1862.

16. *Official Records of the Union and Confederate Navies in the War of the Rebellion* (Washington 1894-1922), Series I, Vol. 14, p. 518.
17. Flag-Officer J. A. Dahlgren report to Secretary of the Navy, 17 March 1865.
18. RAdm D. D. Porter letter to MajGen B. F. Butler, USA, 25 December 1864.
19. Quoted on p. 301, *Mr. Lincoln's Navy*, R. S. West, Jr. (New York 1957).
20. Adm of the Navy George Dewey, *Autobiography of George Dewey* (New York 1913), 135.
21. This and the immediately following quotation are from the report by Capt L. L. Dawson to Commander North Atlantic Squadron, 15 February 1865.
22. *Ibid.*
23. LtCdr K. R. Breese report to Commander North Atlantic Squadron, 16 January 1865.
24. Adm D. D. Porter, *Naval History of the Civil War* (New York 1886), 716.
25. Report by the Secretary of the Confederate Navy, 5 November 1864. Principal sources regarding the CSMC are cited in the bibliography of the present work.
26. *Welles Diary*, 14 May 1864.
27. *Ibid.*, 9 June 1864. Although Welles had good reason to be impatient with the behavior and lack of capacity on the part of several of the senior Marine officers, there is evidence of some prejudice on his part against the Corps. As an example, at the end of the Civil War, Congress passed a law providing for accelerated promotions (not brevets) of Navy and Marine officers who had distinguished themselves during the war. In January 1866, a selection board composed of Admirals Farragut, Davis, Dahlgren, and Porter, presented their recommendations to Secretary Welles, who thereupon suppressed the entire Marine Corps portion of the list, and nominated only the Navy officers recommended by the board. Among those so passed over by Welles was Maj J. L. Broome, Farragut's Marine officer, who thereby ultimately lost his colonelcy and possibly the commandancy itself. Report by Committee on Naval Affairs, House of Representatives, on H.R. 1072, 28 May 1892.
28. Quotation supplied by LtCol Magruder.
29. Col John Harris, *Letters from Naval Officers in Reference to the United States Marine Corps* (Washington 1864). Succeeding quotations from Farragut, Du Pont, Wilkes, and Balch are from the same source.
30. *Ibid.*
31. House Report No. 22, 39th Congress, 2d Session, 21 February 1867.
32. *Ibid.*
33. Capt McLane Tilton letter to Commandant of the Marine Corps, 13 March 1870, brought to my attention by Capt W. A. Merrill.
34. Capt McLane Tilton report to Commander Asiatic Fleet, 16 June 1871.
35. *Ibid.*
36. *Ibid.*
37. Cdr L. A. Kimberly report to Commander Asiatic Fleet, quoted in Collum, *op. cit.*, 206.
38. Col F. M. Wise, *A Marine Tells It to You* (New York 1929), 2-3.
39. Quoted in *United Service Magazine*, September 1882.
40. Lord Charles Beresford letter to 1stLt F. L. Denny, 24 October 1882, quoted in Collum, *op. cit.*, 234.
41. Order by Commander Naval Force, Isthmus of Panama, 16 April 1885.
42. This and the immediately following quotation from General Elliott are found in "On the Isthmus—1885," Col H. C. Reisinger, *Marine Corps Gazette*, December 1928.

43. Quoted in Collum, *op. cit.*, 253. Collum was present on this expedition as a company commander.

44. *Marine Corps Headquarters Bulletin,* February 1944, 10.

45. Collum, *op. cit.*, 193.

46. *Ibid.,* 220.

47. Military Division of the Atlantic G.O. 46, 13 August 1877.

48. This and the succeeding quotation on the training of the detachment are from Capt H. C. Cochrane's report to the Colonel-Commandant, 16 October 1891.

49. Maj R. W. Huntington report to the Colonel-Commandant, 11 October 1892.

50. *Information in Regard to the Marine Corps, op. cit.,* 1.

51. Secretary of the Navy letter, 3 April 1877. The anecdote about Secretary Thompson and the ironclad was told me by my father, Mr. R. D. Heinl, Sr., a fellow townsman of Thompson's, and is confirmed in *The Rise of American Naval Power,* by H. and M. Sprout (Princeton 1939), 181.

52. Quoted in *Marching Along,* John Philip Sousa (Boston 1928), 68.

53. Capt D. P. Mannix report to the Colonel-Commandant, 1 October 1892.

54. Quoted in *U. S. Naval Institute Proceedings,* June 1954, 662.

55. It might almost seem as if Lieut Fullam had found the inspiration for his anti-Marine proposals in the views of Thomas Truxtun who, almost a century earlier, wrote LtCol Burrows, the 2d Commandant, the following irate remarks: "It is high time that a good understanding should take place between the sea officers and Marines. . . . If this cannot be done it may be thought best, to do without Marines hereafter in the ships of the U.S., by adding an equal number of ordinary seamen to the crew of each ship, and training them under a good & Skilful master at arms, so that they would soon become excellent Musqueteers; those men in that case would answer every purpose of marines, by being placed as guards and Centinals & c. They would also under the Sea officers only, be handy in doing duty aloft. . . ." Capt Thomas Truxtun letter to LtCol W. W. Burrows, 15 April 1801, *Naval Documents, Quasi-War with France,* Vol. VII, 187. For Truxtun's idea of what constituted the proper basis for "a good understanding . . . between the sea officers and Marines," see reference 17, Chapter One.

56. Quoted in "The Genesis of FMF Doctrine: 1879-1899," W. H. Russell, *Marine Corps Gazette,* June 1951.

57. MajGen G. F. Elliott endorsement on letter of Cdr W. F. Fullam to Secretary of the Navy, 2 February 1907.

58. Russell, *op. cit., Marine Corps Gazette,* July 1951.

59. Secretary of the Navy letter to CO, USS *Indiana,* 1 November 1895.

60. Information from General Holcomb.

61. Fullam's two articles are: "The System of Naval Training and Discipline Required to Promote Efficiency and Attract Americans," *U. S. Naval Institute Proceedings,* Vol. XVI (1890), 473; and "The Organization, Training, and Discipline of the Navy Personnel as Viewed from the Ship," *U. S. Naval Institute Proceedings,* Vol. XXII (1896) 83. The officers' views cited at this point are from the printed "Discussion" following the 1896 article.

62. RAdm S. B. Luce letter to Col Charles Heywood, 15 February 1894.

63. *U. S. Naval Institute Proceedings,* Vol. XXII (1896).

64. Strength figures for the Corps during

this period vary widely as given in the various histories. This and those following in Chapter Four are from the respective Naval Appropriation Acts for the years in question, which may be found in *Navy Yearbook,* Senate Document No. 140, 59th Congress, 2d Session, 1906

65. Russell, *op. cit.*

66. Quoted in *Recruiters' Bulletin,* January 1918.

67. Quoted from the Naval Appropriation Act for 1891 (Public Law 110, 51st Congress, 2d Session).

68. Wise, *op. cit.,* 2-3.

69. Capt G. C. Reid, testimony Joint Committee on Naval Personnel, 53d Congress, 2d Session, 1894.

CHAPTER FOUR—*EXPEDITIONARY YEARS*

1. *Naval Operations in the War with Spain,* Bureau of Navigation (Washington 1898), 23.

2. BrigGen Dion Williams, "Thirty Years Ago," *Marine Corps Gazette,* March 1928.

3. Adm George Dewey letter to Secretary of the Navy, 14 January 1909, in *Hearings on the Status of the Marine Corps,* House Naval Affairs Committee (Washington 1909), 350.

4. CMC Annual Report, 1898.

5. Secretary of the Navy J. D. Long cable to Commo W. S. Schley, 28 May 1898.

6. Cdr B. H. McCalla letter to Cdr G. C. Reiter, 12 June 1898, in *Naval Operations in the War with Spain, op. cit.,* 491.

7. *Wounds in the Rain,* Stephen Crane (New York 1899), 188-89.

8. Cdr Seaton Schroeder report to Assistant Secretary of the Navy, 8 July 1901.

9. Lt G. A. Merriam, USN, report to CO, USS *Dixie,* 28 July 1898.

10. IstLt C. M. Perkins report to CO, USS *Philadelphia,* 2 April 1899.

11. Wise, *op cit.,* 7.

12. Lowell Thomas, *Old Gimlet Eye* (New York 1933), 10.

13. LtCol G. F. Elliott undated (October 1899) forwarding endorsement to CinC, Asiatic Station, on action report by Capt B. H. Fuller, in Collum, *op cit.,* 376.

14. Wise, *op. cit.,* 17.

15. Quoted in *Soldiers in the Sun,* Capt W. T. Sexton, USA (Harrisburg 1939), 273; also see proceedings of general court-martial, case of Maj L. W. T. Waller, Manila, 5 March 1902, and testimony summarized in the Adjutant General's dispatch to MajGen Chaffee, USA, in *Correspondence Relating to the War with Spain, Including the Insurrection in the Philippine Islands, and the China Relief Expedition* (Washington 1902), 1327-28.

16. Maj L. W. T. Waller statement during general court-martial, Manila, 5 March 1902, in files of the Judge Advocate General, USN.

17. *Ibid.*

18. *Ibid.*

19. *Ibid.*

20. MajGen A. R. Chaffee, USA, to the Adjutant General, 19 April 1902, *Correspondence Relating to the War with Spain,* 1329. BrigGen Owen Seaman, USA, who served under Chaffee in the Boxer Uprising and in the Philippine Insurrection, stated that bad blood between Chaffee and Waller, originating in the Peking relief expedition, was one reason for the Waller trial.

21. Capt J. K. Taussig, USN, "Experiences During the Boxer Rebellion," *U. S. Naval Institute Proceedings,* April 1927.

22. Herbert Hoover, *Years of Adventure* (New York 1952), 52.
23. The strengths of the respective legation guards at Peking are as compiled by LtCol Peter Fleming in *The Siege of Peking* (London 1959), 114.
24. Capt J. T. Myers report to CinC Asiatic Station, 26 September 1900.
25. Taussig, *op. cit.*
26. 1stLt S. D. Butler letter to Mrs. Thomas Butler, 17 June 1900, made available through the kindness of Mr. T. R. Butler, his son.
27. *Ibid.*
28. E. H. Conger (American Minister) dispatch to Secretary of State, 15 June 1900, in *Foreign Relations of the United States, 1900* (Washington 1902), 154.
29. 1stLt S. D. Butler letter to Mrs. Thomas Butler, 2 July 1900, also made available by Mr. T. R. Butler.
30. Maj L. W. T. Waller report to CinC Asiatic Station, 22 June 1900. See also Maj Waller's report of 26 September 1900.
31. RAdm Louis Kempff forwarding endorsement to CinC Asiatic Station, 4 July 1900.
32. Hoover, *op. cit.*
33. Wise, *op. cit.*, 33.
34. Thomas, *op. cit.*, 62.
35. Action report by CO, 9th Infantry, 25 July 1900.
36. Wise, *op. cit.*, 38.
37. RAdm G. C. Remey dispatch to Bureau of Navigation, 24 July 1900.
38. Note by Sir Claude MacDonald contained in notes of investigation by Capt William Crozier, USA, of conduct of Capt Newt Hall at Peking, in files of the Judge Advocate General, case of Capt Hall.
39. Hall file, JAG.
40. *Ibid.*
41. *Ibid.*
42. E. H. Conger (American Minister) dispatch No. 395 to Secretary of State, 17 August 1900.
43. Quoted in Fleming, *op. cit.*, 142.
44. *The Army and Navy Journal*, 1 June 1901.
45. E. H. Conger letter to Capt Henry Leonard, 28 August 1901.
46. Thomas, *op. cit.*, 69.
47. Wise, *op. cit.*, 64-65.
48. 1stLt S. D. Butler letter to Mrs. Thomas Butler, 30 August 1900, made available by Mr. T. R. Butler.
49. CMC Annual Report, 1901.
50. CMC Annual Report, 1903.
51. MajGen J. A. Lejeune, *Reminiscences of a Marine* (Philadelphia 1930), 161.
52. Excerpt from Theodore Roosevelt's speech in Berkeley, Calif., 23 March 1911.
53. Quoted in *The Story of the United States Marines*, J. W. Leonard and F. F. Chitty (Philadelphia 1920), 141.
54. The foregoing section owes much to information from Gen Thomas Holcomb and to "Tradition of Experts," *Marine Corps Gazette*, August 1954, by LtCol J. A. Crown.
55. Statement to the author by MajGen R. C. Berkeley. Gen Holcomb, in similar vein, referred to Col Moses as "that remarkable man."
56. Quotation supplied by Gen Holcomb.
57. MajGen G. F. Elliott endorsement on letter of Cdr W. F. Fullam to Secretary of the Navy, 2 February 1907, *Hearings on the Status of the U. S. Marine Corps, op. cit.*, 25.
58. Chief, Bureau of Navigation, letter to Secretary of the Navy, 16 October 1903.
59. Testimony by MajGen G. F. Elliott to House Naval Affairs Committee, *Hearings on the Status of the U. S. Marine Corps, op. cit.*, 217.
60. Diary entry, 19 November 1908, quoted in *Taft and Roosevelt*, by Maj A. W. Butt (New York 1930).
61. Theodore Roosevelt letter to MajGen Leonard Wood, USA, 26 November

1908, made available through the kindness of Dr. A. D. Chandler, Jr., Theodore Roosevelt Research Project, Massachusetts Institute of Technology.

62. Elliott testimony, House Naval Affairs Committee, *op. cit.*

63. Naval Appropriations Act of 3 March 1909 (35 Stat. 773).

64. RAdm S. B. Luce letter to a friend, 29 March 1909, quoted in *Life and Letters of Rear Admiral S. B. Luce,* by RAdm Albert Gleaves (New York 1925), 348.

65. This and the immediately subsequent quotation are from Capt Butt's letter to his sister, 24 July 1909, in *The Letters of Archie Butt,* by L. F. Abbott (New York 1924).

66. Lejeune, *op. cit.*, 193.

67. MajGen D. C. McDougal letter to Gen R. McC. Pate, 18 January 1956.

68. LtGen J. C. Smith letter to Col R. D. Heinl, Jr., 29 January 1957.

69. Details of this episode may be found in Lejeune, *op. cit.*, 202.

70. *Marine Corps Gazette,* Vol. I, No. 1, March 1916.

71. Gen H. M. Smith, *Coral and Brass* (New York 1949), 19.

72. Lejeune, *op. cit.*, 200.

73. Capt W. S. Sims, USN (Chief Observer) report to CinC Atlantic Fleet, 23 January 1914.

74. *Collier's* Magazine, 9 May 1914.

75. *Harper's Weekly,* Vol. LV, No. 2844, 1912.

76. After General Elliott's retirement in November 1910, the post of Commandant was kept vacant by the Taft administration for more than nine weeks, with Col Biddle administering Marine Corps Headquarters without portfolio, under supervision of the Assistant Secretary of the Navy—an arrangement whereby the office of Commandant was intentionally allowed to lapse, and one which *The Army and*

Navy Journal, 28 January 1911, reported that officers in the Navy Department wanted to make permanent.

77. CMC Annual Report, 1912.

78. Thomas, *op. cit.*, 152.

79. *Ibid.*, 181.

80. Most accounts charge these murders to President Sam's direct order. I have, however, followed the version by Dantès Bellegarde in *La Résistance Haitienne* (Port-au-Prince, 1937), 30.

81. R. B. Davis, Jr. (American Chargé d'Affaires) report to Secretary of State, 12 July 1916; immediately preceding quotation from same source.

82. Col L. W. T. Waller report to RAdm W. B. Caperton, 10 January 1916, on p. 37, *Report on Affairs in the Republic of Haiti* prepared by BrigGen George Barnett for Secretary of the Navy, 11 November 1920.

83. Thomas, *op. cit.*, 186.

84. *Ibid.*, 191

85. Col L. W. T. Waller report to RAdm W. B. Caperton, 9 November 1915, on p. 34, *Report on Affairs in the Republic of Haiti, op. cit.*

86. Thomas, *op. cit.*, 201.

87. Annual Report, American High Commissioner to Haiti, 8 January 1930, 14.

88. Thomas, *op. cit.*, 209.

89. *Washington Post,* 27 December 1916.

90. Wise, *op. cit.*, 144.

91. *Ibid.*, 148-49.

92. *Ibid.*

93. This and the immediately preceding quotation are from memorandum of 11 April 1916 by Col J. A. Lejeune to Capt H. S. Knapp, USN, Joint Board.

94. Quoted in "Perspectives in Public Relations," by Capt R. Lindsay, *Marine Corps Gazette,* January 1956.

95. F. D. Roosevelt letter to his wife, 21 August 1915, in *F.D.R., His Personal Letters,* edited by Elliott Roosevelt, (New York 1948), 283.

96. Col R. W. Huntington action report, appended to CMC Annual Report 1898.
97. J. L. Dix, *The World's Navies in the Boxer Rebellion* (London 1905).
98. Anecdote supplied by Mrs. H. L. Thebaud, who was Col McCawley's niece.

CHAPTER FIVE—*OVER THERE*

1. MajGen George Barnett, "Soldier and Sailor, Too," MSS autobiography in Barnett Papers, now in custody of Marine Corps Museum, Quantico, Va.
2. *The Quantico Leatherneck*, Vol. I, No. 2, 24 October 1917.
3. Barnett, *op. cit.*
4. *Ibid.*, as is the account of Barnett's initial rebuff by the Army Chief of Staff.
5. Josephus Daniels, *The Wilson Era* (Chapel Hill 1946), 150.
6. Woodrow Wilson letter to Secretary of the Navy, 29 May 1917.
7. Quoted in Barnett, *op. cit.*
8. *Ibid.* Even before the departure for France of the first troop convoy, including the 5th Marines, Gen Pershing's forward headquarters and staff had left for France aboard SS *Baltic* on 28 May 1917. Attached to this group was LtCol R. H. Dunlap, the thoughtful and talented Marine artillerist, and Maj Hiram Bearss.
9. Gen J. J. Pershing letter to the Major General Commandant, 10 November 1917, in the Barnett Papers.
10. Maj Frederick Palmer, USA, *America in France* (New York 1918), 97 ff.
11. An unintended consequence of the enforced AEF designation of the Marine Brigade as 4th Infantry Brigade was that the War Department ruled after World War I that the postwar 4th Infantry Brigade of the Army was entitled to all battle honors, streamers, and suchlike, won by the Marines in France, as a result of which the infantrymen of the 1920s and 1930s wore the *fourragères* earned by the Marines. Information supplied by LtGen Ridgely Gaither, USA.
12. Anecdote supplied by Gen Holcomb, to whom Harbord recounted the story while dining in his battalion mess (2d Bn, 6th Mar). Pershing must have been sure of Harbord, for on Doyen's relief he cabled that no other Marine general officer was wanted in France. If one were sent he would not be assigned to the Marine brigade or any other combatant unit. Lejeune, *op. cit.*, 248.
13. Pershing letter to MGC, *op. cit.*
14. MajGen J. G. Harbord, *The American Army in France* (Boston 1936), 264.
15. *Ibid.*, 272.
16. Quoted in *Fix Bayonets!*, Capt John W. Thomason, Jr. (New York 1926), xiii.
17. Wise, *op. cit.*, 202.
18. Quoted in "Dan Daly: Reluctant Hero," E. A. Dieckmann, Sr., *Marine Corps Gazette*, November 1960.
19. Quoted in "Battles Before World War II," Maj C. W. Hoffman, *Marine Corps Gazette*, November 1950.
20. Quoted in "A Brief History of the Fourth Brigade of Marines," Maj E. N. McClellan, *Marine Corps Gazette*, December 1919.
21. Harbord, *op. cit.*, 290-91.
22. F. D. Roosevelt journal entry, 5 August 1918, in *F.D.R., His Personal Letters, op. cit.*, 426.
23. F. D. Roosevelt cable to Secretary of the Navy, 10 August 1918, in Barnett Papers.
24. The complete French text of this

order may be found in McClellan, "History of the Fourth Brigade of Marines," *op. cit.*

25. F. D. Roosevelt journal entry, 3 August 1918, in *F.D.R., His Personal Letters, op. cit.,* **415.**

26. Extract from GHQ Seventh(German) Army Intelligence Office serial 3528, 17 June 1918.

27. Thomason, *op. cit.,* 90.

28. W. A. Carter, *The Tale of a Devil Dog* (Washington 1920), 23.

29. Quoted in *The New Breed,* Maj A. C. Geer (New York 1952), 7.

30. Statement to the author, 5 March 1958.

31. Field Marshal Paul von Hindenburg, *Out of My Life,* quoted in Harbord, *op. cit.,* 337.

32. German Army Intelligence Summary, quoted in *The Leatherneck,* November 1957, 82.

33. Gen J. J. Pershing cable to Secretary of War, 19 June 1918.

34. Thomas, *op. cit.,* 245-46.

35. Barnett, *op. cit.*

36. Metcalf, *op. cit.,* 458. Whether Marine artillery officers were really welcome in the AEF even as individual replacements is open to question. When, after the 10th Marines had finally been benched, Col Dunlap returned to France alone and reported as a replacement, the Chief of Artillery, AEF, refused his services until, on appeal, Pershing himself was reminded of his previous commitment, and Dunlap was then given command of the 17th Field Artillery. Col R. H. Dunlap letter to MGC, 28 February 1919.

37. Barnett, *op. cit.*

38. Dunlap letter, *op. cit.*

39. *Ibid.*

40. Frederick Palmer, *Newton D. Baker* (New York 1931), Vol. II, 222.

41. Lejeune, *op. cit.,* 306.

42. *Ibid.*

43. Carter, *op. cit.,* 66.

44. Thomason, *op. cit.,* 136.

45. LtCol Ernst Otto, *The Battle at Blanc Mont* (Annapolis 1930), 188.

46. Thomason, *op. cit.,* 179.

47. *Ibid.,* 130.

48. Report by CG, V Corps, U. S. Army, 2 November 1918.

49. Lejeune, *op. cit.,* 402.

50. CMC Annual Report, 15 December 1918.

51. Col A. W. Catlin, *With the Help of God and a Few Marines* (New York 1918).

52. Lejeune, *op. cit.,* 300.

53. Woodrow Wilson letter to MajGen Barnett, 14 August 1919.

54. Lt G. G. Strott (HC) USN, *The Medical Department of the United States Navy with the Army and Marine Corps in France in World War I* (Washington 1947), 1.

55. *Ibid.,* 48. Excerpt from log of a battalion surgeon.

56. *Ibid.,* 142.

57. Quoted in *History of Marine Corps Aviation,* Robert Sherrod (Washington 1952), 7.

58. Lt H. B. Mims memorandum to MGC, 8 July 1918.

59. Proclamation by Allied Naval Forces, Vladivostok, 6 July 1918.

60. Statement by Secretary of the Navy Daniels in Navy Department press release, 12 February 1918, in Barnett Papers.

61. All quotations in this paragraph, and other information on this debate, are taken from the *Chicago Tribune,* 19 June 1918.

62. Barnett, *op. cit.*

63. BrigGen George Barnett letter to Col W. C. Dawson, 29 June 1920, in Barnett Papers.

64. Lejeune, *op. cit.,* 461.

65. Col S. L. A. Marshall, *The Soldier's Load and the Mobility of a Nation,* quoted in *Marine Corps Gazette,* August 1951, 4.

CHAPTER SIX—*BETWEEN THE WARS*

1. Capt J. H. Craige, *Black Baghdad* (New York 1933), 93. For a vignette of this outstanding Marine, see *Leatherneck*, September 1931, 17.
2. Wise, *op. cit.*, 311.
3. *Ibid.*, 323.
4. Excerpt from comments by Gen G. C. Thomas on draft of this history.
5. MajGen E. A. Ostermann letter to Col R. D. Heinl, Jr., 15 August 1959.
6. Interview with MajGen E. A. Ostermann, 30 June 1959.
7. Extract from "Daily Diary Report" of Commanding Officer, 1st Marine Brigade, 19 May 1920.
8. J. D. Kuser, *Haiti: Its Dawn of Progress after Years in a Night of Revolution* (Boston 1921), 32 ff.
9. Thomas comments, *op. cit.*
10. "One-Man Armies in Haiti," *Leatherneck*, September 1931, 13.
11. The Marine casualties given here differ from official totals of the Personnel Department, HQMC, and have been reconstructed from those listed mainly by name, in Barnett's *Report on Affairs in the Republic of Haiti, op. cit.*, and other reports of patrol actions. Casualty reporting by the 1st Brigade appears to have been incomplete. An example: in the attack on Port-au-Prince in January 1920, 1stLt G. C. Thomas's patrol sustained seven casualties alone, in addition to others which occurred during the fight, yet the brigade report to Washington listed only three wounded, none in the Thomas patrol.
12. MajGen George Barnett letter to Col J. H. Russell, 2 October 1919, text given in *Report on Affairs in the Republic of Haiti, op. cit.*
13. Dana G. Munro, *The Latin American Republics* (New York 1942), 560.
14. U.S. Special Report, *President's Commission for the Study and Review of conditions in the Republic of Haiti* (Washington 1930).
15. Secretary of the Navy special letter of instruction, 11 November 1921, quoted in *Marine Corps Gazette*, September 1949.
16. CMC Annual Report, 1920.
17. Another barracks at Philadelphia which was occupied in part by Basic School was an oddity of the Josephus Daniels era. Secretary Daniels, a prime egalitarian as between officers and enlisted men, forced the erection, before World War I, of a hybrid structure designed to quarter enlisted men under the same roof as officers and their families. For obvious reasons the experiment was never repeated, although the building was still in use in 1960.
18. Operation Plan 712, Division of Operations and Training, HQMC, 23 July 1921.
19. *Ibid.*
20. MajGen J. A. Lejeune, undated pamphlet reprint from *The Military Engineer*, "The United States Marine Corps."
21. MajGen J. A. Lejeune, address to Naval War College, 14 December 1923.
22. Both quotations from CMC Annual Report, 1922.
23. *Joint Action of the Army and Navy* (Washington 1927), 3, 12.
24. Capt J. W. Thomason, Jr., *Red Pants* (New York 1927), 36.
25. H. L. Stimson and McGeorge Bundy, *On Active Service in Peace and War* (New York 1947), 113.
26. MajGen J. A. Lejeune testimony before Senate Committee on Foreign Relations, 18 February 1928, printed

in *Marine Corps Gazette*, March 1928, 49.

27. There are several versions of the Cabulla shooting, all more or less irreconcilable in detail. This one is based on information from LtGen R. E. Hogaboom.

28. Quoted by Lejeune in his Senate Foreign Relations Committee testimony, *op. cit.*, 59.

29. *Ibid.*, 60.

30. Quoted in "Protection of American Interests," Division of Operations and Training, HQMC, *Marine Corps Gazette*, September 1927.

31. Capt G. D. Hatfield report to CG, 2d Marine Brigade, 20 July 1927.

32. Interview with MajGen R. E. Rowell, Naval Aviation History Unit, Navy Department, 24 October 1946.

33. Maj E. H. Brainard, lecture on Marine Corps aviation at Marine Corps Schools, reprinted in *Marine Corps Gazette*, March 1928.

34. Hatfield action report, *op. cit.*

35. Pvt L. C. Handzlik statement, *Marine Corps Gazette*, March 1929, 25.

36. *Ibid.*, as is the immediately following quotation.

37. 1stLt G. J. O'Shea patrol report, undated, reprinted in *Marine Corps Gazette*, March 1929, 26 ff.

38. *Ibid.*

39. Lejeune, Foreign Relations Committee testimony, *op. cit.*, 53.

40. Maj H. C. Pierce field message 8616 to CG, 2d Marine Brigade, 15 June 1927.

41. Information from LtGen R. E. Hogaboom.

42. Lejeune, Foreign Relations Committee testimony, *op. cit.*, 57.

43. *Ibid.* An example of the mendacious propaganda spread against the Marines in Nicaragua was the widely asserted statement that Quilali was heartlessly levelled in an act of reprisal, like Lidice in World War II.

Actually the town was already abandoned, with knee-high grass in the main street, when first seen on patrol in August 1927 by Capt (GNN) Hogaboom.

44. *Ibid.*, 56.

45. *Ibid.*, 57.

46. BrigGen Logan Feland report to Major General Commandant, quoted in "Coco Patrol," LtCol H. Stiff, *Marine Corps Gazette*, February 1957.

47. H. W. Dodds, "American Supervision of the Nicaraguan Elections," *Foreign Affairs*, April 1929.

48. Maj R. E. Rowell, Annual Report of Aircraft Squadrons, 2d Brigade, U. S. Marine Corps, 20 June 1928.

49. Capt L. B. Puller statement during lecture on Small Wars to Basic School class of 1937.

50. Capt L. B. Puller report to Jefe Director, Guardia Nacional de Nicaragua, 3 October 1932.

51. Anecdote supplied by BrigGen W. R. Wendt, who was an eyewitness.

52. Stimson and Bundy, *op. cit.*, 115.

53. For details and circumstances of Sandino's last moments, see *El Verdadero Sandino, o el Calvario de las Segovias*, A. Somoza (Managua 1936).

54. Quoted in House Document No. 787, "Hearing on Proposed Reduction in Enlisted Strength of Marine Corps," Committee on Naval Affairs, 15 December 1932, 2691, kindly made available by Col. J. R. Blandford.

55. Rowell, Annual Report of Aircraft Squadrons, 2d Brigade, *op. cit.*

56. Sherrod, *Marine Aviation, op. cit.*, 28.

57. The Adjutant General, U. S. Army, letter to CG, Philippine Department, 21 October 1922, quoted by Dr. Louis Morton in "Army and Marines on the China Station: A Study in Military and Political Rivalry," *Pacific Historical Review*, February 1960.

58. Hearings before House Committee on

Appropriations, 12 February 1929.

59. Quoted in "The Story of a Dream," F. A. Ruoff, *Marine Corps Gazette,* February 1950.

60. Information supplied by LtGen J. T. Selden.

61. Thomas, *op cit.,* 301.

62. *Liberty* Magazine, 5 December 1931.

63. Quoted in House Document No. 787, *op. cit.,* 2655.

64. Herbert C. Hoover letter to Col R. D. Heinl, Jr., 22 January 1957.

65. Hearings by the Committee on Appropriations, Naval Appropriations Bill 1934, 6 February 1933, 503. See also House Report No. 2075, 72d Congress, 2d Session, 20 February 1933, and *The Congressional Record,* 23 February 1933, 4627, 4814, and 4843, all made available through the kindness of Col Blandford.

66. Commandant Marine Corps Schools letter to the Major General Commandant, 5 October 1931, subj: "Text for Landing Operations"; MCS memo 30 June 1931, same subject.

67. Gen H. M. Smith, *Coral and Brass* (New York 1949), 59.

68. MajGen J. H. Russell, "The Birth of the Fleet Marine Force," *U. S. Naval Institute Proceedings,* January 1946.

69. J. A. Isely and P. A. Crowl, *The U. S. Marines and Amphibious War* (Princeton 1951), 36.

70. *Ibid.,* 56.

71. FAdm E. J. King and Cdr W. M. Whitehill, *Fleet Admiral King, a Naval Record* (New York 1952), 321.

72. "The Marines' Amphibian," LtCol V. J. Croizat, *Marine Corps Gazette,* June 1953. Also see letter to *Marine Corps Gazette* by Col John Kaluf, September 1953, 8.

73. Quoted in Smith, *Coral and Brass, op. cit.,* 95.

74. Anecdote supplied by General Holcomb.

75. Col J. C. Blizzard, USA, memorandum for War Plans Division, War Department General Staff, 20 May 1942.

76. Original in HQMC archives.

77. Information supplied by General Holcomb and Admiral Stark.

78. See "Barefoot Marines," 1stLt R. A. Owens, *Marine Corps Gazette,* November 1948.

79. BrigGen W. R. Wendt comments on draft of this history.

80. Statement by General Holcomb to author, 13 July 1959.

81. Thomason, *op. cit.,* xx.

82. Anecdote supplied by General Holcomb.

83. Lejeune, *op. cit.,* 94.

CHAPTER SEVEN—. . . *IN MANY A STRIFE*

1. Cecil Woodham-Smith in her review of *The Red Fort, New York Times Book Review,* 21 April 1957, by kind permission of the *New York Times.*

2. MajGen R. C. Mangrum comments on draft of this history.

3. BrigGen S. R. Shaw comments on draft of this history.

4. *Ibid.*

5. The official history of Marine Corps operations in World War II (Vol I, *Pearl Harbor to Guadalcanal,* Hough *et al.*) gives no consolidated Marine Corps casualty figures for the Pearl Harbor attack. My total is the sum of those reported for ships' detachments, Ewa, and a few personally remembered by me within the 4th Defense Battalion. In all probability, a few more wounded should be added.

6. Pearl Harbor action report, CO, USS *West Virginia.*

7. CinCPac letter to CNO, 18 April 1941. This letter is quoted from the Marine Corps monograph, *The Defense of Wake* (Washington 1947), by LtCol R. D. Heinl, Jr. The account of the action on Wake which follows is condensed from the same monograph.

8. JICPOA Item No. 4986, "Translation of Professional Notebook of an Ensign in the Japanese Navy," 25 February 1944.

9. Interrogation of Capt Tadashi Koyama, IJN, Interrogation Nav. No. 83, *Interrogations of Japanese Officials,* U. S. Strategic Bombing Survey (USSBS), (Washington 1946), Vol. II, 371.

10. LtCol C. A. Barninger report to CO, 1st Defense Battalion, 8 October 1945.

11. Quoted in *The Story of Wake Island,* Col James P. S. Devereux, (Philadelphia 1947).

12. Koyama interrogation, *op. cit.*

13. Maj Paul A. Putnam (CO, VFM-211) report to CO, MAG-21, 20 December 1941.

14. 1stLt J. F. Kinney report to CO, 1st Defense Battalion, 12 October 1945.

15. File of dispatch traffic received from Wake, 7-23 December 1941, in HQMC archives.

16. Excerpt from account by a Japanese observer aboard HIJMS *Yubari* in ATIS (SWPA) Enemy Publications No. 6, "Hawaii-Malaya Naval Operations," 27 March 1943, 33.

17. *Ibid.,* 29.

18. Koyama interrogation, *op. cit.*

19. Ancedote supplied by General Holcomb.

20. Quoted in "The Fourth Marines at Corregidor," Hanson W. Baldwin, *Marine Corps Gazette,* November 1946, 15.

21. *Ibid.*

22. Quoted in "Naval Battalion at Mariveles," Col W. F. Prickett, *Marine Corps Gazette,* June 1950. Also see "The Naval Battalion on Bataan," same author, *U. S. Naval Institute Proceedings,* November 1960.

23. Strength figures provided by the Historical Branch, HQMC.

24. "The Fourth Marines at Corregidor," *op. cit., Marine Corps Gazette,* February 1947.

25. Maj H. E. Dalness, USA, "Operations of the 4th Battalion (Provisional) 4th Marine Regiment in the Final Counterattack in the Defense of Corregidor, 5-6 May 1942," monograph original on file at The Infantry School, Ft. Benning.

26. "The Fourth Marines at Corregidor," *op. cit., Marine Corps Gazette,* February 1947. Marine casualties for the 4th Regiment during the Philippine campaign totaled 331 dead or missing and presumed dead, and 357 wounded. Two hundred and thirty-nine more officers and men died in enemy prison camps.

27. Commander in Chief U. S. Fleet (ComInCh) letter to Chief of Staff, U. S. Army, 18 February 1942.

28. ComInCh letter to Chief of Staff, U. S. Army, 2 March 1942.

29. Acting Chief of Staff, U. S. Army, memo to CNO, 9 April 1942.

30. That this point of view was not confined to General McNarney is recorded in Admiral King's memoirs (*Fleet Admiral King,* 321-22) in his account of a conversation with General Marshall on the subject of amphibious warfare: "He [Marshall] appeared to think that landings were easily managed, and that while Marines might be competent in that respect, they were hardly capable of commanding an entire division, with its adjuncts of engineer, communica-

tions, medical, and intelligence units!"

31. Col G. Boyington, *Baa, Baa, Black Sheep,* (New York 1958), 55.

32. Quoted in *Marines At Midway,* LtCol R. D. Heinl, Jr. (Washington 1948), 29.

33. "The Japanese Story of the Battle of Midway," *ONI Review,* May 1947, 72.

34. Interrogation of RAdm Akira Soji, IJN, Interrogation Nav. No. 83, *Interrogations of Japanese Officials, op. cit.,* Vol. II, 363.

35. Col C. A. Larkin letter to BrigGen R. E. Rowell, 15 June 1942; Col James Roosevelt letter to Mr. Robert Sherrod, 26 July 1948, in *Marine Aviation, op. cit.,* 64.

36. ComInCh letter to Chief of Staff, U. S. Army, 26 June 1942.

37. Remark by Gen A. A. Vandegrift to LtCol R. D. Heinl, Jr., 12 March 1948.

38. Message quoted in War Diary, 25th (Japanese) Air Flotilla, August-September 1942.

39. Although this mission was almost certainly the first *call-fire* naval gunfire support by a U. S. ship during the war, the first prearranged gunfire support of any kind appears to have been furnished by the 3-inch guns of USS *Quail,* a minesweeper which fired in support of the operations of the provisional Naval Battalion at Mariveles on Bataan, 29 January 1942.

40. Maj J. L. Zimmerman, *The Guadalcanal Campaign* (Washington 1949), 31.

41. Gen G. C. Thomas comments on draft of this history

42. Isely and Crowl, *op. cit.,* 131.

43. CG South Pacific (SoPac) letter to Chief of Staff, U. S. Army, 11 August 1942.

44. War Diary, Commander Task Force 62, September-October 1942.

45. George McMillan, *The Old Breed* (Washington 1949), 46.

46. VAdm Raizo Tanaka, IJN (Ret.), "Japan's Losing Struggle for Guadalcanal," *U. S. Naval Institute Proceedings,* July and August 1956.

47. Maj C. H. Brush letter to CMC, 15 January 1949.

48. Col C. B. Cates letter to Col John W. Thomason, Jr., 6 September 1942, quoted in preface to first edition, *. . . and a Few Marines,* (New York 1943).

49. Tanaka, *op. cit.*

50. *Ibid.*

51. Cates letter to Thomason, *op. cit.*

52. Capt J. R. Stockman, *The Battle for Tarawa,* (Washington 1947), 6.

53. Smith, *Coral and Brass, op. cit.,* 132.

54. Maj J. N. Renner, quoted in Sherrod, *Marine Aviation, op. cit.,* 83.

55. Mangrum comments, *op. cit.*

56. Sherrod, *Marine Aviation, op. cit.,* 90.

57. Thomas comments, *op. cit.*

58. Sherrod, *Marine Aviation. op. cit.,* 83.

59. *Ibid.,* 82.

60. McMillan, *The Old Breed, op. cit.,* 71.

61. *Ibid.*

62. Quotation supplied by General Edson in March 1947.

63. In his comments on the draft of this history, Major General Mangrum, one of the ablest officers on Guadalcanal, wrote: "If you want to give credit where credit is due, you ought to have more to say about the 11th Marines. This was a magnificent job of shooting."

64. John Hersey, *Into the Valley* (New York 1943), 11.

65. Col S. B. Griffith II, letter to Capt. Clifford Morehouse, undated, 1945, in HQMC archives.

66. 2d (Sendai) Division Op Order 174, 21 October 1942, quoted in *The Guadalcanal Campaign,* Zimmerman, *op. cit.,* 125.

67. Quoted in *The Struggle for Guadal-canal*, RAdm S. E. Morison (Boston 1949), 183.
68. Quoted in Sherrod, *Marine Aviation, op. cit.*, 105.
69. Quoted in R. E. Sherwood, *Roosevelt and Hopkins* (New York 1948), 624-25.
70. Anecdote supplied by LtCol Regan Fuller.
71. Interrogation of Capt Toshikazu Ohmae, IJN, Interrogation Nav. No. 109, *Interrogations of Japanese Officials*, Vol. II, 468.
72. FAdm E. J. King, *The U. S. Navy at War* (Washington 1946), 60.
73. Thomas comments, *op. cit.*
74. Tanaka, *op. cit.*
75. FAdm W. F. Halsey and LtCdr J. Bryan III, *Admiral Halsey's Story* (New York 1947), 131.
76. Gen A. A. Vandegrift personal letter to unknown addressee, 6 December 1942, in HQMC archives.
77. Col F. P. Henderson, "NGF Support in the Solomons," *Marine Corps Gazette*, March, June, and December, 1956.
78. *Ibid.*
79. Capt Ohmae in Interrogation Nav. No. 43, *Interrogations of Japanese Officials*, Vol. I, 177.
80. Zimmerman, *op. cit.*, v.
81. Halsey and Bryan, *op. cit.*, 161.
82. LtCol S. B. Griffith II, "Action at Enogai," *Marine Corps Gazette*, March 1944.
83. Quoted in *Marines in the Central Solomons*, Maj J. N. Rentz (Washington 1952), 135.
84. Statement by MajGen Geiger quoted in *Bougainville and the Northern Solomons*, Maj J. N. Rentz (Washington 1948), 12.
85. Isely and Crowl, *op. cit.*, 176.
86. Quoted in Rentz, *Bougainville, op. cit.*, 106.
87. Henderson, "NGF Support," *op. cit.*
88. *Ibid.*
89. Testimony by Gen T. Holcomb, 13 April 1951, before Senate Armed Services Committee, on S. 677, "Marine Corps Strength and Joint Chiefs of Staff Representation," 35.
90. *Ibid.*
91. All quotations and information in this paragraph from Holcomb testimony, *op. cit.*
92. As late as December 1943, a regular Marine officer on duty at Pensacola had an unsatisfactory fitness report placed on his record by Capt J. B. Lyon, USN, because of his insistence in urging that aviation cadets earmarked for Marine commissions receive at least the rudiments of Marine indoctrination during their pre-commissioning ground-school instruction in the Naval Air Training Command.
93. LtCol F. O. Hough and LtCol J. A. Crown, *The Campaign on New Britain* (Washington 1952), 2.
94. *Ibid.*, 19.
95. MajGen J. T. Selden letter to LtCol F. O. Hough, 7 March 1952, in HQMC archives.
96. Sam Stavisky and Jeremiah O'Leary, quoted in McMillan, *The Old Breed, op. cit.*, 203.
97. Sixth Army Observer reports, Cape Gloucester campaign, 4 and 9 January 1944, in HQMC archives.
98. Quoted in Col D. W. Fuller letter to Maj J. A. Crown, 28 February 1952, in HQMC archives.
99. Sherrod, *Marine Aviation, op. cit.*, 131.
100. LtCol F. H. Schwable memo to LtCol E. C. Dyer, 28 May 1943, quoted in Sherrod, *Marine Aviation, op. cit.*, 162.
101. Statistics compiled from USSBS, *The Allied Campaign Against Rabaul*, and USSBS, *Summary Report (Pacific War)*. In addition, as anyone can see who follows the footnotes, I have relied heavily for facts and conclusions

on Robert Sherrod's truly definitive history of Marine aviation.

102. Sherrod, *Marine Aviation, op. cit.,* 132.

103. Information from *Administration of the Navy Department in World War II,* RAdm J. A. Furer (Washington 1960), 562 ff.

CHAPTER EIGHT—*UNCOMMON VALOR*

1. King and Whitehall, *op. cit.,* 444.
2. Field Marshal Lord Alanbrooke, diary entry 8 April 1943, quoted in *Triumph in the West,* Arthur Bryant (New York 1959), 132.
3. King and Whitehall, *op. cit.,* 440.
4. Commander Southwest Pacific Area (ComSoWesPac) Operation Plan *Reno I,* 25 February 1943.
5. Adm C. W. Nimitz letter to LtGen T. Holcomb, 19 June 1943.
6. Marine Corps participation in the Alaskan campaign was not limited to training the forces. A detachment of VMO-155 (LtCol P. P. Schrider) provided photo coverage at Attu, and its officers gave basic close air support indoctrination to the Navy squadron with which they were embarked in USS *Nassau.* This detachment was the first Marine unit to fly combat missions from a carrier. In addition, Marine shore fire control parties were attached to the Army landing force at Attu, to control both naval gunfire and (when the fog lifted) air support.
7. Smith, *Coral and Brass, op. cit.,* 109.
8. King, *U. S. Navy at War, op. cit.,* 71.
9. CinCPac Operation Report, the Gilberts, November 1943.
10. Quoted in *Tarawa, the Story of a Battle,* Robert Sherrod (New York 1944), 24.
11. Quoted in *Betio Beachhead,* by five Marine Corps combat correspondents (New York 1945), 32.
12. *Ibid.*
13. Sherrod, *Tarawa, op. cit.,* 68.
14. Quoted in Stockman, *op. cit.,* 17.
15. Sherrod, *Tarawa, op. cit.,* 92.
16. Quoted in Stockman, *op. cit.,* 40.
17. Quoted in *Aleutians, Gilberts, and Marshalls, June 1942-April 1944,* RAdm S. E. Morison (Boston 1951), 173.
18. Sherrod, *Tarawa, op. cit.,* 47.
19. *Betio Beachhead, op. cit.,* 158.
20. Stockman, *op. cit.,* 68.
21. *Time* Magazine, 6 December 1943.
22. LtCol R. D. Heinl, Jr., and LtCol J. A. Crown, *The Marshalls: Increasing the Tempo* (Washington 1954), 11.
23. Adm R. K. Turner to CMC, 20 February 1953.
24. The careful simulation on Kahoolawe of Betio's beach defenses was a logical extension of experimental naval gunfire exercises conducted in the Solomons, at the instance of LtCol F. P. Henderson, IMAC naval gunfire officer, in which destroyers, working with 3d Marine Division shore fire control parties, bombarded the undamaged enemy beach-defenses of Kolombangara. See "Naval Gunfire Support in the Solomon Islands Campaign," by LtCol Henderson, unpublished MSS in HQMC archives.
25. Smith, *Coral and Brass, op. cit.,* 142.
26. LtGen R. C. Richardson, USA, memo for Adm C. W. Nimitz, 27 December 1943, in HQMC archives.
27. 4th Marine Division Journal, 1 February 1944.
28. *Ibid.*
29. Quoted in *Baltimore Evening Sun,* 10 February 1944.
30. MajGen W. W. Rogers letter to CMC, 3 February 1948.

31. VAdm R. L. Conolly letter to CMC, 26 November 1952.
32. Adm R. A. Spruance letter to J. A. Isely, 14 January 1949, in Princeton University Library.
33. In November 1943, in preparation for the Marshalls operation, the 22d Marines moved to Maui and became a regimental landing team by virtue of attachment of the 2d Separate Pack Howitzer Battalion and other supporting units.
34. "This unit [wrote Gen Hogaboom in his comments on draft of this history] boarded a wrecked Jap merchantman in the Kwajalein lagoon. The unit commander recognized the value of a complete set of Japanese charts covering the Central Pacific areas. Here in one little package was much of the detailed information we had been seeking since the days of Ellis."
35. Heinl and Crown, op. cit., 142.
36. Ibid., 150.
37. Spruance-Isely letter, op. cit.
38. Smith, Coral and Brass, op. cit., 154. What General Smith, who had been a major general in 1941 when Admiral Turner was only a captain (and had enjoyed relative seniority of either one or two grades over Turner during much of the period prior to 1944) might have added but did not was that an unexplained feature of his and Turner's 1944 promotions to three stars was a Navy Department reversal of their relative ranks: Turner's new date of rank was 4 February 1944 while Smith's was 28 February 1944.
39. In comments on the draft of this history, it has been heatedly pointed out by aviation friends that nowadays aviators are of course line officers, too. Unfortunately for those who write about the Marine Corps, there is no single term to describe the rest of the Corps, corresponding to "aviation," that part which flies. "Ground" not only has an unfortunate tri-elemental ring, suggesting Prussian military terminology, but doesn't include the important non-aviators who serve at sea. In the time-honored phrase, "the line," which for many years colloquially distinguished the rest of the Corps from its aviators (and still survives colloquially if technically erroneously), I resort to the only solution I know.
40. Sherrod, Marine Aviation, op. cit., 325.
41. CO, MAG-1, report, Fleet Landing Exercise 5, 1939, in HQMC archives.
42. Quoted but not attributed in Sherrod, Marine Aviation, op. cit., 327. Admiral Nimitz said practically the same thing in less blunt language when he approved the Marine CVE concept: "[this reorganization] will more firmly integrate Marine Corps aviation within the Marine Corps and is therefore in the interest of the Naval Service." CinCPac 1st endorsement to CMC memo on Marine aviation in the Pacific, undated, quoted in Isely and Crowl, op. cit., 508.
43. King and Whitehall, op. cit., 444 and 532.
44. Both Holland Smith's chief of staff (Erskine) and his G-3 (Hogaboom), on the NTLF staff, had been members of the Quantico Advance Base Problem Team which, before the war, had prepared and presented the Marine Corps Schools Saipan problem at the Naval War College.
45. Isely and Crowl, op. cit., 325.
46. Quoted in NTLF G-2 Report, Operation Forager, 8-9.
47. Quoted in On to Westward, Robert Sherrod (New York 1945), 94.
48. Ibid., 37-38.
49. Smith, Coral and Brass, op. cit., 162.
50. Both the assault division commanders, Generals Watson (2d Division) and Schmidt (4th Division), had landed on D-day.
51. Quoted in Saipan: the Beginning of

the End, Maj C. W. Hoffman (Washington 1950), 101.

52. Col G. W. Kelley, USA, report of action, Saipan, 16-27 June, in Office of Chief of Military History (OCMH), Department of the Army.

53. 27th Infantry Division Intelligence Journal, 21 March 1944. Although 500 enemy was what the 27th Division G-2 believed and reported that the 105th Infantry was up against, postwar studies suggest that the total number of Japanese on Nafutan Point was nearer a thousand. These, however, were predominantly stragglers, all disorganized, and some unarmed. *Campaign in the Marianas,* P. A. Crowl (Washington 1960), 160.

54. Statistics from *New Guinea and the Marianas, March 1944-August 1944,* RAdm S. E. Morison (Boston 1953), 319-321.

55. Col S. Hayashi, IJA (Ret.), and A. D. Coox, *Kogun, the Japanese Army in the Pacific* (Quantico 1959), 110.

56. Sherrod, *On to Westward, op. cit.,* 94.

57. Hoffman, *Saipan, op. cit.,* 128.

58. Hayashi and Coox, *Kogun, op. cit.,* 111.

59. Quoted in Hoffman, *Saipan, op cit.,* 136.

60. MajGen S. Jarman, USA, memo for record, 23 June 1944, in Office of Naval Records and Library (ONRL).

61. Smith, *Coral and Brass, op. cit.,* 173.

62. MajGen S. Jarman, USA, letter to Lt Gen R. C. Richardson, USA, 30 June 1944, in ONRL.

63. Capt J. R. Stockman, "The Taking of Mount Tapotchau," *Marine Corps Gazette,* July 1946.

64. Quoted in Hoffman, *Saipan, op. cit.,* 157.

65. MajGen G. W. Griner, USA, endorsement, 28 June 1944, on report of Nafutan Point operations by CO, 105th Infantry, in ONRL.

66. Smith, *Coral and Brass, op. cit.,* 171.

67. NTLF Memo 9-44, "Occupation of Positions for the Night, and Preparation for Counterattack," 2 July 1944; 1st endorsement by CG, TF 56 (Maj Gen H. M. Smith) on 27th Infantry Division special action report, Saipan, 4 December 1944.

68. Commander Fifth Fleet serial 00418, 19 July 1944, in ONRL.

69. Quoted in Sherrod, *On to Westward, op. cit.,* 141.

70. *Ibid.,* 140.

71. Quoted in Hoffman, *Saipan, op. cit.,* 284.

72. Interrogation of FAdm Osami Nagano, IJN, Interrogation Nav. No. 80, *Interrogations of Japanese Officials,* Vol. II, 356.

73. Interrogation of VAdm Shigeyoshi Miwa, IJN, Interrogation Nav. No. 72, *Interrogations of Japanese Officials,* Vol. II, 298.

74. Smith, *Coral and Brass, op. cit.,* 181.

75. "Proceedings of a Board of Officers . . . to inquire into the relief of Maj Gen Ralph Smith, USA," CG U. S. Army Forces, Central Pacific, 12 July 1944.

76. ComInCh serial 003233 to Chief of Staff, U. S. Army, 6 November 1944, in ONRL.

77. Commander Amphibious Forces Pacific Fleet (ComPhibsPac) serial 00640, 16 July 1944, in ONRL.

78. *Ibid.;* Smith, *Coral and Brass, op. cit.,* 177; CG Expeditionary Troops (MajGen H. M. Smith) serial 00232-3, to Commander Joint Expeditionary Force, 18 July 1944. MajGen Schmidt, commanding the 4th Marine Division, was present during this interview, and confirmed by written endorsement General Holland Smith's account of what was said.

79. ComPhibsPac (VAdm R. K. Turner) serial 00640, 16 July 1944.

80. Seen on original copy, CinCPac serial 002921, 16 September 1944, in ONRL.

81. Adm C. W. Nimitz serial 003506 to

FAdm E. J. King, 27 October 1944, in ONRL.

82. ComInCh serial 003233, *op. cit.*

83. For those who wish to sort out the Saipan controversy for themselves, both the Marine Corps and Army official histories are highly recommended for their objectivity and restraint. See Hoffman, *Saipan,* and Crowl, *Campaign in the Marianas,* both *op. cit.*

84. The XXIV Corps Artillery, which performed outstandingly throughout Saipan and Tinian, had been temporarily assigned to V Amphibious Corps in an exchange for the V Corps Artillery, which was committed, as a result of an intricate series of planning changes, to support Army forces in the Leyte operation.

85. Smith, *Coral and Brass, op. cit.,* 206.

86. Maj F. E. Garretson letter to Maj C. W. Hoffman, 17 August 1950, in HQMC archives.

87. Maj W. McReynolds letter to CMC, 8 January 1951.

88. 1stLt J. G. Lucas, quoted in *The Fourth Marine Division in World War II,* Carl W. Proehl (Washington 1946), 101.

89. 4th Marine Division special action report, Tinian.

90. Quoted in the foreword to *Tinian,* Maj C. W. Hoffman (Washington 1951), iii.

91. Smith, *Coral and Brass, op. cit.,* 201.

92. Quoted in letter from Col W. F. Coleman to CMC, 5 September 1952.

93. Quoted in letter from BrigGen W. J. Scheyer to CMC, 26 September 1952.

94. CinCPac-CinCPOA Item (enemy translation) 10,410, diary of unidentified Japanese soldier.

95. LtCol Hideyuki Takeda, IJA (Ret.), letter to Chief of Military History, Department of the Army, February 1952, in OCMH.

96. Quoted in *The Recapture of Guam,* Maj O. R. Lodge (Washington 1954), 78.

97. Gen L. C. Shepherd, Jr., comments on draft of this history.

98. All the Pacific Fleet shore-based air in the so-called "Forward Area" which immediately followed the advancing conquests of the campaign, came under Army Air Force command, but, at this stage of the war, much of it was Marine. Out of five principal subordinate task groups that made up the force, three were primarily Marine: Air-Defense Command Marianas (Col W. L. McKittrick); Dive Bomber and Fighter Command (BrigGen T. J. Cushman); and Transport Air Group (LtCol T. J. McQuade).

99. Morison, *New Guinea and the Marianas, op. cit.,* 386.

100. Quoted in "The Battle for Banzai Ridge," 1stLt A. A. Frances, *Marine Corps Gazette,* June 1945.

101. *Ibid.*

102. *The Third Marine Division,* 1stLt R. A. Aurthur and 1stLt Kenneth Cohlmia (Washington 1948), 154; also, Lodge, *Guam, op. cit.,* 81.

103. Quoted in Marine Corps Schools lecture, "Case Studies in Naval Gunfire Planning" (GF-701, LtCol R. D. Heinl, Jr.), 1951, in Records Section, Marine Corps Schools.

104. The original proposal for FMFPac functions, drafted by Marine Corps Headquarters, included a provision that FMFPac should be prepared to operate as a task force of two or more corps, with appropriate supporting troops. Adm Nimitz, however, rejected this provision and substituted greatly weakened language to the effect that the CG, FMFPac, might act as a task-force commander when so directed. When Gen Holland Smith tried to force the issue (after the Marianas), Marine Corps Headquarters reversed its earlier position, very likely by direction.

105. Hayashi and Coox, *Kogun, op. cit.,* iii.

106. The genesis of the fire-team concept has been the subject of considerable controversy. The basic concept has been variously credited to Merritt Edson, to Evans Carlson, and to unknown officers in both the 22d and 24th Marines. Regardless of earlier embryonic experiments, the concept seems to have jelled in the field during early 1943, and was tested at Quantico early the next year, under direction of Col S. B. Griffith, a veteran raider, after which adoption was directed. See "Birth of the Fire Team," 1stLt L. M. Holmes, *Marine Corps Gazette,* November 1952, as well as resulting correspondence in the February and March issues of 1953.

107. Fletcher Pratt, *The Marines' War* (New York 1948), 337.

108. In his comments on the draft of this history, LtGen J. T. Selden notes, "As for having no gunfire officer on the staff, that was because higher headquarters paid no attention to our repeated requests. . . ."

109. Pratt, *op. cit.,* 325.

110. Maj F. O. Hough, *Peleliu* (Washington 1950), 25.

111. Quoted in McMillan, *The Old Breed, op. cit.,* 269.

112. Pratt, *op. cit.,* 337.

113. Capt George P. Hunt, USMC, *Coral Comes High,* 58.

114. Quoted in McMillan, *The Old Breed, op. cit.,* 288.

115. *Time* Magazine, 16 October 1944.

116. BrigGen W. A. Wachtler letter to CMC, 1 March 1950.

117. Col W. F. Coleman undated letter to CMC, in HQMC archives.

118. McMillan, *The Old Breed, op. cit.,* 318.

119. Quoted in Hough, *Peleliu, op. cit.,* 77.

120. *Ibid.,* 146.

121. *Ibid.,* 155.

122. Adm J. B. Oldendorf letter to Director of Marine Corps History, 25 March 1950.

123. Halsey and Bryan, *op. cit.,* 231.

124. *Ibid.,* 231.

125. CinCSWPA message, 1 January 1945.

126. Army Air Forces Evaluation Board, "POA Report No. 3." The senior member of this board, which bluntly reported that Navy-Marine close air support doctrine was best, BrigGen M. J. Scanlon, USA, was demoted to colonel after receipt of this report at Army Air Forces Headquarters.

127. LtCol K. B. McCutcheon, "Close Air Support," undated report to CMC, in HQMC archives.

128. Quoted in *The 1st Cavalry Division in World War II,* Maj C. B. Wright, USA, 126.

129. Quoted in War Diary, MAG-24, February 1945.

130. Quoted in War Diary, MAG-32, 10 February 1945.

131. Quoted in Sherrod, *Marine Aviation, op. cit.,* 323.

132. Quoted by LtCol St. Clair McKelway, USA, in *New Yorker* Magazine, June 1945.

133. Maj R. D. Heinl, Jr., "Dark Horse on Iwo," *Marine Corps Gazette,* August 1945.

134. Maj Yoshitaka Horie, IJA (Ret.), "Explanation of Japanese Defense Plan and Battle of Iwo Jima," 25 January 1946, in HQMC archives.

135. Smith, *Coral and Brass, op. cit.,* 255.

136. *Ibid.,* 255.

137. In his comments on the draft of this history, Gen H. M. Smith writes, "When we received orders to prepare for the capture of Iwo Jima I had a conference with Admirals Spruance and Turner at which I stated that the V Amphibious Corps was sufficient to do the job and that I did not think it was fair to Harry Schmidt to have me superimposed above him; that he and

his staff were fully competent to take Iwo Jima. I was informed, in no uncertain terms, that I and my staff would go on Admiral Turner's command ship. I then asked upon whose shoulders would rest the responsibility for the success or failure of the operation. The reply was that the responsibility would be mine. I did not in any way interfere, or give any orders to Schmidt other than [for him] to maintain pressure upon the Japanese once contact was made. . . . The situation was embarrassing to me as well as to Schmidt."

138. ComPhibsPac serial 00232, 26 November, 1944, in HQMC archives.

139. CG FMFPac serial 000182, 26 November 1944, in HQMC archives. The Navy planners' reasons for limiting the bombardment to three days, as given by Adm Morison in *Victory in the Pacific*, 73n, were: (1) that the Tokyo carrier strikes could only keep kamikazes away from Iwo for three days; (2) the bombardment ships available could carry only so much ammunition (Spruance added that it didn't do any more good to fire this in four days than in three, a debatable proposition); and (3) "by the law of diminishing returns, three days' bombardment should accomplish about 90 per cent of the maximum" —hardly a convincing rebuttal to the closely calculated computations of the Marine planners (which Adm Turner said were much the best he had ever seen), calling for ten days' bombardment.

140. This and the immediately following quotation are from "Iwo Jima Before H-Hour," John P. Marquand, *Thirty Years* (Boston 1954), 201.

141. Still another factor which pulled the pre-D-day bombardment's punch was Adm Spruance's decision at the last minute to withdraw the two new battleships, *Washington* and *North Carolina*, armed with 16-inch guns, from Blandy's fire-support group in order to reinforce the antiaircraft strength of Task Force 58 in its Tokyo raid. "I regret this confusion caused in your carefully laid plans," Spruance wrote Turner and Holland Smith, "but I know you and your people will get away with it." Smith, *Coral and Brass, op. cit.*, 247. Diversion of these powerful ships from the Iwo bombardment not only kept their heavy guns out of the fight but, perhaps more important, reduced the amount of ammunition available for pre-D-day bombardment by at least a thousand tons.

142. "Iwo Jima," LtGen Harry Schmidt, in *Hit the Beach!* (New York 1948), 237.

143. Sherrod, *On to Westward, op. cit.*, 159-60.

144. *Ibid.*

145. Marquand, "Iwo Jima Before H-Hour," *op. cit.*

146. Altogether, eight Marine fighting squadrons provided close air support at Iwo Jima from 19 to 22 February inclusive. These were VMF-124, 213 *(Essex)*, 216, 217 *(Hornet)*, 112, 123 *(Bennington)*, 221, and 451 *(Bunker Hill)*. These fighting squadrons had been hastily assigned to carrier duty early in 1945 when the increasing menace of the kamikaze attacks made extra fighters imperative. As the Navy was short on fighter pilots and units at this time, Marine aviation was drafted to fill the breach. Here Marine aviation was fulfilling a classic, long-standing role, that of providing "replacement squadrons for carrier-based naval aircraft," as stated in the 1939 mission assigned to Marine aviation by the Navy General Board.

147. Sherrod, *On to Westward, op. cit.*, 163.

148. Proehl, *Fourth Marine Division, op. cit.,* 149.

149. Sherrod, *On to Westward, op. cit.,* 180.

150. Smith, *Coral and Brass, op. cit.,* 261.

151. 2dLt Cyril P. Zurlinden, Jr., quoted in *The U. S. Marines in Iwo Jima,* Capt Raymond Henry, 1stLt J. G. Lucas, and TSgts W. Keyes Beech, David K. Dempsey, and Alvin M. Josephy, Jr. (Washington 1945), 49.

152. A. R. Matthews, *The Assault* (New York 1947), 48.

153. Quoted in Sherrod, *On to Westward, op. cit.,* 212.

154. 1stLt J. G. Lucas, quoted in Proehl, *Fourth Marine Division, op. cit.,* 155.

155. Quoted in Maj Horie, "Japanese Defense Plan," *op. cit.*

156. Biennial Report, Chief of Staff, U. S. Army, to Secretary of War, 10 October 1945.

157. Statistics from *The AAF Against Japan,* Vern Haughland, 260.

158. Isely and Crowl, *op. cit.,* 432.

159. Commander Fifth Fleet action report, Iwo Jima, 14 June 1945.

160. CinCPOA Communique #300, 16 March 1945, quoted in *Navy Department Communiques 301 to 600, and Pacific Fleet Communiques, March 6, 1943, to May 24, 1945* (Washington 1945), 370.

161. Quoted in "Case Studies in Naval Gunfire Planning," *op. cit.*

162. *Ibid.*

163. Gen G. C. Marshall memo to FAdm E. J. King, 22 November 1944, in ONRL.

164. Quoted by VAdm L. F. Reifsnider in letter to CMC, 21 March 1955.

165. MajGen J. R. Hodge, USA, letter to LtGen R. C. Richardson, USA, 17 April 1945, in OCMH.

166. In an interview, Gen Buckner stated, "It might be lots more fun killing them rapidly, but if you want to prolong the enjoyment you take a little longer to kill them." *New York Times,* 18 May 1945.

167. Quoted in *Washington Star,* 30 May 1945.

168. Comments by Gen Thomas on draft of this history. The information on Gen Bruce's proposal may be found in Crowl, *Campaign in the Marianas,* 317n.

169. Quoted in Sherrod, *Marine Aviation, op. cit.,* 382.

170. *Ibid.,* 393.

171. Commander Task Group 32.1 to ComInCh, 27 September 1945.

172. Quoted in Japanese Monograph No. 135, "Okinawa Operations Record," November 1949, 105, in OCMH.

173. Not to be confused with the better known Coco River patrol under Capt Edson. The Coco River expedition was an ill-fated but heroic attempt, under Capt P. C. Geyer, to descend the Coco from Ocotal in September 1928. See "The Saga of the Coco," Maj E. N. McClellan, *Marine Corps Gazette,* November 1930.

174. *New York Sun,* 11 September 1945. This article was published with the foreknowledge and tacit consent of Admiral King.

CHAPTER NINE—*FIVE YEARS OF CHALLENGE*

1. Although an early arrival, the V Amphibious Corps was not the first American force to reach metropolitan Japan. This honor fell to the 4th Marines, comprising part of a Fleet landing force under BrigGen W. T. Clement, which first set foot on Japanese soil at 0558, on 30 August 1945, at Yokosuka Navy Yard on Tokyo Bay.

2. Only two demobilization incidents involving Marines are known to have occurred, both on Oahu, where the author was on duty as a member of General Geiger's staff, and where agitators from other Services were particularly active (and almost wholly unsuccessful) in attempting to get sailors and Marines to join their cause. In one case, six enlisted men at Ewa signed and abetted publication of a petition, prepared for them by one from another Service, in early 1946. General Geiger promptly confined and reduced all six, and relieved the station commander. A second lesser episode took place one evening at Camp Catlin, where a handful of beery enlisted men demanded to see the camp commander *en masse*. The disturbance was quelled by a bellow from LtCol J. E. Buckley, one of the toughest (and smartest) old-timers in the Corps.

3. CG FMFPac letter to CMC, 21 August 1946.

4. CMC letter to Chairman, Commandant of the Marine Corps' Special Board, 13 September 1946.

5. Chairman, Special Board, report to CMC, 16 December 1946.

6. Marine Corps Historical Branch interview with Col V. H. Krulak, 18 November 1953.

7. James Forrestal *aide-memoire* of conversation with President Truman, 13 June 1945, in *The Forrestal Diaries*, edited by Walter Millis (New York 1951), 62.

8. Quotation supplied by BrigGen M. A. Edson, March 1947.

9. Chief of Staff, Army Air Force, memorandum, 15 March 1946; Chief of Staff, U. S. Army, memoranda of 16 March 1946 and 3 April 1946. Texts are given in House Report No. 961, Committee on Expenditures in the Executive Departments, on H.R. 4214, 1st Session, 80th Congress. Within four years, however, Gen Spaatz recanted his view, expressed in these memoranda, that the Marine Corps should consist only of small, lightly armed units no larger than a regiment. On 17 July 1950, in *Newsweek* Magazine, he demanded, as part of our defense establishment, "Two or three Marine divisions, stationed at strategic locations, ready for quick movement to any part of the world."

10. Chief of Naval Operations memorandum to JCS, 30 March 1946.

11. BrigGen Frank Armstrong, USA, quoted in *Saturday Evening Post*, 5 February 1949, 20. Hanson Baldwin, of the *New York Times*, who investigated this episode at the time, has written me that General Armstrong's caustic remarks were made in a spirit of levity during a pre-Army and Navy game luncheon. Unfortunately, they were widely reported otherwise and therefore did as much damage as if seriously intended.

12. Statement by Gen A. A. Vandegrift to Senate Naval Affairs Committee, 6 May 1946.

13. *New York Sun*, 27 March 1947.

14. The members of the Edson Board were: BrigGen M. A. Edson and G. C. Thomas; Col M. B. Twining and E. C. Dyer; LtCol V. H. Krulak, S. R. Shaw, DeW. Schatzel, J. C. Murray, J. D. Hittle, E. H. Hurst, R. D. Heinl, Jr.; and Maj J. M. Platt, recorder.

15. Millis, *Forrestal Diaries, op. cit.*, 271.

16. National Security Act of 1947 (61 Stat. 495).

17. Millis, *Forrestal Diaries, op. cit.*, 108.

18. *Ibid.*, 188.

19. Information from "Marines in North China," by Historical Branch, G-3, HQMC, 1960.

20. Millis, *Forrestal Diaries, op. cit.*, 179.

21. CO HMX-1, "Operation Packard Two: Amphibious Command Post Exercise," 10-26 May 1948.

22. Remark heard by the author, who was on the scene. It was also reported in the press.

23. Quoted in *Saturday Evening Post,* 20 February 1949, 20.

24. Quoted in HQMC Study, "The Status of the Marine Corps within the Department of the Navy," undated (c. 1956).

25. Complete text of the interchange of correspondence comprising the gentlemen's agreement is given in Senate Armed Services Committee Hearings on S. 677, "Marine Corps Strength and Joint Chiefs of Staff Representation," 82d Congress, 1st Session, 147-49.

26. Adm Louis Denfeld memo for Secretary of the Navy, 11 May 1948, "Restrictions on the Composition and Organization of the Marine Corps." Also see Millis, *Forrestal Diaries, op. cit.,* 392.

27. Gen C. B. Cates memo to Secretary of the Navy, 5 May 1948.

28. Millis, *Forrestal Diaries, op. cit.,* entry of 12 March 1948, 392.

29. The "second land army" phrase originally appears in Chief of Staff, U. S. Army, memo to JCS, 16 March 1946, quoted in House Report 961, *op. cit.* Also see Millis, *Forrestal Diaries, op. cit.,* 224. "The '1478' Papers" was the newspaper and Congressional phrase for the series of memoranda which, in 1946, debated the roles and missions of the Marine Corps and naval aviation. "1478" was their file number.

30. Adm Denfeld memo of 11 May 1948, *op. cit.*

31. CMC memo to CNO, 10 January 1950.

32. Chief of Staff, Army Air Force, memo to JCS, 15 March 1946, quoted in House Report 961, *op. cit.*

33. Gen C. B. Cates statement to House Armed Services Committee, 17 October 1949.

34. Testimony by Secretary Royall before Senate Armed Services Committee, quoted in *U. S. Naval Institute Proceedings,* June 1954, 67.

35. Quotation supplied by Mr. James Stahlman, who was present, to Brig Gen C. C. Jerome, and recorded in memo for record, 19 October 1949, in Cates Papers.

36. Quoted in *Unification and Strategy,* report by House Armed Services Committee, 1 March 1950, 6.

37. Capt Neil K. Dietrich, USN (aide to CNO) memo for Capt Ira Nunn, USN, 14 January 1950, in Cates Papers. Aside from the principle involved, the point later proved to be of some practical importance; when, in 1950, the 1st Marine Brigade was mounting out for Korea, the Marine Corps had to ask Admiral Sherman's permission to organize third platoons for the attenuated rifle companies of the 5th Marines. After due consideration, the admiral approved this purely internal reorganization, and directed Commander in Chief, Pacific Fleet—another admiral—to take the necessary action. See CNO dispatch to CinCPacFlt, this subject, 5 July 1950.

38. *Unification and Strategy, op. cit.,* 40.

39. Quoted in memo from BrigGen J. T. Selden to BrigGen C. C. Jerome, 10 November 1949, in Cates Papers, HQMC archives.

40. Statement by Gen C. B. Cates to House Armed Services Committee, 17 October 1949.

41. Secretary of Defense memo to Secretary of the Navy, 5 April 1949, in Cates Papers, HQMC archives.

42. CMC undated (23 September 1949?), "Statement concerning proposed modification in the Functions of the Armed Forces," in Cates Papers, HQMC archives.

43. C. W. Thayer, *Diplomat* (New York 1959), 119. The first U. S. Marine em-

bassy guard, however, was mounted in Washington, D.C., in 1805. When the Bey of Tunis sent an ambassador to the United States, the government

ordered a sergeant's guard of Marines posted at the embassy "to prevent intrusion." *Naval Documents, Barbary Wars*, Vol. VI, 315.

CHAPTER TEN—". . . *IN THE SNOW OF FAR-OFF NORTHERN LANDS*"

1. Quoted in *The New Breed*, Maj A. C. Geer (New York 1952), 5.
2. I am indebted to General Shepherd, in comments on this history, for the details of this interview.
3. This strike was the first air action of the Marine brigade, but, less than a month before, on 4 July, two F4U photo-planes from MAG-12, temporarily attached to USS *Valley Forge*, scored first blood for the Marine Corps by participating with the Navy's Air Group 5 in a strike on Pyongyang. The MAG-12 detachment, which consisted of 3 officers and 10 enlisted men, continued in action throughout July and until 7 August, when one of their Corsairs was shot down, after which the remaining aircraft and pilots were restricted to photography only. Capt R. N. Welch letter to *Marine Corps Gazette*, September 1952.
4. Quoted in Geer, *The New Breed, op. cit.*, 56.
5. CO, 23d Infantry report, quoted in Marine Corps Board study, *Evaluation of the Influence of Marine Corps Forces on the Course of the Korean War*, I-II-A-35.
6. *New York Times*, 28 June 1951.
7. *London Daily Telegraph*, 1 September 1950.
8. Quotation supplied by Col. H. N. Shea.
9. Complete text of the McDonough-Truman exchange of correspondence is given in *The Congressional Record*, 16 May 1952, 5446-5447.
10. Quoted in *The Sea War in Korea*, Cdr M. W. Cagle and Cdr F. A. Manson (Annapolis 1957), 77.
11. *Ibid.*, 76.
12. VAdm A. D. Struble, quoted in Cagle and Manson, *op. cit.*, 83.
13. *Ibid.*, 81.
14. MajGen O. P. Smith, excerpt from *Notes on the Operations of the 1st Marine Division during the First Nine Months of the Korean War*, MSS, kindly made available by Gen Smith.
15. *Ibid.*
16. Quoted in *The Inchon-Seoul Operation*, Lynn Montross and Capt N. A. Canzona (Washington 1955), 90.
17. ComPhibGroup 1 action report, Inchon operation, ONRL.
18. In his comments on the draft of this history, General O. P. Smith writes: "I was not very happy over the development that brought General MacArthur and the convoy of correspondents to the scene of the ambush of the North Korean tanks and infantry, but my hand was forced. . . . After the General and the correspondents had left the area, Marines flushed 30 North Koreans out of a culvert near where General MacArthur had dismounted from his jeep to view the tanks."
19. This anecdote, with slightly different dialogue, appears in Geer, *The New Breed, op. cit.*, 175. The dialogue given here is as I heard the story in Korea.
20. Quoted in Cagle and Manson, *op. cit.*, 149.

21. MacArthur's operations north of the 38th parallel and up to the Yalu were authorized by JCS message 92801 of 27 September 1950. Two days later, General Marshall, the Secretary of Defense, told MacArthur "to feel unhampered, tactically and strategically" in operations north of the 38th parallel. JCS message 92985 of 29 September 1950.

22. LtCol T. B. Tighe in comment on this history.

23. MajGen C. L. Ruffner, USA, letter to MajGen E. W. Snedeker, 13 January 1956, in HQMC archives.

24. Quoted in Geer, *The New Breed, op. cit.*, 223.

25. MajGen O. P. Smith letter to Gen C. B. Cates, 15 November 1950, in HQMC archives.

26. Quoted in Geer, *The New Breed, op. cit.*, 262.

27. Comment by Gen O. P. Smith on draft of this history.

28. Quoted in *The Chosin Reservoir Campaign*, Lynn Montross and Capt N. A. Canzona (Washington 1957), 261.

29. MajGen O. P. Smith letter to Gen C. B. Cates, 17 December 1950, in HQMC archives.

30. *Ibid.*

31. Quoted in Geer, *The New Breed, op. cit.*, 311.

32. MajGen O. P. Smith letter to LtGen M. H. Silverthorn, 10 February 1951, in Cates Papers, HQMC archives.

33. Quoted in Cagle and Manson, *op. cit.*, 174. Both the wing and division asked for and got the enthusiastic main effort of the fast carriers all through the breakout. When General Harris told General Smith of his efforts to get maximum support for the division, General Smith recounts: "I told him we would like to have in support all the Marine and naval planes we could get; that we had no objection to the participation of Air Force planes, provided they operated outside a ten-mile zone astride the breakout route. Field Harris was as good as his word and rendered us magnificent support." Comment by General Smith on the draft of this history.

34. This phrase was reported in a news broadcast by Robert K. Martin on 7 December 1950 and was soon confused with Wise's "Retreat, Hell!" of 1918. As General Smith commented on the draft of this history, "I have been plagued by 'Retreat, Hell!' ever since Korea. It was simply not in character to describe our situation in those terms." It may be added that, to those who knew General Smith, a quiet-spoken, deliberate man not given to profanity, such a phrase was not "in character" in any case.

35. Quotation from speech by Gen O. P. Smith to Bay Area Chapter, Marine Corps Association, 20 June 1959, made available by General Smith.

36. MajGen O. P. Smith letter to MajGen Field Harris, 20 December 1950, in HQMC archives.

37. Quoted from *Combat Forces Journal* in Geer, *The New Breed, op. cit.*, 190.

38. S. L. A. Marshall, "The Last Barrier," *Marine Corps Gazette*, January 1953.

39. Quoted in "Buttoning Up the Offensive: The Marines in Operation Killer," Lynn Montross, *Marine Corps Gazette*, February 1952.

40. Quoted in "Advance to the 38th Parallel: The Marines in Operation Ripper," Lynn Montross, *Marine Corps Gazette*, March 1952.

41. MajGen O. P. Smith letter to LtGen M. H. Silverthorn, 5 May 1951, made available by General Smith.

42. *Ibid.*

43. Quoted in *The United States Marines*, Lynn Montross (New York 1959), 206.

44. Remark to the author shortly after Col Krulak's return from 1st Marine Division.

45. *Ibid.*

46. From the command-relations point of view, the status of the 1st Wing was nothing if not complicated. The wing commander had been ordered to report in turn to Commander Naval Forces, Far East (ComNavFE), then to Commander Far East Air Forces (CG FEAF), then to CG Fifth Air Force. Within the Naval Forces Far East organization, "when in execution of naval missions," the wing commander operated as Commander Task Force 91; under 5th Air Force, the wing commander was, for the air defense of Korea, Commander, Southern Defense Sector. In addition, the units of the wing performed a wide variety of air operations as ordered by 5th Air Force and coordinated by the Joint Operations Center (JOC) which was supposed to provide a mechanism for meeting and coordinating the air-support requirements of the 8th Army, but signally failed to do so in any fashion satisfactory to front-line units. To confuse the foregoing complex and compartmented relationships further, two Marine aviation units, the helicopter squadron (HMR-161) and division observation squadron (VMO-1) were not under the wing, but under the division. Of course this was where they should have been, but the division, in turn, being under 8th Army, was forcibly and far separated, in everything but spirit, from the Marine air wing.

47. In his comments on the draft of this history, MajGen Mangrum writes, ". . . for the rest of 1951 and well into 1952 the major effort of my Group [MAG-12] and of MAG-33 was devoted to cutting the rail lines in North Korea. Without success, of course. Little by little we were able to increase the percentages of effort devoted to close support of the troops."

48. Quoted in Cagle and Manson, *op. cit.*, 270.

49. Statistics and quotations from *1st Mar Div Report on Close Air Support,* undated folder in Cates Papers, HQMC archives.

50. Quoted in undated letter from MajGen G. C. Thomas to LtGen L. C. Shepherd, Jr., in *1st Mar Div Report on Close Air Support, op. cit.*

51. MajGen G. C. Thomas letter to LtGen L. C. Shepherd, Jr., 4 October 1951, in Cates Papers, HQMC archives.

52. This information, and the immediately following quotation, are from the comments of Gen V. E. Megee on the draft of this history.

53. Senate Armed Services Committee Hearings on S. 677, 7.

54. House Report No. 666, 82d Congress, 1st Session, 10.

55. *New York Times,* 28 June 1951.

56. Quoted by General Selden in comments on draft of this history.

57. In his comments on the draft of this history, MajGen Mangrum, who at the time was 1st Wing liaison officer to headquarters, 5th Air Force, recalls, "I saw much of Gen Van Fleet & Co. Van Fleet was wont frankly to express his relief to all and sundry visitors over having 'that powerful 1st Marine Division in position on [his] vulnerable left flank.'"

58. Martin Russ, *The Last Parallel* (New York 1957), 55.

59. *Ibid.*, 321.

60. LtGen M. B. Twining speech, Navy Day 1956, at Los Angeles, California, before the Navy League of the United States.

CHAPTER ELEVEN—*THINGS PRESENT AND TO COME*

1. Secretary of the Navy R. B. Anderson address to graduates of Marine Corps Schools, 19 September 1953.
2. Statement by the Hon Carl Vinson, MC, 1 May 1956.
3. *New York Times,* 15 November 1959.
4. Quoted in statement by the Chief of Naval Operations to House Armed Services Committee, 8 March 1961.
5. Maj C. M. See, "Suez," *Marine Corps Gazette,* July 1958.
6. Thayer, *op. cit.,* 31.
7. *Army and Navy Journal,* 2 April 1960, 3.
8. Statement by Gen D. M. Shoup, 4 January 1961.
9. The Haitian government's desire for a Marine military mission dated back almost 20 years, such an initial request having been first submitted to the U. S. government in 1939, only five years after the end of the occupation. Unfortunately and, as later events would prove, unwisely, Undersecretary of State Sumner Welles was adamant against the proposal ("Have the Marines march back into Haiti?— Never!" he exploded), but did accede to a small U. S. Army Mission which lapsed in the mid-1940s. Information supplied by the former President of Haiti, S. E. Elie Lescot, and by General Holcomb.
10. Senate Armed Services Committee hearings on S. 677, 105.
11. LtGen Twining Navy Day speech, *op. cit.*
12. Gen L. C. Shepherd, Jr., statement at General Officers' Conference, HQMC, 16 July 1954.
13. Gen Cates statement to House Armed Services Committee, *op. cit.*

BIBLIOGRAPHY

BOOKS

ALDRICH, M. ALMY. *History of the United States Marine Corps*. Boston, 1875.

ALLEN, R. *The Siege of the Peking Legations*. London, 1901.

AMMEN, DANIEL, R. ADM., USN. *The Atlantic Coast*. New York, 1883.

—— *The Old Navy and the New*. Philadelphia, 1891.

APPLEMAN, R. E. *Okinawa: the Last Battle*. Washington, 1948.

AURTHUR, R. A., 1ST LT., USMC and 1ST LT. K. COHLMIA, USMC. *The 3d Marine Division*. Washington, 1948.

BALCH, E. C. *Occupied Haiti*. New York, 1927.

BARDE, ROBERT E., MAJ., USMC. *The History of Marine Corps Competitive Marksmanship*. Marksmanship Branch, G-3 Division, HQMC. Washington, 1961.

BARTLEY, W. S., LT. COL., USMC. *Iwo Jima: Amphibious Epic*. Washington, 1954.

BELLEGARDE, DANTÈS. *La Résistance Haitienne*. Port-au-Prince, 1937.

BEMIS, S. F. *A Diplomatic History of the United States*. New York, 1936.

BLAKENEY, JANE. *Heroes, U. S. Marine Corps, 1861–1955*. Washington, 1957.

BOGGS, C. W., MAJ., USMC. *Marine Aviation in the Philippines*. Washington, 1951.

BOYINGTON, G., COL., USMC. *Baa, Baa, Black Sheep*. New York, 1958.

CAGLE, M. W., CDR., USN, and CDR. F. A. MANSON, USN. *The Sea War in Korea*. Annapolis, 1957.

CARTER, W. A. *The Tale of a Devil Dog*. Washington, 1920.

CASS, B. G., 1ST LT., USMC. *History of the 6th Marine Division*. Washington, 1948.

CATLIN, A. W., COL., USMC. *With the Help of God and a Few Marines*. New York, 1918.

COLLUM, R. S., MAJ., USMC. *The History of the United States Marine Corps*. Philadelphia, editions of 1890 and 1903.

CONDIT, K. W. and E. T. TURNBLADH. *Hold High the Torch*. Washington, 1960.

CONNER, H. M., MAJ., USMC. *The Spearhead*. Washington, 1950.

COOPER, J. F. *Naval History of the United States*. Philadelphia, 1839.

CRAIGE, J. H. CAPT., USMC. *Black Baghdad*. New York, 1933.

—— *Cannibal Cousins*. New York, 1934.

CROWL, P. A. *Campaign in the Marianas*. Washington, 1960.

DAGGETT, E. S., BRIG. GEN., USA. *America in the China Relief Expedition.* Chicago, 1903.

DANIELS, JONATHAN. *The End of Innocence.* Philadelphia, 1954.

DANIELS, JOSEPHUS. *The Wilson Era.* Chapel Hill, 1946.

DECHANT, J. A., CAPT. *Devilbirds.* New York, 1947.

DERBY & JACKSON (publishers). *The Life of Commodore Robert F. Stockton.* New York, 1856.

DEVEREUX, J. P. S., COL., USMC. *The Story of Wake Island.* Philadelphia, 1947.

DEWEY, GEORGE, ADM. OF THE NAVY. *Autobiography of George Dewey.* New York, 1913.

DUTTON, C. J. *Oliver Hazard Perry.* New York, 1935.

EVANS, R. D., R. ADM., USN. *A Sailor's Log.* New York, 1901.

FIELD, CYRIL, COL., RMLI, *Britain's Sea Soldiers.* London, 1924.

FISKE, B. A., R. ADM., USN. *From Midshipman to Rear Admiral.* New York, 1919.

FLEMING, PETER. *The Siege at Peking.* London, 1959.

FURER, J. A., R. ADM., USN. *Administration of the Navy Department in World War II.* Washington, 1959.

GEER, A. C., MAJ., USMC. *The New Breed.* New York, 1952.

———— *Reckless, Pride of the Marines.* New York, 1955.

GIUSTI, ERNEST, MAJ., USMC. *Early Days of the 1st Marines.* USMC Historical Reference Series No. 5. Washington, 1958.

GLEAVES, ALBERT, R. ADM., USN. *Life and Letters of Rear Admiral Stephen B. Luce.* New York, 1925.

GLEIG, G. R. *Narrative of the Campaigns of the British Army at Washington and New Orleans.* London, 1827.

GREENE, F. V., 1ST LT., USA. *The Mississippi.* New York, 1895.

HALSEY, W. F., F. ADM., USN, and LT. CDR. J. BRYAN III, USN. *Admiral Halsey's Story.* New York, 1947.

HAMERSLY, L. R. *The Records of Living Officers of the U. S. Navy and Marine Corps.* Philadelphia, 1890, 1894, 1902.

HAMERSLY, T. H. S. *General Register of the United States Navy and Marine Corps.* Washington, 1882.

HARBORD, J. G., MAJ. GEN., USA. *Leaves from a War Diary.* New York, 1926.

———— *The American Army in France.* Boston, 1936.

HARRIS, JOHN, COL., USMC. *Letters from Naval Officers in Reference to the United States Marine Corps.* Washington, 1864.

HAYASHI, SABURO, COL., IJA (RET.) and A. D. COOX. *Kogun: The Japanese Army in the Pacific War.* Quantico, 1959.

HEINL, R. D., JR., LT. COL., USMC. *The Defense of Wake.* Washington, 1947.

———— *Marines at Midway.* Washington, 1948.

———— and LT. COL. J. A. CROWN, USMC. *The Marshalls: Increasing the Tempo.* Washington, 1954.

HENRI, RAYMOND, CAPT., USMC; 1ST LT. J. G. LUCAS, USMC; T. SGT. W. K. BEECH, USMC; T. SGT. D. K. DEMPSEY, USMC; and T. SGT. A. M. JOSEPHY, JR., USMC. *The U. S. Marines on Iwo Jima.* Washington, 1945.

HERSEY, JOHN. *Into the Valley.* New York, 1943.

HOOKER, MARY. *Behind the Scenes in Peking.* London, 1910.

HOPPIN, J. M. *Life of Andrew Hull Foote, Rear Admiral U. S. Navy.* New York, 1874.

HOUGH, F. O., LT. COL., USMC. *The Assault on Peleliu.* Washington, 1950.

—— *Island War.* New York, 1946.

—— and LT. COL. J. A. CROWN, USMC. *The Campaign on New Britain.* Washington, 1952.

——, MAJ. V. E. LUDWIG, USMC, and H. I. SHAW. *Pearl Harbor to Guadalcanal.* Washington, 1958.

HUNT, G. P., CAPT., USMC. *Coral Comes High.* New York, 1946.

ISELY, J. A. and P. A. CROWL. *The U. S. Marines and Amphibious War.* Princeton, 1951.

JOHNSON, A. W., CAPT., USN. *Brief History of the Organization of the Navy Department.* Washington, 1933.

JOHNSTON, R. W. *Follow Me!* New York, 1948.

KELSEY, CARL. *The American Intervention in Haiti and the Dominican Republic.* Philadelphia, 1922.

KING, E. J., F. ADM., USN. *The U. S. Navy at War, 1941–45.* Washington, 1946.

—— and CDR. W. M. WHITEHILL, USN. *Fleet Admiral King, A Naval Record.* New York, 1952.

KNOX, D. W., COMMODORE, USN. *A History of the United States Navy.* New York, 1948.

LEJEUNE, J. A., MAJ. GEN., USMC. *Reminiscences of a Marine.* Philadelphia, 1930.

LEONARD, J. W. and F. F. CHITTY. *The Story of the United States Marines.* Philadelphia, 1920.

LEWIS, C. L. *Famous American Marines.* Boston, 1950.

LINDSAY, ROBERT, CAPT., USMC. *This High Name.* Madison, Wisconsin, 1956.

LODGE, O. R., MAJ., USMC. *The Recapture of Guam.* Washington, 1954.

LONG, J. D. *The New American Navy.* New York, 1903.

MACLAY, E. S. *A History of the United States Navy.* New York, 1898.

MAHAN, A. T., CAPT., USN (RET.). *Sea Power in Its Relations to the War of 1812.* London, 1905.

MARINE, W. M. *The British Invasion of Maryland, 1812–1815.* Baltimore, 1913.

MARTI, W. H. *Messenger of Destiny.* San Francisco, 1960.

MCCLELLAN, E. N., MAJ., USMC. *The U. S. Marine Corps in World War I.* Washington, 1920.

MCCROCKLIN, J. H. (compiler). *Garde d'Haiti.* Annapolis, 1955.

McKEAN, W. B., BRIG. GEN., USMC. *Ribbon Creek.* New York, 1958.

McMILLAN, GEORGE. *The New Breed.* Washington, 1949.

——, C. P. ZURLINDEN, JR.; A. M. JOSEPHY, JR.; DAVID DEMPSEY; KEYES BEECH; and HERMAN KOGAN. *Uncommon Valor.* Washington, 1946.

MERRILLAT, H. L. *The Island.* Boston, 1944.

METCALF, C. H., LT. COL., USMC. *A History of the United States Marine Corps.* New York, 1939.

MILLER, JOHN, JR. *Guadalcanal, the First Offensive.* Washington, 1949.

MILLIS, WALTER. *The Martial Spirit.* Boston, 1931.

—— *The Forrestal Diaries.* New York, 1951.

—— *Arms and Men.* New York, 1956.

—— *Arms and the State.* New York, 1958.

MONTROSS, LYNN. *The United States Marines.* New York, 1959.

—— and CAPT. N. A. CANZONA, USMC. *U. S. Marine Operations in Korea.* Vols. I, II, and III. Washington, 1954–57.

MORISON, S. E., R. ADM., USNR. *History of United States Naval Operations in World War II.* Boston, 1947–60.

—— *John Paul Jones, A Sailor's Biography.* Boston, 1959.

MORTON, LOUIS. *The Fall of the Philippines.* Washington, 1953.

MUNRO, D. G. *The Latin American Republics, a History.* New York, 1942.

NALTY, B. C. *The Barrier Forts.* Washington, 1958.

—— *The United States Marines in the Civil War.* Washington, 1958.

—— *"At All Times Ready . . ." The Marines at Harper's Ferry.* Washington, 1959.

—— *Guests of the Conquering Lion.* Washington, 1959.

—— *The United States Marines in the War with Spain.* Washington, 1958.

NICHOLS, C. S., MAJ., USMC. and H. I. SHAW. *Okinawa, Victory in the Pacific.* Washington, 1955.

OLIPHANT, NIGEL. *A Diary of the Siege of the Legations in Peking.* London, 1901.

O'SHEEL, PATRICK. *Semper Fidelis.* New York, 1947.

OTTO, ERNST, LT. COL., GERMAN ARMY (RET.). *The Battle at Blanc Mont.* Annapolis, 1930.

PAINE, R. D. *Joshua Barney.* New York, 1924.

PALMER, FREDERICK. *America in France.* New York, 1918.

—— *Newton D. Baker.* New York, 1931.

PAULLIN, C. O. *The Navy of the American Revolution.* New York, 1906.

PEARSON, J. L. (publisher). *Information in Regard to the United States Marine Corps.* Washington, 1875.

PERSHING, J. J., GEN. OF THE ARMIES. *My Experiences in the World War.* New York, 1931.

PIERCE, P. N., LT. COL., USMC, and LT. COL. F. O. HOUGH, USMC. *Compact History of the Marine Corps.* New York, 1960.

PORTER, D. D., ADM., USN. *Naval History of the Civil War.* New York, 1886.

POTTER, E. B. (editor). *The United States and World Sea Power.* Englewood Cliffs, New Jersey, 1955.

PRATT, FLETCHER. *The Marines' War.* New York, 1948.

PROEHL, C. W., CAPT. *The Fourth Marine Division in World War II.* Washington, 1946.

PUTNAM-WEALE, B. L. (pseud. for B. L. SIMPSON). *Indiscreet Letters from Peking.* New York, 1909.

RENTZ, J. N., MAJ., USMCR. *Bougainville and the Northern Solomons.* Washington, 1948.

—— *Marines in the Central Solomons.* Washington, 1952.

REYNOLDS, F. J. *The U. S. Marine Corps from the Revolution to Date.* New York, 1916.

ROOSEVELT, THEODORE. *The Naval War of 1812.* New York, 1882.

ROOSEVELT, ELLIOTT. *F.D.R., His Personal Letters.* New York, 1948.

RUSS, MARTIN. *The Last Parallel.* New York, 1957.

SARGENT, H. H., CAPT., USA. *The Campaign of Santiago de Cuba.* Chicago, 1907.

SCHLEY, W. S., R. ADM., USN. *Forty-Five Years Under the Flag.* New York, 1904.

SEXTON, W. T., CAPT., USA. *Soldiers in the Sun.* Harrisburg, 1939.

SHERROD, ROBERT. *Tarawa, the Story of a Battle.* New York, 1944.

—— *On to Westward.* New York, 1945.

—— *History of Marine Corps Aviation.* Washington, 1952.

SHERWOOD, R. E. *Roosevelt and Hopkins.* New York, 1948.

SMELSER, MARSHALL. *The Congress Founds the Navy, 1787–1798.* Notre Dame, Indiana, 1959.

SMITH, H. M., GEN., USMC. *Coral and Brass.* New York, 1949.

SMITH, J. C., MAJ., USMC. *A Review of the Organization and Operations of the Guardia Nacional de Nicaragua.* Washington, undated.

SMITH, J. H. *The War with Mexico.* New York, 1919.

SOMOZA, A. *El Verdadero Sandino, o el Calvario de las Segovias.* Managua, 1936.

SOUSA, J. P. *Marching Along.* Boston, 1928.

SPAULDING, O. L., COL., USA. *The United States Army in War and Peace.* New York, 1937.

SPEARS, J. R. *The History of Our Navy, 1775–1897.* New York, 1897.

—— *Our Navy in the War with Spain.* New York, 1898.

SPROUT, H. and M. *The Rise of American Naval Power.* Princeton, 1939.

STOCKMAN, J. R., CAPT., USMC. *The Battle for Tarawa.* Washington, 1947.

STRINGER, H. R. *Distinguished Service.* Washington, 1921.

THOMAS, LOWELL. *Old Gimlet Eye.* New York, 1933.

THOMASON, J. W., JR., CAPT., USMC. *Fix Bayonets!* New York, 1926.
TITHERINGTON, R. H. *A History of the Spanish-American War.* New York, 1900.
TREGASKIS, RICHARD. *Guadalcanal Diary.* New York, 1943.
TUCKER, GLENN. *Poltroons and Patriots.* New York, 1954.
VEGA Y PAGAN, E., LT. CDR., Dominican Navy. *Sintesis Historica de la Guardia Nacional Dominicana.* Ciudad Trujillo, D. R., 1953.
WELLES, GIDEON. *Diary of Gideon Welles.* ed. by H. K. Beale. New York, 1960.
WELLES, SUMNER. *Naboth's Vineyard.* New York, 1928.
WEST, R. S., JR. *Mr. Lincoln's Navy.* New York, 1957.
WILCOX, C. M., MAJ. GEN., late CSA. *History of the Mexican War.* Washington, 1892.
WILLIAMS, J. S., *History of the Invasion and Capture of Washington.* New York, 1857.
WILLOCK, ROGER, COL., USMCR. *Lone Star Marine.* Princeton, 1961.
WISE, F. M., COL., USMC. *A Marine Tells It to You.* New York, 1929.
ZIMMERMAN, J. L., LT. COL., USMCR. *The Guadalcanal Campaign.* Washington, 1949.

PERIODICALS

"Action and Patrol Reports, La Paz Centro, Ocotal, Telpaneca, Chipote" (ed. by Division of Operations and Training, HQMC), *Marine Corps Gazette,* 1928–29.
APLINGTON, HENRY, II, LT. COL., USMC. "North China Patrol," *Marine Corps Gazette,* June, 1949.
ASPREY, R. B., CAPT. "Waller of Samar," *Marine Corps Gazette,* May and June, 1961.
BALDWIN, HANSON. "The Fourth Marines at Corregidor," *Marine Corps Gazette,* November, 1946–February, 1947.
BATTERTON, R. J., MAJ., USMC. "You Fight by the Book," *Marine Corps Gazette,* July, 1949.
BRAINARD, E. H., MAJ., USMC. "Marine Corps Aviation," *Marine Corps Gazette,* March, 1928.
BUBECK, A. E. "Colonel Lee and the Marines at Harper's Ferry," *Marine Corps Gazette,* December, 1959.
CARLSON, E. F., CAPT. "Guardia Nacional de Nicaragua," *Marine Corps Gazette,* August, 1937.
CROIZAT, V. J., LT. COL., USMC. "The Marines' Amphibian," *Marine Corps Gazette,* June, 1953.
CROWN, J. A., LT. COL., USMC. "Tradition of Experts," *Marine Corps Gazette,* August, 1954.
CURTIS, P. C., T. SGT., USMC. "Quantico," *Leatherneck,* November, 1957.
DODDS, H. W. "American Supervision of the Nicaraguan Elections," *Foreign Affairs,* April, 1929.

DONNELLY, R. W. "Uniforms and Equipment, Confederate Marines," *Military Collector and Historian,* Spring, 1957.

—— "Battle Honors of Confederate Marines," *Military Affairs,* Spring, 1959.

DUKESHIRE, T. S., CAPT., USN. "The Confederate Marine Corps," *Philatelic Gossip,* April, 1956.

EDSON, M. A., MAJ., USMC. "The Coco Patrol," *Marine Corps Gazette,* November, 1936–February, 1937.

ELLICOTT, JOHN, CAPT., USN (RET.). "Marines at Matachin," *Marine Corps Gazette,* September, 1950.

—— "Marines at Manila Bay," *Marine Corps Gazette,* May, 1953.

ELLIOTT, G. F., MAJ. GEN., USMC. "On the Isthmus, 1885," (as told to Col. H. C. Reisinger), *Marine Corps Gazette,* December, 1928.

EVANS, E. J., M. SGT., USMC. "Time on Target 177 Years," *Marine Corps Gazette,* February, 1954.

FRANCES, A. A., 1ST. LT., USMC. "The Battle for Banzai Ridge," *Marine Corps Gazette,* June, 1945.

GAYLE, G. D., LT. COL., USMC. "Commandants of the Marine Corps," *Marine Corps Gazette,* November, 1950.

GREEN, ISRAEL. "The Capture of John Brown," *North American Review,* December, 1885.

GREENWOOD, J. E., CAPT., USMC. "Seventy-Five Years of Academy Marines," *Shipmate,* November, 1957.

GRIFFITH, S. B., II, LT. COL., USMC. "Action at Enogai," *Marine Corps Gazette,* March, 1944.

HAYNES, F. E., MAJ., USMC. "Left Flank at Iwo," *Marine Corps Gazette,* March, 1953.

HEINL, R. D., JR., LT. COL., USMC. "The Cat with More Than Nine Lives," *U. S. Naval Institute Proceedings,* June, 1954.

—— "Dark Horse on Iwo," *Marine Corps Gazette,* August, 1945.

—— "NGF Training in the Pacific," *Marine Corps Gazette,* June, 1948.

HENDERSON, F. P., COL., USMC. "NGF Support in the Solomons," *Marine Corps Gazette,* March–December, 1956.

HOFFMAN, C. W., MAJ., USMC. "The Marine Band—President's Own," *Marine Corps Gazette,* November, 1950.

HOGABOOM, W. F., 1ST. LT., USMC. "Action Report: Bataan," *Marine Corps Gazette,* April, 1946.

HOLMES, L. M., 1ST. LT., USMC. "Birth of the Fire Team," *Marine Corps Gazette,* November, 1952.

HORIE, YOSHITAKA. "The Last Days of General Kuribayashi," *Marine Corps Gazette,* February, 1955.

HOYLER, H. M., LT. COL., USMC. "The Legal Status of the Marine Corps," *Marine Corps Gazette,* November, 1950.

HYMAN, H. M. "When Congress Considered Abolishing the Marine Corps," *Marine Corps Gazette,* April, 1959.

JOHNSON, M. M., LT. COL., USA. "Marine Weapons: from Musket to M-1," *Marine Corps Gazette,* November, 1950.

LAUGHLIN, PATRICK, MAJ., USMCR. "Rebel Marines," *Marine Corps Gazette,* November, 1953.

LEJEUNE, J. A., MAJ. GEN., USMC. "The Mobile Defense of an Advance Base," *Marine Corps Gazette,* March, 1916.

—— "The United States Marine Corps," *Military Engineer,* 1925.

—— Testimony before Senate Foreign Relations Committee, 18 February 1928, *Marine Corps Gazette,* March, 1928.

MAGRUDER, J. H., III, LT. COL., USMC. "A Touch of Tradition," series in *Marine Corps Gazette,* February–July, 1956; November, 1956; and November, 1957.

Marine Corps Gazette, "The Marine Band," November, 1930.

—— "The Device of the Marine Corps," November, 1930.

—— "Captain Jinks' Horse Marines," November, 1946.

—— "Guarding the Crossroads: The 7th Defense Battalion in Samoa," January, 1944.

MARSHALL, S. L. A., BRIG. GEN., USA. "The Last Barrier," *Marine Corps Gazette,* January and February, 1953.

McCLELLAN, E. N., MAJ., USMC. "A Brief History of the Fourth Brigade of Marines," *Marine Corps Gazette,* December, 1919.

—— "The Battle of Blanc Mont Ridge," *Marine Corps Gazette,* March, 1922.

—— "American Marines in the British Grand Fleet," *Marine Corps Gazette,* June, 1922.

—— "From 1783 to 1798," *Marine Corps Gazette,* September, 1922.

—— "The Naval War with France," *Marine Corps Gazette,* December, 1922.

—— "Saga of the Coco," *Marine Corps Gazette,* November, 1930.

—— "The American Marines, 1740–42," *Marine Corps Gazette,* December, 1929.

MERRILL, W. A., CAPT., USMC. "This Is My Rifle," *Marine Corps Gazette,* December, 1960.

MONTROSS, LYNN. "The Marine Autogiro in Nicaragua," *Marine Corps Gazette,* February, 1953.

MORTON, LOUIS. "Army and Marines on the China Station: A Study in Military and Political Rivalries," *Pacific Historical Review,* February, 1960.

MYERS, LEWIS, CAPT. "Greyclad Marines," *Marine Corps Gazette,* January, 1947.

OLSON, H. C., LT. COL., USMC. "43 Years of Motor Transport," *Marine Corps Gazette,* December, 1952.

OWENS, R. A., 1ST LT., USMC. "Barefoot Marines," *Marine Corps Gazette,* November, 1948.

PHILLIPS, C. A., LT. COL., USMC. "1st MAW in Korea," *Marine Corps Gazette,* May–June, 1947.

PIERCE, P. N., LT. COL., USMC, and CAPT. LEWIS MYERS. "The Seven Years' War," *Marine Corps Gazette,* September, 1948.

PORTER, J. W. "The Corps' Oldest Post," *Marine Corps Gazette,* November, 1950.

PRICKETT, W. F., LT. COL., USMC. "Naval Battalion at Mariveles," *Marine Corps Gazette,* June, 1950.

RANKIN, R. H., LT. COL., USMC. *"Per Mare, Per Terram," Marine Corps Gazette,* April, 1953.

RUNYAN, C. F., MAJ., USMC. "Capt. McLane Tilton and the Korean Incident of 1871," *Marine Corps Gazette,* February and March, 1958.

RUOFF, F. A. "The Story of a Dream," *Marine Corps Gazette,* February, 1950.

RUSSELL, J. H., MAJ. GEN., USMC. "The Birth of the FMF," *U. S. Naval Institute Proceedings,* January, 1946.

——— "A Plea for a Mission and Doctrine," *Marine Corps Gazette,* June, 1916.

RUSSELL, W. H. "The Genesis of Fleet Marine Force Doctrine: 1879-1899," *Marine Corps Gazette,* April–July, 1951; November, 1955.

SANDERSON, C. R., LT. COL., USMC. "The Quartermaster's Department," *Marine Corps Gazette,* March, 1930.

SEE, C. M., MAJ., USMC. "Suez," *Marine Corps Gazette,* July, 1958.

SHEPHERD, L. C., JR., MAJ. GEN., USMC. "Battle for Motobu Peninsula," *Marine Corps Gazette,* August, 1945.

——— "As the President May Direct," *U. S. Naval Institute Proceedings,* March, 1952.

SMITH, H. M., GEN., USMC. "Development of Amphibious Tactics in the U. S. Navy," *Marine Corps Gazette,* June–October, 1948.

SMITH, J. C., LT. GEN., USMC. "Tarawa," *U. S. Naval Institute Proceedings,* November, 1953.

SNODDY, L. F., JR., LT. COL., USMC. "Leatherneck Salesmen," *Marine Corps Gazette,* August, 1955.

TANAKA, RAIZO, V. ADM., IJN (RET.). "Japan's Losing Struggle for Guadalcanal," *U. S. Naval Institute Proceedings,* July and August, 1956.

TAUSSIG, J. K., CAPT., USN. "Experiences During the Boxer Rebellion," *U. S. Naval Institute Proceedings,* April, 1927.

THACKER, J. D. "Marine Uniforms: 1775–1950," *Marine Corps Gazette,* November, 1950.

——— "Highlights of U. S. Marine Corps Activities in the District of Columbia," *Records of the Columbia Historical Society,* Washington, 1952.

TREGASKIS, RICHARD. "The Marine Corps Fights for Its Life," *Saturday Evening Post,* 20 February 1949.

TURNBLADH, E. T., "The Committee on Nova Scotia," *Leatherneck,* November, 1960.

USMC Historical Division. "The Marines' Hymn," *Marine Corps Gazette*, September, 1942.

VAN HOOSE, G. W., MAJ., USMC. "The Confederate States Marine Corps," *Marine Corps Gazette*, September, 1928.

WADE, S. S., BRIG. GEN., USMC. "Operation Bluebat," *Marine Corps Gazette*, July, 1959.

WHYTE, W. H., JR., CAPT. "Hyakutake Meets the Marines," *Marine Corps Gazette*, July and August, 1945.

WILDS, T. "The Japanese Seizure of Guam," *Marine Corps Gazette*, July, 1955.

WILLIAMS, DION, BRIG. GEN., USMC. "Thirty Years Ago," *Marine Corps Gazette*, March, 1928.

ZIMMERMAN, J. L., LT. COL., USMCR. "A Note on the Occupation of Iceland by American Forces," *Political Science Quarterly*, March, 1947.

—— "Force in Readiness," *U. S. Naval Institute Proceedings*, February, 1957.

USMC HISTORICAL REFERENCE PAMPHLETS

CHAMPIE, E. A. *The Marine Corps Recruit Depot, Parris Island, S.C. 1891–1956.* USMC Historical Reference Series No. 8, Washington, 1959.

SHAW, H. I. *The United States Marines in North China, 1945–1949.* USMC Historical Reference Series No. 23, Washington, 1960.

USMC Historical Division. *Brief History of the Marine Corps Recruit Depot, San Diego, California,* Washington, 1956.

—— *Enlisted Ranks and Grades, U. S. Marine Corps, 1775–1958.*

—— *Enlisted Rank Insignia in the U. S. Marine Corps, 1798–1958.*

—— *Home of the Commandants,* Washington, 1956.

U. S. GOVERNMENT DOCUMENTS

Adjutant General, U. S. Army. *Correspondence Relating to the War with Spain, Including the Insurrection in the Philippine Islands and the China Relief Expedition,* Washington, 1902.

American State Papers, Naval Affairs, 1789–1836. Washington, 1834–1861.

Battle Monuments Commission. *American Battlefields in Europe,* Washington, 1927.

Chief, Bureau of Navigation. *Naval Operations in the War with Spain,* Washington, 1898.

Chief, Bureau of Yards and Docks. *Building the Navy's Bases in World War II,* Washington, 1947.

House of Representatives. Armed Services Committee, *Hearings on S. 677,* 23 May 1951.

—— Armed Services Committee, *Report of Investigation: Unification and Strategy,* 1 March 1950.

—— Doc. No. 787, *Hearing on Proposed Reduction in Enlisted Strength of Marine Corps,* 15 December 1932.

—— Naval Affairs Committee, *Hearings on the Status of the U. S. Marine Corps,* January 1909.

—— 39th Congress, 2d Session, *Report No. 22,* 21 February 1867.

—— 80th Congress, 1st Session, *Report No. 961,* 16 July 1947.

—— 82d Congress, 1st Session, *Report No. 666,* 30 June 1951.

Navy Department. *Naval Documents Related to the United States Wars with the Barbary Powers,* Washington, 1939–45.

—— *Naval Documents Related to the Quasi-War Between the United States and France,* Washington, 1935–38.

—— *Official Records of the Union and Confederate Navies in the War of the Rebellion,* Washington, 1894–1922.

Senate. 59th Congress, 2d Session, *Document No. 140,* 1906.

—— 67th Congress, 1st–2d Sessions, *Inquiry into Occupation of Haiti and Santo Domingo,* 1922.

—— 82d Congress, 1st Session, Armed Services Committee, *Hearings on S. 677,* 13–21 April 1951.

—— 82d Congress, 1st Session, *Report No. 308,* 1951.

Special Report, *President's Commission for the Study and Review of Conditions in the Republic of Haiti,* Washington, 1930.

State Department. *Papers Relating to the Foreign Relations of the United States,* Washington.

STEELE, M. F. *American Campaigns, War Department Doc. 324,* Washington, 1909.

Strategic Bombing Survey. *Interrogations of Japanese Officials,* Washington, 1946.

—— *The Allied Campaign Against Rabaul,* Washington, 1946.

—— *Summary Report, Pacific War,* Washington, 1947.

—— *The Campaigns of the Pacific War,* Washington, 1946.

STROTT, G. G., LT. (HC) USN. *Medical Department of the United States Navy in France in World War I* (NavMed 1197), Washington. 1947.

MANUSCRIPTS

BARNETT, GEORGE, MAJ. GEN., USMC. "Soldier and Sailor, Too," MSS autobiography, Barnett Papers, Marine Corps Museum.

BERKELEY, R. C., MAJ. GEN., USMC. MSS autobiography 1959, made available by Maj. Gen. J. P. Berkeley.

ELLSWORTH, H. A., CAPT., USMC. "180 Landings of the United States Marines," mimeographed MSS, Washington, 1934.

McCLELLAN, E. N., MAJ., USMC. "History of the United States Marine Corps," mimeographed bound MSS, Washington, 1925–32.

INDEX